The National Committee of Inquiry into **Higher Educa**

Main Report

Contents

Chairman's foreword

1 We were appointed with bipartisan support by the Secretaries of State for Education and Employment, Wales, Scotland, and Northern Ireland on 10 May 1996 to make recommendations on how the purposes, shape, structure, size and funding of higher education, including support for students, should develop to meet the needs of the United Kingdom over the next 20 years, recognising that higher education embraces teaching, learning, scholarship and research. We were asked to report by the summer of 1997. Our full terms of reference are set out on pages 3 and 4.

2 We now submit our report. In doing so, we thank those who were members of the working groups we created to study and advise on particular issues, and in particular the members of our Scottish Committee, whose advice to us is published as part of our report. We are indebted to all those who gave evidence, both oral and written. We are grateful to those in higher education in this country and in the countries we visited for being so open with us as we sought to inform ourselves and develop policies for the future. Most of all we are indebted to our secretariat and in particular to our secretary, Shirley Trundle, who served us with distinction and far beyond the call of duty. We were indeed fortunate in having such a team.

3 I am personally much indebted to all my colleagues on the Committee, of whom I asked far more than they can have envisaged when they agreed to join it. This report is very much the work of all of us.

4 We begin by setting out our vision for higher education over the next 20 years. This vision is central to our report, and the other chapters are founded on it: our recommendations are designed to enable this vision to become a reality. After briefly outlining the approach we took to our work, we then describe the current state of higher education and the wider economic and social context in which it is now operating. Taking all of this into account, we then set out our view of what the aims and purposes of higher education should be. After this introductory material, we examine the demand for higher education in the United Kingdom, in terms of its level and distribution between different groups in the population and the needs of students. This is followed by a group of chapters in which we consider the main business of higher education institutions: the delivery and content of programmes; standards and the framework of awards; research; and the particular local and regional role of institutions. In the subsequent group of chapters we review staffing and staff development, particularly in relation to teaching; the growing implications of communications and information technology; the way institutions are organised, managed and governed; and the characteristics which differentiate institutions. We then examine the funding needs of institutions, the sources of funding, and what structures and mechanisms should exist for channelling funds to institutions, a graduate contribution and arrangements for supporting students. We end with a discussion of the relationship between Government and higher education, including special features in Scotland, Wales and Northern Ireland, and of the immediate priorities for action.

5 Our report is supported by a range of annexes and appendices, with the first annex containing a list of our recommendations.

An introductory comment

6   We were appointed to advise on the long term development of higher education. But we express here our concern that the long term wellbeing of higher education should not be damaged by the needs of the short-term.

7   We are particularly concerned about planned further reductions in the unit of funding for higher education. If these are carried forward, it would have been halved in 25 years. We believe that this would damage both the quality and effectiveness of higher education. We are also concerned about some other immediate needs, especially in relation to research.

8   We recognise the need for new sources of finance for higher education to respond to these problems and to provide for growth. We therefore recommend that students enter into an obligation to make contributions to the cost of their higher education once they are in work. Inescapably these contributions lie in the future. But there are pressing needs which we identify in the Report in the years 1998/99 and 1999/2000. We urge the Government to respond to these in its decisions on funding, by giving credit for the full value embedded in the commitments given by students to provide for their education. The present public expenditure and accounting practice does not provide for this: it therefore fails to recognise value that is properly recognised in normal commercial accounts, and leads to costly arrangements for securing that value by sale of the loan book, which can be ill afforded.

9   Much of our report is concerned with material things and with the central role of higher education in the economy. It would be surprising were it not so. But throughout we have kept in mind the values that characterise higher education and which are fundamental to any understanding of it. They were well expressed by John Masefield in an address at the University of Sheffield in 1946. Speaking of a university, he said, as we would now say of higher education as a whole:

> 'It is a place where those who hate ignorance may strive to know, where those who perceive truth may strive to make others see; where seekers and learners alike, banded together in the search for knowledge, will honour thought in all its finer ways, will welcome thinkers in distress or in exile, will uphold ever the dignity of thought and learning and will exact standards in these things.'

10   It must continue to be so.

Ron Dearing

The National Committee of Inquiry into Higher Education

Terms of reference and membership

To make recommendations on how the purposes, shape, structure, size and funding of higher education, including support for students, should develop to meet the needs of the United Kingdom over the next 20 years, recognising that higher education embraces teaching, learning, scholarship and research.

The Committee should report by the summer of 1997.
The Committee should take account of the context in Annex A.

The Committee should have regard, within the constraints of the Government's other spending priorities and affordability, to the following principles:

- there should be maximum participation in initial higher education by young and mature students and in lifetime learning by adults, having regard to the needs of individuals, the nation and the future labour market;
- students should be able to choose between a diverse range of courses, institutions, modes and locations of study;
- standards of degrees and other higher education qualifications should be at least maintained, and assured;
- the effectiveness of teaching and learning should be enhanced;
- learning should be increasingly responsive to employment needs and include the development of general skills, widely valued in employment;
- higher education's contribution to basic, strategic and applied research should be maintained and enhanced, particularly in subjects where UK research has attained international standards of excellence or in Technology Foresight priority areas;
- arrangements for student support should be fair and transparent, and support the principles above;
- higher education should be able to recruit, retain and motivate staff of the appropriate calibre;
- value for money and cost-effectiveness should be obtained in the use of resources.

Annex A to the terms of reference

The Committee should take account of the following context:

- demand for higher education from suitably qualified applicants of all ages is growing as more people achieve qualifications at level 3 and more of those who already have higher level qualifications look to upgrade or update them;
- there is a growing diversity of students in higher education with a growing number of mature entrants, part-timers, and women students;
- higher education continues to have a key role in developing the powers of the mind, and in advancing understanding and learning through scholarship and research;

- the UK must now compete in increasingly competitive international markets where the proliferation of knowledge, technological advances and the information revolution mean that labour market demand for those with higher level education and training is growing, particularly in business, and that there is a greater premium on the products of the country's research base;
- many of our international competitors are aiming to improve the contribution their higher education systems make to their economic performance;
- higher education has a key role in delivering national policies and meeting industry's needs for science, engineering and technology in research and postgraduate training;
- a flourishing higher education system is important for all sectors of the economy and essential to the NHS and the education service, supplying qualified manpower, research and innovation, and continuing professional development;
- through scholarship and research, higher education provides a national resource of knowledge and expertise for the benefit of out international competitiveness and quality of life, and provides a basis for responding to social and economic change through innovation and lifelong learning;
- higher education continues to have a role in the nation's social, moral and spiritual life; in transmitting citizenship and culture in all its variety; and in enabling personal development for the benefit of individuals and society as a whole;
- higher education is a major contributor to local, regional and national economic growth and regeneration;
- there are distinctive features of higher education in different parts of the UK;
- links between higher education and other parts of the education and training system, particularly further education, are increasing in importance;
- links between higher education in the UK and elsewhere in the world are growing, as the international mobility of students and staff increases;
- higher education is an important educational export in its own right;
- new technology is opening up the possibility of new forms of teaching and learning, and higher education is increasingly delivered in the work-place and in the home through distance-learning;
- the Government has legislated to enable private financial institutions to offer loans to students on similar terms to those offered by the Student Loans Company;
- there have already been reviews of a number of areas likely to be of interest to the Committee, for example of the national framework of qualifications and of credit accumulation and transfer, of postgraduate education, and of the dual support arrangements for research funding.

Members of the National Committee

Professor John Arbuthnott	Principal and Vice-Chancellor of the University of Strathclyde
Baroness Dean of Thornton-le-Fylde	(formerly Brenda Dean)
Sir Ron Dearing	(Chairman)
Ms Judith Evans	Departmental Director of Personnel Policy, Sainsbury's
Sir Ron Garrick	Managing Director and Chief Executive of Weir Group
Sir Geoffrey Holland	Vice-Chancellor of the University of Exeter
Professor Diana Laurillard	Pro Vice-Chancellor (Technology Development) of the Open University
Mrs Pamela Morris	Headteacher, The Blue School, Wells
Sir Ronald Oxburgh	Rector of Imperial College of Science, Technology and Medicine
Dr David Potter	Chairman of Psion plc
Sir George Quigley	Chairman of Ulster Bank
Sir William Stubbs	Rector of the London Institute
Sir Richard Sykes	Chairman and Chief Executive of Glaxo Wellcome plc
Professor David Watson	Director of the University of Brighton
Professor Sir David Weatherall	Regius Professor of Medicine at the University of Oxford
Professor Adrian Webb	Vice-Chancellor of the University of Glamorgan
Mr Simon Wright	Education and Welfare Officer, Students Union, the University of Wales College of Cardiff

Secretary to the National Committee

Mrs Shirley Trundle	Department for Education and Employment

Chapter 1

A vision for 20 years: the learning society

Introduction

1.1   The purpose of education is life-enhancing: it contributes to the whole quality of life. This recognition of the purpose of higher education in the development of our people, our society, and our economy is central to our vision. In the next century, the economically successful nations will be those which become learning societies: where all are committed, through effective education and training, to lifelong learning.

1.2   So, to be a successful nation in a competitive world, and to maintain a cohesive society and a rich culture, we must invest in education to develop our greatest resource, our people. The challenge to achieve this through the excellence and effectiveness of education is great. As Members of the National Committee of Inquiry we have been privileged to have the opportunity to review and recommend the direction of higher education policy over the next twenty years. None of us doubts the importance or difficulty of our task.

A vision for higher education

1.3   Over the next 20 years, we see higher education gaining in strength through the pursuit of quality and a commitment to standards. Central to our vision of the future is a judgement that the United Kingdom (UK) will need to develop as a learning society. In that learning society, higher education will make a distinctive contribution through teaching at its highest level, the pursuit of scholarship and research, and increasingly through its contribution to lifelong learning. National need and demand from students will require a resumed expansion of student numbers, young and mature, full-time and part-time. But over the next decade, higher education will face challenges as well as opportunities. The effectiveness of its responses to these, and its commitment to quality and standards, will shape its future.

1.4   We believe that the country must have higher education which, through excellence in its diverse purposes, can justifiably claim to be world class. As institutions will increasingly have to operate within an international market for education, they will all be judged by international standards. UK higher education must:
- encourage and enable all students – whether they demonstrate the highest intellectual potential or whether they have struggled to reach the threshold of higher education – to achieve beyond their expectations;
- safeguard the rigour of its awards, ensuring that UK qualifications meet the needs of UK students and have standing throughout the world;
- be at the leading edge of world practice in effective learning and teaching;

- undertake research that matches the best in the world, and make its benefits available to the nation;
- ensure that its support for regional and local communities is at least comparable to that provided by higher education in competitor nations;
- sustain a culture which demands disciplined thinking, encourages curiosity, challenges existing ideas and generates new ones;
- be part of the conscience of a democratic society, founded on respect for the rights of the individual and the responsibilities of the individual to society as a whole;
- be explicit and clear in how it goes about its business, be accountable to students and to society and seek continuously to improve its own performance.

1.5   To achieve this, higher education will depend on:
- professional, committed members of staff who are appropriately trained, respected and rewarded;
- a diverse range of autonomous, well-managed institutions with a commitment to excellence in the achievement of their distinctive missions.

1.6   Institutions of higher education do not and will not fit into simple categories: they do and will emphasise different elements in their chosen purposes and activities: they are and will be diverse. Those which already have an established world reputation should be able to retain their distinctive characters: there should be no pressure on them to change their character. Their aim should be to sustain their outstanding achievements in research, scholarship and teaching. There will also be specialist institutions and individual departments which achieve distinction in the world community of scholars.

1.7   Many institutions will see their distinctive contribution in offering first class teaching. They will find innovative and effective ways to extend the opportunity for learning to a larger and broader section of the community. Some institutions will seek to interact creatively with local and regional communities. Some will see a distinctive role in applying the knowledge gained from research to addressing practical problems. Yet others will challenge their peers in other countries with ideas on some of the world's most profound and challenging problems.

1.8   Such diversity and distinctive missions should be encouraged, valued and fostered by national funding schemes. While there will continue to be competition between institutions, diversity will become the basis for collaboration between complementary institutions to their mutual advantage, and to the advantage of the communities of which they are part.

1.9   Higher education needs continuity in the framework within which it operates to support its achievement of quality and distinctiveness. Government should avoid sudden changes in the funding or scope and direction of higher education. In return, the community, as represented by the government, has a right to expect higher education to be responsive to the developing needs of society and to be as zealous in the use of resources as it is in the pursuit of excellence in teaching and research. In this, higher education should be as ready to question conventions about what is desirable or possible in the way it operates, as it is to question established wisdom through academic enquiry.

The learning society

1.10   The expansion of higher education in the last ten years has contributed greatly to the creation of a learning society, that is, a society in which people in all walks of life recognise the need to continue in education and training throughout their working lives and who see learning as enhancing the quality of life throughout all its stages. But, looking twenty years ahead, the UK must progress further and faster in the creation of such a society to sustain a competitive economy.

1.11   In a global economy, the manufacturers of goods and providers of services can locate or relocate their operations wherever in the world gives them greatest competitive advantage. Competitive pressures are reinforced by the swift pace of innovation and the immediate availability of information through communications technology. When capital, manufacturing processes and service bases can be transferred internationally, the only stable source of competitive advantage (other than natural resources) is a nation's people. Education and training must enable people in an advanced society to compete with the best in the world.

1.12   The pace of change in the work-place will require people to re-equip themselves, as new knowledge and new skills are needed for economies to compete, survive and prosper. A lifelong career in one organisation will become increasingly the exception. People will need the knowledge and skills to control and manage their own working lives.

1.13   This requires a learning society, which embraces both education and training, for people at **all** levels of achievement, before, during and, for continued personal fulfilment, after working life.

1.14   Experience suggests that the long-term demand from industry and commerce will be for higher levels of education and training for their present and future workforce. The UK cannot afford to lag behind its competitors in investing in the intellect and skills of its people. While the United States of America is a strong investor in higher education, and has high rates of participation, the Far East is increasingly setting the pace. In Japan, participation in higher education is already more than ten percentage points higher than in the UK and, with demographic changes, participation by young people there will exceed 50 per cent in 2000-2010 without an increase in total expenditure on higher education. A significant proportion of such participation is at levels below first degree.

1.15   The economic imperative is, therefore, to resume growth. In a 20-year context, participation rates by young people of 40 per cent or beyond have been canvassed by those giving evidence to us. This has already been achieved in Northern Ireland and in Scotland, with participation rates by young people of around 45 per cent. Much of the increase may be among people seeking qualifications below degree level, as in Scotland. Whatever the means of delivery and level of achievement, however, it is clear that growth in participation by traditional young entrants will need to resume. The present cap on continued expansion must be seen as a temporary pause following several years of very fast growth.

1.16   Traditional entry by young people is only one aspect of the need. The other, for the members of a learning society, is the requirement to renew, update and widen their knowledge and skills throughout life. This will influence the system, character and scope of higher education in very many institutions.

1.17   Apart from the economic imperative, there are other influences pointing to resumed growth. Unless we address the under-representation of those from lower socio-economic groups we may face increasingly socially divisive consequences. As a matter of equity, we need to reduce the under-representation of certain ethnic groups and of those with disabilities. Not least, there will be increasing demand for higher education for its own sake by individuals seeking personal development, intellectual challenge, preparation for career change, or refreshment in later life.

The characteristics of higher education in the learning society

1.18   Lifelong learning points to the need, overall, for higher education to:
- be increasingly responsive to the needs of students and of clients (such as employers and those who commission research);
- structure qualifications which can be either free-standing or built-up over time, and which are commonly accepted and widely recognised;
- offer opportunities for credit transfer between courses and institutions;
- adopt a national framework of awards with rigorously maintained standards, with the academic community recognising that the autonomy of institutions can be sustained only within a framework of collective responsibility for standards, supported by the active involvement of professional bodies;
- work in partnership with public and private sector employers;
- respond fully to the need for active policies for developing, retraining and rewarding its own staff;
- maintain its distinctiveness and vitality through linking research and scholarship to teaching;
- take full advantage of the advances in communications and information technology, which will radically alter the shape and delivery of learning throughout the world;
- be explicit about what it is providing through learning programmes, and their expected outcomes, so that students and employers have a better understanding of their purposes and benefits.

Responding to change

1.19   Higher education has responded fully over the last decade to the national need for greater participation. It has managed this in the face of much reduced public funding per student. It has maintained its high reputation for research. The decade has been one of increasing demands upon staff, whether through increasing teaching loads, more effective administration, or through demands for more and ever higher quality research outcomes. They have responded to these demands in the service of society as a whole.

1.20   While traditional but still-relevant values must be safeguarded, higher education will need to continue to adapt to the needs of a rapidly changing world and to new challenges. In a period of discontinuous change, the future cannot be forecast from the past: what is clear is that a policy based on 'more of the same' is not an option. Increasing competition, particularly in the context of lifelong learning, will come from employers and training providers, in partnerships with major institutions of higher education possibly linked to the entertainment and communications industries, and from prestigious institutions overseas making extensive use of distance learning through modern technology.

1.21   The level of investment needed in a learning society is such that we see a need for those who benefit from education and training after the age of 18 to bear a greater share of the costs. As a result, we expect students of all ages will be increasingly discriminating investors in higher education, looking for quality, convenience, and relevance to their needs at a cost they consider affordable and justified by the probable return on their investment of time and money.

A new compact

1.22   At the heart of our vision of higher education is the free-standing institution, which offers teaching to the highest level in an environment of scholarship and independent enquiry. But, collectively and individually, these institutions are becoming ever more central to the economic wellbeing of the nation, localities and individuals. There is a growing bond of interdependence, in which each is looking for much from the other. That interdependence needs to be more clearly recognised by all the participants.

1.23   For the individual student, we see an institution committing itself through a compact which recognises its obligation to provide a high quality service and accurate information to inform students' choices. A student, in return, will invest time, effort and money. At best the outcome will be, through lifelong learning, a relationship which lasts for decades.

1.24   In research, we see higher education taking a more active role in relating the outcomes of research and scholarship to the wider needs of society. We see industry and commerce, and a wide range of public bodies who have need of research, reciprocally making greater use of the knowledge and expertise which resides in higher education institutions. Mechanisms at national and regional level must help develop that relationship. We see an implicit compact between higher education and the world of work, based on how much each has to offer the other and the potential advantage in realising the mutual gain.

1.25   For the state itself, higher education has become a crucial asset. It must recognise what it will gain from ensuring the well-being of higher education. In return, as it has done in the past, higher education as a whole must recognise its obligation to society as a whole.

1.26   We believe that an adaptive, proactive higher education community will serve the UK well. By continuing to address cost and quality, it can make a major and recognised contribution to national competitiveness, which can in turn justify continued expansion. Reciprocally, higher education must be able to look to society for respect for its purposes, for recognition that funding to maintain quality provision reflects the national interest, not just the self-interest of institutions, and for recognition that the purpose of higher education goes beyond the economic to embrace all of life.

1.27   We think in terms of a compact between higher education and society which reflects their strong bond of mutual interdependence: a compact which in certain respects could with advantage be made explicit. A compact which is based on an interpretation of the needs of both sides at national, regional and local level requires continuing dialogue and a framework within which it takes place. It needs to be informed by disinterested advice. It should not be another 35 years before a group like ours looks again systematically at the issues.

1.28   When asked what we should be seeking to achieve in our review, one respondent said:
        '....restore both within the system and in regard to everyone who plans it and uses it, the kind of confidence that the previous Committee managed to establish within the 1960s.[1] Morale within the system is lower than it should be. The confidence of the country is lower than it should be. I hope that what you produce will address both things.'[2]

        We believe that the vision for the future and the recommendations set out in this report should raise both morale and confidence.

Chapter 2

The Committee's approach to its work

2.1 From our first meeting we recognised the scale of the task facing us. Our terms of reference were extensive and the problems we had to address were complex.

2.2 The last such review, by the Robbins Committee, took two and a half years to report on similar issues. In contrast, we had 14 months to complete our work. The way in which we approached the task was conditioned by that constraint: many people, both within and outside higher education, told us that it was important that we should keep to the timetable. This chapter outlines our process: Annex B gives more information.

2.3 One of the problems we had to resolve was the balance between depth and breadth in our work. This mirrored the debates we had about the balance between depth and breadth in higher education programmes. For programmes of learning, one option we identified for combining both depth and breadth in a constrained period of study was to offer breadth across a subject and its related disciplines, and depth in only a limited number of areas of the main subject. That is, in effect, the approach we adopted for our own study. Although this report is wide-ranging in its coverage, we have made a deep examination leading to detailed recommendations in only a limited number of areas. For example, we have not, in general, made a study of individual subjects (such as chemistry or mathematics) although we do have observations to make about certain subjects, where we think this is helpful in illustrating a particular point.

2.4 We made an exception in the case of school teacher education because the Secretaries of State who commissioned this report have special responsibilities for it; teaching is still the single largest employment destination for graduates; and the quality of the teaching force in schools has an important influence on the capabilities of those who subsequently enter higher education. We commissioned a report on teacher education in England and Scotland (Report 10 'Teacher education and training: a study') and have used this material as the basis for some observations and recommendations.

2.5 Across much of the field, however, we have offered a broad outline of the way forward, but have left it to others to advise on how to achieve it.

Table 2.1 – The Committee's work: some statistics

Number of meetings of Committees and Working Groups	90
Number of papers considered by Committees and Working Groups	445
Number of documents prepared by the Secretariat	13,000+
Number of visits to UK higher education institutions	33
Number of overseas visits	8
Number of meetings between Chairman and interested parties	150
Number of individuals and organisations submitting written evidence	840
Number of pages of written evidence	6,000

The proceedings of the Main Committee and the Scottish Committee

2.6　　To promote freedom of discussion, we decided that our papers and our meetings should be confidential during the life of the Committee, but we were committed to listening to the widest range of views and to reviewing as much external evidence as we could.

2.7　　Our papers are being passed to the Public Record Office, to be made available to the public on 1 January 2000.

Working Groups

2.8　　To make rapid progress, and to allow us to tap into a broader range of expertise than we possessed collectively, we established a series of Working Groups, each chaired by a member of our Committee. The Working Groups' memberships are shown in Annex B. We are extremely grateful to all the external members of these groups for the time and thinking they devoted to the task which, in many cases, went well beyond what they had signed up for at the start. The Working Groups were charged with clearing the ground for the Committee, identifying the issues and analysing the options, but not with making recommendations. Their contributions were invaluable, but we take full responsibility for the content and recommendations of this report.

Secretariat

2.9　　We were supported throughout our work by a Secretariat which varied in size from three to twenty staff from a variety of backgrounds. We are grateful to the organisations who were willing to second key members of their staff to us.

Gathering the evidence

2.10   To fulfil our commitment to hear the widest range of views we decided to consult interested parties in a number of different ways. The outcomes of those consultations are reported in the volumes published with this report, and the way in which we carried them out is described in Annex B.

2.11   Our consultations included:
- a major written consultation resulting in 840 responses;
- formal oral evidence from 37 organisations;
- seven consultation conferences;
- a written consultation with major employers resulting in 110 responses;
- seminars with employers from small and medium sized enterprises.

2.12   We commissioned major surveys of 1,270 students currently in higher education and 809 academic staff in higher education. We also arranged small focus group discussions with other staff in higher education. As others were already embarking on relevant studies of graduates, we joined forces with them rather than duplicating their work.

2.13   We were concerned that our work should be as firmly grounded in evidence as possible. We were fortunate that we had a much greater wealth of statistical data and other recent reports to draw on than had the Robbins Committee, although there were some areas where we would have liked better information. We commissioned a number of literature surveys and original pieces of research, and collaborated with other organisations on research projects. We ran several seminars at which experts in various fields informed us about latest thinking and helped us to test the evidence presented to us. The resulting reports are published alongside this report. In publishing the reports we commissioned, we do not endorse every conclusion and recommendation in them. Their contents are the views of their authors, but we wanted the advice and evidence which was available to us to be available to a wider audience as well. Some of the reports contain ideas for further work which might usefully be undertaken. Some also address matters which go beyond our remit: we have not followed these up in our main report but we will draw them to the attention of those with the relevant responsibilities.

2.14   Given our belief that our higher education system needs to match the best in the world, we examined a good deal of evidence about the strengths and weaknesses of alternative approaches. Small groups of members of the Committee visited Australia, France, Germany, Japan, the Netherlands, New Zealand and the United States in order to examine aspects of their higher education systems. In the course of those visits we had discussions with policy makers, representatives of higher education institutions, employers, academics and students, and we visited a range of different types of higher education institution. We are grateful for the help we received from those who organised our visits, and for the warm welcome we received wherever we went.

2.15   We made enquiries about practice in a wide range of other countries through their embassies, and gathered much published material on overseas experience. We were able to read the recent thematic study of the early years of higher education by the Organisation for Economic Co-operation and Development (OECD), including its analysis of higher education in the United Kingdom.

2.16   We visited 33 institutions which provide higher education across the UK and benefited from many informal meetings and discussions with interested organisations and individuals.

Acknowledgements

2.17   Throughout our work, we received tremendous support and commitment to our task from those within and outside higher education. Many gave considerable time and effort to ensuring that we were well informed about the strengths and weaknesses of the present system, and the advantages and disadvantages of options for the future. We cannot name all those who have helped us, but we are greatly indebted to all of them.

Chapter 3

Higher education today

3.1   The last major review of the future of higher education in the United Kingdom, by the Robbins Committee, took place in the early 1960s. Since then, higher education, both in the UK and across the world, has changed dramatically.

3.2   UK higher education can take justifiable pride in what it has achieved over the last 30 years. It has expanded opportunities, changed and adapted as the needs of students and other clients have changed, maintained its international standing in research, introduced new approaches to learning and teaching and to quality assurance, and greatly improved its cost-effectiveness. This success has been achieved through the commitment of those who work in higher education: staff have responded to stiff challenges. The nation can have confidence in its higher education system.

3.3   In proposing a new vision for higher education, we are seeking to build on past achievement and support existing excellence. But there are strains resulting from the pace of change, especially in the last few years, which must be addressed if higher education is to continue to be able to develop and serve the nation well. This chapter identifies the major developments in higher education, summarises the views put to us about the strains in today's arrangements, and concludes with a brief note of the main problems as we see them.

Students

3.4   For the last 35 years, the general trend across the developed world has been for increasing participation in higher education. In the UK there have been periods of rapid growth, in the late 1960s and from 1988 to 1993, with a long pause through the 1970s and early 80s, and our higher education system is now far larger than before the Robbins Committee report. Consistent data about all students are not available for the full period from the early 1960s to the present, but Chart 3.1 shows a complete run of figures for full-time, UK students.

Chart 3.1 – Full-time UK students in higher education in the UK (000s)

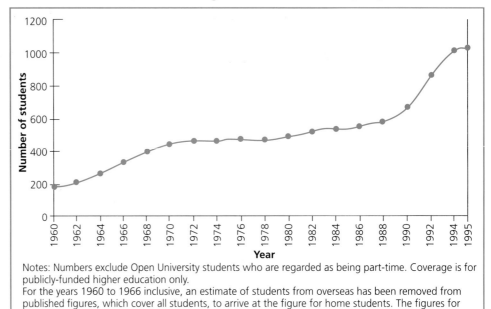

Notes: Numbers exclude Open University students who are regarded as being part-time. Coverage is for publicly-funded higher education only.
For the years 1960 to 1966 inclusive, an estimate of students from overseas has been removed from published figures, which cover all students, to arrive at the figure for home students. The figures for years 1994 and 1995 are provisional.

Source: DfEE

3.5   Forecasts suggest that, if current patterns of participation continue, more than half of today's school leavers will experience higher education at some time in their lives.[1] Higher education will shape individual lives, the economy and society. Such an activity must be the subject of broad and informed consideration and debate.

3.6   In 1996/97 there were more than 1.6 million students studying at higher education level in higher education institutions – over 1.1 million studying full-time or on sandwich programmes and over a half a million part-time. In addition, there are estimated to be in the region of 200,000 higher education students in further education colleges. Historical data on the number of students studying short programmes is incomplete. This is regrettable, as such programmes are likely to be of increasing importance in a learning society.

Chart 3.2 – All students in higher education institutions, 1996/97

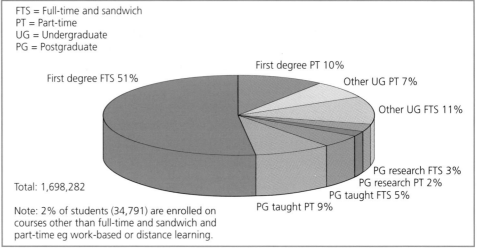

Source: HESA Data Report on student numbers 1996/97

3.7 Whereas the numbers in all categories of students have expanded, postgraduate numbers have grown fastest in recent years. Over the country as a whole, the growth in numbers studying for sub-degree qualifications (described as 'other undergraduate' in Chart 3.3 below) has been slower than growth in first degree numbers especially in the 1960s and 1970s. As a result, the balance of higher education has shifted markedly towards the higher levels.

Chart 3.3 – UK higher education students (excluding Open University) by level of study (000s)

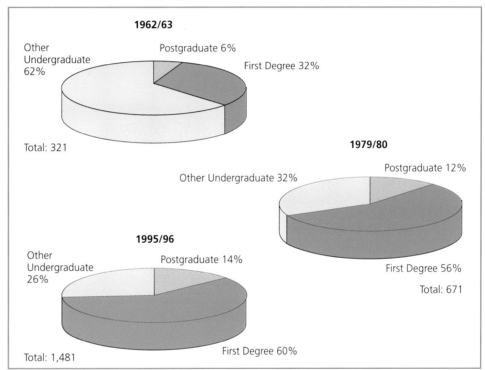

Source: DfEE

3.8 Of particular interest in a society committed to learning throughout life is the incidence of part-time study. Chart 3.4 shows that the overall balance between full and part-time study has not changed significantly over time, but students of the Open University now make up a substantial proportion of all part-time students. Within the totals, there has been a marked increase in the proportion of postgraduate students who study part-time. A high proportion of students who are studying part-time are in employment – some 90 per cent of those in our survey – although the proportion is much lower among Open University students.

Chart 3.4 – UK higher education students by mode of study (000s)

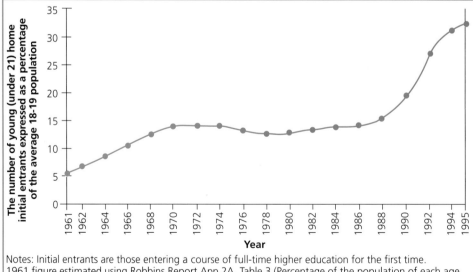

1962/63

UG = undergraduate
PG = postgraduate

Part-time UG & PG 37%

Open University 0%

Full-time UG & PG 63%

Total: 321

1979/80

Part-time UG & PG 28%

Open University 9%

Full-time UG & PG 63%

Total: 741

1995/96

Part-time UG & PG 28%

Open University 7%

Total: 1,597

Full-time UG & PG 65%

Source: DfEE

3.9   In the early 1960s attention focused primarily on young people who entered higher education straight from school. At that time, only one young person in eighteen entered full-time higher education. Today the figure is nearer to one in three for the country as a whole and around 45 per cent in Scotland and Northern Ireland.

Chart 3.5 – Higher education Age Participation Index (API) – GB Institutions

Notes: Initial entrants are those entering a course of full-time higher education for the first time.
1961 figure estimated using Robbins Report App.2A, Table 3 (Percentage of the population of each age receiving higher education GB Oct 1961).
Due to minor change in definition, the years 1961 to 1970 inclusive are not strictly comparable with later years.
Due to minor change in definition, years from 1980 onwards are not strictly comparable with earlier years.

Source: DfEE

Views on growth in higher education

3.10   Those who offered us evidence generally support, in principle, the expansion of higher education that has taken place. They see it as having responded to the needs and aspirations of individuals, contributing to the health of society, and as an economic necessity. There is some concern, however, that too high a proportion of students is aiming for a degree rather than a sub-degree qualification. Schools, colleges and employer organisations are concerned that potential students do not have the right kind of information about programmes and their outcomes to enable them to make good choices. Our conclusions about the future size of higher education are in Chapter 6.

Female students

3.11   An important element in the growth in higher education has been the increase in participation by women. The Robbins report foresaw growth in women's participation but, even by 1979/80, women made up only 37 per cent of students. Since then participation by women has increased rapidly so that they constituted 51 per cent of students in 1995/96. However, in 1996/97, only 39 per cent of first year students studying full-time for research degrees were women.[2]

Chart 3.6 – UK higher education students (excluding Open University) by gender (000s)

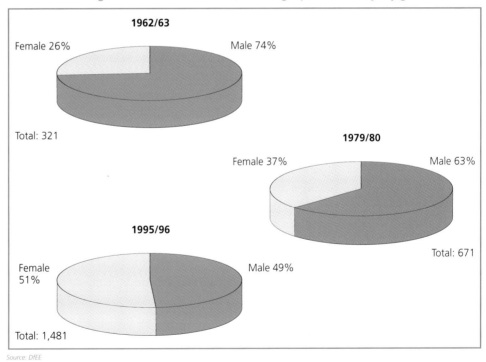

Source: DfEE

Mature students

3.12   The Robbins Committee's remit was confined to full-time higher education, and the main focus of their attention was on young entrants to higher education. In 1979/80 young students (those under the age of 21 on entry to an undergraduate programme, or under the age of 25 on entry to a postgraduate programme) were only just in the majority; by 1995/96, 58 per cent of entrants to higher education were mature. The majority of mature students study part-time.

Chart 3.7 – Entrants to higher education in Great Britain including
Open University (000s)

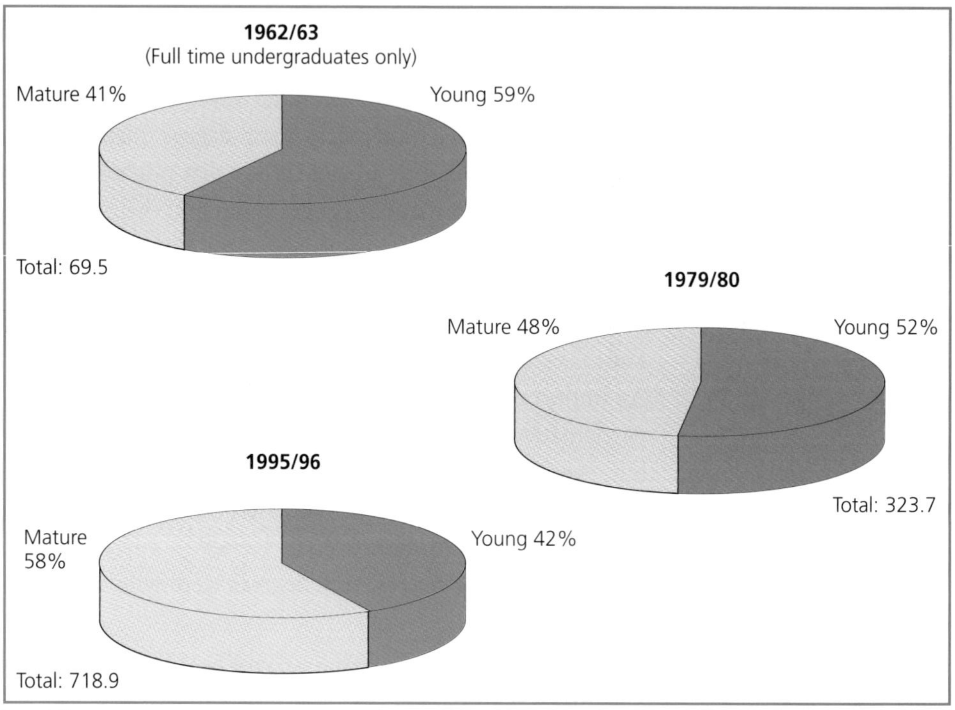

1962/63
(Full time undergraduates only)

Mature 41%   Young 59%

Total: 69.5

1979/80

Mature 48%   Young 52%

Total: 323.7

1995/96

Mature 58%   Young 42%

Total: 718.9

Source: DfEE

Students from ethnic minorities

3.13   In aggregate, students from ethnic minorities are more than proportionately
        represented in higher education, but their profile differs from that of white students: a
        greater proportion of them are mature students, and they are particularly concentrated
        in a few of the 1992 universities. Some individual ethnic minority groups are, however,
        still significantly under-represented in higher education. More information can be
        found in Report 5, 'Widening participation in higher education by ethnic minorities,
        women and alternative students'.

Students from socio-economic groups IV and V[3]

3.14   One characteristic identified in the Robbins report was the under-representation in
        higher education of the children of manual workers. Participation by young people
        from socio-economic groups IV and V (semi-skilled and unskilled) has increased in
        recent years. For example, the participation rate for group V has at least doubled
        between 1991/92 and 1995/96. But their participation rate is still only a fraction
        of that for the children of professional families. This, in part, reflects lower
        achievements at A level and equivalent for socio-economic groups IV and V.

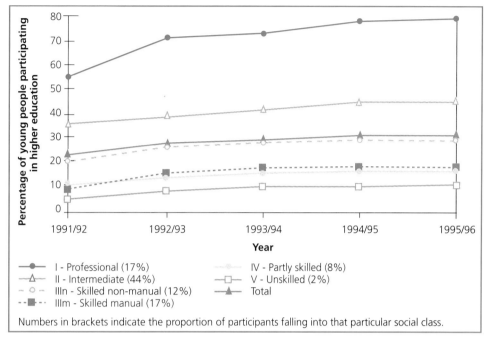

Chart 3.8 – Percentage participation rates for Great Britain by socio-economic group

Percentage of young people participating in higher education

Year

I - Professional (17%)	IV - Partly skilled (8%)
II - Intermediate (44%)	V - Unskilled (2%)
IIIn - Skilled non-manual (12%)	Total
IIIm - Skilled manual (17%)	

Numbers in brackets indicate the proportion of participants falling into that particular social class.

Source: DfEE

Notes:

(1) The API is the number of young (aged <21) home domiciled initial entrants to courses of HE in FE and HE institutions across Great Britain, expressed as the proportion of the average 18 to 19 year old GB population. Initial entrants are those entering full-time & sandwich undergraduate courses of HE for the first time.

(2) Acceptance data from the admissions agencies (UCCA, PCAS and UCAS) provided the distribution of initial entrants by social class.

(3) The 1991 census provided the population distribution by social class – the same distribution is used for all years.

Students with disabilities

3.15 It is difficult to assess how well students with disabilities are represented in higher education. About three per cent of first year students in 1996/97 declared a disability.[4] More information is given in Report 5 and Chapter 7.

Views on access to higher education

3.16 The pattern of participation in higher education was not a dominant theme in evidence. General satisfaction was expressed about the progress made by some groups in the population, but there is continuing concern about the poor representation of those from lower socio-economic groups and the potentially socially divisive effects of the great disparity in educational achievement between different groups in the population. Comments on women and students from ethnic minorities focused on their under-representation at the highest levels of study. Our conclusions about access to higher education for different sections of the population are in Chapter 7.

Entry qualifications

3.17 The traditional qualification for entry to degree study has been two or three GCE A levels (or five Highers in Scotland). These remain the most common form of entry qualification held by full-time undergraduate students. Despite the rapid increase in participation, the average points score for those who enter with A levels has remained broadly unchanged at around 18.[5] A recent study of A level standards over time by the

School Curriculum and Assessment Authority and the Office for Standards in Education concluded that, over the last ten years, in the three subjects investigated:

a) the level of demand had remained broadly the same;

b) the performance required for a given grade had remained broadly the same;

c) there had been a broadening of content so candidates had to be familiar with more material;

d) as a result, there had been reduced emphasis on some topics within subjects, such as reasoning and extended problem-solving in mathematics.[6]

3.18   As the study covered only three subjects – albeit major ones – it was too limited to allow general conclusions to be drawn, but the outcome provides no basis for concluding that entry via A level to higher education has become significantly easier. The combined effects of c) and d) mean, however, that there are subject areas where new entrants to higher education need additional preparation for specialised programmes.

3.19   More students than ever before now enter higher education with qualifications other than A levels or Highers, even though the traditional qualifications still predominate. In 1996/97, 60 per cent of full-time first year students studying for first degrees in higher education institutions had A levels, Highers or other equivalent academic qualifications, two per cent had vocational qualifications at that level, eight per cent already had qualifications at a higher level, four per cent had taken an Access course and 12 per cent had no or lower level qualifications. The highest qualification on entry of the remainder was not recorded.[7]

3.20   Not surprisingly, given that they are, on average, older and have work experience, part-time students have more diverse entry qualifications. The Open University, in particular, has shown that many mature students, with few or no prior educational qualifications, are capable of benefiting from higher education.

Views on the quality of entrants to higher education

3.21   Notwithstanding the evidence about A level standards and the maintenance of average points scores of higher education entrants, some of those who responded to our consultation exercise and many academic staff in our survey (Report 3: 'Academic staff in higher education; their experiences and expectations') express concern about the quality of higher education entrants. Nearly half of staff think that the quality of undergraduate entrants to their department has declined over the last five years. It is not clear whether these concerns relate to the students who are now entering with a wider range of qualifications, to a perceived decline in the quality of those with conventional qualifications, or both. The concerns are particularly strong in respect of certain subject areas. The engineering professional bodies are exercised about the quality of many undergraduate engineers and feel that too many students who would, in the past, have taken a Higher National Diploma are now encouraged to aim for a degree. The report on teacher education and training (Report 10) highlights the modest prior attainments of many of those being trained as teachers. Concerns about the quality of entrants and their implications for standards were a major theme in evidence. Our approach to standards is set out in Chapter 10.

Completion rates

3.22 Completion rates have remained high. Non-completion rates have been difficult to measure until recently because statistical records did not track individual students through the higher education system. Non-completion will become an increasingly difficult concept to measure if more students undertake higher education programmes in a flexible way, over a long period of time. Estimates from the Department for Education and Employment suggest that, for the pre-1992 universities and the 1992 universities in England, drop-out rates did not change significantly over the ten years up to 1994/95, the level ranging from 14 per cent to 18 per cent.[8]

3.23 High completion rates contribute to the UK having one of the highest first degree graduation rates in the world.

Chart 3.9 – Ratio of tertiary graduates to population at the typical age of graduation (times 100) by type of programme (1994)

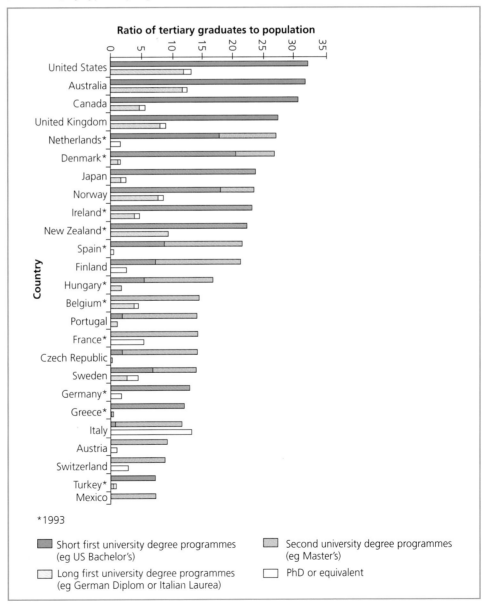

*1993

- ⬛ Short first university degree programmes (eg US Bachelor's)
- ☐ Long first university degree programmes (eg German Diplom or Italian Laurea)
- ▨ Second university degree programmes (eg Master's)
- ☐ PhD or equivalent

Source: OECD Database

Views on completion rates

3.24   The fact that the vast majority of entrants to higher education leave with a recognised award is a tribute to the quality and effectiveness of UK higher education. Many of those who offered us evidence identified the high completion rates in UK higher education as a strength. They are concerned, however, that inadequate funding threatens completion rates, because it reduces the academic support and guidance which institutions can give to students, and because students who receive inadequate financial support may spend too much time in paid employment, jeopardising their academic performance, or may give up higher education altogether.

Subject balance

3.25   Chart 3.10 shows that the balance between subjects studied by full-time students has changed over time. Because of changes in definitions in 1988, two separate sets of data are presented. Although all subjects have grown as total student numbers have grown, the lowest growth is in engineering and technology. The largest increase, in 'medicine', is attributable mainly to increases in the numbers studying subjects allied to medicine.

Chart 3.10 – Full-time UK students in higher education in Great Britain 1979/80 and 1987/88

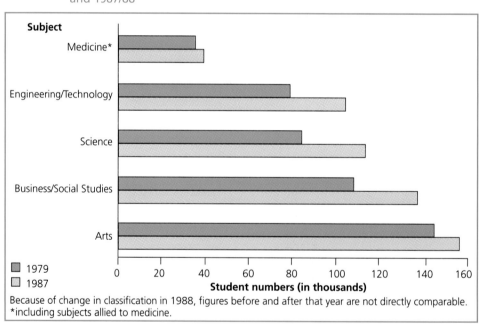

Because of change in classification in 1988, figures before and after that year are not directly comparable.
*including subjects allied to medicine.

Full-time UK students in higher education in Great Britain 1988/89 and 1995/96

Subject

Combined

Medicine*

Engineering/Technology

Science

Business/Social Studies

Arts

■ 1988
□ 1995

0   50   100   150   200   250
Student numbers (in thousands)

Because of change in classification in 1988, figures before and after that year are not directly comparable.
*including subjects allied to medicine.

Source: DfEE

3.26   The balance of subjects studied at first and higher education degree level in the UK is
similar to the pattern across the Organisation of Economic Co-operational
Development (OECD) countries, apart from a lower than average proportion who
have studied medicine and a higher than average proportion who have studied science
and mathematics.

Chart 3.11 – University degrees as a percentage of total degrees by subject category 1994

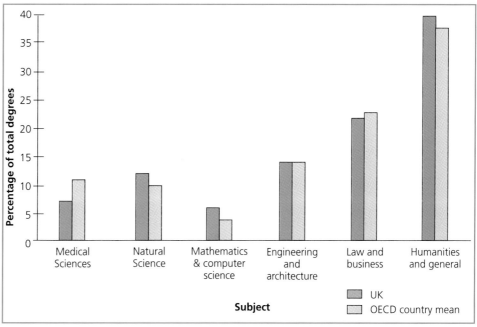

Source: OECD

3.27 Concerns about the balance between subjects of study were expressed by some groups, especially but not exclusively, employers and professional bodies. They perceive a shortage, in particular, of those studying certain branches of engineering and there is concern about the number entering the hard sciences. There are also worries about intakes to teacher training and modern languages programmes. These concerns parallel those about the quality of entrants. Generally speaking, less popular subjects have less demanding entry requirements. A small number of those giving evidence are sceptical as to whether certain vocational studies or new subject areas have a place in higher education. We discuss subject balance in Chapter 6.

Qualifications awarded

3.28 As student numbers have grown, the number obtaining degrees each year and the proportion of graduates in the population has increased. In 1994/95, more than 230,000 first degrees were awarded in the UK and nearly 60,000 sub-degree qualifications.[9] By 2001 there are expected to be just under 4 million graduates in the workforce, double the number in 1981.[10]

Staff

3.29 Higher education is a major UK employer. The Census of Employment recorded 382,000 people employed in higher education in 1995, 1.8 per cent of the total UK workforce in employment.

3.30 There is a shortage of other information about the full range of staff in higher education but Table 3.1 gives national estimates, based on a survey for the Committee of Vice-Chancellors and Principals (CVCP) which covered around 70 institutions.[11]

Table 3.1 – Total employment in higher education institutions by category 1996/97

Category	Full-time	Part-time	Totals
Senior management (Grade 6 and above or equivalent)	5,500	200	5,600
Other management	16,000	1,800	17,900
Teaching staff	71,000	20,900	91,900
Research staff	29,600	3,700	33,300
Secretarial and clerical	44,500	18,600	63,100
Technicians	26,700	3,100	29,800
Security	2,700	200	2,900
Janitorial and cleaning	5,800	18,600	24,400
Catering staff	2,000	5,600	7,600
Residence staff	4,400	8,300	12,600
Workshop etc assistants	1,600	200	1,900
Labourers, gardeners etc	2,900	400	3,300
All other staff	12,600	10,800	23,400
Total	**225,400**	**92,400**	**317,700**

Note: Components may not sum to totals because of rounding

3.31   These figures suggest that only just under 40 per cent of staff are defined, by institutions, as teachers or researchers. Although caution is necessary in interpreting the results, distinctive differences in the pattern of staffing between higher education and the economy as a whole can be identified. The survey for the CVCP produces the comparison shown in Chart 3.12.

Chart 3.12 – Distribution of employment by standard occupational classification

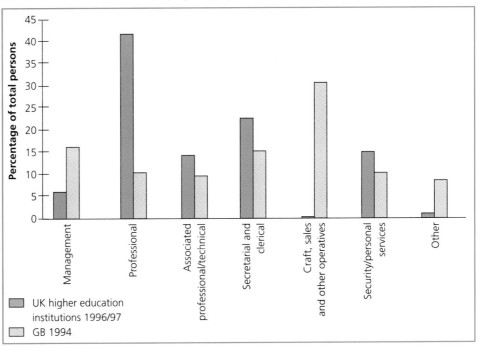

Source:

3.32   The high ratios of professional and associated staff in higher education, as compared with the country in general, are to be expected given the nature of higher education's activities. The relatively high proportion of security and personal services staff probably reflects the large physical estates which institutions have to maintain and the need to service student residences and other facilities. A relatively small proportion of higher education staff is designated as being in management compared to the nation as a whole. This may arise because there is scope for differences of interpretation over whether a senior academic, administrator or professional is regarded primarily as engaged in management or in professional activity. Figures for managerial staff in the Labour Force Survey may also appear high because many self-employed people are automatically classified as managers.

3.33   An analysis of academic staff numbers in higher education institutions is shown in Table 3.2.

Table 3.2 – Academic staff numbers in higher education 1995/96

Course	Full-time '000	Part-time '000	Total '000	Percentage
Male	74	6	80	70
Female	28	6	34	30
Total	103	12	115	100
Percentage	90	10	100	

Source: Higher Education Statistics Agency (HESA)
Note: Components may not sum to totals because of rounding

Use of staff time

3.34   Historical information on academic staff numbers across higher education as a whole does not exist. It is acknowledged though that the increase in academic staff numbers in higher education has been proportionately smaller than the increase in the number of students. Staff have faced increased teaching loads, larger teaching groups and, in many cases, new kinds of student. At the same time, the volume of research carried out has increased significantly. Increased requirements for accountability have led to new demands on staff. Delegation of budgets and management decisions to individual departments have required academics to take on new tasks. Taken together, these developments represent a significant increase in the volume of work for individual academics and a change in its nature. Administrative and support staff have faced the same kind of challenge.

3.35   The survey of academic staff carried out for the Robbins Committee found that, in the early 1960s, during term-time, university teachers spent 38 per cent of their time on teaching, guidance and examining, 28 per cent on research and 14 per cent on administration and meetings with the rest spent on a variety of professional activities.[12] Our survey of academic staff (Report 3), which covered the whole year not just term-time, showed that they now typically spend 35 per cent of their time on teaching, guidance and assessment, 20 per cent on research and 15 per cent on administration and management (30 per cent for professorial staff) with the rest spent on other professional activities. Very little time is spent explicitly on professional development.

Views on use of staff time

3.36   Our survey showed that academic staff are not content with the way they spend their time. They would like to spend less time on administration and management and to transfer the time to research. They would also like more time for professional development and to attend seminars and conferences. Over half of those doing research claim to be doing it outside normal working time. It is also evident from our survey that academic staff are concerned about the quality of support they can offer to students and feel it has declined over the last five years.

3.37   A high level of academic and other support for individual students has long been one of the characteristics of higher education in the UK and is a major factor in enabling this country to maintain good quality, relatively short degree programmes with high completion rates. The increasing strain on such support is therefore a matter of concern to many of those offering us evidence.

3.38   Many administrative and support staff feel that they have had to take on large additional amounts of work, are working far more than their contracted hours, and cannot keep up with what is expected of them.

3.39   In conversation with academics we sometimes found scepticism about the need for the present scale of management activity in higher education, and about its quality. Administrative and support staff are not sceptical about the place of management, but see a need for it to become more effective.

Staff development

3.40   Academics are all committed to keeping abreast of the latest research and ideas in their discipline, but few of them have the opportunity to keep at the forefront of developments in how to teach their subject. According to our survey of staff in higher education (Report 3), only just over half of academics have ever received any training in how to teach and over two thirds of those had received training only at the beginning of their careers. This inevitably means that a large proportion have had no training in, for example, the use of information technology for learning and teaching. Likewise, although many academic staff have significant management responsibilities – for example the financial and personnel responsibilities of a head of department – they rarely have the training to support these functions.

Views on staff development

3.41   A number of those offering us evidence commented on the irony that, in institutions devoted to learning and teaching and to the advancement of knowledge and understanding, so little attention is paid to equipping staff with advanced knowledge and understanding of the processes of learning and teaching. Many see a need to rectify this situation.

3.42   Administrative and support staff are also concerned that they have little access to training and feel that their potential is under-used as a result. Our recommendations on staff development are in Chapter 14.

Career structures

3.43   The terms on which staff are employed have changed over the last few years. Legislation enabled university statutes to be changed to remove academic tenure for new or promoted staff. In addition, an increasing proportion of staff have been recruited on fixed-term contracts. This has been mainly a response to research funding, which is often available only on a short term basis. The concerns about lack of career prospects and job insecurity among young researchers is well-documented. Our survey showed, however, that a significant minority of teaching staff are now employed on fixed-term contracts too (Report 3).

3.44   With certain exceptions, staff perceive promotion opportunities and financial rewards to be associated with long service or research excellence, and not with excellence in teaching, in spite of many institutions' stated commitment to consider research, teaching and administration.

3.45   There is a wide range of non-academic staff employed in higher education and, for some of them, the distinctions from academic staff are becoming increasingly blurred. Many such staff , for example librarians, technicians and computer support staff, are directly involved in guiding and supporting students. With the widespread introduction of modular programmes, administrative staff have taken on new tasks in guiding and tracking students through their choice of programmes.

3.46   Staff with entirely new skills and roles, for example in marketing or contract management, have also been recruited in recent years to support the more commercial orientation of at least some of higher education's activities. Our survey (Report 4: 'Administrative and support staff in higher education: their experiences and expectations') showed that administrative and support staff are frustrated by their lack of opportunity for career progression, the low regard in which administrative and support functions are held, and the feeling that they have responsibility without power.

Pay levels

3.47   Different groups offer different statistics about changes in academic pay levels, depending on which comparators they use. The Association of University Teachers suggests that, while academic salaries have remained largely unchanged in real terms since 1981, other comparable groups have seen increases of between 18 and 50 per cent. The Committee of Vice Chancellors and Principals observes that, while male university teachers' pay grew by 8.6 per cent in real terms between 1961 and 1993, non-manual male workers in general saw their pay increase by 37 per cent. The New Earnings Survey shows that male university teachers increased their pay premium over the average non-manual male worker very substantially between 1979 and 1981 but that it has declined markedly since then (Chart 3.13). The impact of the most recent pay settlement is not included in these figures.

Chart 3.13 – The pay premium for male university teaching professionals compared to all male non-manual employees

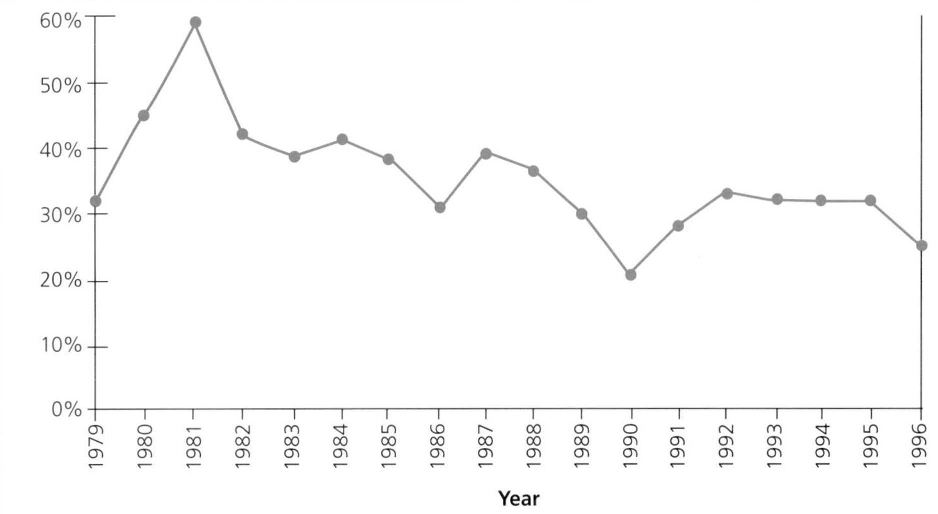

Note: There was a definitional change in 1991, with the inclusion of 'new university' teaching staff

Source: DfEE

3.48   Evidence about comparative pay movements for other staff in higher education is difficult to establish and assess. The higher education employers have recently commissioned a pay comparability study, the results of which were sent to us as we were completing our work. We refer to it in Chapter 14.

Views on pay levels

3.49   Whatever the difficulty in assessing comparative pay, there is no doubt that pay causes widespread dissatisfaction among higher education staff who highlight increased workloads and productivity. Among the academic staff whom we surveyed (Report 3), those who said that they were unlikely to stay in the profession until retirement age cited pay as the biggest single factor likely to make them leave, although this accounted for only 15 per cent of the total. Organisations representing staff in higher education all made strong representations to us about the inadequacy of pay levels. Institutions, as employers, are also concerned about pay levels which they see as having been held down by constraints in public funding. We make recommendations relating to pay determination in Chapter 14.

Learning and teaching

3.50   Students can choose from a much greater array of types of higher education programme now than at the time of the Robbins report. As knowledge has expanded, whole new subject areas (such as molecular biology) have opened up. Preparation for many occupations, for example the professions allied to medicine, now takes place partly in higher education. The recognition of the benefits of cross-disciplinary approaches, for example in area studies, has led to a rich new range of programmes and techniques. As encouraged by the Robbins report, higher education institutions have developed combined honours programmes, allowing students to study more than one subject in depth. The move to modularisation has offered students greater flexibility to combine course elements to build programmes which suit their individual needs and interests.

3.51 Increasingly, institutions are introducing the development of personal transferable skills as part of programmes and many of them mentioned the value of such activity in their evidence to us. Such activity has been spurred by the demands of employers and aided by initiatives such as Enterprise in Higher Education.[13]

3.52 A wider variety of modes of learning is now available. Sandwich programmes, incorporating an element of work experience, have been developed. The work of the Open University has transformed distance learning opportunities. Employers and professional bodies are working with higher education institutions to develop programmes, tailored to the needs of particular occupations or professions, which can largely be taken by students in the workplace.

Views on learning and teaching

3.53 The need for higher education to do more to develop a range of key skills in students, in addition to the cognitive capabilities traditionally associated with higher education, was a major theme of the evidence from employers, both in our own survey (Appendix 4: 'Consultation with employers') and in evidence from representative bodies. Roughly half the employers we surveyed are dissatisfied with the current level of skills exhibited by graduates, but there is little commonality in their concerns about particular skills. The largest single expression of dissatisfaction comes from the 25 per cent who would like graduates to have better communication skills. In our survey of students themselves, the majority feel that their skills have improved during their time in higher education, with the notable exception of numeracy.

3.54 The strongest message conveyed to us by employers in the course of all our work is that they would like more students to have work experience. This is seen as particularly valuable by small firms who cannot afford training or support for a long induction period. They need new members of staff to be able to operate effectively in the workplace almost immediately. While a sandwich year for all is seen as the ideal, the difficulty for both institutions and employers of securing it is recognised. Other less extensive alternatives are endorsed. Students, especially those who have experienced a sandwich year, and senior academic staff express similar views.

3.55 There is widespread recognition among those who offered us evidence that students need to be placed at the centre of the learning process, but less conviction that this happening at the moment. Nonetheless, two thirds of students in our survey (Report 2: 'Full and part-time students in higher education: their experiences and expectations') say that their time at university or college has lived up to their expectations whilst only one in eight say that it has not done so.

Teaching methods

3.56 The learning environment of students today is quite unlike that in the 1960s. The dramatic increase in student numbers, which has not been matched by a proportionate increase in funding, staffing or other resources, has resulted in increased class sizes, decreased class contact time for students, and an increase in students studying off campus. Despite these major changes, the traditional teaching methods of higher education still predominate. The teaching methods experienced by the highest proportions of students in our survey were lectures (98 per cent); seminars and tutorials (91 per cent); essays (82 per cent); and projects and dissertations (82 per cent).

3.57   Although lectures still predominate, our research (Report 3) showed that over the last five years staff have been widening their repertoire of teaching methods.

Table 3.3 – Changes in teaching methods over last five years

Percentage of staff reporting increased use of teaching methods	%
Use of videos	47
Use of distance learning	24
Use of interactive course work	51
Use of multi-media	59
More project work by students	61
More team/group work by students	60
More team/group teaching by staff	37

3.58   The methods of teaching which the fewest students in our survey experienced were individual sessions with teaching staff (30 per cent), work placements as part of a sandwich course (15 per cent), and work experience (16 per cent). These relatively low percentages reflect pressure on resources both in institutions and in the work place. It is hardly surprising therefore that full-time, undergraduate students have very limited appreciation of the environment of employment.

Views on teaching methods

3.59   Students in our survey (Report 2) generally feel that the teaching they receive is well-prepared whether it is presented in the form of lectures, tutorials or seminars. There is rather less satisfaction with computer-based learning packages. Many students are, however, critical of the scale of academic support available to them and especially about the feedback they get on their work. This is a matter of particular concern to part-time students. Our survey of academic staff (Report 3) found that around half of those taking small group sessions feel that the numbers of students is too high and two fifths of the students we surveyed would like more opportunity to learn in small groups.

Resources for learning

3.60   Libraries received little attention in the Robbins report which suggests that they were not a significant cause for concern at that time. It is different today. The expansion of student numbers, the rapid increase in the costs of printed materials, changes in teaching and learning methods, and the additional opportunities and costs presented by information technology have led to the adequacy of library provision becoming a major concern. There is pressure on space and on the supply of books. In some institutions students have limited access to popular texts, supplemented by heavy use of reprographic facilities. In response to these concerns, the Funding Bodies set up a committee, under the chairmanship of Professor Sir Brian Follett, which reported in 1993, and made recommendations on the need for additional library space, the potential role of information technology and the need for collaboration.[14] Even so, nearly half the students in our survey (Report 2) were dissatisfied with library provision. The level of complaint was higher at the 1992 universities and other higher education institutions than in the pre-1992 universities.

3.61   The use of communications and information technology (C&IT) as a tool for teaching and learning has increased rapidly in the last few years. In SuperJANET, the UK has the most advanced academic information technology network in the world. Various projects and initiatives have been carried out, with varying degrees of success, to try to exploit the potential of new technology for learning and teaching. The largest of these, the Teaching and Learning Technology Programme (TLTP), has involved investment of over £32 million by the Funding Bodies to launch over 70 projects to develop computer-based teaching and learning course materials. This has had some beneficial outcomes, and students have reacted positively to the flexibility offered, but communications and information technology are far from being embedded in the day-to-day practice of learning and teaching in most higher education institutions. One barrier is the shortage of staff skilled in developing computer-based course materials, but the main reason is that many academics have had no training and little experience in the use of communications and information technology as an educational tool. Our survey (Report 2) showed that nearly all full-time students have access to the computing facilities at their institution. Their concerns are not so much about access as about the level of support that is available in using the information technology facilities.

Quality of higher education

3.62   The pre-1992 universities have always had their own degree awarding powers. Responsibility for maintaining and assuring the standards of awards has rested with the institutions themselves, assisted by the external examiner system. Until the establishment of the current Funding Councils, there was no external scrutiny of the quality of programmes offered by pre-1992 universities. The polytechnics and colleges of higher education did not have degree awarding powers. Students from these institutions received degrees of the Council for National Academic Awards, set up in response to a recommendation of the Robbins Committee. Programmes at these institutions were inspected by Her Majesty's Inspectors.

3.63   As a result of the 1992 Further and Higher Education Act, there are now two major forms of quality assurance in the UK known as 'audit', carried out by the Higher Education Quality Council, and 'assessment', carried out by the Funding Councils, which cover all higher education institutions. These functions have included a quality enhancement component. The two activities are now being made the responsibility of a single body, the new Quality Assurance Agency (with the exception of assessment in Scotland which remains with the Scottish Higher Education Funding Council). In addition, professional bodies conduct their own accreditation arrangements for particular vocational professional programmes. Higher National provision – Higher National Certificates (HNCs) and Higher National Diplomas (HNDs) – are regulated by Edexcel and the Scottish Qualifications Authority (SQA).[15]

3.64　There has been a clear trend over time, though varying between subjects, for institutions to award an increasing proportion of first and upper second degrees. There are variations in the proportion of higher class degrees awarded by different institutions. One explanation put to us was that degree class is now increasingly dependent on continuous assessment, in which students perform better than in terminal examinations.

Views on quality and standards

3.65　Many of those giving evidence expressed concerns both about the quality of students' experiences and about the standards of degrees. A persistent strand of criticism, which might be characterised as 'more means worse', surfaces when higher education expands. As already mentioned, academic staff are concerned about the amount of support, and therefore quality of experience, which they can offer to students. The students in our survey are, by contrast, generally content with their higher education, but the National Union of Students articulates more concern about the quality of the students' experience, especially the level of support and guidance on academic and non-academic matters.

3.66　There are differences of views over standards. Although most institutions believe national standards should be maintained, there are some, particularly among the pre-1992 universities, who argue that standards differ across the sector and that this is an inevitable consequence of a mass system of higher education which should be formally recognised.

3.67　Employers expressed strong views to us about standards. The Institute of Directors was particularly strong in its comments, suggesting that the growth in participation seen over the last decade is not compatible with the maintenance of standards. Other employer organisations expressed similar views, but less forcefully. The Confederation of British Industry, while expressly supporting wider participation, is concerned that the intellectual demands made on some students (most commonly those of the 1992 universities) may be inadequate and that others (most commonly those of the pre-1992 universities) may not have their generic skills adequately developed. The concerns about standards are greatest in the areas of engineering and science.

The overseas reputation of UK higher education

3.68　Higher education institutions in the United Kingdom have long attracted great respect around the world. The UK remains one of the more popular destinations for students wanting to study overseas. However, there have been a few worrying reports of some loss of confidence overseas about the quality and standards of UK awards. A number of factors could account for this. The increasing trend to franchise provision to overseas institutions has led to some problems where a very small number of institutions have embarked on such ventures without a sufficient understanding of the risks or of how to ensure quality and standards at a distance. It has been suggested that the expansion of UK higher education has weakened arguments about its highly selective entry route supporting the three or four year honours route (Report 11: 'The development of a framework of qualifications: relationship with continental Europe'). Whatever the principal cause of concern, any justified criticisms of UK higher education would be damaging if the cause were not dealt with.

Research

3.69   The mediaeval universities, from which some of the UK's oldest universities are directly descended and from which many other of our higher education institutions take their traditions, were self-governing communities of scholars. The academics in them pursued studies of their own choice and made a living by teaching students. The functional link between teaching and research was regarded as sacrosanct until the expansion of the university system in 1992. Although the number of universities approximately doubled then and student numbers have grown rapidly, funding for research in higher education has not increased correspondingly.

3.70   The large increase in the number of academics has called into question the assumption that all academics should conduct research. The ranks of academic researchers, from PhD students to professors, have expanded greatly. Robbins identified some 22,500 graduate teaching staff involved in research.[16] In 1992, around 43,000 academic staff were entered for the Research Assessment Exercise; by 1996, this had risen to 48,000.

3.71   Further pressure has come from the increase in the cost of research, particularly in the field of science and technology, which has risen faster than the rate of inflation. Together these factors have served to increase the competition for research funds.

Funding of research

3.72   Overall UK spending on research is over £14 billion, with higher education spending making up nearly a fifth of the total.

Table 3.4 – Gross expenditure on research and development in the UK – 1994-95

Source of Funds	Higher education	Industry	Govern-ment	Research Councils	Private non-profit	£ million Total
Funding Councils	1,017		–	–		1,017
Research Councils	570		39	579	85	1,274
Government departments	153	1,130	959	134	51	2,427
Higher education institutions	109	–	–	2		110
UK industry	157	6,841	166	31	213	7,407
UK based charities	354	–	9	38	120	521
Overseas, EU & other	199	1,559	29	35	34	1,857
Total	**2,559**	**9,529**	**1,202**	**819**	**504**	**14,613**

Source: Office for National Statistics (ONS)
Note: Components may not sum to totals because of rounding

3.73 Government expenditure (in real terms) on research and development has decreased since 1985-86. Within this, expenditure by the higher education Funding Bodies and Research Councils has risen by 14.5 per cent, while expenditure by civil departments and on defence (some of which is spent on contracts with higher education institutions) has decreased by 34 per cent.

International comparisons

3.74 Research expenditure in the UK compares unfavourably with competitor countries. Table 3.5 shows that of the G7 countries, the UK – from all sources public and private – spends the third lowest proportion on research as a percentage of Gross Domestic Product (GDP) and its spend on civil research and development is even lower. The UK Government makes one of the smallest contributions of the G7 countries.

Table 3.5 – International comparisons of expenditure on research and development (R&D)

Country	Total spend on R&D as % of GDP 1994	Total spend on R&D as % of GDP – civil only 1994	Government spend on R&D as % of total spend 1993
Japan	2.7(1993)	2.7(1993)	19.6
USA	2.5	2.0	39.2
Germany	2.4	2.4	37.0
France	2.4	2.0	44.3
UK	2.2	1.9	32.7
Canada	1.5	n/a	42.4
Italy	1.2	1.2	45.9

Source: Office for National Statistics (ONS)

3.75   The investment which is made in higher education is used extremely effectively. A report by the Office of Science and Technology shows that: with only about one per cent of the world's population, the UK carries out 5.5 per cent of the world's research effort; the UK science base is the most cost-effective producer of research in the world, as measured by citations per unit of expenditure; in terms of the number of contributions to publications and the number of citations in science, engineering and medicine, the UK comes second only to the US.[17] It also comes second to the US in the number of major prizes and medals won.

3.76   Given the time lag from the conduct of research to publication and citation, today's success is related to past expenditure. More recently there has been a decline in the UK's relative citation rate. This could be a result of the maturing, and therefore relative advancement of science systems elsewhere in the world, or it could relate to current concerns about the research infrastructure in UK universities. There is a general perception that the UK is weaker in applying the results of research than many of its competitors.

Research infrastructure

3.77   The last decade or so has seen an erosion of the nation's research equipment and infrastructure. A recent survey of the state of the equipment in universities found it to be less than adequate.[18] It estimated that £474 million will be needed over the next five years to bring the equipment in the public research base up to a level which will allow it to carry out the volume of research expected to be funded. Nearly 80 per cent of departments reported important areas in which researchers were unable to perform critical experiments because of insufficient equipment funding. Of equipment used for research, 17 per cent had poor or very poor capability, and 60 per cent of the stock had a remaining useful life of five years or less. In particular, top-rated departments accounted for 74 per cent of the need.

3.78   Concerns about equipment and about laboratories and other facilities were reflected strongly in the evidence we received from higher education institutions, some employers and professional bodies.

Research selectivity

3.79   From the mid 1980s it has become accepted that support from the higher education Funding Bodies for research should be allocated selectively between institutions, according to excellence. The Research Assessment Exercises, the first of which took place in 1986 and the fourth in 1996, have been used as the basis for determining excellence. The results have been used over time to concentrate funds on the highest quality departments. In England, for example, five universities received almost one third of the available research funding. The Research Councils also distribute their project grants on a competitive basis, according to judgements from other experts in the field drawn from the UK and abroad. About 50 per cent of Research Council grants are awarded to individuals in 12 universities.

3.80 Most of those submitting evidence to us support the principle of selectivity although some feel that it has not gone far enough, and others that research funding should be more evenly distributed, so that all academics can use research to support their teaching. There are criticisms of the way the Research Assessment Exercise is carried out, in particular that it discourages interdisciplinary research, promotes undue competition instead of collaboration, does not recognise adequately new areas of research, and promotes the use of time and effort for research at the expense of teaching.

Partnerships with industry

3.81 Private sector support for research in universities has risen steadily for the past ten years to £169 million in 1995/96. This is only a small proportion of total research and development expenditure by industry, but this is not surprising given that only 6 per cent of industry's spending is on basic research. The pre-1992 universities have had the most significant growth in industrial research income with a real increase of over 80 per cent in ten years from 1984-85 to 1993-94.

3.82 In their evidence, institutions told us that they are keen to build on this. Several are keen to develop closer links with small and medium sized enterprises (SMEs) but are concerned about the costs involved. For their part, SMEs find it hard to relate to higher education institutions which can seem large, difficult to access and concerned with the long term rather than an SME's immediate concerns. A number of institutions, employers and representative bodies also described successful approaches to overcoming these barriers. Our recommendations on support for different kinds of research are in Chapter 11.

Institutions

3.83 The number and type of institutions offering higher education have changed markedly over 35 years. The Robbins report recorded the existence of 31 universities. Higher education was also provided in some other institutions, principally colleges for the education and training of teachers and institutions of further education. Following the Robbins report, a number of additional universities were created in the 1960s. The same decade saw the establishment of the first polytechnics and of the Open University, now the largest university in the UK as measured by total student enrolments.

3.84 Today there are 176 higher education institutions in the UK of which 115 are titled universities (which include the various constituent parts of both the University of London and the University of Wales).[19] In addition, there are many further education institutions offering higher education programmes, mainly part-time sub-degree programmes. A small number of institutions of higher education are not funded by the higher education Funding Bodies, of which the best known is the University of Buckingham. Historically, the churches have made a contribution to education at all levels and in higher education through 19 colleges with almost 60,000 students.

Views on the number and distribution of institutions

3.85 There was no single clear view put to us about the current pattern of higher education institutions. We heard concerns about certain parts of the country which do not currently have ready access to higher education and suggestions that there should be new universities established or extensions of existing ones into new geographical areas. Others mentioned the apparent inefficiency of having several institutions in some towns and cities. In Northern Ireland there is concern that some 40 per cent of students need to come to Great Britain to receive higher education. Some institutions feel that the criteria for determining the status and titles of institutions are too restrictive. Others are concerned that there is not sufficient control. We discuss these issues in Chapter 16.

Funding and organisation

3.86 Higher education institutions were established in different ways at different times, and their legal status reflects this diversity. Some older universities were established by statute, and some by Royal Charter. The polytechnics and colleges of higher education, formerly under the control of local authorities, are now higher education corporations or companies limited by guarantee. Some institutions, especially those which began as teacher training colleges, have a denominational and charitable basis.

3.87 As a result of the Education Reform Act 1998, the polytechnics and colleges were removed from local authority control and became corporate bodies in their own right. In 1992, 'the binary line' between universities and polytechnics was removed and a new higher education sector was created. Higher education funding councils with responsibility for funding universities and colleges of higher education were established in England, Scotland and Wales to replace the Universities Funding Council and the Polytechnics and Colleges Funding Council. A Northern Ireland Higher Education Council was established to advise the Department of Education Northern Ireland, which provides funding for the universities there.

3.88 Further education colleges in England, Scotland and Wales have also been removed from local authorities and set up as corporations in their own right. Funding arrangements for higher education programmes in these colleges vary in different parts of the UK.

3.89 A number of institutions of both higher and further education put the case for a greater commonality of approach to the funding of further and higher education – with some referring to a preference for a tertiary approach covering further and higher education. The weight of opinion differed in different parts of the country with stronger support for such an approach in Scotland, Wales and Northern Ireland. Our recommendations on funding bodies are in Chapter 22 and Appendix 1.

Diversity

3.90 Institutions of higher education have different profiles of activity. At the risk of over-simplification, universities at one end of the spectrum can be characterised as more heavily engaged in research; having a higher proportion of postgraduate students; and more selective entry requirements for undergraduate students; and playing a predominantly national or international role. Those at the other end tend to concentrate on teaching activities; have a higher proportion of sub-degree students, and to promote the access of non-conventional students; and focus on serving the locality or region. There is a tendency for the pre-1992 and 1992 universities to be concentrated towards opposite ends of the spectrum but there is great and increasing variation, not only between institutions but also between departments within one university. Colleges of higher education are typically smaller and cover a more limited range of subjects than a typical university.

3.91 Most of the growth in higher education student numbers in the last few years has been concentrated in the 1992 universities, colleges of higher education and colleges of further education.

Views on diversity

3.92 Since the abolition of the binary line and the introduction of Funding Councils covering all higher education institutions, there is concern that all institutions are becoming more like each other with a consequent loss of diversity. This has been attributed in part to the funding methodologies for research and teaching, and in part to some convergence of institutional ambitions. All higher education institutions entered the last Research Assessment Exercise, because it is one of the few opportunities for securing additional funding, but many received little or no financial return from it. There are few funding incentives to encourage teaching excellence or activities such as support for local economies.

Funding of higher education

3.93 In 1995-96 total expenditure by higher education institutions was over £10 billion which represented about 1.4 per cent of Gross Domestic Product (GDP). Chart 3.14 shows how public expenditure on higher education by the education departments and Research Councils has increased in real terms by around 45 per cent since 1976.

Chart 3.14 – Public expenditure on higher education in the UK (1995-96 prices)

£ billion

Maintenance and loans
Capital expenditure
Recurrent expenditure & fees

Financial year beginning

Notes: Includes recurrent and capital grants to institutions, publicly funded tuition fees, funding from Research Councils, expenditure on student maintenance grants and net expenditure on student loans.

Source: DfEE

3.94   Chart 3.15 shows how the proportion of GDP devoted to public expenditure on higher education has varied over time. Broadly the same picture emerges from an examination of expenditure as a share of government expenditure or as a share of all education expenditure.

Chart 3.15 – Public expenditure on higher education in the UK as a percentage of GDP

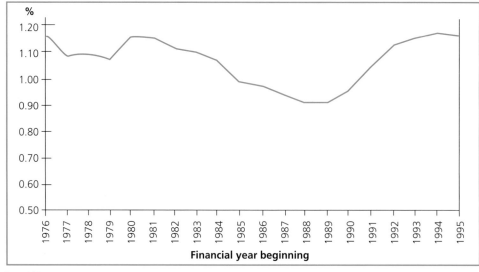

%

1.20
1.10
1.00
0.90
0.80
0.70
0.60
0.50

Financial year beginning

Source: DfEE

3.95   Concern about funding, especially on the part of higher education institutions, was one of the main factors which led to the establishment of our Committee. While growth in student numbers has been accompanied by real growth in total public expenditure on higher education, the level of public funding per student (measured in constant prices) has fallen since at least 1976. Chart 3.16 shows that public funding per student in higher education institutions has fallen by more than 40 per cent since 1976. If the further reductions in the public expenditure plans up to 1999-2000 were added, the cumulative reduction would be around 50 per cent.

Chart 3.16 – Index of public funding per student for higher education 1976-7 to 1995-6

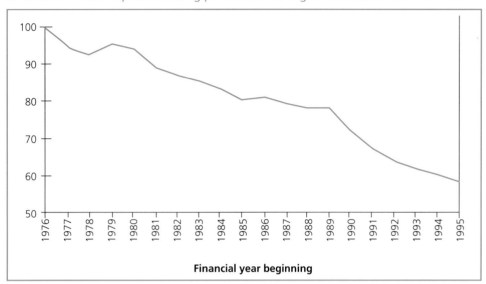

Financial year beginning

Source: DfEE

3.96   While a reduction in unit funding was intended by the Government, institutions themselves contributed to it when, in response to funding incentives, they opted to recruit additional students at lower than average levels of unit funding to maximise their overall income. In response to continuing tight public expenditure allocations for higher education, a number of institutions have recently been considering whether to charge individual undergraduate students supplementary fees.

3.97   Though higher education in the UK is widely perceived as substantially publicly funded, private funding is a significant and growing feature, currently contributing around a third of the income of higher education institutions (see Table 18.1).

3.98   In 1995, 140 institutions reported a surplus or break-even while 41 reported a deficit and the sector as a whole had a surplus of £237 million.[20] In 1996 the number in surplus had declined to 115 while the number in deficit had increased to 66 and the surplus for the sector as a whole had reduced to £112 million. This is equivalent to only just over one per cent of income in that year. The financial position of institutions in different parts of the UK varies as shown in Table 3.6.

Table 3.6 – Income and expenditure by UK country

| Location of institution | Financial Year 1995-1996 | | | |
	Income £ billion	Expenditure £ billion	Surplus/deficit £ billion	%
England	8,745	8,637	108	1.2%
Northern Ireland	220	226	-6	-2.7%
Scotland	1,225	1,221	5	0.4%
Wales	521	515	5	1.0%
Total	**10,711**	**10,599**	**112**	**1.1%**

Source: HESA
Note: Components may not sum to total because of rounding

International comparisons

3.99   International comparisons of expenditure are complex. Chart 3.17 suggests that the UK spends rather a low proportion of gross domestic product (GDP) on higher education. But the UK figures do not include private expenditure on higher education. If this were included the UK figure would probably be nearer to the average at least among European Union countries.

Chart 3.17 – Total expenditure from public, private and international sources for tertiary education institutions plus public subsidies to households

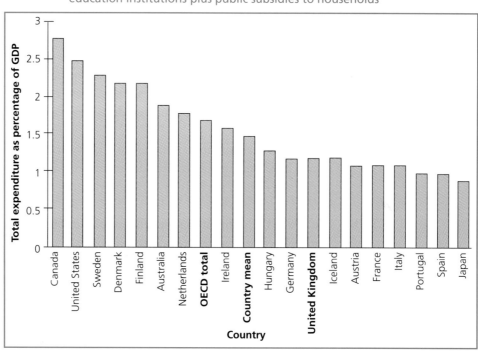

Source: OECD Database

Views on the funding of higher education

3.100   Higher education institutions were very clear in all their evidence to us that additional funding for higher education is needed. They argue that they have improved their cost-effectiveness greatly over several years and that any further improvements would damage the quality of provision. Similar views are expressed by many others who offered us evidence, but some employer organisations and the administrative and support staff in our survey (Report 4) do see scope for the more effective use of existing resources. Studies by the National Audit Office and by the Funding Councils have indicated opportunities in some areas of activity.

3.101   There are widespread concerns that, with financial pressures, institutions have been forced to defer capital investment in equipment and buildings and maintenance, with consequent damage to the infrastructure, and that recent sharp cuts in public support for capital investment will make the position worse. The reductions implied by the current public expenditure plans, which require further substantial cuts in unit funding over the next two years, are a source of major concern in institutions. A number of institutions told us that they are embarking on programmes of redundancies in anticipation.

3.102   Academic staff also see the need for additional funding, and express particular concerns about the limited time they have for research, the inadequate support they can give students and pay levels. Our views on the funding requirements of higher education are summarised in Chapter 17.

Funding routes

3.103   Public funding for institutions flows through a variety of routes.

3.104   Research funding comes in the form of block grants from the Funding Bodies, project grants from the Research Councils, and contracts from government departments and other public bodies. The balance of funding responsibility between block grant and Research Council grants was altered in 1992 and corresponding transfers of funds between them were made.

3.105   Funding for teaching comes mainly from the various government Funding Bodies in the form of block grants, and from local authorities (who are reimbursed by central government) for fees for students who receive mandatory grants. The balance between the two streams of funding has changed over time as the Government has used them as an instrument to influence institutional behaviour. Generally, a greater proportion of funding has flowed through student fees when expansion of the system was sought, and a smaller proportion when consolidation was sought. More recently, the Teacher Training Agency has been established as the source of funding for initial teacher training in England and some institutions have entered contracts with health authorities for the provision of education in nursing.

3.106   Institutions are concerned about the complexities of interacting with a number of public funding bodies which have different accountability arrangements.

Student financial support

3.107   Financial support for students varies widely. The mandatory awards system, which provides financial support towards tuition fees and living costs for mostly full-time undergraduate students, was designed in the late 1950s for an elite system in which a relatively small number of young people were assumed to study full-time while living away from home. The tuition fee element of the mandatory award is currently provided on a non-means tested basis, but up to the early 1970s it was means tested. Parents with a certain level of income were expected to contribute to their student children's fees although the fees were not at that time particularly high as the majority of tuition costs were met through various forms of publicly financed grant to institutions.

3.108   The element of the mandatory award which supports student living costs has always been means tested. Around a third of students receive no maintenance grant because their family income is above the cut-off level, around a third receive a full grant, and the remainder receive a partial grant.

3.109   Since 1991, the grant element of maintenance support has been progressively reduced and replaced by access to a loan which is available on a non-means tested basis. The overall balance between loan and grant reached 50:50 in 1996/97. The take-up of loans was low at first, but has increased as loans have over time made up more of the total package of available support.

3.110   Taking grant and loans together, the level of support for student living costs is much lower now than when mandatory student grants were first introduced in the 1960s. Total support from grants and loans is, however, now broadly at its 1979 levels, as measured against retail prices. Students are nonetheless finding it harder to make ends meet. Most students are no longer entitled to claim social security or housing benefits or other linked benefits, such as free prescriptions. Growth in student numbers has increased competition for accommodation in the vicinity of higher education institutions, driving up rents. At the same time, institutions have been precluded from subsidising student accommodation from their Funding Body grants. Increases in student support have been linked to increases in prices, while earnings have been increasing faster, so students have become poorer relative to the population in general.

3.111   Support for part-time and postgraduate students is far less comprehensive. They have their tuition costs subsidised through the grants paid to institutions by the Funding Bodies, but the majority of them have to pay tuition fees. Only in a few cases are they eligible for publicly financed assistance with the fees, although many of the part-time students in our survey (Report 2) received assistance from their employers. To fill some of the gaps in support, there are Career Development Loans. These are operated by commercial banks, with some public subsidy of the interest rate while the student is studying and with a limited guarantee against default. Most part-time and postgraduate students have to meet their own living costs without public assistance, although some may be able to claim social security benefits.

Views on support for students

3.112   We received many expressions of concern about the inadequacy of financial support for students. Students are concerned that many of them live in poverty, are forced to seek employment for excessive hours in term-time to the detriment of their studies and that some accumulate large debts, not just to the Student Loans Company but to commercial lenders as well.

3.113   We received representations from students and others that the current financial arrangements for supporting part-time students are inequitable, that postgraduate students need access to more financial support and that certain students, for example in dance, drama and alternative medicine, who currently have to pay all or most of their own tuition and living costs are unfairly disadvantaged relative to other students. Our recommendations on student financial support are in Chapters 7, 20 and 21.

Conclusion

3.114   By international standards, UK higher education has generally remained in good shape until now. The OECD review team which studied the UK recently was impressed by the strengths of the system and by its responsiveness.[21] The team also commended the openness and vigour of debate on future policy directions. But there are undoubtedly severe strains in the system which must be addressed urgently if UK higher education is to maintain its quality and international standing.

3.115   In our view, the Government was right to expand higher education between 1988 and 1993. There should be no going back on it. The expansion opened up opportunities to many more people who could benefit from higher education, and kept the UK in the same league as our main competitors in terms of highly educated people in the workforce. The expansion was, however, much faster than the Government had initially envisaged and there was insufficient thought about the potential effects of a progressively reducing unit of funding.

3.116   In effect, the Government committed itself to expansion without ensuring that funding could be made available to support that expansion in the long term. There was scope for institutions to use resources more efficiently and effectively and they have done so. The policy of incremental reductions in the funding per student has, however, not always been conducive to strategic consideration of new ways of delivering higher education which might be both more cost effective and better suited to the current range of students in higher education. Short term needs have driven out long term investment for the future. The results include a backlog of maintenance and inadequate infrastructure for research. Competition between institutions has led to improvements in efficiency, sometimes at the expense of collaboration and co-operation. Student support arrangements reflect past participation patterns rather than current or future ones, and potentially distort students' choices because they subsidise certain patterns of study more than others.

3.117   As the system was enlarged, with strong competition between institutions for students, there was recognition that this would put pressure on teaching quality. Although new quality assurance arrangements were introduced, the systems were burdensome and did not in general pay enough attention to maintaining standards. Neither alternative progression routes nor qualifications for a more diverse range of students have been fully established, running the risk that students are encouraged to embark on programmes for which they are not suited. Abolition of the distinction between universities and polytechnics, and the introduction of a common approach to funding, was necessary to allow all to compete on a level playing field, but the retention of large differences in funding levels which reflect history rather than current needs, and a policy of rewarding excellence in only a limited range of activities, particularly research, has encouraged all institutions to try to achieve in those activities.

3.118   The recommendations in this report are designed to deal with these problems, as well as to equip higher education to be able to respond flexibly to new challenges over the next 20 years.

Chapter 4

The wider context

The changing context for higher education

4.1 In this chapter we explore some of the most significant changes outside higher education since the Robbins report, which help to explain how and why higher education has developed as it has. We then explore the implications of potential changes over the 20 year timescale of our terms of reference for the future development of higher education. We look at the impact of:
- increasing economic integration across the world;
- changes in the labour market;
- the changing structure of the United Kingdom (UK) economy;
- public finances;
- family finances;
- new communications and information technology;
- social and cultural changes;
- demographic patterns;
- environmental changes;
- school and further education;
- developments in higher education elsewhere in the world.

4.2 In doing so, we do not accept a purely instrumental approach to higher education. Its distinctive character must lie in the independent pursuit of knowledge and understanding. But higher education has become central to the economic wellbeing of nations and individuals. The qualities of mind that it develops will be the qualities that society increasingly needs to function effectively. Knowledge is advancing so rapidly that a modern competitive economy depends on its ability to generate that knowledge, engage with it and use it to effect. Above all the country must enable people, in large numbers and throughout life, to equip themselves for a world of work which is characterised by change. Our examination of the future of higher education must therefore cover the changing context in which it will be operating.

4.3 Many of those who enter higher education towards the end of our twenty year time horizon will still be active workers and citizens well into the second half of the next century. We recognise the hazards of attempting to foresee what the world will be like over this timescale. We have taken account of the advice offered to us by government departments in our terms of reference and in their evidence, we have consulted extensively about the developments which others foresee and we have looked at international evidence. This chapter summarises our views on the aspects which we believe are most significant.

4.4 We start with a review of the changing economic context and, in particular, three features of it:
- increasing international economic integration;

■ the changing nature of the labour market in the United Kingdom;

■ the pace, nature and unpredictability of change in the nature of the UK economy.

Increasing economic integration across the world

4.5   Looking back, while the UK has doubled its national income since the time of Robbins, other advanced economies have grown more quickly. We have become relatively poorer.

Table 4.1 – Comparisons of Gross Domestic Product (GDP): 1963–1996

	GDP Per Head 1995: US dollars Current prices and purchasing power parities	Average annual percentage growth rates of GDP 1963–1996
Japan	25,300	5.20
United States	23,400	3.83
Germany	21,900	3.11
France	21,800	3.16
Australia	18,600	3.83
United Kingdom	17,800	2.33

Source: Organisation for Economic Co-operative and Development (OECD)

4.6   This leads to something of a paradox for higher education: on the one hand, the nation feels itself to be poorer and therefore less able to afford to fund higher education; on the other, as the economic necessity for high level education and skills increases, so does the need to maximise the proportion of the population with such education and skills.

4.7   Looking ahead, it seems reasonable to expect increasing integration of the world economy. The economic emergence of less developed countries and the strong commitment they often have to education will have major implications for countries like the UK.

4.8   Table 4.2 shows the scale of the recent economic growth of some developing countries.

Table 4.2 – Average annual percentage increase in Gross National Product per head: 1985–94

	%
Thailand	8.6
Korea	7.8
China	7.8
Singapore	6.1
Indonesia	6.0
Malaysia	5.6
Hong Kong	5.3
Philippines	1.7

Source: OECD

4.9   In analysing economic integration, the Organisation for Economic Co-operation and Development (OECD) Industry Committee has identified three major elements: the organisation of production on a global scale; the acquisition of inputs and services from around the world which reduces costs; and the formation of cross-border alliances and ventures, enabling companies to combine assets, share their costs and penetrate new markets. We have noted a number of additional factors: capital markets have been integrated; the information which allows benchmarking of commercial performance on an international basis is widely available through international travel and better communications; many consumers have the knowledge, information and spending power to make discriminating choices; and more countries have now developed the infrastructure and technological capability to compete against the established industrial centres. The causes of increasing integration are predominantly technological: changes in telecommunications, information technology and transport. Integration has also been fostered by political changes, specifically the promotion of free trade and the reduction in trade protection.

4.10   This is not to deny that nations have always interacted. Trade has increased steadily over many centuries, as shown in Table 4.3, although the position of individual countries varies.

Table 4.3 – Trade as percentage of Gross World Product

Year	%
1500	0.4
1820	1.0
1870	5.0
1913	8.7
1929	9.0
1950	7.0
1973	11.2
1992	13.5

Source: OECD

4.11   But the consequence of increasing integration and the emergence of developing economies is that corporations are increasingly free to locate their operations, research and administration wherever in the world suits them best. While a corporation's headquarters may well remain in its country of origin, it will design, build and market products and services on a global basis. This has changed the relationships between corporations and their suppliers and between corporations and the communities in which they are located; and the balance of available skills and labour cost in any given country that will attract and retain a global corporation.

4.12   As a result, in the UK, as elsewhere, there has been social change, growing income and labour market inequality. Some of the consequences are that:
  ■ there has been downward pressure on pay, particularly for unskilled labour, because corporations can shift their production to the area of cheapest labour;
  ■ there has been upward pressure on the quality of labour input; and on the service provided by employees, and by corporations to their customers;
  ■ competition is increasingly based on quality rather than price;
  ■ people and ideas assume greater significance in economic success because they are less mobile than other investments such as capital, information and technology;
  ■ unemployment rates of unskilled workers relative to skilled workers have increased across the countries of the Organisation for Economic Co-operation and Development, including Britain;
  ■ more, probably smaller, companies whose business is knowledge and ways of handling knowledge and information are needed.

Implications for higher education

4.13   These changes are not transient nor are they applicable only to a small proportion of the modern economy. They are pervasive and persistent. The implications for higher education students, their employers, those who provide higher education, and those who fund it are great.

4.14   In our view, these economic changes have the following main implications for
        higher education:
        ■ high quality, relevant higher education provision will be a key factor in attracting
          and anchoring the operations of global corporations because of the research
          capability of its institutions, and the skills and knowledge it can develop in the
          local workforce;
        ■ institutions will need to be at the forefront in offering opportunities for learning
          throughout life, to individuals and their corporations, so that they can have access
          to the most up-to-date processes and creative strategies;
        ■ institutions will need to meet the aspirations of individuals to re-equip themselves
          for a succession of jobs over a working lifetime and to manage the corresponding
          uncertainty with confidence;
        ■ higher education must continue to provide a steady stream of people with high
          level technical skills and creativity, to meet the premium put on innovation,
          product and service development by the developing relationship between global
          corporations and their suppliers;
        ■ higher education itself will become more strongly an international service, with
          students and employers choosing, on a global basis, the programmes they require,
          delivered in ways and at times that suit them, making use of new communications
          and information technologies;
        ■ higher education institutions may need to learn from the changes in organisational
          structure, decision-making and the approach to lifelong learning made by other
          organisations in order to flourish in a fast-changing global economy;
        ■ above all, this new economic order will place a premium on knowledge.
          Institutions are well-placed to capitalise on higher education's long-standing
          purpose of developing knowledge and understanding. But to do so, they need to
          recognise more consistently that individuals need to be equipped in their initial
          higher education with the knowledge, skills and understanding which they can use
          as a basis to secure further knowledge and skills;
        ■ in addition to a well-educated, highly skilled workforce, the other prerequisite for
          a knowledge-based economy is a research base to provide new knowledge,
          understanding and ideas. High technology companies will choose to locate in those
          countries which have a good supply of trained researchers; which can apply the
          fruits of research; and which offer opportunities to companies for communication
          and collaboration with those involved in basic research.

4.15   The relevance of education to economic survival has been recognised by successive
        governments over the last century and has been a major influence on their education
        and training policies. With the global approach to production and service provision,
        the factors which will determine the economic future of the UK will be the quality,
        relevance, scale, and cost-effectiveness of its education and training, and the
        commitment of its population to lifelong education and training. It will increasingly be
        this element in national life which determines a nation's relative prosperity and its
        ability to offer a high level of employment.

A transformed labour market

4.16   Increasing international economic competition, the emergence of once poor countries as major international competitors, new technology and social, cultural, political and legislative changes have all contributed to major changes in the UK labour market. Significant features include:

- a large rise in the proportion of women who are economically active;[1]
- an increase in the proportion of the labour force who work part-time;[2]
- a shift towards employment in small and medium sized enterprises and self-employment;[3]
- increases in the proportion of professional and skilled jobs and a decrease in the proportion of unskilled jobs;
- decreases in primary and manufacturing employment and an increase in employment in the service sector.

4.17   Other significant changes include, for example, an increase in the number of qualifications and of their use in employment selection. Teaching and chartered accountancy, for example, are now largely graduate entry occupations and it seems likely that other occupations, such as nursing, will move in this direction. This may be seen as an indicator of the need for higher skill levels, although to some extent it is a consequence of the expansion of higher education, and employers and professions seeking to attract their share of talent.

4.18   Looking to the short term future, employment growth is projected to be 0.8 to 0.9% a year over the next few years and all the labour market trends of the last few years are expected to continue.[4] Within jobs there may be a shift away from routine processes within narrowly defined functions and towards teamwork which crosses functional boundaries. If organisations continue to remove layers of management, there will be an increasing range of responsibilities within jobs.

4.19   We recognise the fragility of attempts to forecast the demand for specific skills in the longer term. Recent history is littered with failures to forecast needs successfully, and as the pace of change in industry quickens, the task of forecasting is becoming still more difficult. But, even with the lessons of history to caution us, we believe that the broad direction of change for the long term can be described.

4.20   Looking ahead over the next twenty years, the UK labour market will undergo further fundamental changes. The number of graduates in the workforce is likely to more than double by 2020. Increasingly, graduates will enter jobs not traditionally filled by graduates, causing their jobs to be redefined and reducing the number of layers needed in the organisation. Driven by continuing change in industry and commerce, there will be the further development of what are sometimes called 'portfolio careers'. Many people will change career direction several times in the course of a working life. They will move between employment, self-employment and unemployment. Their relationship with their employing organisation will change. People will be much more involved in managing and shaping their own careers.

4.21 To survive in the labour market of the future, workers will need new sets of skills, to work across conventional boundaries and see connections between processes, functions and disciplines and, in particular, to manage the learning which will support their careers.

Implications for higher education

4.22 Higher education needs to reflect key aspects of such changes in the UK labour market. It will need:

- to equip graduates with the skills and attributes needed to be effective in a changing world of work and upon which to found and manage a number of careers. Graduates will need to be able to identify their own development needs and to be committed to lifelong learning. The balance between specific subject knowledge and a broad educational base and between initial and subsequent higher education qualifications will change;

- to respond to the very different needs of students. Continuing education is likely to continue to grow both absolutely and in its proportionate share of higher education. Employers will, as now, wish to train their staff. They may undertake this in-house or commission it from external providers, including higher education. There will be a range of needs which cannot be met in-house if, as we assume, there is a significant shift towards self-employment, employment in small and medium sized enterprises (SMEs) and more limited-term contracts. As individuals take more responsibility for their own learning and development throughout life, they are likely to look to educational institutions as one of the main sources of advice and help;

- to relate effectively to the labour market, providing support and services to employers, especially SMEs and the self-employed, and encouraging and supporting graduates to develop skills for working life. This will include, in some cases, helping students to develop the attributes of the entrepreneur.

4.23 The SME sector, which we believe to be of increasing importance, needs a distinctive response from higher education institutions in terms of initial skills of graduates and consultancy support. For initial skills, SMEs told us they need graduates who can make an immediate contribution to work as soon as they arrive in the company.[5]

4.24 The small firms population is relatively young: about 20 per cent of those registered for VAT are under two years old and nearly half under five years old.[6] SMEs have a low survival rate and there is a relative absence of fast growing SMEs compared, for example, to the USA.[7]

4.25 There is more scope for more graduates to start their own businesses. Education has a role here, for example as part of a more co-ordinated approach to support for individuals; to offer a supportive environment for individuals in their early months; to give students the chance to experience and learn the skills of entrepreneurship and creativity during their programmes; and to offer postgraduate programmes in which graduates prepare specifically for entrepreneurship. Graduates from certain subject areas, for example graphic design, communication and information technology, are especially likely to be self-employed or employed in very small firms, and it is important that such students are properly prepared for this.

4.26   Students will look to higher education to offer more flexible access – in the workplace and in the home; and in the evenings and at weekends – so that learning can be combined with work. They are also likely to want more short courses and more opportunities to build qualifications flexibly through time from different modules, perhaps from different institutions. Many students will want to continue taking programmes beyond the basic requirements of a degree.

4.27   Higher education has before it the opportunity to take a major part in enabling people, throughout their working lives, to renew old skills and develop new ones. To do so effectively, it will need to be responsive, adaptive and proactive. To the extent it is, individuals and organisations will make full use of its resources. If there is not the will to respond to the needs of lifelong learners, individuals and employers will look elsewhere, to commercial and overseas sources, and employers will develop their own capabilities. There are threats as well as opportunities for institutions.

Changing structure of the economy

4.28   During the 1970s and 1980s, international economic change led to the decline of traditional industries in the United Kingdom such as textiles, heavy engineering, shipbuilding, coal mining and machine tools. Compared with the earlier decades of the post war period, since 1980 the levels of unemployment experienced in Europe have increased markedly as these traditional industries have declined. During the 1980s, the prevailing view was that the United Kingdom was entering a post-industrial phase in which manufacturing would play little significant part. Some commentators projected an economy based purely on services, distribution and tourism. Nevertheless the output of what is classified as manufacturing has not declined in parallel with the employment in the manufacturing sector. Instead, the influence of competition in the global economy has driven great advances in productivity.

4.29   As traditional industries in the United Kingdom have declined, they have been, at least in part, replaced by new industries. These include pharmaceuticals, information technology, biotechnology, communications, and semi-conductors. For example, 40 per cent of European manufacture of personal computers is now carried out in Britain. This in turn has created a local supply industry in many components – for example the design and manufacture of sophisticated printed circuit boards.

4.30   Three features characterise these new industries: the employment of highly skilled designers, engineers, scientists, software specialists, and production personnel; a high rate of technological development: and the capital-intensive nature of the activity. The innovative creation of products, rather than the process of manufacturing, becomes the vital competence for the most advanced economies.

4.31 Many of the approaches and techniques required in the new industries straddle more than one traditional subject area and the disciplinary structures of existing higher education. This poses the question whether higher educational institutions are able to respond, as the context and boundaries of subjects and disciplines change and as the flexibility of thinking required in the economy of tomorrow increases. The prevailing classification of disciplines could serve the UK poorly if it inhibits the development of new programmes of study and if it means that research is focused on areas which are, in economic terms, of limited currency.

4.32 Most importantly, perhaps, it is clear that in this exciting but challenging environment, for many employers, creativity, design, research, development, engineering, marketing and organisational skills matter at least as much as the content of knowledge. For higher education, this presents particular challenges. To be able to work closely with industry, broadly defined, and to ensure that graduates can contribute effectively, the conventional organisation of knowledge and teaching in major areas may need to be transformed. Activities which cross traditional boundaries will become more important. Institutions will need to be more flexible in the way they organise their resources and in their organisational structure. Programmes will need to give students the opportunities and skills to work across disciplines and to develop generic or transferable skills which are valuable in many contexts.

4.33 If higher education cannot respond and develop in this way, it is inevitable that alternative centres of research and advice will gain in strength at higher education's expense.

Pressure on public finances

4.34 In the UK in 1961, general government expenditure as a percentage of gross domestic product (GDP) was about 35 per cent. Today it is around 43 per cent. The balance of public spending has moved significantly over this period too. The proportion spent on social security has risen substantially while the proportion spent on defence has fallen.

4.35 It is impossible to predict what will happen to public finances over a twenty year time horizon. This will depend on government policy on taxation and expenditure, which will, in turn, be driven by voters' preferences, and on the rate of economic growth. It is clear, however, that on present trends the pressure on public expenditure in respect of social security, education and health will continue to increase. Within whatever public spending total is set by government, there will always be hard choices to be made about competing priorities. The present Government has identified education as its first priority but, over a 20 year period, it will undoubtedly be competing with other pressing needs, and within education itself there will be competing needs and changing priorities.

4.36 Although our concern is with higher education, we recognise that if we are to create a learning society, greater investment in education and training at all levels will be needed. If society does not wish to see increases in taxation but instead sees individuals taking greater responsibility for financing services which yield personal benefits, we are led to two conclusions:

- higher education cannot be regarded as something separate from the rest of society's need for investment in lifelong learning;
- individuals will need to take a greater share of financial responsibility for their own learning throughout life.

4.37   There can be no expectation of automatic increases in public financing for any public service despite the benefits which might flow from it. The objective for higher education must be to develop diverse sources of funding so that it has the flexibility to adapt to changing circumstances. The onus will be on higher education to demonstrate that it represents a good investment for individuals and society. It cannot afford to sit back and wait for recognition or to proceed on the assumption that its value is generally recognised: it must be transparent about what it seeks to achieve and what it does achieve.

4.38   Setting clear objectives and finding means for properly evaluating the costs and benefits of alternative priorities will be important if well-based decisions are to be taken in the wider national interest. We also recognise that the pressures on public finances will vary over time and that our recommendations must lead to a system which is flexible enough to cope with variations in the level of public funding for higher education, but which offers institutions a degree of stability in the interests of effective planning and management.

4.39   There have been important changes since Robbins in the nature of the relationship between government and those who receive public funds. There have been moves towards the stronger interplay of market forces, in order to increase competition between providers and thereby encourage efficiency, and an emphasis on standards and accountability. These general trends have been reflected in higher education through the introduction of new funding methodologies, new approaches to quality assurance and an emerging focus on the 'consumer' rather than the 'provider'. Although the emphasis and the mechanisms may change over time, we expect there to be a continuing concern to promote efficiency, informed choice, quality and accountability over the next twenty years.

Family finances

4.40   Families and individuals in the UK have, on average, seen increasing income and wealth over the last 25 years although the figures conceal differences between different groups in the population. Between 1971 and 1990, real disposable income per head rose by nearly 80 per cent and then levelled off.[8]

4.41   Assuming that economic growth continues, family incomes should, in general, continue to do so as well. Such a trend cannot be taken for granted though. Over the last 15 years median male income in the US has dropped by more than five per cent and the incomes of the lowest paid ten per cent have fallen by nearly a fifth.[9] We cannot predict what will happen to income and wealth distribution nor what other calls there may be on family incomes. Some commentators believe that there will be an increasing polarisation between those families with a relatively secure, comfortable income and those without.

Implications for higher education

4.42   If individuals' and families' incomes rise on average, they will potentially be able to invest more of their own resources in higher education and training, if they so choose. However, if, as we assume, pressures on public expenditure increase, it may become increasingly necessary for those who are earning to make their own provision against times when they will not be earning – by investing in personal pensions for retirement, and insuring against unemployment and the need for social care, for example. We do not underestimate the challenge to people's current expectations that would be posed by a combination of these factors and a requirement to contribute more to the costs of higher education and training after compulsory schooling. On the other hand, the information available to us shows that, for most, higher education is an excellent personal investment.

New communications and information technologies

4.43   One of the key factors which has nourished and stimulated the development of a global economy and, increasingly, shared cultures has been the development of information and communication technologies. The rate of technological change over the last 20 years has been astonishing in its rapidity: *'the latest Sega video game costing a few hundred pounds has a higher performance than the original 1976 Cray Super-computer which cost millions of dollars.'*[10]

4.44   The technologies which are being deployed and further developed for the telecommunications industry promise a vast array of future options and possibilities. We expect that over the next 20 years technology will continue to advance strongly, although not necessarily at a constant rate. Information technology products are likely to be faster, cheaper, more available and more capable. The capacity to transmit large amounts of information quickly and cheaply in electronic form has transformed many forms of work. Routine clerical tasks which are computer-based can be performed anywhere in the world so long as there is a labour force with the necessary basic skills and the infrastructure to support computer-based operations. Financial transactions are no longer constrained by time or place. Decision-making has become more complex because it has to be done more quickly, and because more information has to be assimilated first. New ways of doing things can be disseminated almost immediately, requiring great flexibility and adaptability from organisations and individuals if they are to keep up with the best. This, in turn, has changed the skills needed at work and in everyday life. Basic information technology skills are needed in almost all spheres and many jobs require sophisticated information handling skills. This often means much more than simply knowing how to use a computer.

4.45   Within the time horizon of our 20-year perspective, it will be possible for all
        information – whether currently in the form of newspapers, magazines, books, music,
        radio, films, or television – to become available in digital form. We believe that
        developments in communications and information technologies, and particularly the
        storage and transmission of information in digital form, will prove eventually to be
        as revolutionary an innovation as the printing press. The trend in software technology
        will be towards greater user-friendliness. Alternative means for people to interact with
        machines, such as voice recognition, speech synthesis and handwriting recognition are
        likely to become widely available.

4.46   Use of the Internet – a global network of networks – has increased at an astonishing
        rate and looks set to continue to do so. The World Wide Web now connects a
        community of around 50 million people. The application of this technology inside
        organisations, the Intranet, is heralded to transform organisational life through the
        step change increase in access to information it provides.

4.47   Increasingly, anyone will be able to be his or her own publisher with a global audience,
        through the Internet. No-one will have a monopoly on knowledge transmission. But
        everyone will need the skill and discernment to access, select and sort through the
        overwhelming volume of available information. Complex information handling is a
        very high-level skill. Even higher-level skills will continue to be needed for the creation
        of knowledge and to make it intelligible, accessible and manageable for others.

Implications for higher education

4.48   Such changes have important implications for higher education. They affect the types
        of skills which students will have when they enter higher education, their expectations
        of the facilities and learning modes open to them and the types of skills and intellectual
        attributes which those leaving higher education will need to have if they are to operate
        successfully in the modern world. For example, the development of high-level skills in
        handling the large volumes of complex information which can be made available by
        communications technology will be one of the tasks of undergraduate programmes.

4.49   Over the next few years, there is also the potential for new communications and
        information technologies to change radically the way higher education is organised
        and delivered – whether within institutions or in people's homes or workplaces.
        *'Ultimately, anyone with access to a networked computer, anywhere in the world,
        will have at their fingertips the entire gamut of human knowledge – from the
        British Library's archives to the latest pictures beamed back from NASA's
        Voyager space probe, from the latest Hollywood blockbuster movie to the entire
        works of Stockhausen.'*[11]

4.50   To a greater or lesser extent the new technologies will impact upon each of the
        following:
        ■ the organisation and support of teaching and learning programmes and,
          particularly, the development of educational materials;
        ■ research;

- quality assurance of learning, teaching and research;
- the management and administration of higher education institutions;
- the degree to which, and the way in which higher education institutions interact with external organisations.

4.51 Much will depend on the extent to which individuals have ready access to networks and hardware. At present the UK is well-placed with a much higher level of penetration of information technology into everyday life than in most other countries, apart from the United States. In 1995, the sale of personal computers outstripped the sale of televisions for the first time in the US. The UK will not be far behind. In 1995, more than 20 per cent of UK homes had a personal computer and there were 1.4 million cable TV subscribers. By 2000, it is predicted that 44 per cent of homes will have a computer.[12] However, at present the majority of educational software is of American origin and unless the UK can move rapidly it runs the risk of becoming a net purchaser rather than supplier of such services.

Social and cultural changes

4.52 Social and cultural changes over the last thirty years have been profound.

4.53 Since the early 1960s, households and families have become smaller. There are 43 per cent more households now than in 1961 with more elderly people and young men living alone, and more divorces. People are marrying at an older age, an increasing proportion of women are remaining childless and those who do have children have fewer and start their families later in life.[13]

4.54 Young people seek and acquire financial independence from their parents at a younger age and the voting age has been reduced to 18. Women's position in society has changed radically, particularly through their greater involvement in paid employment. The existence of discrimination and the consequent need for equality of opportunity has been recognised by legislation against discrimination by race or gender or against individuals with a disability.

4.55 The proportion of the population who are in lower socio-economic groups has declined and the proportion in higher groups has increased. The disparity in income and wealth between the two groups has increased and there is perceived to be a polarisation of society. This presents great challenges if a cohesive and inclusive society is to be sustained.

4.56 A much wider range of cultural influences is apparent in every day life. There has been a decline in religious observance and in respect for figures and institutions of authority. There is greater scepticism about the ability of science or governments to solve problems. In some respects, there is no longer a shared set of cultural norms or values: in other areas new commonly shared concerns have emerged that were less prominent in the past, for example concern for the environment and for the natural world.

4.57   The extent and rate of cultural transmission has accelerated throughout this century as first radio, and then television, were added to print media as a form of mass communication. Television, in particular, has brought representations of different cultures and lifestyles into almost every home. A breadth of cultural experience which once had to be actively sought and was expensive to attain is now readily available to all.

4.58   In the early 1960s, universities were seen as the highest manifestation of a cultured and civilised society and their standing was unquestioned. Robbins saw the transmission of a common culture as a purpose of higher education. This rested on the largely unchallenged view that there was a common culture, that universities possessed it and were its guardians, and that it could be transmitted. It is a tribute to the universities and colleges of higher education in this country that, while they may not be regarded with the same awe as in the past, they remain popular and respected in a way that many other national institutions would envy. We have been struck by the strong desire of places which do not currently have a local higher education institution to establish or attract one.

Implications for higher education

4.59   The nature of the relationship between traditional institutions and the individuals they serve has changed. There is now greater emphasis on recognition of the individual as customer or consumer. People's expectations of publicly funded services have risen and they no longer accept unquestioningly what is offered. Some of these expectations have been codified in public charters which set out performance standards, including those for higher education. Notwithstanding this, we do not believe that students will in the future see themselves simply as customers of higher education but rather as members of a learning community.

4.60   Future social and cultural changes are at least as hard to predict as economic changes. It is plausible to assume that many of the trends of recent years will continue. Smaller families may be better able to offer financial support to their student offspring but the extent of family breakdowns may limit this. Greater female participation in the workforce together with increasing divorce rates may increase women's propensity to seek higher education, particularly continuing education. Participation rates in higher education have historically been positively correlated with socio-economic status and with the educational level achieved by parents, particularly mothers. Other things being equal, as the proportion of the population who are in professional, managerial and skilled socio-economic groups increases and as the proportion of parents who are themselves graduates rises, there are likely to be more young people who will want to enter higher education. What is harder to predict is how successful the education system for pupils up to the age of 16 will be in raising the attainments and aspirations of those from lower socio-economic groups so that a greater proportion of them will seek higher education.

4.61   As higher education is seen less and less as the preserve of an elite, there may be less agreement about what culture or values it should seek to transmit or, indeed, whether it should seek to 'hand down' a static concept of culture or values. There is, however, still a range of values, such as respect for evidence, rational argument, debate and tolerance of alternative viewpoints, which are characteristic of higher education in this country and generally held by those who teach in it. As the proportion of the population which passes through higher education increases, the greater its potential impact in transmitting such values to society as a whole.

4.62   Over time, higher education institutions have become more open to their local communities and the increase in their number means that more people live within reach of one. Local and regional communities are likely to seek to re-establish the strong links with institutions that often characterised the creation of universities and polytechnics. The motivation for this may be largely economic, in view of the growing significance of higher education institutions to local economies. But strengthened relationships may encourage the creation of a greater role for institutions in the cultural and sporting life of communities, through the joint provision and use of facilities.

Changing age structure of the population

4.63   One of the great immediate challenges facing higher education policy makers in the early 1960s was demographic. At that time the great majority of higher education entrants were young school leavers – 88 per cent of university entrants were under 20. The number of 18 year olds in the population had grown from 600,000 in 1959 to 750,000 in 1964, and a remarkable jump to 960,000 was expected in 1965. Thereafter it was predicted that numbers would fall back steadily over the next five years to the 1964 level.[14] By contrast, in the 1980s, policy makers were preoccupied by an impending sharp reduction in the number of young people in the population. In its 1985 Green Paper on higher education, the government pointed out that the 18 and 19 year old population would fall by 33 per cent between 1984 and 1996 and, even after allowing for an increase in the participation rate from that smaller cohort and for increased participation by mature students, it expected the size of higher education in Great Britain to fall significantly to a low point in the academic year 1996–97 of somewhere between 490,000 and 530,000 full-time and sandwich home and overseas students.[15] In fact, the full-time student population exceeded 1 million in that year.

4.64   We do not face the same kinds of demographic change. Chart 4.1 shows that there will be changes in the size of the relevant age groups but the swings will be much less severe than in the last 20 years.

Chart 4.1 – Demographic trends and forecasts, Great Britain, 1972 – 2029

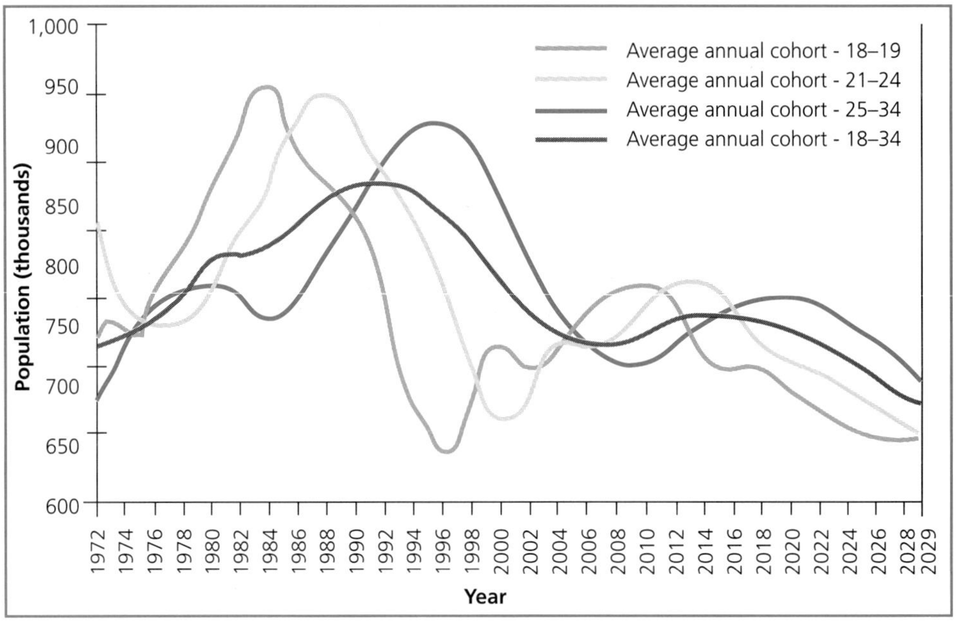

Source: DfEE
Note: Estimated population as at 1 January, age as at previous December.

4.65   As Table 4.4 shows, the most significant demographic change over the next twenty years in the UK, as in other developed countries, is expected to be an increase in the proportion of older people.

Table 4.4 – Age distribution of UK population

UK Population	Actual		Projected
	1961	1995	2021
Total	53m	59m	61m
% under 16	25	21	18
%16 – 34	24	27	23
%35 – 64	39	36	40
% 65+	12	16	19

Source: ONS

Implications for higher education

4.66   As those aged between 18 and 30 currently make up the majority of higher education entrants and are likely to continue to do so well into the future, we have looked at the impact which changes in the proportion of the population in this age range might have on demand for higher education, and also the factors that are likely to influence their wish to engage in higher education in Chapter 6.

4.67   An increase in the proportion of older people in the population will, in the learning society, create an increased demand for adult continuing education, particularly if more people stay in employment beyond current retirement age. The prospective sharp increase in the number of healthy and active much older retired people may create a whole range of expanding demands for learning for pleasure at a variety of levels, including those provided by higher education.

Environmental changes

4.68   Another significant trend over the last 30 years has been an increasing interest in and concern about environmental issues and an increasing realisation of the impact which human activities have on the environment. We expect that over the next 20 years, we shall gain a better understanding of the nature and extent of those changes and that there will be increasing pressure on all countries, particularly developed ones, to modify industrial practices and lifestyles to minimise adverse environmental effects.

Implications for higher education

4.69   If changes in lifestyle become necessary, and particularly if the cost of travelling rises sharply, the demand for home or workplace-based higher education may increase. Technological developments will help to make this feasible. Indeed the continuing advance in communications technology will, of itself, be a major force in advancing the practice of learning at home and in the workplace.

4.70   The Toyne report examined the action which needed to be taken by further and higher education to equip the workforce to assume greater environmental responsibility but a subsequent review suggested that little progress had been made.[16,17]

4.71   Higher education can also contribute to environmental sustainability through research and innovation, for example in the areas of pollution control, energy use and renewable and sustainable resources. Increased environmental concerns may also require changes in research procedures and practices. Greater evaluation of the potential impact of new technologies and of medical and agricultural advances on the environment may be required before they are able to be applied.

School and further education

4.72   The nature of schools and further education – which prepare most of the young people who enter higher education – has changed since the time of Robbins. In 1962, the minimum school leaving age was 15; only 9 per cent of 18 year olds were in full-time education, and only 7 per cent of young people left school with two or more A levels or the equivalent in Scotland. Now the minimum school leaving age is 16; 40 per cent of 18 year olds are in full-time education and, in 1994, 28 per cent of young people in England had two or more A levels and 31 per cent of school leavers in Scotland in 1995 had three or more Highers.

4.73   Under the National Targets, the aim is that by 2000, 60 per cent of young people should, by the age 21, achieve two A levels, an Advanced General National Vocational Qualification (GNVQ) or an National Vocational Qualification (NVQ) Level 3. Whether or not this target is achieved, we are clear that over the timescale we are considering, an increasing proportion of people will obtain qualifications at Level 3 through one route or another, and that many of them will have qualifications beyond the thresholds set by the targets, for example three or four A levels or their equivalent. Furthermore, the Department for Education and Employment has demonstrated that the single most important determinant of later educational success is performance at Level 2, where substantial progress has been made in recent years.[18]

4.74 The introduction of a National Curriculum for 5–16 year olds has ensured breadth of study for all pupils and a greater degree of commonality in the content of their studies. But there is a danger that these benefits will not be fully realised. There are shortages of high quality teachers in key subject areas such as science and technology and, perhaps not unrelated, there is low take up of science subjects post-16.

Implications for higher education

4.75 Having obtained qualifications at Level 3, many are likely to want to progress further and to work towards qualifications at a higher level. Inevitably the demand for higher education will rise, particularly from those with more modest prior academic attainments, although we cannot predict the precise figures.

4.76 A levels have formed the main traditional entry route to higher education although their dominance has declined. The main growth in Level 3 qualifications is expected to be through the GNVQ and NVQ families of qualifications. There are early signs that a large proportion of GNVQ students will seek and gain admittance to higher education. Students may be less likely to see an NVQ as a stepping stone to higher education, although those achieving an NVQ at Level 3 through the recently introduced Modern Apprenticeships at age 19 may wish to consider entering higher education. Those who succeed at Level 3 through a more applied route will have received a different preparation for higher education than those who have taken the traditional routes. They may have different aptitudes and have preferences for different styles of learning. Higher education will need to provide programmes and teaching which are appropriate to these students' needs and aspirations.

4.77 Unless the take up of the physical sciences and mathematics post-16 can be improved, higher education is likely to face continuing difficulty in recruiting well-qualified students to subjects such as physics and engineering. This, in turn, will exacerbate the problems of recruitment to teacher training programmes in science and make it still harder for schools to offer high quality, inspiring teaching in these subjects. In this lies one of the major problems facing education in the UK.

Developments in higher education elsewhere in the world

4.78 Many of the developments in higher education in the UK over the last 20 to 30 years have been mirrored by similar changes in other developed countries, and increasingly in rapidly developing countries too, although at different rates and with differing emphases. There is an increasing emphasis on the role of higher education in serving the needs of the economy. There has been a general move towards mass participation in higher education. Those countries which historically restricted higher education entry in order to meet labour market demand have moved away from this approach.

4.79   Many countries are devolving more power to institutions although in most countries there remains greater control by central authorities than in the UK. Along with the trend towards deregulation has come a greater emphasis on quality assessment. Interest is being shown in new approaches to learning and teaching in some countries, particularly in the potential of information technology.

4.80   There is often assumed to be an indivisible link between teaching and research at the higher education level although most countries have a binary system with research confined to the university sector. Countries are moving in different directions on research funding – some towards concentration on strong research centres and some towards dispersion.

4.81   Some of the greatest differences in approach are in the area of funding. The USA and Asian countries have a long tradition of substantial private contributions to the cost of higher education. Most European countries have a tradition of tuition paid for by the state although some are now reviewing or having to move away from this. Australia and New Zealand have recently required graduates to contribute to their tuition costs. A fuller analysis of developments overseas can be found in Appendix 5 to this report.

Implications for higher education

4.82   We are clear that it is important for our economic future that we match the commitment of our competitors to higher education. That means concentrating on maintaining appropriate levels of participation in both initial and continuing higher education but, at least as important, it means ensuring that the quality of activity and the standards of awards are of world repute. We must benchmark ourselves against international standards in learning and in research.

4.83   The aspirations of many of the developing countries to improve the skill levels of their populations also provide opportunities for UK higher education, both to educate overseas students in the UK and to provide educational services, support and advice overseas. For the long term the greatest new opportunities for attracting overseas students to this country may lie at the postgraduate level.

Conclusion

4.84   This then is the background against which we began our consideration of the aims and purposes of higher education over the next 20 years. Despite this survey of the background, we have no doubt that there are changes and developments which will have an important impact on the future of higher education which we have not managed to identify. This underlines the need for a higher education system which is not only flexible and responsive to immediate external changes but also identifies and plans for the long term strategic goals of the nation. Individual institutions will need to look outwards as well as inwards as they develop their strategies for the future.

Chapter 5

Aims and purposes

Definition of higher education

5.1 After reviewing the context in which our work on higher education should be set, we considered the aims and purposes of higher education and the principles which should guide us. In this chapter we explain the definition of higher education which we adopted, we establish the purposes of higher education and we discuss the principles which were set down for us in our terms of reference.

5.2 Our terms of reference describe higher education as embracing teaching, learning, scholarship and research. These activities are, and should be, at the heart of higher education. But there is a range of associated activities which have increased in significance as higher education has expanded and become a greater element in national life. These include increasingly important contributions to the cultural and business life of local, national and international communities. We have been concerned to take a broad view of the meaning and role of higher education in our work.

5.3 We considered at an early stage the merits of broadening the scope of our studies to encompass 'tertiary' education. This term, which is widely used but not often closely defined, has been variously interpreted to describe:
- all post-compulsory education – which in the UK would be all education at any level after the age of 16;
- all education taken by adults – which in the UK would include a mixture of further education, higher education and adult education taken by those aged 18 and over; or
- all education at a level above that normally achieved at the end of upper secondary schooling – which in the UK would include all education above Level 3 (A level and its equivalents) and equates to our normal definition of higher education.

5.4 We see merit in taking a coherent view of education. Higher education is but one part of an interdependent system of education and training, – it cannot be looked at in isolation. Any dividing line set between further education and higher education, or between higher education and higher level training, is bound to be somewhat arbitrary. This is true particularly for adults – for example, when making a change of career direction a person may need access simultaneously to a range of programmes spanning both higher and further education and training. But we had to set some boundaries to our work. We were conscious that our terms of reference directed us specifically to look at higher education and, even with that, we already faced an enormous task. We decided, therefore, to concentrate our attention on education above Level 3 (ie above A level and the Advanced Level General National Vocational Qualification (GNVQ)) and its equivalents in Scotland. We paid careful attention throughout our work to the relationship between higher education and other levels and forms of education and training.

5.5   We are also clear that our concern is not only with higher education institutions, but with higher education wherever it takes place. Universities and colleges of higher education are currently the main providers of higher education, but there are many other organisations, most notably colleges of further education, and also professional bodies, firms and private training organisations, which offer programmes of education or training at levels equivalent to higher education. In some cases, such provision is clearly identified as higher education and has a direct equivalence in terms of qualifications awarded or academic and professional recognition. Information about the full extent of activities which might be classified as higher education outside the formal education sector is limited and we have not endeavoured, in the time available to us, to survey the full extent of such activity or to make extensive recommendations about its future. However, we have sought to take account of how the role of these activities and their relationship with conventional higher education may change and develop over time.

5.6   In looking at research, we have concentrated on higher education's distinctive contribution to the research base, recognising that higher education constitutes only a part of that base. Private sector companies and research institutes and a range of public sector bodies, as well as universities and colleges, carry out research. We have also considered the relationship between research in higher education and elsewhere, and the relationship between research and the other activities of higher education. We have sought to recognise the importance of research in support of regional and national economies, and the potential for further collaboration with industry and commerce in developing applied research.

Aims and purposes: the history

5.7   The first question which we asked in our written consultation exercise was:
> 'What should be the aims and purposes of higher education over the next twenty years?'

Most of those who responded took as their starting point the Robbins report of 1963.[1] The Robbins Committee identified four aims and objectives of higher education which can be summarised as:
- instruction in skills for employment;
- promoting the general powers of the mind;
- advancing learning;
- transmitting a common culture and common standards of citizenship.

5.8   The Secretary of State for Education and Employment undertook a consultation exercise in the autumn of 1994 which invited views on what changes to the Robbins' aims were needed in the light of modern circumstances. The Education Departments reported to us on the outcome of that consultation exercise which showed that there was still widespread support for the Robbins' aims, but that there needed to be a shift in the balance between them and some amplification and development to reflect the changing context in which higher education now operates.[2]

5.9 In the light of that, the Departments offered us their updated version of the objectives as a basis for our consideration. Their suggested objectives were:

- imparting employment skills;
- providing opportunities for adult lifetime learning to enable individuals, employers and the nation as a whole to adapt to changing circumstances;
- promoting the general powers of the mind;
- advancing learning and research;
- promoting culture and high standards in all aspects of society;
- serving local and regional communities, as well as national interests at home and abroad.

Our views

5.10 The aim of higher education is to enable society to make progress through an understanding of itself and its world: in short, to sustain a learning society. There are numerous ways in which we could classify and describe what we see as the main components of this aim, but, in the interests of clarity, we have summarised four broad purposes. They all overlap and interlink in important ways and are described in more detail below. The first relates specifically to the needs of individuals and the others to society's requirements.

5.11 The four main purposes of higher education are:

- to inspire and enable individuals to develop their capabilities to the highest potential levels throughout life, so that they grow intellectually, are well-equipped for work, can contribute effectively to society and achieve personal fulfilment;
- to increase knowledge and understanding for their own sake and to foster their application to the benefit of the economy and society;
- to serve the needs of an adaptable, sustainable, knowledge-based economy at local, regional and national levels;
- to play a major role in shaping a democratic, civilised, inclusive society.

Inspiring and enabling individuals to develop their capabilities to the highest levels

5.12 Our vision for the future, outlined in Chapter 1, emphasises the need for individuals to be committed to lifelong learning and for our society to become a learning society. Education and training must be embraced by people at all levels of achievement and, to varying degrees, throughout working life and thereafter to enhance leisure and the quality of life.

5.13 Higher education is one player among many in meeting these needs, but it is likely to play an increasing role because:

- as more people throughout the population engage in education and training more will reach levels of attainment which will enable them to progress to higher education;

■ the propensity to engage in continuing education and training is positively correlated with previous educational attainments. The number and proportion of graduates in the workforce is increasing rapidly, which is likely to drive an increased demand for continuing education. A recent survey showed that over 40 per cent of graduates aged between 30 and 34 had undertaken education or training related to their current job within the last four weeks.[3]

5.14   The traditional pattern of an extended, continuous, residential period of higher education taken immediately after school is no longer the predominant pattern of study. In future, a large part of the population will need access to higher education in some form at intervals throughout life. Many will still take a concentrated and lengthy programme of study in higher education, immediately or soon after school or further education, in preparation for entry to work, but this will be seen as only the foundation for the first stage of a career. Such programmes should explicitly prepare students to look forward to, and to manage their learning throughout life – so that they can plan and develop their own careers and gain fulfilment.

5.15   Not all students want, or benefit from, a full-time programme of higher education after school or college. Some will prefer to integrate higher education closely with their career development and job needs. For them, part-time study while in employment will be the preferred option. They will need a longer time than full-time students to reach a particular level and may need the flexibility to build up credits over a long period of years. Nor do all students want to enter higher education at the age of 17 or 18 – students who enter higher education for the first time before the age of 21 are already in the minority in higher education. Students who have work experience bring a greater breadth of experience to their studies and have more focused needs. They may well get more out of higher education as a result.

5.16   In the years since the Robbins report, but particularly over the last decade, we have seen increasing diversity in the backgrounds of those coming into higher education. Looking ahead, this diversity, and with it the range of requirements on higher education, may be expected to increase, especially if, as we urge, a national commitment to lifelong learning is achieved. More students will need to be able to take short programmes at varying levels to meet specific needs. Some graduates will need postgraduate-level programmes to deepen their knowledge and skills. Others may need to take programmes at undergraduate level or in further education to broaden or change their skills. Some will wish to pursue higher education from time to time to enrich the quality of their lives.

5.17   Thus, although all programmes of higher education should have the same general purpose of developing individuals to higher levels of knowledge and understanding, different programmes should include different specific objectives and learning outcomes.

5.18   The Robbins Committee saw two distinct strands to the work of higher education in developing individuals: imparting employment skills and developing the general powers of the mind. Both are important objectives for higher education, but we do not find it helpful to make a clear-cut distinction between them. The single most important capacity employers seek in those with higher education qualifications is intellectual capabilities of a high order. We take the view that any programme of study in higher education should have as one of its primary intentions the development of higher level intellectual skills, knowledge and understanding in its students. We believe there is intrinsic merit in this aim because it both empowers the individual – giving satisfaction and self-esteem as personal potential is realised – and because the development of the general powers of the mind underpins the development of many of the other generic skills so valued by employers, and of importance throughout working life.

5.19   There is a long history of highly vocational programmes in higher education in preparation for professions such as medicine. As more and more aspects of employment have become increasingly complex, it is inevitable and right that at least part of professional preparation should take place in higher education. Higher education must continue to have a role in ensuring an adequate supply for the nation of doctors, engineers, lawyers, teachers, pharmacists, technicians and so on. As the demands on such professions become ever greater, the need for the underpinning of knowledge, skills and understanding provided by higher education becomes more important. The essence of professionalism is a thorough and up-to-date grasp of the fundamental knowledge base of an occupation; sufficient understanding of the underlying theoretical principles to be able to adapt to novel circumstances and to incorporate research findings into practice; and appropriate practical skills and professional values.

5.20   There is also a distinguished tradition of programmes in higher education which give students the chance to pursue, in depth, an academic subject in which they have a great interest, but which is not likely to be used directly in subsequent employment. Such programmes develop high level intellectual skills in their students and this is a proper objective for higher education. But we believe that such programmes should help students to develop other capabilities which they will need beyond higher education. The intellectual attributes developed by higher education are needed in employment but so are other capabilities. Apart from the key skills of communication, numeracy and capability in communications and information technology, those in work increasingly need to be able to be flexible and adaptable, to work in teams, and to manage their own development and career. As we describe in Chapter 9, we believe that all those completing major programmes in higher education should have developed these key skills as well as the practice of planning, managing and taking responsibility for their own learning. All programmes therefore need to recognise and provide for these skills – however specialised their main area of study.

5.21   Higher education also responds to those who want to equip themselves for life in a broad sense. Responding to these students is consistent with our contention that programmes should have specific objectives. Programmes which meet their needs will be concerned with developing the general powers of the mind through one or more areas of study pursued in depth, combined with studies to provide a breadth of knowledge and understanding. Apart from responding to the inclination of the student, such education responds to the need in society, and in work, for people who have a breadth of understanding and an educational basis from which they can build in a range of directions as life develops.

5.22 Furthermore, there is an indivisible link between higher education's role in developing individuals and its service of the nation's wider economic need. Highly educated people will be central to our country's future economic wellbeing. Higher education's importance and influence has grown with the recent increases in participation.

Increasing knowledge and understanding

5.23 Research and scholarship, which extend and re-interpret knowledge, and the transmission and dissemination of that knowledge, are not exclusively the province of higher education institutions, but they are features which distinguish higher education institutions from other parts of the education and training system. Universities once held the position where they were the main sources of knowledge generation and transmission. This position has changed as the number and diversity of institutions devoted to knowledge production and dissemination has increased. Higher education institutions' distinctive continuing role within a democratic society is as independent, questioning institutions unconstrained by any particular political or commercial agenda. Such institutions must be dispassionate, committed to the pursuit of truth and able to reflect on the hardest and most complex issues facing the world. This does not mean that every individual or every institution in higher education has to be actively involved in research, but it does mean that research and scholarship are defining purposes of higher education as a whole. Teaching at higher education level must be informed and enhanced by research and scholarship which is in itself, a reason for supporting research in higher education institutions.

5.24 It is a distinctive feature of an advanced civilisation to seek the advancement of knowledge for its own sake and to satisfy natural human curiosity about the nature of the world. The UK has a good historic record in world class basic research. Over the past century, this country has won a significant number of Nobel prizes. The UK contributes to the sum of human knowledge, well beyond that which might be expected from its size or economic place in the world, although today's output inevitably reflects our historic pattern of investment of time, people and money. We believe that world class research raises the aspirations, capability and confidence of the nation and enriches its culture. This alone justifies an investment in research, even in areas which do not have any obvious long term economic return. As a nation, we need to show that we value inventiveness, curiosity and creativity in people, as they are the source of innovations which can benefit all. The very notion of pure research makes it difficult to predict when an observation becomes useful or applicable. Unless such research is carried out in higher education institutions, it is unlikely to be pursued anywhere else.

5.25 We are also clear, however, that research and innovation are vital to the future wellbeing of our nation – contributing both to economic success and to the quality of life – and that if we do not have a flourishing research base the nation will be poorer, both culturally and economically. The research base in higher education has a particular part to play in the preservation and pursuit of knowledge which provides the fundamental understanding and principles from which applications can be developed to meet the needs of society. Higher education also needs to be involved in developing and applying research findings, in technology and knowledge transfer. This is likely to be achieved most effectively when there is direct interaction and joint working between those in higher education and commercial partners. The research community in higher education has an essential role in the innovation and exploitation cycle.

5.26   Higher education needs to train the next generation of researchers, not just for academia but for industry, commerce and the public services. As the world changes faster and faster, more people need the ability to innovate and to understand how to incorporate research findings into current practice. Over the last century or so, we have been making the transition to a society which is essentially scientifically and technologically based. If we are to maintain such a society in the face of new challenges, such as environmental concerns, pressure on natural resources and an increasing capacity to change the biological basis of the world, we shall need to continue to understand science and technological principles better, and to be able to innovate. As we advance in knowledge the challenges increase in complexity. We shall need to understand biological and environmental systems which are far more complex than those studied so far. We shall need to find ways of living in a society which is stable and civilised, but which can adapt to major changes without becoming inward-looking and isolationist. We shall need to exploit the advantages of science and technology, but with an understanding of their ethical and social implications. Research in the social sciences and humanities has a crucial role to play here.

Serving the needs of the economy

5.27   Discussion of the first two purposes of higher education, developing individuals and increasing knowledge, has already included much on the economic role of higher education. Our studies of other countries have revealed how, all over the world, higher education is increasingly being seen as an essential component of a knowledge-based economy capable of providing people with the quality of life, mental and material, to which they aspire (see Appendix 5). Over the next 20 years we face unparalleled change because of the integration of the world economy described in Chapter 4.

5.28   The education and skills of our people will be our greatest natural resource in the global economy of tomorrow. They must be developed to internationally excellent standards if we are to prosper. A high quality workforce will secure continued and increasing investment in the UK by industry and commerce. Higher education cannot do the task alone: other parts of the education and training sector have a major contribution to make, and some of those giving evidence to us asserted that the UK's comparative weaknesses are not in higher education but at lower levels. Nonetheless, higher education's relative importance is increasing, both in developing the levels of capability that are needed in the world of work and in providing an underpinning research base. The role of higher education in an advanced economy is not just to develop a senior echelon although it must continue to do that: it is increasingly involved in developing the capabilities of people in a whole range of activities.

5.29   Research in higher education contributes materially to the nation's wealth creating capacity. It is important as a part of the research base, which generates much of the basic and strategic research for developments which are directly useful to industry, and public services and commerce. It would be a mistake, however, to rest on a linear model of technology transfer which assumes that the principal direction of causation runs from research outcomes to economic competitiveness. This is too simplistic a model to explain a process where connections are rarely clear. Very often there are long time intervals between a discovery, or the elucidation of a new principle, and its application in revenue-producing products or services. There may be little obvious connection between research in one discipline and the utilisation of its results in an unrelated field. The flow of new knowledge between higher education and industry is increasingly becoming a two-way process: the term 'knowledge exchange' rather than 'technology transfer' is becoming more appropriate.

5.30   Research also contributes in other ways to our economic health and the quality of life. Medical research is designed to lead to advances in medical treatment, which improve the health of the nation. The social sciences can help us to understand better the human aspects of changes in the world and how best to adapt to them. Research in the arts and humanities contributes to growing industries in tourism, entertainment and leisure. Service industries and the public and voluntary services rely on research in areas as diverse as finance, economics and organisational behaviour. Research which is tailored to UK needs may not be done elsewhere in the world.

5.31   As well as producing a stream of basic science with potential for application, higher education provides a supply of trained researchers, of the kind needed to sustain a UK presence of research-based and high technology companies, who locate themselves wherever they see the greatest economic advantage. There is a long history of analysis which suggests that the UK is good at basic research but poor at translating it into workable, wealth-generating applications, although there are signs of improvement. If higher education is to serve the nation's economic needs effectively, it has to contribute, along with industry, commerce and other users of research, to overcoming the UK's weaknesses in this area. The Technology Foresight exercise has identified areas in which it is considered that an international competence will be required in the UK. Some basic research funded by the Research Councils is being focused on these areas; but there is still a need for more effective collaboration between higher education and industry if the full potential is to be realised.

5.32   By conducting research in higher education, the UK gains access to an international network of researchers and information. This enables the UK to understand and adopt the benefits of research findings from across the world.

5.33   Higher education institutions have a major role in their own region or local area. Although, over time, the potential of information technology could lessen the local focus of higher education institutions as developers of individuals, all the evidence we have received suggests that such institutions will have an increasingly important and multifaceted role in their local communities. Close links with local employers can lead to programmes which are designed to meet local needs. Research collaboration, which does not need to be at the leading edge of basic research, can help local firms which do not have their own research capability to solve immediate problems. In some areas, a local higher education institution may provide the only major local concentration of skilled and knowledgeable people, who can, if minded to, offer general advice and support to businesses and a point of access to national and international sources of expertise. Universities and colleges are also major employers themselves and attract students from outside the immediate locality, bringing employment and spending power into an area.

5.34   A strong research base which demonstrates international standards of excellence provides a powerful incentive for inward investment by overseas companies in the UK. There is growing evidence that businesses can be attracted to particular localities by the strength of their research base.

5.35   The other increasingly important economic contribution of higher education is as a generator of foreign exchange earnings. The UK remains one of the most popular destinations for overseas students, who bring with them, not just the fees they pay to higher education institutions in this country, but more general spending power used in the UK economy. Recent estimates suggest such spending exceeds £1 billion. There are also unquantifiable economic and other benefits for the UK in having people in positions of influence throughout the world who have a knowledge of, and links with, the UK. Such people are likely to look naturally to the UK as a potential trading partner or for investment opportunities.

5.36   Such benefits do not arise only from attracting overseas students to study in the UK. There is great potential for selling UK higher education overseas, whether through the establishment of units in other countries, through collaborative working with overseas institutions or, increasingly, through the use of new communications and information technologies. As such technologies continue to develop, the range of services which can be offered will increase and costs should fall. The UK has a great natural advantage in developing these opportunities because of the English language and the expertise it has developed in distance learning, especially through the Open University. But the UK also has strong competitors, notably in the US and Australia. The preconditions of continued success, and the development of what could be an increasing source of national income will be: a commitment to offering a high quality experience; the pursuit of quality; the safeguarding of standards of awards; innovation; collaboration in the provision of world class learning materials; and the reputation of higher education in this country for research, scholarship and teaching.

5.37   Overseas opportunities should not, of course, be seen simply in an economic context. The presence of overseas students, and collaboration with overseas institutions, greatly enriches teaching, scholarship and research in this country. Overseas students bring valuable alternative perspectives and experiences to the educational process and to the social and cultural life of higher institutions. The quality of research in the UK is enhanced by involving the best minds and the greatest breadth of experience from across the world.

Shaping a democratic and civilised society

5.38   Since the time of the Robbins report, the UK has increasingly become a society which includes many cultures and one in which there is active debate about the basis for any system of values. It is a society that is actively engaged in reflection about the place of the UK in the world, particularly in relation to Europe. There is debate about the relationship of the different parts of the UK to each other. In Northern Ireland there is a continuingly frustrated wish for a peaceful basis for communal life.

5.39   In such a society, those in higher education may not see themselves as custodians of a culture and system of values which they are entitled to advocate and transmit on behalf of society. There are, however, values shared throughout higher education and without which higher education, as we understand it, could not exist. Such values include:
   ■ a commitment to the pursuit of truth;
   ■ a responsibility to share knowledge;
   ■ freedom of thought and expression;
   ■ analysing evidence rigorously and using reasoned argument to reach a conclusion;
   ■ a willingness to listen to alternative views and judge them on their merits;
   ■ taking account of how one's own arguments will be perceived by others;
   ■ a commitment to consider the ethical implications of different findings or practices.

5.40   These are values higher education can, and should, share with students. It was put to us at one of our consultation conferences that higher education should see itself as having a distinctive responsibility to act as the conscience of the nation. Others will legitimately claim that they have such a responsibility, but we agree that higher education should see itself as sharing it.

5.41   The Robbins Committee saw higher education as an important compensator for social disadvantage but the expansion of higher education which followed its report did not lead, to the extent it hoped, to significant broadening of the social class composition of higher education. Nonetheless, the rapid expansion of higher education in the last few years has brought an increase in participation by those from socio-economic groups IV and V. We, like Robbins, believe that higher education should promote greater equality of social and economic opportunity, although we recognise that much depends on the earlier stages of education. In areas where young people do not stay in school or college education for long enough, or where they are not being sufficiently prepared for higher education, they are unlikely to put themselves forward. Higher education needs to take active steps to encourage access by under-represented groups.

5.42   Such social objectives are seen as the province of higher education in other countries as well. In reply to our enquiries, the Danish Ministry of Education represented that higher education has to:

> *'assist in creating a sustainable, economically sound, democratic society where few have too much and fewer too little.'*

5.43   Their time in higher education provides students with an opportunity to consider for themselves the values needed in a democratic society; a willingness to debate issues rationally and openly, and a commitment to a pluralistic society, the rule of law and the protection of personal liberties. It also provides the chance to reflect on the vulnerability of such a society and the need for continued support for the values that underpin it. Research in the humanities, for example, develops individuals who are reflective, have a sense of being rooted in a cultural and historical context, and understand the origins and moral nature of the great institutions of our society; the law, religion and education itself.

5.44   Higher education contributes to the health of society by helping it to understand itself, its history, culture and institutions. It is also a hallmark of a civilised society that it pursues knowledge at the highest levels for its own sake and that it seeks knowledge for altruistic, and not only commercial, ends.

5.45   Many institutions of higher education are custodians of part of the nation's cultural riches: in their library holdings, in their art collections and in their museums. While these may be held primarily as a research resource, there is also a duty on higher education to present them and to make them accessible, physically or through suitable interpretation, to members of society. Higher education has a custodial role in conserving what is known. Research that appears arcane today may become useful in the future, when it will be important that the knowledge is accessible.

5.46   There may be less emphasis now on the role of higher education in transmitting a common culture than there was at the time of Robbins, partly because cultures within the UK have become more diverse, and partly because there are so many other forms of cultural transmission available through the mass media. But this reinforces the need for higher education to preserve and transmit those forms and aspects of culture which may be, for the time being, unfashionable or in danger of being overwhelmed by the majority culture. For example, higher education is rightly still involved in transmitting the historic languages and cultures of the various parts of the United Kingdom.

5.47   In the course of our review we often invited comment on the role of higher education in transmitting a common culture. In particular we invited a contribution from Professor Stewart Sutherland, which we offer as a fitting conclusion to this section of our report:

'Higher education's central contribution to civic virtue is first and foremost in the spread of sense and practical wisdom in our society. Sense includes the capacity to distinguish truth from falsehood, knowledge from opinion, and good argument from bad. All of these fall within the tradition which emphasises the cultivation of the powers of the mind as central to all levels of education.

Practical wisdom is the capacity to apply these to the needs of others as well as oneself in the time and place in which one lives.

Democracy presupposes all of these abilities which is why the growth of democracy and the extension of education have always gone hand in hand. This is part and parcel of the responsibility which all citizens share in maintaining common purpose and the degree of common culture which is the foundation of democratic society.

In our time, however, there is an additional and distinctive role for our higher education institutions. A central challenge to democracy is the extension of specialised knowledge and its application to the way in which we live. Increasingly citizens are required to take, or at least to sanction very complex decisions about for example, nuclear power, about the most appropriate monetary system for our society, about complex moral issues surrounding gene therapy or reproductive biology, and so on. To do this with any confidence requires for each of us, to a varying degree, a combination of understanding and trust in the understanding of others. Higher education institutions have a dual responsibility in maintaining and strengthening these pillars of democracy.'

Our terms of reference

5.48   Our terms of reference gave us a substantial list of principles to take into account. We were required to consider all of them *'within the constraints of the Government's other spending priorities and affordability'*. Although we were not in a position to assess other spending priorities, we were advised in April 1997 by the Department for Education and Employment not to expect any increase in higher education's share of the financial resources provided for education, and that there might be a decrease. The Labour Party's Manifesto said there would be no increase in taxpayers' money for higher education. The Liberal Democrats said they would increase taxation to support education but indicated that little of this would be for higher education.

5.49   We discuss below our detailed interpretation of the rest of the principles in our terms of references.

There should be maximum participation in initial higher education by young and mature students and in lifetime learning by adults, having regard to the needs of individuals, the nation and the future labour market.

5.50   We endorse this principle. It is the key to becoming a nation committed to lifelong learning, although there will always be scope for strong debate about the precise nature of the needs and aspirations of individuals and the nation, and experience points to the difficulty of foretelling the future needs of the labour market. The various influences which should shape opportunities for participation in higher education and its size are discussed further in Chapters 6 and 7.

5.51   We are clear that the decisions about which individuals should be admitted to higher education should rest with the individual providers of higher education. They have a responsibility to assess whether an individual student's needs can in principle be appropriately met by a particular programme in higher education. This judgement entails more than a simple criterion of prior educational qualifications. The former University Grants Committee and National Advisory Body for Public Sector Higher Education suggested that qualifications for higher education should be interpreted as broadly as possible and that *courses of higher education should be available to all those who can benefit from them and who wish to do so'*. Although concerned that programmes should be maintained at levels appropriate to higher education, and that entry procedures should test ability to benefit as rigorously for those without formal qualifications as for those with them, the (then) Government accepted this principle, which we also endorse.[4] It recognises the success of those institutions which have enabled mature students with no formal qualifications to obtain higher education qualifications. The realisation of such opportunities is necessary for achievement of our vision of a Learning Society.

5.52   In a system where the providers of higher education are autonomous institutions, there can be no absolute statutory or government-backed guarantee of a place for all who want one. We do, however, believe that student choice should be the main shaper of the system and that institutions must be enabled to respond flexibly.

5.53   We recognise, however, the Government's duty to make decisions about the level of public expenditure and the proportion of public funding which should be devoted to higher education. What is required is a reform of the way in which higher education is funded, to allow greater flexibility in meeting different students' needs, whilst recognising the government's duty to weigh the many deserving calls on the public purse and, within that context, determine within Parliament what public resources should be made available to higher education.

        Students should be able to choose between a diverse range of courses, institutions, modes and locations of study.

5.54   A more diverse student population will require a more diverse range of programmes and access to different types of learning. Forms and styles of learning which were appropriate in the past will need development to meet the needs and develop the potential of a much larger learning population. Those who enter higher education will have widely varying previous experience and qualifications. A young entrant with A levels may be well-prepared academically but lack the breadth of experience and self-management skills of a mature student with employment experience. Those who have taken vocational qualifications before higher education may be more accustomed to projects and team-working than an A level entrant but less used to essay writing. A part-time mature student in employment, and perhaps with a family, will have many more competing pressures on her time than most young full-time students. She is likely to need to study in or near her home or workplace. All these students must have access to higher education which meets their needs. The nature of programmes to meet the increasingly diverse demands of students is discussed further in Chapter 9.

5.55 Diversity must, however, be accompanied by measures to ensure that students and employers understand the nature of the programmes being provided, and the outcomes expected from them, and that qualifications have national standing and are clearly understood.

Standards of degrees and other higher education qualifications should be at least maintained, and assured.

5.56 We attach much importance to this principle, while recognising the difficulty of ensuring it in a large and diverse system, with many different types of student taking varying types of programmes for diverse purposes. Students and employers must be able to rely on the value, quality and standards of qualifications. It is not currently evident to employers why there is not a common definition and understanding of what a degree is in higher education, although in other countries, such as the USA, there is a clear understanding that standards vary widely.

5.57 As access to higher education widens, and students with more modest prior academic attainments or abilities are admitted to higher education, adaptations to programmes and qualifications and new programmes will be needed to meet their needs. If such changes are not made, too many people will be set up to fail in higher education, or there will be a natural pressure to compromise on standards of achievement to allow them to succeed.

5.58 People who have under-performed at school may have few or no academic qualifications to demonstrate their intellectual capacities or knowledge. Such students may be as well-suited as a more conventionally qualified student for a standard degree programme. However, some of them, and some students who have attained modest qualifications at Level 3, although ready to move on to study at a higher level, may not be well-suited to or inclined to embark immediately on a programme designed to lead to a full honours degree within three or four years. In the context of access to lifelong learning, the current emphasis on the initial three- or four-year degree programme may be seen to be misplaced by students from a whole range of backgrounds. Some will see advantages in an initial commitment to a lower level qualification, so long as there is the opportunity to build on it later. We discuss these issues further in Chapter 10.

The effectiveness of teaching and learning should be enhanced.

5.59 We go further. We believe that the UK should aim to be the world leader in effective learning and teaching in higher education. It has, however, become clear to us that complex issues underlie the effectiveness of different approaches to learning and teaching. We want to see the emphasis placed on learning rather than teaching, but the key to this lies in better and different approaches to teaching and guidance. Individual higher education teachers are not well-informed about the effectiveness of different approaches to learning and teaching. We make recommendations designed to address this issue in Chapter 8.

Learning should be increasingly responsive to employment needs and include the development of general skills, widely valued in employment.

5.60   We recognise that many higher education programmes, especially short programmes designed in conjunction with employers, and programmes which have benefited from developments under the Enterprise in Higher Education Initiative, already have preparation for employment as one of their key objectives.[5] We have already noted the crucial role higher education will play in our future economy and believe that, over the system as a whole, even greater attention should be paid to this aspect. Chapter 9 discusses the relationship between programmes and the needs of employers in further detail.

Higher education's contribution to basic, strategic and applied research should be maintained and enhanced particularly in subjects where UK research has attained international standards of excellence or in Technology Foresight priority areas.

5.61   Higher education's contribution to research is one of its primary purposes. Its contribution to a range of types of research needs to be recognised and encouraged. Within that, the main, though not exclusive, focus should be on excellence and on areas of national need, however identified. Our research system needs to be capable of identifying and responding to new needs and areas of research as they open up. Rigid disciplinary boundaries in organisational structures or in relation to funding hamper institutions in exploiting new cross-disciplinary opportunities which are essential for maintaining innovative energy. There is a need for better communication between the academic community and industry, and better understanding on both sides of the other's needs. We make recommendations on the future development of research in higher education in Chapter 11.

Arrangements for student support should be fair and transparent and support the principles above.

5.62   We support this principle and our recommendations are designed to be consistent with it. We make a range of recommendations on financial support in Chapters 7, 20 and 21.

Higher education should be able to recruit, retain and motivate staff of the appropriate calibre.

Value for money and cost-effectiveness should be obtained in the use of resources.

5.63   We strongly support both these statements as necessary conditions which must be met if higher education is to achieve the aims and purposes we have identified within the constraints of the other principles. We make a number of recommendations designed to achieve these conditions in Chapters 14 and 15.

Additional principles

5.64   We considered whether there were other important principles which we should add to those in our terms of reference. We endorsed two further principles.

The various beneficiaries of higher education should share its costs, and public subsidies should be distributed equitably so that individuals are not denied access to higher education through lack of financial means.

5.65   There are many potential beneficiaries of higher education. Individuals achieve, on average, enhanced earning capacities as well as personal satisfaction. Employers have access to a well-qualified workforce. Industry has access to research findings. Everyone in society benefits from wealth creation and improvements to the quality of life generated by higher education.

5.66   Higher education also consumes a significant proportion of national resources and we believe, in principle, that the burden should be shared among the beneficiaries. This principle does not, in itself, imply any fundamental departure from existing practice: the costs of higher education are already shared. The taxpayer meets a large part of the cost through grants to universities and colleges and through support to individual students. Individual students may pay part or all of their own tuition costs if they are studying part-time or at postgraduate level, and employers may pay their employees' fees or allow them paid leave to pursue higher education. Students who study full-time contribute by foregoing the earnings they might have secured if not in higher education, and they may, over time, repay loans for their living costs. Commercial and public sector bodies may pay for contract research, consultancy or other specific services from higher education.

5.67   The more fundamental issue which we have had to address is whether the current balance of cost sharing is the right one. As we indicate in Chapter 18 we have concluded that greater contributions should be forthcoming from graduates in work as the chief beneficiaries.

5.68   At present, individuals who are in similar circumstances and studying in similar ways receive broadly similar levels of support for their maintenance because national arrangements are in place. For tuition, however, public subsidies vary substantially between institutions for programmes which are notionally the same in terms of the expected outcomes and the nature of the experience. We believe any such variations should be explicitly recognised and only continued to the extent that they can be justified.

5.69   Another major consideration is that the cost of higher education is substantial and the benefits which flow from it are unpredictable for the individual and realised over a long time period. We believe it would be unjust and inefficient if those who did not have immediate access to the necessary finance to participate in higher education were, for that reason, denied the chance of receiving any of its benefits.

Those who participate in higher education should receive an experience of assured quality and the users of higher education – both students and employers – should have access to enough information about what is on offer, its standards, quality, costs and intended outcomes, to enable them to make informed choices.

5.70   Both the nation and individuals invest substantial amounts of time and resources in higher education and are entitled to expect a minimum assured quality of experience in return for the sums invested and adequate information to inform their decisions. These are important elements in the new compact we have proposed.

Conclusion

5.71   Having established the purposes of higher education and the principles which should guide its development, we move on in the next group of chapters to explore how these should be given effect in responding to demand for higher education and in the principal activities of higher education, learning, teaching, scholarship and research.

Chapter 6

Future demand for higher education

6.1   Our terms of reference asked us to have regard, within the constraints of the Government's other spending priorities and affordability, to the principle that:

> *'there should be maximum participation in initial higher education by young and mature students and in lifetime learning by adults, having regard to the needs of individuals, the nation and the future labour market'*

6.2   In this chapter, we consider the future demand for higher education from the economy and from individuals over the next 20 years, in response to the social and economic influences outlined in Chapter 4. We turn in the next chapter, Chapter 7, to consider the pattern of participation between those from different social groups and the steps that need to be taken to tackle under-representation by some of these groups. In Chapter 17 we consider the financial implications of future demand for higher education.

6.3   In considering the future demand for higher education we looked at a range of evidence which enabled us to address:

- the economic factors affecting demand for those with higher education qualifications;
- possible scenarios of demand for higher education;
- how the demand for higher education should best be reflected in determining the size and shape of higher education.[1]

Economic factors affecting demand for those with higher education qualifications

6.4   The future demand for those with higher education qualifications will be shaped by the changing structure of the national economy and the labour market, which in turn will be responding to changes in the world economy and the associated competitive challenges. These forces will find their response in the choices made by individuals about participation in higher education and in employer demand for lifelong learning opportunities on behalf of their employees.

The changing structure of the national economy

6.5   The introduction of state education more than a century ago was fundamentally a response to the developing needs of the economy. The history of the last century has been marked by the progressive extension of state education not only as something which is socially desirable and good in its own right, but in response to the needs of an economy which, to sustain its markets, has had progressively to provide more advanced goods and services. The 20th century has seen a remarkable change in the structure of the national economy away from the extractive and basic industries and towards activities characterised by the intensive use of human capital, including advanced manufacture, the creative development of new products, and major new services.

6.6 Powerful world economic forces inescapably tie the United Kingdom (UK) more fully into the world economy. As we show in Chapter 4, one phenomenon is the emergence of the global corporation locating and relocating its operations to wherever there is greatest relative advantage, whether in accessing markets or in accessing the factors affecting production, including in particular the quality of the labour force.

6.7 The UK, in seeking to provide its people with a high and improving standard of living, will be able to do so and remain a major economy only if its people are highly educated and well trained. It must match proportionately the investments made in their people by other nations, and the volume and the quality of their outputs from such education and training. A decade ago we had fallen well behind many other countries of Western Europe in the provision of higher education. Even now, after participation rates by young people have doubled, and the target set by the last Government for a third of young people to participate in full-time higher education by the year 2000 has been largely met, our levels of participation remain behind the United States and Japan. However the stock of graduates in the labour market compares well with many European countries in part because of high graduation rates.[2] There is a long term expectation of growth in higher education in many countries, especially those of the Pacific Rim. Our degree programmes, whilst of high quality and comparable standards, are in the main shorter (other than in Scotland) than those of almost all other nations, largely because of the very specialised nature of the A level examination system.

6.8 There is international consensus that higher level skills are crucial to future economic competitiveness:

> 'The direction is universal participation: 100 per cent participation with fair and equal opportunities to study; in some form of tertiary education; at some stage in the life cycle and not necessarily end on to secondary education; in a wide variety of structures, forms and types of delivery; undertaken on equal terms either part-time or full-time; publicly subsidised but with shared client contributions; closely involving partners in the community; serving multiple purposes – educational, social, cultural and economic.'[3]

6.9 Our visits overseas suggest that, in the long term, other nations will increase their investment in higher education to sustain their economies. There is some emerging economic evidence to support such an approach. First, that countries which are the first to develop new research and technology capabilities gain a long term advantage over their competitors. Secondly, that 'the weight of evidence is increasingly that education is positively associated with income growth and higher education seems to be the most relevant educational variable in more developed countries'. As a matter of economic strategy, we must match international levels of investment to anticipate and respond to the changing structure of the international and national economy.

The changing requirements of the labour market

6.10   Labour market requirements for those with higher education qualifications are changing dramatically. Many of the employer organisations which gave evidence to us support this view. This will affect overall demand. The Confederation of British Industry told us:

> '*as the economy and organisations change, the areas in which graduate skill and qualities add value will multiply...large numbers of graduates are adding value not just in expanding numbers of traditional graduate jobs but also in a widening range of previously non-graduate roles*'.[4]

6.11   There is room for debate as to whether, following the major expansion in higher education that has taken place over recent years, there is need in the immediate future for further expansion and whether the labour market could absorb further increases in the numbers of conventional graduates. A study of the likely future labour market needs for highly skilled workers by the Institute for Employment Research (IER) at the University of Warwick looks ahead to the year 2000.[5] It considers in some detail the likely changes to occupational structures, based on changes in the recent past. The IER research concludes that, up to the year 2000, labour market requirements will largely be met by the current level of higher education participation.

6.12   Another view put to us is that the UK's chief economic need is not for more people with graduate qualifications but rather for more people with lower level post-school qualifications. This view draws on evidence that graduates are now being employed in jobs which were traditionally done by non-graduates, raising the possibility of their under-utilisation, and on the longstanding perception that the UK's comparative international weakness lies at the technician rather than degree level.

6.13   It would indeed be surprising if the labour market did not need time to respond fully to the increased supply of those with higher level qualifications. We are persuaded that jobs are being progressively redefined to utilise graduate skills:

- a recent study for the Department for Education and Employment (DfEE) showed that, even when graduates were recruited into traditionally 'non-graduate' jobs, a large majority (65 per cent) of managers who had taken on increased numbers of graduates thought that the jobs had improved because they were being undertaken by a graduate;[6]
- research by the National Institute of Economic and Social and Research shows that some sectors of the economy have been able to deal more flexibly with additional graduates than others and that redesigning jobs can enable graduates to add value in traditionally non-graduate jobs;[7]
- respondents to our employer questionnaire suggest that '*graduates, as a proportion of total employees, will continue to grow*' and that '*there is scope to increase the proportion of those with first degrees in some industries, although this will partly depend on the response of higher education to employers*';[8]
- Swedish research shows that flexible organisations are more likely to thrive in the international marketplace and that the key to their flexibility is the extent to which they employ highly skilled workers;[9]

- Japanese and USA experience demonstrates an ability to make good use of much higher numbers and proportions of graduates in the economy than is traditionally the case in the UK. Even in the USA, where some 60 per cent of the population has some experience of higher education, graduates attract significantly higher salaries than non-graduates, suggesting that their employers continue to regard them as bringing extra value;[10]
- a survey of graduates by the University of Central England points to strong demand from employers for graduates with the right qualities, notwithstanding recent increases in the flow of graduates to the labour market;[11]
- public policy decisions are transforming certain professions. For example, we were told that in a health service with a new focus on primary care, nurses and those in professions allied to medicine will need the knowledge, skills and aptitudes typically acquired in higher education.[12]

6.14 As to the demand for more people with advanced technical training, we agree that this is an area of national need. We believe that much of the further growth of higher education, at least in the short term, should be in the Higher National Certificate, the Higher National Diploma and other analogous awards. We reflect this in our proposals for the structure of qualifications in Chapter 10 and for the pattern of institutions in Chapter 16. It is expansion at this level that has particularly characterised recent Scottish experience, where participation by young people has reached almost 45 per cent, significantly ahead of England and Wales.

6.15 Chapter 9 also explores in more detail the views of employers about the range of skills and attributes which they require from graduates; and how those views can better be reflected in higher education, based in part on the questionnaire which we sent to a sample of employers.[13] We emphasise in Chapter 12 the importance of higher education institutions ensuring that they are well-informed about local and regional employers' requirements.

Economic benefits to individuals from participating in higher education

6.16 An assessment of the economic benefits to individuals from participating in higher education has been central to our work. These benefits are probably the most significant economic factor affecting demand. They are substantial and consist of:
- employment rates which are, on average, above those for people who were qualified to enter higher education but did not do so;
- pay levels which are, on average, above those for people who were qualified to enter higher education but did not do so.

6.17 We drew on three important studies to assess these benefits and their possible impact on demand:[14]
- research by Analytical Services within the Department for Education and Employment. This studies graduates across a number of economic cycles, from those graduating in 1971 to those graduating in 1995. The 1989 to 1995 results are shown in Report 7, 'Rates of return to higher education';
- research by the Policy Studies Institute (PSI) which looks at young graduates (at ages 23 to 24);[15]

■ research by the Institute for Fiscal Studies (IFS) which uses data for those born in 1958 recorded in the National Child Development Study and examines those who were graduates at the age of 33.[16]

6.18　These three studies show evidence of strong and persistent economic benefits to those with higher education qualifications. First, the Analytical Services research shows that employment rates are higher for those with such qualifications than for those without, particularly for women (Chart 6.1). Employment benefits are apparent for men with higher education qualifications in their mid-30s onwards, and rather earlier for women. The IFS and PSI reports broadly support these findings for the particular ages they study.

Chart 6.1 – Proportion employed by age and qualification

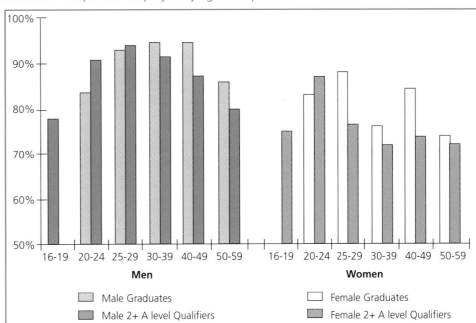

Source: Report 7 – Rates of return to higher education
Note: 2+A level qualifiers refers to those qualified to enter higher education but choosing not to do so

6.19　Secondly, the Institute for Fiscal Studies (IFS) and Analytical Services research show that, on aggregate, those with higher education qualifications enjoy higher levels of pay than those qualified to enter but not entering higher education (Table 6.1). Again, the differences are more significant for women than for men, and increase through the working life.

Table 6.1 – Pay differences for graduates

Report		Pay differences (per cent)
Institute for Fiscal Studies	(at age 33)	21 (men, first degree) 39 (women, first degree)
Analytical Services	(across a working lifetime)	24 (men only)

Source: IFS TITLE, Report 7
The Analytical Services research includes employment, as well as pay differences. The other studies do not. However, for men across lifetime earnings the employment difference is small compared to the pay premium.

6.20 Any reliable measurement of pay premia (rather than raw data about pay differences) needs to discount any differences in pay levels between the two comparator groups which are attributable to innate ability or socio-economic background. Hence, the measurements quoted in Table 6.2 seek to calculate the pay premium which can be attributed uniquely to higher education, rather than to any other factor. The research by Analytical Services and the Institute for Fiscal Studies (IFS) notably agree in their calculations that around 60 to 80 per cent of the pay premia can properly be attributed to higher education. This is persuasive. These two pieces of research find significant pay premia for those with higher education qualifications. This implies that employers place a genuine economic value on higher education qualifications when they pay higher salaries to those who posses such qualifications. The Policy Studies Institute (PSI) data show the lowest difference because of the early point in the career at which the data are collected.

Table 6.2 – Adjusted pay premia for graduates

Report		Pay premia (per cent)
Policy Studies Institute	(at age 23 to 24)	5 (men and women)
Institute for Fiscal Studies	(at age 33)	12 to 18 (men) 34 to 38 (women)
Analytical Services	(across a working lifetime)	14 to 19 (men)

Source: Policy Studies Institute, Institute for Fiscal Studies, Report 7

6.21 The pay premia, however, take no account of the costs to the individual of obtaining their higher education qualification. To arrive at a true measure of the economic benefit to individuals, the pay and employment benefits should be offset against the costs incurred, including opportunity costs. Such calculations are referred to by economists as the 'private rate of return'. The standard method of determining the return, either to the individual or to society as a whole (which we discuss below) of participation in higher education is to regard becoming a student as an investment, incurring costs which are repaid in later life through enhanced earnings. For the individual, the principal costs are any additional maintenance expenditures, tuition fees (if any) and income foregone (the salary the person would have earned if he or she had gone straight into work instead of studying for a degree). The return to the individual's investment consists of a stream of extra earning accumulated over a whole lifetime, or the difference between earnings with a higher education qualification and what a person would have earned without such a qualification. The relevant difference for individuals is that in post-tax earnings. This calculation, by using lifetime earnings, takes account of lower unemployment rates, which is one component of the earnings difference. Once costs and earnings are known, it is possible to calculate a percentage return on the investment.

6.22   The Analytical Services evidence shows that, on average, those with higher education qualifications currently in the labour market enjoy a significant and sustained private rate of return to their investment (Table 6.3).

Table 6.3 – Private rates of return to graduation

All	Men	Women
11–14%	9–11%	14–17%

Source: Report 7

6.23   These private rates of return, were they to be well known by potential students and reasonably certain to continue, would be likely to stimulate sustained high levels of demand for higher education.

6.24   However, in looking forward, it is relevant to consider how far the increase in the stock of those with higher education qualifications in the labour market might depress the pay premia. Even the most recent data, in the Policy Studies Institute research, are really too recent to provide any evidence of the impact on pay premia and rates of return of this latest and large expansion. The supply of those with higher education qualifications will continue to increase well into the next century, even with no further increase in participation rates. But a long term expectation that there will continue to be a pay premium and a private rate of return is supported by the UK's experience in the post-Robbins period. US experience is also encouraging. Although more graduates are entering jobs in the USA which have not, in the past, required a first degree, there continue to be significant labour market benefits for graduates.[17]

6.25   Whether high private rates of return will be sustained depends also on the costs to the individual of acquiring a higher education qualification. At present, these costs are met primarily from public funds for full-time undergraduates, who pay no tuition fees. If this balance is altered, as we discuss in Chapter 18, the private rate of return may fall. The technical advice from Analytical Services (Department for Education and Employment) for future private rates of return is first, that there will be continuing high returns for graduates, even when the graduate stock increases significantly, although at lower levels because of the recent expansion in participation; and secondly, that further expansion will depress these rates in the medium term.[18]

6.26   We take a somewhat more optimistic view. If higher education institutions and employers adopt the recommendations in the rest of our report, we are confident first, that employers will be better placed to make effective use of increased numbers of those with higher education qualifications; secondly, that students will be better placed to make well-informed decisions about their studies; and thirdly, that institutions will be better able to ensure that the programmes and qualifications they provide meet the aspirations and requirements of individuals and employers. On this basis, we conclude that there are likely to be continuing significant economic benefits for individuals from higher education.

Economic benefits to society from participation in higher education

6.27 Having considered the demand from individuals arising from their economic benefits, we also explored the demand that might flow from the economic benefits to society. But it is extremely difficult to quantify such benefits and, therefore, on that basis alone, to quantify how much higher education society might demand and be prepared to fund. We are much more circumspect about this evidence than about that on the economic benefits to graduates themselves, as it is intrinsically more difficult to evaluate and interpret.

6.28 We considered two studies to assess these wider benefits and their possible impact on society's demand for higher education:
  ■ research by the Analytical Services Higher Education Division at the Department for Education and Employment on the social rate of return (Report 7);
  ■ research by Professor Norman Gemmell on externalities (Report 8 'Externalities to higher education: a review of the new growth literature').

6.29 The calculation of the social rate of return is similar to that of the private rate of return in that it seeks to measure a return on investment in teaching in higher education. But it differs from that of the private rate of return in two ways. First, the investment in this calculation is that of the taxpayer, and not the individual student. Many of the costs of higher education, especially for full-time undergraduates, through free tuition and support for living costs, are currently met from public funds. Secondly, the return in this calculation is the additional gross earnings of the graduate, compared to those of a non-graduate. The assumption here is that these additional graduate earnings reflect the additional productivity of graduates compared to non-graduates. This is discussed further in Report 7.

6.30 The Analytical Services research found that the long run social rate of return calculated in this way has run at about seven to nine per cent for the period since Robbins.[19] This is above the six per cent rate regarded by the Treasury as a minimum acceptable return on public investment. As with the private rate of return, the advice from Analytical Services is that the social rate of return may fall for those graduating now, probably to around the Treasury benchmark of six per cent. The social rate of return for those currently in the labour market may remain at around six per cent until about 2015 (although the prospective rate of return for new graduates in that year is likely to be higher).[20] This reduction is likely to be similar to that which immediately followed the Robbins expansion, which caused rates to fall outside the long run range and which was reversed by the mid 1980s, as is shown in Chart 6.2. In our view, the post-Robbins experience of an initial drop followed by reversal and return to the long run rate is likely to be repeated.

Chart 6.2 – The social rate of return, for young men, first degrees

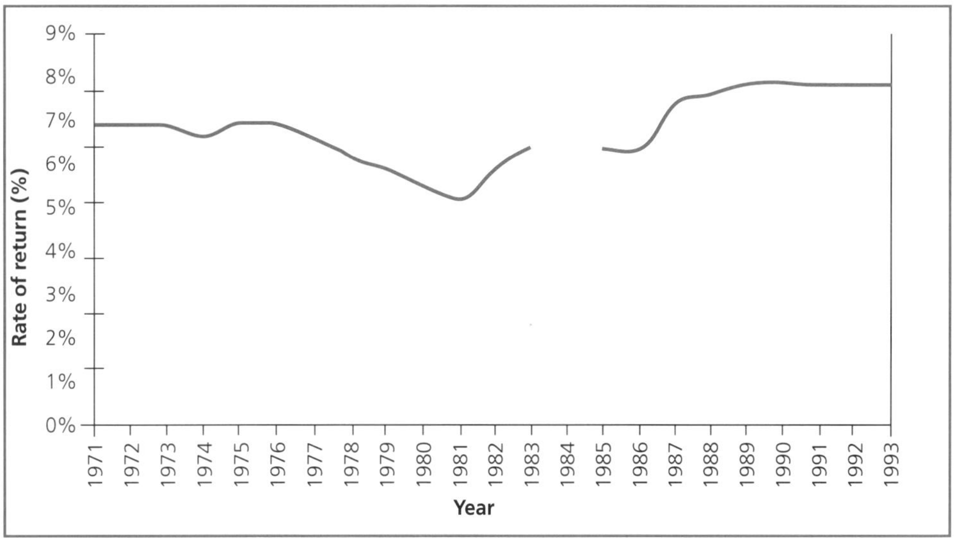

Source: Report 7
Note: measurement changes between 1983 and 1985 mean that figures from 1985 onwards are measured on a lower basis than the figures for earlier years

6.31   Indeed, this projection of future social rates of return could be exceeded if higher education can improve the value of its output to employers (which we explore in more detail in the Chapter 9); and if employers make better use of more people with higher education qualifications and reflect this in the salaries they pay.

6.32   This calculation of the social rate of return, whilst an accepted methodology amongst many economists, rests on the assumption that graduate pay is a robust proxy for graduate productivity. Such calculations may appear to offer a narrow measure of the impact of graduates on the economy. It is possible, for example, that graduates raise the productivity of non-graduate colleagues and help spread technological change. It is also possible that graduate salaries are not actually an accurate reflection of graduates' own productivity if the labour market works imperfectly. This raises the question as to whether the return to society is really higher than the measurable figure of seven-nine per cent. We therefore wanted to explore any social and economic benefits from participation in higher education which are not captured by the measurements of higher salaries and tax payments upon which the social rate of return is calculated.

6.33   We therefore commissioned Professor Gemmell to review the evidence from economists about any externalities to higher education. These refer to any economic benefits which are not captured in graduate salaries and reflected in the standard calculations of the rate of return on which we have drawn. In theory, these might include the economic benefits to society from extra productivity in the economy above that represented in graduate salaries. Professor Gemmell reviews a range of research, including comparisons of growth between different countries; growth in productivity between firms; and evidence on the contribution of levels of skills to productivity. Professor Gemmell draws a number of conclusions:

■ those economic theories in which there are externalities make assumptions which are currently essentially unproven;[21]

- there is some emerging evidence which suggests that higher education can be important *'for the development of innovative research and the ability to acquire and adopt it'*;[22]
- calculations of the social rate of return which include and exclude externality effects differ only slightly. This suggests that externalities are likely to be small.[23]

6.34 The difficulties in identifying any robust or compelling measurement of externalities led us to treat the evidence with caution.

Possible scenarios of demand for higher education

6.35 The return to the individual from gaining a higher education qualification is likely to prompt continuing strong demand for higher education. Individuals are likely to respond to strong labour market signals about employment and salary prospects. But whilst significant, economic factors will not be the sole factors affecting demand.

Demand from young people for full-time initial higher education

6.36 Both the Department for Education and Employment (DfEE)[24] and the Institute for Employment Studies (IES)(in a study commissioned by the CVCP)[25] have made projections of the likely demand from young people for full-time higher education. The components of such forecasts are based on:
- data about the number of young people in the relevant age cohort;
- data about the likely numbers of young people who will gain Level 3 qualifications, the traditional threshold for entry to higher education;
- the current propensity of those with such qualifications to enter higher education.

6.37 The Analytical Services projections suggest that the number of young people in the relevant cohort will increase, thereby potentially increasing demand for higher education. Further, Analytical Services and the IES project an increase in the proportion of the cohort obtaining Level 3 qualifications, including the Advanced General National Vocational Qualification (GNVQ); and an increased propensity for those with this level of qualification to enter higher education. This is largely explained by the changing socio-economic composition of the population, in which, for example, the relative share of those whose children look to enter higher education is increasing. It is also because of the initiatives in schools and further education designed to drive up achievements at 16 plus. These include efforts to improve GCSE results and staying-on rates at 16 plus; the introduction of the GNVQ and the Modern Apprenticeship; the emphasis on achievement in the English Further Education Funding Council's funding methodology; as well as initiatives by individual schools, colleges and higher education institutions. We say more about some of these initiatives in Chapter 7.

6.38 Decisions by young people will, however, be much influenced by the extent to which there continues to be a substantial return on their own investment in higher education; and the extent to which they are aware of this in making their decisions. Inevitably, there are economic cycles which affect graduate employment, especially that for new graduates. The technical advice from Analytical Services suggests that the likely short to medium term decline in the private rate of return following the most recent expansion in participation (as well as any increased costs of participating) will depress demand for places in higher education.

6.39 If the present funding and capacity constraints were lifted, entrants to full-time first degrees and sub-degree programmes could probably rise significantly in response to demographic and social changes: The Institute for Employment Studies (IES) suggests a rise in entrants to full-time first degree programmes of about a quarter by the year 2003.[26] The technical advice from Analytical Services suggests that participation will increase up to 2004 to between 35 and 42 per cent under current funding arrangements.[27]

6.40 Taking a long-term view, we consider that the returns will be such as to stimulate continuing significant demand from young people for full-time initial higher education. In saying this, we have in mind the continuing increase in the severity of the challenge in world markets; that today's level of response will be inadequate in the years ahead; and that the baseline against which calculations of economic return have to be made will itself be changing. This is fundamental to any assessment of the future returns to further expansion of participation in higher education, to our view of the long-term return to individuals, and therefore, on economic grounds alone, to likely demand. We consider that a participation rate of 45 per cent is achievable over the next 20 years.

Demand from older, part-time and postgraduate students

6.41 It is much more difficult to make projections of demand from older, part-time or postgraduate students, in part because these groups are so diverse. It is particularly difficult to know whether the numbers of older first-time entrants will decline, as educational achievement by 18 year olds at Level 3 increases; and, if so, how that will interact with any increase in demand from those who already have a higher education qualification but want to update their skills and knowledge in higher education. Certainly the decline in the size of the first category is likely to be slow; and our analysis of the changing nature of the economy suggests that the increase in the size of the second category may be pronounced. As the Committee of Vice-Chancellors and Principals (CVCP) noted of the second category in its evidence to us, *'such groups could grow at a much faster rate as a consequence of the need for lifelong learning and continuing personal and professional development'*.[28] Responses to our employer questionnaire also suggest that there is scope for an increase in employer usage of higher education to meet their requirements for continuing professional development, including tailor-made courses and company sponsorship of employees, provided the costs and quality are right.[29]

6.42 We received technical advice from Analytical Services (Department for Education and Employment) of projections of demand for part-time and postgraduate study. For postgraduate research qualifications, the projections take account of the constraints recognised in the Review of Postgraduate Education of the availability of supervisors, grants and facilities.[30] For taught postgraduate qualifications, an increase of

40 per cent over the 20 year period is suggested, in line with increasing numbers of those with first degrees, diplomas and certificates, a sizeable percentage but small when compared to total undergraduate numbers.[31] This suggested increase refers to publicly funded students: the advice from Analytical Services further suggests that the adoption of lifelong learning by higher education institutions, employers and students would lead to an additional increase, of non-publicly funded participants.

Conclusions about the future demand for higher education

6.43   In our view, in the longer term, demand for higher education in the UK from the economy and individuals for initial qualifications and lifelong learning is likely to be higher than it is today. We base this conclusion on:

- the nature of the developing competitive environment facing the UK and the consequences that will have for the economy, incomes and the labour market unless we respond to the investment being made in higher education by our main competitors;
- the economic benefits of participation in higher education to be gained for individuals and society;
- the need to maintain high participation at the traditional ages of entry, affected particularly by improving rates of achievement at Level 3;
- the need for the increasing stock of those with higher education qualifications in the labour market to refresh their previous learning and engage in new learning.

6.44   Given the economic requirement for more highly skilled people in the workforce, it would be a high risk policy for the UK not to maintain parity of achievement in higher education with the other main members of the European Union, the USA and also the countries of the Pacific Rim. As we show in the next chapter, Chapter 7, there are also pressing social as well as economic imperatives in the UK to tackle differential participation by some particular social groups.

6.45   We have already endorsed the principle of maximising participation, within public expenditure constraints, consistent with individual, labour market and national needs. We do not see value in setting targets. Rather, we see participation in higher education being determined primarily by informed student demand, subject to the constraints of what can be afforded and by the need for government intervention to ensure that participation in higher education does not fall behind that of our major competitor countries. But in making our proposals for the future development of higher education, we needed to take a view about the kind of increase in participation that it would be prudent to envisage if the UK is to be well-served in terms of maintaining its international competitiveness. In that context, we have noted the relatively high rates of participation by young people in Japan and the USA. We have also noted that rates of around 45 per cent are already being achieved in Scotland and Northern Ireland. Although the technical advice from Analytical Services suggests an increase in participation in initial higher education by about one fifth and comments that any increase in costs to the graduate may reduce this, we think it would be imprudent not to look to a significant expansion in higher education over the next 20 years. We see much of this increase in participation, as in Scotland, being at the sub-degree level.

How best to reflect demand for higher education in determining the size and shape of higher education

Responding to overall demand

6.46 Finally, we considered, in the light of all this evidence, how best to reflect overall demand in determining the size and shape of higher education. Until the cap was imposed on the numbers of full-time undergraduate places, the UK had a system which was driven largely by demand. This accounts for the unprecedented growth over the late 1980s and early 1990s. Total undergraduate student numbers are now capped. We cannot make a firm prediction about levels of demand or total numbers in higher education over the next 20 years, nor do we want to set a specific target. In our view, informed student and employer demand should be the main determinants of the level of participation in the future, but with the state intervening if need be to ensure that levels of participation match those of our major competitor nations.

6.47 We know that employers share our view that there should be no artificial constraint on participation and that an increase needs to be underpinned by responsible employer behaviour. As the Confederation of British Industry stated in its evidence to us:

'the Government's current cap on student numbers in higher education is against the national interest. It should be removed and individual demand made the main determinant of the size of the sector....individual demand is influenced by employer signals. Employers have a clear responsibility to send appropriate signals in terms of salary and career structure'[32]

The balance of subjects

6.48 We also considered how best to reflect demand for different subjects. Some of the employers who responded to our survey identified quite specific areas where they felt they had immediate difficulties in finding graduates.[33] There are many others for whom the subject of study is much less significant. Many employers are concerned less with the subject studied than the skills and attributes of the individual, as developed by their higher education studies. Of course, for individuals, employment prospects may be an important factor in their choice of study, but there will be others, including intellectual excitement and intrinsic satisfaction.

6.49 Given the public investment in higher education, it is a legitimate concern that investment should provide the nation with individuals who have the knowledge, skills and understanding it needs. There are those who, in an effort to ensure a closer fit between what they perceive employers to want and the subjects studied, advocate an extension of manpower planning. The precise achievement of such an objective would require accurate forecasting, intervention in higher education on an unprecedented scale, and significant constraints on student choice. There have never been accurate forecasts of the balance of subjects required. National manpower planning has a poor track record and we do not recommend it, although we recognise that student numbers for some disciplines have always been subject to planning intervention, whether to limit the places in the face of strong demand (veterinary programmes, for example) or to stimulate the demand for places in the face of low demand (teacher training, for example). We say more about this in Chapter 22.

6.50   We believe that the better option is to rely on informed student demand to shape the balance of subjects, with employers articulating their requirements clearly and students having better information about available options and their implications.

6.51   In our view, the overall size and subject balance of higher education should, with the exception of some disciplines where intervention continues to be required, better reflect demand. We therefore make recommendations in other chapters to improve the information available to students; to make their choices more financially neutral as between modes of study and to help institutions better understand local and regional participation (Chapter 7 and 12); and work more closely with employers (Chapter 9). Institutions, employers and students have much to gain from an open exchange of information and comment.

Qualification levels

6.52   The balance of demand between full-time and part-time, and between young and mature learners will be influenced by the extent of public and employer support, and how far individuals are expected to contribute to the costs of higher education. At least initially, we see a large part of the growth taking place at sub-degree level. This is likely better to reflect the aspirations of many of those who may enter this expanded system, large numbers of whom are likely to have non-standard entry qualifications and more diverse aspirations. It will also address the UK's relative international disadvantage at these levels. We make proposals in Chapter 10 for a new qualifications structure which we believe to be best fitted to meet the needs of an expanded system. This will support lifelong learning; include more stopping-off points with real value below the level of the first degree for more initial entrants; enable students to take clearer but flexible pathways including academic and vocational components; and enable students to return to higher education later in life to take study at a higher level. This approach is supported by a major international study of tertiary education which predicts that 'mass' higher education systems need to be accompanied by intermediate qualifications to help reduce drop-out.[34]

Recommendation 1   **We recommend to the Government that it should have a long term strategic aim of responding to increased demand for higher education, much of which we expect to be at sub-degree level; and that to this end, the cap on full-time undergraduate places should be lifted over the next two to three years and the cap on full-time sub-degree places should be lifted immediately.**

Conclusion

6.53   In this chapter we have considered the likely future demand for higher education. In the next chapter we look in some more detail at the need to widen participation in higher education and how this might be achieved.

Chapter 7

Widening participation in higher education

7.1 In this chapter, we review the levels of participation in higher education by different groups in our society and offer recommendations on how low levels of participation by some groups might be increased. Looking back, there is much to celebrate: there have been some remarkable achievements. But substantial problems remain and improvements are required as a matter of priority. For the reasons set out in the previous chapter (Chapter 6), increasing participation in higher education is a necessary and desirable objective of national policy over the next 20 years. This must be accompanied by the objective of reducing the disparities in participation in higher education between groups and ensuring that higher education is responsive to the aspirations and distinctive abilities of individuals.

7.2 In making this statement, we reject the notion that more students will mean a reduction in academic standards. The notion of a limited 'pool of ability' was examined and rejected by the Robbins Committee. We too have examined it and reject it. It is very often true that *'people respond to opportunities that are available'* and, if the recommendations elsewhere in our report are accepted (Chapter 10) widening opportunities can certainly be consistent with maintaining standards.[1]

7.3 We considered a range of evidence[2] which enabled us to address:
- the current pattern of participation, including that by specific groups within the population;
- the causes of differential participation and possible solutions.

The current pattern of participation

7.4 As we saw in Chapter 3, participation in higher education has greatly increased since the time of Robbins. Over the last decade alone there have been major changes in the pattern of participation as the following table demonstrates for full-time first degree students.

Table 7.1 – Trends in student intake (full-time, first degree), per cent

	1986	1995
Women	42	52
Age 21+	15	29
Socio-economic group IIIm-V	23	28
A level entrants	86	74
Ethnic minorities	11	13

Source: Report 6, *Widening Participation in Higher Education for Students from Lower Socio-Economic Groups and Students with Disabilities*

7.5   We welcome the way in which the expansion of higher education during this period has been associated with increased participation by women, by mature students, by students from socio-economic groups III to V, by students with new kinds of entry qualifications, and by students from ethnic minorities.[3] Higher education can bestow material benefits on those who take it up, whether in higher salaries or in having a job rather than being unemployed, as we saw in Chapter 6. As participation increases, the cost of non-participation grows too.[4] Society are higher education institutions have, therefore, a moral obligation to concern themselves with continuing differences in levels of participation by different groups.

Participation by women

7.6   Women's participation overall is now in line with their demographic representation. The percentage of women undergraduates in the UK has doubled since Robbins. But they are unevenly distributed across subjects and levels of study. Women are under-represented in engineering and technology; and more than proportionately represented in the arts and humanities and in the natural sciences. As the Equal Opportunities Commission told us in its evidence, *'degree choice clearly illustrates a gender bias with more than twice as many women as men studying English and French and four times as many men as women studying Physics and Computer Studies'.*[5] Women are under-represented at higher levels of study, especially in research degrees, where only 35 per cent of postgraduate research students are women.[6]

Participation by students from different socio-economic groups

7.7   Participation rates amongst students from the Registrar General's socio-economic groups IV and V rose steeply during the late 1980s and early 1990s across the UK. But the ratio of participation between socio-economic groups did not change significantly. The share of participation in higher education by those from professional and managerial groups (groups I and II) is much higher than their share in the economically active population. The share by those from the three other socio-economic groups is lower than their share in the economically active population, as shown in Chart 7.1.

Chart 7.1 – Percentage of home full-time degree programme entrants, 1994

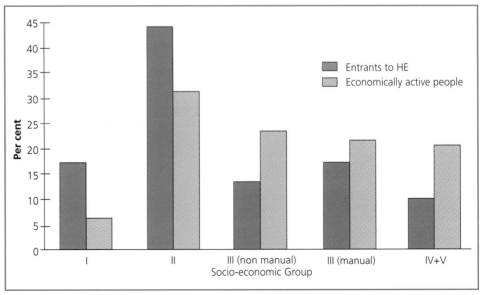

Source: Report 6

7.8   Men from socio-economic groups IV and V are particularly unlikely to participate. Once in higher education, those from socio-economic groups IV and V are more than twice as likely to be studying for a sub-degree qualification as those from groups I and II.[7]

7.9   The relative proportions of young people gaining qualifications for entry to higher education, their A level points scores and their propensity to enter higher education also vary with socio-economic group, as Table 7.2 shows.

Table 7.2 – Level 3 qualifications and entry to higher education, 1993

Socio-economic group	Percentage of 18–19 year olds gaining 2 A Levels or equivalent	Percentage of 18–19 year olds with 2 A Levels or equivalent going to higher education	Mean A Level points score for those achieving 2 A Levels
Highest socio-economic groups	50	77	17
Middle socio-economic groups	27	59	11
Lowest socio-economic groups	16	47	8

Source: Policy Studies Institute[8]

Participation by students from different localities

7.10   Reflecting the differences in participation in higher education between socio-economic groups, participation rates vary widely with students' home location. Here, the discrepancy in the achievements between regions and localities – and in some cases, between schools – is remarkable. In 1992, there was a 16 percentage point difference in the participation rate in full time education for 16 to 19 year olds between the regions with the highest and the lowest post-16 participation rates.[9] Research by the Higher Education Funding Council for England (HEFCE) shows that the probability of a young person entering a higher education institution is strongly related to the nature of the student's more immediate neighbourhood. That probability increases sharply with neighbourhood affluence. The HEFCE has estimated that, if the participation from the neighbourhoods with the lowest rates increased to the national average, an extra 35,000 more young English people would enrol in higher education institutions.[10]

Participation by mature students

7.11   Mature students (those over the age of 21) are well represented: more than half of entrants to higher education are now mature and 30 per cent are over the age of 30. The figures are significantly higher in the 1992 universities than the pre-1992 universities, as Table 7.3 shows.

Table 7.3 – Participation by age of student, by type of university, 1996, per cent

University	18 years and under	20–25 years	26 years and over
Pre-1992	68	37	35
1992	32	63	65

*Source: **Report 5**, Widening participation in higher education by ethnic minorities, women and alternative students*

7.12   Older students are particularly strongly represented among part-time students: 63 per cent of first degree students studying part-time are over 30 and of those 30 and over, 55 per cent study part-time. Chart 7.2 shows the proportion of students who study part-time, by age.

Chart 7.2 – Part-time students, by age, per cent

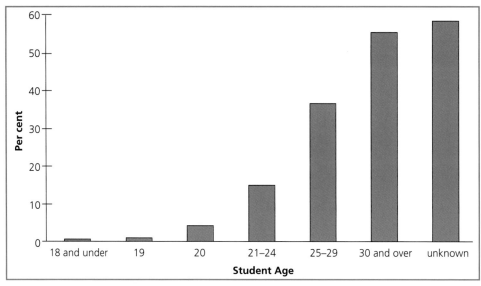

Source: HESA data

7.13   There is debate about the extent to which this participation by mature students helps to redress the under-representation by some groups at younger ages. It is well-known that learning is very unevenly distributed among the adult population. But it would also seem that individuals from those groups which have not, traditionally, participated in higher education at 18 are increasingly doing so at later ages.

Participation by students with disabilities

7.14   There is a shortage of reliable information on which to base a secure judgement on whether participation by students with disabilities matches their presence in the population as a whole. The data available for higher education depends on whether or not students identify themselves as having a disability. Also, the count of students with disabilities is made on a different basis from the count of the general population. More significantly the data does not appear to record those who need assistance in order to study as a result of a disability, rather than those who have a disability irrespective of its impact on their studies.

7.15   The information available suggests that between two and four per cent of students in higher education have a disability.[11] In comparison, the Labour Force Survey shows seven per cent of the 18–30 age group to have a long-standing disability.[12] Estimates for schools indicate that between 2 and 20 per cent of pupils have a learning difficulty and/or disability at any one time during their school career. Just over five per cent of further education college students in England have been recorded as having a learning difficulty and/or disability.[13] Students with disabilities are enrolled disproportionately strongly with the Open University, where the challenges of living away from home, physical access to study and so on, do not apply to the same extent.[14] Overall, it appears that people with disabilities are probably under-represented in most institutions and across higher education as a whole.

Participation by ethnic minority students

7.16   Ethnic minorities as a whole are more than proportionally represented in higher education, compared to the general population. In 1994, 8.2 per cent of the 18 to 20 year olds in higher education were from ethnic minorities compared to 5.2 per cent in the population as a whole (although it has to be noted that the age profile of the ethnic minority population tends to be younger than that for the population as a whole). However, Bangladeshi women, and Afro-Caribbean men remain under-represented in higher education. Table 7.4 shows the available national data.

Table 7.4 – Ethnicity in higher education and the national population, 1994, per cent

Ethnic Group	18–20 years		21–27 years		28–37 years		38–47 years		48 years and over	
White	87.8	(92.7)	83.5	(93.1)	86.4	(93.1)	91.8	(94.8)	93.1	(97.3)
Black	1.7	(1.8)	5.8	(2.1)	7.7	(2.5)	3.7	(1.2)	2.8	(0.9)
Indian	4.5	(2.0)	3.6	(1.8)	1.4	(1.8)	0.9	(1.8)	1.1	(0.8)
Pakistani	2.0	(1.4)	2.4	(1.1)	0.6	(0.8)	0.4	(0.7)	0.3	(0.3)
Other	4.0	(2.1)	4.6	(1.8)	3.9	(1.8)	3.3	(1.5)	2.7	(0.6)
All	100	(100)	100	(100)	100	(100)	100	(100)	100	(100)

Source: Report 5
Note: numbers in parenthesis show the figures for the UK population as a whole

7.17   Ethnic minority students are also represented differentially in different subjects and disciplines, with Afro-Caribbean students being more than proportionately represented in arts and humanities programmes and under-represented on technical programmes. Some professional programmes, such as teacher training, where it might be argued that proportional representation is particularly important, appear to be failing to recruit students proportionately from the various ethnic populations in the UK.[15] Black students are also more likely to study for degree qualifications part-time; and Black students and those from the Indian sub-continent are more likely to study for sub-degree qualifications than the population as a whole.[16]

Participation in different types of institution

7.18   There are pronounced differences in the participation of students from different groups in different types of institution, as Table 7.5 shows. In 1993, 84 per cent of students in the pre-1992 universities had A level qualifications compared to 59 per cent in the 1992 universities. As already mentioned, mature students are more likely to be found in the 1992 universities. Students from ethnic minorities and from socio-economic groups III to V were also more strongly represented in the 1992 universities.

Table 7.5 – Student intake by type of university, 1993, per cent

	Pre-1992 universities	1992 universities
Women	49.6	49.0
Age 21+	17.0	34.2
Social class IIIm-V	22.3	32.4
A level entrants	83.9	58.5
Ethnic minorities	8.5	14.4

Source: Report 5

7.19   We believe that institutions are even-handed between one student and another in their selection and admission against policies and criteria that reflect their missions. And we support diversity of institutional mission. But it has nonetheless been put to us that differences in the outcomes of selection and admissions by institutions may create a two-tier system in which, because of perceptions in the labour market of the relative status of institutions, *'applicants progress from privileged pasts to privileged futures or from less privileged pasts to less secure and lower status futures'*.[17]

The causes of differential participation and possible solutions

7.20   We wish to see participation widened and the differentials between groups reduced significantly over the coming years. Consequently, we have sought to identify the reasons for the differences and the extent to which solutions lie within the influence of higher education. Where they can be addressed by higher education, we have considered to what extent the solution lies in collective initiatives or action. Many institutions already take their responsibilities seriously. Government policy should now ensure that higher education is an active partner in the developing strategy to raise achievement and increase participation, at national, regional and local level.

Wider participation in the context of increased demand for higher education

7.21   The previous chapter argued that employer and individual demand for higher education will increase and that participation should increase to reflect this demand. Within this expansion it should be an objective of policy to see that those groups who are currently under-represented in higher education come to be properly represented: as participation increases so it must widen. Recent history does suggest that, as overall numbers in higher education expand, so participation widens. We believe that this will be true too over the next twenty years. Progress will be greater still if, in adopting our recommendation in the previous chapter (Chapter 6) to respond to demand, priority is given to funding expansion where it is most likely to lead to widened participation. This is most likely to occur in institutions which can demonstrate a commitment to widening participation in the recent past, and have a robust strategy for doing so in the future.

Recommendation 2   **We recommend to the Government and the Funding Bodies that, when allocating funds for the expansion of higher education, they give priority to those institutions which can demonstrate a commitment to widening participation, and have in place a participation strategy, a mechanism for monitoring progress, and provision for review by the governing body of achievement.**

Governing body responsibility

7.22   Many institutions have made great progress in widening participation, and regard this as a key responsibility at the highest level within the institution. Others have left it to dedicated individuals. We are concerned that the current thinking about institutional responsibility for widening participation is contributing to the emerging division between institutions which we described above. This would be a matter of considerable concern. We encourage diversity of missions between institutions and their autonomy. This permeates many of our later recommendations. Some will rightly wish to concentrate on meeting the requirements of a local population and some on meeting national requirements. Nonetheless, and particularly in the context of the new compact which we have advocated, it will be important that institutions individually and collectively command public confidence in the way they address participation matters. Each governing body should have a clear understanding of the local, regional and national trends in participation by different social groups. We therefore propose that each governing body should devise a clear policy about its strategic aims for participation with particular reference to those groups who are known to be under-represented; and that it should monitor admissions and participation against those aims. When developing such strategies, governing bodies should in particular explore discrepancies between their own student population and the wider population; and should benchmark their performance with comparable institutions. They should aim to work closely with other agencies, both national and local, such as local education authorities, schools and further education colleges, Training and Enterprise Councils and employer bodies. In Chapter 17 we recommend a rolling review by governing bodies of their own and the institution's performance. The participation strategy will form part of that review.

Achievement for entry to higher education

7.23   All the available evidence suggests that the largest single determinant of participation in higher education amongst the 18 to 21 year old cohort is educational achievement at 18. The evidence suggests that *'differential participation therefore arises largely because of differences in the proportions of those possessing entry qualifications for HE.'*[18] In turn, the best predictor of educational achievement at 18 is achievement at 16.[19]

7.24   The prime causes of uneven participation by young people therefore lie outside higher education. There are many factors affecting performance and decisions at 16. They reflect the aspirations and attitudes of individual young people, their peers and families; the circumstances at home, and in particular whether there is a strongly supportive attitude to school and homework, with facilities for it. They also reflect the quality of schooling; the availability of other alternative routes, such as youth training or employment; and the attraction of the learning opportunities available at 16.[20] They also reflect the financial circumstances of the family. But this analysis does not, in our view, mean that higher education is powerless to affect participation. Institutions are already helping to raise aspirations, change attitudes, dispel misconceptions, and provide support and encouragement to those that need it.

7.25 We have learnt of many initiatives by higher education institutions designed to tackle earlier achievement, including, for example, the Birmingham 'Compacts' with local schools; Staffordshire University's 'Priority Application Scheme', which gives a guaranteed conditional offer to local pupils; Wolverhampton University's 'inreach' and 'outreach' schemes, which bring young people on to the campus and take the University out to schools; and other schemes which support pupils' revision for their exams and offer undergraduate role models in schools.

7.26 For older students, and those not enrolled at school and college, higher education may appear to be an alien culture. It was suggested to us that: *'there are some groups and communities, geographical and cultural, where the value of education (let alone [higher education]) is not widely recognised. Public images of [higher education] are often quite unlike the reality and the potential benefits of participation are not self evident to people living in communities where no one has previously entered [higher education]'.*[21] Institutions recognise the problems and are responding. For example, the Community University of the Valleys in South Wales is a joint initiative by three universities which supports community groups and projects – many initiated by local women with no experience of higher education; Sunderland University and Gateshead College have launched Learning World within Europe's largest shopping mall, to make learning available in a non-threatening learning environment and at times to suit the learner.

7.27 We endorse such initiatives, the most successful of which recognise the need for institutions to collaborate with schools, colleges and other local agencies; that improvement will require a long term investment of commitment and resources; and that funding needs to be focused in order to be effective. There is much that can be learnt from the existing initiatives and from schools and further education. We consider that the Funding Bodies in further and higher education, local education authorities and representative bodies could usefully jointly identify good practice designed to promote individual access and the enhancement of achievement in those communities with especially low levels of participation.

Recommendation 3 **We recommend that, with immediate effect, the bodies responsible for funding further and higher education in each part of the UK collaborate and fund – possibly jointly – projects designed to address low expectations and achievement and to promote progression to higher education.**

Information and guidance

7.28   For students to make well-informed decisions about the higher education programme that they wish to follow, they need clear information and guidance.[22] This is especially so for applicants with non-traditional entry qualifications, many of whom are first-generation entrants to higher education with a history of previous under-achievement in education.[23] These students may find it particularly difficult to make a successful transition to higher education. One study has suggested of the 'non-A level world' that it *'lacks clear signposts and route maps....progression narratives and outcomes were unpredictable and inconstant. Few students were successful in achieving their original aspirations. Most had successively to re-negotiate new and more attainable plans for the future as the realities of opportunities and constraints became clear'.*[24] Improving counselling and guidance for students is a recurring theme throughout our report, and particular recommendations are made in Chapter 8.

The framework of qualifications

7.29   The availability of sufficient entry and stopping-off points is important to allow students to access learning in a way that best meets their requirements. It has been put to us that *'a major limitation of the UK system of higher education is that students are offered just one contest – they must clear the "high jump" of the three/four year honours degree, or fail'.*[25] We say more in Chapter 8 about the relevance of moving to a post-qualifications admissions system, which, although it would apply to all young entrants and would not be designed specifically to widen participation, would nevertheless put more students on an equal footing and would ensure that students' choices about their participation were better informed.

7.30   The high participation rate in Scotland, which reached 44.2 per cent in 1995/96, is attributed, in part, to the recently-introduced structure of qualifications which supports progression from school, through further education and into higher education; and to the wide scope there to study sub-degree higher education in further education colleges. In Scotland, 40 per cent of higher education is at sub-degree level, compared with 26 per cent in the rest of the UK. This evidence lends support to those who maintain that *'access to [higher education] cannot be widened unless it is part of a web of flexible educational opportunities'.*[26]

7.31   In Chapter 6 we recommended that, in response to demand, a major part of future expansion should be at sub-degree level, through qualifications like the Higher National Certificate and Higher National Diploma. Such courses are provided in both higher and further education institutions. In Chapter 10 we recommend a framework of qualifications which will provide greater flexibility to students who wish to enter and exit higher education at different levels, with a qualification of value. In Chapters 16 and 22, we recommend that future funding arrangements recognise the distinctive mission of further education colleges in offering sub-degree higher education, which is accessible locally. We believe that these recommendations will be fundamental to widening participation in higher education.

Financial disincentives to participation

7.32   The factors which encourage students from traditionally under-represented groups to enrol and subsequently to succeed in higher education are complex. Success in such encouragement requires recognition that, whilst higher education historically was designed for young students, able to study full-time and away from home, this is no longer an accurate representation.

7.33   Responding sensitively and effectively to non-traditional entrants is likely to involve some extra cost to institutions, through guidance and counselling; and in addressing the learning skills and confidence which may need development if a student is to succeed in higher education. Research commissioned by the Higher Education Funding Council for England (HEFCE) from the Institute for Employment Research into the costs of teaching different groups of students found that *'certain groups of students are held to incur higher costs than others, particularly mature students, those with non-traditional qualifications and students with certain disabilities, although such costs tend not to have been quantified'.*[27]

7.34   We therefore adopt the principle that funding arrangements by the Funding Bodies should take into account the financial implications of encouraging wider participation.

7.35   We welcome the funding initiatives which the three Higher Education Funding Councils have already taken to support institutions' efforts to widen participation, by seeking to meet some of the known additional costs which can be incurred for specific activities. We would urge them to continue those efforts and to take further steps, in collaboration with the representative bodies, to disseminate good practice emerging from the initiatives by institutions. We were also interested in the initiative taken by the Further Education Funding Council for Wales (FEFCW) to allocate additional funds to those institutions which enrol students from disadvantaged localities, as represented by their home postcodes. We think there would be merit in the higher education Funding Bodies exploring similar initiatives.

Recommendation 4   **We recommend that the Funding Bodies consider financing, over the next two to three years, pilot projects which allocate additional funds to institutions which enrol students from particularly disadvantaged localities.**

7.36   Turning to funding for individual students, we adopt the principle that funding arrangements for individuals should not exacerbate disincentives to participation. We received many submissions which attested to the inadequacy of the current financial support arrangements. It is likely that any financial disincentives for individuals will bear disproportionately on those from poorer backgrounds and those with greater other financial and domestic commitments. We also considered evidence that students from poorer backgrounds may be more debt-averse than others and that in some cases, financial difficulties are causing students to abandon their studies or to take on excessive part-time work during term-time.[28] We say more about these factors in Chapter 17.

7.37   We believe that, as part of the range of measures necessary to widen participation, there is a pressing case for targeting some additional help where it is most needed. The two most effective ways of doing this might be through the social security system, which is designed to assess individual needs, and through expanding the size and scope of the current Access Funds.

7.38   Access Funds are already provided to institutions to enable them to support students on the basis of an individual assessment of financial need. They have in general proved an effective way of targeting additional support where it is most needed and have shown that institutions are best placed to make that necessary assessment and judgement. But their effectiveness has been limited by the relatively small sums available. Also, the scope of the funds is restricted to full-time students and to those who are already enrolled, rather than those who need some financial assurance before they feel able to enter higher education (for example, where their parents are unwilling to make up the parental contribution). In Chapter 20, we recommend extending the scope of the Access Funds for part-time students.

Recommendation 5   **We recommend to the Government that:**
- **it considers the possibility of restoring to full-time students some entitlement to social security benefits, as part of its forthcoming review of the social security system. This review should include consideration of two particular groups in current difficulty, those who temporarily withdraw from higher education due to illness and those with dependent children aged over 16;**
- **the total available to institutions for Access Funds should be doubled with effect from 1998/99 and that the scope of the funds should be extended to facilitate participation by students who would otherwise be unable to enter higher education.**

7.39   We recommend later that graduates in work should make a greater contribution to the costs of their higher education. We considered the possible impact of this on the level of participation, particularly for students from socio-economic groups III–V. Indications from Australia and New Zealand are that an income contingent loans system (under which the loan is repaid once a graduate's earnings pass a certain threshold) can meet this concern, if the system is properly constructed. However, the precise effect on a particular student in a particular country will be dependent on the level of debt incurred, the nature of the payment terms and also on wider cultural and sociological differences between countries. Some US evidence suggests that requiring graduates to meet more of the costs of their higher education affects the choice of programme. We are therefore sensitive to these issues when we develop our funding recommendations in Chapter 20 and believe that a fair system of contributions from graduates in work should **not** represent a deterrent to participation in higher education.

Participation by people with disabilities

7.40   The measures proposed here are intended to tackle under-representation by each of the social groups identified earlier in the chapter. There remains, however, one group, those with disabilities, for whom these measures are unlikely on their own to give sufficient support and for which we therefore make specific recommendations.

7.41   The Disabled Students Allowance (DSA) has helped many students with disabilities to meet the personal costs which arise from their disability. This is directly material to encouraging their participation in higher education. But the DSA is only available to full-time undergraduates and is subject to a parental means test. We received strong representations about this and consider it to be anomalous.[29] It should also be available to part-time students, graduate students and those with a degree who have subsequently acquired a disability and, as a result, require a second higher education qualification, without a parental means test.

7.42   But providing for students with disabilities may well involve additional costs for institutions as well as individual students. In some cases these costs can be heavy. As the Higher Education Funding Council for England (HEFCE) has commented, *some disabilities appear to be more under-represented than others and these might reflect the nature of the resourcing and support required*.[30] Higher education institutions are currently exempt from the access to goods, facilities and services provisions of Part III of the Disability Discrimination Act 1995 although they are required to produce a disability statement. During the course of the review we received representations that this should no longer be the case. While the requirements of that Act have been carefully drafted to avoid placing unreasonable requirements upon the organisations covered, we can understand why institutions of higher education, in what they feel to be financially straitened circumstances, might be apprehensive about the extension of all of the provisions of the Act to them. We consider that over the long term institutions should seek to honour the spirit of the Disability Discrimination Act.

7.43   We also consider that higher education could do more to adapt its teaching and learning strategies to meet the requirements of some students with disabilities who learn in different ways. We consider that the Institute for Learning and Teaching, recommended in Chapter 8, could usefully consider the requirements of students with disabilities when developing its early work programme.[31]

Recommendation 6   **We recommend:**
- **to the Funding Bodies that they provide funding for institutions to provide learning support for students with disabilities;**
- **to the Institute for Learning and Teaching in Higher Education (see Recommendation 14) that it includes the learning needs of students with disabilities in its research, programme accreditation and advisory activities;**
- **to the Government that it extends the scope of the Disabled Students Allowance so that it is available without a parental means test and to part-time students, postgraduate students and those who have become disabled who wish to obtain a second higher education qualification.**

Data requirements
7.44   An informed implementation of our recommendations requires that their effect on students from different social groups can be identified; and that institutions have available the information necessary on which to base their strategies. Our examination of the pattern of participation has revealed some weaknesses in the current data, in part because the arrangements for collection have been in operation for a limited

period. In a society whose future wellbeing depends so much on the success of its investment in people throughout life is important to have a good database on education. In the past, there have been concerns that a unique record number which learners take with them as they move from school, to further education and higher education might compromise an individual's confidentiality. We would hope that renewed joint discussion by the parties involved might yield a workable solution.

Recommendation 7   **We recommend that further work is done over the medium term, by the further and higher education Funding Bodies, the Higher Education Statistics Agency, and relevant government departments to address the creation of a framework for data about lifelong learning, using a unique student record number.**

Conclusion

7.45   In this chapter, we have analysed the available data about the pattern of participation and made a range of recommendations designed to widen participation by those groups which are currently under-represented in higher education. We have also shown the extent to which the solution to the current under-representation by some social groups requires concerted and long-term attention on a number of fronts. Higher education can therefore play a part, but not solve alone, these wider socio-economic difficulties. It **will** be higher education's responsibility, however, to respond to the increasing diversity of students in the practice of learning and teaching, and we examine this in our next chapter, Chapter 8.

Chapter 8

Students and learning

8.1 In Chapters 5 and 6 we set out our views about the need for increased and wider participation in higher education. We expect greater numbers of students to come from a broader spectrum of cultural backgrounds and abilities. Many of them will be mature students, increasingly aware of the knowledge and skills that are valued in employment. Given this increasing diversity in students, and the progressive development of communications and information technology, the next 20 years will be a period of major change in the practice of learning and teaching in higher education.

8.2 Teachers will have to respond to a changing – and more discerning and demanding – student population. They are more likely to have to work increasingly in partnership – or in competition – with publishers, film-makers and broadcasters as the growth of information technology opens up new ways of learning and teaching. They will be increasingly involved in learning partnerships with major employers. They will need to deliver a learning experience in higher education which enthuses students to become lifelong learners. They will need to encourage all students to aspire to a deep understanding and experience of their area of study at whatever level they are studying.

8.3 The consensus among many educators is that depth of understanding is fostered by an active approach to learning, and by forging the links between theoretical and practical aspects of the subject. For this to be possible, students must have access to more than just the articulation of knowledge in the form of books and lectures. They also need practical experience that rehearses them in the professional or scholarly skills of their field, and the opportunity to develop and express their own understanding and point of view in an environment that gives constructive feedback.

> *'great teachers create a common ground of intellectual commitment. They stimulate active, not passive, learning and encourage students to be critical, creative thinkers, with the capacity to go on learning after their college days are over.'*[1]

8.4 Such a vision puts students at the centre of the learning and teaching process and places new challenges and demands upon teachers. As our terms of reference say: *'the effectiveness of teaching and learning should be enhanced.'* It also places a premium on wider support and guidance for students which enables them to focus their attention fully on their learning. We believe that achievement of our vision will establish the United Kingdom (UK) as a leader in the world of learning and teaching at higher levels. In our view, this must be a national objective.

8.5 In this chapter we develop our ideas on how such a vision can be realised by considering:
- what is distinctive about learning and teaching at the higher education level;
- the challenges for learning and teaching;
- the impact of communications and information technology (C&IT) on learning and teaching;
- how best to support the student learning experience;
- staff development and training for improved learning and teaching.

Distinctive features of learning and teaching in higher education

8.6   At a seminar with prominent researchers specialising in learning in higher education, we sought to identify what is distinctive about learning at the higher level. We heard that it can be defined as the development of understanding and the ability to apply knowledge in a range of situations. This requires information and the opportunity to engage in 'learning conversations' with staff and other students in order to understand and be able to use new concepts in a particular field. A successful student will be able to engage in an effective discussion or debate with others in that field, relying on a common understanding of terms, assumptions, questions, modes of argument, and the body of evidence. Learning also involves acquiring skills, such as analysis and communication, but these in isolation do not constitute learning.

8.7   We have sought to evaluate the often argued need to link teaching with research and scholarship in higher education. Our visits to institutions, in the UK and overseas, have persuaded us of the important role of research and scholarship in informing and enhancing teaching, which we expand upon in Chapter 11. Although research is carried out at different levels and different intensities by different institutions, higher education is characterised by the interest and enthusiasm of staff for pursuing their subject in directions of their choosing. For some staff this may involve studying the corpus of knowledge in a subject or field to gain a broad understanding of the outcomes of research, to analyse and synthesise these outcomes to produce a coherent picture, and from this to identify trends and connections, to draw conclusions and to point out further directions for research. We believe that this form of scholarly investigation, together with research, is a distinctive feature of higher education: they enliven staff, they ensure that teaching and curriculum development is up-to-date, and, more generally, they invigorate higher level learning in our universities and colleges.

Challenges for learning and teaching

8.8   The challenge of the next 20 years is to maintain the distinctiveness of learning at the higher level and to enhance teaching and improve students' learning. Virtually all higher education institutions have mission statements which emphasise the importance of learning and teaching.[2] Many have developed strategies and established committees or units devoted to the development of these activities. In pursuit of a national strategy of excellence, we are convinced that the enhancement and promotion of learning and teaching must be a priority for all of higher education.

8.9   One current barrier is that staff perceive national and institutional policies as actively encouraging and recognising excellence in research, but not in teaching. Although the teaching quality assessments (TQA) carried out by the Funding Bodies, which are designed to measure the effectiveness of teaching, have raised the profile of teaching within institutions, the Research Assessment Exercise (RAE) has been a stronger influence and has deflected attention away from learning and teaching towards research. An analysis of the impact of the 1992 RAE in higher education institutions in

England suggests that it has devalued teaching because research assessment is closely linked to the allocation of large sums of money, whereas teaching assessment is not.[3] The fact that almost every higher education institution in the country entered the exercise – regardless of whether its primary mission was to research or to teach – indicates the influence of the RAE on institutions' activities. In Chapter 11, we develop proposals to redress the imbalance between teaching and research, and to recognise that a distinctive feature of higher education is the link between research, scholarship and teaching.

8.10   Changes to national policy are only part of the answer to a better balance. Our national consultation suggested that, if the quality of students' educational experience is to be maintained or improved, innovative teaching strategies which promote students' learning – many of which are already in place – will have to become widespread. This means that higher education institutions will need to continue to emphasise the centrality of learning and teaching in all their work.

Recommendation 8   **We recommend that, with immediate effect, all institutions of higher education give high priority to developing and implementing learning and teaching strategies which focus on the promotion of students' learning.**

8.11   We recognise the scale of the challenge to institutions in our prescription of national excellence in teaching and the management of learning. The rise in student numbers over the last decade, and the continuing pressure on institutional finances resulting in lower staff to student ratios, has meant larger class sizes and less contact time for students. We note some research that has indicated that students perform worse in large classes, and markedly so in some subject areas, particularly the social sciences.[4] We are aware of how many students, out of necessity, have to seek part-time work during term time, and the effect this may have on their performance.

8.12   The pattern of learning has been changing, with an increasing proportion of time spent outside the classroom in independent study. Administrative and support staff have noticed a change in the delivery of higher education, with a greater emphasis on independent learning. Library staff have told us that they have to spend more time supporting students, and that many students come from school ill-prepared for this form of learning.[5]

8.13   Given the increased time students spend in independent study, the task of planning the time they spend learning becomes ever more important. To manage the learning process for more diverse and greater numbers of students, teachers will have to consider the trade-off between the quantity and the quality of time spent with students. Planning for learning means that designing the forms of instruction which support learning becomes as important as preparing the content of programmes.

8.14   Despite the changes in the learning environment, teaching methods do not appear to have changed considerably. Our survey and other research suggest that lectures are still the most common form of teaching in higher education.[6] Initial findings from research suggest that many staff still see teaching primarily in terms of transmission of information, mainly through lectures.[7] There are many teachers who are ready to adopt different methods of teaching as circumstances change, but others find change hard to accept and do not reflect much on their teaching or consider the basis of good teaching practice. This does not mean that staff are not interested in teaching, but it reflects the lack of incentive to develop teaching knowledge and skills, and the limited opportunities for staff development within departments.

8.15   It is not for us to offer institutions a compendium of learning strategies to enable them to achieve excellence in a world in which it is unrealistic to expect a return to former staff to student ratios. But it seems plain that an effective strategy will involve guiding and enabling students to be effective learners, to understand their own learning styles, and to manage their own learning. We see this as not only directly relevant to enhancing the quality of their learning while in higher education, but also to equipping them to be effective lifelong learners. Staff will increasingly be engaged in the management of students' learning, using a range of appropriate strategies.

8.16   The evidence we have had from employers shows that they value the contribution work experience makes to the development of a range of personal skills and students' understanding of the world of work, which we consider in more detail in Chapter 9. The educational value of such work is enhanced if the student is encouraged and helped by the institution to reflect on the work experience, to make linkages with theory learned in other settings and, thereby, to learn from it. We are, however, concerned at the number of students who, out of necessity, undertake excessive amounts of paid work during term time to the detriment of their studies. At present, the relatively short timescale for study in most UK institutions is justified by the high quality of the learning experience and its outcomes. This could be undermined if students are not able to spend sufficient time studying and are unable to learn from the work experience because of the extent of employment commitments.

8.17   Feedback and assessment are important in helping students to progress and learn from their mistakes. Fewer than half the students responding to our survey were satisfied with the feedback they got from staff about their work. Planning for learning will require teachers to consider carefully how best to provide useful feedback to assist students' ability to think about their work and develop their understanding of the area of study.

8.18   As part of their strategies for learning and teaching, we suggest that all institutions encourage staff to plan for the learning time of students. At a practical level, this could involve:
- making 'planning for learning' an explicit responsibility of heads of department;
- redirecting attention to learning by changing staff contracts (where they exist) to refer to the time spent in support of student learning in its variety of forms rather than simple class contact time;
- considering how students can become active participants in the learning process;
- creating structured opportunities for teachers to examine and evaluate teaching methods;

- considering how communications and information technology (C&IT) can provide support for learning.

8.19   We find it surprising that there has been little strategic research to monitor the consequences of recent changes in the students' learning environment and institutions' teaching activities. Although there is a substantial body of research about student learning, there has been little follow-up work into how some accepted principles might be translated into new teaching practices across disciplines and professional areas. We make a key recommendation on this point later in the chapter (Recommendation 14).

The impact of Communications and Information Technology on learning and teaching

8.20   We estimate in Chapter 13 that up to ten per cent of expenditure in higher education is committed to C&IT. Our concern here is with its potential contribution to learning and teaching. Technological development provides the potential for enhancing the quality of learning for students in an era of attenuated staff to student ratios.

8.21   It is clear to us, however, that personal contact between teacher and student, and between student and student, gives a vitality, originality and excitement that cannot be provided by machine-based learning, however excellent. When free to make a choice, even though it costs more, individuals are likely to choose to receive information and experience in the company of others, rather than alone, and to receive it from a person who is there to respond, even as part of a group. But, through C&IT, it is possible to offer forms of contact and access to some highly effective learning materials that were previously unavailable for many students.

8.22   Over the last 20 years, the higher education sector has undertaken a wide range of experimentation in developing and implementing new technology for learning and teaching. This has been triggered by a succession of publicly funded development programmes, and in the last decade has been underpinned by the network of discipline-based Computers in Teaching Initiative (CTI) centres, now numbering 24, all sited in universities.

Benefits of C&IT to learning and teaching

8.23   From documents submitted to us, and from our visits to UK higher education institutions to see how C&IT is being used to enhance learning and teaching, it is evident that there is much good work to build on. Moreover, from our overseas visits we see good reason for the UK to lead the world in the effective use of C&IT for learning and teaching in higher education. Looking ahead, we see a growing contribution to learning from the extensive use of computer-assisted learning materials, communications technology and new, enhanced delivery systems. We say more about delivery systems in Chapter 13.

8.24   One of the benefits of new technology lies in providing a learning environment that may succeed in improving understanding where other methods have failed. Computer-based programmes, such as tutorials, simulations, exercises, learning tools and educational games can be highly interactive and provide activities that students need to develop their understanding of others' ideas and the articulation of their own.

8.25 Computers can provide access to information and learning materials through the World Wide Web, datastores, electronic journals and other sources. For students with visual, hearing or motor disabilities, communications and information technology (C&IT) can provide enhanced access to such materials. Given the general concerns of students in our survey about access to learning materials, C&IT provides the potential to ease these difficulties.

8.26 By using computer-based learning materials, students can receive immediate feedback to assist with learning complex concepts. Such materials often provide students with an opportunity to generate as many exercises as needed, as a way of supplementing tutor-marked assignments for certain topics. Simulations of experiments can help students to understand complex or dangerous experiments, or replace experiments that would otherwise use live animals, just as simulators for pilots can be as effective as 'flying hours'. A simulation may replace, or simply supplement, the actual experiment itself. Students can repeat simulations as many times as necessary to enhance their understanding of the procedure and outcomes. We recognise, however, that hands-on experience with real experiments, that may not work if students are careless or unlucky, has an important role in developing competencies required in practitioners.

The development of computer-based learning materials

8.27 Despite the potential of C&IT and some major national initiatives, there is as yet little widespread use of computer-based learning materials. This relative lack of use derives in part from the reluctance of some academics to use teaching materials created by others, from the considerable time it takes to redesign programmes to integrate computer-based materials, and from the limited availability of good materials.

8.28 Developing good computer-based learning material is expensive: the Teaching and Learning Technology Programme (TLTP) has spent £32 million, with at least equal contributions from participating institutions. Given the expense of producing high quality courseware, we have noted the comments and advice of a number of expert groups. The House of Lords Select Committee on Science and Technology concluded that *'critical mass is essential for network operators to develop the new advanced applications both in the UK and on a global basis'.*[8] Advice from the Vice Chancellor of the Open University and from an evaluation of TLTP was that courseware developers should concentrate on developing materials and systems that can be used by large numbers of students.[9]

8.29 It is clear that competition in the provision of materials is coming from institutions overseas and from private companies. An American company plans a UK launch of educational provision using television. The Harvard Business School could easily make its Master in Business Administration programme available through the Internet, although as yet it has no plans to do so. The Massachusetts Institute of Technology is developing basic learning materials in physics, mathematics and engineering, which might eventually find a world market.

8.30 Markets will, therefore, have to be gained in the face of strong competition. Institutions, and the UK more widely, have an interest in being at the forefront of developments to sustain and extend the UK's share of the world market in education and provision of learning materials. This will enable the UK to maintain the distinctiveness of home-produced materials rather than becoming dependent on the USA and other countries who will be active participants in the supply of materials.

8.31 With English likely to remain the predominant international language, the UK has a natural advantage. But success will be highly dependent on the quality of learning materials. UK higher education is well-placed, with a good international reputation for the quality and standards of its higher education. This reputation can be built upon in the new and potentially large communications and information technology (C&IT) market. In the interests of promoting and assuring the quality of UK-produced C&IT materials, we believe that there would be advantage in introducing some form of quality control. We make a recommendation on this point (Recommendation 15).

8.32 Few institutions will have the resources and expertise to develop high quality material alone. The Teaching and Learning Technology Programme (TLTP) has encouraged departments to produce materials on a collaborative basis, which has been valuable in bringing staff from different institutions together and in assisting wider use of computer-based materials. We support the discipline-based approach of past initiatives as a good way of pooling expertise, achieving synergy and securing ownership of the products.

8.33 In any future central initiatives, the lessons of the TLTP will need to be taken fully into account. Partnerships between institutions are the most likely basis for progress, especially where they exploit complementary strengths. Future initiatives must secure a commitment from institutions, which might be reflected in a requirement for matching any centrally-provided funding. Partnerships will almost certainly need to involve the publishing, communications or entertainment industries. Partnerships, which at present are predominantly national, may usefully be extended to a multi-national basis to provide the scale of take up necessary to cover the costs of producing high quality material. We make a recommendation on how this should be taken forward (Recommendation 15).

Implications of C&IT for staff and students

8.34 Increased use of new technology will have major implications for the way in which staff and students work. Students will need to develop advanced skills in searching for and selecting valid, relevant and up-to-date information from computer-based storage. They will look to institutions to guide them through the information maze. Students will expect to leave higher education competent and confident in the use of C&IT so that they can use it in their future careers and personal learning. We return to this point in Chapter 9.

8.35   According to our survey of students, the use of computer-based learning packages is, at present, the least satisfactory mode of learning of those asked about. This points to the scale of the task facing institutions in integrating computer-based learning packages into their teaching programmes, in training staff in their use, and most particularly in ensuring that students learn effectively from computer-based materials.

8.36   We have noted during our visits to institutions the growing scale of adoption of C&IT. But its use for learning is still at a developmental stage. For a full and successful integration into learning to take place, staff need to be effective practitioners and skilled in the management of students' learning through C&IT.

Recommendation 9   **We recommend that all institutions should, over the medium term, review the changing role of staff as a result of communications and information technology, and ensure that staff and students receive appropriate training and support to enable them to realise its full potential.**

Supporting the student

Entering higher education

8.37   Entering higher education and choosing the programme to study is a major decision in the life of an individual. Chapters 6 and 7 both argue for the need for better information for students when making such decisions. Even with better information, the current system for the admission of young school and college leavers does not provide sufficient time for students to make the best decisions. They have to make their selection of programmes very early with offers of places made on the basis of predicted performance. Those who do not meet the offer have to enter 'clearing', which requires even faster decisions about which institution and which programme to pursue. It was put to us strongly that this system is not in the best interests of students. We agree.

8.38   As we move towards a system of lifelong learning with greater numbers of adults entering higher education at different points in their lives, the significance of the problems with the existing admissions system will diminish. However, there is still a need to ensure that it supports students to make the best decisions at an important time in their lives.

8.39   A frequently discussed alternative to the existing system is that admission to an institution should be based on actual achievement, rather than predicted results.[10,11] This would assist students since they know more about their abilities (and possibly their interests) having received their examination results and having studied for longer. The main obstacle to this alternative is the relatively short time between the A level/GNVQ/ Higher examination results coming out in mid-August and the start of the academic year in September/October. However, recent changes in the structure and operation of examination boards and the potential for using information technology to speed up processes could make a 'post-qualifications admissions' system feasible.

We recommend that, over the medium term, the representative bodies, in consultation with other relevant agencies, should seek to establish a post-qualification admissions system.

Guidance which supports learning

8.40   We agree with the Higher Education Quality Council (HEQC) that:
> '*Guidance and learner support is an important area of quality that affects student choice and learner autonomy, the development of general skills and the enhancement of effective teaching and learning.*'[12]

8.41   We have noted many examples of good practice in institutional arrangements for guiding students as learners. But there is concern that arrangements are under strain, particularly, in larger institutions, the personal tutor system.[13] This strain is most frequently manifested in lack of consistency in arrangements, staff not being available because of other duties, and inadequate or unclear arrangements for reporting on student progress, especially for students experiencing difficulties. Some marginalisation and a lack of co-ordination between different learner support services in terms of programme planning and development is also apparent in some institutions. We have the impression that learner support has a low profile in some institutional hierarchies.

8.42   A number of institutions have piloted the use of guidelines developed by the HEQC to offer a framework for guidance and learner support. The principles underpinning the guidelines – which we support – are that guidance in higher education should be learner-centred, confidential, impartial, equitable and accessible. Given the width of choice afforded by modularisation, it is important that students should not be left to find a pathway through the matrix of opportunities open to them without adequate guidance.

8.43   We propose that the Quality Assurance Agency should develop a code of practice related to student support and guidance, based on existing codes. Institutions could either adopt the national code or develop their own, which would be expected to be broadly in line with the principles established nationally. We would expect institutions' codes to be available to students and others. In Chapter 10 we discuss the role of the Quality Assurance Agency in ensuring that institutions are following their codes of practice.

Careers education and guidance

8.44   The responses to our student survey showed clearly that students' strongest motivation for entering higher education was their desire to improve their labour market prospects. Good careers advice is essential to them. The representatives of schools and sixth form colleges, in their oral evidence to us, indicated the importance they attached to knowing the success of their former pupils in gaining employment when offering guidance to current pupils on subject and institutional choices. Our survey of students revealed that nearly half of part-time students did not think that the careers service in their institution was relevant to them, which suggests that these services focus primarily on new entrants to employment and are not particularly attuned to the needs of older students.

8.45   Good careers guidance has always been valued by students, but with graduates in work taking increasing responsibility for funding their higher education through loans it will have an added importance. As we see it, those engaged in providing careers guidance have a two-fold role: to provide advice and assistance to students; and to make a contribution to the development of academic programmes. This may mean that programme planning could include consideration of feedback on the destinations of students and the perceptions of students and employers on the employment value of programmes. Those involved in careers guidance could also be closely involved with arrangements for, and monitoring of, student work placements.

8.46   We have encountered a variety of different – and often good – examples of careers education in institutions, including: the introduction of an institution-wide optional module on personal and career development; the introduction of broadly-based skills courses which incorporate careers education; and linking students' personal decision-making, including career decisions, into mainstream academic teaching, assessment and validation procedures. During institutional visits we found good examples of institutions including the success of students in gaining employment as a criterion in their self-evaluation. We saw subject associations taking an interest in this issue. But we also read evidence to the effect that careers guidance was to some extent marginalised.[14]

8.47   An increasingly important aspect of careers advice will be to assist students who wish to start their own businesses. Such a venture requires a range of skills and a student is more likely to succeed if aware of the likely pitfalls and the strategies for dealing with them. We believe that pointing future entrepreneurs to where they can get advice on taking their first steps into business should become a growing role for higher education institutions.

8.48   Good careers advice has a particular importance in helping to ensure sufficient recruitment to certain professions. As Sir Stewart Sutherland's report notes there are problems of recruitment to teacher training programmes in particular 'shortage' subjects (Report 10). The Teacher Training Agency is taking action to address these shortages, but careers guidance also has a role. It should also have a role in addressing the Engineering Institutions' concern that insufficient high quality candidates are applying to the profession.

8.49   Outside higher education, careers guidance has been high on the national agenda, with careers education now mandatory in schools and further education, by legislation (in the former) and through audit and inspection (in the latter). Higher education is outside this framework with institutions left to decide what form their careers guidance should take and what level of resource it should have. In a society committed to lifelong learning, where higher education institutions will have a major role, we question the rationale of separating careers advice in higher education from that provided in the wider context.

8.50   We support the notion of a lifelong guidance service, based on a partnership between the services inside higher education and those outside. In particular, it is important that students in higher education have access to an external, impartial, and independent source of advice.

8.51 Such a service will require proper resourcing: to provide current advice to students advisers must be up-to-date with the latest developments in industry, commerce, business and the public sector. Communications and information technology could also be harnessed to improve the quality and accessibility of careers advice.

Recommendation 11 **We recommend on careers guidance that:**
- **institutions of higher education, over the medium term, integrate their careers services more fully into academic affairs and that the provision of careers education and guidance is reviewed periodically by the Quality Assurance Agency;**
- **the Government, in the medium to long term, should integrate careers advice for lifelong learning, to complement services based inside higher education institutions.**

Other forms of support and guidance for students

8.52 A number of those giving evidence to us, particularly the National Union of Students, emphasised the importance of a range of forms of non-academic support and guidance for students if they are to learn effectively. Students who have financial, health, housing, or childcare problems are unlikely to be able to concentrate fully on their studies. We heard, in particular, that some students are living in extremely poor quality or even dangerous rented accommodation, and that some parents face considerable problems in finding flexible affordable childcare.

8.53 Institutions provide a range of non-academic services for students including financial advice, medical centres and assistance in finding accommodation and nurseries, but we have heard that these are under increasing pressure as student numbers have risen. Students' unions have increasingly sought to supplement such services, or to work in partnership with institutions to provide them.

8.54 In our survey of students, young students were generally content with the services available to them from institutions and students' unions, but part-time students were much less satisfied, often regarding services as irrelevant to their needs. Support services that were originally developed to meet the needs of young people moving away from the parental home for the first time have not necessarily adapted to meet the needs of a more diverse student body.

8.55 Although some of the problems students face are simply those of anyone on a low income, it is not sensible to invest time and resources in education if they cannot be used to good effect. In recognition of this, we believe that there are advantages in students having access to independent advice from a students' union, and also that institutions and unions should collaborate to ensure that they are providing a co-ordinated set of services appropriate to the needs of all students.

Recommendation 12 **We recommend to students' unions and institutions that they review, on a regular basis, the services offered to their students and adapt them as necessary, in particular to meet the needs of part-time students.**

Staff training and development for improved learning and teaching

8.56 Institutions and their staff face a great challenge if our vision that the UK should be at the forefront of world practice in learning and teaching in higher education is to be realised. We recognise the scale of the task at a time of reduced staff to student ratios. The vision will be realised only if there is investment in staff training and development, both initial training and updating throughout an academic career. The skills of effective teachers will need to be valued through the rewards and career framework for academic staff.

8.57 Development of initial training and professional up-dating for teachers will be going with the grain. Many institutions have already embraced a voluntary scheme of teacher accreditation developed by the Staff and Educational Development Association (SEDA). The SEDA scheme recognises institutional programmes and then accredits individual teachers on successful completion of a SEDA-recognised programme.

8.58 We recognise that any form of accreditation of teaching will need to take account of the ways in which high quality teaching is underpinned by scholarship and research. It will need to recognise that different types of students at different institutions have distinctly different learning needs. It will also have to be sufficiently flexible to accommodate the brilliant but unorthodox teachers who do not fit conventional definitions of good teaching.

8.59 We believe that the necessary recognition of teaching in higher education will only be achieved through a national scheme of teacher accreditation to which all institutions voluntarily commit, with strong support from the bodies which represent higher education institutions and academic staff. To cater for differing institutional perspectives and approaches to learning and teaching, we favour the recognition of institutional programmes leading to the accreditation of staff who have successfully completed a recognised programme, along the lines of the SEDA scheme. Institutions might well collaborate in the provision of programmes.

8.60 From the point of view of staff, a national scheme has the merit of providing a professional recognition with standing across the whole of higher education.

8.61 While initial professional development will be the basis for establishing the professionalism of teaching, we consider it essential that staff should be encouraged to enhance and up-date their skills. To that end, we see advantage in establishing an organisation that can accredit training and practice, and recognise excellence in teaching at higher levels of recognised status. Such a body should have national standing, as in other professions. We propose the creation of an **Institute for Learning and Teaching in Higher Education** (Recommendation 14). To encourage teaching of the highest quality, the Institute would confer associate membership, membership and fellowship to recognise superior levels of expertise.

Recommendation 13   We recommend that institutions of higher education begin immediately to develop or seek access to programmes for teacher training of their staff, if they do not have them, and that all institutions seek national accreditation of such programmes from the Institute for Learning and Teaching in Higher Education.

8.62   In Chapter 14, we recommend that new staff should have to achieve associate level in order to complete probation. We expect that all institutions would partake in the scheme within several years if it were seen to be successful and to offer benefits to staff. If institutions are taking their responsibilities for the quality of teaching seriously, they will not want to neglect such an obvious tool.

8.63   The growth in the use of postgraduate students to teach undergraduates has prompted a number of organisations to raise concerns about the adequacy of training and support for postgraduates to be able to provide quality teaching. The practice has obvious benefits for postgraduate students in giving them an opportunity to experience teaching and providing a welcome source of income. A number of institutions use postgraduate students extensively and provide the necessary support and training. We commend such practice to all institutions which use postgraduate students to assist with teaching.

An Institute for Learning and Teaching in Higher Education

8.64   Placing higher education teaching on a more professional basis requires a strong foundation of theoretical and practical research into learning and teaching processes. There is no place, at present, where such a body of knowledge can develop. Moreover, while higher education has increased its class sizes, reduced its teaching time, modularised, accepted students without traditional academic preparation, refocused programmes to prepare students for employment, and so on, it has done so on the basis of little evidence of the consequences and with little strategic research in place to monitor them. There is no agency to fund, commission or co-ordinate such research.

8.65   A wide range of organisations – including institutions of higher education, the Royal Society, the Council for Industry and Higher Education, and the National Union of Students among others – have all declared support for an organisation dedicated to the development of learning and teaching.

8.66   The establishment of such an organisation is a fundamental feature within the interlocking elements of our proposals for change. The functions of the Institute would relate to the enhancement of learning and teaching and fall into three major categories:
■ the accreditation of teacher education programmes, as described above;
■ research and development in learning and teaching;
■ stimulation of innovation in learning and teaching.

8.67   Research into learning and teaching would involve the Institute commissioning rigorous analyses of various aspects of educational and organisational practice and development, especially related to learning and teaching. We would also expect research to be carried out on the impact of national policies on the effectiveness of teaching methods in higher education. We expect that the Institute would develop and maintain a shared knowledge base on learning and teaching and would require effective dissemination of the outcomes of the research.

8.68   It is especially important that research outcomes are used to inform policy and improve practice in learning and teaching. Accordingly, the third role of the Institute would be to use the outcomes of research to stimulate innovation in learning and teaching. Particular activities could include: widening the debate on the curriculum, teaching and assessment with teachers throughout higher education; encouraging – and part-sponsoring – conferences, workshops and seminars designed to disseminate interesting and useful practice across the sector; and producing practitioner-oriented publications. Later in this chapter we recommend a series of tasks for the Institute to provide a focal point for the developing use of communications and information technology for learning and teaching (Recommendation 15).

8.69   We are conscious that there are already a number of providers and agencies with a developmental remit. We do not believe that another organisation should simply be superimposed on the current fragmented pattern. Instead the opportunity should be taken to bring together related functions in a more effective and efficient way which ensures long term development and proper co-ordination. It would also be necessary for the Institute to liaise with bodies such as the General Teaching Councils in Scotland and the rest of the UK, the Further Education Development Agency and the Scottish Further Education Unit. As we recommend (Recommendation 14), the institutional representative bodies – in consultation with the Funding Bodies – should establish the professional Institute for Learning and Teaching in Higher Education.

The Institute and communications and information technology (C&IT)

8.70   An important initial task for the Institute will be to assist the sector in making the best use of information technology. The Institute should become a major resource for institutions regarding the use, procurement and development of computer-based learning materials. It could act as a broker in the development of relationships between commercial sponsors and consortia of institutions. It could also investigate the availability and usefulness of varied sources of funding – for example, the Private Finance Initiative. The Institute would need to have regular contact with the Joint Information Systems Committee (JISC) to ensure coherence in the system and consistency of standards and protocols.

8.71   Computer-based learning materials are valueless unless they are actually used by staff and students. We have already recommended that institutions take steps to assist staff and students to make full use of such tools. We also see a role for a national body to assist in promoting those tools and in the sharing of good practice. The Computers in Teaching Initiative (CTI) has done valuable work in providing institutions with subject-specific advice on technology-based educational practice and by testing and promoting materials. In order to secure greater use of computer-based learning materials, we see a central role for the CTI centres working as part of the Institute.

8.72   The scope for use of computer-based learning materials will vary between subjects and with the level of learning. However, we believe that there is particular scope for the production of packages which can be used widely, in the early stages of undergraduate programmes or for programmes that already have set curricula, such as some Edexcel or Scottish Qualifications Authority programmes. Such material could also be valuable in extending the provision and diversity of the range of higher education to smaller institutions, making it available in the work-place and at home to support lifelong learning. The Institute could take a prime role in the facilitation of this work.

The functions of the Institute

Recommendation 14   **We recommend that the representative bodies, in consultation with the Funding Bodies, should immediately establish a professional Institute for Learning and Teaching in Higher Education. The functions of the Institute would be to accredit programmes of training for higher education teachers; to commission research and development in learning and teaching practices; and to stimulate innovation.**

8.73   As stated earlier, the Institute would confer associate membership, membership and fellowship to recognise high quality teaching. It would also have a significant role in harnessing the development of communications and information technology for more effective and efficient learning and teaching.

Recommendation 15   **We recommend that the Institute should:**
   - **develop, over the medium term, a system of kitemarking to identify good computer-based learning materials;**
   - **co-ordinate the national development, over the medium and long term, of computer-based learning materials, and manage initiatives to develop such materials;**
   - **facilitate discussion between all relevant interest groups on promoting the development of computer-based materials to provide common units or modules, particularly for the early undergraduate years.**

Funding for the Institute

8.74   If the Institute is to do a useful and credible job it will need to be adequately funded. The Funding Bodies already provide some funding for developments in learning and teaching (for example, the Higher Education Funding Council for England provided £8 million over two years for the Fund for the Development of Teaching and Learning, and all the Funding Bodies have contributed some £32 million to the Teaching and Learning Technology Programme over three years). We believe that, in the future, this funding would be better spent by an institutionally-owned body with a co-ordinated and focused mission towards learning and teaching development. Institutions may wish to second staff to the Institute to contribute towards its costs. As a result of co-ordination and coalescence (as appropriate), the organisation should cost less than the current complex arrangements.

8.75   There should be three elements to the funding of the organisation:
- core funding to support the organisation through institutional subscription;
- payment by institutions for specific services;
- public funds from the Funding Bodies or government departments, for example to enable the Institute to launch focused initiatives in learning and teaching development.

Conclusion

8.76   We believe that our proposals will raise the status of teaching across higher education, help the UK to become the world leader in the practice of teaching at higher levels, and emphasise the importance of learning. This should be a national objective to enable the UK to compete effectively in the next century in a world where the quality, relevance and effectiveness of education and training systems will underpin future prosperity. In the next chapter (Chapter 9), we address the nature of programmes that we believe will need to be delivered to underpin a modern economy and to support lifelong learning.

Chapter 9

The nature of programmes

9.1 In this chapter we consider the nature of programmes of higher education and how the achievements of students are assessed and recorded. We address the principle in our terms of reference that: *'learning should be increasingly responsive to employment needs and include the development of general skills, widely valued in employment.'* In doing so, we have had in mind the need to build on the established strengths of higher education, but we have also reflected on the implications of the evidence received from employers about their needs, and on the widening range of demands there will be from individuals in a lifelong learning society.

9.2 These considerations have led us to consider:
- the breadth and depth of programmes;
- skills in higher education programmes;
- the relationship between work and other experience and higher education;
- the assessment and recording of student achievement;
- how to provide information about programmes.

Breadth and depth of programmes

9.3 We have given much thought to the appropriate breadth and depth of programmes, particularly at the undergraduate level. The breadth of programmes was a particular theme for the Robbins Committee. It felt that higher education was constrained by a tradition of relatively narrow educational experiences, and that its requirements drove a similarly narrow focus earlier in the educational system. We believe that, while many students will continue to welcome the opportunity to pursue a relatively narrow field of knowledge in great depth, there will be many others for whom this will be neither attractive, nor useful in future career terms, nor suitable. In a world which changes rapidly, the nation will need people with broad perspectives.

Employers' views about breadth

9.4 Employers emphasised to us in their evidence the importance of high level analytical skills. The development of such skills characterises higher education, and should continue to be one of its primary purposes. Indeed, many employers are seeking individuals with highly specialised knowledge and skills, with the medical and veterinary fields as the most obvious examples. But employers are also concerned about the general capabilities and potential of those with higher education qualifications, not just about the subject they have studied. The recruitment patterns of employers demonstrate that they are often looking for rounded but adaptable people who can successfully tackle a range of tasks and be effective members of a team.

> *'for many years over 40 per cent of jobs advertised for graduates in the UK have been open to applicants from most, if not all, disciplines'.*[1]

9.5   Employers are, therefore, looking for a variety of entrants: some specialists, some generalists. A typical response to our employer questionnaire confirms this:

> 'We will continue to need scientists and engineers ..over the next twenty years. (Applied skills with people management abilities – not pure science.) For other roles we will continue to need broad intellectual skills.'

Breadth and Robbins

9.6   On breadth, the Robbins report said:

> 'There are unquestionably young men and women for whom study that involves penetration in depth is naturally appropriate. They are eager to get to the heart of the subject and to develop powers of rigorous analysis and observation within its ambit. For such students the specialist first degree courses...are an admirable education...Nevertheless there is another sort of mind that at the first degree stage is likely to be more at home in broader fields studied to more moderate depth'[2]

9.7   We agree with Robbins about the need for different types of programmes to suit different types of students. For Robbins, it was not breadth for its own sake which was important, but breadth reflecting long-established and natural groupings of subjects, or new combinations with recognisably organic connections. This is increasingly important as connections across disciplines become more apparent.

Future programmes

9.8   Breadth of study characterises Scottish higher education. We believe that introducing breadth more extensively would assist students to respond to the social, economic and cultural changes they will be facing throughout their lives by assisting them to think divergently and to integrate information and knowledge from a variety of sources. The way ahead is to provide a diverse range of programmes. Within this, specialists need the opportunity to understand their specialism within its context, and breadth – provided it is not identified with shallowness and lack of intellectual rigour – has a place of growing importance. Higher education qualifications which aim to provide breadth must reside within the same framework of qualifications as specialist and professional qualifications, and the matrix of choice must be underpinned by robust standards. In Chapter 10, we propose a framework of qualifications which will allow for flexibility of programme content, yet ensure that the standards of awards are maintained. One implication is that students who choose to specialise later could take longer than at present to reach the current honours degree standard.

9.9   We have already said that informed student demand should become an increasingly important factor in determining what higher education offers. In the light of the evidence we have received, we welcome the extent to which higher education has responded to the developing needs of students and employers. The fact that many undergraduate programmes are now modular (or unitised) means that the development of broad programmes is likely to be relatively straightforward. However, choice and flexibility must be constrained by coherence. In that context, we believe that the range of higher education degree programmes should have the potential for a student to:

- study a single subject degree, where that subject is set in its broader context;
- construct a broad foundation of knowledge and understanding in an area where the student may like to specialise later;
- study a combined degree including a small number of subject areas;
- study a general degree which would cover a wider range of subject areas providing a good advanced general education.

Recommendation 15 **We recommend that all institutions of higher education should, over the medium term, review the programmes they offer:**
- **with a view to securing a better balance between breadth and depth across programmes than currently exists;**
- **so that all undergraduate programmes include sufficient breadth to enable specialists to understand their specialism within its context.**

Barriers to the introduction of breadth

9.10 Opportunities to pursue studies in breadth need to be available for both young and mature people entering higher education. Outside Scotland, the experience of young people entering higher education has been constrained by the close focus of A levels. This is combined with the traditional practice of requiring candidates for higher education to apply to read a specific programme. This is in marked contrast to the USA where near-universal practice is to make an application to the institution. Once admitted, students take a fairly broad range of subjects in their early years, and on the basis of that experience decide on specialisation.

9.11 The majority of students in the United Kingdom (UK) are expected to have identified their speciality when they apply for admission. In the first year, they generally study their chosen subject in broad terms, with greater depth and specialisation occurring throughout the programme. This pattern of higher education, typical of the traditional, elite higher education system, has carried across into the more diverse system of today. We believe that it is not serving all students well. It requires applicants to higher education to be clear at a relatively early age what they want out of higher education, and promotes undue specialisation at school aimed at meeting the admission requirements for particular programmes.

9.12 This approach has been the subject of continuing debate over the last 30 years. Last year the report by Sir Ron Dearing proposed the introduction of an Advanced Diploma which would combine studies in depth to A level standard, with broader studies to the new AS level in four out of five domains of knowledge.[3] This Diploma was intended to provide a strong preparation for higher education programmes, while leaving students who may be clear on the specialisms they wish to pursue in higher education to select closely related A levels. More recently the new Government made a Manifesto commitment to broader A levels.

9.13 Broader programmes are already a popular choice for part-time students: 57 per cent of them are on combined degree programmes, compared to only 12 per cent of full-time students. Clearly, offering choice between breadth and depth, and supporting many different types of broad study, is important if the sector is to provide opportunities for lifelong learning. Institutions that wish to introduce breadth to the early years of higher education programmes could consider admitting students to a faculty or to the institution, rather than to a specific programme, in order to send strong signals to schools and their pupils about the importance that higher education attaches to a broad education.

Skills in higher education programmes

9.14   Our consultations showed that employers want graduates to have a wide range of skills, such as those personal and cognitive capabilities that people use to carry out a wide range of tasks and activities. They include, for example, ability to communicate, to use information technology, to think critically, to use cognitive skills – such as an understanding of methodologies – or practical skills needed for the practice of a profession.

9.15   While our national consultation showed that a range of skills was valued by respondents across all groups, there was no consensus about a definitive list. For example, the Council for Industry and Higher Education (CIHE) identified: continuous learning; behavioural and interpersonal skills; problem identification and solving; information appreciation and management; communication; and general awareness.[4] The Centre for Research into Quality identified a range of personal and interactive attributes as important characteristics for work.[5] The former included: intellect; knowledge; willingness to learn; and self-management and motivation. The latter included: inter-personal skills; team working; and communication.

9.16   Nor did we find a consensus from employers on where the main deficiencies in skills lie, although about a quarter of them complained about the inadequate communication skills of graduate entrants. Our student survey showed that students themselves believed that many of their skills had improved while in higher education, especially their analytical skills. The one exception was numeracy, where only one in three students thought this had improved. Not surprisingly, improvements in numeracy and information technology skills were dependent upon the subjects studied by students.

9.17   Although it may be argued that to devote time to the development of skills is a diversion from a student's main studies, and that the potential list of skills becomes so long that it is self-defeating, we believe that four skills are **key** to the future success of graduates whatever they intend to do in later life. These four are:
- communication skills;
- numeracy;
- the use of information technology;
- learning how to learn.

9.18   These are referred to as **key skills** throughout the remainder of our report. We believe that these **key skills** are relevant throughout life, not simply in employment. We include 'learning how to learn' as a key skill because of the importance we place on creating a learning society at a time when much specific knowledge will quickly become obsolete. Those leaving higher education will need to understand how to learn and how to manage their own learning, and recognise that the process continues throughout life. We propose one means by which students can develop their capability to take responsibility for, and manage their own learning, in Recommendation 20.

9.19 The development of skills is also a prime responsibility of schools and colleges. The 1996 recommendations on qualifications for 16 to 19 year olds encouraged all students to gain a certificate of competence in communication, numeracy, and the practical use of information technology.[6] If higher education places an emphasis on these skills at entry, this will provide a sound basis for their further development.

Recommendation 17   **We recommend to institutions of higher education that, over the medium term, their admission procedures should develop to value good levels of competence in communication, numeracy and the practical use of information technology.**

9.20 Even with such an emphasis in admissions procedures, students will continue to enter higher education with different levels of ability in key skills. This may be particularly true of the increasing numbers of mature students with highly developed skills as a result of experience. Ideally, students should be able to diagnose deficiencies for themselves and decide how to address them.

9.21 We resist the temptation to offer a list of the other types of skills which higher education should seek to develop. Much will depend upon the nature of the programme and the aspirations of students. It must be for each institution and each department, taking account of the starting points and learning objectives of their students, to consider how far programmes should include the development of particular skills. But it is important that institutions are explicit about the skills being developed as part of a programme. In this context, the coherence of programmes becomes especially important: it is neither sensible nor possible for every module or unit to develop every skill. We propose a mechanism so that programmes are explicit about skills at the end of this chapter (Recommendation 21).

Integration of skills into programmes

9.22 Basically, there are two ways in which institutions might include key skills in their programmes: by embedding them in existing programmes as the vehicle for development; or by creating parallel modules of 'skills development'. We have considered both of these approaches in the light of evidence from a project by the Open University (OU), where both methods were used in its programmes and the outcomes evaluated.[7]

9.23 The OU found that the embedded model required the programme to be completely revised to integrate the selected skills. Academic staff provided feedback to students on their skill development in the same way as on the subject being studied. In contrast, the parallel model involved the development of a separate 'bolt-on' skills pack. In this model, staff were not involved in feedback or assessment of students. We summarise the results from the Open University (OU) project in Table 9.1.

Table 9.1 – Summary results of OU skills project

Embedded model	Parallel model
Maximum impact on programme	Minimum impact on programme
Costs of training of subject tutors required	No significant training costs
Redesign of programme required	Skills in additional module
Maximum impact on all students	Many students chose not to complete skills sections
High initial costs, but once running recurrent costs were not significantly different from a programme without a skills element	Lower initial costs, but ongoing costs were incurred

9.24 Given the OU's findings, we consider that in the long term there is considerable advantage in embedding skills into programmes. However, this will require an initial investment to redesign programmes to include skills and to train staff in feedback and assessment techniques. We envisage that institutions' learning strategies will encompass this type of development.

9.25 Many universities and colleges have already made impressive progress in integrating skills into programmes. Some of this work has been spurred by the Enterprise in Higher Education Initiative sponsored by the (former) Employment Department. A recent survey about skills by the Committee of Vice-Chancellors and Principals shows that most universities consider skills development to be a part of their mission and plans for the future.[8] We commend the progress made, and believe that the best practice should now be adopted by all. All institutions of higher education should aim for student achievement in key skills – communication, numeracy, the use of information technology and learning how to learn – to become an outcome for all programmes.

The relationship between work and other experience and higher education provision

9.26 All the evidence that we have reviewed endorses the value of some exposure of the student to the wider world as part of a programme of study. This may be achieved through work experience, involvement in student union activities, or work in community or voluntary settings. We have seen examples of a range of excellent opportunities for students.

The value of experience

9.27 Employers place high value on new recruits having had work experience. Research by the Centre for Quality into Higher Education on graduates and their experiences in work confirms its value:

'If there was to be a single recommendation to come from the research, it would be to encourage all undergraduate programmes to offer students an option of a year-long work placement and employers to be less reluctant to provide placement opportunities.'[9]

9.28   An increasing proportion of graduates is likely to be employed in small and medium sized enterprises. Here, the need for recruits to have had some work experience is particularly relevant, because staff need to be immediately effective in a range of roles.

9.29   For many employers and graduates, work experience makes a real difference, complementing traditional academic skills with a basic understanding of work. This addresses the graduate recruitment problem most often mentioned by employers.

9.30   We conclude that those with higher education qualifications should be familiar with the outside world and be able to reflect constructively on issues related to work, such as how they have managed situations or learned from work experiences. Students can benefit from experience in many different settings, structured and informal, paid and unpaid. Their academic experience should help them understand how experience relates to their personal and future professional development.

How to include work and other experiences in programmes

9.31   We found that institutions welcome opportunities for their students to have work experience. Many institutions devote a great deal of effort to identifying such opportunities, developing relationships with companies and collaborating with them to ensure that the experience is rewarding for both the employer and the student. From discussions with students and staff, we have no doubt of the value of such experience. This is particularly so when the work is treated as a structured part of a programme, and its progress is moderated by both the employer and the institution.

9.32   Many students in higher education have experience of work which is not a structured part of a programme. Mature and part-time students generally arrive with considerable work experience. Younger, full-time students increasingly work part-time during term-time and vacations. The need for work experience in particular programmes, or for particular students, will vary. Arrangements must suit the circumstances of individual students.

Recommendation 18   **We recommend that all institutions should, over the medium term, identify opportunities to increase the extent to which programmes help students to become familiar with work, and help them to reflect on such experience.**

9.33   The question is how to expand opportunities for work experience. A notable example is provided by the Shell Technology Enterprise Programme (STEP), a national scheme which has for a number of years placed undergraduates and some graduates in small and medium sized enterprises for eight weeks during the summer vacation of (generally) the second year of their programme. The experience enables the 'host' management to realise the potential for the business from the recruitment of graduates, and encourages participating undergraduates to explore future career opportunities in the small business sector.

9.34   A recent analysis of STEP has highlighted considerable successes.[10] One year after the STEP programme, 93 per cent of students reported that it had satisfied or exceeded their expectations, 61 per cent felt their academic work had benefited from the skills learnt on the programme, and 45 per cent felt they had gained considerable development of their personal skills. After graduation, STEP undergraduates, particularly women, were significantly more likely to have been offered full-time jobs than otherwise similar undergraduates who had not participated in the programme. One year after STEP, 43 per cent of participating businesses had employed an additional member of staff with a university/college degree.

9.35   The provision of work experience depends on the ability and willingness of employers to offer it, and on their willingness to pay students a reasonable wage. We mention the STEP programme as an illustration of a constructive initiative and urge other major companies to consider what they can do to help students to have work experience. We need the active pursuit of enlightened self-interest.

Recommendation 19   **We recommend that the Government, with immediate effect, works with representative employer and professional organisations to encourage employers to offer more work experience opportunities for students.**

9.36   As part of this process, drawing on examples of good practice, the Government and other bodies might examine the following options:
■ the use of intermediary agencies (such as Chambers of Commerce and trade associations) to identify opportunities for work placements;
■ tax incentives to encourage small enterprises to employ students, by covering part of the cost of managing such programmes;
■ an extension of the STEP scheme by which major employers provide students with short periods of work experience;
■ institutions working actively with local employment agencies to identify opportunities for student employment;
■ encouragement of public sector employers by the Government to expand placements, especially for vacation work.

Assessing and recording student achievement

Assessment

9.37   We have taken a particular interest in the assessment of achievement, because it provides a principal vehicle for ensuring the standards appropriate for awards, as well as influencing the direction and form of student learning. Good assessment of students' knowledge, skills and abilities is crucial to the process of learning. As David Boud, an Australian researcher on education development, has said:
    'Students can escape bad teaching: but they can't avoid bad assessment.'[11]

9.38   The purposes of assessment can be broadly described as formative or summative. The former aims to motivate students by giving them an opportunity to review their progress and by providing feedback on their strengths and weaknesses to help them improve. The latter aims to evaluate achievement against set criteria and/or in relation to the performance of others, and is also used to select individuals for progression and for appointments. Assessment also contributes to an institution's own quality assurance by indicating the extent to which programme providers are achieving their objectives and students are achieving appropriate standards.

9.39   To achieve its purposes, assessment must satisfy three major criteria. It needs to be fair, valid and reliable.

9.40   Continuous assessment has become widespread as modular programmes have been adopted across higher education, which has led to an increase in the burden of assessment for staff.[12] This problem has been compounded by the progressive reduction in the ratio of staff to students, and by the increasingly varied backgrounds of students, who come to institutions with more marked differences in knowledge and in learning styles. With greater numbers of students, staff have less time to assess work and provide meaningful feedback. In our survey students were critical of the feedback they received from academic staff.

9.41   At the same time, staff have come to value an approach involving less reliance upon a terminal examination in the assessment of student achievement.[13] Assessing the performance of students over time and in a variety of ways provides a more realistic and holistic view. Many academics perceive this as a considerable advantage over a set of final examinations taken in a short period of time at the end of a year or more of study.

9.42   Given the importance of assessment, both in terms of its contribution to the quality of a student's learning and to the maintenance of standards, we have been concerned to hear that the process of designing programmes (including relating learning objectives to teaching programmes) is often divorced from anything but the most general consideration of the assessment process.[14] Recent research has indicated that, while in the past there were close links between programme design and assessment, the greater use of modularisation and continuous assessment has resulted in these links becoming fragmented. This has militated against the formation of common understanding and standards, with particular implications for the role of the external examiner. It has been suggested that unless measures for dealing with the challenges posed by new programme developments can be found, the reliability and validity of assessment systems will be damaged. The development of assessment strategies and practices should be a priority for the work of the Institute for Learning and Teaching in Higher Education, which we proposed in Chapter 8.

9.43   We have been impressed with work in Scotland to produce an inventory of assessment practice to assist staff.[15] But we have found it surprising that institutions have not given greater attention to developing and improving assessment and marking practices and to training academic staff. Our proposals for the development of skills and for the greater use of communications and information technology in learning and teaching add to the need for training in assessment techniques. Higher education institutions should ensure that assessment methods become a key part of the initial training and continuing professional development of teaching staff.

Recording achievement

9.44   We have also considered the way in which the achievement of students is recorded by institutions. The evidence we received showed a large minority view, more marked among employers, that the honours classification system had outlived its usefulness. Those who hold this view felt that, while the classification made sense in a small homogenous system where general classifications said something meaningful about a student's achievements, it no longer provided useful information, given the varying aims of degree programmes.

9.45   A number of commentators urged that the honours system should be supplemented by a profiling and transcript system, which would offer employers and others detailed information about the capabilities acquired by students. The Higher Education Quality Council recommended the development of student transcripts to provide greater consistency in presenting information about the achievements of students.[16]

9.46   We see value in the development of such transcripts, and have considered them in the context of a restructured National Record of Achievement of the kind proposed in the report by Sir Nicholas Goodison.[17] This report proposes the introduction of a 'Progress File' designed for people to use throughout their lives. The report suggests that:
         'intelligent use of a record of achievement, as a planning tool for people's personal development throughout their lives, is likely to make a major contribution to the raising of skills and therefore to the economy of the United Kingdom'.

9.47   Building on the Goodison report and on the Dearing recommendation in the review of qualifications of 16 to 19 year olds, more and more young people will be entering higher education in the future having used and completed Progress Files from the age of 14. They will have learned how to manage and plan their own learning, how to match their achievements to possible jobs and further learning opportunities, and will have prepared written applications for interviews. It is, therefore, likely that the effective use of such records could assist the transition from one phase of education to another. For students entering higher education at later stages in their lives – often from employment – the use of a Progress File could help to improve links between formal and informal learning and help people to value what they can do as well as what they know.

9.48   We are convinced that it would be advantageous if institutions of higher education were to contribute to the use of a Progress File as part of a student's academic and personal development. The contents of the File would help students to review and record their past achievement, and encourage them to set targets and plan future development. It would provide a record from which they could construct their curricula vitae to communicate their achievements to prospective employers or education and training institutions. It would provide a basis from which students could seek guidance and advice. We see two major elements to the Progress File:

- an official record of achievement or transcript, provided by institutions;
- a means by which students can monitor, build and reflect upon their own personal development.

9.49 We have considered the extent to which there should be a common format across higher education providers for the first element, the transcript. It is likely that both students and employers will become impatient if faced with a plethora of different formats for the presentation and summation of achievement. On the other hand, different institutions offer students very different higher education experiences. We believe a common format should be developed, within which individual institutions can produce their own transcripts. We expect the transcripts to convey a standard set of information, including final award; modules covered, with individual marks; and results of any other assessed activity (work placements, for example).

9.50 The second element of the File would include material which demonstrated progress and achievement in key and other skills and recorded informal and work-based learning. The File would need to be structured to enable students to manage the information they want to record, store and update. It is likely that information technology will be a powerful tool in the use and updating of individual Progress Files.

9.51 There is a danger that the reservoir of materials within the Files may become dysfunctional unless it is used skilfully and selectively: otherwise potential employers could be overwhelmed by information and job seekers put at a disadvantage. If students are in the habit from the age of 14 of using the information stored in the File, it is likely that they will select the most relevant evidence for an interview in order to present themselves more effectively than individuals with no systematic approach to cataloguing achievement. Students will need encouragement to focus on the File, which may require them to be related in some way to assessment and progression. This suggests that staff should integrate the development of the Progress Files into the academic process, which in turn leads to training and development needs for staff. It will be for individual institutions to develop ways of ensuring that students are encouraged to exploit the full potential of their personal records.

9.52 We expect that employers will always want some form of brief indication about the achievement of students, especially when they are overwhelmed with applications. We do not, therefore, recommend the early withdrawal of the degree classification system. However, we do hope that as the Progress File approach is adopted nationally – including the development of transcripts – and its utility is confirmed, the present classification system may become increasingly redundant. Indeed, we envisage that in due course the honours classification system will be replaced by awards and awards with distinction. This will provide a clear indication to employers and others where achievement has been of a higher order.

Recommendation 20   We recommend that institutions of higher education, over the medium term, develop a Progress File. The File should consist of two elements:

- ■ a transcript recording student achievement which should follow a common format devised by institutions collectively through their representative bodies;
- ■ a means by which students can monitor, build and reflect upon their personal development.

Information about programmes

9.53   In this chapter, we have outlined our vision for the developing nature of programmes in higher education. We have emphasised a desire for diversity and choice to meet the varying needs of students with different interests and at different stages in their lives. In Chapter 10, we argue the case for additional stopping-off points as part of the qualifications framework. In Chapters 6, 7 and 22 we stress the importance of clear and explicit information for students so that they can make informed choices about their studies and the levels they are aiming to achieve. Drawing these strands together, we believe that clear descriptions of programmes should be developed so that students are able to compare different offerings and make sensible choices about the programmes they wish to take.

Recommendation 21   We recommend that institutions of higher education begin immediately to develop, for each programme they offer, a 'programme specification' which identifies potential stopping-off points and gives the intended outcomes of the programme in terms of:

- ■ the knowledge and understanding that a student will be expected to have upon completion;
- ■ key skills: communication, numeracy, the use of information technology and learning how to learn;
- ■ cognitive skills, such as an understanding of methodologies or ability in critical analysis;
- ■ subject specific skills, such as laboratory skills.

9.54   Such programme specifications could usefully replace some of the prospectus material that is presently produced. They will provide a basis for employers and students to understand the level – or standard – that programmes are aiming to reach in different areas. Students and others will need to be able to rely on the accuracy of the information provided in the programme specifications. In the next chapter, we develop our ideas on how the programme specification can become a vehicle for clearer understandings about the content and standards of programmes and how its reliability can be assured.

Chapter 10

Qualifications and standards

10.1   The maintenance and assurance of standards of awards and quality of provision across higher education has been one of the most important aspects of our work. One of our terms of reference stated that: *'standards of degrees and other higher education qualifications should be at least maintained, and assured.'*

10.2   Students need to be clear about the requirements of the programmes to which they are committed, and about the levels of achievement expected of them. Employers want higher education to be more explicit about what they can expect from candidates for jobs, whether they have worked at sub-degree, degree, or postgraduate level. Existing arrangements for safeguarding standards are insufficiently clear to carry conviction with those who perceive present quality and standards to be unsatisfactory. We believe there is much to be gained by greater explicitness and clarity about standards and the levels of achievement required for different awards.

10.3   We believe the best progress will be made by building upon existing practice, recognising that each institution is responsible for its own standards, but at the same time engaging the whole academic community in sharing a collective responsibility for standards and quality of provision. This needs to incorporate a clarity of approach which enables those inside and outside higher education to have confidence in the effectiveness and fairness of the arrangements. Uniformity of programmes and national curricula, one possible approach to the development of national standards, would deny higher education the vitality, excitement and challenge that comes from institutions consciously pursuing distinctive purposes, with academics having scope to pursue their own scholarship and enthusiasms in their teaching. The task facing higher education is to reconcile that desirable diversity with achievement of reasonable consistency in standards of awards.

10.4   For some programmes, however, the setting of some form of core national curriculum may be appropriate, for example in medicine where doctors need to be trained to consistent standards, and in teacher training where the existence of the national curriculum in schools demands a degree of consistency.

10.5   In this chapter we address:
- the present position on qualifications and standards;
- the development of a framework of qualifications;
- the standards of awards;
- quality assurance of provision;
- the role of the Quality Assurance Agency.

The present position on quality and standards

10.6   In Chapter 3 we described the ways in which quality is assured at the national level and the changes to existing mechanisms as a result of the creation of the new Quality Assurance Agency. Institutions of higher education and their staff have demonstrated great commitment to ensuring the quality of provision over the last decade, at a time of an expansion of student numbers unmatched by increases in funding. Indeed, the systems in the United Kingdom (UK) for assuring the quality of higher education provision are among the most rigorous in the world.

10.7   But the expansion of student numbers has put the existing quality assurance arrangements under strain. The system of external examiners alone cannot guarantee comparability of standards across a diverse mass system of higher education. In some areas professional bodies are expressing concern about present arrangements. There have been a few highly publicised cases where concerns exist about the adequacy of arrangements to ensure that quality and standards are safeguarded where an institution franchises programmes to another, whether in this country or overseas. We are also concerned about the low level of confidence among some employers about standards of qualifications awarded.

10.8   We believe there is a need to develop quality assurance practices which allow for diversity throughout the system, yet ensure that diversity is not an excuse for low standards or unacceptable quality. In listing these strains on the system and making a range of proposals, our concern is to maintain the high global reputation which higher education in the UK has justifiably earned. We are no less concerned to ensure that students who commit themselves to several years of study can be assured that the awards they earn continue to be respected and valued. The importance of these issues becomes the greater as we look forward to further growth in the number of students in higher education.

A national framework of qualifications

10.9   An important element in our approach to standards is a framework of qualifications broad enough to cover the whole range of achievement, consistent in terminology, and well understood within and outside higher education.

10.10   At present, there is no consistent rationale for the structure or nomenclature of awards across higher education. Most substantively, at the **postgraduate level**, the terms postgraduate diploma and certificate have little common meaning across institutions. There is considerable confusion about the 'M' (Masters) title which is awarded for a variety of types of programmes. For example, the awarding of a Masters degree can be for:
   - the fourth year (or the fifth year in Scotland) of an undergraduate programme – essentially advanced undergraduate work (MEng etc.);
   - a postgraduate conversion programme (where the standard of the programme is sometimes below that of an undergraduate programme in the same subject);

- an undergraduate degree awarded by one of the four Scottish ancient universities;
- a specialist programme of one/two years in duration (such as the MSc, MA);
- no additional work, as in the Oxbridge tradition.

10.11   Not surprisingly, the Harris report on postgraduate education (see also Chapter 11) concluded that, although there had always been diversity in postgraduate titles, it had reached the point of being unhelpful, and that in a number of cases it was positively misleading.[1] We concluded that this situation had arisen as a result of a 'market system' operating during a period of increased demand for postgraduate qualifications without an adequate framework or control mechanism. The problem of reliance on such a market system is that by the time the market has corrected the worst examples of ambiguous standards, damage may have been done to the whole sector.

10.12   This is a salutary warning for undergraduate education. If greater market influences were to be introduced without an adequate framework or mechanisms to ensure the consistent use of titles and corresponding level of award, great damage could be done.

10.13   At the **degree level** in England, there is a strong perception that a three-year ordinary degree represents a failed honours degree. In Scotland, the three-year ordinary or general degree has more standing, with about 30 per cent of all students graduating with this degree, the majority through choice.

10.14   At the **sub-degree level**, there are differences in the use of award titles across the UK. The most obvious difference is that between the Higher National Certificate (HNC) and the Higher National Diploma (HND) in Scotland and in England. In Scotland, the HNC is awarded after one (successful) year and the HND is awarded after two. Both can be studied full- or part-time. In contrast, in England, the HNC is essentially the part-time, work-based equivalent of the full-time HND.

10.15   A number of organisations have proposed the development of a framework to provide clarity on levels of achievement and to show the progression pathways for students. The Royal Society, in its report 'Higher Education Futures', proposed a qualification structure based on a clear progression from 'certificate of higher education' through 'diploma' and 'degree' to enhanced and extended first degrees.[2] In response to the need for clarity in the vast range of vocational qualifications, the National Council for Vocational Qualifications (NCVQ) has developed a five level framework which is being progressively introduced in England, Wales and Northern Ireland. The Dearing report on qualifications for 16 to 19 year olds proposed a national framework covering awards and pathways to achievement up to level 3, which covers both academic and vocational awards in England, Wales and Northern Ireland.[3] The Scottish Qualifications Authority is taking similar steps in Scotland through the implementation of Higher Still.

10.16   The Higher Education Quality Council (HEQC), as part of its work on the standards of degrees, recommended the development of a consistent awards framework, possibly linked to credits and levels, that would provide a rationale for different types of award and clarify the relationship between awards at different levels. In its evidence to us, Committee of Vice-Chancellors and Pricipals (CVCP) called for:

> 'The long-term goal for the UK must be a new education and training framework encompassing all post-16 further and higher level training and qualifications. Such a framework would offer clear pathways for students, encourage progression, and contribute to wider international recognition of qualifications.'[4]

10.17   We agree with those who have represented the need for a framework of qualifications providing greater clarity to the meaning of awards at the higher levels, and we have addressed the nature of a national framework. In so doing, we have considered:
- the extent to which the framework should be national, encompassing the different qualifications of Scotland, England, Wales and Northern Ireland;
- the relationship of vocational and academic qualifications within such a framework;
- the types of qualifications that it should contain, and whether there is a case for additional 'stopping-off' points below first degree;
- whether the framework should be based on credit points;
- the European implications of such a framework.

Should there be a UK-wide framework?

10.18   We have considered the possibility of a framework which is truly national in nature. In the long term – say five to ten years – we think that it may be possible and advantageous for there to be a UK framework of qualifications, encompassing England, Scotland, Wales and Northern Ireland. However, given the historic differences in educational traditions, it will be necessary, in the short term, to have separate frameworks for Scotland and for the rest of the UK. In the meantime, it may be practicable to map the Scottish arrangements on to those for the rest of the UK. Proceeding in this way makes it possible to recognise distinctive practice in Scotland, while enabling students to understand where they are within the structure and potential options open to them UK-wide. This approach would also allow institutions throughout the UK to develop a range of programmes to cater for different types of students – with, for example, the rest of the UK developing some programmes which are similar to those in Scotland, and vice versa. What happens in Scotland may depend ultimately on what is decided about school leaving qualifications and the extent to which the Advanced Highers are adopted.

10.19   We have, therefore, concluded that it would be in the long term interests of the UK to establish a national framework, but that sufficient and necessary conditions do not at present appertain.

Vocational and academic qualifications

10.20   The distinction between vocational and 'academic' work has never been clear cut. University education, in its origins, had an academic purpose in preparing young men for a religious vocation. Medicine has long been an esteemed element in higher education, and our consultation has confirmed that, particularly in view of the increased importance of the basic biomedical sciences and the increasing breadth of knowledge of the social sciences and ethical issues that will be required of the profession in the future, the training of doctors must remain firmly embedded in higher education institutions in a research environment. The training of nurses has been extensively incorporated into higher education in recent years. Dentistry, veterinary science and a range of paramedical qualifications are pursued through higher education. The training of teachers is a long-established element in higher education. The engineering and other professional bodies accredit university degree programmes. The HND and the HNC, as vocational qualifications, are also a well-established part of higher education.

10.21 Although there are distinct differences in the purpose of academic and vocational pathways, to regard them separately and in isolation is at variance with the facts. We see advantages in creating a framework which encompasses both pathways. In particular, we see the potential for National Vocational Qualifications (NVQs) and their Scottish equivalents, Scottish Vocational Qualifications (SVQs) at levels 4 and 5 to integrate with provision in higher education.

10.22 Recent developments have acknowledged that the development and assessment of knowledge and understanding was under-emphasised in early work on S/NVQs. At the higher levels, there is a particular need to ensure the adequate specification and assessment of knowledge and understanding which, for practical reasons may need to be separately assessed from their application in the workplace. This reappraisal leads to the prospect of an enlarged role for colleges and universities in delivery and assessment of S/NVQ.

10.23 It also means that, through appropriate programme development and assessment, taking account of the academic and S/NVQ approaches, a student could receive multiple outcomes from one learning process. For example, a legal conversion programme could lead to a Diploma in Legal Practice, a number of NVQ units towards an NVQ 4, and credits towards a masters degree. This would mean that a student could build up a portfolio of experience, shown by credits and units, which could be used and supplemented where necessary.

10.24 We have, therefore, concluded that with the redevelopment of the S/NVQ (to include an adequate specification of the underpinning knowledge and understanding) it would be possible to accommodate vocational and academic qualifications within the framework. We welcome this development as fundamental to the incorporation of the S/NVQ within the framework.

The qualifications within the framework

10.25 The last Government asked us to consider whether General National Vocational Qualifications (GNVQ) should be extended beyond the present Advanced level to levels comparable with NVQ levels 4 and 5. Introduced in 1992, the Advanced GNVQ provides an alternative (or an addition) to GCE A levels for the increasing number of young people staying in full-time education beyond age 16. Numbers registering for Advanced GNVQs have grown, from just under 4,000 in 1992/93 to approximately 84,000 in 1996/97. In consequence, GNVQs entrants are an increasing proportion of higher education students. Undergraduates with GNVQs are located in greater proportions in the 1992 universities.

10.26   In September 1995, the National Council for Vocational Qualifications (NCVQ) issued a consultation document to education and training agencies, institutions, employers, lead bodies and related interest groups on the need to extend the GNVQ framework in England, Wales and Northern Ireland to levels 4 and 5.[5] We have taken account of that document and the responses to it in arriving at our views.[6] We note that there are no plans to introduce General Scottish Vocational Qualifications (GSVQs) above level 3 in Scotland as the Higher Still qualifications and HND will cover these areas.

10.27   We conclude that while there are some benefits to be gained from introducing GNVQs at level 4 (and possibly level 5), there are significant reasons for **not** doing so, as given below.

■ The case for introducing GNVQs at the Foundation, Intermediate and Advanced levels – to widen choice by providing a distinctive approach to the acquisition of knowledge and understanding – does not apply with the same force to the higher levels where there is already a wide range of choice.

■ Many of those in higher education consulted by the National Council for Vocational Qualifications (NCVQ) about higher level GNVQs believed that existing qualifications achieved the aims set for GNVQs; while a third were in favour, over half were against its introduction.

■ It is not clear what employer demand there might be for higher level GNVQs. A recent survey of employers for the Association of Graduate Recruiters found that, while employers wanted skills relevant to work and an understanding of the world of work, there was '*no evident desire for an undergraduate education to become more closely linked to specific vocational qualifications.*'[7]

■ The NCVQ is changing its criteria for NVQs, which may make it easier for existing vocational qualifications offered by institutions of higher education to be incorporated into the NCVQ framework, irrespective of whether they take the form and structure of existing GNVQs.

■ The development of key and core skills, a distinctive feature of GNVQs, is already being extended into other programmes of higher education, with the potential for further development.

10.28   We are fully supportive of the Foundation, Intermediate and Advanced GNVQs, which are an apt response to a clear need. The indications are that the Advanced GNVQ will provide a valuable stream of entrants to higher education. We are not, however, in favour of the creation of new awards unless they demonstrably meet an identified need.

10.29   The report 'Choosing to Change' proposed the introduction of an Associate Degree as an additional level of successful achievement below first degree.[8] Our enquiries found minimal support for the introduction of such a qualification. It is seen as devaluing the term 'degree' and thought likely to become a second class qualification which would not be credible with employers or overseas, especially in mainland Europe. There was, moreover, suspicion that it was a cost-driven proposal paving the way to a 'two-year entitlement', so that students would be persuaded that it was a normal endpoint for a majority of undergraduates.

10.30   On the other hand, there was support in evidence to us for opportunities for students to gain national recognition for achievement at a range of levels, rather than a uniform expectation that all students would aspire to the same qualification, typically a degree. There is concern that enrolling most students on to degree programmes as the terminal qualification – rather than offering recognised stages of achievement along the way – could result in failure rather than success for many students as higher education expands. In the context of lifelong learning, much of which will be spread over time, it is desirable to be able to recognise worthwhile steps to achievement by awards that are valued in their own right. The National Union of Students (NUS) told us:

> *Recognition, with a qualification, of study equivalent to one or two years of current full-time study would be a significant step forward in allowing flexible study and facilitating lifelong learning.*[9]

10.31   We, therefore, support the development of recognised exit points within a framework of qualifications, but not the introduction of additional qualifications such as higher level GNVQs or an associate degree.

Credits and the framework

10.32   The report 'Choosing to Change' recommended the creation of a national framework of qualifications based on credit points at different levels.[10] We have considered the arguments put forward in that report, as well as the responses to consultation on it.[11]

10.33   There have already been a number of attempts to develop national credit frameworks. The first was developed in 1986 by the Council for National Academic Awards (CNAA). This scheme was designed to facilitate inter-institutional student mobility, to encourage wider access, to develop the recognition of prior achievement and to assist with the transfer of employees between work and higher education through the accreditation of work-based learning and employee training.

10.34   Progress elsewhere in the UK has outstripped that in England. In Scotland, the Scottish Credit Accumulation and Transfer (SCOTCAT) framework covers five levels at present (four at undergraduate and one at postgraduate level), and as a result of work through the Scottish Advisory Committee on Credit and Access (SACCA), there are plans to develop eight linked levels, starting from the HNC (at around the age of 17) up to postgraduate (Masters) level.[12]

10.35   In Wales, a credit framework has been developed, with agreement on the principles of the framework from all Welsh institutions. In Northern Ireland, a project is well advanced for a comprehensive Credit Accumulation and Transfer (CAT) system embracing the whole of further and higher education.

10.36   The majority of higher education institutions now have, or plan to introduce, a CAT scheme: some 70 per cent allow credit for work-based and other experiential learning. But there is wide variation in the arrangements made by institutions. There is, as yet, little inter-institutional credit transfer within higher education. Although there is no reliable basis upon which to make an assessment of the extent of transfer or the demand for it, it is likely that credit transfer will be particularly relevant to part-time students who may have to move with their jobs, than to traditional full-time students who will expect to complete a programme within one institution within a specific time period.

10.37   In responses to our consultation, there was widespread support for the credit rating of all programmes and for the introduction of a national Credit Accumulation and Transfer (CAT) system. Support for a credit system is connected to the concept of flexibility in provision, which will allow a wider array of awards, a range of delivery systems, flexibility in modes of study and work-based delivery. The support for credit systems ranged beyond the higher education sector, with bodies such as the Confederation of British Industry, the National Union of Students and the Further Education Development Agency explicitly supporting the idea.

10.38   There has now been sufficient experience of the building up of credits for the higher education sector to have made an informed judgement of the value of this approach. In the light of that experience, the weight of opinion is that a credit-based approach is the right way forward. We agree and support such an approach to underpin a framework of qualifications.

The framework and Europe

10.39   To help us consider the implications of developing a framework of qualifications in the context of mainland Europe, we commissioned the Higher Education Quality Council (HEQC) to consider a range of issues. The HEQC's conclusions are contained in Report 11.

10.40   There are four major messages from the report. First, UK awards are not perceived as national awards in mainland Europe because they are awarded by individual institutions. Second, the establishment of a UK framework of qualifications would be likely to lessen some current problems of international recognition of qualifications, and to enhance confidence in standards. Third, a typical continental degree tends to be defined as a programme of a minimum of four years of study, although the levels of achievement for such programmes are not defined. Fourth, the expansion of UK higher education has weakened the argument, previously accepted in Europe, that highly selective entry for UK students supported the standing of the three-year honours degree.

10.41   On the basis of this work, we conclude that the development of a framework would contribute to the recognition and standing of UK awards throughout Europe, and the world.

The basis of a national framework of qualifications

10.42   We believe that, in the long term, there should be a national framework of qualifications to provide a structure which, will be common across the UK. The framework should be comprehensible to all inside and outside higher education. This means placing a limit on the number of award titles.

Chart 10.1 – A qualifications framework

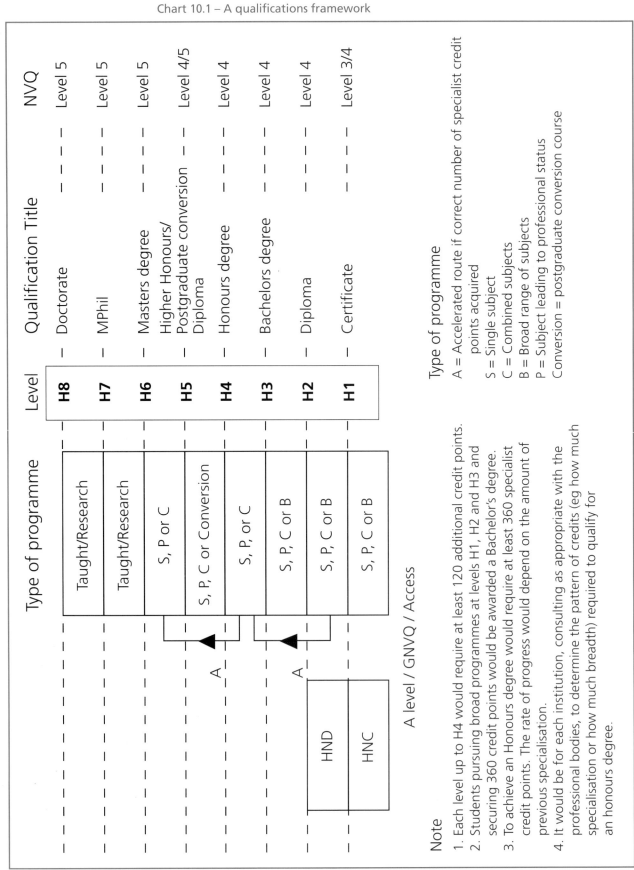

Level	Qualification Title		NVQ
H8	Doctorate	—	Level 5
H7	MPhil	—	Level 5
H6	Masters degree	—	Level 5
H5	Higher Honours/ Postgraduate conversion Diploma	—	Level 4/5
H4	Honours degree	—	Level 4
H3	Bachelors degree	—	Level 4
H2	Diploma	—	Level 4
H1	Certificate	—	Level 3/4

Type of programme

H8	Taught/Research
H7	Taught/Research
H6	S, P or C
H5	S, P, C or Conversion
H4	S, P, or C
H3	S, P, C or B
H2	S, P, C or B
H1	S, P, C or B

A level / GNVQ / Access

HND

HNC

Type of programme

A = Accelerated route if correct number of specialist credit points acquired
S = Single subject
C = Combined subjects
B = Broad range of subjects
P = Subject leading to professional status
Conversion = postgraduate conversion course

Note

1. Each level up to H4 would require at least 120 additional credit points.
2. Students pursuing broad programmes at levels H1, H2 and H3 and securing 360 credit points would be awarded a Bachelor's degree.
3. To achieve an Honours degree would require at least 360 specialist credit points. The rate of progress would depend on the amount of previous specialisation.
4. It would be for each institution, consulting as appropriate with the professional bodies, to determine the pattern of credits (eg how much specialisation or how much breadth) required to qualify for an honours degree.

10.43 Such a framework will:
- cater for a wide range of aspirations and achievement;
- have recognised standards;
- enable students to progress through higher levels, as well as move between programmes as appropriate;
- enable attainment to be recognised, providing it can be reliably assessed;
- articulate with other areas of tertiary education;
- encompass vocational and academic qualifications;
- have standing here and abroad.

10.44 The main elements of the framework will be:
- standardised nomenclature for awards;
- agreed and common credit points at relevant levels;
- the inclusion of additional and recognised 'stopping-off' points.

10.45 We propose a framework of qualifications for institutions in England, Wales and Northern Ireland ('other UK' institutions), as shown in Chart 10.1. It describes higher education qualifications in terms of levels of achievement – from H1 to H8. It is based on credit points, which means that different levels can be regarded as equivalent, although achievement will not guarantee automatic progression to a higher level or entry to any one institution at a particular level. The final responsibility for admissions and progression will rest, as now, with the receiving institution, and decisions will depend upon the appropriateness of the credits achieved and the prerequisites for particular pathways.

Recommendation 22 **We recommend that the Government, the representative bodies, the Quality Assurance Agency, other awarding bodies and the organisations which oversee them, should endorse immediately the framework for higher education qualifications that we have proposed.**

10.46 The framework entails a number of changes to existing programmes to clarify the pathways available to students. Higher National (HN) programmes should be structured so that the HNC is at level H1, and the HND at level H2. This represents the adoption throughout the UK of present practice in Scotland. This does not mean that we want to see an end to the type of programme which currently leads to an HNC. We support a diversity of routes to level H2, including those based full-time in higher education as well as part-time, work-based routes, so long as all lead to similar levels of achievement and people understand this. But, in encouraging the practice of lifelong learning, we see value in the Scottish practice of having a recognised qualification which represents the equivalent of one year's full-time work (the HNC) and one denoting the equivalent of two year's work (the HND).

10.47 At level H4, we believe that the title 'Honours' should be clearly understood to denote a level achieved in a single subject, a professional area or related subjects, which would include the existing combined honours programmes. We recognise that it will be difficult to define precisely what constitutes sufficient depth for the honours degree title to be justified. The external examiner system will have a significant role to play.

However, as we explained in Chapter 9, we believe that there is a need for a diverse range of programmes, including those that are considerably broader than, but as rigorous as, existing ones. These will warrant the title Bachelor's degree at level H3. We intend the framework of qualifications to allow for such flexibility, whilst ensuring the standards of all qualifications are maintained and achievements are clear to students and to employers.

10.48   For postgraduate provision, we propose that advanced undergraduate education (such as the present MEng and the MPharm) should be called 'Higher Honours' so as to distinguish them from Masters level programmes. We welcome and endorse the recommendations made in the Harris report about the need for standardised nomenclature for programmes above degree level, and propose that developmental work in this area be continued in relation to the framework for higher education qualifications to ensure that there is consistency and clear progression.

10.49   The framework is designed to provide clarity and to cater for the diversity of higher education and professional development. We intend that those responsible for the different subject or professional areas should use the framework to identify and describe the various pathways available for qualifications in their areas. We have taken the examples of engineers, teachers and doctors to show how particular qualifications might articulate within this qualifications framework. This is not intended to be prescriptive: those responsible for these subjects should decide exactly where the qualifications fit.

10.50   For engineers, the Engineering Council's proposals for Standards and Routes to Registration (SARTOR 1996) envisage four different qualifications: an HND, leading to Engineering Technician status; an ordinary BEng degree leading to Incorporated Engineer status; and a BEng (hons) and an MEng, both of which lead, after different additional criteria have been met, to Chartered status. In the framework, the HND would be awarded at H2 level, the ordinary BEng at H3, the BEng (hons) at H4 and the MEng, which would be re-titled Higher Honours, at H5. Given what we propose on programme specifications and standards, we believe that having clearly defined exit points at recognised levels will remove the need to specify entry criteria as a guarantee of standards as suggested by SARTOR.

10.51   For teachers, the one-year Postgraduate Certificate of Education (PGCE) would be awarded at level H5, reflecting the fact that it is a postgraduate conversion qualification. The BEd programme would be awarded at level H4 (see Chart 10.2). In medicine, most students currently receive a conjoint degree of Bachelor of Medicine and Bachelor of Surgery. The specialism and advanced level of study required means that it would be awarded at level H5.

10.52   It is fundamental to our approach that awards should be based on achievement rather than on the length of study required. Progress should depend on the aptitude, aspirations, diligence and interests of students and the credits acquired. Several examples of possible routes through the framework are provided in Chart 10.2. The first example is a student reading for an English degree, with relevant A levels, who would enter an honours degree programme and progress to level H4, achieving an honours degree in three years by the accelerated route.

Chart 10.2 – Examples of routes through the framework

Student A had always been interested in English and wanted to study it in depth in higher education. Having acquired the relevant A levels, she entered higher education as a full-time student and followed the single subject route and left with an honours degree at level H4. She takes no breaks and completes her honours degree in three years by the accelerated route.

Student B was interested in science, but less sure about the specific area she wanted to study. She entered higher education and studied a General Sciences programme up to level H2 on a full-time basis. She left full-time studies with a diploma having got a job as a technician in a laboratory. She continued her studies on a part-time basis sponsored by her employer focusing on biology and acquired an honours degree at level H4.

Student C, following a Short Service Commission in the Army, wanted to retrain as a primary school teacher, specialising in education of young children. He enrolled on a BEd programme, which enabled him to study for a profession and acquire a range of subject knowledge. He left with an honours degree at level H4. Later, in order to progress in his career and update his skills, he enrolled on a part-time MEd programme. This took him up to level H6.

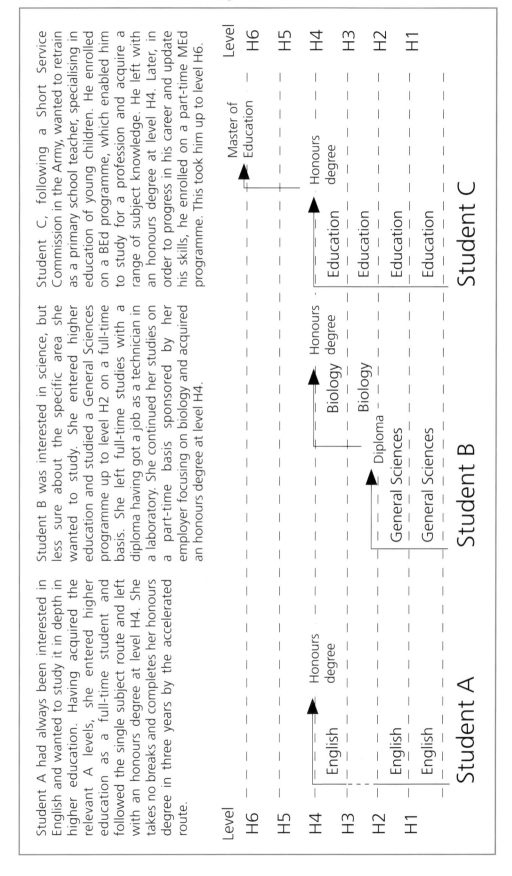

10.53   Another example is a student with a wide interest in the sciences who wished to postpone choosing the area she wanted to study in depth. She might choose to study a 'General Sciences' programme and follow that route through levels H1 and H2, leaving with a Diploma at level H2. She might later begin to study biology in greater depth with the aim of achieving an honours degree at level H4. This would be equivalent to the 'two-plus-two' route. Alternatively she might have left upon completion of level H3 with a Bachelors degree.

Standards of awards

10.54   The introduction of a framework of qualifications underpins the development of robust and recognised standards. There is national concern about the maintenance of standards of achievement at all levels of education. A recent review of A level standards concluded that, although standards had not changed, the arrangements for safeguarding standards needed strengthening. Frequent comparisons are made between the standards achieved by younger pupils in this country and abroad, and those achieved by one school compared with another.

10.55   There is similar concern about the standard required for the award of higher education degrees. Given the large increase in the number of students taking degrees over the last 20 years, and a marked rise in the proportion awarded First or Upper Second class honours, many think that it is not plausible to say that standards have not declined.[13] There is also a widely held view that degree standards are not uniform and that they cannot be in a mass system.

10.56   The argument that there are differences between institutions is not new. The Robbins Committee argued that it was unavoidable that there should be differences in achievement and reputation between institutions. In its view, the key issue was that, where differences existed, they should rest clearly on differences of function, not on acknowledged excellence in the discharge of functions. While the issue is not new, it is inescapable that with progression towards mass higher education, the range of functions adopted by institutions has widened.

10.57   We have not attempted to make an independent investigation of the standards of degrees and the evidence we received did not provide a firm base on which to conclude whether they have fallen over time. The Higher Education Quality Council (HEQC) has argued that there is no straightforward or dependable way of reaching a conclusion on this. Nevertheless, we are sensitive to the public concern that exists about standards and to the significant body of opinion in higher education which holds that, at the broad subject level, little precise comparability of standards exists, except perhaps where there is an external validating or accrediting body.

10.58   In its interim report on graduate standards, the HEQC has pointed to *'inconsistencies and other weaknesses in the actual practice of external examining'*,[14] and in its evidence to us the HEQC stated:

> *'The Council's work does make it clear, that the consequence of current changes in higher education is that traditional understandings of what a degree is no longer hold good...essential aspects of the academic infrastructure that used to support confidence in shared standards have been undermined, with resultant problems of understanding for students, employers, research councils and academics themselves, since the existing frames of reference no longer match reality.'* [15]

10.59   At the postgraduate level, we have heard some concerns about the comparability and consistency of standards of postgraduate programmes across the higher education sector. The most extreme example is the Masters in Business Administration (MBA). Here, the awarding institution has become the prime recognition point for students and employers, rather than the course and its content.

10.60   Against such concerns, we have debated whether it is important, or necessary, for UK higher education awards to have a meaning which is commonly accepted and recognised. One option would be for UK awards to go in the direction of a number of other countries, such as Japan and the USA. In these countries, there is no national attempt to have awards of common standards across institutions or subjects, except in some professional areas. Instead, there is an informal ranking of institutions, with parents, students, academics and employers knowing, at least in broad terms, the relative status of each.

10.61   We also considered practice in Australia, where an academic standards programme was introduced about ten years ago with a view to ensuring that the class of an honours degree should signify something similar for an award in the relevant field by any of the Australian universities. Expert panels were established to review the standards of awards in the main subject areas and, over a period of years, the interaction between academics has enabled views to crystallise on the essentials of an honours degree and the appropriate standards that ought to be applied.

10.62   We have been impressed by the approach that has been attempted in Australia, and share the view that there is advantage in awards reflecting a national approach to standards. We consider that national recognition and standing of UK programmes is to the advantage of all those concerned about higher education.

■ It is owed to the **student** – who is typically committing three or more years of life, spending money on higher education and foregoing years of potential earnings – to offer a quality of both experience and award that have standing and meaning in the market-place, both in this country and abroad.

■ If the **higher education sector** is to be truly committed to the concept of lifelong learning, students will need to be able to take advantage of a national system of credit accumulation and transfer. Transfer will not be possible without some level of national currency of the credit acquired by the student.

- **Staff** in higher education institutions want to have pride in their work, and if they are going to give their best, they need to have confidence in the standing of their institution. There would be little satisfaction for staff in an institution whose awards were not well regarded.

- **Higher education institutions** in the UK have a valuable business in attracting students from other parts of the world, and a developing business in providing educational services in other countries. Over the next 20 years, higher education is likely to become increasingly international, promoted by information technology. There are distinct benefits from this. It enriches the learning experience for UK students through interaction with students from other countries. At the financial level, overseas students are a welcome source of income to institutions, as well as to the national balance of payments. For the long term, with the prospect of higher education becoming progressively an international activity, with active competition between institutions and nations for students, the award of degrees with recognised value represents a competitive advantage. Conversely, loss of international recognition of UK degrees would be a competitive disadvantage to higher education as a whole.

- The evidence received from **employers** shows a wish for threshold standards in awards. For example, the CBI, among other bodies, urges that learning outcomes be explicitly stated:
  'some learning outcomes must be made compulsory in the form of threshold standards for degrees. The threshold would include key skills as well as knowledge/technical skills to an appropriately high standard. Public funding would be dependent on institutions ensuring these thresholds.'[16]

10.63 We conclude that UK awards at all levels, and especially the first degree, must be nationally recognised and widely understood.

10.64 To this end, building on work already in train, institutions need to be more explicit and publicly accessible about the standards of attainment required for different programmes and awards. It would be both impractical and undesirable to try to achieve close matching of standards across the whole of higher education in all its diversity. What is practicable is to develop threshold or minimum standards which set an agreed level of expectations of awards, and we are convinced that this should be done now.

10.65 From the evidence put to us, it appears that the need for these threshold standards is more urgent in some subjects than in others. The Engineering Council has expressed acute concerns about standards in engineering which we agree need to be urgently addressed. It would be consistent with the approach outlined in this chapter that this should be done by giving immediate consideration to developing threshold standards for engineering and that, as a priority, attention should focus initially on developing outcome standards for level H1 which is broadly equivalent to the first year (in full-time terms). This would set a threshold for further progression through subsequent levels and would also set standards for those providing guidance to students contemplating a career in engineering. This might be done most rapidly by recognising the Edexcel HNC which we propose, as a threshold qualification for entry to level H2 for those who had entered level H1 with lower qualification levels than those expected by SARTOR. It will be for the Engineering Council to consider this approach as an alternative to its SARTOR 96 proposals for tightening entry criteria to programmes. It might also be sensible to consider developing additional access courses to engineering.

10.66   We are attracted to the proposition that standards should be developed by the academic community itself, through formal groupings for the main areas of study. We also think that achievement and expectations, at the threshold and at the highest end of the spectrum for different programme types, should be identified by these groups. In many cases, subject associations and professional bodies will play a role developing benchmarks. We make a recommendation on this point (Recommendation 25).

10.67   This benchmark information could be used by institutions as part of their programme approval process to set degree (and other award) standards. In addition, it should be used by external examiners to validate whether programmes are within the agreed standards for particular awards. This will require institutions to be explicit about the required standards for awards and to make this information publicly available. We make a recommendation on how higher education institutions, assisted by the Quality Assurance Agency, can take these proposals forward (Recommendation 25).

Quality assurance

Quality assurance of the student learning experience

10.68   The Teaching Quality Assessments (TQA) introduced by the Funding Bodies have raised the profile of teaching within institutions and have served a useful purpose. But, given that the vast majority of outcomes have been satisfactory, we are not convinced that it would be the best use of scarce resources to continue the system in the long term. Moreover, we believe that it is exceedingly difficult for the TQA process to review the quality of learning and teaching itself, rather than proxies for learning and teaching, such as available resources or lecture presentation. The utility of such a system is also likely to wane as institutions 'learn' how to achieve high ratings. While, therefore, we see value in completing the current round of assessments, for the longer term we see the way forward lying in the development of common standards, specified and verified through a strengthened external examiner system, supported by a lighter approach to quality assessment. For this to happen, it would be a pre-condition that:

- institutions are explicit about the content of, and terminal standards required for, the awards they offer, with students and employers having accurate and clear information about programmes;
- institutions are prepared to adopt national codes of practice (analogous to those prepared by the Higher Education Quality Council (HEQC) and other organisations) to support quality provision with guidance for students, overseas students, and others.

10.69   If institutions are willing to develop in this way, so that it is clear to all stakeholders what they can expect from higher education, we believe that it will be possible to restore a 'qualified trust' between higher education institutions, students and the public funders of higher education. If students, employers or staff in institutions have justified complaints or concerns about the quality of educational provision, there will have to be means to take action to protect them and the wider reputation of higher education. The way in which this compact for providing high quality education can be taken forward is given in Recommendation 24.

Aspects of quality relating to postgraduate students

10.70   We have already noted our concerns about the breakdown in consistency of the use of postgraduate qualification titles, and have made a recommendation to rectify this as part of the development of a framework of qualifications. Our recommendation is similar to that in the 'Review of postgraduate education' (the Harris report).

10.71   The Harris report recommended that a national code of practice for the quality of postgraduate provision be developed, to which all institutions should subscribe, monitored through the new Quality Assurance Agency, with compliance ensured by making it a condition of funding. We endorse this recommendation, and in Chapter 11, we consider how it will apply to postgraduate research students. In Recommendation 24, we describe the functions of the Quality Assurance Agency and its role in reviewing the quality of provision through the development of codes of practice.

Quality assurance of collaborative provision

10.72   There is a wide range of collaborative and partnership arrangements. We say more about the scope, size and reasons for collaboration in Chapter 16. Here we consider collaborative arrangements for: accreditation; validation; and franchising. **Accreditation** is the process by which an institution without degree awarding powers is given authority by a body with those powers to validate, deliver and control the quality of programmes. This arrangement is typically found where a partnership has matured over a number of years and the degree awarding body has a high level of confidence in the practices and standards of the accredited institution. **Validation** is similar to accreditation, but relates only to specific programmes. **Franchising** occurs when a degree awarding body (such as a university) authorises another institution (usually a further education institution) to teach an approved programme, whilst itself keeping control of the programme content, delivery, assessment and quality assurance.

10.73   For franchised provision, funding is directed from the franchiser to the franchisee. Franchising is common practice in England, Wales and Northern Ireland where further education institutions (the franchisees) offer programmes to students that are designed, quality assured and funded by a higher education institution (the franchiser). Although there is some franchising in Scotland, the practice is less common. Arrangements where higher education institutions in the UK franchise programmes to institutions in other countries are becoming more widespread.

10.74   For all collaborative provision, we are concerned that the quality of the experience for the student, and the standard of achievement required for an award, should match that in the parent institution. As the practice of franchising has been expanding rapidly, we have concerns that some further education institutions, seeking to provide a wide range of options for students, may be extending themselves too broadly and entering into too many relationships to be able to ensure quality and standards.

10.75 The Higher Education Quality Council (HEQC) has been auditing collaborative provision in the UK and overseas. The UK audits have identified a number of areas for improvement in collaborative audit arrangements, such as clearer statements about the aims and purposes of different kinds of collaboration and formal processes to ensure the active management of remote provision, once in operation.[17] More recent international audits have generally presented a reassuring picture, in that the delivery of UK awards overseas was found to be undertaken with serious regard for quality and standards, and with evident commitment from the partners involved.[18] Overseas students, in particular, were enthusiastic about the provision on offer, and those students who studied franchised programmes before transferring to the UK were found to perform extremely well when compared to their UK counterparts. However, some findings were negative and have attracted the attention of the media both here and overseas. These adverse findings included: variability in the coverage and application of quality assurance policies; over-delegation of responsibility to franchisees; difficulties in managing quality assurance in the context of different languages, cultures and higher education systems; and an occasional willingness for UK higher education institutions to accept a learning environment which would not be considered suitable in the UK.

10.76 We believe that in the interests of extending opportunity and encouraging lifelong learning, franchising should continue, but only on the strict understanding that it must not prejudice the assurance of quality and maintenance of standards. To that end, there needs to be a proper contractual arrangement between the franchiser and franchisee which describes clearly the responsibilities of the partners. We would expect further education colleges to enter into partnership with only one higher education institution, unless there were exceptional circumstances relating to geographical proximity or subject provision. Such an exception would have to be approved by the Quality Assurance Agency.

10.77 We consider that 'serial franchising', where one institution validates or franchises provision to another, which in turn franchises this provision elsewhere, must cease at once. This arrangement makes it difficult for different parties to have clear responsibilities and to ensure quality of provision. The appropriate Funding Bodies should proscribe such practice.

Recommendation 23   We recommend that:
- the Quality Assurance Agency should specify criteria for franchising arrangements;
- these criteria should rule out serial franchising, and include a normal presumption that the franchisee should have only one higher education partner;
- franchising partners should jointly review and, if necessary, amend existing arrangements to ensure that they meet the criteria, and should both certify to the Agency that arrangements conform with the criteria;
- there should be periodic checks by the Agency on the operation of franchise arrangements to verify compliance;

■ after 2001, no franchising should take place either in the UK or abroad except where compliance with the criteria has been certified by the Quality Assurance Agency.

10.78   As far as we are aware, the UK is the only country that conducts audits of its international collaborative provision. More must be made of this as a positive point for UK higher education internationally. Once these new arrangements are in place, it would be advantageous to inform the governments of other countries.

The role of the Quality Assurance Agency

10.79   In this chapter and previously, we have made a range of proposals about the safeguarding of quality and standards, which can be summarised as follows:
■ the adoption of a framework of qualifications based on agreed credits and levels of achievement;
■ the development of recognised standards of awards;
■ a learning experience for students which enables them to meet the standards of the award;
■ clear and accurate information for students, employers and others about the content, standards and delivery of programmes;
■ confidence, internally and externally, that standards are assured and that the quality of education supports those standards through a system which is easy to understand and not burdensome to operate;
■ the potential for action to be taken swiftly to protect students (and the reputation of higher education more widely) if problems with regard to standards or quality occur.

10.80   We have considered how such a programme of change, consisting of a number of interdependent elements, can be carried forward throughout the higher education sector. Clearly, any approach will need to be owned by, and carry the support of, the institutions themselves. Moreover, there is a need for the process to be strategically managed if good progress is to be made to a reasonable timescale. Fragmented responsibility for overseeing implementation would blur the vision, could produce ill-co-ordinated initiatives and could cause frustration within institutions.

10.81   For that reason, we consider that much of the work should be carried out through a single organisation. The new Quality Assurance Agency would be appropriate, since its primary function is to assure the quality of higher education provision and the standards of its awards. The Agency will operate initially in England, Wales and Northern Ireland. We agree with our Scottish Committee that the Scottish institutions should join the Agency, and that, once its criteria for joining are met, the Scottish Higher Education Funding Council should contract with the Agency for relevant services.

10.82   The report which led to the establishment of the Quality Assurance Agency,[19] and the recommendations coming from the HEQC's Graduate Standards Programme, outlined a range of tasks for the Agency. Our recommendations add up to a somewhat different agenda for the Agency, but one which we believe it should embrace vigorously.

10.83   We propose three main functions for the Quality Assurance Agency:
- quality assurance and public information;
- standards verification;
- the maintenance of the qualifications framework

10.84   As part of these functions, the Agency will need to conduct external scrutiny of institutional practice relating to quality or standards following serious complaints or on the basis of other verifiable evidence of serious institutional failing. Examples might include where the quality of support available to students is inadequate, or where an institution is offering substandard awards. The Funding Bodies should be enabled to withdraw funding if the complaint is upheld and appropriate remedial action is not forthcoming. The Agency will, therefore, need to develop a fair and robust system for complaints relating to educational provision.

10.85   In England, the quality assurance arrangements for the provision of teacher training require separate consideration, because of the involvement of the Teacher Training Agency (TTA) and the Office for Standards in Education (OFSTED) in the process. The establishment of a General Teaching Council (GTC) may further complicate the picture. We propose that the Government review the respective responsibilities of the various agencies involved in the quality assurance of teacher training when considering the future role of a General Teaching Council (GTC). (Recommendation 87)

Quality assurance and public information

10.86   This function of the Agency would include developing a robust system of public information and assurance about the nature of higher education provision, as reflected in programme specifications (see Chapter 9) and the arrangements for ensuring quality and standards.

10.87   As we have already discussed, it would include the development of codes of practice relating to particular areas of activity, such as collaborative provision, postgraduate work, and guidance. Institutions would adopt the codes of practice, and their adherence to them would be reviewed through periodic (perhaps five-yearly) institutional reviews organised by the Agency. This process of external review will help institutions seeking to examine their own practices.

10.88   There will also be a quality assurance task for the Agency in reviewing whether the research funds, which (as we propose in Chapter 11) should be disbursed to improve teaching, are fulfilling their function.

10.89   The Quality Assurance Agency will be responsible for advising on the award of degree-awarding powers. It will, therefore, need to ensure that it is able to exercise this responsibility with rigour and consistency. In Chapter 16 we consider the case for the QAA also advising on the removal of these powers.

10.90   The development of this function will require communication with the various clients of higher education to ensure that there is confidence in its quality, and with the institutions themselves, whose support is essential to deliver our vision. In particular, institutions will need to believe that, by ensuring that outputs meet acceptable standards, they will be left to take more responsibility for ensuring the quality of the process.

Standards verification

10.91   This function will involve the Agency in providing mechanisms for programme outcomes to be identified, and managing an enhanced external examiner system. We have already proposed the establishment of formal groupings of academics to identify expectations for awards and achievements at the threshold and highest end of the spectrum for different types of programme. The Agency should arrange for this work to be done.

10.92   Professional bodies and subject associations should be brought into the dialogue, although there will be a need for firm control so that particular interest groups do not place costly and unnecessary requirements on institutions. The work carried out by Higher Education Quality Council (HEQC) on 'graduateness' could provide a useful starting point for developing a common language and understanding about standards of awards at different levels.

10.93   The second major function will be to manage a strengthened external examiner system. We propose the creation of a UK-wide pool of recognised academic staff from which all universities and other degree-awarding institutions must select external examiners. Examiners should be academics of high standing and integrity who are sufficiently specialised within degree disciplines. The pool could be created through nomination by institutions of appropriately qualified staff, with a small panel – managed by the Agency – to approve the inclusion of any individual on the nationally recognised list.

10.94   The remit of the external examiner will need to be consistent across the UK, necessitating thorough familiarisation, training and preparation, including a trainee/apprentice model for new external examiners. Examiners will need to be fully aware of the aims, teaching methods and approach of programmes under examination. This will require considerable interaction with departments to develop familiarity with entire programmes and how they are constructed from modules throughout the various levels. A further role for the Agency, which would support the work of external examiners, would be to encourage institutions to maintain archive scripts to facilitate the maintenance of standards over time.

10.95   The extended external examiner remit involves additional resources. Institutions will need to release members of staff for extended periods of time throughout the academic year, possibly up to 60 working days a year. For experienced academics to devote such a substantial period to external examiner duties, there must be full institutional co-operation and reward for the individuals. The duties could be linked to a period of research or scholarship time so that individuals are not concerned about being out of date when returning to regular duties. Appointments as external examiners should be for no more than three years in any five-year cycle, with phased exits. External examiners should come together, say in groups of three or five, to review independently a range of papers against standards.

10.96   An important continuing function of the Quality Assurance Agency will be to develop the framework of qualifications, and to provide information and advice to institutions, professional bodies and subject areas on how best to articulate with it. A key role for the Agency will be to assist institutions to credit rate all their programmes, and then develop and operate the Credit Accumulation and Transfer (CAT) Scheme.

The responsibilities of the Quality Assurance Agency

Recommendation 24   **We recommend that the representative bodies and Funding Bodies amend the remit of the Quality Assurance Agency to include:**

- **quality assurance and public information;**
- **standards verification;**
- **the maintenance of the qualifications framework;**
- **a requirement that the arrangements for these are encompassed in a code of practice which every institution should be required formally to adopt, by 2001/02, as a condition of public funding.**

Recommendation 25   **We recommend to the Quality Assurance Agency that its early work should include:**

- **to work with institutions to establish small, expert teams to provide benchmark information on standards, in particular threshold standards, operating within the framework of qualifications, and completing the task by 2000;**
- **to work with universities and other degree-awarding institutions to create, within three years, a UK-wide pool of academic staff recognised by the Quality Assurance Agency, from which institutions must select external examiners;**
- **to develop a fair and robust system for complaints relating to educational provision;**
- **to review the arrangements in place for granting degree-awarding powers.**

10.97   Our recommendations involve a considerably smaller burden on institutions than the existing regime of subject-based quality assessments and institution-wide quality audits, which could result in several visits from national bodies to review quality each year, not including accreditation reviews carried out by professional bodies.

10.98   The Agency will be concerned about the standards and quality of higher education delivered in further education colleges. The HNC and HND have developed particularly strongly in these colleges under the aegis of Edexcel in England and Wales. In the future, Edexcel will continue to accredit further education institutions to make these awards and overall quality control will rest with the Qualifications and Curriculum Authority (QCA) established under the 1997 Education Act. Comparable arrangements for assuring the quality of these awards are being made in Scotland and Northern Ireland. Oversight of HNC and HND provision in higher education institutions will rest with the Quality Assurance Agency (QAA).

10.99   If both of the new quality bodies are to be involved in oversight of Higher National provision, there will need to be a good working relationship between them to ensure that common standards apply in further and higher education. Not only is this desirable in its own right, it is also desirable to facilitate progression from Higher desirable in its own right, it is also desirable to facilitate progression from Higher National programmes to degree programmes, and to prevent bureaucratic demands on institutions delivering these programmes.

10.100   The QAA will need to monitor developments in quality and standards in this country and throughout the world, and be open to new approaches. In particular, it must safeguard against the development of a burdensome bureaucracy and itself be subject to review after a period of not less than five years to ensure that all is well. It must also ensure that the membership of its Board represents the interests of students adequately and that it is not inward-looking.

Recommendation 26   **We recommend to the representative bodies and the Funding Bodies that the Board of the Quality Assurance Agency should, as soon as possible, include a student and an international member.**

10.101   The QAA will play a key role in the safeguarding of quality and standards in higher education across the UK. Over the next few years, it will have a significant task in developing the new system of quality and standards assurance to be introduced in 2001/02. In the meantime, existing assessment and audit cycles should be completed under the Agency's auspices by 2001, or earlier if possible.

10.102   The diversity of programme provision and of students will continue be a valued element in higher education. We welcome choice, flexibility and wide access. However, we seek to encourage diversity within a framework where qualifications are widely understood, standards are high and respected, and the quality of teaching and student learning is amongst the best in the world. In the absence of the infrastructure and arrangements of the kind we propose, pressures for increased and direct intervention from outside higher education system will intensify.

Chapter 11

Supporting research and scholarship

11.1 In Chapter 1, we set out our view that higher education in the United Kingdom (UK) must undertake research which matches the best in the world and make its benefits available to the nation. In this chapter we address the principle in our terms of reference that: *'higher education's contribution to basic, strategic and applied research should be enhanced and maintained, particularly in subjects where UK research has attained international standards of excellence or in Technology Foresight priority areas.'*

11.2 Within the aims and purposes of higher education, which we set out in Chapter 5, there were four main roles for research and reasons for supporting it in higher education institutions:
- to add to the sum of human knowledge and understanding;
- to inform and enhance teaching;
- to generate useful knowledge and inventions in support of wealth creation and an improved quality of life;
- to create an environment in which researchers can be encouraged and given a high level of training.

11.3 All of these roles for research are important, and historically, when pressure on research funds and demands for accountability were not as intense as today, it did not prove necessary to distinguish between them. Now, given the importance of research to the economy and to society, the extreme pressure on the available funds for research, and the importance (and desire) for higher education institutions to be involved in research, there is a need to recognise the different roles of research and support them appropriately.

11.4 Public funding for research comes to institutions from two main routes: the Research Councils and the higher education Funding Bodies. This is the 'dual support' system of research funding. There are important differences in the ways in which the two organisations allocate funds. The Research Council funds are essentially prospective and are earmarked: the Councils respond to proposals or design programmes to carry out future work and their funds are allocated to a particular researcher. In contrast, the Funding Bodies provide research funds selectively on the basis of performance over the previous four years as measured by the Research Assessment Exercise (RAE). Block grants from the Funding Bodies allocated to institutions contain a research component that is retrospective and not earmarked.

11.5 A key question facing us was whether, in relation to its contribution to national competitiveness, sufficient funds are available for research in higher education and whether research infrastructure[1] is adequate to support it. Although the funding needs of the various purposes we have identified differ, without adequate funding and provision for infrastructure none of the purposes can be properly achieved.

11.6   As we have shown in Chapter 3, public expenditure on research in higher education has hardly risen over the past decade, and internationally, expenditure on research in the UK compares unfavourably with competitor countries. The lack of increased investment by Government in research is surprising over a decade when the opportunities for discovery and technological progress have continued to expand rapidly and global competition has increased.

11.7   Despite the lack of investment, the international standing of UK research, as measured by the frequency with which it is cited by others, has remained competitive.[2] It is likely, however, that the UK's recent success in scientific research reflects past levels of expenditure. Recently, the UK has seen a decline in its share of world publications and citations which indicates that it may be falling behind.

11.8   In this chapter, we address:
■ the principles for funding research;
■ future arrangements for funding research;
■ wider impacts of research funding;
■ the creation of multiple funding streams to support research and scholarship.

Throughout the chapter, we make a series of interconnecting proposals on how research should be funded in the future.

Principles for funding research

11.9   Most of those offering evidence to us identified some concerns about the existing funding mechanisms for research. Those most strongly expressed were that:
■ the current state of the research infrastructure is inadequate to support research and train the next generation of researchers needed to maintain our international competitiveness;
■ the Funding Bodies procedures reward institutions for excellence in research and not teaching which leads individuals, departments and institutions to focus on research activity to the detriment of teaching.

11.10   Other issues raised were that current arrangements do not sufficiently support or reward:
■ applied research, research with industry, and research which supports local and regional economies;
■ collaborative activities within and between institutions;
■ research in the arts and humanities.

11.11   It is also evident that research, particularly in the fields of science, engineering and technology, is expensive. It is an international activity and the UK's researchers are working in an increasingly competitive global environment. These factors mean that the UK cannot expect to be pre-eminent in all research fields, and that higher education institutions can no longer expect to have a research capability in all areas. Public investment in research has reflected this position by allocating research funds on a selective basis. Such targeting of funds must continue if creative researchers in higher education institutions are to compete in their fields with the best in the world. The basis for funding research should be to fund excellence wherever it is located – in a department, a team or even the lone outstanding scholar.

11.12   We remain concerned, however, that funds available to support research are barely sufficient. The regrettable, but unavoidable consequence of any further reduction in the research funds available to the Funding Bodies would mean that selectivity of funding would have to be increased so that the best groups were funded at a level that enabled them to be fully viable and competitive with their peers. As we look forward 20 years we would expect to see an increase in Government funding for research. If this was not forthcoming, selectivity would have to be increased further.

11.13   In the light of these factors, we established a set of principles against which future research funding arrangements should be judged. These principles are that:
- excellence should be supported;
- adequate funding for infrastructure to support high quality research and training should be provided;
- whatever research is selected for support, it must be fully funded;
- funding policies to support research should, as far as possible, promote, not devalue teaching;
- different types of research should be supported by different streams of funding – including support for applied and regional work;
- funding streams and mechanisms should be clear and transparent.

Future arrangements for funding research

11.14   In the light of views given to us and on the basis of the above principles, we have examined a number of aspects of the dual support arrangements. These include the balance of funding responsibility between the Funding Bodies and Research Councils, the support for infrastructure, and the support for the humanities and art and design.

The strains on the dual support system

11.15   It is becoming increasingly clear that the working of the dual funding system is less than adequate to meet the needs of a modern research base. The National Academies Policy Advisory Group concluded that the dual support system has shown remarkable adaptability and durability under great strain, but that strain has been carried mainly by the rundown of institutional infrastructure (eg libraries, experimental equipment, and building maintenance).[3] It has also led to an increasing number of researchers on short term contracts, some of whom undertake significant amounts of teaching, and many of whom are reported to be in circumstances which are financially straitened and insecure.

11.16   In recent years, the volume of research in higher education has increased without a commensurate increase in funding levels to support infrastructure. An overall increase in research activity, due to increased amounts of project work, has been achieved through longer working hours for academic staff, more time being devoted to research at the expense of teaching, under-investment in new and replacement equipment, and to a lesser extent, improved operational and financial management of research.[4]

11.17 The increase in volume of research has placed considerable pressures on the infrastructure available to conduct the work. One of the key purposes of the allocations from the Funding Bodies is to contribute to the costs of the infrastructure of projects funded by sponsors such as the Research Councils, the charities, industry and the European Union (EU). However, there is a widespread view that a gap exists between the costs of the research and the combined funding available through the dual support system. A number of organisations have attempted to measure the size of the gap by looking at the amount of research project money gained by institutions and the extent to which institutions have received adequate funding for indirect costs for the work. Estimates of the size of the funding gap for research range from £137 million to £720 million.[5]

11.18 The indirect costs which institutions incur in carrying out Research Council projects are not always adequately met. Although Research Council grants include a nationally applied figure of 45 per cent of staff costs (recently increased from 40 per cent), which is intended as a contribution to the indirect costs of the work,[6] a recent report by Coopers & Lybrand found that at a number of institutions the levels of indirect costs required were in the range of 55 to 65 per cent of staff costs.[7] (These figures exclude academic salaries, premises and central computing costs).

11.19 A related problem is that the indirect cost contribution from non-government sources has not been sufficient to meet the full costs of research, particularly in the case of charity and EU grants. Charities have traditionally taken the position that public funds were provided to meet the indirect costs of their work, but have sometimes been relatively generous in assessing direct costs, and, in some cases, have contributed to the costs of buildings. The recent growth in research funding from charities, has led to problems for institutions that receive large amounts of funding from charities. We judge that the charities may be willing to share more of the indirect costs of research with institutions if there is greater clarity in how the costs arise. Given the increasing importance of the charities, especially medical charities, in funding research, it will be important for the Government to involve them at an early stage in strategic decision-making about research in higher education institutions.

11.20 Funding secured by institutions from the EU does not meet the full indirect costs of research. UK institutions have been particularly successful in securing EU grants and, as a consequence, face problems in finding the indirect costs from their own resources. In 1990, the House of Commons Education, Science and Arts Committee recommended that a fund be established from which any higher education institution winning an EU research contract could claim a contribution towards the indirect costs which would bring it on to a financial par with a Research Council grant.[8] The Higher Education Funding Council for England has indicated that it would be able to contribute to EU grant indirect costs by adjusting its formula for funding research. We urge all the Funding Bodies to consider such a development.

11.21   An associated problem with indirect costs – which should be in the hands of institutions to solve – is the indirect cost payment from industry for contract research services. This differs from collaborative work with industry where it reasonable to expect some costs to be shared. For contract research, industry negotiates the price of the research with higher education institutions on an individual basis. The existence of a national (average) Research Council indirect cost figure results in some of them seeking to pay only this amount, when the real figure is significantly higher.

The future of dual support

11.22   Given the strains in the existing dual support system, it is reasonable to ask whether at least a greater fraction, if not all, of the Funding Body research funds should be directed through the Research Councils. Several arguments have been put to us in support of such an approach.

■ Higher education institutions do not, in all cases, give priority to providing appropriate infrastructure for individual peer-reviewed research projects funded by the Research Councils. They are not transparent in the use they make of Funding Body allocations and they do not necessarily pass to departments what they have 'earned' from the Funding Bodies through the Research Assessment Exercise (RAE).[9]

■ The RAE is not the best mechanism for identifying excellence in research because it is insufficiently selective given that research is largely done by groups and not by departments. It does not treat interdisciplinary areas adequately and it indirectly discourages collaboration.

■ The Research Councils are the best judges of priorities within the fields for which they are responsible and conduct extensive consultation exercises on the basis of which they formulate policy.

11.23   We have sympathy with some of these arguments. However, we heard a large body of opinion, virtually unanimous in the case of institutions most involved in research, and from the National Academies Policy Advisory Group,[10] that a dual support system, albeit modified, should be retained. The arguments are that Funding Body research money provides institutions with an essential degree of flexibility in managing their research, and provides the departmental structure and ethos which develop and sustain Research Council projects. It allows institutions, as employers of those who carry out research, to cope with the sometimes short term and unpredictable character of Research Council funding, and somewhat eases the national problem of career management of contract research workers. We heard strong arguments that it was not only the right of institutions, but also their duty to manage their research income in the wider interests of research, and this might indeed include revitalising departments that were in decline, or initiating new interdisciplinary initiatives that were possible on their campus. The accusation of lack of transparency was vigorously contested.

11.24   A second, more broadly based, argument was that it is healthy for research in the country as a whole to have multiple streams of funding. Limiting the number of streams could result in short term thinking, with the major provider of funds becoming preoccupied with themes or trends that are of particular interest to the Government of the day. Funding Body research funding provides the only way of funding the unconventional or unfashionable field, or the unknown researcher who does not yet have the reputation to compete successfully for Research Council grants. A number of institutions expressed the concern that, because some Research Councils have their own research institutes, there was a conflict of interest, and these institutes were (or could be, in the future) favoured in the allocation of research funds, to the detriment of research in institutions of higher education.

11.25 More generally, we heard that there was real merit in a national system of research funding that was partly retrospective (ie based on track record as is the Research Assessment Exercise) and partly prospective (ie responsive mode Research Council funding).

11.26 There must be proper infrastructural support for projects funded by the Research Councils. At the same time, we see merit in a diversity of funding sources, and in institutions having a degree of discretion over how their research money is spent. We believe that departments have a legitimate role in the promotion of research; we have seen examples of departments that, under good leadership, have developed fine traditions of research and research student training. We have not seen evidence that a departmental structure inhibits interdisciplinary work.

11.27 The relative vigour and cost-effectiveness of UK research over the last decade appears to have been sustained by the two streams of government funding, and we propose that they should continue, albeit in modified form. We do not believe that the national interest is best served by transferring all research funding from the Funding Bodies to the Research Councils. However, we do think that there is a need to introduce greater clarity into the funding responsibilities of the different organisations.

11.28 Research Council funding for peer reviewed individual projects is vital to support high quality research allocated on a competitive basis throughout the UK. Such work should be adequately funded and supported in a way which is clear and transparent to those inside and outside the Research Councils. Furthermore, research groups that are able to win Research Council grants, but happen to be located in departments or institutions with a poor overall performance in the Research Assessment Exercise must be able to obtain sufficient institutional infrastructure support to perform the work.

11.29 We propose, therefore, that all Research Council grants should cover realistic indirect costs and include the costs of premises, infrastructural services and central computing, but exclude the salary costs of academic staff. The indirect cost element should relate as closely as possible to the true reasonable cost to the institution in carrying out the research. We propose that the present rate met by the Research Councils of 45 per cent on staff costs should be increased to 60 per cent, or such higher rate up to 100 per cent as the institution can justify (which would include a sum to cover capital depreciation of buildings and equipment). This will provide a powerful incentive to institutions to understand their costs properly and will ensure that institutions which are research active can maintain the infrastructure they require over the long term. It would also increase the awareness of the costs of research, which would assist institutions in their negotiations with industry or other funding partners who wished to commission research.

11.30   We estimate that around an additional £110 million per annum is required to meet the full costs of the grants allocated by the Research Councils. If Research Councils are given this additional funding responsibility, they must ensure that the projects they fund are adequately supported, and that the temptation to fund as much research as possible, at the expense of proper investment in the infrastructure, is strenuously avoided.

11.31   There are three possible ways to meet the additional costs of the Research Council grants. Our favoured option would be for an increase in Government funding to the Research Councils. An alternative approach would be to reduce the overall volume of research, but this would not be in the long term interests of the UK given the economic, social and cultural importance of research. A third solution would be to transfer the shortfall (around £110 million) from the Funding Bodies to the Research Councils. It is worth noting that the Research Councils experienced some difficulty in implementing the 1992 funding transfer and any future transfer would have to be carefully monitored. Such a transfer would obviously constrain the research funds directly allocated by the Funding Bodies and would have a differential impact on individual institutions depending on the relative importance of the funding they receive from the Research Councils and the Funding Bodies.

Infrastructure

11.32   An immediate problem which affects the UK's research capability is the serious state of the infrastructure and equipment needed to do it. Experimental work has to be carried out in modern laboratories that in some cases have been specially built or modified for the purpose. Special needs may arise from the requirements of equipment, from better understanding of laboratory hazards, and more stringent health and safety requirements. In recent years, there has been virtually no direct funding available to institutions to refurbish old building stock or to bring laboratories up to modern standards. We have already discussed the infrastructure funding gap, and in *Chapter 3* we described the outcomes of a recent survey that found the state of research equipment in universities to be inadequate.

11.33   Concern about infrastructure is not confined to those in higher education institutions. Multinational companies are dissatisfied with the state of research facilities and equipment in higher education institutions and have told us of their serious concerns. Some are relocating their collaborative projects with universities outside the UK as a direct result of decay in the research infrastructure.[11] During our visits to institutions, we came across a number of examples where the poor quality of infrastructure had resulted in major research universities losing international company research contracts to overseas universities.

11.34   Inadequate investment in infrastructure means that potential areas of growth are not being developed adequately. For example, the biomedical field has experienced a change in emphasis from whole-patient or whole-animal research to molecular and cell biology, but very few of the UK medical schools have the plant or equipment to become internationally competitive in this new and extremely fast-moving field. The

Forum on Infrastructure of Health and Life Sciences has concluded that the infrastructure problem has now become chronic and requires an urgent solution.[12]

11.35   When the previous Government made a 30 per cent cut in capital budgets in 1996-97, it suggested that the Private Finance Initiative (PFI) could meet the gap. Whilst it might be realistic for the PFI to support those facilities which are clearly revenue producing, such as residential accommodation and conference facilities, it is unworkable for major research and teaching equipment and laboratory facilities which have little revenue earning capacity, and are rapidly depreciating assets. The Council on Science and Technology sees only limited application of the PFI in this area because of the typically short life of such equipment.[13] As a consequence, the capital cut has simply exacerbated the research infrastructure problems.

11.36   The Joint Research Equipment Initiative (JREI), introduced in February 1996, has provided funds for research equipment in areas of research relevant to Technology Foresight priorities, where industry contributes to the cost. In 1996-97, JREI provided £50 million for equipment, including the contribution from industry. Although welcome, this is insufficient and is not directed at all infrastructure needs.

11.37   Without a major injection of funds to improve the infrastructure of the UK's top quality research departments, we do not believe the future competitiveness of the UK research base can be secured. Although the problem is immediate, a one-off injection of resources would not solve the problem over the long term. Rather, a continuous process needs to be put in place to prevent the deterioration of infrastructure in these departments in the future. We recommend later that a fund be established to provide loans at very low interest rates for research infrastructure (Recommendation 34).

11.38   We are convinced that this is an area where it ought to be possible to seek collaboration between all the major parties, including the Government, the Research Councils, the Funding Bodies, industry, and the research charities, who rely on a well-provided infrastructure to underpin their own investment in research.

11.39   We judge that it would be desirable, with the help of Government commitment, to secure a revolving fund of £400 to £500 million in due course. The fund would support departments or institutions with a track record of conducting top quality research. Repayments of the loan should be made from the enhanced indirect cost rate proposed earlier.

11.40   The establishment of a fund, with contributions from several sources, would require a joint management committee or board to enable the various parties to maintain accountability for their investments. To avoid all of the expenditure being counted against the Public Sector Borrowing Requirement, we understand that it would be important that the power to appoint to the managing body did not rest solely with the Secretary of State and that the Government did not require the board to operate as a Non-Departmental Public Body.

Communications and Information Technology (C&IT)

11.41   An increasingly important element of the infrastructure for research is Communications and Information Technology (C&IT). C&IT has enhanced communication between researchers and provides better access to information such as large information datasets, data-centres and on-line journals. High performance computers are used to model and visualise virtual and remote environments as well as to manipulate information and data. There is less concern about current levels of investment in C&IT compared to other aspects of infrastructure, although continued investment is be needed to keep the UK at the forefront in the use of new technologies for research.

11.42   The Funding Bodies, through the Joint Information Systems Committee (JISC), have supported initiatives to provide services for researchers, such as electronic databases, electronic journals, image databanks and document delivery projects covering a range of disciplines. Funding of such services is significant but finite, and other means of funding them will need to be found if they are to continue. The Funding Bodies should continue to manage and fund these projects, although we suggest that a proportion of the costs should be recouped by charging institutions for services on a volume-of-usage basis, to be recouped, in part, from enhanced Research Council indirect costs. This would result in the provision of demand-driven services which would help to ensure that they are high quality, effective and useful.

Recommendation 27   **We recommend that the Funding Bodies, through the Joint Information Systems Committee (JISC), should continue to manage and fund, on a permanent basis, quality and cost-effective Communications and Information Technology (C&IT) services for researchers and should, in due course, introduce charges for services on a volume-of-usage basis.**

11.43   The provision of a high quality broadband network is essential for much research[14] with the UK Joint Academic Network (JANET), SuperJANET, and their successors, being important to collaborative research across institutions. The UK higher education sector is privileged in its access to an advanced broadband infrastructure. However, its success and the increasing demands on the system have placed it under considerable strain, particularly in communicating with centres overseas. The National Science Foundation in the USA has developed a mechanism to cope with this problem by introducing a graded system with different classes of access ranging from 'overnight express' to 'third class', depending on the importance of the communication. It has been suggested that the UK could adopt a similar system.[15] Other ways to reduce the pressure on international bandwidth include 'caching' (where retrieved data from overseas is stored temporarily locally for use shortly by others) and 'mirroring' (where a duplicate or mirror copy of such data is held locally). These processes are already practised to a limited extent, but the growing use of networks by researchers and their likely increased future use for teaching may mean that these techniques alone will be insufficient to provide sufficient bandwidth to meet all needs.

Recommendation 28   We recommend to the Funding Bodies that the Joint Information Systems Committee (JISC) should be invited to report, within a year, on options to provide sufficient protected international bandwidth to support UK research.

11.44   The business community is increasingly seeking access to SuperJANET, which would not be possible without significant upgrading of its capacity. Nevertheless, it would be worth exploring whether business could pay for the required upgrade, as a part of its contribution to using the network, to ensure that network connections are adequate.[16]

Funding research in the arts and the humanities

11.45   The arts and humanities do not have a Research Council, which puts them at a disadvantage as they do not have direct involvement in high level discussions about research funding and policy. Given the substantial contribution they make to the social and economic prosperity of the nation, we considered a number of options to ensure that research in the arts and humanities is adequately supported.

11.46   At present, research in the humanities is supported through the Humanities Research Board (HRB) of the British Academy which disburses funds for research and for studentships on behalf of the Government. The Student Awards Agency for Scotland (SAAS) fulfills a similar function for Scottish residents pursuing advanced postgraduate degrees in the arts and humanities. The disbursement of funds in other disciplines (including some of those embraced by the British Academy) is through the Research Councils.

11.47   The situation in the arts is more complicated. One contribution to the debate about research in the arts has differentiated:
- research *into* the arts;
- research *through* the arts;
- research *for* the arts.[17]

11.48   Research into art and design, such as musical criticism, history of drama, and visual analysis, employs methods close to those of the humanities and could reasonably be assessed by the same processes and by the same criteria. Research through art and design includes materials research, action research and industrial design and its use in other ways for the development of new products, some of which could be covered by the Industrial Partnership Development Fund (See Recommendation 34). Research for art and design is the most complex, and includes painting, drawing, and composing. This has been described as:

> '*research where the end product is an artefact where the thinking is...embodied in the artefact, where the goal is not primarily communicable knowledge in the sense of verbal communication, but in the sense of visual or iconic or imagistic communication.*'[18]

In the past, this type of research has not attracted very much public support, and has been the responsibility of the Arts Council.

11.49   Although it would be possible to retain the Humanities Research Board (HRB) and to give it additional responsibility and funds to support research into the arts, we see a number of good reasons for not doing so. We note a tension between two present roles of the British Academy – as an agent of government through its responsibility for public funds distributed by the HRB in one particular area of its activity, and as a learned body responsible for providing an independent voice across the much wider spectrum of the humanities and social sciences. The addition of arts funding to its portfolio would add to this tension.

11.50   We favour establishing a new Arts and Humanities Research Council (AHRC). This body would replace the HRB and have a broader coverage to include research into, through and for the arts. The Committee of Vice-Chancellors and Principals has recommended the creation of such a Council as part of the structure of the Office of Science and Technology, suggesting that it should be funded through a transfer of funds from the Funding Bodies. We agree that such a Council should be established but it should be funded by transfers from the HRB and additional public funding. Establishing an AHRC should not result in a large and expensive bureaucracy. We believe, therefore, that it should be located with one of the other Research Councils, to gain the benefits of sharing indirect costs, expertise and relevant best practice.

11.51   We heard from practitioners in the arts and humanities that they believe research in their fields is unfairly treated in comparison with other areas. Arguments have been advanced concerning the importance of the arts and humanities for both the economy of the country and the wellbeing of society. We invited Professor John Laver, Vice Principal (Research) of the University of Edinburgh, and Chairman of the Humanities Research Board, to produce a paper about levels of research investment in the arts and humanities. His report is at Appendix 3.

11.52   Drawing on our previous arguments, we believe that those in the arts and humanities should have both the opportunity and time to pursue basic and applied research and advanced scholarship in their fields and that this is necessary to inform and to enhance their teaching. In some respects, the technological advances that we have discussed elsewhere will have proportionally greater influence in subjects that depend on library access and on bodies of data, than in some of the sciences. The wide availability of work stations that give access to libraries world wide can transform research in the arts and humanities, and in the USA has clearly done so.

11.53   It follows, therefore, that the same information technology infrastructure is needed for these subjects as for experimental ones and proper provision must be made for this. Beyond this, a number of arts and humanities subjects involve field work that require funding as for the social or natural sciences. Other subjects that are regionally based may require researchers to travel. It is also advantageous for workers in every field to extend their network of acquaintances beyond the Internet and to meet at learned discussions and conferences.

11.54   In short, academic staff in the arts and humanities have research needs that go beyond the basic infrastructure that may be expected in a modern institution of higher education.

11.55 Current funding through the Humanities Research Board of the British Academy runs at £21.5 million per annum, of which £19 million provides scholarships and bursaries, leaving approximately £2.5 million for the support of advanced research. We believe that the overall sum should be increased both to meet present purposes better and to recognise new responsibilities for the arts.

11.56 We judge that total funding for an Arts and Humanities Research Council (AHRC) might appropriately be set between £45 and £50 million per year. This takes into account allocations to the other Research Councils, and the fact that a substantial proportion of humanities research is carried out by individual researchers with correspondingly lower costs. The AHRC budget would serve four purposes:

- a substantial proportion of the funds would be to increase the level of funding for supporting advanced research in the humanities and arts, including exploiting the advantages offered by the latest technology;
- to provide a funding stream to support research into and through art and design where no such stream of funding currently exists;
- to increase the level of funding available to support scholarships and bursaries in the humanities to regain the 1995/96 levels and so avoid a decrease in the number which can be awarded;
- to provide studentships in the practical arts.

11.57 This means that around £25 million in additional funds is required, built up over three years as a transitional arrangement to allow the new Council to develop its operations over time and to allow a growing number of researchers to gain greater experience of collaborative research without abruptly distorting the research patterns of the whole field. The implications are that the British Academy would withdraw from its role of distributing funds for grants and studentships through the Humanities Research Board. As part of the transition arrangements, care will need to be taken to protect the financial position of the British Academy. We believe that this would provide the Academy with an opportunity to focus its full attention on the needs of the humanities and social sciences, as does the Royal Society for the sciences. The Royal Society receives Government Grant-in-aid support for the science base and makes research awards in academia. We suggest that the British Academy is treated in the same way.

Recommendation 29 **We recommend to the Government that a new Arts and Humanities Research Council (AHRC) should be established as soon as possible.**

Informing and enhancing teaching

11.58 In Chapters 8, 9 and 10 we have set out our vision of the UK as a world leader in learning and teaching in higher education and, at the beginning of this chapter, we identified informing and enhancing teaching as one of the main purposes of research in higher education. The link between high quality teaching and research is one that has been argued by many of those giving evidence to us. Indeed, a motivation for many people entering the higher education profession is to pursue a subject of interest and to enthuse others in that subject through teaching. We have also noted, however, that current arrangements for funding higher education mean that, although a greater volume of funding is associated with teaching than with research, the principal means to win additional funds is through research performance. We also note that, for individuals, promotion, recognition and rewards within institutions tend to encourage academics to focus on research activities, and that national and international academic reputations are built upon success in research.

11.59 From the mid-1980s, it became apparent that the research funding aspirations of all higher education institutions could not be satisfied – this became even more true when the number of universities doubled in 1992. As we stated earlier, we see no alternative to continuing to target funds towards the best research, which means that some parts of higher education will receive only limited amounts of research funding, or none at all.

11.60 Notwithstanding arguments in favour of research selectivity, which we support, in the evidence we have received a total separation of research from teaching in higher education institutions finds little support. In Chapter 8, we identified the impact of scholarly activity and research on teaching as a distinctive feature of higher education. There is near-universal rejection of the idea that some institutions of higher education should be 'teaching only' institutions. For the majority of respondents, such an institution would simply not be a 'university' in any legitimate sense of that term.

11.61 In this context, our visit to the USA helped us to distinguish between research which was a 'corporate' activity and 'private' research (which includes scholarship). Corporate research is carried out in major US research universities with considerable pressure placed on staff to win major grants and contracts to support research (and even their own salaries). These institutions have large graduate schools and play a major role in the development and training of future researchers. This research ethos is quite different from that in 'teaching' universities which have teaching of the highest quality to degree level as their principal purpose, yet require most of their teaching staff to engage in research, primarily to support their teaching. Research carried out in these institutions is essentially a private activity, with the main research resource given to staff being time. If staff need facilities beyond those that are readily available on campus in connection with undergraduate teaching, they are expected to collaborate with colleagues in neighbouring institutions. Electronic communication with colleagues and access to libraries are used extensively.

11.62 These 'teaching' institutions believe that it is important for their academic staff to be close to the frontier of their subjects, since this adds to the authority and vitality of their teaching. Staff are expected to spend less of their time doing research than in 'research' universities. Yet, the recognition of research enables the institutions to attract high quality teaching staff who also produce good publications, which add to the reputation of the institution.

11.63 We commented earlier on the financial incentives for institutions in the UK to promote research. It is evident that in parts of the higher education system 'research' is believed to be the only hallmark of a 'proper academic'. For both these reasons, academic staff feel under pressure to undertake research for which they may not have been trained and are not, in all cases, suited. This is particularly true of some staff in the 1992 universities and the higher education colleges. We think that this situation serves neither research, nor teaching well. The main concerns are the downgrading and devaluing of teaching with consequences for the morale of individuals and institutions.[19, 20] Too many departments are being entered for the Research Assessment Exercise (RAE) when they have little prospect of achieving funding from it. This does not make for the effective use of time or resources by institutions or the Funding Bodies. Departments need to be encouraged and enabled to take strategic decisions about their role in research.

11.64   We suggest that this could be achieved by making it attractive for departments or institutions who feel that their main strength is in teaching, to opt out of the RAE and receive instead a modest per capita allocation of funds (for example, no less than £500 per capita) related to the number of their permanent teaching staff. This would provide a sum which institutions could make available to staff for private research and scholarship in support of their teaching (eg for travel to use other facilities or to conferences, to provide additional computer terminals for Internet access and for collaboration with colleagues elsewhere). Research funds through this route should be available only to departments that are teaching up to first degree level (level H4).

11.65   We suggest that institutions should, in future, enter departments for the Research Assessment Exercise only if they believe that their research is of a quality that equates to levels of national excellence, showing some evidence of international evidence (3a rating under the current ratings).[21] Those achieving this standard or better should receive funds as at present. Any department which enters and achieves a grade 1 or 2 should receive neither the RAE funding, nor should it be eligible for the per capita funding. In order not to discourage departments with a developing strength in research, those departments that come just under the 3a line, and achieve a 3b rating, should not be required to forfeit the per capita funding.

11.66   Per capita funding for research should be met from the funds released by not funding departments rated below 3a in the RAE (a total of around £30 million in the 1996 RAE). Assessment of the effectiveness of the use of per capita research funds in support of teaching should be included in the work of the Quality Assurance Agency. Funding would be withdrawn where it was not being used effectively. The per capita funding would be distributed to institutions for them to make decisions about where the funding would be best used, in the same way as the Funding Body research funding.

11.67   To summarise, we recommend later that the next Research Assessment Exercise is amended to encourage institutions to make strategic decisions about whether to enter departments for the Exercise, or whether to seek a lower level of non-competitive funding to support research and scholarship which underpins teaching (Recommendation 34). We hope that such measures will help to enhance the status of good teaching.

11.68   The importance of attention to teaching is no less important for institutions that enter the majority of the staff into the RAE. Although such institutions generally have a good record in this respect, we propose that the Funding Bodies ensure that financial incentives for research do not lead to the neglect of teaching in the interests of research. This could be achieved by reducing the multiplier associated with the Research Assessment Exercise within the funding formula where there are concerns about the quality of teaching. The Funding Bodies and the Quality Assurance Agency could usefully consider how this could be taken forward.

Supporting wealth creation and an improved quality of life

11.69 We have already said that supporting wealth creation and an improved quality of life should be an important purpose of research in higher education. In Chapter 3, we described the record of higher education institutions in increasing their research links with industry. At present, UK industry spends approximately £180 million on research in higher education institutions.[22] This is approximately the same proportion of research funding received by institutions in the USA from its industry.[23]

11.70 Given that industry spends over £9 billion on research and development, it is evident that higher education secures only a small proportion of this. However, only six per cent of industry's research and development work is in basic research and 32 per cent of it is in applied research.[24] The major part of industry's expenditure is classified as experimental development, which draws on existing knowledge to produce new products, devices or processes, or improving those already produced. Generally, work of this kind is not appropriately carried out in institutions of higher education. Therefore, it is more realistic to suggest that industry presently spends around five per cent of its research budget (of research that is relevant to higher education) in higher education. If, as we envisage, the relationship between industry and higher education deepens over the next two decades through the growing recognition of the mutual advantage of collaboration, the aim should be to double this figure. However, this will only be achieved if UK higher education institutions are able to offer relevant research supported by adequate infrastructure.

11.71 There is a variety of sources of public funds which can support such research. Although the Research Assessment Exercise is intended to identify excellent research of all kinds, it does not assess applied research well.[25, 26] Various other national funding initiatives have been introduced to promote collaboration between academic researchers and industrialists. These include Co-operative Awards in Science and Engineering, LINK, Realising Our Potential Awards, the Teaching Company Scheme, Faraday Partnerships, Focus Technical and so on. We have concerns – which have been echoed by many industrialists and academics – that such a large number of schemes is confusing. We believe that there would be value in reviewing the extent to which these schemes provide a coherent framework for the promotion of research interactions. Many of these initiatives involve significant contributions from industry. In response to representation made by some in industry, we suggest that, in future, Government departments should consult with industry before introducing shared cost schemes.

11.72 Against a background in which few sectors of UK industry invest as heavily in research by comparison with their competitors,[27] and one in which it is Government policy to encourage all industry, especially small and medium sized enterprises (SMEs), it is appropriate to have a funding stream that actively promotes collaboration between higher education institutions and industry and commerce.

11.73   We recommend later the creation of a dedicated funding stream to be known as **the Industrial Partnership Development Fund** (IPDF) (Recommendation 34). The purpose of this fund would be to support applied research initiatives in partnership with small and large scale industry, both services and manufacturing. It would be the umbrella for all national initiatives designed to encourage applied research, providing a clear focus and strategy to the allocation of the fund so that industries, higher education and others are clear about the strategy and related funding provision.

11.74   We envisage that the Industrial Partnership Development Fund (IPDF) would be administered by the Department for Trade and Industry (DTI), the Welsh Office Industry and Training Department in Wales and the Scottish Office Education and Industry Department in Scotland. Funding would normally be on a 50:50 basis with the IPDF meeting the higher education institution side of the costs. It would receive joint proposals from an industry/institution grouping that might have any number of partners. It would go some way to meeting the concerns of those who feel that, in the present very severe competition for research funds, the more modest, but nevertheless useful and worthwhile applied research projects are unlikely to be supported through existing channels.

11.75   We understand from the DTI that about £50 million per annum is spent on schemes for industry/higher education interaction. We propose that some, or all, of this funding should be rolled into the IPDF within which some of the existing schemes could be retained, if desired. The fund could be administered, at least in part, on a regional basis and we say more about this in Chapter 12.

11.76   We are especially impressed with the Teaching Company Scheme (TCS) and the success it has had in developing connections between small and medium sized enterprises (SMEs) and institutions of higher education. However, we do not support the idea, as has been suggested, that the RAE should be used as a criterion for decisions about TCS funding. We do not believe that the RAE is measuring competence in TCS-type activity and is, therefore, an unsuitable criterion. We would see development of the TCS as a function of the IPDF.

11.77   We see the IPDF as furthering our long term objective of encouraging industry to make greater use of research capabilities to be found in institutions and to double their present spend in higher education. Over time, we believe that the funds available to the scheme should grow to about £100 million per annum, and that making the additional funds available would be a worthwhile investment for the Government.

11.78   We have referred to the need for higher education institutions to develop a strategic approach to collaboration with industry. Industries, too, will have an active and essential role in the formation of links. Some industries have taken initiatives in the national debate and led by example. For others, their involvement, for entirely understandable reasons, has been less close. Whatever the size of the company, working with higher education institutions can be useful to both sides, but it necessarily involves a commitment of time and money.

Recommendation 30   **We recommend that companies should take a strategic view of their relationship with higher education and apply the same level of planning to it that they give to other aspects of their operations.**

From research to products

11.79   It is widely asserted that the UK carries out research which is of the highest international standards, but that its ability to bring the new knowledge generated by such research through to exploitation, by its application to create innovative products, has not been as good. The nation's competitiveness in the world market-place will be greatly enhanced by a greater capacity to make leading edge research and technology readily accessible for the various possible end-users.

11.80   A key feature to improve the entrepreneurial environment in higher education would be to ensure that institutions are professional in their approach to intellectual property rights and have a knowledge of how to do licensing deals. Research staff will need to have a basic understanding of intellectual property rights, be able to appreciate the commercial problems of exploitation of their inventions and be realistic in their demands. We make recommendations about staff development in Chapter 14.

11.81   A major problem for the transition from research to products is the 'development gap': the stage in the innovation process when laboratory work has been completed but prospects for product development have not been proven. This is the stage at which it is most difficult to attract venture capital. One response by some higher education institutions has been to take money from reserves to fund research to cross this development gap. But this is risky for institutions – such entrepreneurial ventures involving high risks have not been part of the traditional role of higher education institutions. Nor is it part of their expertise to judge the commercial potential of a discovery.

11.82   Another approach is for institutions to form consortia and share the risk more widely. The chances of success have been increased by some universities setting up 'technology incubator units'. Such units may offer laboratory space, support services and commercial advice for a limited period of time (eg three years) at advantageous rates. The 'incubator' environment enables researchers to develop commercial aspects of their work, develop understanding and expertise in a commercial environment and prove the concept of their inventions. Some ideas will no doubt fail, but a minority may turn out to have real commercial potential and spawn viable spin-off companies. In Chapter 12, we recommend the further establishment of incubator units.

Training future researchers

11.83   We identified the fourth purpose of research as training future researchers. At its best, research training in the UK rivals any in the world. Such best practice must be generalised to ensure that the UK is producing sufficient numbers of well trained researchers, to ensure that programmes which attract public funding are delivering value for money, and to protect the interests of the students who are taking them.

11.84   The requirements of research training include an understanding of a range of research methods, and competence in relevant technical skills, as well as the development of professional skills. For industry – and other forms of employment – professional skills include the ability to operate effectively in a commercial environment, to be able to communicate ideas in writing and orally to a variety of audiences, to work effectively in teams as well as independently, and to develop high level planning and self-management skills. The great majority of PhD students will already be proficient in basic aspects of information technology. However, it may be necessary to make special provision for some students who may previously have had limited experience in this area.

Recommendation 31   **We recommend to institutions of higher education that they should, over the next two years, review their postgraduate research training to ensure that they include, in addition to understanding of a range of research methods and training in appropriate technical skills, the development of professional skills, such as communication, self-management and planning.**

11.85   Provision for research students needs not only to have the appropriate content, but to be of high quality. We have already recommended in Chapter 10 that institutions should follow a code of practice for postgraduate training, the operation of which would be overseen by the Quality Assurance Agency. Individual institutions could either adopt the national code of practice, or develop their own, which will be expected to satisfy the same general objectives as the Agency's code. The Quality Assurance Agency will need to take account of the views of the Research Councils, the conclusions of the 'Review of Postgraduate Education' (the Harris report), and, of course, the institutions that have long and proven records in postgraduate education. In the event of serious, long term shortcomings in provision, the Agency could make its findings public and inform the Funding Bodies and the Research Councils.

11.86   The Research Councils will wish to be assured of the quality of departments when they allocate studentships. We particularly commend the practice of the Economic and Social Research Council in this area.

11.87   The Harris report emphasised that it was of prime importance that research training is carried out in academic departments that were themselves carrying out high quality research, although this did not guarantee good research training. In this context, we support the spirit of the recommendation in the Harris report (that Funding Body support for postgraduates should be limited to those institutions receiving high ratings in the Research Assessment Executive (RAE)). However, we believe that the RAE score is only one of the measures of the quality of the research environment and its suitability for training new researchers. We would wish to see Funding Bodies taking a wider view of the elements of a high quality training environment for postgraduate research students.

The structure of postgraduate degrees

11.88   The Harris report on postgraduate education argued that it is not always clear to students and future employers what it means to have been awarded a particular qualification. As we have argued in Chapter 10 there is a need to provide clarification of the titles, levels and aims of different programmes. The framework of postgraduate awards also needs to provide a clear pathway of progression with different levels reflecting different levels of attainment.

11.89   The MRes degree was proposed as a means of giving students the opportunity to see whether they were suited to research and to provide institutions with a fairer and more reliable means of assessing their prospects. It was also intended to be a valuable year in itself in which students would have gained good experience – including opportunity to gain personal, transferable skills, technical and research skills, contacts with industry and career awareness – as well as a recognised qualification. Some employers and institutions consider that, in its present form, it does not always meet the different demands of students using it as a staging post on the way to a PhD, or for those who wish to use it as a solid basis for entry into a career in industry. However, evidence emerging from studies of the pilot MRes programmes shows that there is demand for it from students and employers and that it fulfills a number of useful functions.[28] We endorse the continuation of the MRes with the condition that its utility should continue to be reviewed with changes introduced as necessary.

11.90   The MPhil, which can be a prerequisite for PhD acceptance, might meet the needs of students who want to progress their research training beyond an MRes, but do not want to complete a full PhD programme. For the MPhil to be an honourable stopping-off point, there is a need to resolve current concern in the academic community about whether the MPhil is in practice a qualification in its own right, or a qualification awarded to those who fail to satisfy the examiners at PhD level. Its position must be strengthened, and it should be seen as a qualification in its own right: it should be taken as an end in itself and should be awarded for achievement of a standard of research performance. Students submitting a PhD of inadequate standard should be failed and not be awarded an MPhil as a consolation prize. All institutions should have sufficiently rigorous procedures in place to assess the student at the MPhil stage in the process. The national framework that we have proposed in Chapter 10 encompasses postgraduate qualifications and will enable departments to describe to students and employers the nature of qualifications in the framework.

Career structures for researchers

11.91   The postdoctorate stage is an important developmental stage in the career of a researcher. It is, however, a fairly ambiguous one insofar as the PhD is a full professional qualification and holders of the degree may occupy a range of different positions in an institution, all of which may be described as 'postdoctoral'. These may range from positions in which the holder is essentially a free agent, able to develop his or her own ideas, to positions in which the person is employed to do a specific job, perhaps in connection with a research contract for industry. The majority fall between these two extremes. Many postdoctoral workers aspire to a permanent teaching position, but only a minority achieve this goal. Others will choose to move into research in industry or a government research laboratory. Others may decide, after several years, to enter another related profession or leave research altogether.

11.92   Until recently, relatively little attention was paid to specific career development training for postdoctoral workers. They were not denied such opportunities, but they were generally expected to be responsible for their own personal development. We believe that training programmes using a series of postdoctoral positions in high quality research departments are appropriate, providing they are truly regarded as training positions. They should include elements of formal and informal training, not only research skills, but should also encourage scholarship, development of teaching and assessment of skills at the higher education level and supervision of research students. This will equip postdoctorate researchers for careers as researchers in industry or higher education institutions, or as higher education teachers of quality. The importance of training postdoctoratal staff with teaching responsibilities relates to our discussion about accreditation in Chapter 8.

11.93   Academic research careers for graduate scientists have been the subject of a Select Committee review which concluded that there was a major problem arising from the increase in number of researchers on short term contracts.[29] The Committee recognised that such appointments have very little appeal for the most able, and also that the quality of research could be undermined if these researchers did not have the prospect of a more secure career. The problem arises primarily from the short term nature of the funding for research and the inability of institutions, in the current tight funding regime, to commit themselves to long term employment contracts for such people. The report suggested that longer term fellowships, the earmarking of funds to bridge gaps between contracts, and providing sound policies for the career management would help higher education institutions to appoint and retrain high quality individuals.

11.94   The organisations that represent higher education institutions and the Research Councils, charities and the Royal Society have agreed a Concordat to provide a framework for the career management of contract staff, which sets standards for conditions of employment of researchers employed by universities and colleges on fixed term or similar contracts and funded through research grants or analogous schemes. It requires that institutions will make available to postdoctoral workers a range of training opportunities that will better prepare them for subsequent employment, both inside and outside higher education. We welcome the Concordat, but recognise that it is too early to judge its effectiveness. Long term support and career development plans are central to supporting research staff in higher education. In Chapter 14, we emphasise the importance of institutions having human resources strategies that cover the varying needs of all staff.

Wider impacts of research funding

11.95   As long as public funding for higher education institutions is limited it will have to be allocated on a selective basis. This will lead to some concentration of research effort in particular, but also to the concentration of research facilities in particular places. Individual departments that house expensive and major pieces of equipment cannot expect to have them available for their exclusive use. We believe that academic research groups will need to develop a stronger sense of co-operation and partnership in order to maximise the benefit from expenditure on plant, equipment and expertise.

11.96   We also believe that part of the privilege of working in a department selectively funded for research is an obligation to provide reasonable access and support to committed and qualified individuals from other institutions. This is not just a matter of access to equipment, but of allowing them to benefit from, and contribute to, the life of a research community.

11.97   We have been told that the Research Assessment Executive (RAE) discourages collaboration. We have not, however, come across any convincing evidence that collaboration was genuinely inhibited to a serious extent by the exercise. Nonetheless, we consider it important that collaboration is not inhibited in any way. In Chapter 16, we discuss collaboration in broad terms and propose that national funding mechanisms do not block any such activity.

Interdisciplinary research

11.98   A widespread view in the evidence to us was that the competitive nature of the RAE and its strong subject focus has discouraged interdisciplinary work. In spite of the assurances made by the Funding Bodies that assessment panels will *'give special attention to the special nature of interdisciplinary research and its assessment'*, and in spite of the growth in interdisciplinary research, there seems to be little confidence that it is assessed well. We have also concerns that the RAE requires the separation of academic areas that are naturally grouped, thus making it difficult for departments to submit useful information about developments in a coherent area to the exercise.

11.99   This is a more significant problem than those relating to collaboration. Many important research advances are made, and will continue to be made, across the boundaries of traditional fields. It is, of course, hard to prove that the RAE is blocking interdisciplinary research since institutions are conducting such work. It is also true that this criticism could be made not only of the RAE, but also of nearly all of the traditional funding processes, including those often used by Research Councils. The important point is that it could be serious for UK research if funding procedures contained an inherent disincentive to interdisciplinary work. The problem is not easy and we have not had time to study it in detail, but it is of sufficient importance to merit serious investigation by a body, such as the Royal Society. The investigation would need to establish whether the problem was both real and serious and, if so, what possible remedies might be available.

Recommendation 32   **We recommend that the Funding Bodies and the Research Councils commission a study to evaluate the funding of interdisciplinary research, including the incentives and disincentives. The report should be ready to inform the next Research Assessment Exercise.**

International benchmarking of research excellence

11.100   We observe that although it has imperfections, the Research Assessment Exercise (RAE) has achieved general acceptance within the academic community and, considering the large sums of public money that are allocated, is relatively cost-effective. One imperfection, that the exercise is largely carried out without the advice of experts from abroad, is relatively easily corrected. The Research Councils regularly make use of international referees and members on their various committees, and the RAE recently carried out in Hong Kong had no difficulty in securing committee members from abroad. The presence of overseas members would reinforce community confidence in RAE panel judgments.

Recommendation 33   **We recommend to the Funding Bodies, that in the interests of transparency and applying international standards properly, the practice of including one or more international members in all Research Assessment Exercise (RAE) panels, wherever possible, should be introduced to the next RAE.**

Multiple funding streams to support research and scholarship

11.101   At the start of this chapter we set out six principles for future research funding. Throughout the chapter we have developed our ideas about how best to support the different roles of research, taking the principles into account. As a result of our proposals, five discrete and separate funding streams should be available for the future support of research:

- project and programme provision that is fully supported by the Research Councils;
- research funds from the Funding Bodies to support institutional decisions about research priorities with the use of such funds to be assessed retrospectively in the RAE;
- funding on a per capita basis to support scholarship and research that underpins teaching;
- an Industrial Partnership Development Fund to support applied research that attracts matching funds from industry and contributes to regional and economic development;
- a loan fund to maintain the infrastructure to support top quality research.

11.102   As we have suggested throughout this chapter, in order to be able to fund these different streams changes will have to be made to existing funding mechanisms.

Recommendation 34   We recommend:

- to the Government that, with immediate effect, projects and programmes funded by the Research Councils meet their full indirect costs and the costs of premises and central computing, preferably through the provision of additional resources;

- to the Funding Bodies that the next Research Assessment Exercise is amended to encourage institutions to make strategic decisions about whether to enter departments for the Exercise or whether to seek a lower level of non-competitive funding to support research and scholarship which underpins teaching;

- to the Government that an Industrial Partnership Development Fund is established immediately to attract matching funds from industry, and to contribute to regional and economic development;

- to the Government that it promotes and enables, as soon as possible, the establishment of a revolving loan fund of £400 to £500 million, financed jointly by public and private research sponsors, to support infrastructure in a limited number of top quality research departments which can demonstrate a real need.

An Advisory Council on national research policy

11.103   Our recommendations place additional responsibilities with the Research Councils – and thus with the Office of Science and Technology within the Department of Trade and Industry. The proposed Arts and Humanities Research Council would also reside within this structure. In addition, we have recommended the provision of research funds through multiple streams. At national level, the oversight of research policy and funding does not appear to lie clearly with any single body. It is also the case that the principles of research support employed by Funding Bodies may be different from those of the Research Councils. We believe that there is need of some independent oversight of these new arrangements.

11.104   We also note a concern on the part of some institutions that the Research Councils may be insufficiently accountable for their policies and practices in the management of research. Although the Councils themselves carry out internal reviews of various aspects of their activities, there does not appear to be a mechanism for any external and open review of the overall effectiveness of their programmes and appropriateness of their funding procedures. The Councils are to be commended on the efforts they have made to reduce their administrative costs, but it seems that this has led, in some cases, to the introduction of procedures that do not carry the full confidence of the research community.

11.105   We are hesitant to suggest the setting up of a new body insofar as we have not had time to understand fully the working of either the Council for Science and Technology or the Science and Engineering Base Co-ordinating Committee. We do, however, see a need for an independent body that is able to take an objective overview of these new arrangements for research support in higher education to point out where they are failing, to identify inconsistencies in the policies of different public bodies, and to make its voice heard at the highest level.

11.106 The new body would have a Chair independent of Government, its name should reflect its research remit (including the arts and humanities) and it should constitute a broad group of academics and industrialists. Although there would be advantages if the body gave public advice, we judge that it would be more frank about the state of research if it were private.

Recommendation 35 **We recommend to the Government that it should establish, as soon as possible, a high level independent body to advise the Government on the direction of national policies for the public funding of research in higher education, on the distribution and level of such funding, and on the performance of the public bodies responsible for distributing it.**

Chapter 12

The local and regional role of higher education

Introduction

12.1 In Chapter 5 we identified one of the purposes of higher education as:
'to serve the needs of an adaptable, sustainable, knowledge-based economy at local, regional and national levels'.

12.2 While many institutions are national and international in their outlook, they have also developed an importance in a local and regional context that could not have been foreseen at the time of the Robbins report. This is not simply a consequence of the much increased scale of higher education: it also reflects the centrality of higher education to the future economic and social wellbeing of communities, and the changing structure of the economy.

12.3 In this chapter we examine:
- attempts to measure the local and regional impact of higher education;
- how institutions are actively engaging in their localities and regions;
- how this role might be encouraged and enhanced so that institutional engagement is both more systematic and more powerful.

12.4 We commissioned a report on 'Higher Education and the Regions' (Report 9), which examines the issues in some detail. In this evidence and elsewhere we found different perspectives in the United Kingdom (UK) about the significance of the region. For some, the region in England is a geographical area which, often for historical reasons, has a real identity. For others, the word refers to the government administrative regions of England, with regional offices but with no roots in history. For people in Wales, Scotland and Northern Ireland it refers to their home territory. For the institutions themselves, the identification with the three national regions is strong. In England regional identification varies from one part of the country to another, being strong, for example, in the North East, but less so in the Midlands. Throughout the UK, however, there is a widespread recognition of the importance of higher education institutions to local communities, of the contribution they make to them and of their growing mutual interest.

12.5 In this chapter we are concerned with those aspects of higher education to which locality and proximity are important. Some of these activities will be at a very local level, others will be more geographically dispersed. In England, we have found that these activities seldom take place within defined administrative boundaries. In Scotland, Wales and Northern Ireland, while there is activity at a local level, the national region is a natural focus for much activity. To avoid confusion, in this chapter we have adopted the phrase 'local and regional' as a generic term to cover the range of activities we are describing. We use the term 'region' to describe the administrative regions of England, 'locality' to refer to smaller areas and 'national region' to describe Scotland, Wales and Northern Ireland.

12.6   The evidence points to a growing realisation of the importance of higher education to the locality of which it is part. Professor Robert Reich, the former US Secretary of Labor, has suggested:

> 'the skills of a nation's workforce and the quality of its infrastructure are what makes it unique and uniquely attractive in the world economy ... so important are these public amenities, in particular the university and the airport, that their presence would stimulate some collective symbolic analytical effort, even on a parched desert or frozen tundra. A world class university and an international airport combine the basic rudiments of global symbolic analysis: brains and quick access to the rest of the world'.[1]

12.7   The evidence from the UK suggests that the extent of the local and regional involvement of institutions is currently patchy, but that it needs to turn to active and systematic engagement. While throughout this report we advocate institutional autonomy and diversity, with institutions free to identify for themselves the balance between consciously local, national or international roles, we are clear that each locality or region needs the engagement of higher education. The form of this will rightly differ from institution to institution. We exemplify below the ways in which institutions are already engaged and conclude with recommendations which will help institutions enhance the effectiveness of their local and regional engagement to the mutual benefit of themselves and their localities.

Measuring the local and regional impact of higher education

12.8   In recent years, as we have suggested, there has been a growing emphasis on the local and regional role of higher education, to the extent that over three-quarters of institutions now refer to local and/or regional objectives in their strategic plans. At the same time there have been a number of attempts to measure the impact of higher education at local and regional level.[2]

12.9   These studies have shown that higher education providers make a significant economic contribution simply by their existence in a locality, whether or not they adopt an explicit mission to generate local or regional economic activity or to play a part in the cultural life of their locality or region. This reflects their size, both relative and absolute, in the local and regional economy, and is enhanced by the multiplier effect which they exert (ie the additional economic activity generated for every unit of expenditure by the institution). A recent study by the Cardiff Business School found that total spending by Welsh higher education institutions in 1995/96 exceeded half a billion pounds including £280 million on wages for over 14,000 staff and £100 million on Welsh goods and services. The total impact on the Welsh economy of this expenditure, including the multiplier effect, was estimated at just over £1 billion. The study also estimated that the multiplier effect of this spending, acting through local sourcing and local income effects, created or supported a further 10,500 jobs in Wales.[3]

12.10   There is debate about some of the assessments that have been made in the past of the impact on local economies of higher education institutions. Professor Goddard of Newcastle University and his team, in their report for the Committee of Vice Chancellors and Principals, cast doubt on some of the more ambitious calculations made from time to time.[4] Others have drawn attention to some of the burdens institutions inevitably place on a local economy in terms of road congestion and their use of other services. But the evidence is clear that higher education is now a significant and sometimes a major element in local and regional economies. Professor Goddard's report suggests that expenditure by higher education staff and students alone is responsible for an extra one per cent of local employment. The range of its contribution is in fact very wide, extending to support through research and consultancy, attracting investment and providing new sources of employment, meeting labour market needs, supporting lifelong learning, and as centres of culture contributing to the quality of life in their localities.

Active engagement by institutions in their localities and regions

12.11   In addition to being substantial sources of economic activity, higher education institutions make a proactive contribution to local and regional economies. Some commentators place these kinds of activity at the heart of global economic change:

'the shift to knowledge-intensive capitalisation goes beyond the particular business and management strategies of individual firms. It involves the development of new inputs and a broader infrastructure at the regional level on which individual firms and production complexes can draw. The nature of this economic transformation makes regions key economic units in the global economy ... the new age of capitalism has shifted the nexus of competition to ideas ... regions must adopt the principles of knowledge creation and continuous learning; they must in effect become learning regions.'[5]

12.12   Others consider such analyses to be exaggerated. But all the evidence we considered suggested that there is a powerful mutuality of interest between higher education and society and that there is much to be gained by fostering the active engagement of institutions with localities and regions.

Research and consultancy

12.13   As centres of research and scholarship, the potential for institutions to contribute through providing research and consultancy services to local companies is clear. The responses to our employer consultation (Appendix 4) confirmed that many of them use higher education for these services, and our staff survey (Report 3) showed that many staff see consultancy as one of their roles. Institutions actively seek research contracts from companies, and welcome company sponsored research students who address a specific industrial problem with support from the institution. Many institutions have established science parks and incubator units designed to attract and support research-based industry and commerce, and also to provide opportunities for their own researchers to become research-based entrepreneurs. In spite of the often inevitable difference in the purposes and timescales of research in higher education institutions and in the world of commerce, there has increasingly been a mutual recognition of the advantages of partnerships, and a will on the part of higher education to seek them.

12.14   In Scotland, Wales and Northern Ireland the development agencies established to foster industrial and commercial regeneration have explicitly promoted the commercial development of academic research, as illustrated in the following examples:

■ a 'commercialisation' hub at Edinburgh University based on the CONNECT model in California, which aims to provide a single focus for researchers from across Scottish institutions, investors and businesses;

■ the MediCentre at the University of Wales College of Medicine, in which industrial partners work alongside academic departments which are developing new approaches to treating diseases and delivering healthcare, thereby helping small and medium sized enterprises take advantage of research findings;

■ QUBIS Ltd at the Queen's University Belfast, which identifies and exploits commercially viable research through the formation of new companies.

12.15   In England, in the North Eastern region, which is probably typical of the more proactive clusters of higher education institutions, there has been a distinctively regional as well as local approach to research and consultancy support for industry. In response to an analysis of the region's needs, its universities have established a European Process Industry Competitiveness Centre, a Centre for Achievement in Manufacturing and Management, a Centre for Low Volume Engineering, and a Northern Informatics Application Agency. To provide an easy point of access for small firms to all the universities of the North East they have established a 'Knowledge House', which is financed by the universities of the region, the Open University and the European Regional Development Fund (ERDF).

12.16   There are other notable examples in the North West and London, which provide incubator units, and bridges between employer needs and the traditional research and consultancy services of institutions. The longest established exemplar in the UK is probably the cluster of largely scientific companies known as the 'Cambridge phenomenon', where an exceptional number of companies have formed themselves as spin-offs of the university either by using university research or by involving academics. In Cambridge, *'the presence of the University and associated research institutions lies at the root of the Phenomenon. The long history of internationally leading research has resulted in a concentrated accumulation locally of skills, knowledge and facilities, which were the initial foundation on which high technology enterprise became established in the area'*.[6] Most recently, Microsoft is reported to have been in discussion with Cambridge University about setting up a research base in the area.

12.17   In all these examples, which do not comprise an exhaustive list, there is:

- an attempt to provide a common point of contact for otherwise scattered or diffuse companies to find their way into the complex organisation of the higher education institution;
- provision of a semi-sheltered environment in which concepts can be proved, risks can be moderated, expertise shared and support given on a sufficient scale to make the investment worthwhile and viable;
- careful investigation of the respective requirements and strengths of the academic and industrial partners to ensure real mutual interest and generate added value.

Attracting inward investment

12.18   The attraction of overseas inward investment has been one of the core elements of economic development in the UK in the 1980s and 1990s. The UK attracts about 40 per cent of investment from the United States of America (USA) in the European Union, and it has long been one of the leading locations for overseas investment from all parts of the world. The cumulative value of inward investment increased from $28 billion in 1978 to over $200 billion in 1995.[7] Foreign owned companies account for some 40 per cent of UK manufactured exports, and inward investment is estimated to have created 500,000 jobs in the last decade. But the context for inward investment is changing rapidly, as other countries compete more vigorously for initial inward investment, and the UK needs to compete strongly to retain the inward investment it has attracted and to continue its past successful record. The provision for education and training can be crucial to success.

12.19   This is further illustrated by USA experience. The area around Spartanburg and Greenville, South Carolina, has become home to more than 215 companies from 18 countries, 74 of which have their USA headquarters there. While these cities make an unlikely centre for international industry, they have the highest diversified foreign investment per head in the USA. South Carolina's principal attraction is the competence of its workforce, heavily sponsored by the state, which offers free, customised technical training of prospective workers and supervisors of companies that bring new investment.[8]

12.20   In this country, higher education played a part in the recent decision of a major Korean company to locate in South Wales, with institutions heavily involved in the discussions with the company leading to its decision. The institutions of the North East were actively engaged in encouraging major electronics companies from Japan and Germany to locate there, despite the area not having any history of producing micro-electronic components. In return, one of them has established a chair at the University of Newcastle.

12.21   'Locate in Scotland', the joint Scottish Enterprise/Scottish Office inward investment agency, consults extensively with Scottish higher education institutions in order to gather information for their marketing campaigns. In their promotional material they quote a number of companies who have recently invested in Scotland (including companies from Japan and the USA) and told us that the quality of the workforce and the number and quality of graduates were factors in those decisions to locate there.

The Industrial Development Board fulfils a similar function in Northern Ireland, with notable examples of companies attracted by the availability of high quality graduates from the two universities.

12.22   In a climate in which major investment decisions of national significance are taken by global corporations, higher education institutions have been crucial in helping to secure the 'footloose' corporation. As one eminent American commentator has written, *'In the future, success will come to those companies, large and small, that can meet global standards and tap into global networks. And it will come to those cities, states and regions that do the best job of linking the businesses that operate within them to the global economy.'*[9] These examples suggest that successful engagement is characterised by institutions which are proactive and can act together to provide the necessary volume, quality and range of provision; and which can demonstrate consistency of purpose.

Meeting labour market and skills needs

12.23   Higher education institutions typically attract students from all parts of the UK, especially to their full-time undergraduate programmes. They are, therefore, engaged in responding to national as well as regional and local needs. But while the relationship with the local labour market varies between one institution and another, in a society committed to lifelong learning, their contribution to meeting local needs, both of individuals and companies, will be a growing one. For some years now, many institutions have been producing tailor-made programmes for local businesses. The University of Portsmouth, for example, offers a degree programme for people who work in local companies, which incorporates credits towards the degree based upon the individual's learning at work and his or her previous qualifications, organised and delivered in a way that fits in with the individual's employment. In other cases, an institution may enter into a relationship with a single company to provide a tailor-made programme which responds to the company's needs both in the immediate locality and more widely. Particularly in the context of lifelong learning, such partnerships between organisations and institutions will be an increasing feature of higher education. The employers responding to our survey told us that they envisage their links becoming both more focused and more exclusive.

12.24   Higher education institutions have a particular role in the provision of teacher education and training, and in fulfilling this role need to work closely with schools in their area. We endorse Sir Stewart Sutherland's conclusion in his report on teacher education and training (Report 10) that the most effective initial teacher training provision is likely to come from a close partnership between schools and higher education institutions. Schools and higher education institutions will also need to work closely together to define appropriate provision for continuing professional development, perhaps developing a national framework and regional centres for delivery, as suggested in Sir Stewart's report.

12.25   There have been a number of initiatives at national and local levels to encourage institutions to respond to regional and local needs, often involving. Training and Enterprise Councils, local authorities and Development Companies. The Department for Education and Employment has established a Higher Education Regional Development Fund with a budget of £2.7 million for 1997/98 whose purpose is to support projects to encourage institutions to produce more 'relevant' skills among students, and to encourage employers (and in particular local small and medium sized enterprises) to make greater use of the services of institutions in both teaching and research. As we noted in Chapter 9, the Shell STEP programme provides carefully-matched and low-cost placements for students in small and medium sized enterprises (SMEs), and in a recent study three-quarters of employers reported that the placement had a beneficial impact on their businesses.[10] This model has been adapted by a consortium of the institutions in Liverpool to create Business Bridge, a flexible programme which places undergraduates into local SMEs, on a part-time basis during term and full-time during the vacations.

Supporting lifelong learning

12.26 We have already stressed the growing importance of lifelong learning. We attach much importance to the development of distance learning through advances in communications and information technology, and expect this to have a major place in the practice of lifelong learning. Nonetheless, as we made clear in Chapter 7 when discussing widening participation, we have no doubt about the value of access to local institutions which are in close touch with local people and local needs. There may well be, over the 20 year period we have been asked to consider, a material shift in the balance of provision between the traditional young full-time student, and the adult engaged in lifelong learning. This suggests to us that not only will institutions provide, as they have historically done, programmes in the liberal arts and respond to leisure interests, but there will be an increasing opportunity and need for institutions to provide programmes that respond to specifically local social and economic needs for lifelong learning.

12.27 The accessibility of higher education will be increasingly important. Franchising of programmes of higher education to colleges of further education (which is discussed in Chapters 10 and 16) is one way in which provision is being made more widely available for those in communities or from backgrounds for whom geographic or psychological distance is a barrier to participation. Various initiatives exist to reach small and scattered communities in Wales and Northern Ireland, for example. In England, institutions such as the University of Central Lancashire and the University of Warwick are seeking to reach communities where there is not a tradition of entry to higher or further education through local networks with partner colleges which facilitate progression. Others, such as the Universities of Sheffield, Sunderland and Wolverhampton, are encouraging people from such communities to come into and find out about higher education. In Chapter 7, we noted how students themselves can have a valued role as mentors in local schools, or in the schools from which they originate.

Engaging in cultural and community development

12.28 As centres of culture and learning higher education institutions are part of the cultural life of their communities. They have extensive recreational and sporting facilities which are often made available to the community, and in several cases are jointly provided with the local authority. The University of Central Lancashire, for example, recently entered a successful partnership with Preston Borough Council to bid for £8 million in Lottery funding for an outdoor multi-sport complex, to include football pitches, a cycle track and a floodlit athletics track. An important feature of this bid was widespread public consultation and there is now a 'community use agreement' which sets out how the complex will be shared between the university and the local community.

12.29   Several institutions act as hosts to major international arts festivals and many more have theatres which stage student and other productions; 63 per cent of universities have theatres which are open to the public.[11] The presence of university staff and students and their demand for cultural events is often of crucial importance to the viability of such events and facilities in an area.

12.30   Institutions have played an important part in providing public museums and art galleries, as well as in many cases access to lectures and libraries. There are believed to be around 300 university collections, large and small, many of which have been designated by the Museums and Galleries Commission as being of undoubted national distinction. Many of these are open to the public.

12.31   The student body can also make a significant contribution to the local community. There are over 100 Student Community Action groups across the country, often organised by students unions, providing volunteers who work with existing organisations in the voluntary sector, as well as providing invaluable experience for students.

12.32   The institutions in Wales, through research and scholarship, make a particular contribution to the protection and nurturing of the country's linguistic and cultural heritage. There are programmes in the Welsh language, literature and culture, and some limited opportunities for students to study other subjects using the Welsh language as the medium of study. Demand for both these forms of provision is likely to increase in response to the requirement that all children should be taught the Welsh language at Key Stages 2 and 3 of the National Curriculum, and by 1999, Key Stage 4 too.

12.33   Institutions, therefore, offer much to the cultural life of their localities and we see every advantage in further developing this contribution to the extent that funding can be made available. Professor Robson's report to us (Report 9) notes that such provision can be significant in attracting students to enrol at institutions and to stay in the locality once they graduate. We would encourage initiatives which identify collaborative opportunities between higher education institutions and local authorities to bid for Lottery funding to support joint projects.

Discussion and recommendations

12.34   These examples of current practice and recent developments demonstrate the ways in which higher education is already having a major beneficial impact on the lives of local and regional areas.

12.35   Our analysis points to the greater benefits to be gained from a more active engagement by higher education institutions. We believe that regional and local engagement should be a clear element in the role of higher education over the next 20 years. Each institution should be clear about its mission in relation to local communities and regions as part of the compact that we advocate between higher education and society. We recommend in Chapter 15 that institutions ensure they have in place mechanisms through which community interests can be taken into account in their decision-making, and our recommendations about the best way of matching supply and demand in Chapter 6 should ensure closer articulation with local employers. But if higher education is to make its full potential contribution to meeting the research needs and skills requirements of localities and regions, and if those localities and regions are to play a part in the future development of higher education, there needs to be some development of present structures and of the funding which is available. We therefore make a number of recommendations to encourage this.

Regional structures

12.36   Stronger regional structures for the administration of government and for funding have emerged in recent years, often driven by European Union developments. In 1994, the previous Government established Integrated Regional Offices (IROs) in England, bringing together the regional arms of four Departments (Environment, Transport, Trade and Industry and Employment and subsequently Education), together with the single regeneration budget (SRB) which is distributed on a regional basis. £900 million was allocated through the SRB in 1996/97 to support projects which will run for up to seven years. European Union funding is also allocated on a regional basis, both from the European Regional Development Fund and from the European Social Fund. These funds are especially valuable in providing support to capital projects in those regions designated as priority areas. In 1996, over £300 million was allocated to higher education institutions for projects providing, amongst other things, new library facilities, postgraduate facilities and infrastructure for information technology.[12]

12.37   In some parts of England, as we noted above, the government administrative regions do not reflect distinct industrial, social, cultural or national entities, nor are they nourished by the well-resourced types of development agencies with the broad regeneration functions that exist in the three national regions, or by designated European funding. This means that, whilst institutions throughout England identify with their localities, many of them do not relate in any substantive functional way to the administrative region of which they are part. Their ability to engage with their communities has also often been hampered by the large number of different bodies with remits for economic development.

12.38   We have noted the proposals that the role of the English regions should be enhanced by creating regional chambers, whose roles would include developing an economic strategy for the region and helping to establish regional development agencies.[13] We hope that this will be associated with initiatives to clarify and rationalise the work of the various bodies involved in economic development.

Recommendation 36   We recommend to the Government that institutions of higher education should be represented on the regional bodies which it establishes, and that the Further Education Funding Council regional committees should include a member from higher education.

12.39   Given the likely development of regional centres of decision-taking in England, higher education needs to assess how best to relate to them. We note that the Higher Education Funding Council for England (HEFCE) announced in April this year its intention to appoint a number of new senior staff to liaise with regional bodies and to discuss strategic and policy issues with institutions on a regional basis. We understand that these staff are to act as brokers, helping institutions to capitalise on opportunities for local and regional partnerships with Training and Enterprise Councils, commercial companies and local authorities.

12.40   To enable the higher education institutions in a region to make an effective contribution to the work of the evolving regional organ of Government, we believe that they will need to act collectively, and therefore suggest that the higher education institutions in each region convene their own consultative forum of institutional heads or other senior staff, so that they can relate effectively to the new structure.

Funding for regional activities

12.41   Whilst the new regional chambers will be able to influence higher education development by indicative planning and promoting collaboration, there will also be a need for dedicated funding to promote certain types of activity involving higher education institutions.

12.42   A number of sources of funding are already available. For activities directly involving higher education, funds are available this year from the Higher Education Regional Development Fund (HERDF), and we believe that this funding stream should continue. As with other public funding available to promote regional development, we believe that there should be a requirement for matched funds from other sources.

12.43   As plans for new regional structures of government develop, consideration should be given to bringing together a variety of different sources of funding. There may be some merit, for example, in closer links between the Further Education Funding Council's Competitiveness Fund and the HERDF. We recommended in Chapter 11 a new research fund, the Industrial Partnership Development Fund (IPDF), and we expect regional needs to be one of the considerations taken into account in allocating funds. We would expect that at a regional level, Regional Development Agencies would be involved and would contribute to funding applied research in their areas.

Recommendation 37   We recommend to the Government that funding should continue to be available after April 1998, when the present provision from the Higher Education Regional Development Fund is due to cease, to support human capital projects which enable higher education to be responsive to the needs of local industry and commerce.

12.44   Many projects will require a combination of human capital and research capital and in these cases it will make sense for joint bids to be made against both the Industrial Partnership and the Higher Education Development Fund. Bringing these two kinds of activity together, one focused on applied research and one on people and skills, would create a powerful mechanism to allow regions to shape the balance between technology transfer and labour market issues as they judge right for their particular requirements.

12.45   Whatever other regional funds are available, higher education, as a key regional player, will need to be involved in bidding (in partnership with others) for funding to support specific activities. We urge that consideration is given to putting all such funds, both those specifically for higher education and others, onto a longer term, more stable basis.

12.46   We have noted the initiative by the institutions in the North East to establish in different institutions regional centres of excellence in specific aspects of industrial activity particularly relevant to the region, and we commend this approach to institutions in other localities and regions. The development of such centres might be one area to which Regional Development Agencies could contribute.

12.47   Although we argue for a greater emphasis on the regional role of institutions, we believe that the main funding for institutions throughout England should continue to come on a national basis from the Higher Education Funding Council for England, rather than being allocated regionally. We believe that imposing a regional structure on core funding for teaching or research in England would be unnecessarily cumbersome, and would ignore the fact that teaching and research are, in the main, national (and international) activities.

The institutions and small and medium sized enterprises

12.48   It is material to the future development of the national, regional and local economies that the long standing problems of bringing small and medium sized enterprises into more effective contact with the resources of institutions of higher education is tackled more successfully than hitherto.

12.49   Many institutions across the UK have taken initiatives to build bridges, but the problem for institutions and small and medium sized enterprises is great. We suggest that there may be advantage in building on the initiatives already taking place through the creation of a national 'Knowledge House', operated at local and regional levels. This would enable small firms to access a point of inquiry in their local higher education institutions, by using one national telephone number. They would then be able to obtain information about research, technology applications, programmes, science parks, consultancy services, the Teaching Company Scheme, and other resources which are available in the locality. Such a national telephone number, well supported by promotional activity and building on existing work by some institutions and agencies including Business Link, could be a valuable basis for bringing small and medium sized enterprises into much better contact with higher education.

Recommendation 38 We recommend to higher education institutions and their representative bodies that they examine, with representatives of industry, ways of giving firms, especially small and medium sized enterprises, easy and co-ordinated access to information about higher education services in their area.

Encouraging entrepreneurship

12.50 It has been suggested to us that, when considering their career options, those with higher education qualifications too often think only in terms of becoming an employee. It is less common for them to think in terms of starting their own businesses. We believe that, in order that their skills benefit the nation's economy, more people gaining higher education qualifications should be encouraged to start their own ventures. It is very often argued that the dynamic of the economy comes from its small firms and therefore that we need to foster a flow of our ablest people into entrepreneurship. We recommended in Chapter 8 that careers services should improve their advice to students in this area.

12.51 We believe that institutions can contribute to their local and regional economy by helping more graduates start their own businesses in the surrounding area. We referred in Chapter 11 to the way incubator units can reduce the financial risks to institutions and to entrepreneurs in supporting new ventures. Within the incubator environment, researchers are able to prove their concepts and to develop commercial aspects of their work and expertise in product development and exploitation, but finding funds for such incubators is difficult: it may come from Regional Development Funds, local councils, venture capital companies and from institutions themselves. However, we believe that the issue of funding for such units merits further consideration by the Government, preferably through a dedicated source of funding to support joint ventures with the private sector. There is a long-standing problem in finding small sums of equity funding since the risks for start-up ventures are high and the costs of evaluating proposals for financial institutions can make them unattractive. We believe that there is, therefore, a case for a small fund to provide such equity funding for projects in higher education, possibly linked to the Industrial Partnership Development Fund as a source of funding for the initial stages of the research.

Recommendation 39 We recommend:
- to the Government that it considers establishing a modest fund to provide equity funding to institutions to support members of staff or students in taking forward business ideas developed in the institution, and to support the creation of incubator units;
- to higher education institutions that they establish more technology incubator units within or close to the institution, within which start-up companies can be fostered for a limited period until they are able to stand alone.

12.52 We also believe that more could be done to foster entrepreneurship through the development of innovative programmes. In Chapter 9 we described projects which give students work experience, particularly in small and medium sized enterprises, and these can help here. But a specific entrepreneurial focus is also required. When we visited Babson College in the USA we were impressed by the MBA programme they were running in entrepreneurship, where all the teachers had current or recent business experience and students were given a lump sum at the beginning of the programme to start a business which they had to repay at the end of the programme, with all profits going to charity. It might also be possible to develop postgraduate programmes which enable students to develop a business idea while working towards a suitable qualification.

Recommendation 40   **We recommend to higher education institutions that they consider the scope for encouraging entrepreneurship through innovative approaches to programme design and through specialist postgraduate programmes.**

Incentives within institutions

12.53   While specific funds can help to stimulate activities, the success of particular initiatives often depends on the individuals involved. If individual members of staff within institutions do not feel that their efforts in this area will be recognised and rewarded, then little progress will be made. We therefore believe that institutions, if they wish to make local and regional activities a priority, should consider how to reflect this in their reward systems for staff. We discuss a revised system of incentives in Chapter 14.

Chapter 13

Communications and Information Technology

13.1   As will be clear from other chapters in this report, we believe that the innovative exploitation of Communications and Information Technology (C&IT)[1] holds out much promise for improving the quality, flexibility and effectiveness of higher education. The potential benefits will extend to, and affect the practice of, learning and teaching and research. C&IT is also, we argue, needed to support high quality, efficient management in higher education institutions. There is scope to reduce costs in the future and the potential is great, but implementation requires investment in terms of time, thought and resources in the short term. We say more about the possibilities afforded to management by C&IT in Chapter 15.

13.2   In Chapter 8 we have shown how the concept of the higher education experience will need to be altered radically. A growing range of higher education experiences will be offered by institutions, in providing for a more diverse student body, by tailoring learning experiences to the needs of individuals or groups of individuals. C&IT will have a central role in maintaining the quality of higher education in an era when there are likely to be continuing pressures on costs and a need to respond to an increasing demand for places in institutions. We have, however, sought to ensure that our recommendations are led by educational imperative and not by technology.

13.3   We believe that, for the majority of students, over the next ten years the delivery of some course materials and much of the organisation and communication of course arrangements will be conducted by computer. Just as most people will come to expect to be connected to, and to make use of, world communications networks in their daily lives, all students will expect continuous access to the network of the institution(s) at which they are studying, as a crucial link into the learning environment.

13.4   C&IT will overcome barriers to higher education, providing improved access and increased effectiveness, particularly in terms of lifelong learning. Physical and temporal obstacles to access for students will be overcome with the help of technology. Those from remote areas, or with work or family commitments need not be disadvantaged. Technology will also allow the particular requirements of students with disabilities to be more effectively met by institutions.

13.5   The global community, through the medium of C&IT, is already a reality for researchers. C&IT will also help the development of local research groups, linking those researchers in less well-endowed departments with their better-resourced neighbours. It will bring benefits to scholars in the arts and humanities as well as researchers in science and technology.

13.6   Researchers are already beginning to have access to major pieces of equipment and large data banks on a world-wide basis, and this is a facility they will increasingly

13.6   Researchers are already beginning to have access to major pieces of equipment and large data banks on a world-wide basis, and this is a facility they will increasingly require and expect. As the knowledge base increases in volume and sophistication, the requirement for such connections will increase. However, the need to duplicate scarce or expensive equipment and resources, including datasets, should be reduced by prudent exploitation of Communications and Information Technology (C&IT). Electronic journals serving a world-wide network of researchers will be common.

13.7   Over the next decade, higher educational services will become an internationally tradable commodity within an increasingly competitive global market. For some programmes, United Kingdom (UK) institutions will rely heavily on C&IT to teach across continents. Within the UK, by the end of the first decade of the next century, a 'knowledge economy'[2] will have developed in which institutions collaborate in the production and transmission of educational programmes and learning materials on a 'make or buy' basis. We must expect and encourage the development and delivery of core programmes and components of programmes, and sharing and exchange of specialist provision, to become commonplace.

13.8   The development of a world market in learning materials, based on C&IT, will provide scope to higher education institutions to become major participants in this arena. This in turn might lead to the formation of trading partnerships between institutions for the provision of infrastructure, services and content. Such partnerships could include major companies in the communications, media and publishing industries.

13.9   As in other industries and businesses, C&IT is affecting the management and administration of higher education institutions, and is assisting institutions to manage increasingly complex activities and services such as finance, personnel, admissions, time-tabling, data collection, estates management, catering and conferencing. Progress in the successful use of C&IT for these purposes has been mixed but higher education institutions should aim to improve their economy and efficiency by making more effective and extensive use of C&IT (see Chapter 15).

13.10   While the effective adoption of C&IT in higher education requires appropriate technology, adequate resources and staff development, success depends on the effective management of change. The development and implementation of an integrated C&IT strategy will be one of the main challenges facing managers of higher education institutions.

13.11   The key issues are, therefore, the materials available and the use which is made of technology. These must be addressed in order to realise our vision and are discussed in the appropriate chapters of our report in some detail. In this chapter we focus on:
    ■ the need for leadership through a clearly articulated C&IT strategy;
    ■ C&IT infrastucture.

Management, leadership and strategy

13.12 The UK enjoys a good Communications and Information Technology (C&IT) infrastructure. The content – in terms of materials and use of this infrastructure – continues to develop. The challenge to leaders in higher education will be to harness both the communications infrastructure, and the growing and developing collections of high-quality learning materials, within a management strategy capable of being responsive to the needs of staff, students and other stakeholders in higher education. Chart 13.1 shows that effective management through the development of information strategies and through programmes of training and support is at the heart of the effective use of C&IT in higher education. An effective communications and information strategy bears very directly on the success achieved by an institution in establishing itself in the nascent world market for higher education through the medium of C&IT.

Chart 13.1 – Effective use of Communications and Information Technology in higher education

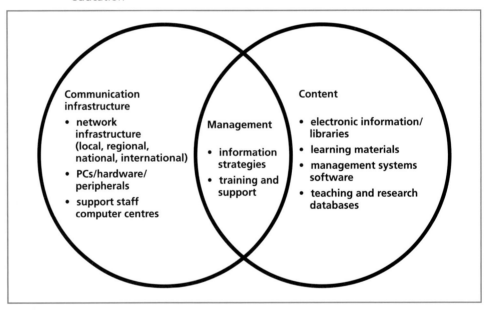

Expenditure

13.13 Implementation of a successful C&IT strategy will require considerable expenditure as well as technological expertise and management. We believe strongly, however, that such expenditure is critical to the delivery of institutions' missions and can only become more so in future. With the diversity of institutions of higher education, needs and levels of spending on C&IT will vary. A detailed audit has not been possible, but we estimate that the UK higher education sector currently spends between £800 million and £1 billion a year (see Table 13.1) in total on C&IT – ie up to ten per cent of total higher education turnover.

Table 13.1 – Estimated annual expenditure by UK higher education on C&IT[3]

Category[2]	£ millon
Central initiatives	60 – 70
HEI central spend	200 – 250
HEI department spend	400 – 550
HEI overheads	100 – 160
HEI courseware	20 – 50
TOTAL	**780 – 1080**

Source: Dr Malcolm Read – Joint Information Systems Committee Secretary

13.14   Such expenditure reflects a strong reliance by higher education institutions on sophisticated high quality Communications and Information Technology (C&IT). New developments will require new patterns of expenditure but the C&IT industry, with which we have consulted extensively, predicts that the costs of computing power and connection will fall. With such high levels of expenditure on C&IT, a major task for management in institutions will be obtaining maximum value for money from it. We note in Chapter 15 that, although there is widespread use of C&IT systems in management and administrative processes, institutions are not near to exploiting fully this potential.

13.15   The successful exploitation of C&IT will require a rethink of institutional priorities and a change of institutional culture. The leadership given by senior management will be critical. Many institutions could realise significant savings by adopting, and adhering to, a minimum sub-set of open standards for hardware and software. Adopting such standards will lead to the need for less C&IT support, less training and improved mobility of clerical, administrative and technical support staff.

13.16   A standard approach to the acquisition and delivery of electronic information (for example through an Intranet[4]) is also needed. Examples would include: techniques to improve the management of the teaching and assessment process; avoiding the duplication of administrative data; computerising student admissions; and drawing together foundation and remedial teaching materials. Other opportunities for savings exist through, for example, the institution-wide use of a single smart card.

13.17   Although we do not underestimate the size of this task, we believe the existing C&IT resources could be used more effectively if institutional managers developed and implemented a coherent and comprehensive C&IT strategy. We are aware that the benefits of such an approach are often seen at the institutional level, rather than in the department which sponsors them, and this needs to be recognised.

Strategy

13.18   The full exploitation of C&IT by higher education institutions in the pursuit of their missions will require senior management to take an imaginative leap. A strategy will need to embrace competition and collaboration in bringing about change. Such strategies should cover information resources, the facilitation of staff/student communication, the development (purchase or production) of learning and teaching materials and other content, and the development of effective management information systems in an integrated manner. We acknowledge that the Funding Bodies currently require institutions to have information strategies and, as part of their strategic planning process, these will form a good basis for extension to all aspects of Communications and Information Technology (C&IT), as we recommend. We therefore propose that the Funding Bodies should encourage institutional management to review their C&IT strategy, and its implementation, as a matter of urgency and importance.

Recommendation 41   **We recommend that all higher education institutions in the UK should have in place overarching communications and information strategies by 1999/2000.**

13.19   We believe that the creation of C&IT strategies will create a focus for debate within institutions and throughout the sector. Central initiatives can help, but they alone cannot deliver our vision of higher education for the next century. Institutions themselves must do that through ownership of their C&IT strategies.

13.20   Central initiatives such as those promoted through the Joint Information Systems Committee (JISC) and Teaching and Learning Technology Programme (TLTP) have been instrumental in advancing the sector's use of C&IT. However, projects initiated through central initiatives are not always carried forward when funding stops. To avoid this loss of momentum it is necessary for institutions to acquire a sense of ownership in such projects. In future, such initiatives should learn the lessons of previous schemes and focus funding on the cost-effective implementation of systems that demonstrably meet identified needs. Exit strategies, and the requirement for a financial contribution on the part of the institution, should also be considered. Thus, we believe that all centrally funded initiatives to foster the use of C&IT should incorporate strategies to secure continued development when the central funding ceases.

13.21   On our visit to the USA we were particularly impressed by the communications infrastructure developed and adopted by the Harvard Business School. This Intranet-based system of teaching and administration was established across the entire School *'due to determined management, including at the highest level, and a dedicated and skilled implementation team.'*[5] We have noted that *'a very significant element in the success of the project was due to top-down enforcement by a technically expert Dean.'*[6] Such a system provides an exemplar for what could be achieved in other institutions, and we are aware that many institutions in the UK are experimenting with Intranetting. The management of UK higher education institutions is less 'top-down' than that of many in the USA, however, and the pure Harvard Business School approach, which also relied on considerable investment, might not transfer completely to large multi-faculty UK institutions. We suggest that the funding bodies consider funding five or six projects in institutions, aimed at capitalising fully on Intranet capabilities, with a view to disseminating advice to the rest of the sector. The proposed Millennium Information and Communication Technology Fund might be a source of additional funding for these pilots.

13.22 We believe, however, that the adoption of Communications and Information Technology (C&IT) is too big, too expensive, and too fundamental to the operation of the institution as a whole to be decided at faculty level. We also think that institutional staff would welcome a strong lead from management in this unknown and uncertain area. While we are not advocating central direction in all such matters, it is very important for top management to take a lead on the overarching infrastructure issues, which should create a flexible environment within which staff can deliver high quality teaching and research more effectively.

13.23 To help achieve this, we believe it will be necessary for institutions to introduce managers who have both a deep understanding of C&IT, and its application to higher education, and senior management experience. There is a shortage of such individuals within higher education. They would therefore have to be bought in or developed by institutions themselves.

Recommendation 42 **We recommend that all higher education institutions should develop managers who combine a deep understanding of Communications and Information Technology with senior management experience.**

Networking

13.24 We have observed that, through the Funding Bodies, higher education has in place an enviable infrastructure in the shape of the Joint Academic Network – JANET, which is one of the most technologically advanced networks in the world. The network, and a range of network services, is managed on behalf of the four UK higher education Funding Bodies by the Joint Information Systems Committee (JISC).

13.25 All higher education institutions in the UK are linked into the network by high-speed connections, as are about 90 further education institutions. An estimated 90 per cent of all significant sites of higher education currently have their own access to JANET.[7] Networks (local, national and international) are impacting upon higher education in a number of ways: as a source of information and software; as a marketing tool; to support learning and teaching; to support research; and for a wide variety of administrative and management purposes. JANET traffic has risen 25-fold, from approximately 40 Gigabytes (40,000,000,000 bytes) a day three years ago, to around 1 Terabyte (1,000,000,000,000 bytes) a day in 1997.[8]

13.26 Academic researchers have identified the need for improved international bandwidth to meet the needs of an increasingly international research environment.[9] We recognise that networks, previously most heavily used by the research community, are now also being more regularly used to support learning and teaching and other activities and that this might eventually reduce access to networks needed by researchers. We believe that increased investment in the network capacity will be essential if researchers are to continue to make good use of centrally provided high performance computing. The networking needs of the research community are discussed further in Chapter 11.

13.27 JANET is extensively used. A recent survey of academic staff connected to JANET found that 98 per cent used electronic mail at least once a week and 92 per cent reported that they found it 'essential' or 'very useful'. Use of and benefit from other technologies, such as video-conferencing, was found to be less widespread and was identified by only a minority of respondents, but the study noted that this *'probably reflects the availability of the technology rather than…the number of users who would use the facilities if they were more widely available'*.[10]

Metropolitan Area Networks (MANs)[11]

13.28　The MANs connect a number of institutions, and sites within those institutions, at regional level, and permit very high speed, sophisticated, high quality network communications. Existing MANs are also connected to each other through the SuperJANET[12] network. The Committee of Scottish Higher Education Principals told us that the Scottish MANs give Scottish higher education *'a considerable lead over most other countries – including the US'* – in terms of high quality connectivity between higher education institutions.[13] Furthermore, we have considered and acknowledge that Scotland has attained a *'world-beating network at a very small incremental cost above that of an adequate network'*.[14]

13.29　Metropolitan Area Networks (MANs) offer a platform for closer links and collaboration between local institutions, local industry and, potentially, colleges of further education on a regional basis. Scottish higher education institutions envisage that MANs will support extensive inter-institutional collaborative projects as part of a programme of strategic change. Although new MANs are being planned and built, there are still significant areas of the UK which are not covered. We, therefore, commend the further development of MANs where the Funding Bodies and institutions consider that these are technically and financially sensible.

Information resources

13.30　There is a growing range of electronic information available over JANET. This material is becoming increasingly important for both learning and research in the higher education community. For example the ISI (Institute of Scientific Information) bibliographic dataset is used by 103 institutions and the IBSS (International Bibliography of the Social Sciences) has 120 subscribing higher education institutions. There is a steady growth of usage of around 70 per cent per annum. Coherent collections of subject-based datasets are also being generated through the electronic libraries (eLib) programme, designed to lead to a distributed national electronic resource for higher education. There are also promising developments in the creation of electronic versions of journals resulting from the joint Funding Bodies' pilot Site Licence initiative.[15]

13.31　Multi-media electronic information available over the network can provide valuable and important building blocks for course material. We see this as a development of growing importance and value. Close liaison is therefore needed between providers of such material and the proposed Institute for Learning and Teaching in Higher Education and, in particular, with any company created to produce, commission and market on-line learning and teaching materials (see Chapter 8).

13.32   C&IT will have a profound effect upon the relationship between the higher education sector and the publishing industry. We welcome the initiative by the Joint Information Systems Committee (JISC) and the Publishers Association to establish a series of working parties to consider how these changes might best be effected. We believe that institutions will need to become more professional and proficient in the production and distribution of electronic publications. We suggest that, as an output from eLib, there should be a detailed assessment of this matter and provision of advice to the sector about electronic publications, for teaching and research accordingly.

Intellectual property rights and copyright

13.33   We have noted the JISC's suggestion that higher education institutions should become more interested in the ownership of the copyright of learned journal articles produced by academics in their employment, not as a means of earning money but as a means of saving expenditure.[16]

13.34   We have also noted that current copyright legislation (the Copyright, Designs and Patents Act, 1988) precludes the use by individuals of copyright digital information without clearance by the copyright owner, which may take weeks. These delays hamper the speed of interaction between student and teacher and make unnecessary demands on staff time. We are, therefore, of the view that there must be provision for the free and immediate use by teachers and researchers of copyright digital information.

Recommendation 43   **We recommend to the Government that it should review existing copyright legislation and consider how it might be amended to facilitate greater ease of use of copyright materials in digital form by teachers and researchers.**

Future networking

13.35   We have considered how networking can be more fully exploited by the higher education community. To gain the full benefits of Communications and Information Technology (C&IT), all significant centres of higher education will require access to a satisfactory pervasive network.

13.36   As a significant proportion of higher education is delivered in further education colleges, we consider that **all** further education institutions should have access to the higher education network, either directly or via a secondary connection to a local higher education institution. This is in keeping with the report of the Learning and Technology Committee of the Further Education Funding Council for England which recommended that a third party owned, flexible bandwidth communications network, managed on behalf of the further education sector and linking all colleges, should be established.[17] This should be extended UK-wide and the appropriate Funding Bodies should work together to develop suitable networks.

13.37   To realise the wider benefits of C&IT there is a strong case for greater connectivity between the higher education sector and other organisations and sectors, such as schools, community colleges, Training and Enterprise Councils and Local Enterprise Companies, the National Health Service and other national organisations such as the British Library. Links are possible through Internet service providers but there is a case for strengthening these links through higher bandwidth connections to enable access to more sophisticated applications available on JANET.

Recommendation 44   **We recommend to the Government and the Funding Bodies that, to harness and maximise the benefits of Communications and Information Technology, they should secure appropriate network connectivity to all sites of higher education delivery and further education colleges by 1999/2000, and to other relevant bodies over the medium term.**

Future cost trends

13.38   The predicted demand and growth in network traffic and requirement for enhanced bandwidth will result in significant additional costs, year-on-year, to the sector, and the Joint Information Systems Committee (JISC) has signalled the introduction of tariffs in the future. We are not opposed in principle to the introduction of tariffs, provided that such tariffs offer value for money to customers and do not unreasonably limit access to quality materials and services to those customers least able to pay. Cost should not be an obstacle to pervasive broadband access, nor should it inhibit growth in the use and availability of quality learning materials and information resources. Our immediate concern is that the swift and sudden introduction of tariffs would have a dampening and damaging effect on development and use of such materials. We therefore consider that the introduction of tariffs should be withheld until 2000/2001 and that thereafter tariffs should be phased in. Meanwhile, institutions should take steps to ensure that network usage is efficient.

13.39   As students gradually require increased access to networks, it will become more important for institutions to supply networking to student residences (as many are already doing) and to offer dial-up connectivity to students in their own homes. In the case of provision in institutions, there will need to be some control over the amount of costs and, therefore, usage, as there are few economies of scale to be had. Eventually, students at home will have connectivity provided by Internet service providers and fund their own access, just as many currently fund their own travel to their place of study. We suggest a period of subsidy and gradual migration to user provision as a means of managing the transitional phase.

Recommendation 45   **We recommend that institutions of higher education, collectively or individually as appropriate, should negotiate reduced tariffs from telecommunications providers on behalf of students as soon as possible.**

13.40   SuperJANET has now successfully established the potential of multi-service networking.[18] We believe there is now a requirement to make such a network available throughout the higher education community, at an affordable price, to enable the widespread use of Communications and Information Technology (C&IT)-based learning and teaching materials to supplement existing modes of teaching.

13.41   Table 13.2 provides an estimate of likely costs of our recommendations on networks. These have been prepared on the basis of the current year by the JISC and are indicative only at this stage.

Table 13.2 – Network costs £ million

	1997-1998		1998-1999		1999-2000		2000-2001	
	Central costs	Costs to be met by insti-tutions	Central costs	Costs to be met by insti-tutions	Central costs	Costs to be met by insti-tutions	Central costs	Costs to be met by insti-tutions
JANET	£17.5	£2.5	£21.0	£3.0	£24.0	£4.0	£22.0	£8.0
Extend MANs[19]	£4.0	£2.0	£4.5	£4.0	£3.0	£3.0	£1.0	£3.0
Extend JANET/ SuperJANET to all HE sites	0	£2.0	0	£4.0	0	£5.0	0	£5.0
Extend JANET to FE[20]	n/a		£9.0		£12.0		£15.0	

Source: Dr Malcolm Read, Secretary, Joint Informations Systems Committee

13.42 The Funding Bodies are already planning substantial expenditure on networking through the Joint Information Systems Committee, and the expenditure outlined in the table falls within that budget.

Student Portable Computer

13.43 Over the next ten years, all higher education institutions will, and should, progressively move significant aspects of administration and learning and teaching to the computer medium. They should be planning for this now. The development of powerful paperback-sized 'notebook' computers, capable of sending and receiving e-mail and accessing the Internet, is envisaged within the next few years.[21] We expect that this technology will be harnessed by students and institutions for learning and teaching and administration through the development of a Student Portable Computer (SPC).

13.44 The SPC will store basic course information and enable the student to undertake a significant amount of work off-line (for example drafting of assignments). It will also allow the student, via a network connection, to access electronic information (such as timetables, course materials and library catalogues), to submit assignments, and to communicate with tutors and other students. It is possible that the SPC might be a fully mobile device accessing the network through wireless technology. We found, on our visit to the USA in January 1997, that an SPC (usually an industry-standard laptop computer) is already a requirement for courses at a number of institutions. The same requirement applies to some UK programmes.

13.45 To use their SPCs effectively in this way, to communicate and send and receive information, students will require daily access to the network. There will, therefore, need to be adequate provision of network connection ports in institutions into which students can plug their SPCs and there should be provision of dial-up connectivity for off-campus students at each institution.

13.46 At least in the short term, the widespread availability of SPCs will not obviate the need for Networked Desktop Computers within the campus. An SPC is unlikely to be powerful enough or suitable for all applications. For example, larger and better quality screens and keyboards, or a faster processor, may be needed for many purposes. Some applications will require better network speeds than would be typically available to a student at home or in halls of residence.

13.47   As access to a Student Portable Computer (SPC) becomes a standard requirement for a student, we envisage that it will represent part of a growing market for such hardware, comparable with the mobile phone market which has burgeoned in recent years. Thus the SPC will be a relatively standard product in an open and competitive market.

13.48   Table 13.3 shows how the costs of the SPC might be apportioned over time. We are assuming it will retail at about £500. Although the price of the basic SPC can be expected to fall, students may choose, and some may need, a higher performance machine which costs more.

13.49   We suggest that the SPC is funded by students themselves with some assistance for the transitional phasing of its introduction from the National Lottery. We note that the proposed Millennium Information and Communication Technology Fund may come into being in 2000 to distribute around £300 million per annum. In the interests of keeping prices as low as possible for the student purchaser we also propose that institutions assume a role in the distribution of the SPC and that the Government should give consideration to allowing tax credits for hardware suppliers of this product.

Networked Desktop Computer

13.50   Networked Desktop Computers (NDCs) need to be of a sufficiently high technical specification to make full use of the network and networked services, and permit the use of the latest interactive multimedia learning and teaching materials and other applications (whether accessed via the network or CD-ROM). They must, therefore, incorporate up-to-date sound, video and graphics technology.

13.51   Existing evidence suggests that, at present, the ratio of students to desktop computers in higher education institutions is only slightly better than 15:1 across the UK.[22] In the short term, student access to NDCs needs to be improved across the sector as a whole. The required ratio will vary from institution to institution, depending on such factors as subjects taught, types of student and learning and teaching methods. A ratio of 10:1 would be a good standard at present but this needs to improve to 8:1, particularly where an institution makes extensive use of on-line learning materials and electronic information services. We expect that, as such methods become widespread, a ratio of 5:1, or better, will be necessary for multi-faculty institutions. Students will need information about the adequacy of an institution's provision of equipment for their use and must know in advance of study what expectations there are of students providing their own access.

Recommendation 46 **We recommend that by 2000/01 higher education institutions should ensure that all students have open access to a Networked Desktop Computer, and expect that by 2005/06 all students will be required to have access to their own portable computer.**

13.52   Institutions should publish details of the student: Networked Desktop Computer (NDC) ratios in their institution to inform student choice on entry. This in itself might prove to be a stimulus for improved provision of access to NDCs as Communications and Information Technology (C&IT) takes a larger role in curricula and students' need for access to electronic information grows.

13.53   Access and space issues will arise as a result and consideration will need to be given to how existing space, designed to accommodate traditional learning and teaching methods and library storage, can be freed up and remodelled. This activity should feature in the C&IT strategies we are suggesting institutions should devise. Table 13.3 shows the costs of reaching a ratio of 8:1 by 1999/2000 and 5:1 by the end of 2001/02.

Table 13.3 – Hardware costs £ million

	1998-1999	1999-2000	2000-2001	2001-2002	2002-2003	2003-2004
HEI-provided NDC[23] @ £2,800 per unit	100	100	90	90	60	60
Student-provided SPC[24] @ £500 per unit	20	75	125	150	150	150

13.54   Expenditure on institutionally provided hardware reduces from 2002-2003 to take account of the uptake of Student Portable Computers (SPCs). Provision will need to be made, however, for increased network ports and links. We suggest that this expenditure can be met from within existing institutional budgets.

Value-added tax

13.55   Value-added tax (VAT) is payable, at the full rate, on electronically published materials, but no VAT is currently charged on printed materials. The current arrangements inhibit the development and use of electronic materials as an alternative to print-based materials. To minimise this adverse effect the rate of VAT levied on electronic materials should be reduced and maintained at the lowest level possible. Assuming no change in European Union law, however, we suggest that if VAT is levied on print-based materials in the future, the level of VAT levied on electronic educational materials should not exceed that levied on print-based materials.

Misuse and abuse

13.56   C&IT brings with it the potential for improper and illegal behaviour. Institutions need to ensure that users understand what constitutes acceptable use. An important step is to publish a code of acceptable practice and behaviour for users. Without such a code it is difficult for institutions to invoke disciplinary procedures where appropriate. We suggest that all institutions of higher education should adopt policies on abuse and misuse of Communications and Information Technology (C&IT) facilities.

Conclusion

13.57   We have been impressed by the high standard of Communications and Information Technology (C&IT) provision in UK higher education and the enthusiasm of the many dedicated experts who are pioneering its extended use. We believe that the successful exploitation of C&IT is pivotal to the success and health of higher education in the future, as it has been since the first computers were built at Manchester and Cambridge. We do not consider that the barriers to this are financial, indeed the sector already spends a significant amount in pursuit of such activities. We consider that this expenditure warrants closer attention at the institutional level. What will be required, however, is a fundamental rethink of institutional priorities, an equally essential change of culture, and well-informed leadership. Above all, there remains an urgent need for institutions to understand better and respond to the challenges and opportunities of the emerging information age.

Chapter 14

Staff in higher education

Introduction

14.1 Realisation of the vision for higher education that we have developed throughout our report is wholly dependent on the people in higher education. We therefore turn in this chapter to the policies and practices needed in institutions to enable staff to respond to what lies ahead and to provide a framework for their future employment. Our terms of reference included the following principle:

'that higher education should be able to recruit, retain and motivate staff of the appropriate calibre'.

14.2 An effective, fairly remunerated, professional and well-motivated workforce lies at the heart of the high quality system of higher education which this country will continue to need. We deal elsewhere with other matters of concern to staff: participation in governance; grievance procedures; academic freedom; and the development of teaching as a profession.

14.3 In making recommendations on these matters we have drawn on the evidence put to us by, and on behalf of, academic and other staff.

14.4 We discussed in Chapter 3 the wide range of staff employed by universities, and their numbers across the United Kingdom (UK). They form a significant percentage (1.8 per cent) of the total UK workforce in employment. The groupings and terminology used by institutions to describe different staff vary, depending on institutional policy. Broadly, the categories reflect the groupings for the collective bargaining arrangements that still prevail, but there is a growing recognition of the inadequacy of these types of categorisation. In pre-1992 universities the categories are: academic staff; academic and related staff; technical staff; clerical staff; manual staff; and computer operators. The categories in the 1992 universities are: lecturers; researchers; administrative, professional, technical and clerical (APT&C) staff; and manual staff.

Career patterns and changing roles

14.5 The skills associated with academic work: teaching, scholarship, research, and administration, have traditionally been acquired within higher education itself. Possession of a good first degree and a postgraduate research qualification have been the traditional entry qualifications for academic staff.

14.6 Promotion is based on criteria devised by individual institutions, but they are generally perceived as rewarding research rather than teaching. Some institutions are changing this emphasis, and seek to reward other aspects of academic work, particularly excellence in teaching, but also managerial skills and leadership abilities. Nevertheless, our survey of academic staff indicates that only three per cent believe that the present system rewards excellence in teaching. We agree that there is currently inadequate recognition of teaching excellence, and make proposals to help change this in paragraph 14.29.

14.7   In the pre-1992 universities, since the abolition of the University Grants Committee's restriction of a maximum ratio of 40 per cent senior (ie those staff holding posts at senior lecturer level and above) to junior academic teaching staff, universities have been able to recruit staff to suit their own institutional plans. Nationally, the ratio is approximately 46 per cent, but we have been told that in some institutions senior academic teaching staff ratios of 50 to 60 per cent are now not uncommon. This has helped to offset the relatively modest general pay increases for academic staff, and it has also tended to lift the general career grade expectation of academic staff in pre-1992 universities to the level of senior lecturer. This is significant when attempting to judge whether changes in pay in higher education have matched changes elsewhere. In the 1992 universities the comparable national ratio is only 25 per cent.

14.8   It is important that promotion is seen not simply as a reward for past achievement but also as an ongoing expectation of the need to assume greater responsibility or perform in a different way. It is not clear whether the responsibilities and/or performance of academic teaching staff on higher grades currently always match the higher levels of reward they receive. Long incremental salary scales, with semi-automatic increments, together with the culture of 'gradism', can lead to less attention being paid to individual performance than is desirable or fair. Some institutions are responding by moving away from the staff appraisal and development schemes introduced in the late 1980s and early 1990s, which do not link individual performance to appropriate rewards or to remedial action to improve performance. They are gradually developing schemes which match their own human resource requirements and institutional mission.

14.9   Pre-1992 universities also face limitations on staff deployment through contractual arrangements for academic and academic-related staff recruited before 1987, which guarantee grading and employment. Some institutions cite this as a serious obstacle to greater efficiency, and may have as many as a third of their staff employed on such terms. The costs associated with moving away from them have dissuaded most institutions from tackling this issue, but for some it is a significant problem.

14.10   The recent changes in higher education suggest that career opportunities for non-academic staff working in areas such as libraries, computer support, technical support, and administration are widening, as universities restructure and identify new types of services and activities to offer students and other customers. The growing emphasis on learning rather than teaching in higher education means that students can be expected to place increasing demands upon support staff to provide them with advice and guidance. As we discussed in Chapter 8, comments made by support staff in the survey we commissioned confirm this trend. Library staff, for instance, refer to students starting to behave more like 'customers', and being more demanding in the services they seek, particularly if they are self-funding or mature students. Administrative and support staff report a growing involvement in learning and teaching functions, for example, in preparing materials for self-directed learning, and training students to use new equipment or data sources. The task of 'teaching students how to learn' was one they had previously seen as being the responsibility of academics.

14.11   With an increasing growth of partnerships and collaborative arrangements between higher education and other organisations in the public and private sectors, career structures in higher education are likely to become more diverse and less predictable. In its evidence to us, the Universities and Colleges Employers Association (UCEA) referred to outdated ways of organising staff into hierarchies (eg unskilled, semi-skilled, technician etc). The UCEA has recommended moving away from this and adopting approaches based on organisational review and job design. The UCEA leads a consortium developing computerised job evaluation analysis to assist with tasks such as job design, performance appraisal and rewards systems, and equal opportunities practices.

14.12   In the long term, we believe future career patterns might be expected to show some of the following characteristics:
- more staff transfers and secondments between higher education institutions and other organisations, with individual staff developing and managing their own career portfolios, combining teaching, research, scholarship, and public service as appropriate, at different periods in their lives;
- a smaller proportion of an institution's staff remaining as core employees, but a need to ensure continuity in management, administration and learning;
- the erosion of historic staff categories and pay structures and also of the distinction between academic and support staff;
- more flexible criteria for promotion which reflect the wider range of relevant skills that staff can offer, and which take into account our proposed accreditation arrangements;
- increased institutional collaboration, offering staff more opportunities to develop their skills and widen their experience.

14.13   Such changes will offer academic staff the opportunity to re-interpret their traditional role if they wish to do so. The likelihood is that there will be a greater range of opportunities, with staff undertaking different combinations of functions at different stages of their careers, depending on the development of institutional missions and their personal career aspirations. The changes will also offer new opportunities to support staff to be involved in providing advice and guidance to students. To support and prepare staff for these new working patterns, more focused and appropriate training and staff development activities will be necessary; these are discussed below.

Managing new employment patterns

14.14   In submissions to us the case was made for radical changes in the way higher education institutions manage their staff in the light of the new demands being made upon them. The Association for Learning Technology noted:

'In circumstances where communications and information technology has changed the nature of learning and teaching, there is a need to review and redefine the roles of academic staff and support staff within HEIs.'

14.15   Similarly, in evidence to us higher education personnel professionals looked ahead to:
- the distinctions between staff groups becoming increasingly irrelevant as staff move across functions (see paragraph 14.10);
- an emphasis on building up effective teams to utilise fully staff skills from across an institution;
- the need to develop better tools to enable institutions to organise, develop, assess and reward staff.

14.16   We agree that such developments are likely and necessary. Similarly, we are in no doubt about the increased pressures currently facing staff in higher education, or about their achievements over the last few years. Increasing workloads and outputs at a time of declining unit resources have been a feature across the system as we discussed in Chapter 3. Our surveys indicate that higher education staff are concerned that the quality of support they can provide to students is not as high as they would like, and in many cases has declined over the past five years. Academic staff experience greater teaching commitments with larger groups, pressure to research and publish, and fewer opportunities to offer individual support to students (Report 3). The changing approaches to learning and teaching discussed in Chapter 8 (eg modularisation, resource-based learning), have added to the workloads of non-academic staff.

14.17   A survey carried out among academic staff in one English institution found 25 per cent of respondents reported the reason for stress to be *'too much work – no time to complete it'*.[1] Our survey of academic staff indicated that stress levels were a significant consideration and it was the second most frequently cited reason for those staff seeking to leave higher education before the normal retirement age. There was a marked difference between pre-1992 and 1992 universities, however, with stress factors being of more concern to staff in the former.

Staff development

14.18   Although for the future we see Communications and Information Technology (C&IT) providing a valuable addition to institutional resources for learning and teaching, and as a means of maintaining quality at a time of attenuated staff to student ratios, we are conscious that time is needed to develop and exploit its potential.

14.19   Training and support in the use of C&IT is an issue in its own right. In such training we imagine that institutions will wish to draw on materials already developed in the sector such as the Netskills project at the University of Newcastle and the TalisMAN activities being carried out by Heriot-Watt University on behalf of the Scottish institutions. Job descriptions, reward structures and career patterns will need to be reviewed to take into account the developments in C&IT, and stimulate their use. As we recommended in Chapter 8 there is a particular need for institutions to recruit or develop staff with experience in C&IT and management skills, many of whom are in short supply at present.

14.20   The challenge to staff goes much wider than the use of Communications and Information Technology (C&IT). The growth in lifelong learning, new partnerships with employers, and closer links with the economic life of localities and regions will all require staff to widen their roles. It will also require institutions to reassess the link between the achievement of such institutional priorities and reward systems for staff.

14.21   As the Universities Personnel Association said in its evidence, managing in a higher education environment requires skills, many of which are best learnt in that environment, and the sector must be prepared to put in place programmes that enable it to develop its own support specialists. Similarly, the Higher Education Quality Council's evidence specified the need to develop project management skills at unit, department and faculty levels, as well as strategic management skills. The National Audit Office made a similar point in its report (see Chapter 16), and, in our surveys, administrative and support staff referred to inefficient use of money and equipment resulting in duplication and fragmentation in services. It is clear from this evidence that institutions must ensure that, over the medium term, managers in departments have the necessary range of management expertise and skills to contribute to corporate improvements in value for money.

14.22   Our survey of administrative and support staff showed that they shared the perception of the personnel professionals that traditional definitions of roles are breaking down, and they are being involved in a wider range of functions than in the past.

14.23   All this points to the need for action to improve individual and institutional effectiveness through staff development. The opportunity for development should be welcomed by staff as demonstrating the institution's commitment to them and as a means of preparing them for career advancement.

14.24   Staff often perceive a lack of commitment towards and inadequate funding for their personal development. Whether or not the perception is accurate, it needs to be addressed by institutions. It may be that there would be benefit in institutions identifying their expenditure on staff development in their annual reports. This has the merit of ensuring that the issue receives continuing attention by senior management and the governing body. We are aware of definitional problems, but it merits consideration by institutions. We have noted the adoption by many organisations of Investors in People schemes, and the, as yet, modest progress they have made in higher education. Only a small number of higher education institutions have received the award, although a number of others are working towards it, and some have found it more appropriate to adopt a staged programme, taking each department or faculty one by one, to achieve institution-wide coverage. It may be that Investors in People is not well suited for all higher education institutions, but the principles and practices that inform it are sound and relevant. To the extent that Investors in People schemes need adaptation, it may be possible for the Institute for Learning and Teaching in Higher Education to redevelop it to reflect the needs of higher education.

14.25   We recognise that many institutions have human resource development policies which serve them well. But, in view of the pace of change, the increasing range of demands being placed on staff, and the centrality of their contribution they will need to be kept under review, to ensure that they support institutional priorities. For instance, in Chapter 11 we discussed the importance of protecting Intellectual Property Rights (IPR), and we would expect institutions to take into consideration the need to develop expertise in managing IPR, and if appropriate, to employ professional staff capable of carrying out this function.

Recommendation 47

We recommend that, over the next year, all institutions should:
- **review and update their staff development policies to ensure they address the changing roles of staff;**
- **publish their policies and make them readily available for all staff;**
- **consider whether to seek the Investors in People award;**

14.26   Such reviews should include explicit consideration of the developmental needs outlined in the paragraphs above.

14.27   We are sensitive to the risk that what would be seen as good practice in staff development, appraisal and counselling in most of industry and commerce, could be construed in an academic institution as trespassing on, or undermining academic freedom. This is not our wish: our concern is that while academic freedom should be respected, staff are helped to realise their full potential; that where there are problems they are addressed; that staff are assisted to respond with best effect to the opportunities and challenges facing higher education; and that they are, and feel valued, as members of the community of the institution.

Academic/professional accreditation

14.28   In Chapter 8 we made clear our belief that higher education teaching needs to have higher status and be regarded as a profession of standing. To support this we have proposed the establishment of a professional Institute for Learning and Teaching in Higher Education, one of whose roles would be to accredit programmes of higher education teaching training. There is widespread support for a system of accreditation, as our staff survey and the responses to our consultation indicated.

14.29   The Institute would provide the basis for a nationally recognised system of professional qualifications for higher education teachers based on a probationary period, and followed up with appropriate continuing professional development at later career stages. Differing levels of expertise would be recognised by different forms of membership of the Institute, from associate member through to Fellowship for those attaining the highest levels of excellence in teaching.

14.30   We have considered whether such qualifications should become compulsory for higher education teachers but have concluded that a degree of flexibility is needed. Some disciplines rightly make substantial use of part-time teachers, for example, professional practitioners who deliver parts of programmes. It would not be appropriate to insist that they are trained to the same level as a full-time higher education teacher. It should, however, become the norm that all permanent staff with teaching responsibilities achieve at least associate membership of the Institute before completion of probation and continue to keep their skills up-to-date throughout their careers. We hope that, over time, most existing staff will also seek recognition of their teaching skills.

Recommendation 48   **We recommend to institutions that, over the medium term, it should become the normal requirement that all new full-time academic staff with teaching responsibilities are required to achieve at least associate membership of the Institute for Learning and Teaching in Higher Education, for the successful completion of probation.**

14.31   The Institute for Learning and Teaching would be concerned with all aspects of teaching and its pedagogy, and as we discussed in Chapter 9, would give priority to developing assessment practices and strategies, which would become a key part of the initial training and continuing professional development of teaching staff. It was also suggested to us that accreditation arrangements should encompass all aspects of 'academic practice', for example, management/administration, use of Communications and Information Technology (C&IT), and research. We would support this approach as a means of ensuring quality, enhancing public perceptions of higher education, and improving its self-perception.

Use of short term contracts for academic staff

14.32   Greater reliance on short term contract staff (particularly for research), has been highlighted in staff association surveys and by the House of Lords Select Committee on Science and Technology.[2] If not properly managed, this practice may have a detrimental effect on the quality of higher education institutions' activities. Loss of expertise as staff on short term contracts look for stable employment may lead to inefficiencies in research, and impair the quality of teaching. Career planning is difficult and the uncertainty may act as a disincentive for people to enter the profession, or remain in it, in the absence of more senior level posts. This can be a particular issue in areas such as the biomedical sciences where alternative career paths are readily available.

14.33   We recognise however, that short term contracts can be beneficial for both sides, if managed carefully. They provide the flexibility needed for projects whose funding cannot be guaranteed long term, thus enabling institutions to avoid making commitments they cannot fulfil.

14.34   Arrangements such as the Concordat between the Committee of Vice-Chancellors and Principals (CVCP), the Research Councils, the Royal Society, the British Academy, the Standing Conference of Principals and the Committee of Higher Education Principals should help alleviate past problems. As the Concordat has only been in operation since September 1996, no assessment of its impact has yet been made. After a reasonable period of experience, the CVCP and the Research Councils will need to review its effectiveness and, if necessary to consider whether an alternative approach is needed. For more senior level research posts, the Research Councils might consider earmarking certain funding to be distributed on a competitive basis to inter-departmental groups to fund specific individuals for their research careers. This funding would not be indefinite, but would be sufficiently long term to retain talented individuals.

Use of part-time/hourly paid staff for teaching

14.35   Institutional policies vary on the use of part-time and hourly paid staff. Some
          institutions do not employ staff on an hourly basis, instead using part-time contracts
          which enable the staff concerned to enjoy similar benefits to those offered to full-time
          staff. Table 14.1 below shows the pattern in 1994/5 and 1995/6, suggesting an
          increase of over 20 per cent in each of the two categories of staff.

Table 14.1 – Number of part-time and hourly paid staff

Mode of Employment	Teaching		Research		Teaching and Research		Totals	
	94/95	95/96	94/95	95/96	94/95	95/96	94/95	95/96
Part-Time	1,521	2,076	3,133	4,065	5,418	6,569	10,072	12,710
Casual*	1,624	1,942	9	14	196	297	1,829	2,253

Source: HESA   * = hourly paid

14.36   Evidence from the National Association of Teachers in Further and Higher Education
          (NATFHE) refers to the increasing use of part-time and hourly paid staff for teaching.
          Hourly paid staff often do not benefit from agreed conditions of service, and may be
          excluded from staff appraisal and development and training programmes, and
          programme planning and delivery mechanisms. The extensive use of casual staff can
          also mean that full-time staff spend much of their time managing part-time staff. There
          is a concern that, in the long term, a trend towards increased use of casual staff will
          adversely affect the quality of the student experience. We recognise the need for good
          management of these staff groups, and an approach that is sensitive to particular
          circumstances, for instance for those vocationally-oriented programmes where
          practitioners from business and other organisations contribute on a part-time basis, or
          as needed. Opportunities for part-time working may also be welcome to certain groups
          of staff, eg those with family responsibilities, thus enhancing equal opportunities.

14.37   The use of postgraduate students for undergraduate teaching has also been referred to
          us by both the Association of University Teachers (AUT) and the National Union of
          Students (NUS) as an issue of concern, and in their submissions they recommend clear
          guidelines for their use. Some institutions use postgraduate students extensively,
          formalising the relationship with suitable employment contracts and providing the
          necessary support and training.

14.38   The practice has obvious benefits for postgraduate students, in giving them an
          opportunity to experience teaching first hand and in providing a welcome source of
          income. Sixty per cent of the students in our survey had participated in seminars run by
          postgraduate students and less than one in ten believed that postgraduate teaching
          assistants were used too frequently. The practice is common in other countries, eg USA,
          and it can be a desirable development if managed in a systematic way with quality
          control and support mechanisms, and with appropriate training and development.

Equal opportunities

14.39   Although higher education has made good progress in recent years in providing equal opportunities for different types of students, the record on staff is less good, although some progress has been made. The 1994 survey of universities undertaken by the Commission on University Career Opportunity revealed that while 93 per cent of university sector institutions had adopted equal opportunities policies, only 37 per cent had adopted plans for creating equal opportunities. Women, ethnic minorities and the disabled are all significantly under-represented among higher education staff, except, in some cases, at the most junior levels.

14.40   While higher education institutions are not atypical of employers in this respect, such inequalities run counter to the claimed values of higher education. The Equal Opportunities Commission and the Commission for Racial Equality both suggested to us that the key to making progress is awareness and training and an effective human resources policy in each institution.

Recommendation 49   **We recommend that all institutions should, as part of their human resources policy, maintain equal opportunities policies, and, over the medium term, should identify and remove barriers which inhibit recruitment and progression for particular groups and monitor and publish their progress towards greater equality of opportunity for all groups.**

The employment framework

14.41   Enabling the sector to deliver our vision for higher education means constructing a framework for employment that addresses quality, stability, diversity and flexibility in the recruitment and retention of staff. The current employment framework and the rather under-developed staffing policies of many institutions are barriers to effective practice. These need to be addressed.

Pay levels

14.42   The report by the Independent Pay Commission, set up as part of the 1996/97 pay settlement between employers and the eight staff unions, provides a source of well-researched material about the relativity between pay in higher education and in the rest of the economy. However, this information only became available to us towards the end of our work. We note the findings which suggest that the majority, but by no means all, staff in higher education are paid substantially below comparable private and public sector market levels, and the concerns of higher education employers and trades unions about the possible effects this may have on staff recruitment, retention, morale and motivation.

14.43   In evidence to us, the view that academic staff salary levels have declined in comparison with other non-manual workers was expressed. The level of the decline is subject to debate, as different comparators and base years are used by different parties. Trades unions, the Department for Education and Employment (DfEE) and the Committee of Vice-Chancellors and Principals (CVCP) have provided their own examples:

- the AUT, in its evidence, compares the cumulative percentage change of the salary in academics since 1981 to that of MPs, civil service principals, clinical lecturers, hospital senior registrars and school teachers. This analysis shows that, while academic salaries are largely unchanged in real terms in the period, those of the other groups have risen by between 18 and 50 per cent;
- the CVCP compares the growth in the pay of male university teachers in the period 1961-1993 (8.6 per cent growth) with that of non-manual men (37.1 per cent growth), male further education teachers (9.4 per cent growth), NHS nurses (29.4 per cent growth) and a range of other groups;
- the DfEE has used New Earnings Survey data to show that male university teachers were earning 30 per cent more than the average male non-manual workers in 1995, the same premium as in 1979.

14.44 Most evidence does suggest that there has been a relative decline in academic salaries over the long term. On the other hand, as we comment in paragraph 14.7, there has been a marked increase in the proportion of senior posts. These two factors cannot be regarded as independent: grading inflation may have offset a relative decline in levels of salary for some staff. The more fundamental issue is whether or not the absolute level of pay is sufficient to recruit, motivate and retain staff of the required quality. We have received no evidence of widespread recruitment and retention problems, although specific examples have been cited, particularly in relation to attracting people of the quality needed in certain disciplines and functions. Society has so much at stake in achieving our vision of being world class in higher education teaching, that it needs to establish whether salary levels are appropriate. It also needs to be satisfied, in view of the scale of resources required by higher education, that staff are being used to the best possible advantage.

14.45 The evidence on pay levels of some other groups of staff is not clear cut. Both the Transport and General Workers Union evidence, and that of UNISON, referred to a basic weekly wage for full-time manual and ancillary workers in pre-1992 universities of £133.70 per week, and suggested that this was unacceptably low. However, in some areas national pay scales for manual and ancillary staff exceed local pay rates, leading institutions to contract out functions in order to achieve greatest cost effectiveness.

Future pay determination: the options

14.46 In evidence to us, the case has been made for a review of the mechanisms for pay determination. Recent disputes and protracted pay negotiations suggest that the present collective bargaining arrangements may not be appropriate, and that the sector may well need to agree on a more flexible approach which caters for the widening range of institutions and types of staff.

14.47 Some argue that the type of minimum national agreements prevailing in higher education offer the worst of all possible worlds: they do not provide the detailed framework of terms and conditions needed by institutions, nor is there an incentive for institutions to develop their own frameworks. This, it is argued, inhibits the development of institutional human resource strategies. However, the system does not prevent those institutions willing and able to experiment with more attractive pay packages from doing so if they have the human resources expertise, the managerial will, and the resources. On the other hand, few institutions are, at present, equipped to carry out local pay bargaining for academic staff.

14.48   The arguments which have been put to us in support of national pay bargaining, local pay bargaining, a statutory pay review body and a standing pay review body are set out below. There is wide support for an independent review of academic pay, although views differ as to whether it should be a one-off review, or the basis for setting up a statutory pay review body. Some 43 per cent of academic staff in our survey identified a pay review body as their preferred method of salary settlement, and 25 per cent, a review body supplemented by local negotiations.

14.49   The arguments put to us for maintaining national bargaining are:
■ academic staff are part of a national employment market;
■ locally negotiated discretionary payments are already part of the practice, and provide flexibility;
■ the cost of training local staff to carry out local negotiations is high, and the ongoing costs for higher education management of local pay bargaining would be high;
■ it assists harmonisation between the pre-1992 and 1992 universities;
■ union negotiators facing independent institutions would be able to lever pay up by quoting one institution against another.

14.50   The arguments put to us for opting for local bargaining are:
■ as independent institutions, institutions of higher education are responsible for their own affairs;
■ institutions have their own priorities, missions, and levels of resource, all of which require differential practices with respect to pay;
■ ability to pay varies, as do institutional priorities.

14.51   An alternative arrangement would be a statutory standing pay review body. The Association of University Teachers advocates this approach for academic and academic-related staff.

14.52   Some of the arguments for establishing a standing pay review body are:
■ a one-off pay rise to deal with any present underpayment would be eroded in future years;
■ annual negotiations inhibit the establishment of academics as mature professionals with professional standards in quality and ethics;
■ industrial style negotiations are inappropriate and have not yielded results;
■ it would be a way of bringing to bear an informed obligation on the Government to provide adequate funding.

14.53   A standing body would offer the benefit of independence, but unless its recommendations were to be fully funded by Government, institutions might find they were unable to implement them. It is, therefore, inconsistent with the autonomy of financially responsible institutions and loses the benefits of local bargaining summarised above.

14.54   Whatever view may be taken of the merits of the different options, we do not believe that the issue of remuneration should be looked at in isolation. Significant changes to ways of working will be needed as higher education responds to changing needs and opportunities. These changes will necessarily affect the jobs which individuals are doing, the skills they require, and levels of remuneration. To the extent that higher levels are justified, there is the question of how institutions can meet the cost. The employment framework of all higher education staff, not just academics, needs to be addressed. We recognise the advantages of a fundamental forward-looking review of the framework for determining remuneration in the context of working practices.

Recommendation 50   **We recommend to the higher education employers that they appoint, after consultation with staff representatives, an independent review committee to report by April 1998 on the framework for determining pay and conditions of service. The Chairman should be appointed on the nomination of the Government.**

14.55   We suggest the following terms of reference for the review committee:
'In the light of the changes in higher education proposed in the National Committee of Inquiry's report, and the need to ensure the future wellbeing of higher education, to review and assess the options, and make recommendations for all staff in higher education on:
■ the framework for negotiating pay and terms and conditions of service;
■ whether pay levels, for all or any group, need adjustment;

with a view to achieving:
■ new ways of working as outlined in the National Committee's report;
■ a link between conditions of service and remuneration;
■ arrangements which respect the autonomy and diversity of institutions and the need of each to ensure its own financial wellbeing and the quality of its provision;
■ appropriate transitional arrangements.'

14.56   The individuals selected for membership of the review committee should be drawn from within and outside higher education. They would need to be familiar with modern employment practices, and those from higher education should be able to reflect the views of a range of staff, including those represented by unions and those not so represented. We would envisage the committee reporting to employers and informing the Government.

14.57   The terms of reference do not preclude the review committee proposing a standing review body, but we have not proposed that option because the review committee needs to carry out the work necessary to come to a conclusion as to the best way forward for the future wellbeing of the sector. Additionally, our long term vision is one of autonomous institutions taking increasing responsibility for determining their own futures. However, the recommendations of the review committee would provide an informed basis for subsequent negotiation.

Superannuation

14.58 Superannuation arrangements in higher education are not uniform: there are different schemes for different staff groups, and for different institutions. The main pension schemes for higher education academic staff are the Teachers' Superannuation Scheme (TSS) (and its Scottish equivalent STSS) and the Universities Superannuation Scheme (USS). Although consideration was given to bringing the two schemes together when the binary line was removed, there were considerable difficulties – most obviously the enormous one-off payment which would be required to buy all the TSS staff into the USS. While the existence of two schemes is not causing severe difficulties, it seems desirable that there should be progressive inclusion of all academic staff in a single scheme. This might be achieved after the next re-valuation of the TSS in 2001, when it is expected that employer contributions will increase to a level similar to that of USS. With the employer differential between the two schemes removed, all new entrants could be offered membership of the USS, so achieving, over time, the long term objective of a single system for academic staff.

Recommendation 51 **We recommend to the Government, institutions, and the representative bodies of higher education, that, over the long term, the superannuation arrangements for academic staff should be harmonised by directing all new entrants to the Universities Superannuation Scheme.**

Conclusion

14.59 In Chapter 3, we referred to the achievements in higher education over the last 30 years, and the commitment of staff in a period of declining resources. In the future, the contribution that **all** staff make to the quality of the student experience will need to be recognised and rewarded, and effective, sensitive, management strategies adopted to achieve the changes we anticipate. Higher education institutions are complex organisations, in receipt of large amounts of public funding. Effective management is crucial in ensuring quality, effectiveness and economy in the use of resources as well as proper accountability. These issues are considered in the next chapter.

Chapter 15

Management and governance of higher education institutions

15.1 In previous chapters we have explored the challenges for higher education over the next 20 years. We have advocated increasing and widening participation (Chapter 7); a new emphasis on learning and on defining threshold standards for awards (Chapter 10); new ways of funding excellence across the range of research (Chapter 11); a new understanding of the local and regional potential of higher education (Chapter 12); and we have emphasised the importance of more effective and imaginative staff policies and practices (Chapter 14). We have described these issues within the framework of a new compact for higher education, in which the Government, students, employers and institutions will each play their part. In this chapter, we turn to ways in which managers and governing bodies of institutions can best contribute to the work of higher education.

15.2 Our terms of reference asked us to consider how
'value for money and cost-effectiveness should be obtained in the use of resources'.

15.3 We consider in particular some of the steps institutions need to take to manage and govern themselves over the next twenty years in order to realise the ambitions which we believe they will share with us. The effectiveness of any organisation depends in the long term upon the effectiveness of its management and the arrangements for its governance. This applies particularly during periods of change and especially to higher education institutions in the years ahead. The quality of their management and governance will therefore be a matter for continuing attention.

15.4 Our recommendations on the management and governance of institutions are guided by three essential principles:
- institutional autonomy should be respected. Whilst we take it as axiomatic that government will set the policy framework for higher education nationally, we equally take it as axiomatic that the strategic direction and management of individual institutions should be vested wholly in the governance and management structure of autonomous universities and colleges;
- academic freedom within the law should be respected. By this we mean the respect for the disinterested pursuit of knowledge wherever it leads. This too is axiomatic, but needs to be managed responsibly by individual academics and institutions;
- institutional governance should be conducted openly and should be responsive to constituencies internal and external to the institution.

15.5 Whilst acting to support these principles, institutions should govern and manage themselves to obtain maximum efficiency and effectiveness.

15.6   Those from whom we received evidence demonstrated ways in which the management and governance arrangements now in place are working well and highlighted many achievements. But they also identified ways in which the arrangements could – and need to – be improved if the agenda defined in our report is to be tackled to best effect. This applies particularly to the use of resources in institutions, where sustained effort is required. It applies, too, to institutional governance, where often the arrangements tend to be complex and not well-understood by students, staff and those outside the institution, and do not necessarily seem designed to equip institutions well to address future challenges. We have considered two main issues:
■ improving the use and management of resources in institutions;
■ enabling governance to become more effective.

Improving the use and management of resources in institutions

15.7   We began by acknowledging the huge reduction in costs achieved by higher education in recent years and we express elsewhere our concern that an immediate further reduction could be damaging to the long term effectiveness of higher education. We make recommendations accordingly. Nevertheless, looking ahead to the next 20 years, a sustained effort to improve the effective and efficient use of resources by institutions is required to secure the long term future of an expanding higher education system. Institutions need to satisfy government, students and other funders that they are making a contribution to the total costs of higher education by continually seeking better value from their resources. This is a requirement in almost all aspects of national life and is part of the new compact with higher education. Here, we examine what has been achieved in recent years and some of the ways in which institutions can make the necessary further adjustments.

15.8   The demands on institutions' staff, estates, and equipment and other resources has increased markedly as the number of students has risen faster than the level of public funding. In some areas, such as libraries, this has caused severe problems for students. The efficient use of resources has been promoted by the Funding Bodies. For example, institutions share their strategic plans, including an estates strategy, with the three Higher Education Funding Councils, including an estates strategy; and the financial memoranda require institutions to secure value for money in the use of their assets and to follow a maintenance plan for their estates. Several institutions have developed ambitious projects to redevelop their estates, guided by the need to maximise efficiency in their utilisation and running costs as well as their suitability for new learning and teaching methods.

15.9   The efficiency gains achieved across higher education have only been possible because staff productivity has increased and because institutions are using all their resources more intensively. This increasing efficiency has reflected the contribution made through an increasingly professional approach to resource management. To maintain the quality of provision will require a continuing commitment. The National Audit Office (NAO) has noted that institutions have achieved improvements in value for money, but that scope for further improvement remains.[1] It told us that institutions *'need to apply a wide range of management skills and experience if they are to survive and prosper, particularly at a time of tight financial constraints'.* [2]

15.10   The evidence about how much has been achieved – and how much more could be achieved – varies. We were told that *'the sector considers that it is both sensitive to maximising cost effectiveness and is deploying advanced managerial disciplines and techniques so as to extract the highest efficiency levels'.*[3] The international evidence suggests that the reduction of costs has been pursued more vigorously in the United Kingdom (UK) than elsewhere in recent years, but that, our costs are comparable with those generally found overseas. There is also a difference of opinion about the extent of the achievements and the potential for further efficiencies. Those from outside the sector tend to believe that there is further scope for efficiency gains. Some of these respondents are prepared to countenance more systematic sharing of resources and the rationalisation of institutions as a way of improving efficiency. There are certainly examples where institutions continue to adopt traditional and isolated approaches rather than taking a forward-looking, strategic assessment of their developing requirements. Experience in other sectors suggests that, to a varying extent, institutions might be able to move to a different cost curve (that is, where the unit costs of teaching become significantly lower because of a different use of resources) were they able and willing to adopt more radical models for some of their work. This is explained in more detail in Appendix 2.

Staff

15.11   Staffing is the largest single cost to institutions, at about 58 per cent of all expenditure. Increased participation has been achieved largely through pressure on the ratio of teaching staff to students. It is true that much higher ratios are to be found in a number of other countries, but the UK compensates for the comparatively short length of its degree programmes by the quality of provision and high completion rates. We do not consider that further incremental increases in this ratio can be consistent with a resumption in growth and maintained standards without the development of new learning and teaching methods. In particular, continuing pressure on the ratio will be dysfunctional unless the benefits from the extended use of Communications and Information Technology are realised.

15.12   We have discussed elsewhere (Chapter 14) the increased commitment and improved management which are necessary for staff development and training, especially in the practice of teaching and the management of learning. In learning and teaching, more institutions would gain from a more corporate approach in which staff with management responsibilities are fully engaged and able to contribute. Whilst we would expect some differences in practice, few institutions appear to have undertaken any rigorous analysis or comparative studies of the best approach to delivering their learning objectives and the resources required. Too often, programme directors and heads of department have inadequate training and are not engaged sufficiently in the quest to achieve greater effectiveness in the use of resources. The National Audit Office (NAO) comments both that *'the problem may be compounded by the substantial delegation of decision-making within institutions'*[4] and that *'a key issue has often been the need to enhance the contribution that academic departments within institutions can make to help the institutions to achieve corporate improvements in value for money'.*[5] This suggests a need for training and information for those academics with management responsibilities.

15.13   The whole approach to programme design and the most effective means of delivering programme objectives needs the constructive involvement of institutional management to promote best practice. Management, at all levels, needs to put greater emphasis on resource management and ensure that the necessary investments are made in the measures designed to achieve longer term gains. A series of studies of different practices across institutions would contribute to thinking in institutions, and subsequently to the development of useful benchmarks. Institutions should review current departmental approaches to teaching techniques in order to identify the relative costs of differing forms of delivery, with the longer term objective of inter-institutional costs comparators and benchmarks.

Estates

15.14   Institutions' expenditure on buildings and estates represents 12 per cent of total expenditure across higher education, the second biggest single component of their costs. The estate has been valued at £30 billion. It is thus relevant to explore every option for managing these assets well. The potential for further growth in participation, and the implications of the progressive extension of lifelong learning, resource-based learning and different learning and teaching methods, give extra incentives to do so. Mature learners in particular, but also, to an increasing extent, younger people, will in future want to take their programmes in shorter and more intermittent blocks, irrespective of conventional academic terms. Increasing numbers of students will need access to central facilities outside traditional working hours. Consequently, the prevailing model of a standard academic year, a single admissions round and a long summer vacation will be increasingly inappropriate for students and institutions. Imaginative solutions will therefore continue to be required to tackle the constraint that can be presented by a particular configuration or use of space.

15.15   Estimates (based in part on work by the National Audit Office [NAO]) suggest that the utilisation of teaching space is currently about 20 to 30 per cent. The NAO acknowledges that there **are** legitimate constraints, including the need for specialist accommodation for certain activities, other demands on student and staff time and the suitability of institutions' estates. Whilst the NAO states that improvements can be made, it acknowledges that a target of 50 per cent would be challenging.[6] If utilisation could be raised to 35 per cent, which the Association of University Directors of Estates has suggested is efficient, this would support a significant increase in student numbers broadly within the present approach to the academic year.[7]

15.16   We considered two options to promote the highest possible level of estates usage. The first is notional capital charging. This has been developed in the Health Service. It rests on charging institutions a notional rent on their publicly-funded assets and redistributing the surplus from asset-rich to asset-poor institutions. However, there are a number of difficulties, including: legal doubts about the applicability of the approach to some of the assets involved; serious difficulties in properly attributing the source of the funding for certain assets; the absence of a uniform basis of asset valuation; and doubts about the possibility of uniform implementation, given the sector's diversity and the flexible way in which it has begun to use its accommodation.

15.17   Unpublished research by the Higher Education Funding Council for England (HEFCE) concluded that capital charging was unlikely to offer sufficiently large gains over the current approaches already being encouraged and developed within individual institutions and that any gains would not outweigh the costs of implementation. We agree with this view.

15.18   The second option is to extend the academic year. Those who have advocated this option in the past have done so largely on the basis of the apparent anomaly of institutions in which full-time undergraduate teaching, traditionally the primary purpose of an institution as well as the major use of space, conventionally takes place for only 24 to 36 weeks a year. Of course, this is to some extent a partial view: institutions **do** operate throughout the year, with important activities taking place in the absence of students. Many of these activities make a substantial financial contribution to their budgets, and institutions already often teach extensively outside conventional 'office hours'. Increasingly, advocacy of change rests as much on the decreasing educational suitability of the model of the traditional academic year as on the possible opportunity costs to higher education.

15.19   Extending the teaching year would deliver teaching in more hours, days and weeks of the year. Particularly for part-time students, more teaching at weekends and in the evening would reflect students' increasing employment during their studies. It would allow the possibility of a longer first semester or the introduction of three semesters. We noted international practice, in which the Netherlands, for example, has a teaching year of 42 weeks (see Appendix 5). We were mindful of the detailed consideration given to this matter in reports by Lord Flowers[8] and Professor Maxwell Irvine.[9] Their studies concluded that there are genuine difficulties in further extending the teaching year. These include: avoiding an unreasonable lengthening of academics' working year; respecting the time needed for research and other academic activities; effecting parallel changes in the admissions timetable; the possible loss by some institutions of valuable summer conference income; student preferences; and that some mature students with dependants would be likely to find summer study particularly problematic. We acknowledge these difficulties, some of which lie largely within the power of higher education to tackle and some of which do not.

15.20   Pilots of a revised academic year have been run recently at two English institutions and one in Northern Ireland and over a longer period at two Scottish institutions. They are designed mainly for part-time students and work-based learning and are therefore limited in the scale and nature of the activity. Further experiments have probably been discouraged by the current cap on full-time undergraduate student numbers and the current funding methodology, which have left institutions little headroom to finance summer teaching. The experience suggests that unit costs increase initially, and that savings accrue later, when student numbers increase. These institutions also suggest that a general summer semester is not sustainable without the critical mass of students necessary to ensure a positive learning experience for them and realistic unit costs for institutions.

15.21 However, there may be more persuasive imperatives in the future. Financially, in the absence of public funding for additions to the estate, institutions will need to consider where the balance of advantage lies in the span of the year over which their assets are used for teaching. Educationally, there may also be student demand for change and it is likely that Communications and Information Technology will alter dramatically the way space is used. Given these factors, major expansion of the estate across the sector might not prove a good or necessary long term investment and different ways of using space are likely to emerge.

15.22 Institutions are already introducing other flexible learning opportunities for those not on traditional three or four year programmes. This trend will continue. For example, summer teaching could be used for bridging modules from one level or subject to another, repeat modules, remedial work, access activity, additional modules, or 'outreach' and 'inreach' for school pupils.

15.23 Summer teaching will need to be developed sensitively and with careful preparation and incentives for the staff involved. There will be difficult logistical issues in matching staff deployment to student requirements and in balancing the various staff responsibilities throughout the year. Costs and benefits will need to be broadly equivalent. An extended academic year need not mean that teaching is extended throughout the year for each academic. Many will welcome more flexible learning and teaching patterns in which there will be different ways of organising the time for research and other activities.

15.24 We therefore support the Flowers and Irvine conclusions that an effort of will in higher education could – and should – be applied to address many of the difficulties identified in extending the academic year more systematically. Different models for using the full year and institutions' estates more intensively will maximise student choice and increase lifelong learning opportunities. These may be particularly relevant to institutions which are not heavily engaged in research, although we would expect all institutions to give attention to the possibilities We consider that, over the medium term, institutions should examine, in consultation with students and staff, new approaches to the academic year, with a view to finding ways of better meeting students' diverse needs and increasing participation without a proportionate increase in costs. Later on, we also propose that institutions review this matter as part of the review of their strategic objectives and progress which we recommend below.

Equipment and other resources

15.25 There is continued scope for further incremental change in the use of other resources for learning, teaching and research, both within and between institutions. We make recommendations about collaboration in Chapter 16. There is considerable variation in the way institutions are using these other resources and the costs that they incur.

This suggests that some institutions, if not the sector as a whole, can achieve more. There are a number of persuasive examples:

- treasury management strategies, which manage cash flows, banking, and short and long term savings, are only in place in a minority of institutions. The resulting variation in costs is considerable, with bank charges per £ million turnover ranging from £95 to £1,143 and average rates of interest from one and a half per cent below the base rate upwards;[10]

- procurement strategies vary considerably. These can make a 25 per cent difference in costs.[11] It is estimated that institutions could save five per cent of their non-pay expenditure through better purchasing, equivalent to £30 million in the pre-1992 universities alone;[12]

- it has been estimated that energy and utilities expenditure could yield savings of ten to 20 per cent;[13]

- many institutions are not good at attributing the costs of research. The National Audit Office (NAO) found that a quarter of all institutions did not know the full overhead costs of their research contract work and were therefore not in a position to know whether or not they were recovering their costs.[14]

15.26   To tackle these matters, institutions need better basic information and analytical tools for allocating to users the costs of accommodation and other overheads. The NAO told us that *'the application of space management techniques at institutions in Wales was variable with, for instance, only one institution having a full system of computerised central timetabling and one charging users for the space they occupied'*.[15] There are considerable differences in the comparative costs of undergraduate teaching, but little real understanding or assessment of the costs of different forms of delivery, and no particular connection between differences in the pattern of spend and the particular specification for the student.[16]

15.27   The recommendations we have made earlier (Chapter 11) should ensure that research is supported by an adequate infrastructure. Such changes will however, only achieve the results necessary if institutions themselves have a thorough understanding of research costs and if the internal costing of research and budget allocations are transparent to staff. This is not the case in all institutions.

Recommendation 52   **We recommend to institutions that, over the medium term, they develop and implement arrangements which allow staff and external bodies to have access to and understand the true costs of research.**

15.28   We have already recommended in Chapter 14 that heads of department are helped to develop management expertise and skills to help them contribute to securing value for money. We also make recommendations in Chapter 16 to encourage collaboration to improve educational effectiveness and efficiency.

Communications and Information Technology in managing institutions

15.29   We explored the potential of Communications and Information Technology (C&IT) in learning and teaching in Chapter 13. The full potential of C&IT in managing institutions has also yet to be realised. There are likely to be significant cost benefits from its increased use. We looked at how far institutions have systems in place and are currently getting the maximum benefit from them. A survey conducted for us by the Universities and Colleges Information Systems Association (UCISA) showed that over 75 per cent of the 50 respondent institutions have in place an integrated C&IT system in each of the areas of personnel management, finance and accounting, and student registration. However, the prevalence of such systems falls markedly in the areas of managing research and consultancy, institutional statistics and estates management. In the last of these categories, only 13 of the institutions have systems in place, even though, as we showed earlier, this represents the second largest cost to institutions. The institutions in the survey also told us that they are not exploiting their systems fully, and are probably using only about 40 to 60 per cent of the capacity of the systems in those areas where utilisation is highest.[17]

15.30   Institutions seem to us to lack ready recourse to relevant advice on best practice; to have varying standards of hardware and software; to have varying understanding and commitment by senior management; and often not to have equipped their middle managers in academic departments with important management information and training in using C&IT. Despite these difficulties, institutions report many effective and important uses of C&IT. For example, digital recording of student information is making storage, update, and retrieval easier; and electronic mail provides staff and students with instant dissemination of decisions, timetable changes, and vital information on health and safety matters.

15.31   Over the next 20 years, C&IT will provide increasing opportunities to improve institutional effectiveness and efficiency. A continuing challenge to institutional managers will be to realise the potential and to ensure that the systems they introduce are used to full effect. Furthermore, there will be new and essential tasks that institutions will be unable to perform without significantly enhanced usage of their hardware and software. Some of the other developments advocated in our report will depend on institutions securing fuller benefits from C&IT in their management. For example:
- institutions and those that fund their teaching are likely to want to know more about patterns of student participation and achievement;
- tracking student progress through one institution, or several, and throughout lifelong learning, will assume a greater significance;
- the single 'learner record' which we advocated in Chapter 8 will require better exploitation of the common language capacity of C&IT across institutions, within and outside the higher education sector;
- the use of on-line registration of students and the use of 'smart cards' to secure access to facilities and, in some cases, payment for them by students, are likely to proliferate;
- the need to demonstrate maximum value for money to a wider range of stakeholders, as part of the new compact, will demand better ways of analysing costs and the way institutional resources are used;
- maximising the use of space by developing fully computerised central timetabling.

Recommendation 53   We recommend that the Committee of Vice-Chancellors and Principals, in collaboration with other institutional representative bodies, reviews the functions of the Universities and Colleges Information Systems Association to ensure that it can promote the implementation of Communications and Information Technology in management information systems.

Enabling governance to become more effective

15.32   The recommendations we have made in the first half of this chapter depend, at a strategic level, on effective institutional governance. Institutional governance differs from institutional management: it is concerned with deciding overall policy, guidance and review rather than executive management or operational delivery. As the Committee of University Chairmen's guidance for governors states

> 'institutions of higher education are legally independent corporate institutions which have a common purpose of providing teaching and undertaking research. The council or board of governors is the executive governing body of the institution and carries responsibility for ensuring the effective management of the institution and for planning its future development. It has ultimate responsibility for all the affairs of the institution'.[18]

15.33   This description of a governing body makes clear that it is the ultimate decision-making body in an institution. These decisions reflect its responsibility for the institution's strategic direction, reputation, financial wellbeing, the well being of staff and students, and, in association with the Senate or Academic Board, for establishing and maintaining high standards of academic conduct and probity. The governing body should ensure that accountability for implementation is delegated appropriately; that there are suitable fora for stakeholders to express their opinions; and (as we recommend below) that it reviews and reports on progress against the strategic direction. As bodies with public responsibilities, there are also important accountabilities. The National Audit Office (NAO), focusing very much on financial accountability and probity, advised us:

> 'the council or board of governors of a higher education institution is the executive governing body and is responsible for ensuring that the conditions made in relation to all forms of Government grant are met. In particular, governors are required to ensure the overall financial health of the institution, the proper stewardship of public funds, value for money in spending and the adequacy of arrangements for account and audit.'[19]

15.34   In making our recommendations, we are conscious that the current structures of institutional governance vary considerably across the sector. They have different histories and circumstances, which we respect. We have no intention of seeking to bring about uniformity. Governance arrangements should continue to reflect the diversity of institutions in the higher education sector. But, having looked across the current diversity of structures of governance, we **do** consider that often institutions may be able to achieve greater clarity and transparency in their governance structures, as well as greater effectiveness in the way they govern themselves. This we regard as their decision-making requirement. They also need to have in place mechanisms which ensure they are in touch with those inside and outside the institution who can contribute to and have a legitimate interest in its work. This we regard as their consultative obligation.

15.35 Institutional governing bodies have responded with vigour to the growing external expectations of higher education, particularly for increased transparency, probity, accountability and efficiency. The recent instances of difficulty have been few and we share the view of the Committee on Standards in Public Life (the Nolan Committee) that these do not represent any wider evidence of failure.[20] Governors have been helped considerably in interpreting their responsibilities by the guidance for governors prepared by the Committee of Chairmen of governing bodies in England and Wales[21] and also in Scotland.[22] It is important that this guidance is kept up-to-date.

15.36 Higher education has benefited greatly during the last decade from the work of its governing bodies and the leadership of its vice chancellors and principals. Their achievements have had insufficient recognition. We are concerned to place on record how much is due to the way they have responded to pressing national needs to expand higher education, maintain standards and yet work with a continually reducing unit of resource. Their task has made particularly heavy demands on the office-bearers in governing bodies who generously give of their time and expertise on a voluntary basis: this has made a real difference. Our concern is to make proposals to enhance the effectiveness of the framework within they work without presuming to assert that one approach is right for all institutions in all circumstances.

A code of practice for institutional governance

15.37 However, we recognise that the recommendations in the rest of our report suggest a degree of change for institutions more profound even than that experienced during the recent expansion: to sustain standards; become still more cost-effective; put greater emphasis on learning and on teaching quality; be better attuned to the external environment; and extend provision to new student populations. They therefore need excellent governance, to steer the institution towards its strategic direction. Whilst many of the present governance arrangements have served institutions well, we believe these arrangements merit review. The guidance for governing body members referred to in paragraph 15.35 has been invaluable. But we do not think it addresses a number of important structural matters; nor that it emphasises sufficiently the importance of academic governance and governors' responsibility for their own performance and that of their institutions. These assume a greater significance in the light of our report. We consider that these matters mean there is merit in deriving a code of practice for governance, and that institutions should report in their annual report on their compliance with the code.

Purposes of the code

15.38 The purposes of the code we propose are straightforward. First, to ensure that institutions' governing bodies can make their decisions in a way which is effective, transparent and timely. Secondly, to provide a basis for familiarity with the governance arrangements within institutions. Thirdly, to ensure there is appropriate membership of the ultimate decision-making body. Fourthly, to ensure that governing bodies can meet their obligations to their wider constituencies inside and outside the institution. The code therefore aims to assist institutions with what we regard as their decision-making requirement and their consultative obligation.

Components of the code

15.39   The code of practice for institutional governance which we propose has the following components:
- unambiguous identity of the governing body;
- clarity of decision making;
- appropriate membership and size of the governing body;
- arrangements for engaging formally with external constituencies;
- a rolling review of the effectiveness of the governing body and institution;
- reporting annually on institutional performance;
- arrangements to address grievances by students and staff;
- effective academic governance.

Status of the code

15.40   We stressed earlier our commitment to institutional diversity and autonomy. The proposed code of practice does not prescribe particular arrangements to be adopted uniformly by institutions. Rather, we urge that institutions ensure they have in place arrangements which suit their own individual circumstances and address each of the components; and which thereby enable them to demonstrate that the components of the code are in place. There will be many different ways of doing this, to suit the history and aspirations of each institution. To emphasise the importance we attach to governance matters, we believe the code should be a priority and that institutions should report on the ways in which they are complying with it in their annual reports. We say more about this below.

15.41   We believe that the components of the code express the current obligations on members of governing bodies and do not add to those obligations.

Unambiguous identity of the governing body

15.42   The first component of the code concerns effective, transparent and timely decision-making by governing bodies. This requires that each institution understands where the ultimate authority for decision-making lies within the institution and therefore that the identity of the governing body is unambiguous. Correspondingly, it is important that the accountability for decisions taken on behalf of the institution is clearly understood. Otherwise, the decision-making requirements upon institutions cannot be met. Authority and accountability rest with the governing body. However, in a number of institutions in England there is doubt about where the ultimate decision-making authority lies. This is particularly so in some of the pre-1992 universities where the Charter and Statutes were prepared for another age. In many of these, there is a Court and a Council (using the English terminology). In some of these, the Court arguably retains the decision-making powers and this appears to us to be increasingly anachronistic. In some, the respective duties and powers of the Court and the Council are not always clearly defined or understood in the contemporary context. We think this is unsustainable.

Recommendation 54 **We recommend that the Government, together with representative bodies, should, within three years, establish whether the identity of the governing body in each institution is clear and undisputed. Where it is not, the Government should take action to clarify the position, ensuring that the Council is the ultimate decision-making body, and that the Court has a wider representative role, to inform decision-making but not to take decisions.**

Clarity of decision making

15.43 In an environment of change, when speed of decision making can be critical, the need for clarity of responsibility for decision making extends beyond the governing body itself. This will contribute to achieving the second purpose of the code. One responsibility of governing bodies is to ensure that the accountabilities of individuals and of committees which support institutional decision making are well defined. This needs to include a clear understanding of which powers are retained by the governing body and which are devolved to other committees. We say more about academic decision making later in this Chapter.

Appropriate membership and size of the governing body

15.44 The third purpose of the code concerns ensuring appropriate membership of the governing body. We heard much evidence, and we are strongly of the view, that the quality of membership of the governing body is crucial. Legitimate institutional governance requires that members of the governing body are appointed on the basis of merit, taking account of any necessary balance of expertise and interests and the institution's requirements. Members are individually and collectively responsible for the decisions taken by the governing body. Institutions' evidence to us strongly endorsed the role of lay members in governing bodies, such that *the clear view is that such a presence is valuable and indeed could be more utilised by institutions themselves*.[23] We endorse the findings of the Committee on Standards in Public Life (the Nolan Committee), and would commend to all institutions that *best practice in appointing members of governing bodies is to select on the basis of merit and skills subject to the need to achieve a balance of relevant skills and backgrounds on the board*.[24] This means that governing body membership should not be determined by external appointments or offices held but on the expertise and capacity of the individual.

15.45 Effective governing bodies will have a majority of lay members. They will need nominations committees or an equivalent mechanism to ensure they find members of the highest individual calibre. We would urge employers to contribute to the work of governing bodies by responding sympathetically to approaches for their staff to serve as members and by helping them to make a meaningful contribution. Governing bodies will also want to ensure a balance of new and more experienced members. We therefore consider that governing body members should not serve for more than two terms, usually three to four years each, unless they also hold office. Once appointed, members must act in the best interests of the institution and not as delegates of a particular constituency. There should be a register of members' interests.

15.46   Effective governing bodies will also, to have legitimacy, include as full members some who are drawn from the students and staff of the institution. In some institutions, this is currently optional. We also heard of some institutions where student and staff members find it difficult to discharge their responsibilities towards the institution rather than the groups from which they are drawn. They may need training to help them become confident and effective governors.

15.47   The appointment of a person to chair a governing body is obviously crucial. Particular arrangements are required. We consider that nomination should usually be made by a committee of members excluding the current holder of the post, and the appointment made by the whole governing body. External involvement in this process, for example, of a senior layperson from another governing body, can be useful. Some appointments are subject to annual confirmation, within the span of a notional term of office which lasts three to four years. There can be advantage in retaining an individual as to chair the governing body for more than one term, but governing bodies should not make such a decision routinely. We can see no circumstances in which an individual should chair a governing body for more than two terms of three to four years, although this could reasonably follow service as a ordinary member.

Recommendation 55   **We recommend to the Government that it takes action so that:**
- **individuals may not serve as members of a governing body for more than two terms, unless they also hold office;**
- **it is a requirement for the governing body at each institution to include student and staff membership and a majority of lay members;**
- **an individual may not chair a governing body for more than two terms of office.**

15.48   The influence of the vice chancellor over institutions is great. Consequently, arrangements for the appointment of the vice chancellor, who is sometimes the only executive member of the governing body, must command public confidence. The individual appointed must command the confidence of the governing body, and the Academic Board or Senate, which they will chair. Selecting the vice chancellor and helping him or her to achieve the institution's goals is perhaps the most important single task of a governing body. Also, governing bodies need to ensure that the vice chancellor is enabled to be fully effective in the leadership of the institution, has clear objectives and is held accountable for their achievement. Provision of this clear framework of authority and accountability is a duty of a governing body. Without it, the institution is disadvantaged and its performance can be adversely affected.

15.49   It follows from the decision making responsibilities of the governing body that governance needs to be vested in a body whose size is conducive to effective decision-making. We do not believe that, over the next 20 years, very large governing bodies will be conducive to the proper exercise of individual and collective responsibility, to individual liability or to institutional effectiveness. Currently, there are wide differences in the size of the governing bodies across the sector. The Further and Higher Education

Act 1992 sets a membership of between 12 and 25 for the governing bodies of the 1992 universities. We think there are very good reasons for governing bodies not to be over-large, specifically, above the range of 12 to 25 members prescribed in the Further and Higher Education Act 1992. We think, therefore, a ceiling of 25 should be the general practice for institutions. Where a governing body exceeds that number, it should consider this matter as part of the periodic review we recommend below.

15.50   For the pre-1992 institutions, where larger governing bodies or their equivalent are common, we were advised that it can be difficult to make changes to the size of the governing body, even when the institution might wish to do so. This is in part because the sensitivities of individuals and external bodies can be involved and in part because the institution would require an amendment to be made to its charter. This can require the agreement of both the court and the council. Also, once a proposal is made by an institution, the procedures for it to be agreed involve the Department for Education and Employment and the Privy Council. This can all be very slow.

Recommendation 56   **We recommend that the Government takes the lead, with the Privy Council, in discussions with institutional representatives to introduce, within three years, revised procedures capable of responding more quickly to an institution requesting a change in the size of its governing body. The intention should be to ensure a response within one year.**

Arrangements for engaging formally with external constituencies

15.51   The final purpose of the Code is to ensure that institutions meet their obligations to their wider constituencies. They therefore need to have in place a mechanism by which external constituencies can contribute their opinion and advice in a systematic and transparent way. Institutions' decisions are likely to be better-informed where they have the capacity to draw on, and to take account of, the views of these constituencies. The Committee on Standards in Public Life discussed this more general need for *'responsiveness to the community'*[25] and the guidance by the Committee of University Chairmen expresses this need when it states that *'ways should be found by which the public or the local community can comment on matters to do with the university that concern them'.*[26] In our view, the importance of this engagement with local and regional communities, and those who can speak on their behalf, will increase in the future.

15.52   Lay membership of the governing body is one way of recognising the value of such engagement. This, however, is not sufficient. Institutions will need a mechanism which provides an interface with the wider community. Many institutions already reflect this in their governance structure and practice. For many pre-1992 institutions, this is done through the court (or council in Scotland) which includes in its membership individuals from local communities, agencies and organisations. Several of the 1992 universities have put in place equivalent arrangements. There are a number of useful models. Some are 'membership bodies' in which particular interests are represented and others are open to anyone with a legitimate interest. In our view, an effective advisory Court or equivalent should complement an effective council or governing body (in the English terminology). Whilst the Council or governing body must be responsible for the strategic direction and decisions of the institution, the Court, or similar body, can act as a sounding-board and mirror for the institution in its relationships with the wider community of interests.

15.53   As part of the review of the effectiveness of an institution and its governing body, which we describe below, each institution should therefore ensure that it has in place a mechanism or body which enables it to draw on the views of relevant constituencies to inform its strategic development. Such a body could have a standing membership which reflects relevant constituencies external to the institution, although other models may work well. In the pre-1992 universities in England and Wales we expect this role to be taken by the court, although its membership may need to be reviewed. For such a court to have public confidence, the membership should be drawn very largely from the external communities with which the institution interacts. The powers of such a body should include being able to ask for information, to comment, to advise, or to invite the governing body to review a decision. This body should not have any decision-making powers.

A review of the effectiveness of the governing body and of the institution

15.54   The performance of an institution is at the centre of a governing body's responsibilities. A powerful regulatory framework is already in place, through the financial memoranda between the institutions and the funding bodies and a range of audit requirements, with which a governing body must comply. But we believe it is necessary to recommend a new and stronger focus within institutions, in which governors periodically review the performance of the governing body and the institution across a wider spectrum than that captured by the current regulatory framework. Institutions should put in place an all-embracing and systematic review, involving the senate or academic board, so that, over a five-year period, the following strategic matters are reviewed:
- a participation strategy which addresses participation by those under-represented in the institution (see Chapter 7);
- a reassessment of the staff development strategy (Chapter 14);
- determining and reassessing a formal framework for engaging with external consistencies (this chapter);
- the size of the governing body and its effectiveness for decision-making (this chapter);
- arrangements for making academic awards in the institution's name (this chapter).

15.55   The review as a whole is likely to be more effective if governing bodies adopt a set of defined, qualitative, quantitative, internal and external indicators which they find appropriate to the mission of the individual institution. We do not envisage a lengthy set of prescriptive indicators imposed across the sector and we acknowledge the efforts made over a number of years to produce definitive measures of institutional efficiency and effectiveness. Nonetheless, each institution would gain from adopting its own set of key indicators by which it can measure the institution's progress against its objectives and through which the governing body can be confident about its own performance. These indicators should include teaching and research; financial health; human resources; student and external feedback; commercial activities; the institution's estates, infrastructure and other services. Benchmarks which enable governing bodies to compare their achievements with those of similar institutions, some of which may be international, will also be essential to ensure that UK institutions are able to aspire to world class standards. Those with governance responsibilities should have access to external guidance and expertise to assist them in carrying out such a review.

Recommendation 57

We recommend that each governing body should systematically review, at least once every five years, with appropriate external assistance and benchmarks:
- **its own effectiveness and, where there is in excess of 25 members, show good reason why a larger body is needed for its effectiveness;**
- **the arrangements for discharging its obligations to the institution's external constituencies;**
- **all major aspects of the institution's performance, including the participation strategy.**

The outcomes of the review should be published in an institution's annual report. The Funding Bodies should make such a review a condition of public funding.

Recommendation 58

We recommend that, over the medium term, to assist governing bodies in carrying out their systematic reviews Funding Bodies and representative bodies develop appropriate performance indicators and benchmarks for families of institutions with similar characteristics and aspirations.

Reporting annually on institutional performance

15.56   Pressures for greater openness are considerable and should be respected. As stated in the analysis of evidence to us, *'institutions are in receipt of public money and provide public services. Internal governance should be open and accountable'*.[27] In our view, institutions' annual reports can be an invaluable source of information about institutions' performance. Company annual reports could be one model to underpin greater consistency in the information made available by institutions. Following corporate sector experience, they could also usefully report on how an institution's governing body is complying with the components of the code of practice.[28] For example, they should identify any members whose terms of membership exceed the parameters described above, and give reasons where this occurs. In this way, the governing body's review, as reported in the annual report, will form an essential part of the accountability of the institution towards its constituencies, and could usefully be made public at meetings of the wider consultative body described in paragraph 53.

Recommendation 59

We recommend to the Funding Bodies that they require institutions, as a condition of public funding, to publish annual reports which describe the outcomes of the governing body's review and report on other aspects of compliance with the code of practice.

Arrangements to address complaints by students

15.57   Inevitably, there will be occasions when students complaint to an institution, for example, complaints about academic judgements of their work or the quality of their experience. It is essential for good governance and achievement of the first, second and fourth purposes of the code, that all complaints are dealt with fairly, transparently and in a timely way. (We say more about complaints by staff in paragraphs 15.66 and 15.67.)

15.58   We were told that complaints from students are likely to increase, particularly as assessment criteria become more explicit and student expectations and financial commitments increase.[29] We noted the evidence of increasing disputes between institutions and their students, about both academic and non-academic matters, including litigation[30]; and concerns from staff and students about the way in which some cases have been handled.[31]

15.59   A working party set up by the Committee of Vice-Chancellors and Principals (CVCP) has undertaken some detailed work, focusing on those complaints from students which do not involve academic judgements. We have not sought to duplicate its careful efforts. Our chief concern is that students' complaints are – and are seen to be – taken seriously. When the internal procedures within an institution are exhausted, the student should have access to an independent individual not involved in the original decision, who can review the way the case has been handled and, in non-academic matters, the decision that has been taken. Where the complaint is particularly serious, the independent individual should be drawn from outside the institution. These procedures need to be accessible, widely understood by staff and students and operated equitably and in a timely manner. They are not intended to involve disproportionate costs or staff time for institutions. We support the use of reconciliation and possibly formal arbitration. We also urge that institutions report on the use made of the procedures from time to time in their annual report. If such procedures are adopted throughout the sector, we think an 'ombuds'-style function is not required. We urge institutions to review their current procedures in the light of the CVCP working party report and our report.

Recommendation 60   **We recommend to institutions that, over the next two years, they review and, if necessary, amend their arrangements for handling complaints from students, to ensure that: they reflect the principles of natural justice; they are transparent and timely; they include procedures for reconciliation and arbitration; they include an independent, external element; and they are managed by a senior member of staff.**

Effective academic governance

15.60   Effective academic governance is essential to the vitality of our higher education institutions and to the individual and collective maintenance of standards by the institutions. It rests on:
- academic freedom within the law, properly understood and combined with academic responsibility;
- rigorous attention to the standard of awards made in an institution's name and the procedures by which they are awarded;
- suitable provision in employment contracts for 'whistleblowing'.

15.61   Looking first at academic freedom, the Education Reform Act 1988 and guidance in the Model Articles of Government define individual academic freedom as: *'freedom within the law to question and test received wisdom and to put forward new ideas and controversial and unpopular opinions, without placing themselves in jeopardy of losing their jobs'.*[32]

15.62   This formulation endeavours to capture in law something which we believe to be fundamental to higher education. The issue can be complex but the underlying principles may be stated simply. These are that:

- individual academic freedom requires from society some basic commitment and support *'to sustain an environment within which academic freedom might be effectively exercised'*[33] and therefore to support research or publication even where this is controversial or unpopular. But there is nonetheless no such thing as an absolute entitlement to public funding to pursue any idea chosen by any academic;

- individual and collective academic freedom confers responsibilities as well as rights. Within their institution or discipline, academics should be bound by proper regard for their colleagues and by the usual rules of professional academic engagement;

- outside the institution or discipline, individual academics, as well as their institutions, share a duty of accountability, both for their work and as stewards of public resources. There is a duty to explain publicly and to professional and academic peers what is being attempted and achieved with those resources.

15.63   The Committee on Standards in Public Life (the Nolan Committee) reported the view that *'the culture of debate and question, so fundamental to teaching and scholarship (and equally helpful for high standards of conduct) continued to be taken very seriously in the vast majority of institutions'*.[34] Some of those giving evidence to us suggested that the scope of individual academic freedom has contracted in recent years as a result of growing pressures on the availability of public funds and the necessity to account more clearly for the use of those funds. In our view, academic freedom is alive and well but must continue to be respected on the basis set out here, within the law.

15.64   Secondly, we looked at the attention given to the standards of awards made in institutions' names. As we show in Chapter 16, higher education institutions are significantly defined by their capacity to make academic awards which have national currency and bear their name. Successful institutions are characterised by a full and mutually respectful partnership between academic and non-academic members of the institution, in which the academic members of each institution individually and collectively take full responsibility for maintaining the standards of those awards. In both the pre-1992 and 1992 universities these responsibilities are vested by charter or statute in senates and academic boards. Whilst members of the academic board or senate carry particular responsibilities, these are shared by those involved in other bodies and committees within the institution, including examination boards, research boards, faculty committees and validation panels. A duty of care applies to the exercise of powers to make all awards made in an institution's name.

15.65   We have been disturbed by the few instances where audit and other investigations have shown this duty of care to have broken down, and where the proper procedures have not been adhered to. The powers relating to an institution's academic work, clearly vested in senates or academic boards should not be bypassed by senior managers or the governing body. Academic boards and senates must ensure that they have a clear account of their responsibilities to guide their decisions and behaviour, that their members are clear about their responsibilities, individually and collectively, and that this is respected by the governing body. Academic boards and senates, in their contribution to the review of institutional performance described earlier, should periodically review their arrangements for making all awards in the name of the institution, including those offered through partnership and franchise arrangements in the UK and overseas.

15.66 Thirdly, we considered suitable provision in employment contracts for what is commonly known as 'whistleblowing', that is, where an individual member of staff feels so strongly that important matters of legitimate wider concern are going astray within the institution's senior management or governance that he or she decides to bring them to a wider audience. We noted the perception that some institutions have developed excessive secrecy about matters which are of legitimate public interest. Bodies representing academic staff expressed to us a concern about a shift which they perceive in management emphasis within institutions. This is said to have *'brought in its wake a potential diminution of academic freedom such that individual staff are less free to speak out on matters in ways which might be held to be injurious to their institution'*.[35]

15.67 We support the findings of the Committee on Standards in Public Life (the Nolan Committee) the finding that individual members of staff (not only academic members) should be able to speak freely within the law about matters relevant to the academic operation of the institution and should be protected when they do so. 'Whistleblowing' within the law where it seeks to expose honestly judged malpractice or wrongdoing should never be a disciplinary matter. The use of confidentiality clauses, which seek to prevent individuals from speaking out for these purposes, have no place within higher education institutions, other than in exceptional instances where commercial confidentiality may be at stake. They are contrary to the public interest when they seek to inhibit exposure of maladministration or malpractice with public funds. But in our view this is no different, in principle, from the conduct of other public services and, as in those services, there should remain an important constraint on individuals: they must exercise this freedom *'lawfully, without malice and in the public interest'*.[36] We endorse the Nolan Committee's recommendation that institutions review the use of confidentiality clauses and restrict their use to cases of clear commercial confidentiality. Institutions would also be well-advised to have in place arrangements which give confidence to staff in responding to their serious concerns or complaints about the conduct of the institution's governance or senior management.

Conclusion

15.68   In this chapter we have paid tribute to the efforts of staff, managers and governors of higher education institutions in their use of resources in recent years, but we have highlighted the scope for further improvements. We have also proposed a code of practice for governors, which would serve to clarify and consolidate some of the current best practice and better enable institutions to discharge their requirements for decision making as well as their representative obligations.

Chapter 16

The pattern of institutions which provide higher education

16.1   Our terms of reference ask us to make recommendations on the shape and structure of higher education; and to have regard, when so doing, to the principle that *'students should be able to choose between a diverse range of courses,* **institutions**, *modes and* **locations** *of study'* (emphasis added). This we refer to as the pattern of institutions. In Chapter 3 we described the changes since the Robbins Report to the pattern of institutions which provide higher education. In Chapter 20 we discuss funding for students at privately funded institutions. In this chapter, we consider the pattern of institutions that will be required over the next 20 years in order to deliver the necessary volume and range of higher education which we have described elsewhere.

16.2   In so doing, we take account of the distinctive features of higher education in different parts of the United Kingdom (UK); of the increasingly important links between higher education institutions and other parts of the education and training system, especially further education; and the impact of new forms of provision, including in the workplace and home, as a result of new technology and distance learning. Our work has been informed by evidence from a range of institutions and bodies.[1]

16.3   There are issues which go to the heart of the capacity of the system to deliver higher education in the way we have described. The distribution, style and title of institutions are matters of concern. Membership of an institution is one of the defining characteristics of many students' experience of higher education. To many other people, higher education is defined in important ways by the institutions which deliver it and by the names by which those institutions are known. The presence of a higher education institution and its standing is of material significance to any locality. It is important, therefore, that the UK has the pattern of institutions, in terms of their number, type and distribution, which it needs; and that the future pattern has public confidence.

16.4   We respect the tradition established by Robbins, and which has informed subsequent policy developments, that *'the pattern [of institutions] must provide for organic growth ...it must neither force their development at an intolerable pace nor leave them undisturbed when foresight would indicate the need for action'.*[2] In this chapter we make recommendations that support both organic growth and intervention. But we think both should be supported by a number of principles, which we develop under the following headings:

- the diversity and autonomy of institutions;
- clarity of institutional status;
- the scope and distribution of institutions providing publicly-funded higher education across the United Kingdom;
- higher education offered by further education colleges;
- the scope for collaboration between institutions.

The diversity and autonomy of institutions

16.5   We have inherited institutions of very different sizes, with different strengths, different patterns of participation, different offerings by level and subject of study, different local, regional and national orientations, different legal status and governance arrangements and different histories. Some are of very recent origin; some are ancient foundations; most owe no allegiance to any particular group in society; others are church foundations. All of these factors influence the pattern of institutional provision and the institutions' individual and collective characters and strategic aspirations.

16.6   Such diversity has considerable strengths, especially in providing for student choice; in programme and pedagogic innovation; in the ability of institutions to capture the energy and commitment of staff; and in the ability of the sector as a whole to meet the wide range of expectations now relevant to higher education. Indeed, institutional diversity has been one of the important defining characteristics of the United Kingdom's higher education system and, with the concomitant flexibility and autonomy of mission afforded to institutions, is one of the features which distinguishes the UK from some of its international comparators.

16.7   In addition, the systems in Scotland, Wales, Northern Ireland and England all have features which link them in important and distinctive ways to the particular circumstances of each country. We say more about some of these features in Chapter 23 and Appendix 1. In all four countries, however, provision is concentrated in three types of institution: universities; higher education colleges; and further education colleges providing higher education. Their pattern can be seen in the following charts.

Chart 16.1 – Total higher education enrolment by type of institution (England 1994/95)

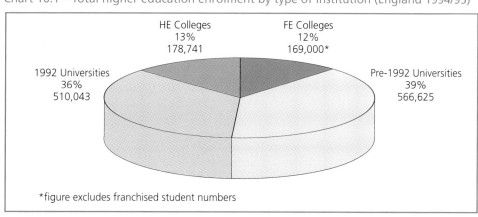

HE Colleges
13%
178,741

FE Colleges
12%
169,000*

1992 Universities
36%
510,043

Pre-1992 Universities
39%
566,625

*figure excludes franchised student numbers

Source: DfEE – HESA Dataset
FEFC Strategic Plans

Chart 16.2 – Total higher education enrolment by type of institution (Scotland 1994/95)

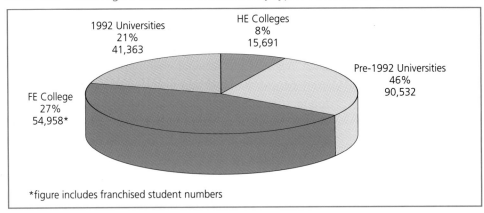

1992 Universities
21%
41,363

HE Colleges
8%
15,691

Pre-1992 Universities
46%
90,532

FE College
27%
54,958*

*figure includes franchised student numbers

Source: Report of the Scottish Committee – Annex 9, Table 2

Chart 16.3 – Total higher education enrolment by type of institution (Wales 1994/95)

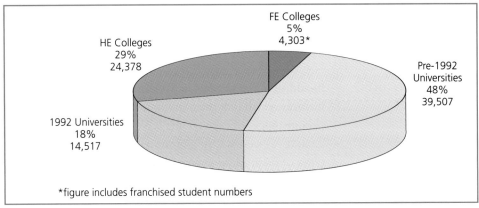

FE Colleges
5%
4,303*

HE Colleges
29%
24,378

Pre-1992
Universities
48%
39,507

1992 Universities
18%
14,517

*figure includes franchised student numbers

Source: DfEE – HESA Dataset

Chart 16.4 – Total higher education enrolment by type of institution (Northern Ireland 1994/95)

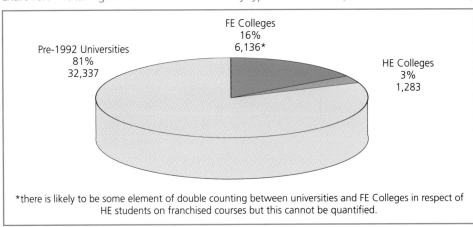

FE Colleges
16%
6,136*

Pre-1992 Universities
81%
32,337

HE Colleges
3%
1,283

*there is likely to be some element of double counting between universities and FE Colleges in respect of HE students on franchised courses but this cannot be quantified.

Source: DfEE – HESA Dataset
DENI, Statistics and Research Branch

16.8   Those who gave evidence attested to the value of this diversity and argued persuasively that the need for it would increase rather than decrease in future. One institution told us 'diversity is a growing element of life, business, commerce, industry and human endeavour in the late 20th century. The diversity in demand that that generates for

higher education has to be matched by diversity in education and research provision'.[3]
The Organisation of Economic Co-operation and Development (OECD) endorsed this
view, noting that *'a system growing and responding to the needs of an increasingly
heterogeneous group of students must work actively to maintain its diversity – and
offer choice to intending students'.*[4] Our recommendations about widening
participation (Chapter 7), the regional role of higher education (Chapter 12), a new
qualifications framework (Chapter 10) and alternative research funding arrangements
(Chapter 11) all point to the likelihood of increased diversity between institutions.

16.9   In the UK, institutional diversity goes hand in hand with institutional autonomy. We
explored in Chapter 15, measures which would underpin the responsible exercise of
autonomy by institutions through their governing bodies. Our advocacy of and
procedures for involving external constituencies in that chapter should help ensure that
institutions exercise their autonomy in a fully informed way.

16.10   But there are two forces which we fear may be starting to affect adversely the proper
diversity of provision. The first, which we explore in the rest of this section, is the
unintended pressure towards institutional homogeneity. The second, which we explore
in the next two sections of the chapter, is a latent danger of declining institutional self-
discipline.

16.11   First, there is the pressure towards institutional homogeneity. We heard from those
who lead and work in the institutions that they consider that current funding
arrangements are tending to promote homogeneity, and that institutions, whilst
autonomous, are increasingly making similar choices in response to the range of
funding options available to them. We were told that:
- the availability of significant amounts of funding for research on a competitive
  basis and the high value placed on it have together encouraged institutions to seek
  to engage in research to attract these funds, sometimes at some expense to other
  activities;
- financial uncertainty has encouraged institutions to spread their risks and therefore
  to dilute the distinctiveness of their missions;
- Funding Bodies, in seeking to be even-handed in their funding methodologies, are
  unconsciously reducing the scope for diversity;
- institutions perceive no explicit financial reward or incentive for pursuing a
  distinctive mission. The increasing range of society's expectations of higher
  education carry with them the danger of institutional 'mission overload' rather
  than a mission which is distinctive yet manageable. It was suggested that:
  *'one of the biggest dangers is that institutions are being over-loaded with an ever
  increasing and ultimately unmanageable list of competing economic and social
  objectives... Not all institutions will be trying to do all these things but too [many]
  are already attempting to undertake a range of roles that generate demands that
  their managerial systems and expertise are inadequate to cope with'.*[5]

16.12   It is difficult to judge how far such comments reflect reality. The Chief Executive of the
Higher Education Funding Council for England reminded us that there is already in
place a range of funding initiatives which acknowledges differences between

institutions; ensures that minority subjects continue to be offered; and which, through selective funding for policy priorities, enables institutions to build on their strengths. He also pointed out that there is no reason why similar inputs should result in similar outputs; and that competitive pressures are themselves a safeguard against conformity.[6] On the other hand, there is clearly a perceived danger that competition could lead to conformity of mission and the Organisation of Economic Co-operation and Development thematic review noted that there may be some risk of this.[7]

16.13   Our own judgement, from visits and discussion, is that there is in fact considerable diversity between institutions, and that this diversity is a strength in responding to the increasingly diverse needs of students as participation in higher education widens, and in providing genuine choices for students.

Recommendation 61   **We recommend to the Government and the Funding Bodies that diversity of institutional mission, consistent with high quality delivery and the responsible exercise of institutional autonomy, should continue to be an important element of the United Kingdom's higher education system; and that this should be reflected in the funding arrangements for institutions.**

16.14   This principle is already reflected in a number of recommendations elsewhere in our report:

- the recommendation in Chapter 12 for new funding arrangements for regional activity and applied research through the Industrial Partnership Development Fund is intended to reward different kinds and levels of research activity and give them a high public focus;
- the recommendation in Chapter 11 for funding explicitly in support of scholarship in parallel to support for research in the Research Assessment Exercise shows the value we place on this kind of activity;
- the recommendation in Chapter 15 that institutional governing bodies should undertake regular reviews of effectiveness should place a greater onus upon them to identify and monitor progress towards their own aspirations;
- the recommendations in Chapter 12 on the local and regional role of higher education should also reward those institutions which have adopted such a mission;
- the recommendation in Chapter 20 that graduates in employment should contribute to the costs of their higher education should also encourage diversity by reducing the extent to which institutions are dependent on one source of public funds for teaching. It creates a greater incentive for institutions to respond to the requirements of students who are likely to become more diverse. As Professor Martin Cave has suggested, *'if students did pay tuition, it is reasonable to expect that they would impose their own discipline as purchasers on institutions,'* which might lead to greater *'product differentiation'*.[8]

Clarity of institutional status

16.15   The second pressure on the pattern of institutions comes from an apparent weakening in the responsibility and self-discipline exercised by some institutions. Our endorsement of institutional autonomy and diversity carries with it a presumption of institutional responsibility and self-discipline. We feel bound to take into account a number of recent failures in this respect: diversity must be complemented by discipline.

16.16   The first discipline, as we explored in Chapter 10, is the maintenance of standards by each institution. UK higher education will benefit from a clearer specification of standards for its output. In our proposals this will be a part of higher education's compact with students and the rest of society. Institutional autonomy and diversity should be exercised in a way that safeguards standards and the quality of the student experience of higher education at each institution.

16.17   The second discipline which concerns us here is the title and name used by institutions to describe themselves to students and others. In the interests of public understanding there needs to be clarity and consistency in the use of both institutional titles (that is, how the Privy Council or Secretary of State has named the institution) **and** the use of institutional names (that is, how the institution describes itself to students and the wider public). At present, titles and names do not always match. Nor do they always define sufficiently clearly membership of a particular institutional category. While a number of institutions have adopted names which they feel properly reflect their status, some of these might be described as owing more to aspiration than to the present facts. It has been put to us that a small number of institutions have exploited a perceived difference in the law concerning the name under which they operate and the law concerning the legal title. This applies particularly to the use in public statements of the word 'university' within the name of institutions which do not carry that legal title and to the use of descriptors such as 'university sector' which have no legal basis. This is confusing and misleading for students and others. It also leads to weakened public confidence in the sector.

16.18   We consider it an important principle that there should be recognised criteria associated with each institutional title and type of institutional category. It should be made clear to institutions that the requirements of the Business Names Act 1985 and the Further and Higher Education Act 1992 restrict the use of names and titles. There should no longer be scope for any discrepancy between the legal title of the institution and the name it uses where this would be misleading.

Recommendation 62   **We recommend to the Government that it takes action as soon as possible to end the scope for a confusion between the title and the name used by institutions, either through clarifying the legal position or by ensuring that conditions can be placed on the flow of public funds so that these go only to those institutions which agree to restrict their use of a name and title to that to which they are legally entitled.**

16.19   The prevailing structure of institutions in the United Kingdom is the product of two recent pieces of legislation which caused significant change to the category and legal status of large numbers of institutions. The Education Reform Act 1988 made the polytechnics and colleges corporate bodies and removed them from the auspices of the local education authorities. The Further and Higher Education Act 1992 in effect re-created the polytechnics as universities, bestowing on them the defining characteristics of a university: the power to award their own taught and research degrees.

16.20   In other countries we visited, especially elsewhere in Europe, publicly-funded institutions appear to have a more fixed pattern, determined centrally; there are clearly understood institutional types and titles; and there appear to be no mechanisms by which individual institutions can, through their own actions, seek to change matters. By contrast, the UK higher education sector has benefited from Robbins' emphasis on organic growth. It has afforded institutions freedom to develop in the light of prevailing circumstances and their own objectives. The 1992 Act gives the Secretary of State and Privy Council powers to make a formal change in an institution's title or category, in response to their aspirations. Within this framework, and in the context of recent growth, some institutions have sought changes in their category and some proposals have been made to establish additional universities. As a result, the reality is, in some ways, less clear-cut than the legislation would imply.

The characteristics of universities

16.21   In our view, the important defining characteristic of a university is the power to award taught and research degrees which then carry the university's name. This was recognised when the Further and Higher Education Act 1992 enabled the polytechnics to obtain degree-awarding powers and to acquire the title and status of universities. Subsequently, numerical criteria have been developed to help assess the cases made by non-university institutions to acquire university status. These numerical criteria refer to the size of the institution and to the spread of academic disciplines offered. We think that these numerical criteria threaten to distort some aspects of institutional behaviour, as institutions seek to acquire a status they perceive to be particularly valuable.

16.22   In addition to the numerical criteria, non-university institutions seeking university status are expected to have taught degree awarding powers and research degree awarding powers and to have demonstrated their ability to maintain degree standards when using these powers for three years. Representatives of a number of institutions that would wish to be accorded this status told us that they found the current situation unhelpful because it leads students and others to misconstrue their academic standing. These institutions, each of which has been granted taught degree awarding powers, stated that they already had sufficient other evidence about the quality of their research to render the three year waiting period subsequent to the granting of research degree awarding powers an unnecessary, if not irrelevant, precaution.

16.23   Binding the award of university status directly to the power to award degrees bearing the institution's name means that the arrangements for awarding those powers are particularly important. We urge in Chapter 10 that the Quality Assurance Agency review these arrangements, on which advice to the Secretary of State and Privy Council is based. In our view, it is important to safeguard the use by universities of the power to make awards which have the general standing and national and international currency of a degree. We have emphasised the importance of the way these powers are discharged within institutions in Chapter 15.

16.24   The debate about the university title is sensitive: we would not wish to disappoint the hard work of a small number of institutions which are very close to satisfying the present criteria for the award of university status and which might feel themselves aggrieved were the rules to be changed now. Their aspirations should continue to be tested against the present criteria. But we do see advantage, after the rapid developments of recent years, in a period of relative stability in the number of universities, with the award of university status used more sparingly, related less to the achievement of the present numerical criteria and more in recognition of a distinctive role and characteristics.

16.25   We also see advantages for amalgamations of institutions, particularly of smaller institutions. The strength of such cases would be judged against educational criteria, including whether this is likely to make for better quality, and financial criteria, including cost-effectiveness. Individual institutions are not necessarily disinterested judges of such matters. We make these comments out of recognition that, with so much happening so quickly, there has been no opportunity to stand back and reflect on the needs of the sector overall, as well as the aspirations and achievements of individual institutions. There has been little incentive in circumstances of growth for some institutions to consider whether, in the best interests of higher education, they should merge with another institution. We think it is timely for such consideration but we have not, however, had time during our review to go into this issue in any detail and we do not make any specific recommendations.

Recommendation 63   **We recommend to the Government that, in the medium term, there is no change to the current criteria for university status; but that, for the future, there should be a period of relative stability in the number of universities, with the weight accorded to the numerical criteria reduced and greater emphasis placed on a distinctive role and characteristics in awarding this status; and that the Government should give notice of this.**

16.26   It was also suggested to us that, whilst the criteria for achieving the university title should be made less burdensome, equally, it should be possible for the powers to award degrees to be removed from an institution, and that this precaution would actually serve to strengthen the important protection of the essential characteristics of universities. The Higher Education Quality Council drew to our attention to apparent anomaly that, whilst the removal of degree awarding powers appears to be possible in Scotland for the 1992 universities, this does not appear to be the case in England or Wales, nor to apply to chartered universities.[9] We think this should be changed, although we are sensitive to the historic powers granted by individual charters.

Recommendation 64   **We recommend to the Government that it takes action, either by amending the powers of the Privy Council or by ensuring that conditions can be placed on the flow of public funds, to enable the removal of degree awarding powers where the Quality Assurance Agency demonstrates that the power to award degrees has been seriously abused.**

16.27 The previous Government asked us to consider the use of 'university college' titles. We took evidence from a second group of institutional representatives seeking some discipline in the pattern of institutions by the creation of a new and tightly specified category, the 'university college'. We also heard from the chair of the working party set up by the Committee of Vice-Chancellors and Principals to explore this matter.

16.28 At present, the 'university college' title applies legally only to those institutions which are constitutionally part of a university, such as University College, London; or where a pre-1992 university has bestowed the title under one of its Charter powers. However, the name is currently being used much more widely by institutions which have taken no legal steps to secure a change in their title. There is concern about the proliferation of the use of the name and variants of it, especially by further education colleges, some of which obtain use of the name under the terms of a university's charter. We agree that the use of the 'university college' designation should be limited by clear criteria to give unambiguous meaning to its use.

16.29 Those who advocate a new legal category of institution using the 'university college' title argue that it would recognise that there is a group of colleges of higher education which offer programmes of the same standing and standards as universities. This, we were told, would better reflect their true nature, properly denote the quality of their provision, and accurately depict the rigour of their quality assurance arrangements. They argue that it would thereby serve to correct mis-perceptions amongst students and others, whom they feel tend to believe that colleges of higher education are of lesser standing and quality than universities and therefore discriminate against them in their decisions. These colleges believe that a new title is needed for a new category, to recognise a particular facet of institutional diversity: the extent to which they share defining characteristic of universities and yet remain colleges. They have become particularly concerned that the 'university college' title is being used by some institutions with no legal claim to it and that it has become misleading.

16.30 Titles incorporating the word 'university' must be applied consistently and be widely understood in the UK and overseas. To that end, there should be a restriction on the use of the 'university college' title. On the basis for authorising the use of the title 'university college', the arguments are balanced between three options: restricting the usage to institutions which are a constituent part of a university; extending the usage to those institutions which have in their own right taught degree awarding powers; and applying it to colleges of higher and possibly also further education which have a particular relationship with one university. We prefer the second of these (although we recognise that particular circumstances may apply in Northern Ireland and we say more about this in Appendix 1). In our view, there is a convincing case to be made for creating a new category of institution which would have clearly defined characteristics, denoted by similarity to universities yet respecting the distinctive 'college' feel.

16.31 We do not feel competent to address the question of the powers of some pre-1992 university charters, although we consider it inappropriate that they should use those powers in relation to further education colleges which remain separate corporate bodies. We also have reservations about the use of the powers by a chartered university in respect of colleges of higher education where these do not have degree awarding powers and where they remain separate corporate bodies. Our preference would be for the institutions concerned to agree to a different title and name with the Government, representative bodies and the funding bodies.

Recommendation 65

We recommend to the Government that it takes action, either by clarifying the legal position or by ensuring that conditions can be placed on the flow of public funds, to restrict the use of the title 'University College' to those institutions which are in every sense a college which is part of a university under the control of the university's governing body; and to those higher education institutions which have been granted taught degree awarding powers.

The scope and distribution of institutions providing publicly funded higher education

16.32   The current pattern of institutional provision is the product of historical and legislative circumstance rather than of any overall rationale, based on location, distribution through the United Kingdom, size or type. It is therefore to an extent an accident of history which counties, towns or cities have a university, or indeed more than one; which have colleges of higher education; which have specialist monotechnics; and which have none of these. There is little doubt that an approach guided by strategic co-ordination whether by individual institutions or by an intermediary body, would have yielded a very different pattern, and possibly a more economical one if measured solely in terms of the costs of provision. However, it is also likely that such co-ordination might have limited institutions' creative enthusiasm, innovation and enterprise; and that the necessary expansion and diversity established over the last decade would not have been achieved at such modest capital cost or with such willingness.

Proposals to establish new universities

16.33   A number of proposals exist to establish new universities beyond those to change the status of a college of higher education to a university. Looking at the general issues raised, there appears to be no systematic basis for decision-making. The cases often rest on broad socio-economic grounds, emphasising anticipated local and regional impact of the kind we explored in Chapter 12 and on perceived inadequacies in the distribution of universities between regions (if not in the distribution of higher education opportunities). For example, students from some English counties must travel outside their home county to find a university place, and sometimes a higher education programme. Advocates of additional local provision argue that a local university would retain highly skilled young people and thereby boost the local economy. We understand this view.

16.34   We were struck by the reliance which the further education sector is able to place on the legal duty on their Funding Council (England and Wales) or Secretary of State (Scotland) to secure facilities for further education which are 'sufficient' and 'adequate'. This gives a clear locus for consideration of whether the current distribution of further education provision is appropriate. We think this precedent could be helpful in developing a more robust and transparent mechanism for considering cases in higher education, where, by contrast, proposals appear to rest on individual initiative, in some cases, through proposals for Lottery funding, and in others, from a local authority. This is unsatisfactory. We would urge the Funding Bodies, sector bodies, representatives of relevant local interests and the Government to come together to agree criteria against which such cases can be decided and funding allocated. Questions which we would consider relevant to such decisions would include:

■ whether the need could be well met by an existing university or college, by an existing institution becoming a college of an existing university, or by existing institutions working together to meet a currently un-met requirement for higher education;

■ the extent to which funding would be available from non-Government sources to support a university institution;

■ the level of provision in relation to regional needs;

■ the likely standing of the institution.

16.35   In applying these criteria, educational requirements should come first : if broader social and economic considerations are found to be overriding, or sufficient by themselves for setting up a new higher education facility, then the costs of so doing should be shared by other relevant government departments and agencies.

Recommendation 66   **We recommend to the Government and the Funding Bodies that there is greater clarity about where responsibility lies for decisions about the establishment of new universities; and that criteria are developed for deciding such cases and allocating public funding.**

16.36   We would also urge that, where there is limited provision for higher education in a locality and where, in response, several institutions may have ambitions to make provision available, the Government and the Funding Bodies should seek to secure an outcome which is most likely to serve the causes of effectiveness and quality. Multiple provision, where each of the institutions meets part of the local demand, is unlikely to achieve that; and we would favour a collaborative solution or single provider.

Corporate providers of higher education

16.37   A number of corporate sector organisations notified us of their intentions to establish what they refer to as their own 'universities' or 'virtual' universities. Some of these are ambitious and exciting ideas for harnessing the learning needs of company employees and embracing lifelong learning. Some are working closely with existing universities. We welcome this commitment to education and training. But we have reservations about the use of the 'university' name in this way, as the proposals usually concern company-specific training and much of it is not at a higher education level, valuable though it clearly is to the companies concerned. Above all, the defining characteristic of awarding degrees, a power granted by the Privy Council, would not be met.

16.38   We also welcome the thinking which lies behind the proposed 'university for industry'. It accords with the belief that informs the whole of our report: the need to create a learning society which is inclusive rather than exclusive, and with learning practised throughout life, rather than concentrated heavily on the earlier years. But as we understand this proposal, it is aimed mainly at learning up to about level 3 in the national framework of qualifications, and will act more as a major national contractor and facilitator than a provider of programmes. We have referred earlier to the importance we place on names and titles having clear meaning and public confidence. We would encourage those who want to develop models of the kind described here to consider alternative titles which might better convey their true nature and prestige.

Higher education offered by further education colleges

16.39   In many cases, local requirements for sub-degree higher education can be met particularly well by further education colleges, whether as direct providers or in a partnership with a higher education institution. Delivery throughout the UK of higher education by further education colleges is extensive and important in many communities. It is predominantly sub-degree and often of a vocational nature. It can be especially important for students regarded as 'non-traditional' to higher education institutions many of whom need to be able to study near their homes. A number of further education colleges have developed particular expertise in this level of provision. In 1994/95, some 13 per cent of higher education was delivered by further education colleges in the UK (27 per cent in Scotland). At twelve colleges in England, directly-funded higher education represented more than 1,000 student places and between 35 and 50 per cent of the total places funded in the colleges. As we suggest in Chapters 6 and 7, it is likely that demand for such provision will increase over the next twenty years.

16.40   In a number of the further education colleges in England and Wales, higher education provision is not directly funded but delivered on a franchised basis from a higher education institution. Many of these arrangements are intended to deliver higher education to those in remote geographic areas or for whom higher education institutions can be remote culturally and historically. There are some concerns about the quality assurance arrangements in some cases, particularly where one college engages in franchise relationships with several higher education institutions ('multiple franchising') and where the franchisee in turn franchises funds to a third party ('serial franchising'). These concerns refer in particular to the possibility of ensuring rigour in the quality assurance arrangements and to the ability of the parties involved to account adequately for the public funds involved. We have already recommended in Chapter 6 that there is scope for an immediate growth in sub-degree provision and we see much of the future expansion of higher education being at this level. In Chapter 10 we set out our recommendations for a new qualifications framework which will promote progression between the levels within higher education, and recommendations about the proper limits on franchising, within a framework to be established by the Quality Assurance Agency.

16.41   We are keen to see directly-funded sub-degree higher education develop as a special mission for further education colleges. In general, over time, we see much more of this level of provision being offered in these colleges, although we recognise that particular circumstances might apply in some cases. We also see no case for expanding degree or postgraduate level work in further education colleges. In our view, this extra discipline to the level of higher education qualifications offered by further and higher education institutions will offer each sector distinctive opportunities and best meet growing individual, local and national needs, although we recognise there may be different circumstances in the different countries of the UK.

Recommendation 67   **We recommend to the Government and the Funding Bodies that, in the medium term, priority in growth in sub-degree provision should be accorded to further education colleges; and that, wherever possible:**

- **more sub-degree provision should take place in further education colleges;**
- **higher education provision in further education colleges should be funded directly;**
- **there should be no growth in degree level qualifications offered by further education colleges.**

The scope for collaboration between institutions

16.42   We have already made a number of recommendations in this report which will further encourage institutions to collaborate, for example, in their research and the use of large scale, expensive equipment. In our view, the scope and need for collaboration will increase in future. It will derive strongly from the extended use of communications and information technology and from a stronger emphasis on the local and regional role of institutions. The framework for higher education qualifications will prompt dialogue about standards and the accumulation and transferability of credits at different levels. Lifelong learning and wider participation in higher education will foster collaboration between further and higher education institutions. Pressure on funding will stimulate joint purchasing and sharing of resources. As the Organisation of Economic Co-operation and Development (OECD) noted in its report, there are strong educational and wider policy imperatives here and organisation of *'co-operation amongst institutions is needed in order to strengthen pathways for students, to further develop cross-crediting and credit transfer, to produce clear articulation and improved transition arrangements and to achieve greater impact for example in regional development'*.[10]

16.43   Some of those giving evidence told us that collaboration is discouraged by the current funding arrangements and that the funding and assessment methodologies are seen as particular barriers to collaboration.

16.44   We also heard that collaboration, especially across the current higher/further education boundary, needs to increase to improve the range of response to individual requirements. The Committee of Vice-Chancellors and Principals suggested that:

'smooth connections ... will enable students to move freely between the two sectors in either direction, whether to advance the level of their learning or to add to their knowledge and skills. Students will increasingly be concerned not with sectors of education and their boundaries but with the accessibility, affordability, quality and relevance of the provision offered' [11]

16.45   Some of those giving evidence extend the debate about qualifications frameworks and institutional collaboration to suggest that the post-16 education system outside schools should be redefined as a single tertiary system. Some institutions are developing formal proposals to merge with others in order to create a new (in the UK) kind of tertiary institution. Others suggest that a single tertiary funding body should be created, even though the institutions which it would fund might continue to offer either mainly higher education or mainly further education. We have already recommended in Chapter 7 that there is scope for more joint working – and joint funding – by the Funding Bodies responsible for further and higher education, specifically in that case to increase achievement at NVQ level 3. We say more about the structure of the Funding Bodies themselves in Chapter 22.

16.46   Finally, we were advised that greater collaboration between institutions would be the corollary of an enhanced emphasis on diversity between institutions. Instead of seeking to undertake every activity themselves, institutions might form strategic alliances designed to cover a range of activities across the alliance:

'British universities have considerable autonomy.... movement in future should be towards even greater autonomy but inter-institutional agreements and arrangements are likely to be more sophisticated in order to meet future educational and research needs...' [12]

16.47   It is as difficult to prove that institutions are discouraged from collaborating by the current funding methodology as it is to prove that diversity is threatened by the same methodology. As the Committee of Vice-Chancellors and Principals (CVCP) pointed out in reporting on a survey carried out for us, *'collaboration is an integral part of academic activity. Individual academics have always sought partners within and across their subject disciplines or administrative roles, at other universities both at home and abroad'.* [13] Nonetheless, there is a strong weight of feeling that competitive pressures have gone too far in promoting a climate which is antipathetic to collaboration, even where there would be strong educational or financial grounds in favour of individuals, departments or institutions working together. However, we did note a difference of view, even amongst institutions, about the best way to tackle these matters. Some urged pump-priming; some were sceptical about financial incentives; some pointed out that institutions can and do already engage in collaboration.

16.48   Collaboration matters. It may, in some case, make the difference between institutional success and failure. But it needs to apply throughout institutions, from individuals to management teams. There needs to be more encouragement within institutions, for example to support faculty teams to develop their ideas and evaluate the costs and potential of collaboration, and incentives to staff. At institutional level too, governing bodies should include a review of collaboration in the review of performance recommended in Chapter 15. At national level, there is scope for more imaginative funding arrangements which would help institutions to get over the initial costs that can sometimes arise from collaboration before the longer term economies arise. Collaboration could be particularly fruitful in the provision and use of libraries, both between institutions and with major national collections like the British Library and student support services. We heard of some impressive examples but more needs to be done to disseminate these. We think that the Funding Bodies might usefully consider bringing forward part of institutions' allocations and offsetting this against future funding, where institutions make strongly-founded proposals with clear educational and financial benefits that cannot otherwise be realised. It will also be important that the new quality assurance arrangements to be developed by the Quality Assurance Agency do not discourage collaboration between institutions where this would lead to improvements in learning and teaching.

Recommendation 68   **We recommend to the Funding Bodies and the Research Councils that they review their mainstream teaching and research funding arrangements to ensure these do not discourage collaboration between institutions; and that, where appropriate, they encourage collaboration. We recommend to the Funding Bodies that they be prepared to use their funds on a revolving basis, bringing forward and offsetting annual allocations in support of collaboration which has a strong educational and financial rationale.**

Recommendation 69   **We recommend to the Quality Assurance Agency that, as it develops its arrangements, it ensures that these arrangements do not discourage collaboration between institutions.**

Conclusion

16.49   In this chapter we have explored aspects of the pattern of institutions that require attention if it is to equip the UK for the next 20 years. In the remaining chapters we make recommendations on how learning in these institutions can be funded and how their continued necessary separation from government can be secured.

Chapter 17

The funding requirement

17.1   In our work, we were conscious that a major factor leading to the establishment of the Committee was widespread concern about the funding of higher education, particularly if growth in student numbers was to be resumed. In Chapters 17 to 21 we examine the funding of higher education. We are conscious that the issues are complex and some of the arguments are lengthy and technical, so throughout these chapters we have highlighted key conclusions in green bold type to provide some signposts.

17.2   It was clear from evidence submitted by all groups that these concerns related in particular to the ability of institutions to maintain the quality of their teaching and research in the face of continued downwards pressure on the level of public funding per student. The previous Government's solution of imposing a cap on student numbers was seen as unsustainable in relation to potential national needs beyond the short term.

17.3   Given the available evidence, it was inevitable that institutions should spell out concerns centred on the short term funding issues. The Higher Education Funding Council for England (HEFCE) reported for example that, in the 1996 forecasts, 78 (or nearly 55 per cent) of English higher education institutions were expected to be in deficit by the end of 1999/2000.[1] We also understand from the Higher Education Funding Council for Wales (HEFCW) that out of 14 higher education institutions in Wales 10 were, in their 1996 financial forecasts, expecting to be in deficit by the end of 1998-99. Several institutions also told us about the programmes of redundancies they were entering into in anticipation of the planned cuts of 6.5 per cent in public funding over the next two years.

17.4   Futhermore our terms of reference invited us to examine how higher education might develop to meet the needs of the UK over the next 20 years, taking into consideration a wide range of principles related to higher education. These principles were prefaced by the general statement that:
   "The Committee should have regard, within the constraints of the Government's other spending priorities and affordability......"

17.5   With this in mind, we have looked critically at all the potential demands for additional funding arising from the proposals we have developed. This chapter provides an assessment of what we judge to be the unavoidable additional costs of providing a higher education system over the next 20 years which will be able both to sustain the UK's economic competitiveness and to meet the legitimate aspirations of its citizens to improve their qualifications and employability. The next chapter examines how these additional costs might be shared between the principal stakeholders – taxpayers, students and their families, graduates, employers and institutions themselves.

17.6   Our terms of reference asked us to look at the contribution of higher education on a 20 year timescale. As the Committee of Vice-Chancellors and Principals (CVCP) put it to us in oral evidence, there is a real danger that the potential long term contribution of the higher education system may be undermined by short term decisions by institutions in the face of current funding pressures. We have, therefore, sought to identify the most serious short term needs. This has implications for the timescale for introducing the new approaches to funding considered in subsequent chapters.

The current position

17.7 To provide a base for assessing the future funding requirements for higher education, we considered the current level of public funding and the sources of funding (public and private) supporting institutional expenditure on higher education and supporting students.

17.8 Such an assessment has to take into account the several streams of public funding for higher education and for student support. These include:

- funding for higher education institutions through the three higher education funding councils and the Department of Education Northern Ireland (DENI);
- funding for higher education institutions provided through fees paid on behalf of students and known as mandatory and discretionary award fee payments, and postgraduate fee payments;
- funding for the living costs – 'maintenance' – of full-time undergraduate students through loans and grants;
- funding for the maintenance of postgraduate students through grants.

Institutional income

17.9 Table 17.1 below sets out the various income streams of higher education institutions in the UK in 1995-96.

Table 17.1 – Higher education institutions: sources of funds 1995-96

	£million	% of total
A. Public sources		
Funding Council grants		
Teaching	2,919	27.3
Research	803	7.5
Other	328	3.1
Capital	346	3.2
FE grants	56	0.5
Total	**4,452**	**41.6**
Academic fees full-time home plus European Union (EU)	1,346[a]	12.6
Research grants		
Office of Science and Technology	532	5.0
Other public sources (incl EU)	417	3.9
Income from public sources for other services	376	3.5
Total public sources	**7,123**	**66.5**
B. Private sources		
Overseas fees	507	4.7
Part-time fees and other fees	656[b]	6.1
Research: UK Charities	338	3.2
UK Industry	170	1.6
Other	97	0.9
Other income from private sources		
Services rendered	334	3.1
Catering and residence	722	6.7
Other (including endowment income)	764	7.1
Total private sources	**3,588**	**33.4**
Total public and private	**10,711**	**100**

Source: Higher Education Statistics Agency : Resources of Higher Education Institutions 1995-96 and DfEE

Notes: a. Includes fees of research students on publicly funded research studentships and discretionary award fee payments;
b. Includes income from further education fees of £17 million.
Components may not sum to totals because of rounding.

17.10 These figures exclude the funding for higher education programmes provided in further education colleges other than those franchised by higher education institutions. Other higher education programmes in further education colleges are funded by different routes in the different countries of the UK.

- in England
  full-time sub-degree programmes and all higher level programmes in further education colleges are funded by the Higher Education Funding Council for England and by mandatory award fees; other, mainly part-time, sub-degree level work is funded directly by the Further Education Funding Council;

- in Wales
  a small number (about 500) of higher education places in further education colleges in Wales are funded directly by the Higher Education Funding Council for Wales;

- in Scotland
  all higher education work in further education colleges is funded directly by the Scottish Office Education and Industry Department (SOEID) alongside funding for further education students.

Higher education provided in further education institutions

In 1995-96 there were 250,000 higher education students enrolled at further education colleges of which 10 per cent were on (mainly sub-degree) programmes franchised by higher education institutions. Excluding the funding for these latter students, total public expenditure on higher education in further education colleges is estimated at some £300 million in 1995-96.[2]

Expenditure on student maintenance

17.11 Table 17.2 below sets out the provisional out-turn of expenditure in 1995/96 (academic year) on student maintenance.

Table 17.2 – Expenditure on student maintenance 1995/96[3] (excluding fees)

	Expenditure (£m)	Student numbers (000)
Mandatory Awards		
England and Wales	1,074	786
Scotland	163	107
Northern Ireland	45	38
Total (UK)	**1,282**	**931**
Student loans (UK)		
Loans advanced	701	560
Loan repayments	(66)	–
Net student loans	635	
Access Funds	27	66
Discretionary awards	11	11
Postgraduate awards	146	19
Total	**2,101**	**–**

Source: DfEE and Student Loans Company

17.12 The current public expenditure plans assume that in 1997-98 expenditure on maintenance grants, at £966 million, will still exceed expenditure on loans at £851 million net of repayments. This reflects the fact that not all students eligible for loans take them out.

Planned public expenditure on higher education 1996-97 to 1999-2000

17.13 At the heart of the debate about the short term funding difficulties facing institutions are the public expenditure plans for the years up to 1999-2000 announced by the previous Government in the November 1996 Budget. Table 17.3 below brings together the current planned public expenditure figures for institutional funding for the years 1996-97 to 1999-2000 for the UK as a whole. The components underlying these figures are, of course, the responsibility of different Secretaries of State.

Table 17.3 – Public expenditure plans, institutional funding[a] for higher education[4] 1995-96 to 1999-2000

	1995-96	1996-97	£ million 1997-98	1998-99	1999-2000
England					
Funding Council grant	3,729	3,615	3,667	3,627	3,535
Full-time tuition fees	967	965	988	1047	1047
Scotland					
Funding Council grant	542	535	545	526	526
Full-time tuition fees	119	119	121	123	123
Wales					
Funding Council grant	239	241	235	228	228
Full-time tuition fees	65	66	65	68	71
Northern Ireland					
Block grant	117	115	113	109	109
Full-time tuition fees	32	33	33	34	36
Total central grant	4,627	4,506	4,560	4,490	4,398
Total full-time tuition fees	1,183	1,183	1,207	1,272	1,277
Total funding (cash prices)[b]	**5,810**	**5,689**	**5,767**	**5,762**	**5,675**
Total funding at 1995-96 prices (£million)	5,810	5,550	5,516	5,403	5,217
Student numbers full-time equivalents (000s)	1,178	1,196	1,197	1,205	1,209
Funding per FTE student (£)	4,932	4,640	4,608	4,484	4,315
Real terms reduction (%)		5.9	0.7	2.7	3.8

Source : England DFEE/HEFCE, Wales HEFCW, Scotland SHEFC, Northern Ireland DENI

Note: a. Includes capital funding
b cash prices are the prices prevailing in the year in question.

17.14 The year on year pattern of reduction varies from country to country within the UK, but the overall reduction from 1997-98 to 1999-2000 of about 6.5 per cent is a consistent feature across the UK. The public expenditure figures include block grant for both teaching and research. On the basis of allocations in 1995-96 (Table 17.1 above), about 17 per cent can be assumed to be allocated for research.[5]

17.15   There are currently significant differences in the average levels of funding for higher education from the Funding Councils in England, Scotland and Wales. Detailed work reported to us by the Scottish Higher Education Funding Council (SHEFC) suggests that the unit of funding in 1996-97 was about ten per cent higher in Scotland than in England. The Higher Education Funding Council for Wales (HEFCW) carried out a preliminary assessment which suggested its average unit of funding was significantly lower than the average unit of funding in England. HEFCW is, we understand, now carrying out more detailed work along the lines of that undertaken by the SHEFC. These comparisons take no account, however, of possible differences arising from the different approaches to funding higher education programmes in further education colleges in the three countries, described in paragraph 17.10, which have been excluded from these calculations.

Short term funding requirements

Reducing the pressure on the unit of funding

17.16   The essential consideration that we have addressed is how far a reduction of 6.5 per cent over two years in the unit of funding, in addition to the more than 40 per cent reduction achieved since 1976, is sustainable without significant damage to the quality of the student experience and to the research base. This reduction of 6.5 per cent includes the full impact of the Government's decision to reduce substantially from 1995-96 onwards capital funding for equipment purchases and the refurbishment of institutions' estates, and the decision by Government and the Funding Bodies to stop separately identifying capital funding from 1997-98 onwards. Institutions are now expected to meet such costs in full from their general recurrent funding.

17.17   We believe that, over time, with further growth in student numbers, institutions can reduce their costs further. But a 6.5 per cent reduction in unit funding is not achievable in two years without putting quality unacceptably at risk. How much and how fast institutions are able to reduce their costs will depend, in part, on their ability to exploit opportunities for expansion and exploit the potential of communications and information technology. This issue is considered further in paragraphs 17.40 to 17.45.

17.18   We cannot, on the other hand, ignore the general pressure on all publicly-funded organisations to improve their cost-effectiveness. Higher education institutions, notwithstanding their notable achievements in this respect over the last 20 years, cannot be exempt. We have, for example, in Chapter 15 identified some of the current differences in costs between institutions which could be reduced. Some of the international comparisons that have been made on our behalf also raise questions about the cost base that merit further consideration.[6, 7]

17.19   On balance, and making the best judgement we can on the basis of the patchy information available, we have concluded that institutions, with their current organisation and approaches to learning and teaching, should be able to deliver a one per cent reduction in costs in both 1998-99 and 1999-2000. To alleviate the pressure on institutions to this extent would require additional funding, compared with current spending plans, of just over £100 million in 1998-99 and £270 million in 1999-2000.

Capital funding

17.20   Analysis carried out for us by the Higher Education Funding Council for England (HEFCE)[8] suggests that the shortfall in capital expenditure is likely to be £250 million per annum given the accumulated backlog both in the refurbishment of the estate and replacing equipment, and the need for investment in communications and information technology of the kind that has been identified in Chapter 13. The question of the sources of funding for capital investment for institutions are discussed further in Chapter 19

17.21   To respond to the urgent need for action to remedy the state of the research infrastructure in our top quality research departments, we consider that a separate initiative is needed of the scale we have identified in Chapter 11. We have in mind the need for a sum of between £400 and £500 million.

17.22   We therefore, propose a revolving fund specifically devoted to addressing the need through loans at a low rate of interest and funded equally by the Government, Funding and Research Councils out of their budgets, industry and charities (see Chapter 11). Each of these sources might be invited to contribute **£50 million in each of two years,** with the contributions from each of the four parties being contingent on matching funding from the others. As described in Chapter 11 we envisage the fund being managed by trustees, with tightly drawn terms of reference agreed by the contributors, and specifically earmarked for a limited number of top quality research departments.

17.23   The analysis by the HEFCE suggests that even with the kind of short term measures we have proposed to limit the reduction in the unit of funding and address the backlog of investment in research infrastructure there is still likely, within the overall identified requirement of £250 million to be a shortfall of £150 million a year in capital expenditure in the next two years.[9]

Staff salaries

17.24   If our recommendation in Chapter 14 for a review of staff pay and conditions is accepted, there could be increased pressure on costs. For every one per cent real increase in academic staff pay, there would be an increase in costs for higher education institutions of around £35 million a year and for every one per cent increase in the pay bill for all staff there would be an increase of around £60 million. An assessment of the short term funding needs for staff salaries can only be made when the review has completed its work.

Student support

17.25   In Chapters 7 and 20 we propose changes to the levels of support to students. We propose in particular:
■ improved support for part-time students in receipt of benefit;

- a doubling of the Access Funds to target additional support for living costs on students with the greatest hardship and a widening of the scope of the Funds;
- a widening of the scope and removal of the means testing of the disabled students allowance.

17.26   These measures taken together would cost an additional £30 million in 1998-99 and an additional £45 million in 1999-2000.[9]

Resumed growth in student numbers

17.27   In Chapter 6 we recommended that the cap on full-time undergraduate numbers should be withdrawn over the next two to three years and for sub-degree programmes in 1998/99. To support this growth, we judge that £20 million is required in 1998/99 and £50 million in 1999-2000.

Summary of short term funding priorities

17.28   We have identified a range of short term funding needs: to relieve the pressure on unit funding; to begin to restore the infrastructure; to improve student support and to resume growth in student numbers. These items total some £350 million in 1998-99 and £565 million in 1999-2000. The first priority is to ease the pressure on the unit of funding as proposed in paragraphs 17.16 to 17.19.

17.29   We have received no indication that higher education can look to public funding to ease the current planned pressure. It is essential, therefore, that our proposals to seek a contribution from graduates in work which we make in Chapter 20 should be brought into effect for the start of the academic year 1998-99. Since for the most part the proposals will involve loan finance, it follows that the treatment of loan finance within public accounts is a major issue. This issue is addressed in Chapter 20.

Long term funding requirements

17.30   In our analysis of how the system of higher education might develop over the next 20 years we have identified six main elements which will give rise to a requirement for significant additional funding. These elements are:
- growth in student load, described in paragraph 17.32;
- aspects of lifelong learning;
- refurbishment of the estate and replacement of obsolete equipment (particularly in the light of developments in the communications and information technology field);
- research, including infrastructure and regional development;
- improved maintenance support for students;
- increasing higher education pay in line with earnings elsewhere in the economy.

17.31   The estimates of the funding requirements in the following paragraphs are those we have been able readily to calculate. They are intended to be illustrative but have been measured against levels for 1997-98 in the current public expenditure plans.

Growth in student load

17.32   Overall student load in the system is made up of two main factors:
- student numbers and patterns of attendance, allowing for wastage;
- programme length.

The effect of these factors on the cost of student load will be affected by efforts by institutions to improve their efficiency and introduce new approaches to learning and teaching.

Student numbers and patterns of attendance

17.33   We have argued in Chapters 6 and 7 for a significantly higher level of participation in higher education 20 years from now. We do not propose a specific target, but in order to model student load we look to 45 per cent full-time participation by 18 and 19 year olds. Participation rates of 45 per cent have been achieved already in Scotland and Northern Ireland. For part-time undergraduates, we envisage an increase of 35 per cent in full-time equivalant student numbers over the next 20 years. For postgraduate study, consistent with 45 per cent full-time participation rates by 18 and 19 year olds, we envisage a growth in demand of 40 per cent.[10] We have assumed, as we said in Chapter 6, that growth in postgraduate research students will be constrained by the availability of research supervisors and research studentships, and that these numbers will, as a consequence, rise only slowly.

17.34   In total, full-time equivalent student numbers would increase from around 1.2 million to 1.6 million over the next 20 years. This is shown in Chart 17.1 and Table 17.4.

Chart 17.1 – Full-time undergraduate numbers and total all student numbers

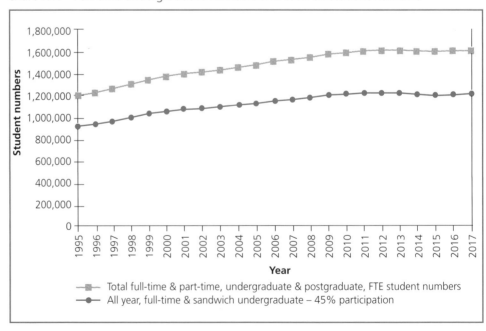

Source: DfEE

Table 17.4 – Student numbers

	1995-96	2005-2006	2015-2016
Undergraduate full-time (000s)	914	1,134	1,214
Undergraduate part-time (FTE 000s)	140	161	189
Total undergraduate (FTE 000s)	1,054	1,295	1,303
Postgraduate (FTE 000s)	141	175	194
Total all students (FTE 000s)	1,194 [12]	1,470	1,598
Percentage increase in FTE	–	23.1	33.8

17.35 Using the 1997-98 unit of funding (£4,608 per full-time equivalent student (at 1995-96 prices) and, after discounting by 17 per cent to allow for the funding attributable to research) the total additional cost to institutions of this growth by 2015 is estimated to be about £1.4 billion at 1995-96 prices. The discount for research would be less if there was a significant expansion at degree level given our views (see Chapter 11) about the importance of research underpinning high quality teaching at higher levels. Student support for the additional 300,000 full-time undergraduates at £250 [13] per student in 1995-96 prices, gives a total additional outlay of £750 million. The total cost of this is about **£2.1 billion** (at 1995-96 prices). This takes no account of the additional income that would flow from the additional students repaying loans under the current scheme. The amount of that is dependent on the Government's decision on whether to sell the student loan book on a continuing basis. This issue is considered further in paragraph 17.83.

Programme length

17.36 The recommendations we have made in Chapters 6 and 7 about the pattern of future demand are likely to lead to a reduction in the average overall length of different programmes as more students – at least for their initial qualifications – choose sub-degree programmes. This has been the experience in Scotland. The qualifications framework proposed in Chapter 10 will facilitate this. Some of those with sub-degree qualifications will subsequently wish to complete a degree programme, but might choose to do so by a variety of routes – part-time, full-time or distance learning.

17.37 A further factor which may encourage more individuals to spend shorter periods of time undertaking study, at least in the initial stages of their higher education, would be a decision to seek increased contributions from graduates towards the cost of the higher education they have received.

17.38 We believe that half of the total growth in initial full-time participation could be in one year and two year programmes. Overall we estimate that a shift in the pattern towards more students on shorter sub-degree programmes might lead to a ten per cent reduction in the average length of study, with a corresponding reduction in the cost of expansion. Chart 17.2 shows the impact of shorter average length of study on the data presented in Chart 17.1.

Chart 17.2 – Full-time undergraduate numbers and total numbers: central scenario compared with increased participation in sub-degree programmes

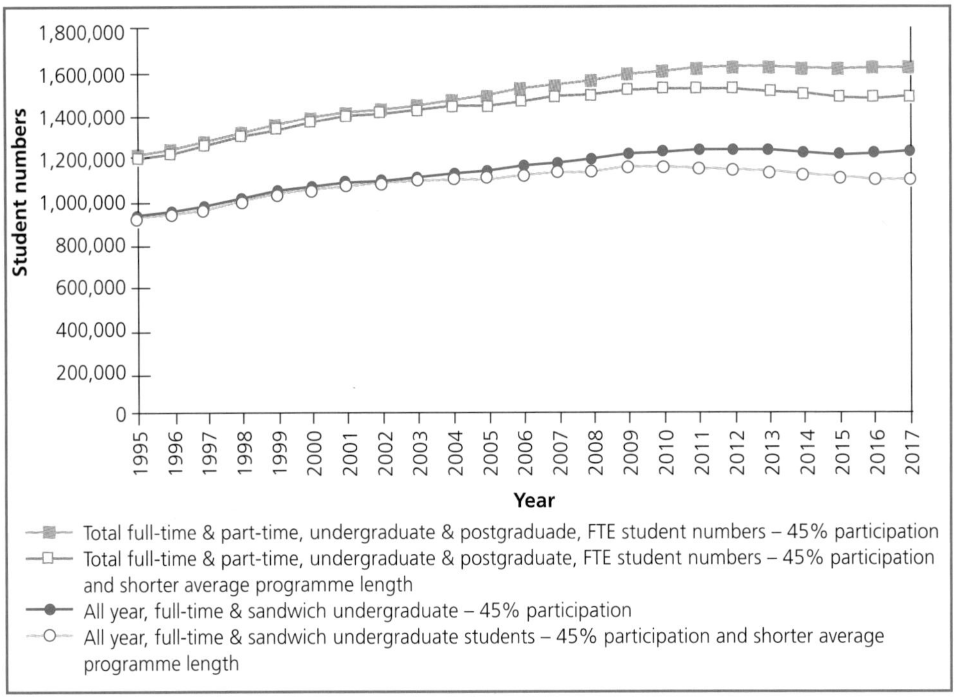

Source: DfEE

17.39   Such changes to programme length would reduce the additional demand for funding by around **£520 million** per annum in the long term: **£420 million in reduced institutional funding and £100 million in reduced student support funding.**

New approaches to learning and teaching

17.40   In Chapter 8 we referred to the initiatives with new technology for learning and teaching that higher education has undertaken. Many of these initiatives were set up in the expectation that using new technology would lead to more cost-effective teaching; they have almost invariably led to higher costs, with greater efficiency still a promise for the future. In the recent rapid expansion, there has been a shift from teaching methods with high variable costs to those with lower variable costs – usually from small group teaching to large group teaching, and from individual supervision to group supervision. Methods of learning and teaching which require a generous staff to student ratio are being used less, with a resulting impact on the nature of the student learning experience.

17.41   The objective is to find more efficient teaching methods that allow institutions to expand numbers without a reduction in the quality of the learning experience or in standards.

17.42   In 20 years time, there will be a wider range of approaches to the delivery of higher education prompted by the developments in communications and information technology (C&IT) identified in Chapter 13. The average cost of provision is likely to be reduced without necessarily reducing the quality of experience for students. An example of the type of cost comparison modelling which leads to this conclusion is presented in Appendix 2. We envisage savings of £200 **million** a year in the long term.

Improved efficiency

17.43 New C&IT can deliver greater efficiency only if it is linked to improving the quality of student learning and amortises development costs over large student numbers. This is one way of securing a step change in the relationship between costs and outputs. Even on current approaches to teaching, there is a range of costs which institutions find difficult to explain in terms of different expected outcomes.[14]

17.44 There is some scope for achieving greater cost-effectiveness through greater collaboration between institutions, which will lead to some rationalisation of practice in institutions serving a locality. We make recommendations in Chapter 16 to address this.

17.45 We conclude that across the whole higher education system it will be possible to deliver the 6.5 per cent reduction in expenditure anticipated in the spending plans of the previous Government over the next seven years, provided that:
- growth is resumed in the system;
- the additional capital investment which we have identified is implemented;
- there is investment in all staff to help meet the challenge they face.

After allowing for further savings (bringing the total to 10%) by 2015-16 the savings delivered would be **£365 million in 2005/06 and £580 million in 2015/16.**

17.46 The discussions so far for improvements in efficiency have taken no account of the impact of changes in relative prices. We have noted, for example, that it has been the practice of government over recent years:
- to increase average levels of student support in line with the Retail Price Index (RPI);
- to calculate the 'efficiency gain' required of institutions in relation to the forecast Gross Domestic Product (GDP) deflator – the Treasury's measure of overall notification with the economy.

17.47 Average earnings have risen by 34 per cent more than prices since 1979. Under the Government's approach to uprating institutional funding and student support the higher rate of growth has imposed an additional pressure on institutions' costs and made students poorer relative to those in work. The implications of a continued growth in earnings realtive to prices for institutional funding and student support are considered further below.

Conclusion on the additional costs of growth

17.48 On the assumptions outlined above about the level of growth, the achievable reductions in unit costs and the proportion of the growth in numbers being on one and two year programmes, the funding requirement for growth against the current planned baseline trended forward from 1997-98 would be as shown in Table 17.5.

Table 17.5 – Estimated cost of growth

	£million	
	2005-2006	2015-2016
Cost at 1995-96 prices	1,400	2,100
savings from		
more students on shorter courses	(200)	(520)
reductions in units of funding	(365)	(580)
new approaches to teaching	–	(200)
Total reduction	**(565)**	**(1,300)**
Net additional cost	**835**	**800**

Lifelong learning

17.49   The above analysis shows little real change from the present pattern of provision and funding, except for overall growth. There are strong economic social, and cultural pressures, at least amongst certain sectors of the population, for higher education to be undertaken full-time, immediately post-school. That will not change quickly. Nevertheless, as Table 17.6 indicates, there is already a wide range of other students in higher education.

Table 17.6 – Qualification aim: comparison between full-time and part-time students across the UK 1995/96 (including the Open University)

	Full-time and sandwich		Part-time	
	Student numbers	% of total	Student numbers	% of total
A. Postgraduate				
Research	47.2	4.3	27.2	5.2
Taught (degree)	48.5	4.4	84.8	16.4
Taught (professional)				
(1) PGCE	19.2	1.7	4.7	0.9
(2) Other	18.2	1.6	62.8	12.1
Taught (other)	1.5	0.1	2.9	0.6
Total postgraduate	**134.6**	**12.2**	**182.4**	**35.2**
B. Undergraduate				
First Degree	860.4	77.8	174.0	33.6
HND/HNC	55.2	5.0	20.5	4.0
DipHE	24.0	2.2	7.8	1.5
Cert HE	0.7	0.1	16.8	3.2
Professional	1.3	0.1	13.5	2.6
Foundation course	2.5	0.2	2.8	0.5
Other sub-degree	27.9	2.5	100.7	19.4
Total undergraduate	**972**	**87.8**	**336.1**	**64.8**
Total undergraduate + postgraduate	**1,106.6**	**100.0**	**518.5**	**100.0**

Source: HESA
Note: components may not sum to totals because of rounding.

17.50   We conclude from these figures that the higher education system in the UK already has a firm base from which to develop as a system of lifelong learning. Further pressures for lifelong learning will come from:

- individuals who wish to combine periods of part-time and full-time study to suit their circumstances;
- individuals who are unemployed and seek mid-career retraining;
- individuals who are employed and whose career developments (or the changing nature of their jobs) require continuing professional development;
- adults with no higher education experience;
- individuals who seek higher education for its own sake.

17.51   All are clearly represented within the existing higher education student population, particularly among part-time and postgraduate students.

Part-time students

17.52   There was strong support from those submitting evidence to us for part-time students to receive the same public funding support as full-time students. Part-time students are currently supported by the block grant from Funding Bodies on a similar basis to full-time students (Table 17.7), but have to pay their own fees and support themselves during study (unless they are unemployed, when they may retain access to benefits such as the Jobseeker's Allowance (JSA) provided they meet certain conditions relating, for example, to availability for work. On the other hand, our survey of students (Report 2: 'Full and part-time students in higher education: their experiences and expectations') indicated that currently about 35 per cent of part-time students have their fees paid for them by their employers, (although the proportion is much lower at the Open University which is the institution with the largest enrolment of part-time undergraduate students). We also note that some 90 per cent of part-time students in our survey are in employment.

Table 17.7 – Public tuition subsidies for different types of students funded by the Higher Education Funding Council for England, 1996-97

Type of Student	Student Numbersa (000)	Funding Council Grant (£million)	1996-97 Publicly funded Tuition fees (£million)	Total (£million)	Public Expenditure/ FTE student (£)
A. Full-time					
undergraduate	705	1,662	965	2,627	3,726
postgraduate (taught)	39	92	–	92	2,359
postgraduate (research)	30	59	46	105	3,500
B. Part-time					
undergraduate numbers FTE	139	265	–	265	1,906
postgraduate numbers FTE (taught)	44	95	–	95	2,160
postgraduate numbers FTE (research)	12	26	–	26	2,166

a The conversion factor to full-time equivalent for part-time students is about 0.4.

Source: HEFCE allocations 1996-97 and DfEE for tuition fees.

17.53   Our preferred approach to removing inequities in the funding of part-time study is one that links closely to our approach to seeking a contribution from full-time students considered in the next two chapters. We are attracted to the model currently operating in the English further education sector, where full-time and part-time students over 18 years old are charged a fee, but institutions may remit the fee for those students in receipt of JSA or family benefits and then claim back the funding foregone from the Further Education Funding Council.

17.54   We estimate that providing equitable treatment of part-time undergraduate students in terms of fee support might cost an extra **£50 million** a year at 1995-96 prices.[15]

Postgraduate study

17.55   For postgraduate study a high proportion of full-time research postgraduate students already have studentships which provide maintenance support and pay programme fees. Most taught postgraduate students (both full-time and part-time), although subsidised by Funding Body block grant, pay fees which are, to a significant extent, determined on the basis of what the market will bear. Although some postgraduate students avail themselves of career development loans (CDLs) to meet fees and their living costs, the vast majority of students on taught postgraduate courses either borrow commercially or are supported by their employers.[16]

17.56   As shown in Table 17.6, 14 per cent of full-time postgraduates and a third of part-time postgraduates, are on professional programmes (excluding Postgraduate Certificate of Education (PGCE) courses). In this area in particular we would expect substantial growth in the next 20 years. A system of lifelong learning must include increased opportunities at the highest level of study for Continuing Professional Development (CPD). These programmes will tend to be of shorter duration and more tailored to the needs of individuals or groups of employees than traditional Masters programmes, although many institutions are now moving to modularise postgraduate Masters programmes in parallel with the modularisation of their undergraduate programmes. Much of this development of CPD will need to be carried out in collaboration with employers, and increasingly the teaching maybe provided on employers' premises.

17.57   Any projection based on the current pattern of postgraduate provision would significantly underestimate the volume of demand for CPD if higher education plays a full part in the development of lifelong learning.

17.58   However, there are strong arguments in favour of growth in CPD provision being funded by the principal beneficiaries – employers and individuals (particularly if they are in work). Individual Learning Accounts (ILAs), discussed further in Chapter 21 could offer a valuable approach to funding this type of programme. We have excluded the potential additional load from CPD in calculating the overall funding requirement because it should, in our view, essentially be **self-funding in the longer term**.

Capital expenditure

17.59 The Government's decision to impose further significant year on year reductions in the unit of funding from 1995-96, and essentially to withdraw long term capital funding, has put a dual pressure on expenditure on refurbishment of the estate; on replacing out-of-date equipment and on investing in new communications and information technology equipment.

17.60 Two recent surveys of research equipment and teaching equipment have indicated the difficulties faced by institutions in replacing equipment on a regular basis.[17, 18] Against this background it is difficult to see how, without additional funding, institutions can be expected to contribute to ensuring that students have access to networked desktop computers as we recommend in Chapter 13.

17.61 If expenditure on infrastructure is foregone, there will be an increase in the proportion of accommodation that is either unfit for its purpose or possibly at risk of closure under health and safety legislation. Institutions will also be unable to give their students access to modern materials and may be frustrated in their attempts to deliver savings because they are unable to invest in the hardware and software required to provide alternative lower cost approaches to teaching.

17.62 We consider further in Chapter 19 how the Funding Bodies might seek to use the funds available to them as effectively as possible in support of investment in the existing estate through a loans scheme.

17.63 On the other hand, the responsibility for funding net additions to estates should rest firmly with institutions themselves either through borrowing, financed by the income stream which the addition to the estate generates, or through using accumulated reserves. The main exception should be where higher education institutions are required to meet costs of developments which serve wider public purposes (for example in medical schools). In those cases, capital grants should be available for higher education institutions.

17.64 We have discussed these issues with the Funding Bodies and concluded that, even if it proves possible, as we have proposed, to spread the planned reduction of the unit of funding over the next seven years and introduce a research infrastructure fund, a shortfall of some **£250 million** per annum in capital funding will remain.

Research

17.65 The establishment of a revolving fund would deal with the need to address the backlog of investment in research infrastructure in top quality research departments. In Chapter 11, we identify three other areas which require increased investment if the UK is to secure the full benefit of its research activity:

■ full funding of project costs by Research Councils requiring around **£110 million** a year;

- additional funding to promote industrial partnership in the Industrial Partnership Development Fund (IPDF), requiring an additional £50 **million** in the long term;
- the establishment of an Arts and Humanities Research Council (AHRC) with additional funding rising to around £25 **million** a year.

17.66   We have not considered the possibility of additional improvements in productivity in research since in general we are looking to provide a more secure base for the current volume of research activity. We consider below, however, the pressures for increased research funding to underpin increased volumes of students on degree programmes.

Improved maintenance support for students

17.67   As we noted in Chapter 7, many representations were made to us about the inadequacy of the 'grant plus loan' package and student hardship. Three main concerns were expressed: that significant numbers of students were living in unhealthy conditions; that an increasing number were being forced to abandon their studies for financial reasons; and that others were having to undertake so much paid work during term time that it was markedly affecting their studies.

17.68   This largely anecdotal evidence was supported by evidence from the Policy Studies Institute's survey of students' income and expenditure in 1995/96.[19] This showed that, on average, students' spending exceeded their income on average from grants (including the assessed parental contribution) and government loans by about £1000 each year.

17.69   To establish the reasons for this, we looked at trends in the value of student support since the introduction of mandatory awards in 1962. We found that although the level of the overall grant plus loan package had fallen in real terms since 1962, it had kept pace with price inflation since 1979. However, as we noted earlier, earnings for those in work have risen 34 per cent more than prices since 1979. Had the value of the total 'grant plus loan' package been increased in line with the rise in real earnings, the total would be £1000 higher per year than it is now.

17.70   Most students cope by supplementing their grant and student loan with earnings, commercial borrowing and additional family support. But in some cases, financial worries are the sole or a major contributing factor in students' deciding to abandon their studies. It is always difficult to establish the real reasons for drop-out, and we note that there has been no significant rise in the overall drop-out rate in recent years.[20]

17.71   Full-time students are now commonly undertaking paid work in term time.[21] While it is valuable for students to gain work experience during vacations, and to supplement their income by undertaking some part-time work during term-time, we believe that students should not have to work a substantial number of hours during term time to meet their basic living costs. Whereas students could ease the pressure caused by working through a combination of full- and part-time studies, there are, as we consider in Chapter 20, significant obstacles to doing so.

17.72 Finally, we were concerned about the extent to which students are graduating with significant levels of commercial debt on top of their student loan debt. We have no difficulty with the idea of students choosing to borrow from the commercial sector with real interest rates to finance non-essential expenditure. We are concerned however, that the combined value of the grant and state student loan together should not fall behind a level adequate to meet students' necessary expenditure.

17.73 There is, therefore, a case for a modest increase in the level of student support for all full-time undergraduates. However, the cost would be substantial: an increase of only £250 in the loan element would cost an estimated £175 million per annum in the short term on current take up levels. Given other pressures on the system, we recognise that funds are unlikely to be available for an across the board increase of this kind over the next few years. We also found that these pressures bear more on some students than others. On balance, those from socio-economic groups IIIm to V are worse placed financially than those from groups I to IIIn. This is because the former have less income from sources other than public support, and because other demands on their income are higher.

17.74 We have also looked at the arrangements and levels of support available for student living costs in other countries. There are varying mixtures of grants and loans for student support in Europe with near universal means testing of such support. The levels of support, even for the poorest students, tend to be significantly below UK levels, but with the Nordic countries being more generous than those in Southern Europe.

17.75 We advocate, therefore, that any increase in support for student maintenance should be targeted. That is why we recommended in Chapter 7 that the Government should review students' access to benefits, increase the size and widen the scope of the Access Funds.

17.76 In addition we think it important, to avoid exacerbating the kind of problems which many current students face, that the overall level of student support is kept under review. In particular we believe it is essential to look both at movements in prices and in earnings.

Recommendation 70 **We recommend to the Government that it reviews annually the total level of support for student living costs taking into account the movements of both prices and earnings.**

17.77 It is not possible to be certain what real increase in the student support for living costs might result from such a review. By way of illustration a one per cent real increase in each year would cost **£16 million in 1998/99** and an additional **£400 million by 2015/16** before taking into account any increase in student loan receipts from the increased level of the available loan.

17.78 In the longer term, we believe that there is a case for higher education institutions to play a greater role in providing financial support to students and that an enlarged role for the Access Funds will provide a basis for such developments. We estimate that an additional **£40 million** is required each year in current prices for increased Access Funds and for widening of scope and removal of the means-test of the disabled students allowance as we discussed in relation to short term needs.

Higher education pay

17.79   As we noted earlier the Government uprates institutional public funding by the Gross Domestic Product (GDP) deflator before applying required reductions in unit funding. Institutions have a significantly higher proportion of their expenditure on pay than is the case in the general economy. A real increase in earnings therefore imposes further pressure on institutions' ability to meet reductions in units of funding. Over the long term we believe it would be reasonable for staff achieving the expected increases in productivity to benefit from some real increase in their wages and salaries. In estimating the long term funding requirement of higher education we have thought it right to assume from 2004-2005 that there will be a real increase in wages and salaries costs of one per cent per year. **By the year 2015-2016 we estimate the additional cost would be £600 million.**

17.80   We have not, however, allowed for any increase in salaries or wages that may arise from the review that we have proposed in Chapter 14.

Summary of long term requirements

17.81   Table 17.8 below summarises the additional funding requirements for growth, to reset the current baseline and to meet our key key priorities.

Table 17.8 – Summary of additional annual funding requirements in 20 years time compared to current expenditure

	£million (recurrent) 2015-2016)
Increased numbers	2,100
Potential offsetting savings	(1,300)
Equity for part-time undergraduate students	50
Refurbishing the estate and replacing and improving equipment (including C&IT equipment)	250
Research:	
■ Project overheads	110
■ Industrial partnership	50
■ Arts and Humanities Research Council	25
Improved student support	40[a]
Real growth in salaries	600
Total	**1,925**

a. This includes £20 million per annum for increase in the access funds, £20 million for disabled student allowances.

17.82   These estimates exclude a number of elements:

- we do not believe that our proposal in Chapter 8 for a new Institute for Learning and Teaching in Higher Education and for new procedures for the assurance of quality and standards, discussed in Chapter 10, should lead to any significant net increase in the funding requirement;
- we believe that very significant investment is required in all staff to help them meet the challenges ahead. Although such investment would, in our view, amount to at least one per cent of the salary bill (£60 million in 1995-96 prices) it is not clear how far this could be met by re-targeting existing expenditure;
- we have made no allowance for ongoing increased costs from the immediate review of pay and conditions we have proposed;
- we have not included the possible cost of student support rising in real terms relative to prices. A cumulative one per cent real increase would cost £400 million by the end of 20 years;
- as we noted, earlier we have not assumend any increase in the research element of the funding provided by the Funding Bodies. If some at least of the growth in student numbers we expect to see over the next 20 years is on higher level programmes, our conclusion in Chapter 11 that such higher level work needs to be underpinned by research would imply some increase in research funding. If one quarter of the growth was in higher level programmes, the additional requirements for research funding would be £100 million per annum at 1995-96 prices.

17.83   As we noted in paragraph 17.35 the funding requirement has been measured against the current public expenditure plans trended forward from 1997-98. These plans include an assumption that the existing student loan book will be sold. If the Government did not proceed with the sale, there would be loan repayments of £600 million available by 2015-2016 (together with a further £100 million from the increased student numbers in the system which we expect) to contribute to the funding requirements we have identified. Not selling the loan book would, however, leave a large gap in the short term public expenditure plans. We discuss these issues further in Chapter 20.

Conclusion

17.84   We are satisfied that the funding requirements we have identified are necessary to secure the high quality, internationally competitive system we would wish to see. We believe the requirements to be modest in the longer term, bearing in mind the expected growth in Gross Domestic Product (GDP) of two per cent a year on a long term basis. We consider in the next chapter how the funding requirements might be met.

Chapter 18

Who should pay for higher education?

Introduction

18.1   Our vision is for a world class higher education system based on high quality learning and teaching, which combines rigour and economic relevance. In the previous chapter we estimated the future costs of such a system and identified a gap between those costs and the current level of public and private funding. We are convinced that the gap is real and cannot be closed simply by further efficiency savings on the part of institutions.

18.2   Throughout our report we have emphasised our belief that the long term wellbeing of higher education rests on establishing a new compact between society, as represented by the Government, students and their families, employers and providing institutions. Each member of the compact needs to play their part and we have shown in the preceding chapters ways in which this can be done. The compact implies that each of the stakeholders both contributes to, and receives benefits from, higher education. This notion is represented schematically in Table 18.1 overleaf.

18.3   In this chapter, we consider the compact in relation to paying for higher education. To establish how each group might reasonably be expected to contribute to the costs of higher education, we therefore consider:
- who currently pays for higher education institutions;
- who currently pays for students to attend higher education institutions;
- who currently benefits from higher education;
- who should pay for higher education in the future.

18.4   We also consider how far the contributions of the stakeholders, taken together, may be expected to meet the overall growth in funding which is needed to bridge the funding gap.

Who currently pays for higher education institutions?

18.5   The sources of income for higher education institutions' activities are shown in Table 18.2.

Table 18.1 – Higher education: a new compact

	Contribution	Benefits
Society and taxpayers, as represented by the Government	■ A fair proportion of public spending and national income devoted to higher education. ■ Greater stability in the public funding and framework for higher education.	■ A highly skilled, adaptable workforce. ■ Research findings to underpin a knowledge-based economy. ■ Informed, flexible, effective citizens. ■ A greater share of higher education costs met by individual beneficiaries.
Students and graduates	■ A greater financial contribution than now to the costs of tuition and living costs (especially for those from richer backgrounds). ■ Time and effort applied to learning.	■ More chances to participate in a larger system. ■ Better information and guidance to inform choices. ■ A high quality learning experience. ■ A clear statement of learning outcomes. ■ Rigorously assured awards which have standing across the UK and overseas. ■ Fairer income contingent arrangements for making a financial contribution when in work. ■ Better support for part-time study. ■ Larger Access Funds.
Institutions	■ Collective commitment to rigorous assurance of quality and standards. ■ New approaches to learning and teaching. ■ Continual search for more cost-effective approaches to the delivery of higher education. ■ Commitment to developing and supporting staff.	■ A new source of funding for teaching and the possibility of resumed expansion. ■ New funding streams for research which recognise different purposes. ■ Greater recognition from society of the value of higher education. ■ Greater stability in funding.
Higher education staff	■ Commitment to excellence. ■ Willingness to seek and adopt new ways of doing things.	■ Greater recognition (financial and non-financial) of the value of all of their work, not just research. ■ Proper recognition of their profession. ■ Access to training and development opportunities. ■ Fair pay.
Employers	■ More investment in training of employees. ■ Increased contribution to infrastructure of research. ■ More work experience opportunities for students. ■ Greater support for employees serving on institutions' governing bodies.	■ More highly educated people in the workforce. ■ Clearer understanding of what higher education is offering. ■ More opportunities for collaborative working with higher education. ■ Better accessibility to higher education resources for small and medium size enterprises. ■ Outcomes of research.
The families of students	■ Possible contribution to costs	■ Better higher education opportunities for their children. ■ Better, more flexible, higher education opportunities for mature students.

Table 18.2 – Source of income of higher education institutions by activity type 1995-96

	Public Funds	Individ-uals	Source of Income £million (per cent) Industry/ Commerce	Charities	Other[a]	Total
Teaching	4,265	411[b]	–[c]	–[d]	752[e]	5,428
(per cent of total)	(78.6)	(7.6)	(-)	(-)	(13.9)	(100)
Research	1,752	–	170	338	97	2,357
(per cent of total)	(74.3)	(-)	(7.2)	(14.3)	(4.1)	(100)
Other activities[f]	1,106[g]	722[h]	122	–	976[i]	2,926
(per cent of total)	(37.8)	(24.7)	(4.2)	–	(33.3)	(100)
Total	**7,123**	**1,133**	**292**	**338**	**1,825**	**10,711**
(per cent of total)	**(66.5)**	**(10.6)**	**(2.7)**	**(3.2)**	**(17.0)**	**(100)**

Source: HESA
(Components may not sum to totals because of rounding)

Notes:

a.   'Other' includes 'other general income', and 'other income for services rendered'.

b.   A proportion of this will be met by employers.

c.   There will be some contribution from employers included within the 'individuals' total including, in particular, fees for company-based training and continuing professional development.

d.   There will be some scholarship income from charities probably included in the 'other' column.

e.   Includes overseas student fees and contract services for core activities other than research. It will also include fee income from those on full-time undergraduate courses but not in receipt of mandatory awards.

f.   Includes some activities which support teaching and research.

g.   Includes income from health and hospital authorities for nurse training.

h.   Income from catering and residence operations. A part of this will be from conference trade, and a part funded from student maintenance, including parental contributions.

i.   Includes endowment income and interest receivable totalling £263m in 1995-96.

Public funding

18.6   This table shows that total income for higher education institutions from public sources in 1995-96 amounted to some £7 billion. This public funding is borne by those in all socio-economic groups as they contribute to general taxation. Nonetheless, it appears that the percentage of Gross Domestic Product spent on UK higher education is significantly lower than that of some of our major competitors (although with our relatively low dropout rates and short courses our system of higher education is more efficient). International comparisons of expenditure levels on higher education are not straightforward because of differences in definitions.

Private funding

18.7   Table 18.2 shows that higher education institutions already receive significant sums, about a third of their total income in 1995–96, from sources other than the Government. We recognise, for example, the funding contribution from employers. In addition to their contribution to fees for some part-time students, included in Table 18.2, employers contribute in ways which are not shown on the table, including:

■   supporting the living costs of some individual full-time undergraduates through sponsorship;

■ providing work placement opportunities for students on sandwich courses or projects for other students.

Who currently pays for students to attend higher education institutions?

18.8 A significant part of the total costs of higher education currently falls to individuals and their families, whether through meeting living costs in whole or in part, or the payment of fees towards the cost of tuition.

18.9 The parental/spouse's contribution to students' living costs is a significant source of private funding to higher education. Table 18.3 shows that parents/spouses were expected to contribute £700 million in 1995/96, under the current mandatory awards system with its parental means test. This averaged £760 per award holder.

Table 18.3 – Assessed parental/individual contribution for mandatory award holders 1991/92 to 1995/96

	1991-92[a]	1992-93[a]	1993-94	1994-95	1995-96
Average assessed parental contribution (£) per student	990	940	880	813	762
Mandatory award holders[b] (0000) (UK)	659	771	855	903	916
Total assessed parental contribution (£m)	**652**	**725**	**752**	**734**	**698**

Source: DfEE
a Numbers of madatory award holders in Scotland and Northern Ireland in 1991/92 and 1992/93 have been estimated using their proportions in the later years.
b Excludes placement year sandwich students who receive no maintenance support in their placement year.

18.10 In practice, the contribution by parents/spouses to students' living costs tends to exceed the assessed contribution.[1] Some of this parental contribution, as well as a proportion of the publicly funded support for maintenance, will be recorded within the £722m of income received by institutions from their catering and residence operations in 1995-96 (Table 18.2). These funds from students' parents and spouses represent an important contribution to the costs of higher education. Indeed, we estimate that, if they are added, together with the public funds for maintenance support of some £2.1 billion, to the funding for institutions shown in Table 18.2, the total private and public income of higher education institutions probably increases by about £2 billion (after taking into account the double counting of expenditure on catering and residence in institutions) to at least £13 billion in 1995-96, or about 1.8 per cent of Gross Domestic Product.[2]

18.11 The contributions from public and private sector sources set out in Tables 18.2, 17.2 and 18.3 can be summarised, as in Chart 18.1.

Chart 18.1 – Sources for funding for higher education, per cent

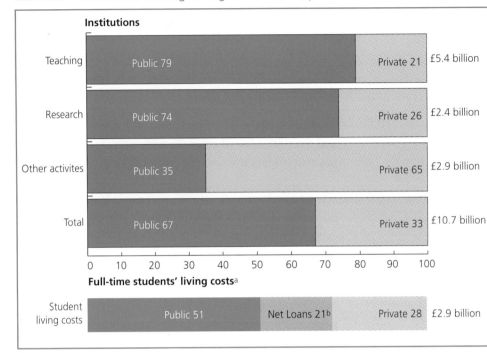

Note: a including parental contributions in excess of assessed contributions

   b loans are shown separately because they are counted as public funding when they are advanced but eventually a
   high proportion will be repaid from private sources.

Who currently benefits from higher education?

18.12   We have also considered who benefits from higher education. The benefits of higher
         education are not necessarily shared equitably between those who currently pay for it.
         Who benefits depends strongly on the activity concerned. The main beneficiaries of
         higher education tuition, for example, differ from the main beneficiaries of higher
         education research.

18.13   As we say in Chapter 6, the evidence of measurable benefits from higher education
         shows that graduates are certainly major beneficiaries. The studies reported there
         demonstrate a strong link – in aggregate – between participation in full-time
         undergraduate education and the relative subsequent earnings potential of an
         individual. Compared to those without higher education qualifications who were
         qualified to enter higher education, those with higher education qualifications:
         ■ have higher employment rates;
         ■ enjoy higher salaries;
         ■ enjoy an average private rate of return of some 11 to 14 per cent.

18.14   This provides a strong positive incentive for individuals to commit themselves to a
         programme of higher education. Accordingly, we suggest in Chapter 6 that such
         information should be generally available to students, and will be a key factor in
         sustaining high levels of demand for higher education. We have summarised the overall
         position. Not all individual graduates will benefit to this extent.

18.15   As we described in Chapter 6 we are persuaded that those with higher education qualifications will continue to enjoy salary premia over those without, even with a significant increase in the numbers of graduates. This is certainly the lesson of the North American experience, where there continues to be significant labour market benefits for graduates.[3]

18.16   We also noted in Chapter 7 that the pattern of participation in higher education by those from different socio-economic groups does not currently reflect the socio-economic composition of the population. Those from socio-economic groups IV and V have much lower participation rates than those from socio-economic groups I and II. The benefits of participation which flow to those with higher education qualifications are thus distributed unequally across the population.[4] However, as we showed earlier, whereas public funding for higher education is drawn from the whole population through general taxation, benefits go primarily to those from socio-economic groups I to IIIn. The one exception to this pattern is the maintenance grant which, because it is means tested, benefits students from lower income households. Its current value is about £1 billion a year. We say more about this in Chapter 20.

18.17   We found in Chapter 6 that it is more difficult to calculate the full economic benefits to the state from its investment in higher education teaching than to calculate the rates of return to individuals. Estimates suggest that the return for the state's investment in teaching has been 7 to 9 per cent over a number of years. But with recent expansion in provision, this is now estimated to have fallen to around 6 per cent and is expected to stay at around that level for the next few years. While this is significantly below the private rate of return to graduates, it matches the requirement which the Treasury sets for returns from public expenditure. It also excludes any other economic benefits beyond those reflected in the earnings differentials of those who have higher education qualifications, although we do conclude in Chapter 6 that the identification of these other benefits, let alone their quantification, remains elusive and we have therefore treated the evidence with caution.

18.18   Higher education, both through its principal purposes and through its rich diversity, contributes directly to the national wellbeing. As we argue in Chapter 5, higher education provides a crucial underpinning to a modern participative democracy and contributes directly to the maintenance and development of our national culture. Such intangible contributions are not of the kind that lend themselves to ready quantification since they are arguably priceless assets.

18.19   Employers, too, are major beneficiaries of higher education through the skills which those with higher education qualifications bring to the organisations which employ them, and, in the long term, from research findings.

18.20   No company manufacturing high technology products or providing high level services in the rapidly developing services sector would have a sustainable business without its share of highly qualified staff. With a movement to a knowledge-based economy that depends even more on the knowledge and skill of individual workers, this is likely to be increasingly the case as we advance into the next century. That is a premise upon which much of this report is built.

Who should pay for higher education in the future?

18.21   Our assessment of the national economic and cultural importance of higher education supports our conclusion that the state must remain a major source of funding for higher education in the future. The social rate of return, whilst in many ways an unsatisfactory way of measuring the return to the state from its investment in higher education, does tell us that that return at least meets the conventional test for public expenditure, as applied by the Treasury.

18.22   But we conclude that there is a more subtle and more powerful rationale for the state's continued involvement in funding higher education. This rationale has three elements:

- Society as a whole has a direct interest in ensuring that the United Kingdom has the level of participation in higher education which it needs for sustained economic and social viability and, therefore, to match those of its competitors. This has been a recurring theme of our report. This means that the state needs to ensure that higher education provision is adequate and receives the levels of funding needed to support the necessary levels of participation. Whilst the measurable financial benefits from higher education qualifications accrue largely to individuals, the costs of a shortfall in the numbers of those obtaining such qualifications will fall to the UK as a whole and its citizens.

- Firms and individuals are most likely to engage primarily in training specific to their immediate needs. There is therefore a danger that, if left to employers or individuals, the nature and level of higher education will not best serve the long term needs of the economy as a whole; and there will be under-investment. The state alone is able to ensure that tomorrow's workforce is equipped with the widest range of skills and attributes.

- The state must also make sure that access to higher education is socially just, and that talent is not wasted.

18.23   We have noted the Government's desire over the long term to increase the proportion of national wealth devoted to education and training. We fully support that ambition and believe it is in the national interest that, over the long term, public spending on higher education should rise in real terms.

Recommendation 71   **We recommend to the Government that, over the long term, public spending on higher education should increase with the growth in Gross Domestic Product.**

18.24   There is overwhelming evidence that those with higher education qualifications are the main beneficiaries from higher education in the form of improved employment prospects and pay. Individuals who benefit in this way are not drawn proportionately from the socio-economic groups that currently fund higher education through general taxation. We conclude, therefore, that graduates in employment should make a greater contribution to the costs of higher education in the future. While we believe the economy as a whole, and those who employ graduates, are also substantial beneficiaries, even though these benefits have proved elusive to quantify, the greatest benefit accrues to graduates themselves. On average, they receive an excellent return for their investment in higher education and we draw on this in our subsequent recommendations in Chapter 20.

18.25   Employers form an essential element in the compact on which our approach is based. We have recognised the contribution they already make to higher education but there are ways in which, in their own longer term interest, we would seek an enhanced contribution. We make recommendations elsewhere to encourage employers to create greater opportunities for work experience and to encourage them to sponsor increased numbers of students (Chapter 9). We also make recommendations on their contribution to research (Chapter 11). However, the greatest contribution by employers, other than through tax, is to the costs of education and training of their workforce. Support for continuing study and development will need to develop further in the years ahead to support lifelong learning and maintain the competitiveness of the UK. Respondents to our employer survey (Appendix 4) suggest that they will increase their use of higher education as an investment in their staff, if the programmes are responsive to their needs, of good quality and competitively priced.

Conclusion

18.26   A common theme from many, but not all, of those submitting evidence to us, was the need to consider new approaches to funding of higher education to supplement that from the taxpayer. As Report 1 on our national consultation states:
  'the general view on funding coming through the submissions is that the responsibility for funding the system should be shared between the government, students and employers; that the funding arrangements should make possible such a balance; and that the funding system should help increase the flexibility of the system.'

18.27   This is consistent with the principle we established in Chapter 5:
  'The various beneficiaries of higher education should share its costs and public funding should be distributed equitably so that individuals are not denied access to higher education through lack of financial means.'

18.28   The need to supplement public funding has been given sharper focus first by the publicly-stated views of the main national political parties that, notwithstanding the priority they afford to education, higher education could not expect additional public funding, at least in the short-term. The evidence in the preceding chapter about the funding gap confronting higher education forces the conclusion that new approaches must be found. A consideration of the beneficiaries of higher education suggests that, on grounds of equity, it is right to turn to graduates in work to contribute more of the costs of their higher education. The evidence on the measurable benefits from higher education does not, however, provide a basis for determining what precise share should be borne by the graduate and what share borne by the state or others. But we do conclude that there is a strong basis for seeking an increased contribution from graduates in work towards the cost of their higher education, and we look in Chapter 20 at ways in which this can be done.

Chapter 19

Funding learning and teaching

19.1 In Chapters 17 and 18 we referred to a common theme in our discussions: the sharing of the costs of higher education between taxpayers in general (the state), individuals and their families, graduates in work and employers. We have also argued that institutions have an essential contribution to make in providing higher education in a cost-effective fashion. It will be clear that we see the state as having a continuing substantial involvement in the funding of higher education. In this chapter we consider the methods of delivery of public funds to institutions. At one level, the proposals put forward are independent of whether or not the graduate in work is to make a contribution towards the costs of higher education, but we examine how the public funding element and a contribution from graduates in work might in practice interact.

19.2 The current funding systems, developed originally to support an elite system, have been adapted to support a much more diverse range of institutions, much larger numbers of students, and a much higher expectation of what can be delivered from the research infrastructure. We have been conscious of the need to take account of this experience in devising funding arrangements which are capable of delivering the kind of higher education system which the UK will need over the next 20 years. In particular, we have sought to take account of the prospective need for further expansion of initial higher education, of the need to promote lifelong learning, and of how an approach in which student choices shape the system could support our long term vision of higher education. We also took the view that funding should promote the wider objectives of higher education rather than, as is currently the case, funding driving those objectives.

19.3 In this chapter we therefore:
- review existing arrangements for distributing funds to institutions;
- establish the principles which should govern such arrangements in the future;
- examine the relative merits of a 'block grant' approach for funding tuition and a system in which public funding flows to institutions on the basis of student choice;
- examine the administrative implications of our proposals;
- consider the circumstances in which it would be acceptable for different levels of public support to be given to different programmes of higher education ('differential pricing');
- consider the financing of capital investment.

Existing arrangements for distributing public funds to institutions

19.4 Public funding for tuition in higher education flows to institutions through two main routes:
- block grants, covering all eligible higher education students (full-time, part-time, undergraduate and postgraduate) paid out through Funding Bodies, principally the Higher Education Funding Council for England, the Scottish Higher Education Funding Council, the Higher Education Funding Council for Wales, the Department of Education Northern Ireland and the Teacher Training Agency;

■ funding which, more directly, follows the student. This takes the form of tuition fees paid to the institution at which study is being undertaken as part of each eligible full-time undergraduate's mandatory grant. The mandatory grant fee levels are determined annually by the Government which reimburses local education authorities for the fee payments they make. There are no publicly funded fees for part-time or postgraduate taught students other than those taking the Postgraduate Certificate of Education (PGCE).

19.5   Governments have, from time to time, adjusted the balance between block grants and tuition fees to achieve their policy objectives. For instance, by providing more money in the form of tuition fees, in the late 1980s and early 1990s, the Government encouraged institutions to admit more students, without any increase in block grants. The increased income from tuition fees provided the opportunity for institutions to increase their total income, so obtaining the growth in participation sought by the Government at a reduced unit cost. In contrast, channelling a greater proportion of funds through the block grants of the Funding Bodies gives greater central control over public expenditure, and over the distribution of funds between individual institutions. In the mid 1990s, when the Government sought to stop growth, it shifted the balance back towards the Funding Bodies' grant, and imposed a system of capping full-time student numbers, leaving individual institutions very little room for manoeuvre in their recruitment of full-time students.

19.6   The methods which the Funding Bodies use to distribute their block grants can themselves have a substantial effect on the behaviour and financial stability of institutions. The Funding Bodies use student numbers as one of the main drivers in their allocation methods for funding tuition, and take account of the different costs of providing different subjects. Such approaches are usually described as formula funding. When the current Funding Bodies were set up, there were wide differences in the unit of funding enjoyed by different institutions which owed more to history than to any rational assessment of the relative costs or value of institutions' offerings. The Funding Bodies have adopted different methods of allocating funds between institutions but all have sought, to differing extents, to bring about some convergence in funding levels for different institutions.

19.7   The Teacher Training Agency has created a direct link between funding decisions and assessments of quality. Although the other Funding Bodies have in reserve the power to remove funding from any activity which they assess as being of inadequate quality, they have not needed to use the power. Institutions have, in most cases, rectified shortcomings or, in a few cases, have chosen to close down a programme.

19.8   Although the majority of funding provided through block grants is distributed by a formula funding approach, each Funding Body holds back some of its grant – to support centrally determined priorities. In practice this has been done principally:
    ■ to provide a single national approach to key developments for example the development of SuperJANET, the higher education information superhighway;

- to provide for historical differences in costs beyond the control of individual institutions, the extra costs of providing minority subjects or the costs of maintaining national museums and galleries;
- to promote new developments in teaching and learning.

The Funding Bodies have also used their discretion to ameliorate the effects of major year on year funding changes on individual institutions. This has been particularly significant after each Research Assessment Exercise, the outcome of which can have a major impact on an individual institution's research funding.

Funding principles

19.9   In advising on funding arrangements over the next 20 years we have, within the general framework of promoting equity of access amongst individuals irrespective of social background, taken the following factors into consideration;
- promoting responsiveness to informed student demand by institutions and other providers;
- aligning, as far as possible, the funding arrangements for part-time and full-time undergraduates;
- promoting a reasonable degree of stability in the system and reducing its vulnerability to fluctuations in the economic cycle or to changes in Government policy;
- helping to sustain standards, so that UK institutions continue to measure up to their international competitors;
- maximising the return on public investment in higher education for the nation's economic development, and incentivising improved cost-effectiveness among providers;
- supporting institutional collaboration, on a regional, national and international basis, where appropriate.

19.10   No single approach to funding can meet all these concerns, and our recommendations have turned on the relative weight attached to them, and the broader desirability that proposals on funding should promote the wider purposes of higher education and of society as a whole.

19.11   It is essential within any approach to funding to define what programmes of study are eligible for funding and which providers of eligible programmes should be included.

What is eligible for public funding for higher education?

19.12   The current legal framework on the eligibility of programmes for funding (and consequent funding arrangements) varies across the UK. There are particular differences in where the responsibility for funding higher education sub-degree work lies. In Scotland, for example, the Scottish Office Education and Industry Department funds all higher education provided in further education colleges. In England, the Higher Education Funding Council for England funds 'prescribed' sub-degree higher education (principally full-time HNDs) in further education colleges but the Further

Education Funding Council funds 'non-prescribed' higher education (mainly HNCs and other part-time study). Across the United Kingdom as a whole, there is currently no common practice in many part-time or postgraduate areas as to whether institutions charge students the full cost or whether they use Funding Body grant to subsidise the fees they charge. This is particularly the case for some postgraduate professional courses.

19.13   Chapter 22 considers the arguments for determining and clarifying funding responsibilities along either institutional lines or on the basis of level of provision, and the case for adopting different approaches in the different national regions of the UK.

19.14   We have not been able in the time available to us to investigate properly the issues surrounding public support for professional courses, especially those at postgraduate level. In general, though, we believe that programmes of study leading to a professional qualification which is a requirement of employment should be funded by employers and individuals, and that the government should discourage tendencies for the length of publicly funded programmes to be extended to meet professional requirements. Such extensions should raise the question of employer contributions.

Which institutions and other providers are in the group which receives public funds?

19.15   Currently, there is a recognised group of institutions eligible to receive public funds from the higher education Funding Bodies. A number of private institutions outside this group would like to be eligible to receive such funding. While we believe that there must be scope for admitting new institutions to the publicly funded group, and for extending the coverage of existing institutions, the availability of funding as well as need will always be relevant criteria to such enlargement. There are also other important conditions that should be satisfied before an institution becomes eligible for public funding from the Funding Bodies. These include openness of access by students, compliance with requirements on standards and quality assurance, and conformity with the conditions for public funding that apply to existing institutions. Institutions seeking public funding would need to show that there was a good prospect of their being able to satisfy these conditions on a continuing basis.

19.16   It has been put to us, however, that individuals who wish to study some subjects such as drama, dance and stage management are disadvantaged because the majority of the provision for these subjects is in institutions that are not currently in receipt of public funds. We believe that the appropriate approach in this case would be to provide public support to the students themselves rather than to the institutions that make the provision. This is considered further in Chapter 20.

Proposals for funding tuition

19.17   We have examined the relative merits of the two main available systems of delivering public funding for tuition to institutions:

■ a 'block grant' system;

■ a system in which funds follow the student.

to see how well they met the principles in 19.9. The alternatives are examined in more detail in Report 14, 'Methods for funding tuition', but their main features are summarised below.

19.18   In a 'block grant' model an institution contracts with a Funding Body to provide a specified quantity of higher education. The contract can specify to varying degrees the precise nature and mix of provision which is to be made. The level of funding in the block grant can vary accordingly to the type of student, the programme of study, and the length and intensity of study. Providing an institution meets the terms of its contract and if the Funding Body does not prevent it from doing so, it can be free to recruit above its student number target but it does not receive any additional public funding through block grants for doing so.

19.19   A system in which funds follow the student can be based on private funding or public funding or a mix of the two. Its essence is that an institution's income is directly related to its success in recruiting students. If public funding is the basis for such a system, the student might carry proxy funds, such as a credit or voucher. The real money value which the institution received when it cashed the proxy could vary according to the nature of the programme chosen by the student.

19.20   As we noted in 19.4, the current UK system for funding higher education tuition combines the two approaches: for full-time undergraduates block grant, and publicly funded fees which follow the student; and for most other students block grant, and private fees at a level set by the institution. The way in which the block grant element is determined varies somewhat across the countries of the United Kingdom.

19.21   It is a feature of the present system that all public funding for the vast majority of part-time and postgraduate students is provided through block grants, and the publicly-funded fee supports only full-time undergraduates.

19.22   The main advantage of a block grant approach, at least in the short term, is the certainty it offers on the level of public expenditure on higher education which will be incurred each year. The Government can make a decision about the level of funding it wishes to devote to supporting higher education tuition before the start of the financial year in the knowledge that it is unlikely to be exceeded. The Funding Bodies can set their contracts with institutions to match the available level of funding. As this approach gives the Funding Bodies the power of being monopoly purchasers – 'monopsonists' – it puts them in a powerful position to push down the cost of higher education, which they can do more effectively than individual student purchasers could. A block grant approach, depending on how it is operated, can offer institutions a degree of stability in their funding. It also gives the Funding Bodies a strong lever to use for the maintenance of quality and standards. It empowers the Funding Bodies to promote particular types of study differentially.

19.23   The main disadvantages of the block grant approach are its inflexibility and insensitivity to student demand. The Funding Body determines to a large extent what subjects students can study, and at what institution. It can, of course, endeavour to adjust its contracts in the light of perceived student demand, but central approaches can never be as sensitive and flexible as individual decisions of students and institutions.

19.24   By contrast, in a model in which public funding follows the students' choices, those choices determine the shape of the system and institutions are encouraged to respond in order to maintain or increase recruitment and income. As responsiveness to students' changing needs is a key aspect of the Committee's vision, this approach is very attractive for the long term. It recognises that students are individuals with a wide range of needs. In the longer term, in a learning society, we expect that students will want to move in and out of the system much more frequently, and a funding system which mirrors student decisions can reflect this more easily than a block grant system.

19.25   The full realisation of this potential requires that an appropriate share of the block grant which currently provides for students on part-time and postgraduate courses is converted into funding that follows student choice as well as the share that supports full-time undergraduate students: otherwise part-time and postgraduate students will be yet more disadvantaged compared to full-time undergraduate students.

19.26   The main potential disadvantages of an approach in which funding follows the student are that:
   ■ the Government has no ready means of controlling public expenditure on higher education within a financial year;
   ■ the individual student will not be as powerful a purchaser as a central funding body, which may reduce the pressure on institutions to be as cost-effective as possible;
   ■ the individual student may not be well-informed enough to make good decisions, and in particular may be unable to avoid poor quality or low standard offerings.

19.27   We believe that our proposals in Chapters 8, 9 and 10, for better information and guidance for potential students, for clearer specifications of programmes of study, and arrangements for the tighter assurance of quality and standards will help to minimise the last of these problems.

19.28   General pressure on institutions to reduce costs will continue to be applied through a squeeze on the total of public funds. However, the impact of continued severe pressure across the board coupled with common funding levels for particular kinds of provision could lead to some institutions seeking a higher per capita payment on the ground that their higher costs are justified. We consider this issue of differential prices for programmes in more detail in paragraphs 19.41 to 19.47.

19.29   This leaves the issue of the control of public expenditure. Experience in the early 1990s showed that when an increasing proportion of public funding flowed with full-time undergraduate students there were substantial increases in demand, and in spending on fees and student living cost support, beyond that allowed for in public expenditure plans. This, in turn, led to the Government's decision from 1994/95 to introduce a consolidation of numbers through the use of individual institutional caps on full-time undergraduate numbers. The Treasury's concern about open-ended payments related to demand will have been exacerbated by recent experience in the further education sector.

19.30   There are several ways of approaching this problem. Public expenditure could be controlled by limiting the number of credits or vouchers an institution could cash in any one year, but this would be tantamount to keeping a student number cap. Alternatively, the value at which the voucher or credit was cashed could be determined once the full number of units to be cashed was known. This would, however, present institutions with great uncertainty, and would enable those who wanted to expand at a low unit cost to drive down unit funding across all institutions, including those which were unable or unwilling to expand.

19.31   We believe that the best way forward would be through gradual but steady progress towards more public funding flowing with the student. Over the long term, we believe that a gradual shift would allow a much better understanding, on the part of the government and the Funding Bodies, of the year to year changes in demand for higher education, and of the propensity of institutions to respond to those changes. Reasonable year on year fluctuations should be accepted by the government but it would be desirable to retain a reduced element of block grant to allow intervention by the government to influence the level of demand if, for example, participation in higher education was falling behind that in competitor countries. In practice, the balance can only be struck on the basis of experience during the transition.

Recommendation 72   **We recommend to the Government that it shifts the balance of funding, in a planned way, away from block grant towards a system in which funding follows the student, assessing the impact of each successive shift on institutional behaviour and the control of public expenditure, with a target of distributing at least 60 per cent of total public funding to institutions according to student choice by 2003.**

Contributions from individuals

19.32   This recommendation must, however, be seen in the context of the option we consider in Chapter 20 for seeking an increased contribution from individuals, on full-time undergraduate courses, towards the cost of higher education. Most of the options involve a contribution to the cost of tuition from individuals either in the form of loan repayments (or contributions) once they have entered employment or from them or their families at the time of study. If one of these proposals is accepted, the individual contribution would flow to the institution immediately and the individual would enter into a loan agreement with the agency making the loans. Within the total of funding for tuition it would be necessary to determine a new balance of block grant, the element of public funding flowing to the institution on the basis of student choice, alongside the loan-backed student contribution. We would favour the student contribution leading to a reduction in the block grant element as a step in the direction outlined in our recommendation above.

19.33   In the evidence submitted to us by institutions, an ongoing message was that, almost as difficult as the levels of reduction in funding, was the suddenness with which the changes were introduced and the frequency of changes. While we do not believe that higher education can or should be wholly insulated from the vagaries which affect the economy as a whole, we believe that higher education requires a greater degree of certainty about its levels of funding beyond the year ahead than is provided by the current public expenditure planning process. We think that the three years as presented in each year's public expenditure settlement should be seen as firm provision to enable institutions to plan more effectively. The annual debate would then be about the new year within the PES programme. Such an approach would, in our view, fit much better with institutions' own strategic planning cycles.

Recommendation 73   **We recommend to the Government that the public funding for higher education institutions should be determined on a rolling three year basis.**

19.34   In examining the contributions of the various parties to higher education we concluded in Chapter 18 that the time is now right for the establishment of a new compact between the state, individuals and their families, graduates and institutions. The state, in providing the degree of stability and commitment to its own funding could expect in return that institutions would continue to seek out ways of managing their affairs and delivering their services to improve cost effectiveness and value for money. Students, in accepting their obligation as graduates in work to contribute, would expect a similar commitment from institutions, and a commitment from Government only to change the level of contributions following a proper procedure for review and public debate.

Administrative arrangements

19.35   The task of distributing to institutions those public funds which come with the individual undergraduate student is, at present, part of the system of administering mandatory awards carried out in England and Wales by local education authorities and by the Student Awards Agency for Scotland and the Education and Library Board in Northern Ireland. We consider in Chapter 21 the various mechanisms for supporting students and enabling graduates to make a contribution once they are in work, and recommend the establishment of a single Student Support Agency (SSA) which might in the longer term form the basis of a system of individual learning accounts (ILAs) appropriate for higher education.

19.36   We describe the principal functions of the SSA in Chapter 21. In summary we would see it bringing together both the individual loan-borne contribution to the funding of tuition **and** the publicly funded grant element related to full-time undergraduate student choice. In this role it would be well placed to keep track of individuals' use of their entitlement to public support through loans and grants which we believe is an essential function in any system of lifelong learning. Within that context, we describe in Chapter 21 how these functions could be met through a system of ILAs.

19.37   As we have noted, all the public support for the majority of part-time and postgraduate taught students is currently provided by the block grant. We consider further in Chapter 20 the issues about overall levels of public support for different types of student. However, we note that in the process of transferring part of the block grants to payments based on individual choice, provision will be needed to cover payments for part-time and postgraduate students, not covered by the current mandatory award sysem for full-time undergraduates. This, together with the contribution from graduates in work proposed in Chapter 20, offers the best way, within the resources available, of giving students a sensible choice between part-time and full-time study.

19.38   The publicly funded fee element of the mandatory award is currently paid termly, but its level is determined on the basis of a year of study. In future, individuals should be able to study full-time for periods of less than a year with funding to match. Ideally, this should be linked to a common national credit framework. Until such time as there is a robust national system of credits and a credit tracking system, the basic unit of funding will, however, almost certainly have to be linked to a year.

Transitional arrangements

19.39   Moving from the current mixed system of funding towards a system in which money follows the student will require some complex administrative changes, as well as behavioural changes by individuals and institutions. As we have suggested, a gradual process, which gives all parties time to prepare would be needed, coupled with close monitoring of the impact on student and institutional behaviour. The transitional stages might be as follows:

- determine the changes required in mandatory award fee payments and/or block grants to match individual contributions (Chapters 20 and 21);
- transfer resources to the proposed Student Support Agency (SSA) so that it can make loan advances for individual contributions;
- transfer the flow of remaining mandatory award fees away from local education authorities to the proposed single Student Support Agency (SSA) (Chapter 21);
- transfer an increasing proportion of block grant, with provision for eligible part-time and postgraduate students, into per capita payments paid by the SSA;
- devise arrangements for students to receive (in the form of cash or a convertible proxy) an increasing proportion of the per capita payments.

Funding Bodies

19.40   The changes discussed in this chapter impact on the way the Funding Bodies operate at present, and their future role. We discuss these further in Chapter 22.

Differential funding

19.41   Part of our inheritance is substantial differences in levels of public funding between one institution of higher education and another for what is nominally comparable provision. This reflects in part the different responses made by institutions to secure additional funded places at 'marginal prices': sometimes as a result of a clear choice between different strategies available to institutions, sometimes as a result of specific circumstances that constrained institutional choice. It also reflects, in part, the different attitudes taken by individual local authorities to appropriate levels of funding for the former polytechnics for which they were responsible.

19.42 The Scottish Higher Education Funding Council (SHEFC) has made significant progress in reducing such differentials for teaching in Scotland, as has the Teacher Training Agency for the programmes it funds in England. The Higher Education Funding Council for England has proposed to limit the differentials in England to between plus and minus 5 per cent of the average level, but at our request deferred action pending this report.

19.43 Apart from these differences between institutions, there are differences in the levels of funding between the various parts of the United Kingdom, with the level being higher in Scotland than in England, and higher in England than in Wales.

19.44 There are legitimate reasons for some variations in the levels of payment made from the public purse for programmes to reflect, for example, marked differences in the public inheritance of institutions and the extra costs of operating in London. We believe that such differentiation should occur only where there are clear grounds for it.

Recommendation 74 **We recommend to the Government that variations in the level of public funding for teaching, outside modest margins, should occur only where:**
- **there is an approved difference in the provision;**
- **society, through the Secretary of State or his or her agent, concludes, after examining an exceptionally high level of funding, that in relation to other funding needs in higher education, it represents a good use of resources.**

19.45 The application of such principles would support the policies adopted by the Scottish Higher Education Funding Council, by the Teacher Training Agency and those proposed by the Higher Education Funding Council for England. All movement towards an approved range of acceptable differences should be made gradually so that institutions have time to adapt.

19.46 The college fees in Oxford and Cambridge represent a substantial addition to the standard funding for institutions of higher education. We propose that the Government reviews them against the two principles we have proposed.

19.47 These comments apply to differences in the funding of courses. We have dealt elsewhere in the report with circumstances where different levels of funding may be appropriate for some students.

Differential fees

19.48   In 19.31 we recommended that there should be a progressive channelling of more of the cost of tuition through the student and away from the block grants provided by the Funding Bodies. In its evidence to us the Confederation of British Industry developed this limited step towards a more market based approach. It suggested:

■ *'HE qualified applicants are issued with cash credits, equal to existing government course funding (banded according to subject).*

■ *Universities could charge tuition fees above the value of the credit, if their quality merited it (income contingent loans would be available to students paying such fees).*

■ *Universities which could deliver the threshold learning outcomes at less than the cost of the credit can charge a lower price to students. The students would receive 'change' from the credit which they could put towards their maintenance costs. Efficient institutions would thus be more attractive to students.*

■ *Every three or four years Government would calculate the average price being charged by institutions (excluding institutions charging top-up fees across each subject), and reduce the value of the credit in line with that average. This would ensure that, where efficiency gains had been made, over the long term this would benefit public expenditure.'*

19.49   There would be safeguards for quality in that only institutions accredited as delivering at least threshold learning outcomes would be eligible for inclusion in the scheme.

19.50   We are aware that a number of institutions would support some opportunity for differential charging for undergraduate programmes in the interests of the quality of the provision they offer. But this is a legitimate concern for all institutions feeling the pressure, of what, on present plans, amounts to a reduction in the unit of funding for teaching of nearly 50 per cent of its level, measured in real terms, of 25 years ago. Our principal concern is with the wellbeing of the whole sector rather than of individual institutions and that is why we have made recommendations to reduce the cuts in funding in the present funding plans.

19.51   It would be a matter for concern if differential fees were introduced in response to an overall deficiency in the level of publicly approved funding for full-time students in higher education. But, for the long term, we do not, however, rule out the possibility of different levels of fee charging by institutions provided that:

■ there are in place the kind of arrangements for safeguarding quality and standards that we propose in Chapter 10;

■ the level of funding provided through the public purse and through standard loan-supported contributions from graduates in work is sufficient to maintain the quality of UK higher education;

■ the fee does not attract additional public funding, including publicly provided loans, except where, under the principles we have outlined above, the Government considers it justified;

- any institution introducing a differential level of fee provides sufficient bursaries to ensure there is equality of access so that no able student is denied access to an institution of his or her choice through lack of funds;
- such differential fee charging is not a widespread feature of the system.

Capital funding

19.52   In Chapter 17 we concluded that institutions would face a shortfall of some £250 million a year in capital funding even if it proved possible to limit the squeeze on public funding to one per cent per annum. This shortfall in capital funding is not related to the need for new buildings but to the need to refurbish existing buildings (to improve fitness for purpose); to replace equipment for teaching and research in a regular cycle; and to increase investment in Communications and Information Technology (C&IT).

19.53   This arises in part because of the previous Government's decision that, in future, institutions should fund refurbishment and replacement activities from within their general revenue stream even though the public contribution to that revenue stream was being reduced. The shortfall also reflects a longstanding under-investment in refurbishment and replacement.

19.54   The position varies, however, between institutions. We have noted that there are considerable differences in the age, condition and fitness for purpose of institutions' estates reflecting, in particular, the very varied inheritance of the 1992 universities. In Chapter 15 we considered capital charging as a way of helping to address these imbalances, but concluded that it would not be a suitable mechanism for that purpose in the higher education sector.

19.55   The Private Finance Initiative (PFI) has not so far proved of particular relevance to meeting higher education's core needs for capital investment. A report from the Committee of Vice-Chancellors and Principals (CVCP) and the Department for Education and Employment (DfEE) confirmed this.[1] If PFI-style arrangements are to make a real contribution they will need to recognise the long lead time for any return on the investment and the difficulties of financing major projects within the current level of revenue resource in the higher education sector. We have seen that the Government is seeking to reinvigorate the PFI in the light of a report prepared for them by Mr Malcolm Baker.[2] The recommendations in the report for the streamlining of the procedures have been accepted and should help higher education to use the PFI where it is appropriate to do so.

19.56   The Pearce Report suggested that the higher education sector should explore other innovative approaches to funding.[3] Experience since 1992 and in the US suggests, however, that innovative approaches such as bonds are at best long term options and then initially only for institutions in a very strong financial position. Furthermore, such approaches carry high risks if all the financial consequences are not fully assessed at the outset.

19.57   We have concluded, therefore, that there is an inescapable requirement for some additional public funding for capital investment in order to retain the value of institutions' existing assets in the short and medium term. We have already proposed in Chapter 11 that the serious shortcomings in the current research infrastructure in departments of research excellence should be funded on a partnership basis between Government and other organisations that may use higher education facilities.

19.58   We have also noted with interest in this context the Higher Education Funding Council for England's decision to provide some capital funding from 1998-99 to meet the most urgent capital needs in English institutions to make good the poor building inheritance of the 1992 universities and to deal with the requirements for upgrading laboratories to meet the requirements of Health and Safety legislation.

19.59   We understand that these schemes have in part been made possible through recycling of grants and we believe that this provides a useful precedent for future schemes.

Recommendation 75   **We recommend to the Funding Bodies that they should explore the possibility of setting aside some of their total grant, as soon as possible, to establish revolving loan schemes to fund:**

- **projects to refurbish buildings (to improve fitness for purpose) or to undertake large scale long term maintenance projects;**
- **expensive equipment purchases (for teaching or research);**
- **collaborative projects which will facilitate access for staff and students in a region to teaching or research facilities which could not otherwise be provided on a viable basis.**

19.60   Any funding awarded would need to be selective, and designed to support only those institutions able to indicate satisfactory/best practice in managing these assets. At the same time, the Funding Bodies, in consultation with institutions should continue to promote understanding and expertise about the Private Finance Initiative, particularly in relation to procuring teaching and research equipment. The priority should be to develop managerial and technical expertise in the sector, in preparation for the future.

Chapter 20

Student support and graduate contributions

20.1 If our vision of a learning society is to be realised, students will have, as we make clear in Chapter 18, to make a greater investment in their own futures. It is also necessary, if our vision is to be realised, for the state to provide equitable financial support for students who want to study in different ways or whose personal circumstances require it.

20.2 The country should have a student support system which, as far as possible:
- is equitable and encourages broadly based participation;
- requires those with the means to do so to make a fair contribution to the costs of their higher education;
- supports lifelong learning by
  - making the choices between full and part-time, and between continuous and discontinuous study financially neutral;
  - reducing the disparity between support for students at further and higher education levels;
- is easy to understand, administratively efficient and cost-effective.

20.3 This is not straightforward to achieve given the diversity of students and study patterns which need support.

20.4 As we have already shown, more funding is needed for higher education. Levelling up the support for those types of students or patterns of study which are not currently well-supported would be very expensive, and impossible to achieve within the constraints of public funding. It might also risk substituting public subsidies for contributions which are currently coming from employers towards part-time study. Reducing support for those groups who are currently better supported could lead to severe financial problems for individuals, especially if they had not had time to prepare for changes and might thereby reduce participation, especially by students from the least well off backgrounds. Consequent changes in behaviour could be destabilising in their effects on institutions. Our recommendations have, therefore, been tempered by pragmatism.

20.5 In this chapter we examine how far it is feasible to provide better support to certain groups of students:
- part-time undergraduates;
- postgraduates;
- students in institutions which are not publicly funded;
- students whose study is not continuous.

In the light of our conclusion that graduates in work who have benefited from a full-time undergraduate course should make a greater financial contribution in the future, we then consider:

- the need for payments to be on an income contingent basis;
- the relative merits of:
  - a graduate tax;
  - a deferred contribution scheme;
  - contributions supported by loans;
- the relative merits of four specific options for contributions supported by loans;
- various approaches to increasing the money which loan supported schemes can provide for higher education over the short term;
- certain special cases.

Part-time undergraduates

20.6   As we have already noted, one message which emerged very strongly from the evidence we received was concern about the inequity of treatment between full and part-time students, in terms of the level of public support for tuition costs. For the full-time undergraduate student tuition is currently free, while for the part-time student a fee is generally charged (though some institutions waive the fee in certain circumstances). These fees do not generally cover the full cost of part-time courses which are still heavily subsidised through the Funding Bodies' block grants. As will become evident later in this chapter, there is a good case for expecting graduates from full-time programmes to make a contribution to their tuition costs, not just, as now, to their living costs. If the Government accepted the case and implemented the proposal, the disparity in treatment between full and part-time undergraduates would be much reduced.

20.7   We have considered whether part-time students should have access to loans to meet a contribution to the tuition costs of their higher education in the light of our later recommendation that full-time students should be supported in this way. We are conscious of the potentially heavy cost to the public purse involved in making subsidised loans universally available to part-time students, given that the vast majority of this group currently pay fees despite the unavailability of loans (other than Career Development Loans, which are subject to credit-vetting and to partly commercial terms). As we noted in Chapter 18, many part-time students currently have their fees paid by their employers – a contribution which we would certainly wish to see maintained. We cannot recommend that these costs, even on a loan basis, are transferred to the Exchequer. One solution would be to make loans available only to those part-time students on low incomes. Means testing of a substantial number of part-time students would, however, be very labour intensive to administer.

20.8   An alternative to providing loans to help part-time students to meet their contribution to tuition would be to waive the fee altogether for students in certain low income groups. A number of higher education institutions already adopt this approach. It would mirror the position in further education in England, where adult students in receipt of Jobseeker's Allowance (JSA) or certain family benefits are excused the fee charged to other students, and the funding shortfall is made up by the Funding Council. Although this would not help those part-time students who are on low incomes but not on benefit, it would provide an incentive to part-time study by the unemployed, and is likely to be relatively straightforward and cost-effective to administer.

20.9   We believe it is important that the Government puts in place arrangements to ensure that part-time students who are in receipt of benefits are not prevented from entering higher education because they cannot afford the fees. On balance, we have concluded that the most appropriate approach would be a scheme where the Funding Bodies provide funding to allow institutions to remit fees for certain students. We estimate that the cost in 1998/99 would be some £15 million, and that the long term cost would be some £50 million a year.

20.10   Part-time undergraduates are currently treated differently from their full-time counterparts in respect of living costs as well. Part-time students – other than a small number on part-time teacher training courses – are ineligible for mandatory grants and student loans, and for payments from the Access Funds (funds for relieving hardship at the discretion of individual institutions). They are however eligible for social security benefits, including the Jobseeker's Allowance (JSA), so long as they meet certain conditions relating, in particular, to availability for work.

20.11   We have considered whether loan or grant arrangements for supporting full-time students' living costs might be extended to part-time students but have concluded that there is a high proportion of part-time students who are in employment and therefore able to support themselves. Moreover it would be extremely expensive. Given the other requirements for additional funding which we have identified, we do not believe that this should be a priority call on any additional funding for higher education. We are concerned, however, that the current social security benefit rules are acting as a disincentive to part-time study for those who might reasonably be assumed to have the most to gain: those who are unemployed.

20.12   We have already recommended that the size of the Access Funds should be doubled and we believe that the scope of those enlarged Funds should be widened to include part-time students.

Recommendation 76   We recommend to the Government that:
- from 1998/99 it should enable institutions to waive tuition fees for part-time students in receipt of Jobseeker's Allowance or certain family benefits;
- as part of its forthcoming review of the social security system, it should review the interaction between entitlement to benefits and part-time study, with a view to ensuring that there are no financial disincentives to part-time study by the unemployed or those on low incomes;
- it should extend eligibility for Access Fund payments to part-time students from 1998/99, and additional funding should be made available for this purpose.

Postgraduates

20.13   There has been rapid growth in the last few years in the number of students on taught postgraduate courses – both full-time and part-time. Such students are subsidised by the Funding Bodies but, in the most cases, also pay a fee from their own resources. We see this contribution as desirable and would not want to disturb it, particularly when there is already a scheme, the Career Development Loan Scheme, which benefits some postgraduates. We received a few representations that postgraduates should be entitled to support for their living costs on the same basis as undergraduate students. Although we see merit in the Government ensuring, as for undergraduates, that the unemployed are not discouraged, we do not see any further extension of living cost support for postgraduates as a priority.

20.14   We also heard concerns about the potential impact of increased contributions being required towards the cost of undergraduate study. Some felt that graduates with debts would be discouraged from further study. We believe that the answer to this lies in the design of mechanisms for the collection of contributions which are sensitive to an individual graduate's circumstances, and do not over-burden those on low incomes.

Students in institutions which are not publicly funded

20.15   We received a number of representations about the position of students studying dance, drama and related subjects and the previous Government asked us to advise on this subject. The problem arises because provision for these subjects is made mainly in institutions which do not receive public funding. The same is true of a number of other subjects, for example, some forms of alternative medicine. In some cases the students in question are eligible for mandatory awards, but the fee paid through mandatory awards covers only a fraction of the cost of tuition, and the student has to bear the rest. Others may receive discretionary grants from local education authorities, but these have greatly reduced in number in recent years and whether a student can get one depends on where he or she lives. The situation is further complicated by the fact that much of the provision is at further education level, but some is at higher education level. Although the former is technically outside our remit, we did not feel it was sensible to look at the higher education provision in isolation.

20.16   We suggest in Chapter 19 that additional institutions should be brought into the public funding net only if they can meet certain stringent criteria. We think it unlikely that many of the institutions currently outside the net would be able or willing to meet the criteria. This leaves their students unfairly disadvantaged relative to others who have chosen other subjects, for example music, which are catered for mainly in the publicly funded sector.

20.17   The previous Government had already accepted that there is a problem and had established an interim bursary scheme for dance and drama students. We believe that a long term solution involving public funding is the only way to secure equity for these students. We propose that the Government should provide a limited number of vouchers (or bursaries or scholarships) with the number offered being related to some assessment of the national need for people trained in the relevant area. The vouchers should be valid only at non-profit-making institutions whose quality and standards have been independently attested, for example by the Quality Assurance Agency. The vouchers should be large enough to cover the reasonable costs of tuition, as determined by the Government. Once students are over 18 they should be required to contribute the same sum each year towards the cost of tuition as higher education students, with the assistance of a loan, and should be eligible for living cost support on the same basis as full-time undergraduate higher education students.

Recommendation 77   **We recommend to the Government that, once the interim bursary scheme expires, it establishes permanent arrangements for the equitable support of students of dance, drama and stage management at institutions which are not in receipt of public funds.**

Discontinuous study

20.18   We have made proposals for a new qualifications framework based on credit points to enable students to accumulate credits towards an award over time. Such a framework supports discontinuous periods of study. It is also feasible for the Funding Bodies to support such study through their block grants. Current student support arrangements for full-time undergraduates make it difficult, however, for students to stop studying for a while and then to return. Generally, if they do, they lose their entitlement to a mandatory award. In future, there must be a framework to support individuals to study to degree level (H4) in a flexible way. In order to allow the Government to control public expenditure, there has to be some limit on a student's overall entitlement to public subsidies. The control at the moment comes from the rule that a student may not receive more than one mandatory award. The recommendation in Chapter 7 for the introduction of a unique student record number and the recommendation in Chapter 21 for a single Student Support Agency, should make it feasible, in future, to track an individual's use of their entitlement, even if they interrupt their study.

Contributions from graduates in work

20.19   As we show in Chapter 17, more resources are needed for higher education. We now turn to consider how graduates of full-time programmes, who are in work, could make a greater contribution to the overall costs of their higher education. While the evidence discussed in Chapter 18 provides a strong case for graduates in general contributing towards the costs of higher education, it provides no means of quantifying what their share should be or whether they should contribute to living costs or tuition costs. In looking at options we have therefore taken a largely pragmatic approach, having regard to:

■ the burden on graduates and the extent to which individuals might be deterred from participating in higher eduction;

- equity and comparability in relation to arrangements for other sectors of education, particularly for adult students in further education;
- the amount of money which would be raised and how clearly the sums raised could be reserved to support increased expenditure on higher education.

Income contingency

20.20 For many who gave evidence, the first of these was of paramount importance. While the average graduate receives a good financial return from higher education, not all do. Some will experience periods of unemployment, some will need to take career breaks and some will have low paid jobs for most of their lives.

20.21 There was almost universal agreement amongst those we consulted – including student representatives – that the solution to these problems was to replace the current arrangements for the repayment of maintenance loans, with their fixed term mortgage-style repayments, with an income contingent system in which payments are based on a percentage of the graduate's income. The main advantage of such schemes – which are usually described as 'income contingent' schemes – is that they fix monthly payments at a level judged to be affordable in relation to an individual graduate's income. Instead of all graduates with an outstanding loan of a certain size paying the same monthly amount once their income has reached a threshold, those on the lowest incomes pay the least each month and those on higher income pay more. The higher a graduate's income, the sooner he or she will complete their payment. Unlike the current arrangements, income contingent schemes provide reassurance to those entering higher education that they will not face unmanageable repayment burdens, whatever their post-graduation income.

20.22 The current student loans scheme for living costs is based on mortgage-style repayments, but with deferment for those on lower incomes. Once a graduate's earning reach 85 per cent of national average earnings (£15,792 in 1996/97), payments start continue over a fixed period – five years for those with up to four loans, and seven years for those with five or more loans. The monthly amount repaid depends on the total size of the debt rather than on the borrower's income (once it exceeds the threshold for payments). We understand that, when the loans scheme was first introduced, the Government's intention was the payment periods would be extended over time as the average level of debt increased, in order to keep monthly payment levels manageable. However, to date, no such extensions have been implemented.

20.23 Many of those we consulted felt that these arrangements do no sufficiently recognise differences in graduates' incomes, and that if graduates were required to make a greater contribution under present payment arrangements, this would create a major barrier to participation. While the relatively high threshold protects the position of graduates on low incomes, there was a general consensus that significantly longer payment periods would be necessary in the future to prevent payment causing real financial problems for many graduates. In addition, a number of those submitting evidence drew attention to the burdensome nature of the payment regime for those whose income only marginally exceeds the threshold. This is illustrated in Table 20.1, which shows that the heaviest burdens in terms of percentages of income fall on those with incomes just above the threshold. In practice, graduates are not currently making payments of this order because the recent shift from grants to loans has only just been completed and it has not yet been possible to accumulate debts of as much as £5,000. Once the current loans scheme reaches a steady state there will, however, be graduates in this position unless the terms for payment are changed.

Table 20.1 – Graduate loan repayments as percentage of gross income under the current student loans scheme (£5,000 loan)

Income	Loan repayment as % of Income
Up to £15,792	0
£16,000	6.3
£18,000	5.6
£20,000	5.0
£25,000	4.0
£30,000	3.3

20.24   These points apply equally whether a contribution from graduates in work is for living costs or tuition costs. We strongly support the weight of opinion in the evidence that any contributions should be on an income contingent basis in future.

Recommendation 78   **We recommend to the Government that it introduces, by 1998/99, income contingent terms for the payment of any contribution towards living costs or tuition costs sought from graduates in work.**

Graduate tax

20.25   One obvious way of achieving an income contingent contribution would be through a graduate tax.

20.26   Under this option all those who had undertaken a publicly-subsidised programme of higher education study would be liable to pay an income tax supplement. This could, in principle, apply at all tax levels or be applied at a separate threshold (or thresholds) from the standard bands of income tax. It could, in principle, be extended to existing as well as future graduates. We have not examined that extension further because of the apparent difficulty of defining a 'graduate' retrospectively and then identifying all individuals caught by the definition.

20.27   We were attracted to the option of a tax on future graduates because:
■ it leaves tuition free at the point of delivery;
■ it has a natural income contingency and can be made more progressive than income tax itself if desired;

- over the long term it could raise more revenue (for example, £2.3 billion in the long term from a two per cent additional tax rate on all future graduates throughout life) than any other options which meet the criteria in paragraph 20.2;
- it would appear in principle to be relatively simple to collect.

20.28 However it also has a number of drawbacks:
- it provides no mechanism for those who might wish to pay at the time they receive the tuition (to avoid tax) and thereby foregoes any short-term benefits to the Exchequer, institutions, or graduates;
- it is open-ended: those graduates who are particularly successful will be expected to contribute large sums in total (even if their success has little to do with their higher education) which may encourage avoidance of the tax;
- it would provide no safeguard that higher education would receive any benefits from the contributions, since to provide such safeguards would cut across the general principle that tax revenue is not earmarked for particular services;
- defining what length or type of higher education study made an individual liable for a 'graduate' supplementary tax would be difficult;
- it would not be straightforward (or necessarily desirable) to secure alignment with funding arrangements for further education;
- there is no experience of graduate tax systems elsewhere in the world.

20.29 We have concluded the disadvantages are such that we do not support a graduate tax as the means of providing contributions from those who have undertaken courses of study in higher education. However, we consider further below options which have some features of a graduate tax.

A deferred contribution option

20.30 We have considered a deferred contibution option which has some features of both a graduate tax and a loan scheme but develops to its fullest extent the notion of a 'contribution'. The contribution in this model does not link payment to a specific loan or debt, although a ceiling would be placed on the maximum level of contribution so that it was not open-ended like a graduate tax. Within the capped ceiling a graduate in work would make a return to society according to his or her earnings over a pre-determined number of years.

20.31 There are various ways in which such a scheme could be devised. For example, under one version:
- in return for tuition free at the point of consumption, students would enter an agreement to contribute a given percentage of income above a specified level once they were in employment;
- the percentage of income would be related to the number of units of tuition taken;
- the contribution would be made for a maximum number of years (for example, 20 years);
- the total contribution would be limited (at maximum, to a sum not exceeding the full average cost of tuition, or some defined percentage of that);

20.32   This scheme shares the advantages of a graduate tax, for example in the income raising potential, and has two additional advantages:
- the contribution is limited in time and maximum amount and is not an open-ended tax;
- the commitment would be entered into at the time of study so that it would be easier to administer than a graduate tax.

20.33   The main disadvantage to the scheme is that it would not produce an additonal flow of money for higher education in the short term, so we considered whether there were variants of it which would do so. One option would be to give individuals the choice of either paying a pre-determined proportion of the costs of their higher education up front or of making contributions once in work, on the same basis as outlined above. But the sums they produced would be modest in the short term.

20.34   Both these options merit consideration for the medium term, but they require time for development and broad informed debate about how they would be implemented.

Contributions supported by loans

20.35   Contributions from graduates in work via loan repayments in their income contingent form, enjoyed a large measure of support from those submitting evidence to us. That support was mainly focused on an option under which the current grants for students' living costs would be converted into loans. Loan-based schemes would enable individuals to choose either, if they had the resources, to make the required contribution at the time of study, or to take out a loan which would be repayable after graduation. The detailed basis of such loans and their implications for individuals are considered in Chapter 21. In carrying out our analysis, we have sought to take account not only of the existing student loan scheme run by the Student Loan Company in support of student living costs, but also of the particular experience of Australia and New Zealand in seeking graduate contributions. We also looked at the work of the National Commission on Education, although they did not have the benefit of the facilities for modelling options which we have developed.[1]

20.36   Loan-based contribution schemes have the following principal benefits:
- the levels of payment can readily be related progressively to income;
- they provide naturally for individuals and their families who wish to pay at the time of study. Such up-front payments could, in principle, be further incentivised depending on the precise details of the loan scheme;
- the commitment is limited: once the loan is repaid the individual no longer contributes;
- loan schemes could be incorporated into a wider scheme for enabling individuals participating in post-18 education to contribute;
- loan schemes are already an accepted element of student support and they have been shown to work elsewhere in the world.

20.37 The principal disadvantages are:

- income contingency means that graduates on lower incomes may never repay all of their loans, and that the initial receipts will be modest;
- loans, as opposed to grants, may have a disincentive effect on the willingness of individuals from socio-economic groups IV and V to participate in higher education;
- the level of debt for those on modest incomes is sensitive to the level of interest charged;
- on the present treatment of loan payments within the public accounts, this option might increase public sector costs in the short term, unless the debt could be sold (we consider this issue in paragraphs 20.96 to 20.97).

Alternative forms of contributions supported by loans

20.38 In the evidence submitted to us there was a widespread view that, if graduates were to contribute more, this should be achieved by transferring the whole of the funding for students' living costs, which is currently made up of a mixture of grants and loans, to 100 per cent loans. There was opposition to the extension of student or graduate contributions to include tuition costs. Others felt that tuition contributions should be resorted to only if, after transferring support for students' living costs from grants to loans, there was still a shortfall in higher education funding.

20.39 This opposition to seeking a contribution towards tuition costs from graduates was despite the recognition that additional public funding for higher education was unlikely to be available, in the short term at least. Many of those submitting evidence to us wanted greater equity of treatment between full and part-time undergraduate students. But they did not see this being achieved by asking full-time students to make a similar contribution to that already made by part-time students.

20.40 We do not underestimate the strength of feeling on the issue of seeking a contribution towards tuition costs: nor do we dispute the logic of the arguments put forward. A detailed assessment of the issues has, however, convinced us that the arguments in favour of a contribution to tuition costs from graduates in work are strong, if not widely appreciated. They relate to equity between social groups, broadening participation, equity with part-time students in higher education and in further education, strengthening the student role in higher education, and identifying a new source of income that can be ring-fenced for higher education.

20.41 We have, therefore, analysed the implications of a range of options against the criteria set out in paragraph 20.2. There is a wide array of options from which to choose, ranging from asking graduates to contribute only to their living costs through to asking all graduates to contribute to their tuition costs. We have chosen to examine four options in depth.

20.42 Under Option A, which we call the 'maintenance contribution' option, students would no longer be eligible for grants to support their living costs (apart from some specific exceptions such as the Disabled Student's Allowance). Living costs would be supported entirely through loans, which would be available equally to all eligible students, regardless of family income. No contribution to tuition costs would be sought: as now tuition would be funded 100 per cent by public grants.

20.43   At the other end of the spectrum is Option D, which we have called the 'tuition contribution with restoration of maintenance grants' option. In this option, support for students' living costs would be restored to the arrangements which prevailed before the introduction of the current student loan scheme. This means that support for living costs would take the form of a grant equal in value to the current grant plus loans package, and would be means tested against parental income. All graduates would be expected to make a flat rate contribution to their tuition costs, either at the point of study or, once they were in work, by repaying a loan on income contingent terms.

20.44   Between these two options we have two others. Option B is the 'tuition contribution' option. This keeps support for living costs in its current form, that is half in the form of universally available loans (but in future to be repaid on an income contingent basis), and half in the form of means tested grants. All graduates would be required to make a flat rate contribution of about 25 per cent to tuition costs, at the time of study or by repaying a loan on an income contingent basis when in work.

20.45   Option C is the 'means-tested tuition contribution' option. This would have the same arrangements for living costs as the 'maintenance contribution' Option A, that is all support for living costs would be in the form of loans available to all students (apart from specific allowances such as the Disabled Students' Allowance which would continue as grants). In addition, students would make a contribution of up to 25 per cent to tuition costs, the size of which would be dependent on parental (or the students' own) income. No loans would be available to meet the tuition costs.

These four options are summarised in Table 20.2 and in pictorial form in Chart 20.1.

Table 20.2 – Graduate contribution options

	Living costs support	Tuition contribution
Existing system	50% means tested grant 50% loan	None
Option A Maintenance contribution	100% income contingent loan	None
Option B Tuition contribution	50% means tested grant 50% income contingent loan	25% contribution with income contingent loan
Option C Means tested tuition contribution	100% income contingent loan	25% means tested contribution with no loan
Option D Tuition contribution with restoration of maintenance grants	100% means tested grant	25% contribution with income contingent loan

The options compared

20.46 The options differ principally in four respects:
- the impact on individuals and their families at the time of study;
- the impact on graduates;
- the differential impact on different social groups which arises from the redistribution of remaining public grants;
- the funds generated and therefore the potential impact on the system.

20.47 More information about how we modelled the impact of these options can be found in Report 12 ('Options for funding higher education: modelling and policy analysis').

Family contributions

20.48 Table 20.3 shows the range of the required family contributions for a student studying for three years away from home outside London. This excludes any voluntary contributions which parents might make to allow their student offspring to avoid taking out a publicly backed loan, or simply to top up their living allowance.

Table 20.3 – Assumed parental/family contributions for three years study under different options

	Existing system	Maintenance contribution A	Tuition contribution B	Means tested tuition contribution C	Tuition contribution with restoration of maintenance grant D
Higher income families (£)	5,000	0	5,000	3,000	10,000
Middle income families (£)	2,000	0	2,000	1,200	4,000
Lower income families (£)	0	0	0	0	0

Notes: Under current arrangements, families with a residual income of less than £16,580 are not assumed to make any contribution; those on residual incomes above around £35,000 are assumed to make the maximum contribution; and those on residual incomes in between contribute on a sliding scale. In the table a 'middle income family' could, on current scales, have an income in the range £20–25,000. Residual income is gross taxable income minus certain allowances eg for dependent adults other than the spouse, interest payments which qualify for tax relief etc. For simplicity rounded figures are presented. Maximum public support for living costs is assumed to be £10,000 over three years and the tuition contribution, where appropriate, is assumed to be £1,000 a year.

20.49 This table illustrates that the 'maintenance contribution' Option A differs distinctively from the other options in completely removing the obligations on middle and higher income parents or families to contribute, and transfers that obligation to graduates. In comparison with the present arrangements, the 'tuition contribution with restoration of maintenance grants' Option D substantially increases the contribution required from parents or spouses whose incomes are above the means testing threshold, including those on middle incomes.

20.50 In practice, it is unlikely that all parents in the middle and higher income categories would be able to make these extra contributions, particularly if they were introduced quickly so that families had not had time to save for the additional contribution. Some

Chart 20.1 – Comparison of options

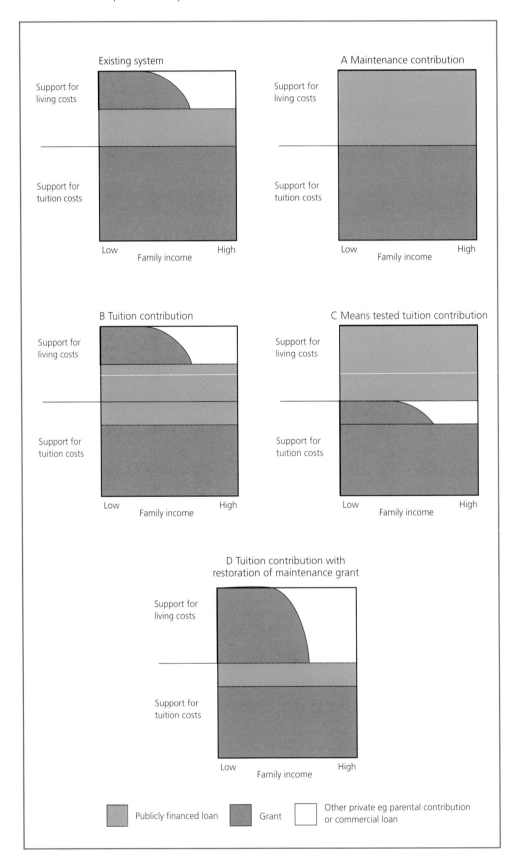

of them would probably themselves borrow or underwrite commercial loans for their children.

Graduate commitments

20.51 With income contingent repayment arrangements, the liability a graduate carries forward is a contingent one – contingent on the ability to pay. In this sense, the liability is a new form of financial instrument, and we choose to refer to it as the 'graduate commitment' rather than as an irrevocable debt. Nonetheless, graduates will still be concerned about the total level of the financial commitments (including commercial debt) incurred over their time in higher education, as this will affect how long it will take them to complete their payments, and will need to be considered alongside debts, such as mortgages for house purchase, which they may wish to take on. Clearly, whether a particular level of commitment is worrying for a graduate will also depend on the graduate's income. More details about what proportion of graduates would have high debt to income ratios under each option can be found in Report 12. Our view is that none of the commitments implied by the options should be unmanageable for graduates.

20.52 The level of graduate commitment will depend on the precise details of the contribution scheme selected and on any commercial loans taken out by individuals. Table 20.4 below sets out the maximum public loan commitment for graduates who have followed three years of study away from home outside London. Some students would be likely to have commercial debts on top of these.

Table 20.4 – Graduate commitment for three years study (£)

Existing system	Maintenance contribution	Tuition contribution	Means-tested tuition contribution	Tuition contribution with restoration of maintenance grants
	A	B	C	D
5,000	10,000	8,000	10,000	3,000

20.53 This table complements Table 20.3 in showing the shift in burdens from individuals and their families to graduates, and vice versa in the case of Option D.

20.54 Chart 20.2 shows how the average graduate's outstanding commitment would change as a percentage of income over time under the existing system (but with income contingent payments) and under the 'tuition contribution' Option B. To give a sense of the size of the burden, the chart also shows the debt burden associated with a typical residential mortgage. None of the options appears to produce an unmanageable commitment.

Chart 20.2 – Average graduate commitment as a percentage of income

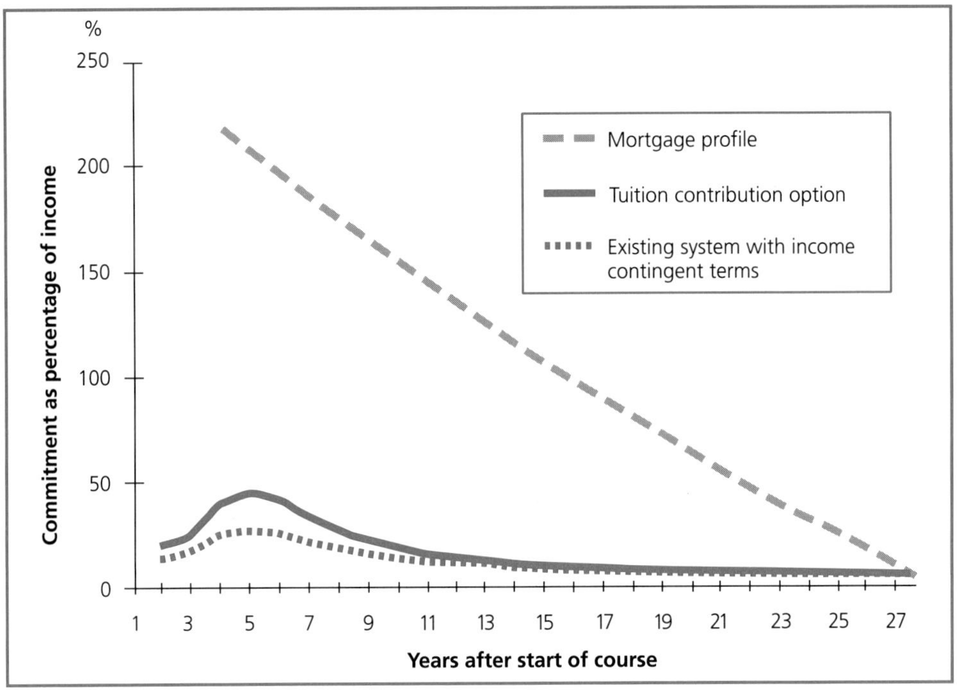

Source: Report 12

The distribution of subsidies between different social groups

20.55   Important though these implications are, we think it is essential to consider the impact of the different options on individuals and families from different income groups, if we are to understand the relative distribution of public subsidies. While recognising that socio-economic grouping and level of income are not directly comparable, we have noted in Chapter 7 that individuals from socio-economic groups IV and V have the lowest propensity to participate in higher education. This is not solely a financial issue, but financial factors are likely to be more important for individuals from these groups who are qualified to enter higher education than it is for those from socio-economic groups I and II. We are concerned about the potential impact on participation of reduced public subsidies for students from the poorest families. In particular, we would be reluctant to see any reduction in public subsidies for the students from the poorest families being used, in effect, to increase subsidies to the better-off.

20.56   Chart 20.3 shows, for the year 2006/07, how subsidies would be distributed between groups under current arrangements.

Chart 20.3 – Public subsidies for higher education under existing system by socio-economic group

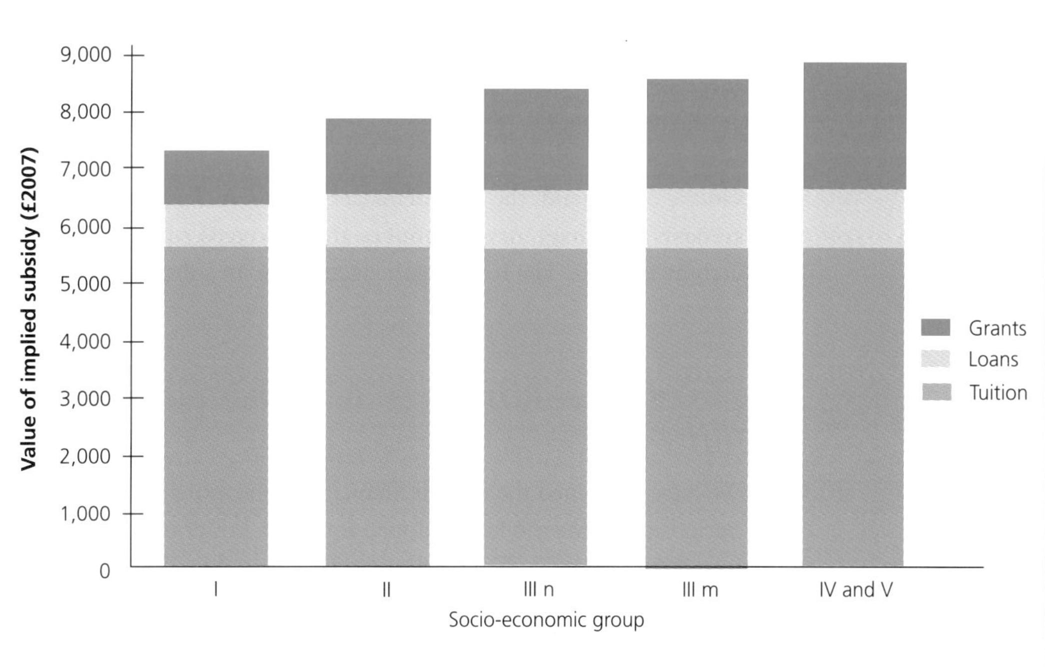

Source Report 12

20.57   Table 20.5 summarises the impact on public subsidies for the poorest and most well-off under the four options, compared to the current position.

Table 20.5 – Effect of options on distribution of public subsidies for three years study compared to present policies

	Students from high income families	Students from low income families
A Maintenance contribution	Increased public subsidy through availability of additional £5,000 living cost loans at a subsidised rate.	Decreased public subsidy as living cost grants of £5,000 replaced by loans at a subsidised rate.
B Tuition contribution	Decreased public subsidy, through £3,000 tuition contribution, backed by a subsidised loan.	Decreased public subsidy, through £3,000 tuition contribution, backed by a subsidised loan.
C Means tested tuition contribution	Depends precisely on the balance between the increased public subsidy on living cost loans and the level of the new tuition contribution.	Decreased public subsidy as living cost grants of £5,000 replaced by loans at a subsidised rate.
D Tuition contribution with restoration of maintenance grant	Decreased public subsidy through loss of £5,000 subsidised loans for maintenance and new tuition contribution of £3,000, although the latter is mitigated by access to a subsidised loan.	Depends on the precise balance between increased public subsidy in 100 per cent grant for living costs and loss of public subsidy in having to contribute £3,000 to tuition backed by a subsidised loan. Likely to be an increase in public subsidy.

20.58   Only Option D is likely, in practice, to secure a shift in the current balance of public subsidies from the families of the most well-off to the poorest students. Even under this option, if the tuition contribution was increased there might well be some decrease in public subsidy for the students from the poorest families. This result is hardly surprising since the overall objective is to increase the contribution made by individual graduates in work.

20.59   On the other hand, the 'maintenance' Option A clearly increases public subsidies to students from high income families at the expense of the students from the lower income families. The former gain access to loan subsidies while the latter lose grant.

Financial contribution to higher education of the different options

20.60   We have examined the overall financial implications for the Exchequer of the different options using the model developed for us by London Economics. More details can be found in Report 12. The results are summarised in Table 20.6:
■ on the present cash accounting base;
■ on the resource accounting base which will be introduced in 2001-02.

Table 20.6 – Financial effects of options compared to existing arrangements.

A. Cash accounting					
	£million net contribution to public finances by academic year in 1995-96 prices				
	Year 1	Year 2	Year 3	Year 8	Year 18
A Maintenance contribution	(200)	(300)	(400)	(50)	800
B Tuition contribution	50	100	150	500	1,100
C Means tested tuition contribution	0	0	50	400	1,450
D Tuition contribution with restoration of maintenance grant	200	300	450	650	600
B. Resource accounting					
A Maintenance contribution	350	500	700	450	100
B Tution contribution	350	550	750	700	900
C Means tested tuition contribution	550	850	1,100	950	750
D Tuition contribution with restoration of maintenance grant	100	150	150	300	800

Notes:
Figures in brackets are net additional costs to the Exchequer.
Cash accounting costs all loans advanced as public expenditure in the year they are made and all repayments as negative public expenditure in the year they are received. Resource accounting counts as public expenditure in the current account only the implied subsidies in the loans (including interest subsidies, provision for default and other types of non-payment).

20.61   In looking at the figures it is important to appreciate that they are sensitive to underlying assumptions, especially for the short term the assumption about what proportion of students would take up loans. We have assumed that take up rates would rise modestly if an additional contribution was sought from individuals. Over the long term the figures are sensitive for example to assumptions about student numbers and rates of student support.

20.62   The table illustrates two points:
- most crucially, none of the options by themselves generates the level of contributions needed to meet the funding requirement which we have identified in Chapter 17 for a high quality internationally competitive higher education system;
- resource accounting for loans expenditure represents a better basis for understanding the continuing subsidy in publicly funded loans (this is discussed further in paragraphs 20.87 to 20.89).

20.63   Option A produces low yields on both a cash and a resource accounting basis. The particularly poor long term performance of Option A under resource accounting may appear surprising. Option A includes the highest overall level of student debt, which means that many graduates would repay over an extended period. As a consequence, it also includes the greatest continuing subsidy in the form of a zero real interest rate. Under resource accounting the difference between the interest rate charged to graduates and the cost of Government borrowing is scored fully and brings the funding released by Option A down to a modest level. We discuss in Chapter 21 the merits of a modest real rate of interest which would make Option A more attractive when measured in resource accounting terms.

20.64   In Option C, which also includes high levels of graduate debt, the impact of the interest rate subsidy is offset by the continuing flow of tuition contributions from higher income families which are not supported by loans. Option A gives, therefore, a useful illustration of a general point. Simply increasing the size of the graduate contribution will not, if it is supported by income contingent loans, necessarily increase the flow of funds to the Exchequer or higher education. Higher repayments from some graduates may be offset by long term interest rate subsidies to others.

20.65   We have concluded that any option which comes close to releasing the public funds necessary to meet the funding requirements identified in Chapter 17 would produce either an unacceptable burden on graduates and on families of modest means, or would lead to a level of graduate commitment, regardless of income contingent payments, such that demand for higher education and participation would be seriously affected. Indeed, one of the implications of income contingent payments is that they limit the rate at which resources flow from graduates, regardless of the level of graduate commitment. We consider the implications of this conclusion below. It is essentially a consequence of the relative high level of continuing grant subsidy inherent in any scheme which protects graduates who remain on low incomes throughout their careers, and ultimately forgives their commitments. This is an important finding which we do not believe is generally understood in the public debate on these issues.

Preferred options

20.66   Making a decision on a preferred option involves a judgement about the relative weight to be given to the various criteria in paragraph 20.20. It also requires a careful scrutiny of the evidence. In going through that process we all changed and developed our views: we did not end up where we started.

20.67   As the figures show, seeking an increased contribution from graduates towards living costs, as in Option A:
- takes away subsidies from the poorest families and provides more substantial loans to others;
- increases public expenditure in the short term;
- releases modest or low resources for higher education in the long term.

This led us to focus on options involving a contribution by graduates to tuition costs.

20.68   The evidence drives us to favour options which involve a contribution by graduates in work to their tuition costs for three further reasons.
- First, we believe that tuition contributions will enable students to be more demanding of institutions if they are making a direct contribution to the costs of their tuition. We have been told by higher education staff that part-time and postgraduate students who pay fees already take this approach.
- Secondly, a requirement to contribute to tuition costs for full-time students helps level the playing field with part-time study and thus enables students to take rational decisions between the two. It also brings higher education students closer to the position of adult further education students.
- Thirdly, we believe that there will be a clearer expectation that, if graduates contribute to tuition costs, they should receive the benefits, in the sense that the public funding released should be spent on higher education. This is an important element of the new compact, described in Chapter 18, which underlies our thinking. We fear that if public subsidies for maintenance are reduced, the funding released would not be redirected to higher education institutions.

20.69   Option C produces a high yield in the long term on a cash accounting basis and is more equitable than Option A. But higher income parents are required to pay for their student children's tuition when we feel that this should be a responsibility of the graduate. Option D is equitable in concentrating subsidies on those from low income families, but, like Option C, expects a substantial contribution to come from higher income parents.

20.70   Having considered the main features of the four options, our own preference is, on balance, the tuition contribution Option B. In our view this option produces the best balance between seeking a continuing contribution from higher income individuals and their families and from graduates once they have completed their course of study and entered employment.

Level of graduate contribution to tuition

20.71   If graduates are to be expected to make a contribution to tuition costs, we thought it essential to try and identify a rationale for the level of that contribution. In their evidence to us, opponents of student contributions to tuition costs were concerned about the essentially open-ended nature of the arrangement.

20.72   We were attracted by the approach adopted in the further education sector in England in which students over 18 years of age are assumed to pay a fee equivalent to 25 per cent of the average level of funding across all subjects. The options we have examined include ones in which the contribution is a flat rate for each year of study and others in which the contribution is means tested.

20.73   We believe that a standard contribution should be charged, regardless of subject of study. The risk otherwise is that students, particularly perhaps those from poorer families, would choose cheaper subjects, rather than those which met their, or the nation's needs. Differential contributions by subject could cause particular problems in the areas of science and engineering where there is already a shortage of good applicants. Our preferred approach would ensure that access to prestigious or popular programmes continued to be determined by academic merit, and not by ability to pay.

20.74   We also considered whether the contribution should be the same for all years of study or should be lower in the first year or two, to encourage access to higher education and take up of programmes to levels H1 and H2, that is at sub-degree level. To balance this a higher contribution would have to be charged in subsequent years. We concluded that we preferred the simplicity of a standard contribution for all years of study.

20.75   We have considered the concerns of students and others that with a graduate contribution scheme, it would be open to any government to increase unilaterally the proportion of tuition costs paid by graduates. We believe that this concern is based on experience of the Australian Higher Education Contributions Scheme (HECs), and the corresponding New Zealand scheme, where graduate contributions were increased suddenly. In a democracy no Government can tie the hands of its successors on such matters, but we believe that the issue is so important that any changes should be subject to rigorous public review. We believe that an independent Committee should be appointed to review any proposal to increase the proportion of the tuition cost to be met by a graduate and that any such increase should be subject to the affirmative resolution of both Houses of Parliament.

Recommendation 79   **On a balance of considerations, we recommend to the Government that it introduces arrangements for graduates in work to make a flat rate contribution of around 25 per cent of the average cost of higher education tuition, through an income contingent mechanism, and that it ensures that the proportion of tuition costs to be met by the contribution cannot be increased without an independent review and an affirmative resolution of both Houses of Parliament. The contributions made by graduates in this way should be reserved for meeting the needs of higher education.**

Means testing

20.76   In the light of our conclusion that graduate contributions alone cannot reasonably be expected to fill the funding gap, we have considered the question of means testing carefully because of its scope to release substantial additional resources from individuals and their families for higher education. One argument suggests that, because all students are adults, support for their higher education should not be dependent on their family income. It is, after all, graduates themselves who benefit, not their parents. An alternative view accepts that parents who can afford it should have a continuing obligation to their children until they graduate. Being pragmatic, we do not see that it is practical to dispense with means testing altogether. The 'maintenance' Option A which we have explored shows that the effect of doing so is, on current accounting rules, to increase public expenditure sharply in the short term. Even our tuition contribution Option B, which retains means testing for half of the support for living costs, does not generate large savings in the short term under current accounting rules.

20.77   If a means testing approach were adopted, one approach would be to means test access to the new 50 per cent living cost loan made available under Option A. This would, however, generate little additional money for higher education, especially in the short term. We have therefore explored the impact of adding additional means tests to two of our Options, B and C. The means tested version of Option B would subject the existing loan for half of students' living costs and the loan for the tuition contribution to a means test against parental income. The position of students from lower income families would be unchanged. In contrast those from higher income families would receive no public support for living costs or the tuition contribution at all.

20.78   The means tested version of Option C would subject half the loan for living costs to a means test. Students from poorer families would continue to be eligible for 100 per cent loans for living costs while those from higher income families would have to look to their parents for half their living cost as well as their tuition contribution. These two variants are summarised in Table 20.7.

Table 20.7 – Student support under graduate contribution options with additional means test

	Living costs	Tuition contribution
Option B with additional means test	50% means tested grant 50% means tested income contingent loan	25% contribution supported by means tested income contingent loan
Option C with additional means test	50% means tested income contingent loan 50% non-means tested income contingent loan	25% means tested contribution

20.79   Requiring additional contributions would bear heavily on many families, who would struggle to find contributions of this magnitude. The annual contributions are larger in some cases than those we exemplify in Chapter 21 for graduates themselves when on the same income. Table 20.8 shows the implied additional contributions on a comparable basis to Table 20.3.

Table 20.8 – parental/family contributions for three years study under additional means tested options

	Option B with additional means test	Option C with additional means test
Higher income families (£)	13,000	8,000
Middle income families (£)	5,200	3,200
Lower income families (£)	0	0

20.80   It is inevitable that some parents would be unable or unwilling to provide the necessary funding especially if the change were introduced in 1998. They might, instead, underwrite a commercial loan taken out by the student, but students in that position would not secure anything like such favourable loan terms as would be attached to publicly-subsidised loans. Other students whose parents could not help in this way would probably be denied access to higher education. This is the situation which pertained in respect of living costs before 1990, and which the current student loans scheme was designed, in part, to redress.

20.81   On balance we believe that the weight of the arguments is in favour of not means testing access to loans. We are particularly concerned that it would have a significant impact on the participation rate. However, we recognise that means testing would release substantial additional funds in both the short and the long term, and that it is an option which the Government may have to consider if it cannot solve the short term funding problems in any other way. The decision on its acceptability to society is essentially a political one.

20.82   Table 20.9 shows the effect of the means testing options on public expenditure.

Table 20.9 – Financial effects of means testing options compared to existing arrangements

Cash accounting	£million net contribution to public finances by academic year in 1995-96 prices		
	Year 1	Year 8	Year 18
Option B with additional means test	250	950	1,400
Option C with additional means test	300	1,200	2,100

Resource accounting	£million net contribution to public finances by academic year in 1995-96 prices		
	Year 1	Year 8	Year 18
Option B with additional means test	400	1,000	1,400
Option C with additional means test	600	1,400	1,700

20.83   Both these options come closer to delivering the sort of resources required by higher education. But they do so at the expense of sharply increasing the contribution which parents have to make. For the long term, we believe it would be more equitable for taxpayers in general, rather than the parents of students, to meet some of the cost of an expansion of higher education.

Encouraging advance payment

20.84   In practice, a proportion of students will choose to pay any contribution to tuition in advance rather than to take out a loan. This is a choice which should be open to those with the means to exercise it. It would be possible to encourage advance payment and therefore maximise short term savings by offering a discount to those who chose this option, as is done in Australia. In equity terms the discount could be justified to the extent that it represented the discounted present value of the subsidy inherent in the preferential rate of interest available to students who paid their contribution over a number of years. However, it would also involve unnecessary costs insofar as the discount would be available to students who might anyway have paid in advance.

20.85   Alternatively, the introduction of a modest real rate of interest should have the effect of encouraging advance payment and reducing loan take up rates. Table 20.10 shows what resources Option B, the tuition contribution option, would realise if a 2.5 per cent real rate of interest led to a modest reduction in loan take up rates. We discuss rates further in Chapter 21.

Table 20.10 – Financial effect of real rate of interest on tuition contribution Option B compared to existing arrangements, £million by academic year

	Year 1	Year 8	Year 18
Cash accounting	100	650	1,350
Resource accounting	350	850	1,200

20.86   Given the need to release substantial resources in the short term, as described in Chapter 17, we believe that the Government should structure any new arrangements for contributions to tuition costs so as to maximise the proportion of students who pay in advance rather than taking up a loan. Means testing the access to the loan or introducing a real interest rate would increase this proportion without additional incentives being offered. If neither of these options is pursued, we believe that there is a strong case for the introduction of a discount along the lines of the Australian model. Further detailed work would be necessary to determine the appropriate level of discount and ensure that the arrangements provided value for money over the longer term, as well as releasing additional funds in the short term.

Technical features of loans in relation to the Public Sector Borrowing Requirement (PSBR)

20.87   A fundamental problem with the Government providing loans to students is the way in which they are treated in the national accounts. Under the current arrangements for Government accounting – cash accounting – the full value of loans is scored in the same way as grants, when the loan is advanced. Repayments are subsequently counted as negative public expenditure. This means that options which change existing grants into loans do not produce any short term savings in public expenditure apart from those caused by less than 100 per cent of eligible students taking up loans.

20.88 The introduction of resource based budgeting for public finances in 2001-02 should help to clarify the fact that loans are not equivalent to grants. Under resource accounting only the implied subsidies in the loans advanced are taken into the accounts. As shown by some of the options exemplified earlier, these implied subsidies can be large and can make some options which are apparently attractive look much less satisfactory over the long term. We believe resource accounting offers a better approach to understanding the true financial implications of loans schemes. Even with resource accounting, however, if the Government continues to treat loan advances in the same way as other current expenditure in the definition of the PSBR, there will still be a problem.

20.89 We have noted that the UK adopts a broader definition of PSBR than a number of other countries and a broader one than it is required to adopt under the Maastricht criteria. When we visited the Netherlands, for example, we learnt that student loans there do not count against the PSBR. We are very concerned that the constraints of the definition of the PSBR may force the adoption of solutions which ease short term problems, but which are poor value for money for the nation over the long term. We are even more concerned that the value being lost would come out of the contributions we feel it necessary to seek from graduates in work.

Recommendation 80 **We recommend to the Government that it looks urgently at alternative and internationally accepted approaches to national accounting which do not treat the repayable part of loans in the same way as grants to students.**

20.90 We recognise that this review will need to take place against the background of the wider economic context, but we see no merit in the present practice of treating loans in the same way as grants. It misleads rather than informs.

Securing private finance for loans

20.91 Faced with the problems created by cash accounting and the PSBR definition, the previous Government sought to find a way of using private capital to finance loan expenditure. Put simply this can be done either:
- by having private financial institutions (eg banks) advance the loan from their own funds in return for a government subsidy to recognise that not all loans will, because of policy decisions, be repaid; or
- by the Government advancing the loans which it then sells to the private sector at a discount (or with a subsidy to the purchaser).

20.92 The previous Government's experience with the 'twin-track' scheme, which would have involved both the Student Loans Company and the banks lending to students, demonstrated how hard it is to involve the private sector in heavily regulated and subsidised lending schemes at a price which offers any advantage to the taxpayer. We spent some time investigating whether we could design a loans scheme which was more like a commercial scheme and, therefore, more likely to be attractive to private sector lenders. In doing so, we still held to the principle that there should be income contingent repayment arrangements. We found that moving to a rate of interest which is close to a commercial rate of interest (the current scheme has an interest rate equivalent only to the Retail Prices Index) created certain problems. The protection of income contingent arrangements for the low paid means that a significant minority of graduates would be making repayments which did not even cover the interest on their loan, let alone repay the debt. Their debts would, therefore, continue to grow through life becoming, in some cases, very large before write-off. Even though individuals would be protected from unreasonable debt-servicing burdens, we felt that the possibility of an ever-rising debt would be a deterrent to participation in higher education. Although the same difficulty can arise with any real rate of interest, it is severe with commercial interest rates. We were told that the Australians had considered real interest rates for their Higher Education Contributions scheme, but had rejected them for the same reasons.

20.93   We also considered whether a mutual scheme might help to make a contributions scheme more attractive as a commercial proposition. Under a mutual scheme, all those taking out loans would be liable to pay not only the sum borrowed, but the sum borrowed plus a premium of perhaps 20 per cent to cover the payment of the commitments of those who will never earn enough to pay their commitments. It would seek to deal with two of the main problems with loan schemes:
- the percentage of individuals who will never repay their loans, which represents a loss of income;
- the impossibility of individuals, or those making loans, identifying in advance who is unlikely to pay.

20.94   This approach also increases the amount paid by those graduates on higher incomes; and may thereby provide an incentive for individuals who are confident about their future earning potential to pay up front. While this might be desirable in terms of short term increases in funding, it risks undermining the basis of the loan scheme by negative selection. Only those with the poorest prospects would take out the loan, which would increase the size of the mutual premium required to cover non-repayment. This would encourage even more of those with better prospects to opt out, leading to a scheme which was unstable. To avoid this, it would be possible to require all students, whether they took out a loan or not, to make a 20 per cent contribution to the loan fund. That would, however, be simply equivalent to requiring a higher contribution from all.

20.95   Although we find the concept of the mutual scheme attractive, we have concluded that it is unlikely to provide a funding approach that is stable in the long term. In the light of these considerations, we have concluded that the twin-track approach has fundamental difficulties that cannot be readily overcome.

20.96   Another way of securing private capital to finance loans would involve selling the rights to repayments of the government-provided loans. It is difficult to see what intrinsic merits such an approach might have, other than achieving short term PSBR savings. In the long term this approach would cost more. This is mainly because the student loan debt is a novel financial asset, which potential purchasers would be likely to discount heavily until a clear track record is available. It also reflects the fact that the Government itself can always borrow money more cheaply than commercial institutions, and that the purchasers would be looking to make a profit. At the time of writing we do not know whether the present Government intends to proceed with the debt sales planned by the previous Government. In Chapter 21 we recommend using the Inland Revenue system to collect graduate contributions. We have been advised that the Office of National Statistics, which is responsible for interpreting international classifications of the PSBR, is likely to take the view that sales of loans whose repayments are collected via the tax system would not be classified as private sector activity. Such loans would stay on the government's balance sheet, thus defeating the very purpose of the sales.

20.97   For the purposes of exemplifying options, we have assumed generally that student loan debt will not be sold. We recognise, however, that if changes in accounting practice are not feasible, debt sales may be a necessary, if undesirable, short term feature. We would, however, make two comments:

- the sale of the loan book may well represent poor value for money if the discounting is high;
- to classify a loan as public expenditure because the repayments are collected on an agency basis through the Inland Revenue, even though much of the risk of non-payment is borne by the private sector owners of the repayment rights, seems to be at variance with the substance of the matter.

Special cases

Loan access

20.98   Full-time students aged over 50 when they start their programme are currently ineligible for student loans on two grounds: first, that they are more likely than younger students to have other resources from which to support themselves; and secondly, that they have a lower future earnings potential than younger students (and therefore are less likely to pay their commitments). These arguments apply equally to loans to meet any new contribution to tuition costs. Indeed the increase in the total contribution required and the introduction of income contingent payments would reduce the likelihood of older students paying the entire contribution before retirement.

20.99   We recognise that a requirement on the over 50s to pay a contribution to tuition costs without access to a loan facility would make participation in higher education difficult for some students in this age group. But, on the other hand, older students would have an unfair advantage over their younger colleagues if they were given loans which, for the most part, they were not required to repay. We do believe, however, that such students should be entitled to the fee remission arrangements we have recommended earlier in this chapter.

Students on longer courses

20.100   We are conscious that the introduction of a flat rate annual contribution to tuition costs would bear particularly heavily on students taking longer than average courses, including those studying for the teaching and medical professions and a high proportion of students on degree courses in Scotland.

20.101   In a limited number of cases study over a period of four years or more is essential in order to gain entry to certain occupations, and it is right that students should not be discouraged from embarking on the necessary course of study – or prevented from completing it – because of financial considerations. On the other hand, we believe it is important (for the reasons set out in Chapter 19) that any drift towards an increase in the average length of course should be discouraged. There are also many cases where a student's choice to undertake, say, a fourth year of undergraduate study is based on a sound expectation that this will increase his or her later earnings potential. For these reasons we believe, on balance, that it would **not** be right to put in place any across the board measures to limit the contribution required from students on longer courses.

20.102   So long as income contingent payment arrangements along the lines which we have recommended earlier in this chapter are adopted, we believe that students will, on the whole, be willing to make a somewhat larger investment where that is necessary to achieve a particular goal (such as entry to their chosen profession). Where the purpose of the additional years of study is less clear, it is right that students should be encouraged to question whether they provide value for money. Having said that, we believe that there is scope for providing additional targeted support to ensure that there is no adverse impact on recruitment to occupations requiring a longer than average period of study. We believe the best approach would be for the appropriate professional bodies and, in the case of relevant public service professions, like teaching and medicine, the Government to establish bursary or similar incentive schemes for students wishing to study for occupations requiring four years or more of study.

20.103   Our Scottish Committee, while supporting our preference for Option B, the tuition contribution option, is concerned about its impact on Scottish students, many of whom will choose to undertake a four year Honours degree. They have suggested that the Secretary of State for Scotland should consider the implications of the proposed arrangements for equity for students studying for comparable degrees across the UK.

Recommendation 81   **We recommend to the Government that Scottish students who have had only one year's education after statutory schooling, many of whom under current arrangements would choose to take a four year honours degree, should not make a tuition contribution for one of their years in higher education. Beyond that, this would be a matter for consideration by the Secretary of State for Scotland.**

The living away from home allowance

20.104   An issue closely related to the overall adequacy of support for students' living costs is whether it is necessary or appropriate for the taxpayer to continue to pay for students to live away from home (through the London and 'elsewhere' rates of grant and loan). We recognise that for many students the opportunity to broaden their horizons by leaving the home environment and living amongst their peers is an important and valued part of the higher education experience. However, given limited resources it is arguable that this experience, however valuable, is not one which should be gained at the expense of the taxpayer. All other things being equal, there is a strong case for arguing at least that this element of support should be provided entirely through loan rather than grant.

20.105   However, there are still large areas of the UK where there is no higher education provider within daily travelling distance, or where the available provision is insufficient or inappropriate in nature. This is a particular problem in relation to Northern Ireland where some 40 per cent of young people are obliged to travel outside the Province to study and is shared by a number of other parts of the UK, including Cornwall, Cumbria and parts of East Anglia. Moreover, the diversity of the system – which we would wish to encourage – means that even where there is an institution within travelling distance it may not provide the particular programme which the student wishes to study. To remove the living away from home allowance for such students would seem harsh, and would have some adverse effect on participation in such areas. It could also have severe consequences for certain campus-based institutions and specialist institutions which rely on a national intake.

20.106   For these reasons we do not recommend any changes on this front in the short term. However, we believe that the Government should keep this issue under review with a view, once the pattern of provision is more evenly spread, to providing only loan rather than grant support to students wishing to study away from home.

Students from elsewhere in the European Union

20.107   Under European law, all European Union (EU) countries are obliged to allow EU nationals access to their higher education provision on the same basis as their own nationals. This requirement applies to tuition facilities but not to public support for living costs. Accordingly, EU nationals are entitled to free tuition and payment of the fee element of the mandatory award so long as they meet the same conditions as a UK student. A large number of EU students take advantage of this position but rather few UK students take advantage of the reciprocal right to study free in EU countries. The net result is that the UK is subsidising higher education provision for a number of EU countries. The introduction of an across the board tuition contribution for UK students would also apply to EU students studying in the UK and might help to rectify the current imbalance in flows. We understand, however, that the UK would probably be obliged to give EU nationals access to any loans made available to UK students to support their tuition contributions. Collection of payments from those who returned to their own country on graduation might be difficult, but this would also be true for UK graduates who go to work overseas.

Conclusion

20.108 Having proposed that individuals who have taken full-time undergraduate courses should be required to make a contribution to their tuition costs, we believe that it is also incumbent on us to make proposals about the nature of the arrangements to support them in making that contribution, and, in particular, to consider how student support arrangements might develop in the long term to support genuine lifelong learning. We take this forward in Chapter 21.

Chapter 21

Enabling individuals to make their contribution

21.1   The previous chapter concluded that graduates will have to contribute more to the cost of their higher education, and makes various recommendations about how they should be encouraged to do so. In the short term at least, an option based on commitments repaid on an income contingent basis by graduates once they are in work should be adopted.

21.2   In this chapter we consider:
- the nature of such a commitment scheme;
- the administrative arrangements required;
- potential longer term developments.

The nature of the commitment scheme

21.3   We are convinced that an increased contribution from graduates can be sought only if payment is income contingent.

21.4   An income contingent graduate contribution scheme (the Higher Education Contribution Scheme, or HECS) has existed for some years in Australia, enabling graduates to contribute to the cost of their higher education. It has attracted international attention, primarily because it has produced significant additional revenue for the higher education system while not deterring access for those from lower socio-economic backgrounds or minority groups.[1] Recent changes to the scheme announced by the Australian government to increase the repayment levels for graduates have been controversial, but previously the scheme had been largely accepted by the student population as equitable.

21.5   As our aim was also a scheme which produces additional resources for higher education and ensures that access does not suffer, we looked carefully at the Australian model in its original form. The relevant features of the scheme are as follows:
- students make a contribution to the cost of their courses which, until the recent changes, amounted to about 23 per cent of the average cost of tuition. Contributions are paid into an independent trust fund and the proceeds are channelled into higher education;
- students have the choice of paying in advance, in which case a discount of 25 per cent is offered, or of deferring payment by taking out a loan;
- where payment is deferred, graduates begin repaying their loans once their income reaches a set threshold. Until the recent changes, this threshold was the average taxable income of Australians in paid work;

- once over the threshold, graduates pay a fixed percentage of their income. Until 1996, the percentage payment rate began at three per cent for those just over the threshold, rising to a maximum of five per cent for those on higher incomes. These payment rates have been significantly increased as a result of the recent changes to the scheme;
- loans are indexed to inflation, but do not attract a real interest rate;
- payments are collected through the tax system.

21.6 In terms of social attitudes, or the amount of additional resource which is needed for higher education, the circumstances of the United Kingdom (UK) in 1997 may not be the same as those of Australia in 1988. Nevertheless, we believe that many features of the Australian scheme, in its original form, would translate well to the UK.

Amount of contribution and discounts for advance payment

21.7 We have already stated in Chapter 20 that in a scheme involving contributions to tuition costs, a contribution of about 25 per cent of teaching costs would be appropriate. This is broadly in line with the Australian scheme. It also corresponds with the contribution normally made by students aged over 18 in further education in England. We have also suggested in Chapter 20 that the Government should consider the case for offering a discount for advance payment of the contribution.

Contribution threshold

21.8 The key question is the income level at which graduates should begin contributing. As graduates are being asked to contribute on the grounds that they receive a personal benefit from higher education in the form of increased earnings, it can be argued that they should not be asked to contribute unless and until that benefit has been received – for example, when their earnings exceed the national average (as in Australia). This, however, ignores the fact that an individual may already be benefiting from higher education at a lower earnings level, for example through being in work rather than unemployed. Higher threshold levels have a substantial impact on the flow of additional resources for higher education. Even the current UK student loan repayment threshold of 85 per cent of national average earnings has a material effect on the income stream, with a high proportion of graduates allowed to defer their repayments. At the end of the financial year 1996-97 almost half of all borrowers from the Student Loans Company (SLC) who would otherwise be due to repay were deferring their repayments.

21.9 Some of those who submitted evidence argued strongly that the contribution threshold should be set significantly lower than at present.[2] They noted that if there is a high threshold, those who are above it have to pay a relatively high proportion of their income to produce a reasonable income stream for higher education. If the threshold is set at a lower level, the burden of contribution is spread across a larger number of graduates, but it is still possible to collect more from the higher earners and ensure that contribution levels are manageable for all. Commercial experience suggests that getting borrowers into the habit of making small regular payments is an effective way of reducing the number of defaulters.

21.10   It has been suggested that the appropriate contribution threshold would be the level of earnings at which national insurance becomes payable, currently £61 per week, or £3,172 per year.³ We are convinced that this would be too low. The result would be either to push many graduates at this income level into reliance on benefits (if contributions were taken into account in assessing benefit eligibility) or to disadvantage this group when compared to others at a similar income level. The contributions obtained from graduates on incomes this low would, in any case, be insignificant.

21.11   We have concluded that the threshold for contributions should be set lower than under the current loans scheme, but significantly higher than the threshold for national insurance payments. The decision about thresholds needs to be taken alongside a decision about rates of contribution discussed below and about whether there should be a cap on the level of contributions from high earners. Two options are exemplified: one under which the threshold is set at 100 per cent of average graduate starting salaries (some £10,500 in 1995-96 prices), and one in which it is set at £5,000 in 1995-96 prices but with a low rate of contribution.

Rates of contribution

21.12   There are three related issues to be resolved in determining the percentage rates at which graduates should make their contribution:
   ■ whether all graduates should pay the same percentage contribution rate once their income exceeds the threshold, or whether the percentage rate should increase for those on higher incomes;
   ■ whether contributions should be at a flat rate (applying to all income) or a marginal rate (applying to income above a threshold, as with income tax);
   ■ the actual levels at which the rates should be set;
   ■ whether there is a ceiling fixed to contributions from those on high incomes.

21.13   On the first of these, we believe there is a case for contribution rates to be fixed on a progressive basis as in Australia, so that those on higher incomes pay a higher percentage of their income. This is both equitable, in that the largest monthly contributions come from those who can most afford them, and will maximise the resources released for higher education. In most cases it will affect only the speed at which graduates make their contribution, rather than the total size of it. However, allowing those on low incomes to pay more slowly will mean that some of this group will not pay their full contribution by the time their commitment is cancelled.

21.14   One way of maximising the extent to which contributions rise with income would be for contribution rates to apply to marginal rather than total income, in the same way as income tax (though not necessarily using the same thresholds). This means that no payment is required on any income below the threshold, even when total income exceeds the threshold. The percentage payment rate is charged only on that part of a graduate's income which exceeds the threshold. So if a marginal repayment rate of 10 per cent is charged on income over £10,000, a graduate earning £11,000 would pay £100 (10 per cent of £1,000) rather than £1,100 (10 per cent of £11,000). This avoids the 'cliff edge' problem which arises when a contribution based on total income is triggered once a graduate reaches the threshold.

21.15 The most appropriate thresholds and contribution rates will need to be determined by taking into account both what is manageable for graduates and the income stream needed for higher education. For exemplification, we have modelled two schemes. In the first, graduates pay 12.5 per cent of marginal income above a threshold of the average graduate starting salary (£10,500 pa in 1995-96 prices). In the second, graduates pay five per cent of marginal income above £5000, and 10 per cent above £10,000. Contributions would not vary with the size of a graduate's commitment. Table 21.1 shows the impact of each of these on graduates. It also shows the payment burden a graduate with a £9,000 loan would have under the current loan scheme if its terms were unchanged. The advantages of the income contingent arrangements are clear: they produce a progressive contribution regime, and modest average contribution rates, payable until a graduate has fulfilled his or her commitment.

Table 21.1 – Comparison of graduate contribution levels

Graduate income level	12.5% of marginal income above £10,500		5% of marginal income between £5,000 and £10,000 and 10% above £10,000		Current loan scheme (£9,000 loan)	
	Annual repay-ment	% of total income	Annual repay-ment	% of total income	Annual repay-ment	% of total income
£ 5,000	0	0	0	0	0	0
£ 6,000	0	0	£ 50	0.8	0	0
£ 8,000	0	0	£ 150	1.9	0	0
£10,000	0	0	£ 250	2.5	0	0
£12,000	£ 188	1.6	£ 450	3.75	0	0
£15,000	£ 563	3.8	£ 750	5.0	0	0
£18,000*	£ 938	5.2	£1,050	5.8	£1,920	10.7
£20,000	£1,188	5.9	£1,250	6.3	£1,920	9.6
£25,000	£1,813	7.3	£1,750	7.0	£1,920	7.7
£30,000	£2,438	8.1	£2,250	7.5	£1,920	6.4

* national average earnings

21.16 Contributions of the level indicated for those on the highest incomes suggest that it may be necessary to cash limit their annual level, for example at £2,000 a year, or seven per cent of total income. It will be necessary to consider this issue in the light of the particular scheme selected. Similarly, provision should also be available for graduates wishing to make early payments in full.

21.17 Table 21.2 shows, however, how much impact a higher threshold has on the resources released for higher education. The higher threshold, even in combination with a higher marginal rate, does not yield as high an income stream as the lower thresholds option.

Because of this, we have used the lower thresholds in exemplifying our main funding options.

Table 21.2 – £ million net contribution to public finances by academic year

% of marginal income	year 1	year 8	year 18
12.5%: high threshold	0	350	750
5% and 10%: low threshold	50	500	1,100

Interest rates

21.18   The largest element of subsidy in the current student loans scheme is the interest rate subsidy (ie the difference between the Retail Prices Index-linked rate of interest charged to students, and the cost to the Government of borrowing the funds). Some of those who submitted evidence to us argued that this 'hidden' subsidy should be reduced, or even removed entirely, and the funds released used to provide more targeted support.

21.19   There are a number of arguments for this approach:
■ it would produce a material increase in revenue from loan contributions over the medium to long term. However, this would be limited by the introduction of an income contingent contributions regime. This is because the contributions which individuals make under an income contingent scheme are determined by their income, rather than the interest rate: for those on low incomes, the effect of an increase in the interest rate is to substitute contributions to interest for the contribution to repayment of principal, so ultimately a larger proportion of principal is written off on cancellation;
■ if the interest rate was set at a level which met the Government's cost of borrowing, there would be no ongoing subsidy paid by the Government, other than the eventual cost of default or cancellation. It would, therefore, matter less if contributions were spread over a longer period than now;
■ if access to the scheme is not means tested, and the interest rate is heavily subsidised, there is a real risk that students who do not need the facility will make use of it anyway and reinvest the money to secure a net financial gain. Real interest rates would reduce the subsidy and this risk (thus also reducing costs).

21.20   Real interest rates can, however, have the effect of increasing the burden for those on lower incomes. To avoid that, it would be possible to prevent the level of graduates' outstanding obligations increasing in real terms, while their incomes were too low for them to make contributions, by charging a zero real interest rate during those periods. Those on low incomes would also be protected because, although the size of their outstanding loans might rise over their working lives, their monthly contributions would be capped, and the outstanding debt would ultimately be cancelled (see paragraphs 21.23 and 21.24).

21.21   Those on low incomes who paid in full, however, would pay more in total than those on high incomes who paid their total contribution quickly. With a zero real interest rate, by contrast, the highest subsidies go to those on the lowest incomes. The existence of a real rate might be a disincentive to participation by students worried about escalation of debt after graduation.

21.22 Clearly there is a balance of considerations. The differences in income to the Government, and in charges to graduates, from rates of interest of 2.5 and 5 per cent amount to some £100 million a year initially, rising to £200 – £300 million a year in 20 years' time. Providing contributions are income contingent, and that rates of interest are limited to 2.5 per cent (ie the rate of inflation) during the years of studentship or during periods of sickness or unemployment, the burden for graduates in work need not be heavy. But that has to be balanced against the potential risk of discouraging participation in higher education. This risk led us to the view that any rate of interest should be linked to the rate of inflation.

Cancellation

21.23 Under the current student loans scheme, liability to repay is cancelled after 25 years or when the graduate reaches the age of 50, whichever is the sooner.[4]

21.24 The purpose of an income contingent scheme is to spread contributions over whatever period is necessary to ensure that they remain manageable, whatever the graduate's income. On that basis, it is reasonable to contemplate contributions for graduates on low incomes, or who take time out from the labour force, continuing over the whole of their working lives. We suggest therefore that liability to repay should be cancelled at the common retirement age of 65. As under the current arrangements, cancellation should be permitted only where the graduate has not defaulted on payments which were due to be paid earlier.

Administrative arrangements

21.25 Current arrangements for administering student support for living costs and tuition are complex, and involve a large number of agencies. In part, this reflects the number of distinct activities involved, but it also reflects the historical accidents of the way the system has developed.

21.26 There are at least six distinct procedures that will need to be carried out, if our recommendations are accepted. These are:
- assessing students' eligibility for public support;
- means testing and paying grants for student living costs;
- payment of any public money for tuition which follows the student;
- advancing (and if necessary means testing) loans for student living costs;
- advancing loans for tuition contributions;
- collection of loan repayments (or graduate contributions) for both living costs and tuition.

21.27 Current arrangements can be confusing to students who have to make applications to a local education authority (or a central body in Scotland or an Education and Library Board in Northern Ireland) for a mandatory award, to the Student Loans Company

(SLC) for a loan, and to the institution which confirms their enrolment on an eligible programme and thus their eligibility for a loan. Institutions have to interact with over a hundred local authorities, the central awards agencies and the SLC. As new funding arrangements are introduced, it should be an objective to simplify the procedures for both students and institutions. In paragraphs 21.51 to 21.65, we examine some options to achieve this objective, including individual learning accounts (ILAs).

Assessing student eligibility and paying maintenance grants

21.28   At present there are two main aspects of assessing students' eligibility for public support. The first centres on whether they are personally eligible, for example, whether they meet the residence requirements or have previously had a mandatory award. The second centres on whether they are enrolled on an eligible programme. This task is largely carried out by local education authorities (LEAs), the Student Awards Agency for Scotland (SAAS) and the Education and Library Boards in Northern Ireland, with the help of institutions. The Student Loans Company (SLC) relies on such assessments to determine loan eligibility in most cases, but has to undertake further work with institutions in some cases because the eligibility criteria for grants and for loans are not identical. It would be simpler for students if they had to interact with only one body.

Public money which follows the student

21.29   LEAs and the central awards agencies also pay a per capita mandatory award fee, which is not means tested, to institutions on behalf of all qualified individuals. This is the current element of public funding which follows the student.

21.30   Among those who commented to us on the administration of mandatory award payments, many were of the view that it is inefficient for LEAs to be involved in the payment of fees or grants. We were concerned, in addition, about the impact on cost-effectiveness of the establishment of even more, and smaller LEAs as a result of local government reorganisation. This involves duplication of functions and still more authorities for each institution to invoice for fee payments.

21.31   We have noted with interest the central administration of mandatory awards in Scotland and the administration of public loans for all UK students by the SLC. We believe, on the basis of this experience, that it would be sensible to bring these functions within a single administration. We consider this further at paragraphs 21.51 to 21.56.

21.32   We proposed in Chapter 19 that there should continue to be an element of public funding, separate from the Funding Bodies' responsibilities, which flows with student choice, that this should cover part-time and postgraduate students, and that it should be a function of a Student Support Agency.

21.33   Such a development will require careful preparation if it is to deliver the kind of benefits we expect.

Making loans for student living costs

21.34   Despite some continuing concerns in the evidence submitted to us about the effectiveness of the SLC, we believe that these concerns stemmed from certain administrative and management problems in the SLC's early days. Evidence from the SLC's own surveys of customer satisfaction indicates a very favourable opinion of its processes, although those in repayment or deferment have slightly less positive views than current borrowers.[5]

21.35   As long as student loans remain in the public sector and universally available, it makes good sense to have a single administration of those loans. Furthermore, in the light of the Student Loans Company's progress in refining its administrative systems, it should form the nucleus of any future student support agency.

Advancing loans for tuition

21.36   A number of the options we identified in Chapter 20 would involve either a flat rate contribution to tuition costs backed by loans, or a means-tested individual contribution. We suggested that a flat rate contributions scheme should exist for individuals who wished to pay at the time of study, perhaps with the incentive of a discount for doing so.

21.37   We envisage that, for all options involving a contribution, whether backed by a loan or not, payment of the contribution would be a condition of admission to the programme of study. For those individuals paying at the time of study, there would be a direct financial transaction with the institution.

21.38   If individuals needed to take out a loan to cover their contribution it would be sensible, if our earlier conclusion about the improved effectiveness of the SLC is accepted, for loans for tuition to be made by the SLC as well. However, loans for the tuition contribution would be different in kind from living costs loans. They would be for a specific purpose, rather than the more general purposes of supporting students' living expenses. It would be essential, therefore, to have in place arrangements to ensure the funds are used for the intended purpose but leave the authority to make payments with individual students. The best available model for this is the process of transfer of funds for house purchase backed by a mortgage. The individual controls the transfer of the funds through his or her signature, but does not physically have access to the funds. The SLC would pay the funds to an institution on the signature of the individual, who would at the same time make a contractual commitment to contribute once earning enough to do so.

21.39   Although loans for living costs and a loan to support a contribution to tuition costs are different in kind, the application process ought to be combined to ensure simplicity for students and to avoid administrative duplication.

Collecting contributions from graduates in work

21.40   Our view that contributions should be made on an income contingent basis makes the collection of payments more complicated than under the current loan system. At present, once a graduate's income exceeds the deferment threshold the annual rate of payment is one-fifth (or one-seventh) of the loan debt, irrespective of income. The payments are made by direct debit signed at the time the loan was taken out. We have suggested that in future, contributions are made on marginal income above the threshold (see paragraph 21.14).

21.41   If future contributions are to be genuinely income contingent, a new system will be needed. A number of those submitting evidence to us, drawing on the work of Dr Barr and Mr Crawford at the London School of Economics and Political Science, suggested that the National Insurance Contributions Scheme (NICs) offers an existing mechanism which could be readily adapted to collect student loan repayments.[6] The proposals put to us by Barr and Crawford were part of a package which included not only the collection of contributions via NICs, but also:
- income contingent contributions;
- charging real interest rates when graduates start to contribute;
- the sale of the loan book to the private sector through securitisation.[7]

21.42   The principal benefits claimed for the use of the NICs are:
- more efficient administration by 'piggy backing' on an existing collection mechanism;
- a lower default rate than achieved by collection through the Student Loans Company (SLC);
- the lower and upper income thresholds used by the National Insurance system would ensure some small contributions, from those on low incomes and cap the annual contribution required from high earners.

21.43   We have already explained in paragraph 21.10 why we think the National Insurance (NI) lower threshold is too low for graduate contributions. Using the NI system would also introduce an unnecessary layer of administrative activity. Currently the Inland Revenue collects tax and NI contributions together from employers and then passes the NI contributions to the Contributions Agency. There would be no advantage in the Inland Revenue passing graduate contributions through the Contributions Agency en route to the SLC. We have therefore examined three alternatives:

a   using the Inland Revenue to collect contributions;

b   using the SLC to collect repayments, with information on individuals' income verified by the Inland Revenue;

c   using the SLC alone.

It is important to appreciate that using the Inland Revenue to collect graduate contributions is not the same as introducing a graduate tax. Under all the options, the SLC would continue to make the loans and be accountable for contributions.

21.44   Under Option a, the SLC would supply the Inland Revenue with the name and NI number of all individuals who had taken out income contingent loans. As the graduate contributions would not be tax, special arrangements would be necessary to ensure the appropriate level of additional deductions from earnings by employers for graduates in paid employment. As with tax, alternative arrangements would be necessary for the self-employed.

21.45   We have been advised by the Inland Revenue that a requirement on employers to deduct graduate contributions from an individual's wages/salary could be implemented in broadly two ways:

- either by providing employers with separate deduction tables, to allow them to calculate the relevant amount to deduct in each pay period;
- or by adjusting an individual's tax code to collect a particular amount during the course of a tax year.

21.46   For self-employed graduates, repayments would form part of the self-assessed return, and would be collected with income tax.

21.47   The other two Options (b and c) would both involve the Student Loans Company (SLC) in collecting income contingent contributions direct from individuals. This would add considerably to the administrative burden on the SLC, in that it would need to establish, in advance, the projected income of every individual, not just those seeking deferment, and would have to send out revised contribution schedules. In addition, it would need to review every individual's actual income each year. The principal difference between Options b and c is that under Option b the Inland Revenue would provide details of the student's income for the year, either on a sample basis or more widely. For individuals not making tax returns, this might require the Revenue to contact individuals direct or to bring them into self-assessment.

21.48   The main advantage in using the Inland Revenue is that it already has in place mechanisms for assessing income and securing payments from virtually all members of the working population. It would be burdensome for individuals, and administratively inefficient, to have those arrangements duplicated by the SLC. A system which is simple and efficient is far more likely to be acceptable to graduates and to reduce the risk of defaults. There would, however, be costs involved in using the Inland Revenue including:

- a compliance burden on employers;
- amendments to the Inland Revenue's computer systems;
- removing student loans from the purview of the Consumer Credit Act;[8]
- resolving the issue of employer default and liability.[9]

21.49   In our view, the balance of advantage lies strongly with using the Inland Revenue as the collection mechanism.

Recommendation 82   **We recommend to the Government that the Inland Revenue should be used as the principal route for the collection of income contingent contributions from graduates in work, on behalf of the Student Loans Company.**

21.50   There will inevitably be some individuals outside the tax system, particularly those working abroad. The SLC will need to continue to be responsible for securing contributions from such individuals.

Longer term arrangements

21.51 Only full-time undergraduate students are covered by the existing arrangements for student living costs and tuition support, ie fees, paid by local authorities. Over time, if individuals are to move in and out of the system more often, and perhaps to mix periods of full-time study with part-time study or to move at different rates through the levels of the qualifications framework, there is a strong case for rationalising and simplifying the administrative arrangements for supporting students and graduates. We have examined two types of approach:

■ the establishment of a single Student Support Agency;

■ the establishment of a series of individual learning accounts (ILAs) perhaps within the context of a Learning Bank.

A single Student Support Agency

21.52 As we noted both in Chapter 19 and paragraphs 21.25 to 21.31, we are concerned about the implications of having up to 160 separate LEAs in England and Wales involved in the administration and payment of student maintenance grants and the payment of the per capita mandatory award fee to higher education institutions. The difficulty is particularly acute because institutions have to invoice separately each LEA from which they have students and other awards agencies for Scotland and Northern Ireland. The separation of the arrangements for grants and loans, and their different requirements, make it difficult for students to relate effectively to the different processes. There would be merit in bringing these functions together, to provide students with a single point of access to a comprehensive service.

21.53 On the basis of the experience of the Student Loans Company (SLC) and the Student Awards Agency for Scotland (SAAS) we have concluded that a single Student Support Agency would be both desirable and feasible. Such an agency could absorb the current functions of LEAs in England and Wales in relation to assessing eligibility, means testing and payment of grant, and the per capita element of public funding to institutions which follows student choice. It could also absorb the functions of the SLC.

21.54 Although ultimately the number of individuals on the books and the number of transactions handled by a single Student Support Agency would be very large, it would provide:

■ a one-stop-shop for students for the administration of funds in support of their living costs and tuition;

■ proper records of how much public support individuals receive over time for higher education study;

■ a single point of contact for institutions in receipt of individual contributions and the per capita element of public funding based on student choice.

21.55 The main challenge for such an agency would be to improve on the standards of service currently provided to students and institutions by the best of the local education authorities and the existing SLC. There would be a particular need to avoid becoming too distant. One possible approach would be to have branch offices on university campuses or in metropolitan centres, although new technology and changing customer expectations might allow the agency to rely largely on telephone and electronic communications rather than face to face contact. The Agency would also need to work with Government to develop appropriate means of tracking the movement of students in and out of higher education, and developing an understanding of patterns of study, in a lifelong learning system.

21.56 One approach, which appears to us promising, would be to build on the SLC. We believe, however, that such a development needs to be planned and implemented in a staged way, to enable new systems to be developed and tested. The priority should be to implement new arrangements for income contingent graduate contributions. The transfer of functions from LEAs to the new Student Support Agency should take place once new arrangements for graduate contributions are effectively implemented.

Recommendation 83 **We recommend to the Government that it establishes, as soon as possible, a unified Student Support Agency with responsibility for:**
- **assessing the eligibility of individuals for various kinds of public support;**
- **administering graduate contributions on an income contingent basis;**
- **means testing and paying grants for students' living costs;**
- **making per capita tuition payments to institutions according to the number of students they enrol.**

Individual Learning Accounts and a Learning Bank

21.57 We were invited by the Labour Party at the time of our establishment to explore the possibility of using a system of Individual Learning Accounts (ILAs) or a Learning Bank as a means of channelling funds (both public and private) into higher education. The proposal was first raised in the Report of the Commission on Social Justice.[10] Our thinking on this idea was informed by a report which we commissioned (Report 13: 'Individual learning accounts and a learning bank') and by other recent work on the use of individual learning accounts to support training and development opportunities for those in work.[11, 12]

21.58 Paragraph 18 of Report 13 defines an ILA as:
- *an accumulation fund: providing opportunities for investment by allowing individuals, their families, the state and/or employers to deposit cash sums into the ILA with a view to accumulating funds for the purchase of lifelong learning and to meet the repayment of outstanding loans and overdrafts;*
- *a distribution fund: providing a facility for individual discretionary control of funds by permitting individual access to, and control over, the distribution funds with the account, circumscribed by the purchase limitations and other rules governing the account;*
- *a loan/overdraft facility: allowing individuals access to loans from public or private sources with which to meet the costs of tuition fees and/or personal maintenance when purchasing a course or learning opportunities;*
- *a repayment mechanism: providing for secure and equitable repayments of loans, debts, overdrafts and so forth.*

As the report notes, each of these elements, taken separately, could probably be secured through existing arrangements but, taken together, they promise a unique solution. The three latter functions line up closely with the functions which we have identified for the single Student Support Agency. It is of interest that others have emphasised the importance of individual control on the withdrawal of funds to support learning, as an essential feature of a system of individual contributions. Our thinking is consistent with this.

Increasing individual contributions

21.59 The first function of Individual Learning Accounts (ILAs), that of providing an accumulation fund, is different in kind from the other three. We see it as desirable to build on the individual propensity to save for lifetime events, for example through pension or private school fees plans, to encourage family, individual and intergenerational savings towards the costs of higher education. A good deal of such support is currently provided informally. Gifts to, and savings withdrawn by, full-time undergraduates nearly doubled from £392 in 1988-89 (the year before the introduction of the Student Loans Scheme) to £782 in 1995-96.[13]

21.60 We examined two approaches to incentivising savings for higher education:
- a savings scheme with tax relief, as now available for pension plans, such as a modified Personal Equity Plan (PEP) or a Tax Exempt Special Savings Account (TESSA);
- a long term savings bond, with the incentive of a Government contribution when the bond is cashed in, provided it is used to support learning.

21.61 On balance, we are inclined to support the conclusion of Report 13 that using ILAs to incentivise savings is unlikely **of itself** to bring significant additional finance into higher education. Moreover, unlike savings for other purposes, savings for higher education carry a risk that the individual will not qualify to participate. Nevertheless, we believe that the prospect that individuals will have to make a higher contribution, and the increased expectation of several mid-career changes requiring training, will lead individuals and their families to seek tax efficient ways of saving to support career development.

Employer contributions

21.62 The other key difference between an Individual Learning Account (ILA) model and the single Student Support Agency is the possible role of employer contributions. While some employers do provide significant support for full-time undergraduates through sponsorship arrangements and industrial placements, these are very different from the kind of support they provide to their employees for training and development.

21.63 The possible contribution by employers to Individual Learning Accounts (ILAs) is part of a much wider group of issues about the burden on employers of employment and training policies.[14, 15] Compulsory contributions by employers to ILAs or training levies would simply add to employment costs. It is questionable, however, whether individuals as employees would have an incentive to make contributions into ILAs for their future training needs, if they could not be sure that employer and/or state contributions would be forthcoming. Nevertheless, we are convinced that ILAs have the potential to provide a more assured basis for individuals and their employers to fund continuing professional development both within higher education and elsewhere.

ILAs and student choice

21.64 One potentially important feature of ILAs is that they provide individuals with real discretion over resources distribution. We have noted, both in Chapter 19 and in this chapter, that it would be desirable for a greater element of institutional funding to be linked to student choice. There would be no real advantage in using ILAs, rather than other arrangements, if individuals continued to behave as they do now, taking a continuous course at a single institution. If, as we believe, it will become more common for individuals to re-order their attendance to meet domestic or employment circumstances, student choice could have an increasingly marked impact on institutional behaviour, and ILAs could support this.

A Learning Bank

21.65 A Learning Bank is essentially a collection of ILAs or other types of learning account. It could, in principle, administer all the functions identified above for ILAs. However, we have concluded that a good deal more work is required to define the exact nature and purposes of ILAs, and to sell the concept to individuals, employers and others, before the precise administrative framework can be determined. Moreover, we are of the view that, within the context of higher education, the Learning Bank and the single Student Support Agency are essentially different approaches to the same end.

Conclusion

21.66 Much of the discussion in this chapter has focused on administrative matters and the way in which arrangements can be responsive to individual needs. It is clear that, whatever approach is taken, the state has a major continuing role, both through its contribution to the funding of higher education, and through the framework it sets for the interactions between institutions and individuals. In the next chapter, we explore the nature of the continuing relationship between government and higher education.

Chapter 22

Government and higher education institutions

22.1   In this report we have advocated a new compact between higher education, the state, students and employers. We have explored aspects of that compact, including the duty on institutions to strive constantly for value for money, their obligations to students, and the need for them to listen to and explain themselves to a wide constituency of interests. We also propose that graduates in work should be responsible for contributing to the costs of their learning. In this chapter we say more about the role of the state in this new compact and specifically, the ways in which the government should relate to higher education institutions.

22.2   We have also emphasised the importance of institutional autonomy and diversity, in Chapter 16. That emphasis has implications for the relationship between institutions and government.

22.3   In our discussion of the funding options in Chapters 19 and 21 we consider the mechanism for distributing teaching funds to institutions and the need for society, through government and its various agencies, to respond to the needs of higher education if their mutual interests are to be well served. In Chapter 21, we discuss the administrative arrangements necessary to enable individuals to contribute more to the costs of their higher education. In the short term, these include arrangements for assessing students' eligibility for public support, making loans and collecting the repayments. In the longer term, that chapter suggests that a unified Student Support Agency be established which would undertake responsibility for assessing eligibility and administering all the tasks associated with making payments to students and which would have an increasing role in channelling public support for teaching to institutions. It further suggests that such an Agency might subsequently assume the role of a Learning Bank with Individual Learning Accounts.

22.4   In this chapter we focus on the best way of distributing block grant for teaching and research in the light of the evidence submitted to us. In particular, we consider the structure of the Funding Bodies responsible for funding higher and further education; and the case for periodic high level advice on higher education to the Government. We offer views on the following issues:
   - changes in the relationship between higher education institutions and government;
   - the case for intermediary funding bodies;
   - the functions of intermediary funding bodies;
   - the structure of the intermediary funding bodies;
   - the need for independent high level advice on higher education to the Government.

22.5   In doing so, we have adopted a number of principles, which we consider important in informing the details of the arrangements put in place for the relationship between government and higher education institutions. These are that:

- institutional diversity and autonomy should be respected, consistent with the requirements of the nation;
- intermediary bodies should continue to be placed between the government and institutions to allocate a proportion of public funds;
- in responding to public needs, the government must be properly informed about the current and future prospects for the sector.

Changes in the relationship between higher education institutions and government

22.6   This report demonstrates the ways in which higher education has now become of national economic importance, and that its place in the national economy will grow. This means that, even were it not to be a major source of funding, the Government would wish to concern itself with higher education, as it has so strongly in the last decade. It will, for example, and as we acknowledge in Chapter 6, want to intervene if it considers that the level of participation in higher education in the United Kingdom is falling behind its main competitors. It will be concerned about the effectiveness and value for money of such a major activity; about its standards and standing in the world; about the way it is able to relate to society as a whole; and about its contribution to the nation's research and development effort. At the local and regional level, higher education is assuming greater importance to cultural and economic life, pointing to a progressive strengthening of regional ties, including the regional aim of government, which we explore in Chapter 12.

22.7   All these considerations point to the need to strengthen the relationship between higher education and its students and the wider community of interests that draws on its services. On the other hand, the greater the scale of higher education the greater the dangers of excessive government involvement and unmanageable expectations. Moreover, the very scale of higher education has already raised the need to identify alternative sources of funding, leading to our proposals for contributions from graduates in work and to an emphasis on stronger and more extensive partnerships with industry. The more diverse the institutions making up the higher education sector, the more devolved decision-making is likely to be. New questions are being asked about the extent to which at regional, if not at national level, there is advantage in more thought being given to ways in which the complementary roles of higher and further education can best be developed.

22.8   Against this background we have re-thought aspects of the functions and structures of the intermediary Funding Bodies.

The case for intermediary funding bodies

22.9   A distinctive element in the relationship between the Government, as a major source of funding, and the higher education institutions, has been the inter-position between the two of Funding Bodies, established under statute with defined functions and responsibilities. This is not a characteristic of the publicly-funded higher education institutions in all the other countries we visited, where public funding may be negotiated directly between the institution and its government; where academic salaries may be determined by the government; where the addition of a professorial post may require government approval; and where the government may have powers to appoint some members of governing bodies.

22.10 The independence, responsiveness and effectiveness of UK higher education institutions owes much to the well-established tradition of the government distancing itself from institutions and entrusting the high-level administration of the public financial to independent bodies of standing, the Funding Councils (other than in Northern Ireland, where funding is allocated directly from the government, with advice from an advisory Council). While the government can attach general conditions to the funding it provides, it may not attach conditions to the funding of individual institutions. We are wholly convinced and firmly commend to the Government that there should continue to be an arm's length relationship between government, both nationally and regionally, and the higher education system, so as to assure the autonomy of institutions within a broad framework of public policy.

22.11 The Organisation for Economic Co-operation and Development (OECD) highlighted the UK tradition of intermediary or 'buffer' bodies alongside institutional autonomy in its recent review of tertiary education, noting that the autonomy of institutions is a very important, traditional and admirable characteristic of the UK university system and that several Continental European systems are in this respect moving towards the United Kingdom system.[1]

22.12 We conclude that there should continue to be intermediary bodies, such as the present Funding Councils, with the functions described below. It follows that an intermediary body is required for Northern Ireland in order to put higher education there on the same footing as in the rest of the United Kingdom, and we say more about this in Appendix 1.

Recommendation 84   **We recommend to the Government that the tradition of institutional separation from national and sub-national levels of government is firmly maintained; and that this principle is extended to Northern Ireland.**

The functions of intermediary funding bodies

22.13 Despite the legal framework in the UK which prevents government intervention in the life of individual institutions, the OECD review comments that, while no evidence was brought before it of deliberate attempts to erode institutional autonomy, *'there are obvious pressures that individually may be slight but collectively could impede the development of institutions if left unchecked.'*[2] We noted in Chapter 16 that there is widespread concern about the effect of current funding arrangements on the diversity of institutions. Balance and fine judgement are necessary if real autonomy is to be maintained. The development of accountability mechanisms and funding incentives, whilst proper elements in the relationship between society, as a major provider of resources, and institutions, should be handled with sensitivity to institutional differences so that it does not lead to an unhelpful loss of diversity. As we showed in Chapter 16 this institutional diversity is a major strength of the UK system, but a number of those giving evidence to us believe that some convergence between institutional missions has already begun.

Funding for teaching

22.14 We are concerned that, as we progress further towards a mass system of higher education, the Funding Bodies responsible for allocating block grant for teaching to institutions may not be able to promote the diversity and responsiveness to student requirements that will increasingly be needed, whilst also being seen to act even-handedly in their stewardship of public money. In principle, individual contracts with institutions might be an attractive alternative to the current largely formula-driven funding methodology for teaching. But, applied in any general way, we fear this would make for very real difficulties in providing and demonstrating equity of treatment, consistency of criteria and transparency of application, which are essential characteristics in the way block grant is allocated. Nonetheless, we do not think this precludes reflection of the renewed focus on institutional diversity, as advocated in Chapter 16, with a somewhat more mission-oriented relationship between the Funding Bodies and institutions.

22.15 Instead of a funding system rooted wholly in individual contracts between the Funding Bodies and institutions, we see the effectiveness, diversity and responsiveness that society rightly expects from higher education institutions coming increasingly from the interplay of market forces. This will be encouraged by the stronger exercise of informed and responsible student choice and from institutions generating a greater proportion of their income from contracts for services, research and teaching.

22.16 Looking at the role of informed student choice, our assessment in Chapter 20 that an increased contribution to the cost of higher education teaching should come from graduates in work is influenced by our view that:
- the ends of higher education and the needs of society will be best served if funding for institutions comes increasingly through the student, with the student having a real understanding of the costs involved;
- the institutions are likely to have a stronger focus on their missions if they are required to be more obviously responsive to diverse student demand.

22.17 We have already stated in Chapter 6 that we consider that student supply and demand should be the predominant influence on the size and shape of the overall system and in Chapter 19 that we are attracted in the long term to a funding system which mirrors student decisions more readily than the current block grant.

22.18 However, it will be important to ensure that student choice is indeed well informed. Otherwise, moves in the direction of a greater share of the block grant funding flowing through the student will not be effective. For those who are young entrants to higher education, this requires the schools and colleges where they study to have much better information than at present on institutions, departments and the programmes they offer. The present institutional prospectus is helpful, but its purpose is substantially promotional. The representatives of schools and colleges who gave evidence to us made clear that they consider the information currently available to be inadequate to enable them to offer well informed guidance on the programmes offered by institutions, and how far these meet the aspirations and abilities of their pupils and students. This was also clear when we talked to secondary school pupils. Apart from information on programmes, potential students need to know about the costs and likely benefits of higher education, including employment prospects. If employed graduates are to repay more of the costs of their studies, potential students will need to know the financial implications of their choices and the sources of funding and other resources available to support their learning. Simultaneously, information technology should make it more likely that relevant and up to date information, sometimes interactive, can be available to potential students through schools, colleges and the providers of careers guidance, without the need for individual institutions to maintain and keep up to date large archives of material. The recomendations we make in Chapters 8 and 9 on specifications for the various programmes offered by institutions and a clearer framework for the qualifications available should be helpful here.

Recommendation 85

We recommend to the Government that, with immediate effect, it brings together the representative bodies of students, schools, colleges, higher education institutions and the organisations offering careers services to identify what better information is needed by students about higher education opportunities, their costs and benefits; and to work together to improve timely dissemination of the information.

22.19   We recommend in Chapter 20 that the contribution from graduates in work should amount to approximately 25 per cent of the average cost of tuition. This will mean, when added to the element which is already allocated by the current Funding Bodies on the basis of student numbers and the fee element paid by local education authorities, that just over half of the average cost of a full-time undergraduate programme will flow with the student. In addition, we envisage that over time, some substantial part of the funding for tuition that is not to be met retrospectively by these graduates when in employment, should transfer from the Funding Bodies to students, in the form of vouchers or proxy fees. This would encourage the student to see him/herself as an investor in receipt of a service, and to seek, as an investor, value for money and a good return from the investment.

22.20   But we also see value in a balance of public funding for teaching continuing to flow through the Funding Bodies, as the block grant does currently. This is because only the Funding Bodies, by virtue of their size and market position, can act as the expert buyer of services, able to exert appropriate influence on the quality, effectiveness and price of higher education.

22.21   The first function for intermediary Funding Bodies for the foreseeable future is therefore to continue to contribute to the funding of teaching activities.

Influencing the supply and demand for higher education

22.22   The second function of the Funding Bodies is to help to influence the overall levels of supply and demand for higher education. They may also need to exert influence in particular programme areas or disciplines.

22.23   As we noted in Chapter 6, there are historically some disciplines where higher education places are filled easily and targets relative to the best estimates of national need are met, such as medicine; and others where there are long-standing shortfalls, such as teacher training. We are satisfied that mechanisms are required which set targets or determine limits for a small number of disciplines which are particularly costly to provide and/or where the state is the major employer and we believe that such mechanisms should be robust and transparent, as recommended for initial teacher education in Report 10, 'Teacher education and training: a study'. In general, as we set out in Chapter 6, informed student demand should be the prime determinant of the balance of student numbers pursuing each discipline. Nonetheless, the intermediary funding bodies will have a role in reflecting imbalances between supply and demand for different disciplines within higher education and trying to bring these more into balance by adjusting funding incentives as necessary. As the Organisation of Economic Co-operation and Development thematic review noted, *'there is a particular problem of "steering" demand'* and this will be a perennial problem of any higher education system, when central planning is to be eschewed, as we argued it should be in Chapter 6.[3]

Promoting and ensuring the good use of public funds

22.24   The third function for intermediary Funding Bodies is promoting and ensuring the good use of public funds. To that end, they need to monitor the financial wellbeing of higher education institutions and act to safeguard the interests of students should an institution for any reason be unable to continue. The greater interplay of market forces we propose may tend to reduce the certainty with which institutions can look ahead. It may increase the risk of an institution finding itself in financial difficulty. A number of those giving evidence to us urged that the Funding Councils be more prepared to step in earlier in support of an ailing institution, to offer guidance, short of additional financial support. We see merit in that proposition, not least as a means of safeguarding the interests of students. As for the financial wellbeing of institutions, we see continued merit in the chief executives of the intermediary Funding Bodies having responsibility as Accounting Officer for the public funds allocated through them and for representing the institutions' financial health to the Government, within the annual public expenditure round. We make recommendations in Chapter 15 for a systematic review by governing bodies, which would be a condition of public funding, and we believe that will do much to further promote and ensure the good use of public funds by institutions.

Supporting government policies

22.25   The fourth function for the intermediary Funding Bodies is to act in support of government policies, in the medium term flowing from the advice of the independent body to which we refer at the end of this chapter; or to pursue other policies, properly formulated. We have already made a number of recomendations elsewhere in the report which require some new or refined funding incentives, such as policies to widen participation in Chapter 7. We have also made recomendations which envisage conditions being attached to the funds allocated by the Funding Bodies, including strategic reviews by governing bodies (including their strategies for participation) in Chapter 15; and discipline in the use of institutional titles in Chapter 16.

Funding dual support for research

22.26   The fifth function for the intermediary Funding Bodies will be to continue to fund research under the dual support arrangements. We have discussed this in detail in Chapter 11 and have there recommended certain changes to the way in which this funding is allocated by the Funding Bodies.

The structure of the intermediary Funding Bodies

22.27   We have considered the extent to which, in a society where people through their working lives may well move between further and higher education and where part of the provision of higher education will be through colleges of further education, it is desirable to maintain separate funding bodies for further and higher education.

22.28   A number of those giving evidence to us had strong views on this matter, some noting that the boundaries between further and higher education are already blurred and likely to become more so, and they argued that this should be reflected in the structure of the Funding Bodies in England, Wales, Scotland and Northern Ireland.

22.29   The arrangements in each country are currently very different:
- in England, two Funding Bodies, one for higher education and the other for further education, each served by its own executive, fund further and higher education irrespective of the sector in which the institutions are located;
- in Wales, two Funding Bodies served by one executive similarly divide their funding responsibilities according to the level of study;
- in Scotland, one Funding Body funds all the provision in higher education institutions and the Scottish Office Education and Industry Department funds all the provision in further education colleges;
- in Northern Ireland, higher education is funded directly by the Department for Education (DENI), with advice from the Northern Ireland Higher Education Council, while further education is funded by the five Education and Library Boards (although the further education colleges are likely to be incorporated shortly and funded directly from DENI).

22.30   In their evidence to us, all the Funding Councils, the Committee of Vice-Chancellors and Principals and others, foresaw a strengthening of links between the two sectors of post-compulsory education, in the context that *'the long term goal for the UK must be a new education and training framework encompassing all post-16 further and higher level learning and qualifications.*[4] The Scottish Higher Education Funding Council (SHEFC) advocated a single tertiary funding council on the grounds that this would *'provide an integrated approach to funding and quality assurance for all higher and further education institutions and which would have the capacity to meet the needs of a wide range of institutions and a diverse spectrum of provision'.*[5] The SHEFC also suggested that employers would find it easier to deal with a single tertiary education sector.

22.31   The Higher Education Funding Council for Wales, however, urged a continuation of present arrangements in that country, on the basis that it was working well.

22.32   In England, the general consensus amongst those giving evidence to us was that, while there is scope for more co-operation between the two Funding Councils, a single body would be too large to work properly or to represent the range of interests adequately. While the Funding Bodies and others, such as the Training and Enterprise Council National Council and institutional representative bodies, acknowledged that further blurring of the boundary between further and higher education was inevitable and that the respective funding responsibilities should be sorted out, they did not advocate a single Funding Body.

22.33   In Northern Ireland, we were advised that, in its particular circumstances, the best option, at least initially, would be to introduce two Funding Bodies with one executive, together with a Tertiary Education Forum to offer an oversight of both sectors (see Appendix 1).

22.34   We are mindful of the advice we received in evidence and we therefore support different arrangements which suit the particular circumstances of each country. In each of Scotland, Wales and Northern Ireland, therefore, we consider that the most appropriate arrangement is two separate Funding Bodies with a single executive.

22.35   In England, in view of the scale of higher and further education, the number of institutions, and the need for a Funding Body to be able to relate effectively to them, we consider that separate Funding Bodies for higher and further education should be continued. But, as we have previously indicated, there should be stronger arrangements for liaison at regional level, particularly to assist in widening participation.

22.36   As for the funding responsibilities of these bodies, we considered how these should be divided between the bodies responsible for higher and for further education. We have previously recommended in Chapter 16 that further education colleges be given the opportunity to develop their particular role for the delivery of sub-degree higher education. We therefore considered what division of the funding responsibilities would be more likely to support the development of vibrant and flourishing sub-degree provision in further education colleges.

22.37   Two main options were put to us. The first option is that sub-degree provision in further education colleges should be funded by the further education Funding Body, with degree-level provision in those colleges and all provision in higher education institutions funded by the higher education Funding Body. The second option is that all higher education, whether in further education colleges or higher education institutions, should be funded by the higher education Funding Body. This is closest to the current English model. We noted the views of the Scottish Committee that the former should obtain on the grounds that this is most likely to ensure successful sub-degree provision. This option would also be supported by those who regard this provision as essentially advanced further education, by virtue of its local delivery and largely vocational nature.

22.38   Set against that is the view that the English model should prevail since only this could force a consideration of the relative costs of similar provision across all the providing institutions, be they in the further or higher education sector; that this would place the enhanced responsibility for funding sub-degree provision squarely alongside that for other higher education; that it would not confuse delivery of sub-degree higher education with the remaining legal duty for further education of the Further Education Funding Councils; that it would be essentially a tidying-up of the current arrangements; and that the development of the sort of sub-degree qualifications with value which we advocate in Chapter 9 could only be achieved within the higher education context. We think that these considerations have force and therefore, on balance, in England and Wales, that funding for higher education in further education colleges should flow through the higher education Funding Body. In Scotland and Northern Ireland, we respect the preference expressed for the first option.

Recommendation 86   **We recommend to the Government that the division of responsibility between the further and higher education Funding Bodies in England and Wales should be such that the higher education Funding Bodies are responsible for funding all provision defined as higher education.**

22.39   Also in England, concerns have been expressed to us about the effects for some institutions of having a separate intermediary body responsible for funding teacher education. We have considered this matter and conclude that the Teacher Training Agency (TTA) should maintain its funding responsibilities in England, as discussed in Report 10. Nonetheless the TTA and the Higher Education Funding Council for England need to consider the means by which they could work more closely together; and careful thought also needs to be given to the relationship between the duties and powers of the TTA if a General Teaching Council is established. We do not recommend the creation of a TTA-equivalent body elsewhere in the UK, where the current arrangements appear to be working satisfactorily.

Recommendation 87   **We recommend to the Government that the Teacher Training Agency continue its remit in respect of teacher training in England but that the respective responsibilities of the Higher Education Funding Council for England and the Teacher Training Agency are reviewed in drawing up proposals for the role of a General Teaching Council.**

Intermediary bodies with non-financial functions

22.40   Elsewhere, we have made recommendations about some of the intermediary bodies
with non-financial functions:

- for quality and standards we welcome the establishment of the Quality Assurance
  Agency. We have made recommendations in Chapter 10 about the extensive tasks
  facing the new Agency;

- we have recommended the establishment of a new Institute for Learning and
  Teaching in Higher Education to raise the status and professionalism of higher
  education teaching (Chapter 8);

- for research we have recommended the creation of an advisory committee whose
  chair has access to the Prime Minister and whose role is to advise the Government
  on research policy (Chapter 11).

22.41   It will be particularly important that the higher education Funding Bodies and the
Quality Assurance Agency work together closely. The former will discontinue their
present roles in assessing the quality of teaching. However, there would be merit in
their funding allocations being explicitly informed by judgements reached by the
Quality Assurance Agency where that Agency finds that an institution is failing to
meet the threshold standards or is otherwise not in compliance with the code of
practice, described in Chapter 10.

The need for a higher level strategic review for higher education to advise the Government on an ongoing basis

22.42   For overall policy guidance on higher education, it should not be another 33 years
before there is another major inquiry into higher education. Events are moving too
quickly for any inquiry to be able to see far into the future and there is so much more
at stake than 30 years ago. We have therefore considered the case for creating a high-
level standing advisory committee. This is the course recommended by our Committee
on Scotland for that country, in the form of the Scottish Forum on Higher Education,
which would meet at the invitation of the Secretary of State for Scotland to advise on
strategic issues. For the UK as a whole, it will be especially important that there is
opportunity for review in depth, from time to time. The first task of this review must
be to reflect on the progress made in implementing our recommendations and on their
impact, including the effects on longer programmes; and which subsequently will be
charged, above all, with considering the level of support needed by students and the
level of contributions from graduates in employment.

Recommendation 88   **We recommend to the Government that, in five years' time and subsequently every ten
years, it constitutes a UK-wide independent advisory committee with the task of
assessing the state of higher education; advising the Government on its financing and
on ways in which, in future years, it can best respond to national needs; on any action
that may be needed to safeguard the character and autonomy of institutions; and, in
particular, on any changes required in the level of student support and contributions
from graduates in employment.**

Conclusion

22.43   In this chapter we have reiterated, in the light of earlier chapters, the importance of the UK's tradition of intermediary bodies between higher education and government. We have reflected on the appropriate functions and structures for these intermediary bodies in the context of our earlier recommendations. We have also noted that precise details of the arrangements in each country might well differ, depending on individual circumstances. We turn in Chapter 23 to a more detailed understanding of the those circumstances in Northern Ireland, Scotland and Wales.

Chapter 23

Higher education in Scotland, Wales and Northern Ireland

23.1   Our terms of reference relate to the whole of the United Kingdom (UK) and our recommendations are intended to be of general application. We are, however, conscious of the distinctive needs and traditions of higher education in different parts of the UK and the Secretaries of State for Scotland, Northern Ireland and Wales will wish to consider the extent to which they need to be modified to meet the circumstances of those countries.

23.2   The provision in Northern Ireland and Wales corresponds, in the main, to that in England, but bearing in mind the distinctive nature of the education structure and qualifications systems, the legal framework, and the administrative funding arrangements in Scotland, Ministers agreed that we should establish a Scottish Committee to consider issues particular to Scotland and to advise us accordingly. The report of the Scottish Committee is published as part of this report in a separate volume.

23.3   No such special arrangements were thought necessary for Wales and Northern Ireland, but it quickly became apparent that there was a major issue of long term concern in relation to Northern Ireland, namely the need for 40 per cent of young people from the Province to look for higher education elsewhere. With the help of Sir George Quigley we have produced an appendix (Appendix 1) commenting in detail on the particular issues that arise in that part of the UK.

23.4   Here we summarise some distinctive characteristics of the provision of higher education in Scotland, Wales and Northern Ireland. Before looking at each of these in turn, we identify those features they have in common and which differentiate them from England. The first of these, as we noted in Chapter 12, is the extent to which institutions in these countries have close links with their local and regional communities, both economically and more widely. We have suggested that this stronger regional engagement reflects: the size of the community; a strong national regional identity; distinctive administrative structures; well-developed and supported agencies with economic development objectives; and the provision of funding related to the achievement of these objectives. In England, the extent of regional identity is generally less than in Scotland, Wales, or Northern Ireland, and the development agencies have a much smaller role.

23.5   The relatively small number of institutions in Scotland, Wales and Northern Ireland makes for a close relationship between them, fostered by a sense of identity and a clear perception of their ability to contribute to each country's wellbeing, both culturally and economically. There are rivalries between institutions, but the personal relationships that are fostered by the smallness of their number leads to the identification of the benefits of collaboration and a willingness to exploit them. It would be wrong to make sharply distinctive generalisations, but the sense of community is a relevant element in the way institutions relate to regional issues and to one another.

23.6   Another distinguishing feature is the way in which teacher education is delivered. In England a distinctive feature is the existence of the Teacher Training Agency, which has responsibility for funding initial teacher training provision in higher education. Its remit does not extend to Wales, Scotland and Northern Ireland and we do not propose that it should. Yet another distinguishing feature is to be found in the arrangements for funding and we believe that continuing differences are justified by the relative scale of the task in England.

Scotland

23.7   There are now 23 institutions of higher education in Scotland, including 13 universities, 9 colleges and the Open University. Four of the universities in Scotland are over 400 years old and many of the others trace their origins to the eighteenth and nineteenth centuries. The higher education sector has approximately 160,000 full-time equivalent (FTE) students, with institutions ranging in size from the universities of Edinburgh, Glasgow and Strathclyde which each have over 16,000 FTE students to the Royal Scottish Academy of Music and Drama which has only 400 FTE students. Institutions also vary widely in their provision at undergraduate level, with Medicine and Dentistry being pursued only in the pre-1992 universities, and the largest proportion of business and administration programmes being studied in the 1992 universities. Over a quarter of all higher education provision in Scotland is provided by the further education sector, mostly at sub-degree level.

23.8   The most distinctive feature of Scottish higher education is the provision made for breadth in post-compulsory education and the tradition of students being able to enter higher education one year earlier than in other parts of the United Kingdom, although many choose instead to stay at school for an additional year. In comparison with the two to three A levels usually taking two years elsewhere, in Scotland students will often take up to five or six Highers after one year. This breadth at school articulates with the provision of higher education itself, where it is possible to study for a broad-based three year ordinary degree, or for a more specialised degree awarded after four years of study.

23.9   The emphasis on breadth means that entry to many higher education institutions is to the faculty, rather than to the subject, with students choosing to specialise only at the end of their second year. This flexibility means that students can change subject more easily than elsewhere in the UK.

23.10   The distinctive articulation between secondary and higher education is one of the reasons why 95 per cent of Scottish full-time undergraduates under the age of 21 choose to stay in Scotland. Given that 12,700 students from the rest of the UK also enter Scottish institutions, Scotland is an overall net importer of students.

23.11   As we noted in Chapter 6, the participation rate is high. At 44.2 per cent in 1995/96, this is much higher than in England, and we have taken this as an indication of what could be achieved across the UK as a whole. We have also noted as relevant to developments in the rest of the UK that most of the recent expansion in Scotland was at sub degree level in the Higher National Certificate and the Higher National Diploma.

23.12   The relatively small size of the sector, and the close co-operation which this engenders, has enabled the development of the Scottish Credit Accumulation and Transfer Scheme, to which all the Scottish higher education institutions are signatories. In Chapter 10 we recommended the development of a framework of qualifications. We hope that in time, the framework will become truly national, but recognise that in the short term the distinctiveness of education in Scotland will require some differences in approach.

23.13   As already noted, institutions in all three countries have strong links with their regions. In Scotland this has its roots in history. In contrast to most of the rest of the United Kingdom, Scotland has benefited from having universities in its main centres of population for several centuries. Since the industrial revolution they have contributed to economic development and they have long-standing links with their local communities.

Wales

23.14   Welsh higher education represents roughly five per cent of the higher education sector in the UK and corresponds with the percentage of the UK's population resident in Wales. The pattern of education is broadly similar to that in England, with the three year undergraduate honours degree forming the core. Its character is heavily influenced by the cross-border flows of students, with approximately half of the student population in Welsh institutions coming from England. This is mirrored by a similar proportion of those domiciled in Wales, who enter higher education, doing so outside Wales. Overall, Wales is marginally a net gainer.

23.15   Historically, Welsh higher education does not have the ancient foundations of England or Scotland: its first institution – St David's College, Lampeter – was established in 1827. Only in 1893 was an independent university with its own charter established, formed from the college at Aberystwyth and colleges at Bangor and Cardiff, as a federal institution – the University of Wales. The federal university, sometimes seen as a symbol of national identity, is now composed of eight institutions. Until the advent of the Open University in 1970 and the granting of university status to the Polytechnic of Wales, which became the University of Glamorgan in 1992, no other university existed within the Principality.

23.16   In relation to the size of the population, Welsh institutions are relatively numerous, although they tend to be small. This means that there is a higher education institution in almost every region, contributing significantly to the culture, language, economy and society of the areas in which they lie. One consequence of their relatively small size is a good level of collaboration and integration between institutions. The so-called 'University of the Valleys' is a prime example of collaborative effort to promote access in the valleys and opportunities for adult learners from some of the most socially and economically disadvantaged communities in Britain.

23.17 The location of institutions in small towns and rural areas means that they have a very significant impact on their local economies, and they are in some cases the largest employer in the area. The local economy is more dependent on their continuing existence than might commonly be the case elsewhere. Their location also makes them dependent on receiving students from outside the immediate vicinity. This means that much of the full-time higher education is fully residential. As a result, Welsh higher education institutions are especially vulnerable to changes in student support arrangements which might encourage full-time students to study closer to home. This is a consideration we took into account in framing our recommendations in Chapter 20.

23.18 Funding per student provided by the Welsh Office to Welsh higher education in 1997-98 was lower than that in England, and very significantly lower than that in Scotland, despite the call on funds as a result of Welsh language requirements. Past research performance of Welsh institutions has fallen below the rest of the UK, but recent support from the Higher Education Funding Council for Wales (HEFCW) resulted in better outcomes in the 1996 Research Assessment Exercise. Given the importance of research to attracting inward investment and encouraging indigenous economic growth, there is a desire to increase the volume of the research base in Wales.

23.19 The manufacturing sector makes a proportionately greater contribution to Welsh Gross Domestic Product than in other parts of the UK, and small and medium sized enterprises play a larger role in sustaining the economic and employment base.[1] Both of these characteristics of the economy affect the way institutions interact with industry, as does the existence of a range of regional bodies which encourage partnership with industry to provide training, development, consultancy support and research which can contribute towards the economic prosperity of Wales.

23.20 Wales is culturally distinct, most notably in having two working languages, English and Welsh, and a separate Welsh language television channel (S4C). It is also reflected in the existence of BBC (Wales), the Welsh National Opera Company, the Welsh Arts Council, the National Library of Wales, the National Museum of Wales, and other national institutions.

23.21 Higher education has a major role in sustaining the Welsh language, literature and culture, through research and scholarship. Through programmes in the Welsh language and literature, and through Welsh-medium provision, for which the Higher Education Funding Council for Wales has set aside substantial sums of money, it helps ensure that the Welsh economy has sufficient Welsh language speakers to meet the requirements of the Welsh Language Act. Welsh higher education institutions have developed programmes ranging from television production to graphic arts and from computer aided design to creative writing to support the rapidly growing Welsh media industries.

23.22 The Welsh Language Act establishes the right of individuals to communicate in the language of their choice. Higher education institutions are required to make appropriate provision to meet this need, for example by employing Welsh speakers, having translating facilities and providing dual language publications. These requirements and the Welsh-medium provision both have cost implications which need to be reflected in funding regimes.

23.23 The complementarity of higher and further education in Wales represents an area of particular interest in the light of developments in recent years. The Further and Higher Education Funding Councils are served by a single Chief Executive who, together with his staff working as a joint executive, serves both Councils. Although the two Councils are provided with separate budgets and pursue their own policies under the guidance of the Secretary of State, it has been possible to develop common approaches in terms of the relationships of the councils with their respective institutions and in terms of strategies for working with industry. The two councils have common processes for monitoring the financial health of institutions and for audit and work within common operational standards. The chief executive and his staff are able to represent both sectors in discussion on, for example, economic development and training support. This has proved particularly important in providing support for major investors from overseas. The two Welsh councils, from their joint executive, can address the whole range of further and higher education support for industry.

23.24 It is noteworthy that both Councils distribute funds, wholly or in part, on the basis of the credits for which students work. This makes the emergence of a single all-Wales post-16 credit framework a distinct possibility. The Higher Education Credit Initiative – Wales produced the first such UK agreed system of cross-institutional arrangements for accreditation.

23.25 A particular feature of post-16 education in Wales is the franchising arrangements with further education colleges for the delivery of higher education provision, where the funding comes through the higher education institution. The development of franchised provision was given particular encouragement by the Wales Advisory Board in the late 1980s and early 1990s, a policy which was endorsed by both councils in 1992, and which has led to substantial growth in part-time sub-degree vocational provision in Wales from 1,864 enrolments in 1992/93 to 3,387 enrolments in 1996/97. This in turn has fostered fruitful relationships between higher education institutions and further education colleges, which form the basis for initiatives designed to increase access to higher education and bring it closer to the work place. We do not intend that Recommendation 67 in Chapter 22 should prevent the continuation of this pattern of higher education within further education colleges in Wales.

23.26 Finally we note that in the delivery of initial teacher training (ITT), the Welsh institutions do not share some of the current concerns of those in England. The compactness of the sector helps all those involved to work together in the spirit of partnership, for example through the 'All Wales Higher Education ITT liaison group'. The funding for ITT is channelled together with the rest of the funding for higher education through the HEFCW, which the institutions see as a distinct advantage.

Northern Ireland

23.27 Higher education in the Province is provided by two universities (which in their distinctive missions exemplify the diversity of higher education), by two colleges of education and, to varying degrees, in the region's 17 institutes of further education. Programmes in the institutes of further education are predominantly vocational. Northern Ireland also constitutes a region of the Open University. Student enrolments total 40,000. 32,000 of these are registered with its two universities. Some 85 per cent of the students enrolled at the two universities come from Northern Ireland.

23.28 Northern Ireland differs fundamentally from other parts of the UK in its lack of sufficient higher education places within easy reach of students. In 1995, students domiciled in Northern Ireland and accepted for university entrance constituted 3.5 per cent of all accepted UK applicants, but Northern Ireland provides only 2.1 per cent of the university places. The age participation rate in Northern Ireland (at around 42 per cent) is, as in Scotland, high but there are only 0.62 places per accepted applicant, whereas Scotland has 1.18.

23.29 We believe that students can benefit from study in a different environment and it is right that those who wish to study outside Northern Ireland should be free to do so. A considerable proportion of the 40 per cent of students who now study away do not, however, do this from choice but because the limitation on the number of places and the relatively high standard of entry to the two local universities obliges them to do so. Many of those obliged to study away from home will be from lower income groups, who can least afford the additional expenditure which this will entail. This is an undesirable situation, given the importance we attach to wider participation in Chapter 7.

23.30 We recognise that there are also areas of England, for example Cornwall and Cumbria, with a low number of places per accepted applicant. However, we believe that the geographical separation of Northern Ireland from the rest of the UK makes the issue particularly important.

23.31 The exceptionally high proportion of students in Northern Ireland that need to go elsewhere for their higher education leads us in Appendix 1 to recommend the examination of options which would increase the provision of places in a cost-effective way and which involve no compromising of quality or standards.

23.32 Northern Ireland is also different in the way its economic and social life is affected by the acute divisions which impair its ability to reach its full economic potential. Whilst it has a vigorous small and medium sized enterprise sector, it is characterised by having very few large enterprises, few of whose headquarters are in the Province. Inward investment is keenly sought but, with notable exceptions, can be deterred by the outsider's perception of a region which is disturbed and unstable. This challenging context offers higher education institutions the opportunity, to which they have not been slow to respond, to acquire a distinctive regional role.

23.33   In Chapter 9 we recommended that students should be given more opportunity to pursue programmes characterised by breadth rather than depth, and we pointed out that this has implications for the nature of the school curriculum for 16-19 year olds, and for the admissions policies of universities. Northern Ireland could provide an appropriate place for schools and universities to pioneer collaborative projects involving the schools and colleges. We, therefore, encourage the Secretary of State for Northern Ireland to consider adopting the breadth plus depth approach recommended in the Dearing Report on 16-19 year olds as one of the bases for entrance to universities in Northern Ireland.

23.34   A distinctive characteristic of the research scene in the Province is the large contribution which universities make to the total research effort. This reflects the size and nature of the industrial base and the absence of any other significant research capabilities. The universities, through their research and their support for small to medium sized enterprises in particular, can help strengthen that base.

23.35   Unfortunately as a result of cuts announced following the last public expenditure round, the universities in the current year will have 16 per cent less and, in subsequent years, 24 per cent less available for research through the block grant, as a result of the progressive reduction in the NIDevR component. Given the implications for the universities and the strategic economic significance of a strong research capability, we recommend in Appendix 1 that the scale and nature of funding for research in Northern Ireland universities should be assessed.

23.36   The case for regarding higher education, wherever it is delivered, as an integrated tertiary sector is particularly strong in Northern Ireland. The sector is relatively small and identifying the opportunities for co-operation to mutual benefit should be relatively easy. Our recommendations in Chapter 10 on the framework of qualifications and a Credit Accumulation and Transfer System are germane to the smooth functioning of a tertiary sector, and to the construction of well signposted pathways into and through it. Machinery is needed to ensure that all the relevant interests can participate in devising a strategy for a tertiary sector which plays a significant regional role. Unlike Great Britain, there are no intermediary funding bodies in Northern Ireland. The universities are at present funded directly by the Department of Education Northern Ireland and the institutes of further education by the Education and Library Boards. We made recommendations about the creation of intermediary bodies in Chapter 22 and Appendix 1.

23.37   We have also noted the differences in the approach to teacher education and training, and in particular the high average A level points of those who enrol on these programmes in Northern Ireland. The Department of Education Northern Ireland is currently putting in place an integrated, three stage process of teacher education which embraces initial training, induction and the early years of continuing professional development. At the end of initial training all teachers are given a 'career-entry profile', on the basis of which their induction and in-service training can be planned. Such arrangements should facilitate the development of genuine partnerships between employers, schools and higher education institutions.

23.38 Northern Ireland, as the smallest part of the UK, is an area in which it may be particularly opportune to innovate and pioneer. Within its institutions there are already to be found admirable examples of best practice and forward thinking which go with the grain of much of what we propose in this Report. We believe that the tertiary sector has the potential to expand successfully to meet a greater proportion of local need and to play an increasingly effective regional role.

Conclusion

23.39 Our report is intended to apply to the whole of the UK. We are conscious that there are notable differences between the regions of England, and that some of the problems of provision of higher education that we identified in Northern Ireland apply to some counties of England. We thought it right to recognise in particular the distinctive elements of higher education in Scotland, Wales and Northern Ireland, each of which have distinctive histories and form part of the responsibilities of the Secretaries of State for their parts of the UK. In taking forward the recommendations in our report, it will be for the respective Secretaries of State to decide whether there are particular circumstances which require a somewhat modified approach.

Chapter 24

Next steps

24.1   This report sets out a major programme of change for higher education over the next twenty years. Our vision for the future is clear. Although our outlook has been to the long term, our detailed recommendations necessarily focus on the first steps towards that vision. We hope that the legacy of our work will be a higher education system which is well-placed to develop and respond as new challenges and circumstances arise, including those which we cannot foresee from the perspective of 1997. Our recommendations add up to a coherent package for the future of higher education. We do not intend that those to whom they are addressed should choose to implement only some of them. The new compact requires commitment from all sides.

24.2   We have addressed our recommendations to those who should, in our view, be responsible for taking them forward. Where it is possible to set a specific timescale for the necessary action, we have done so. Some of our recommendations require organisations to undertake substantial developmental work before they can be implemented, and some are of less immediate urgency than others. We are conscious of the need not to overload organisations with too many tasks at once: it is often better to focus energy and attention on the most important and urgent work, but that does not mean that our recommendations for the medium and longer term can be ignored. Recommendations which we have described as for implementation 'over the medium term' are those which should generally be implemented within the next three to five years, although work in preparation for that may well need to start immediately. Those recommendations which we suggest should be implemented 'over the long term' are those which require even more substantial preparatory work or the prior implementation of other recommendations before they can be put into effect. Most of them are unlikely to be implemented in less than five years.

24.3   The recommendations are addressed to a wide range of bodies who have varying responsibilities in relation to higher education. Table 24.1 shows the allocation.

Table 24.1 – Organisations to whom recommendations are addressed

Organisation	Recommendation number
The Government	1, 2, 5, 6, 7, 11, 19, 22, 29, 34, 35, 36, 37, 39, 43, 44, 51, 54, 55, 56, 61, 62, 63, 64, 65, 66, 67, 70, 71, 72, 73, 74, 76, 77, 78, 79, 80, 81, 82, 83, 84, 85, 86, 87, 88, 90, 91, 92, 93
Higher Education Funding Bodies	2, 3, 4, 6, 7, 14, 24, 26, 27, 28, 32, 33, 34, 44, 57, 58, 59, 61, 67, 68, 75
Further Education Funding Bodies	3, 7
The Institute for Learning and Teaching in Higher Education	6, 13, 15
The Higher Education Statistics Agency	7
Institutions and their governing bodies	8, 9, 11, 12, 13, 16, 17, 18, 20, 21, 31, 38, 39, 40, 41, 42, 45, 46, 47, 48, 49, 50, 51, 52, 57, 60
Representative bodies of Higher Education	10, 14, 22, 24, 26, 38, 51, 53, 54, 58
The Quality Assurance Agency	11, 22, 23, 25, 69
Students' union	12
Employer representative bodies	19, 38
Awarding bodies and the organisations which oversee them	22
Franchising partners	23
Companies	30
Research Councils	32, 68

24.4   We give below some guidance on the immediate priorities for action.

Funding

24.5   As we have identified in Chapter 17, there is an immediate short term problem with the funding of higher education. If this is not addressed by the Government, there is a real danger that some institutions will be severely damaged and that others will take unilateral action, for example through the introduction of top-up fees, which together will make it impossible for our long term vision to be realised.

24.6   If the Government accepts our proposals on funding, it will need to introduce primary legislation because it does not currently have the power to make loans available in support of students' tuition costs or to give effect to our proposals for income-contingent collection of loan repayments through the Inland Revenue. Introduction of the relevant legislation must be the priority if additional resources are to flow to higher education in 1998-99. We are encouraged that the Government has already indicated its intention of introducing early legislation.

24.7   The same degree of urgency will need to be applied to the complex process of implementation. If implementation on this timescale cannot be achieved, alternative means of providing additional resources in the short term will have to be found, but the options are not attractive. We have already explained why short term moves to remove student loans from the public sector are unlikely to represent good value for money. The only other immediate source of resources, apart from the taxpayer, is the parents of students.

24.8   Our proposals on funding do not stand in isolation. They are part of a new compact between all the stakeholders of higher education. The Government must therefore commit itself just as firmly and with the same urgency to the other elements of that compact, if all who are involved in higher education are to be encouraged to play their part. This means that the early legislation we propose must include for a procedure to govern any review of the contribution to be made by graduates. It must also ensure that new arrangements are well-publicised and explained clearly to prospective students and their families.

24.9   Universities and colleges have pressed hard for a solution to the funding crisis which they perceive. We have made proposals which should place them on a firmer financial footing. But institutions need to take urgent action too. They owe it to students and to the taxpayer to make sure that they make the best possible use of the available resources. They must secure appropriate management and cost information systems to support this as quickly as possible. They will need the help of the Funding Bodies and their representative bodies to ensure that all know what the best can do. Work on developing appropriate benchmarks is urgent. They must ensure that their governance arrangements enable them to carry this forward

Quality and standards

24.10   In return for additional contributions from graduates, institutions must make much clearer what they are offering to students. They must work continually to improve the quality of teaching and they must approach the mutual assurance of standards with real commitment. Anything less would be to sell their students short. The immediate requirement from institutions is that, acting collectively, they give the Quality Assurance Agency all the support and facilities it needs to be fully effective and that they establish the Institute for Learning and Teaching in Higher Education, and give it also the necessary support and facilities. Edexcel will also need to work closely with institutions and the Quality Assurance Agency to bring the Higher National provision in line with our proposed framework.

24.11   Our recommendations place great expectations on the new Quality Assurance Agency. The bodies which established the Agency need urgently to review and amend its remit if it is to assume the role we propose for it. It needs the support of the whole sector in its tasks and it will need to embark very rapidly on its programme of work. New systems for the assurance of quality and standards must be in place and seen to be effective within a short space of time. If they are not, the Government will be justified in intervening to protect the interests of students.

Research

24.12   The priorities in research are to begin to rectify the deficiencies of the infrastructure and to establish new arrangements which encourage strategic decisions by institutions to concentrate on their strengths. The Government will need to take immediate steps to secure private sector contributions for the rolling loan fund for infrastructure. The Funding Bodies need to set the rules for the next Research Assessment Exercise quickly so that institutions can begin now to plan their preparation for it.

Staff in higher education

24.13   Staff in higher education have achieved much in recent years and our Report expects that they will continue to be dedicated, professional and adaptable. They must be given appropriate support in this. Our recommendations for more systematic staff development and training, and especially for accreditation of teaching staff need to be pursued as a matter of urgency by individual institutions and by the sector collectively. The overall review of pay and conditions of service which we recommend should also be set up as soon as possible, in order to try to avoid a repetition of the unsatisfactory pay negotiations seen this year.

Higher education's local and regional role

24.14   We assume that the Government will be taking early steps to introduce new regional structures. As it does so, it needs to take account of our recommendation that higher education should be represented on the new structures and it must ensure that higher education can play its full part in economic regeneration.

Conclusion

24.15   We know, from all the contacts we have had in our work, that the value and importance of higher education is widely recognised. We also know that those within higher education are committed to its wellbeing and are willing to embrace change. If all that good will, energy and professionalism can be focused on the developments proposed in this report, we are convinced that UK higher education will match the best in the world over the next 20 years.

Annex A

List of recommendations

Chapter 6

1   We recommend to the Government that it should have a long term strategic aim of responding to increased demand for higher education, much of which we expect to be at sub-degree level; and that to this end, the cap on full-time undergraduate places should be lifted over the next two to three years and the cap on full-time sub-degree places should be lifted immediately.

Chapter 7

2   We recommend to the Government and the Funding Bodies that, when allocating funds for the expansion of higher education, they give priority to those institutions which can demonstrate a commitment to widening participation, and have in place a participation strategy, a mechanism for monitoring progress, and provision for review by the governing body of achievement.

3   We recommend that, with immediate effect, the bodies responsible for funding further and higher education in each part of the UK collaborate and fund – possibly jointly – projects designed to address low expectations and achievement and to promote progression to higher education.

4   We recommend that the Funding Bodies consider financing, over the next two to three years, pilot projects which allocate additional funds to institutions which enrol students from particularly disadvantaged localities.

5   We recommend to the Government that:
- it considers the possibility of restoring to full-time students some entitlement to social security benefits, as part of its forthcoming review of the social security system. This review should include consideration of two particular groups in current difficulty, those who temporarily withdraw from higher education due to illness and those with dependent children aged over 16;
- the total available to institutions for Access Funds should be doubled with effect from 1998/99 and that the scope of the funds should be extended to facilitate participation by students who would otherwise be unable to enter higher education.

6   We recommend:
- to the Funding Bodies that they provide funding for institutions to provide learning support for students with disabilities;
- to the Institute for Learning and Teaching in Higher Education (see Recommendation 14) that it includes the learning needs of students with disabilities in its research, programme accreditation and advisory activities;

- to the Government that it extends the scope of the Disabled Students Allowance so that it is available without a parental means test and to part-time students, postgraduate students and those who have become disabled who wish to obtain a second higher education qualification.

7   We recommend that further work is done over the medium term, by the further and higher education Funding Bodies, the Higher Education Statistics Agency, and relevant government departments to address the creation of a framework for data about lifelong learning, using a unique student record number.

Chapter 8

8   We recommend that, with immediate effect, all institutions of higher education give high priority to developing and implementing learning and teaching strategies which focus on the promotion of students' learning.

9   We recommend that all institutions should, over the medium term, review the changing role of staff as a result of Communications and Information Technology, and ensure that staff and students receive appropriate training and support to enable them to realise its full potential.

10   We recommend that, over the medium term, the representative bodies, in consultation with other relevant agencies, should seek to establish a post-qualification admissions system.

11   We recommend that:
- institutions of higher education, over the medium term, integrate their careers services more fully into academic affairs and that the provision of careers education and guidance is reviewed periodically by the Quality Assurance Agency;
- the Government, in the medium to long term, should integrate careers advice for lifelong learning, to complement services based inside higher education institutions.

12   We recommend to students' unions and institutions that they review, on a regular basis, the services offered to their students and adapt them as necessary, in particular to meet the needs of part-time students.

13   We recommend that institutions of higher education begin immediately to develop or seek access to programmes for teacher training of their staff, if they do not have them, and that all institutions seek national accreditation of such programmes from the Institute for Learning and Teaching in Higher Education.

14   We recommend that the representative bodies, in consultation with the Funding Bodies, should immediately establish a professional Institute for Learning and Teaching in Higher Education. The functions of the Institute would be to accredit programmes of training for higher education teachers; to commission research and development in learning and teaching practices; and to stimulate innovation.

15   We recommend that the Institute should:
- develop, over the medium term, a system of kitemarking to identify good computer-based learning materials;
- co-ordinate the national development, over the medium and long term, of computer-based learning materials, and manage initiatives to develop such materials;
- facilitate discussion between all relevant interest groups on promoting the development of computer-based materials to provide common units or modules, particularly for the early undergraduate years.

Chapter 9

16   We recommend that all institutions of higher education should, over the medium term, review the programmes they offer:
- with a view to securing a better balance between breadth and depth across programmes than currently exists;
- so that all undergraduate programmes include sufficient breadth to enable specialists to understand their specialism within its context.

17   We recommend to institutions of higher education that, over the medium term, their admission procedures should develop to value good levels of competence in communication, numeracy and the practical use of information technology.

18   We recommend that all institutions should, over the medium term, identify opportunities to increase the extent to which programmes help students to become familiar with work, and help them to reflect on such experience.

19   We recommend that the Government, with immediate effect, works with representative employer and professional organisations to encourage employers to offer more work experience opportunities for students.

20   We recommend that institutions of higher education, over the medium term, develop a Progress File. The File should consist of two elements:
- a transcript recording student achievement which should follow a common format devised by institutions collectively through their representative bodies;
- a means by which students can monitor, build and reflect upon their personal development.

21   We recommend that institutions of higher education begin immediately to develop, for each programme they offer, a 'programme specification' which identifies potential stopping-off points and gives the intended outcomes of the programme in terms of:
- the knowledge and understanding that a student will be expected to have upon completion;
- key skills: communication, numeracy, the use of information technology and learning how to learn;
- cognitive skills, such as an understanding of methodologies or ability in critical analysis;
- subject specific skills, such as laboratory skills.

22   We recommend that the Government, the representative bodies, the Quality Assurance Agency, other awarding bodies and the organisations which oversee them, should endorse immediately the framework for higher education qualifications that we have proposed.

23   We recommend that:
- the Quality Assurance Agency should specify criteria for franchising arrangements;
- these criteria should rule out serial franchising, and include a normal presumption that the franchisee should have only one higher education partner;
- franchising partners should jointly review and, if necessary, amend existing arrangements to ensure that they meet the criteria, and should both certify to the Agency that arrangements conform with the criteria;
- there should be periodic checks by the Agency on the operation of franchise arrangements to verify compliance;
- after 2001, no franchising should take place either in the UK or abroad except where compliance with the criteria has been certified by the Quality Assurance Agency.

24   We recommend that the representative bodies and Funding Bodies amend the remit of the Quality Assurance Agency to include:
- quality assurance and public information;
- standards verification;
- the maintenance of the qualifications framework;
- a requirement that the arrangements for these are encompassed in a code of practice which every institution should be required formally to adopt, by 2001/02, as a condition of public funding.

25   We recommend to the Quality Assurance Agency that its early work should include:
- to work with institutions to establish small, expert teams to provide benchmark information on standards, in particular threshold standards, operating within the framework of qualifications, and completing the task by 2000;
- to work with universities and other degree-awarding institutions to create, within three years, a UK-wide pool of academic staff recognised by the Quality Assurance Agency, from which institutions must select external examiners;
- to develop a fair and robust system for complaints relating to educational provision;
- to review the arrangements in place for granting degree-awarding powers.

26   We recommend to the representative bodies and the Funding Bodies that the Board of the Quality Assurance Agency should, as soon as possible, include a student and an international member.

Chapter 11

27   We recommend that the Funding Bodies, through the Joint Information Systems Committee (JISC), should continue to manage and fund, on a permanent basis, quality and cost-effective Communications and Information Technology (C&IT) services for researchers and should, in due course, introduce charges for services on a volume-of-usage basis.

28   We recommend to the Funding Bodies that the Joint Information Systems Committee (JISC) should be invited to report, within a year, on options to provide sufficient protected international bandwidth to support UK research.

29   We recommend to the Government that a new Arts and Humanities Research Council (AHRC) should be established as soon as possible.

30   We recommend that companies should take a strategic view of their relationship with higher education and apply the same level of planning to it that they give to other aspects of their operations.

31   We recommend to institutions of higher education that they should, over the next two years, review their postgraduate research training to ensure that they include, in addition to understanding of a range of research methods and training in appropriate technical skills, the development of professional skills, such as communication, self-management and planning.

32   We recommend that the Funding Bodies and the Research Councils commission a study to evaluate the funding of interdisciplinary research, including the incentives and disincentives. The report should be ready to inform the next Research Assessment Exercise.

33   We recommend to the Funding Bodies that, in the interests of transparency and applying international standards properly, the practice of including one or more international members in all Research Assessment Exercise (RAE) panels, wherever possible, should be introduced to the next RAE.

34   We recommend:
- to the Government that, with immediate effect, projects and programmes funded by the Research Councils meet their full indirect costs and the costs of premises and central computing, preferably through the provision of additional resources;
- to the Funding Bodies that the next Research Assessment Exercise is amended to encourage institutions to make strategic decisions about whether to enter departments for the Exercise or whether to seek a lower level of non-competitive funding to support research and scholarship which underpins teaching;
- to the Government that an Industrial Partnership Development Fund is established immediately to attract matching funds from industry, and to contribute to regional and economic development;
- to the Government that it promotes and enables, as soon as possible, the establishment of a revolving loan fund of £400 to £500 million, financed jointly by public and private research sponsors, to support infrastructure in a limited number of top quality research departments which can demonstrate a real need.

35   We recommend to the Government that it should establish, as soon as possible, a high level independent body to advise the Government on the direction of national policies for the public funding of research in higher education, on the distribution and level of such funding, and on the performance of the public bodies responsible for distributing it.

Chapter 12

36 We recommend to the Government that institutions of higher education should be represented on the regional bodies which it establishes, and that the Further Education Funding Council regional committees should include a member from higher education.

37 We recommend to the Government that funding should continue to be available after April 1998, when the present provision from the Higher Education Regional Development Fund is due to cease, to support human capital projects which enable higher education to be responsive to the needs of local industry and commerce.

38 We recommend to higher education institutions and their representative bodies that they examine, with representatives of industry, ways of giving firms, especially small and medium sized enterprises, easy and co-ordinated access to information about higher education services in their area.

39 We recommend:
- to the Government that it considers establishing a modest fund to provide equity funding to institutions to support members of staff or students in taking forward business ideas developed in the institution, and to support the creation of incubator units;
- to higher education institutions that they establish more technology incubator units within or close to the institution, within which start-up companies can be fostered for a limited period until they are able to stand alone.

40 We recommend to higher education institutions that they consider the scope for encouraging entrepreneurship through innovative approaches to programme design and through specialist postgraduate programmes.

Chapter 13

41 We recommend that all higher education institutions in the UK should have in place overarching communications and information strategies by 1999/2000.

42 We recommend that all higher education institutions should develop managers who combine a deep understanding of Communications and Information Technology with senior management experience.

43 We recommend to the Government that it should review existing copyright legislation and consider how it might be amended to facilitate greater ease of use of copyright materials in digital form by teachers and researchers.

44 We recommend to the Government and the Funding Bodies that, to harness and maximise the benefits of Communications and Information Technology, they should secure appropriate network connectivity to all sites of higher education delivery and further education colleges by 1999/2000, and to other relevant bodies over the medium term.

45   We recommend that institutions of higher education, collectively or individually as
      appropriate, should negotiate reduced tariffs from telecommunications providers on
      behalf of students as soon as possible.

46   We recommend that by 2000/01 higher education institutions should ensure that all
      students have open access to a Networked Desktop Computer, and expect that by
      2005/06 all students will be required to have access to their own portable computer.

Chapter 14

47   We recommend that, over the next year, all institutions should:
      ■ review and update their staff development policies to ensure they address the
        changing roles of staff;
      ■ publish their policies and make them readily available for all staff;
      ■ consider whether to seek the Investors in People award.

48   We recommend to institutions that, over the medium term, it should become the
      normal requirement that all new full-time academic staff with teaching responsibilities
      are required to achieve at least associate membership of the Institute for Learning and
      Teaching in Higher Education, for the successful completion of probation.

49   We recommend that all institutions should, as part of their human resources policy,
      maintain equal opportunities policies, and, over the medium term, should identify and
      remove barriers which inhibit recruitment and progression for particular groups and
      monitor and publish their progress towards greater equality of opportunity for all
      groups.

50   We recommend to the higher education employers that they appoint, after consultation
      with staff representatives, an independent review committee to report by April 1998
      on the framework for determining pay and conditions of service. The Chairman
      should be appointed on the nomination of the Government.

51   We recommend to the Government, institutions, and the representative bodies of
      higher education, that, over the long term, the superannuation arrangements for
      academic staff should be harmonised by directing all new entrants to the Universities
      Superannuation Scheme.

Chapter 15

52   We recommend to institutions that, over the medium term, they develop and
      implement arrangements which allow staff and external bodies to have access to and
      understand the true costs of research.

53   We recommend that the Committee of Vice-Chancellors and Principals, in
      collaboration with other institutional representative bodies, reviews the functions of
      the Universities and Colleges Information Systems Association to ensure that it can
      promote the implementation of Communications and Information Technology in
      management information systems.

54   We recommend that the Government, together with representative bodies, should, within three years, establish whether the identity of the governing body in each institution is clear and undisputed. Where it is not, the Government should take action to clarify the position, ensuring that the Council is the ultimate decision-making body, and that the Court has a wider representative role, to inform decision-making but not to take decisions.

55   We recommend to the Government that it takes action so that:
■ individuals may not serve as members of a governing body for more than two terms, unless they also hold office;
■ it is a requirement for the governing body at each institution to include student and staff membership and a majority of lay members;
■ an individual may not chair a governing body for more than two terms of office.

56   We recommend that the Government takes the lead, with the Privy Council, in discussions with institutional representatives to introduce, within three years, revised procedures capable of responding more quickly to an institution requesting a change in the size of its governing body. The intention should be to ensure a response within one year.

57   We recommend that each governing body should systematically review, at least once every five years, with appropriate external assistance and benchmarks:
■ its own effectiveness and, where there is in excess of 25 members, show good reason why a larger body is needed for its effectiveness;
■ the arrangements for discharging its obligations to the institution's external constituencies;
■ all major aspects of the institution's performance, including the participation strategy.
The outcomes of the review should be published in an institution's annual report. The Funding Bodies should make such a review a condition of public funding.

58   We recommend that, over the medium term, to assist governing bodies in carrying out their systematic reviews Funding Bodies and representative bodies develop appropriate performance indicators and benchmarks for families of institutions with similar characteristics and aspirations.

59   We recommend to the Funding Bodies that they require institutions, as a condition of public funding, to publish annual reports which describe the outcomes of the governing body's review and report on other aspects of compliance with the code of practice on governance.

60   We recommend to institutions that, over the next two years, they review and, if necessary, amend their arrangements for handling complaints from students, to ensure that: they reflect the principles of natural justice; they are transparent and timely; they include procedures for reconciliation and arbitration; they include an independent, external element; and they are managed by a senior member of staff.

Chapter 16

61   We recommend to the Government and the Funding Bodies that diversity of institutional mission, consistent with high quality delivery and the responsible exercise of institutional autonomy, should continue to be an important element of the United Kingdom's higher education system; and that this should be reflected in the funding arrangements for institutions.

62   We recommend to the Government that it takes action as soon as possible to end the scope for a confusion between the title and the name used by institutions, either through clarifying the legal position or by ensuring that conditions can be placed on the flow of public funds so that these go only to those institutions which agree to restrict their use of a name and title to that to which they are legally entitled.

63   We recommend to the Government that, in the medium term, there is no change to the current criteria for university status; but that, for the future, there should be a period of relative stability in the number of universities with the weight accorded to the numerical criteria reduced and greater emphasis placed on a distinctive role and characteristics in awarding this status; and that the Government should give notice of this.

64   We recommend to the Government that it takes action, either by amending the powers of the Privy Council or by ensuring that conditions can be placed on the flow of public funds, to enable the removal of degree-awarding powers where the Quality Assurance Agency demonstrates that the power to award degrees has been seriously abused.

65   We recommend to the Government that it takes action, either by clarifying the legal position or by ensuring that conditions can be placed on the flow of public funds, to restrict the use of the title 'University College' to those institutions which are in every sense a college which is part of a university under the control of the university's governing body; and to those higher education institutions which have been granted taught degree awarding powers.

66   We recommend to the Government and the Funding Bodies that there is greater clarity about where responsibility lies for decisions about the establishment of new universities; and that criteria are developed for deciding such cases and allocating public funding.

67   We recommend to the Government and the Funding Bodies that, in the medium term, priority in growth in sub-degree provision should be accorded to further education colleges; and that, wherever possible:
■ more sub-degree provision should take place in further education colleges;
■ higher education provision in further education colleges should be funded directly;
■ there should be no growth in degree level qualifications offered by further education colleges.

68   We recommend to the Funding Bodies and the Research Councils that they review
      their mainstream teaching and research funding arrangements to ensure they do not
      discourage collaboration between institutions; and that, where appropriate, they
      encourage collaboration. We recommend to the Funding Bodies that they be prepared
      to use their funds on a revolving basis, bringing forward and offsetting annual
      allocations in support of collaboration which has a strong educational and financial
      rationale.

69   We recommend to the Quality Assurance Agency that, as it develops its arrangements,
      it ensures that these arrangements do not discourage collaboration between
      institutions.

      Chapter 17
70   We recommend to the Government that it reviews annually the total level of support
      for student living costs taking into account the movement of both prices and earnings.

      Chapter 18
71   We recommend to the Government that, over the long term, public spending on higher
      education should increase with the growth in Gross Domestic Product.

      Chapter 19
72   We recommend to the Government that it shifts the balance of funding, in a planned
      way, away from block grant towards a system in which funding follows the student,
      assessing the impact of each successive shift on institutional behaviour and the control
      of public expenditure, with a target of distributing at least 60 per cent of total public
      funding to institutions according to student choice by 2003.

73   We recommend to the Government that the public funding for higher education
      institutions should be determined on a rolling three year basis.

74   We recommend to the Government that variations in the level of public funding for
      teaching, outside modest margins, should occur only where:
      ■ there is an approved difference in the provision;
      ■ society, through the Secretary of State or his or her agent, concludes, after
        examining an exceptionally high level of funding, that in relation to other funding
        needs in higher education, it represents a good use of resources.

75   We recommend to the Funding Bodies that they should explore the possibility of
      setting aside some of their total grant, as soon as possible, to establish revolving loan
      schemes to fund:
      ■ projects to refurbish buildings (to improve fitness for purpose) or to undertake
        large scale long term maintenance projects;
      ■ expensive equipment purchases (for teaching or research);
      ■ collaborative projects which will facilitate access for staff and students in a region
        to teaching or research facilities which could not otherwise be provided on a
        viable basis.

Chapter 20

76   We recommend to the Government that:

■ from 1998/99 it should enable institutions to waive tuition fees for part-time students in receipt of Jobseeker's Allowance or certain family benefits;

■ as part of its forthcoming review of the social security system, it should review the interaction between entitlement to benefits and part-time study, with a view to ensuring that there are no financial disincentives to part-time study by the unemployed or those on low incomes;

■ it should extend eligibility for Access Fund payments to part-time students from 1998/99, and additional funding should be made available for this purpose.

77   We recommend to the Government that, once the interim bursary scheme expires, it establishes permanent arrangements for the equitable support of students of dance, drama and stage management at institutions which are not in receipt of public funds.

78   We recommend to the Government that it introduces, by 1998/99, income contingent terms for the payment of any contribution towards living costs or tuition costs sought from graduates in work.

79   On a balance of considerations, we recommend to the Government that it introduces arrangements for graduates in work to make a flat rate contribution of around 25 per cent of the average cost of higher education tuition, through an income contingent mechanism, and that it ensures that the proportion of tuition costs to be met by the contribution cannot be increased without an independent review and an affirmative resolution of both Houses of Parliament. The contributions made by graduates in work in this way should be reserved for meeting the needs of higher education.

80   We recommend to the Government that it looks urgently at alternative and internationally accepted approaches to national accounting which do not treat the repayable part of loans in the same way as grants to students.

81   We recommend to the Government that Scottish students who have had only one year's education after statutory schooling, many of whom under current arrangements would choose to take a four year honours degree, should not make a tuition contribution for one of their years in higher education. Beyond that, this would be a matter for consideration by the Secretary of State for Scotland.

Chapter 21

82   We recommend to the Government that the Inland Revenue should be used as the principal route for the collection of income contingent contributions from graduates in work, on behalf of the Student Loans Company.

83   We recommend to the Government that it establishes, as soon as possible, a unified Student Support Agency with responsibility for:

■ assessing the eligibility of individuals for various kinds of public support;

■ administering graduate contributions on an income contingent basis;

- means testing and paying grants for students' living costs;
- making per capita tuition payments to institutions according to the number of students they enrol.

Chapter 22

84 We recommend to the Government that the tradition of institutional separation from national and sub-national levels of government is firmly maintained; and that this principle is extended to Northern Ireland.

85 We recommend to the Government that, with immediate effect, it brings together the representative bodies of students, schools, colleges, higher education institutions and the organisations offering careers services to identify what better information is needed by students about higher education opportunities, their costs and benefits; and to work together to improve timely dissemination of the information.

86 We recommend to the Government that the division of responsibility between the further and higher education Funding Bodies in England and Wales should be such that the higher education Funding Bodies are responsible for funding all provision defined as higher education.

87 We recommend to the Government that the Teacher Training Agency continue its remit in respect of teacher training in England but that the respective responsibilities of the Higher Education Funding Council for England and the Teacher Training Agency are reviewed in drawing up proposals for the role of a General Teaching Council.

88 We recommend to the Government that, in five years' time and subsequently every ten years, it constitutes a UK-wide independent advisory committee with the task of assessing the state of higher education; advising the Government on its financing and on ways in which, in future years, it can best respond to national needs; on any action that may be needed to safeguard the character and autonomy of institutions; and, in particular, on any changes required in the level of student support and contributions from graduates in employment.

Chapter 23
NONE

Chapter 24
NONE

Appendix 1

89 We recommend that higher education institutions in Northern Ireland, in close collaboration with all the relevant external players, steadily enhance their regional role, taking full advantage of the special potential for the development of strong regional networks.

90   We recommend to the Government that options be examined for substantially increasing the number of higher education places in Northern Ireland in a cost-effective way which involves no compromise in quality and standards.

91   We recommend to the Government and institutions that consideration be given to adopting the Dearing 16–19 year olds option as one of the bases for entrance to universities in Northern Ireland.

92   We recommend to the Government that the scale and nature of funding for research in Northern Ireland universities should be assessed afresh in the context of the Province's strategy for economic development and of the recommendations in Chapter 11.

93   We recommend to the Government that there be constituted in Northern Ireland a Tertiary Education Forum, a Higher Education Funding Council and a Further Education Funding Council.

Annex B

How the Committee carried out its work

Working Groups

1.   The membership of each of the Committee's Working Groups is given below.

Economic Role of Higher Education

Professor John Arbuthnott*
Professor Mark Blaug   Visiting Professor of Economics, University of Exeter
Dr John Bridge   Chief Executive, Northern Development Company
Professor Martin Cave   Vice-Principal and Professor of Economics, Brunel
                             University
Ms Judith Evans*
Sir Geoffrey Holland*
Dr David Potter*   Chair
Jill Wilson   Managing Director, Manor Properties
Elizabeth Maddison   Secretary

Teaching, Quality and Standards

Dr Madeleine Atkins   Dean, University of Newcastle
Ann Bailey   Head of Education and Training Affairs, Engineering
                            Employers Federation
John Bolton   Principal, Blackburn College
Mrs Pamela Morris*
Sir Ron Oxburgh*
Sir George Quigley*   Chair
Professor David Watson*
Professor Adrian Webb*
Dr John Rea   Principal, College of St Mark and St John, Plymouth
Simon Wright*
Clare Matterson   Secretary

Information Technology

Professor John Arbuthnott* Chair
Sophie Ansell   President, University of Sheffield Union of Students
Professor Diana Laurillard*
Sir Ron Oxburgh*
Dr David Potter*
Sir William Stubbs*
Jane Denholm   Secretary

Research

Ewan Gillon	Postgraduate Research Student, Department of Management and Social Sciences, Queen Margaret College, Edinburgh
Professor John Laver	Vice-Principal (Research), University of Edinburgh
Dr Anthony Ledwith	Director of Group Research, Pilkington plc
Professor Howard Newby	Vice-Chancellor, University of Southampton
Sir Ron Oxburgh*	
Sir Richard Sykes *	*Chair*
Professor Sir David Weatherall*	
Professor David Watson*	
Professor Adrian Webb*	
Clare Matterson	Secretary

Staff and Use of Resources

Baroness Brenda Dean*	*Chair*
Professor David Chiddick	Pro Vice-Chancellor, De Montfort University
Sir Geoffrey Holland*	
David Holmes	Registrar, University of Birmingham
Professor Diana Laurillard*	
Hon. Mrs Sara Morrison	Director, General Electric Company
Dr Robert Smith	Vice-Chancellor and Chief Executive, Kingston University
Simon Wright*	
Michael Yuille	Director of Finance, University of Aberdeen
Eve Jagusiewicz	Secretary

Funding of Higher Education and Student Support

Professor Sir Eric Ash	Department of Physics, University College London
Sir John Cassels	
Baroness Brenda Dean*	
Fred Goodwin	Chief Executive, Clydesdale Bank plc
Sir Geoffrey Holland*	*Chair*
Eddie Newcomb	Registrar and Secretary, University of Manchester
Sir Ron Oxburgh*	
Andrew Pople	Managing Director of Retail Division Abbey National plc
Sir William Stubbs*	
Professor Adrian Webb*	
Simon Wright*	
Nigel Brown	Funding Consultant
Eve Jagusiewicz	Secretary

The Structure and Governance of Higher Education

Professor Ewan Brown, CBE	Director, Noble Gossart Limited
Richard Coldwell	Head of Government and Overseas Relations, National Grid
Dame Elizabeth Esteve-Coll DBE	Vice-Chancellor, University of East Anglia
Ms Judith Evans*	Chair, Governance sub-group
Julian Gizzi	Partner, Beachcroft Stanleys Solicitors
Professor Martin Harris CBE	Vice-Chancellor, University of Manchester
Caroline Neville	Principal, City College – Norwich
Sir William Stubbs*	*Chair*
Professor Peter Townsend	Pro-Vice Chancellor of Administration, University of Wales – Swansea
Professor David Watson* *Structure sub-group*	
Barbary Cook *Governance sub-group*	President, Oxford University Students Union
Simon Caffrey	President, Leeds Metropolitan University Students Union
Michael Shattock, OBE	Registrar, University of Warwick
Elizabeth Maddison	Secretary

*Members of the National Committee of Inquiry into Higher Education

2. Those who worked full or part-time in membership of the Secretariat are listed below, together with, where appropriate, the names of the organisations from which they were seconded.

Secretary to the Committee:
Shirley Trundle (Department for Education and Employment)

Policy Advisers:
Chris Boys (National Council for Vocational Qualifications)
Nigel Brown, Funding Consultant
Jane Denholm (Scottish Higher Education Funding Council)
Angus Gray, Private Secretary to the Chairman (Department for Education and Employment)
Eve Jagusiewicz (Anglia Polytechnic University)
Andrea Kupferman-Hall (Higher Education Quality Council)
Clare Matterson (Coopers & Lybrand)
Elizabeth Maddison (Further Education Funding Council)
Jacquie Spatcher (Department for Education and Employment)

Assistant Policy Advisers:
Conrad Benefield (Department for Education and Employment)
Richard Hill
Chris Kirk (Department for Education and Employment)
Bridget Tighe

Support Manager:
Steven Suckling (School Curriculum and Assessment Authority)

Support team:
Joyce Ajumobi, Support Assistant (Department for Education and Employment)
Cheryl Buckingham, Support Assistant
Anna Caseldine, Personal Assistant
Sharon Cooper, Personal Assistant to the Secretary of the Committee (Department for Education and Employment)
Judith Dutton, Support Assistant
Gaylene Eichstead, Support Assistant
Bianca Harrison, Personal Assistant
Shaila Hussein, Senior Personal Assistant to the Chairman (School Curriculum and Assessment Authority)
Lisa Misraoui, Personal Assistant
Jan Peters, Personal Assistant
James Pettigrew, Support Assistant
Kareena Sanderson, Personal Assistant

Media Adviser
Tony Millns, (School Curriculum and Assessment Authority)

Written consultation exercise

3.   One of our first actions – and one with which many readers of this report will have had some involvement – was to embark on a large-scale written consultation exercise. A substantial questionnaire was issued to around 2000 organisations and individuals in July 1996, with a deadline for responses of 15 November. It was also made available on the World Wide Web. We were delighted with the response. Not only were there a large number of replies – 840 – but a great deal of careful thought had gone into them. Many of the organisations who responded set up arrangements of their own to ensure that their responses reflected the views of their members. But we were also pleased that so many individuals took the trouble to send in contributions.

4.   A shorter version of the main consultation questionnaire was sent to a representative sample of schools with pupils in the 16-19 age range. The response to this aspect of our consultation was disappointing – only 18 out of the 300 who were sent a questionnaire replied. We have not attempted therefore to draw any conclusions about the views of schools from this exercise but their responses were included in the wider analysis of the evidence.

5.   Every piece of evidence submitted was sent to at least one member of the Committee, so that we all had a good sense of the nature of the responses coming in and could draw the attention of our colleagues to particularly pertinent contributions. To give us a wider sense of the main themes emerging and the balance of opinion, we commissioned a team from the University of London Institute of Education, led by Professor Ron Barnett, to analyse the responses for us. The report from the Institute is

being published with this report (Report 1). Their analysis included most responses which arrived after the 15 November deadline except those received in late December and beyond. The latter were fed into the Committee's work on an ad hoc basis depending on the issues raised in them.

6.   A few of those who submitted evidence asked for it to be kept confidential. All other written submissions are being placed in the Public Record Office and will be available for scrutiny shortly. In addition the University of London Institute of Education library has a full set of the non-confidential responses in its archive.

Oral evidence

7.   Because of time constraints we could not take oral evidence from all those who might have liked to appear before us. Twenty-nine organisations were invited to give evidence to a panel of members in London, and a further eight were seen by a panel of Scottish Committee members in Edinburgh. Full transcripts of those oral evidence sessions were taken and circulated to all members of the Committee. Copies are being placed in the Public Record Office.

Association of Colleges
Association of Metropolitan Authorities & Association of County Councils
Association of Scottish Colleges
Association of University Teachers
Biotechnology & Biological Science Research Council
British Academy
British Chambers of Commerce
Commission for Racial Equality
Committee of Scottish Higher Education Principals
Committee of Vice Chancellors and Principals
Confederation of British Industry
Convention of Scottish Local Authorities
Economic and Social Research Council
Educational Institute for Scotland
Engineering and Physical Sciences Research Council
Equal Opportunities Commission
Further Education Funding Council
General Teaching Council for Scotland
Higher Education Funding Council For England
Higher Education Funding Council For Wales
Highlands & Islands Enterprise

Institute of Directors
Medical Research Council
National Association of Teachers in Further and Higher Education
National Bureau for Students with Disabilities
National Union of Students
Natural Environment Research Council
Northern Ireland Higher Education Council
Particle Physics and Astronomy Research Council
Royal Society of Edinburgh
Scottish Enterprise
Scottish Higher Education Funding Council
Seven Associations Working Party
Standing Conference of Principals
Teacher Training Agency
Training & Enterprise Council National Council
Trades Union Congress

Consultation conferences

8.   Although our written consultation exercise was extensive, we also wanted to debate issues in more depth with a range of people. To do this, we arranged seven consultation conferences:

Leicester	31 October 1996
Exeter	1 November 1996
Manchester	28 November 1996
London	3 February 1997
Belfast	17 February 1997
Edinburgh	18 February 1997
Newport	24 February 1997

9.   We invited a range of people to each including:
   academics, senior staff and students from higher education institutions;
   staff from further education colleges;
   employers;
   representatives of Training and Enterprise Councils, Government Offices and development agencies.

10.   Although there was generally an enthusiastic response to the conferences, we found it hard to persuade employers to attend, despite issuing invitations to them through a variety of routes.

11. We started each conference with a plenary session where the Chairman outlined some issues for discussion. At most, though not all, of the conferences those present then divided into small groups to talk about a particular set of issues of which they had had prior notification. Each small group was chaired by a member of the Committee, of one of its Working Groups or of the Secretariat, and a note of the discussion was kept. At the end of each conference, the Chairman summarised the main points which had arisen and offered the opportunity for further questions and debate. We all received summaries of the discussions.

Seminars for small and medium sized enterprises

12. We knew that small and medium sized enterprises (SMEs) have little time for filling in questionnaires, but that their views were crucial because of their growing importance as a source of jobs for those with higher education qualifications. We asked a range of Training and Enterprise Councils (TECs) to arrange small seminars with groups of SMEs at times and places they felt were convenient. Six such seminars were held as follows:

16 September 1996	North and Central London TECs
20 September 1996	Leeds TEC
7 October 1996	Tyneside TEC
8 October 1996	Herts TEC
9 October 1996	Cheltenham and Gloucester LEC
9 December 1996	Stirling TEC

13. Each seminar was attended by at least one Committee member and a member of the Secretariat, who kept a record of the main points arising. At the end of each seminar the SMEs were given a copy of our employer questionnaire and asked to complete it. Completed responses were added to the analysis described below in paragraph 18.

Surveys

Students

14. We were grateful to student organisations such as the National Union of Students and SKILL for the effort they put into assembling evidence on behalf of students. To find out more about what individual students felt about their experience of higher education, we commissioned a large-scale survey of full and part-time undergraduate students in their second or subsequent year of higher education. The result of that survey, carried out by the Policy Studies Institute, is in Report 2.

Those who have higher education qualifications

15. Important as the views of current students are, we also wanted to know how those who had been through higher education had fared since and what they felt, in retrospect, about their higher education. We found that others were already planning work in this area so, rather than duplicate what they were doing, we worked in co-

operation with them. The Association of Graduate Recruiters (AGR), the Council for Industry and Higher Education (CIHE) and the Department for Education and Employment funded a survey of graduates in employment with a wide range of different types of employer. We are grateful to them for allowing members of our Secretariat to join the steering committee for that project and to influence the questions which were asked in the study, which was carried out by Professor Lee Harvey and colleagues at the Centre for Research into Quality, University of Central England. The findings of that study have been published.[1]

16. The Higher Education Funding Council for England had already planned a large-scale survey of two English graduate cohorts from 1985 and 1990. We agreed to contribute funding so that the survey could be extended to cover the UK, holders of Higher National Diplomas and graduates of the Open University and the University of Buckingham. Most of the results of that survey have been published[2] in respect of the Open University and the University of Buckingham because confidentiality assurances were given at the beginning of the survey. Committee Members have, however, seen the results of that part of the survey and its findings have been taken into account in our work.

Staff in higher education

17. The unions representing staff in higher education gave us written and oral evidence and were interviewed by our Working Group which looked at staff matters. We also conducted two surveys to find out the views of staff. The Policy Studies Institute carried out both surveys for us. The first was a large-scale telephone interview survey of 800 academic staff. The second was a small study of support staff which used focus groups. The results of the surveys can be found in Reports 3 and 4 respectively.

Employers

18. Since we found it difficult to attract a good representation of employers to our consultative conferences, we used other approaches to find out their views. The large-scale study by the Association of Graduate Recruiters[3], mentioned above, examined the views of graduates in work and also of their employers. To complement that survey, which concentrated mainly on the changing world of graduate career opportunities and the range of knowledge, skills and attributes that will help graduates to acquire jobs, we sent our own questionnaire which dealt with skills, research and development and continuing professional development to a range of large and small employers. Although our sample was not statistically representative, it gave us a good flavour of employers' views and showed quite clearly that employers have very diverse views and requirements. An analysis of the results of the survey can be found in Appendix 4.

Other research commissioned by the Committee

19. We made use of a wide range of statistical information from the Higher Education Statistics Agency which is now publishing the first comprehensive and comparable information on higher education. Previously, data from the various parts of the higher education system were collected separately by a range of different organisations including the then Department for Education and Employment, the Universities Statistical Record and the then Scottish Office Education Department. While the establishment of a unified set of statistics is a welcome advance, we were inevitably handicapped by the lack of a consistent series of figures over several years under the new arrangements.

20. We also had the benefit of research, analysis and modelling by economists and statisticians from the Department for Education and Employment on the economic returns achieved from investment in higher education and projections of student numbers. Evidence on the labour market demand for graduates, returns to higher education and the economic impact of higher education on regions was tested with a group of economists at a seminar held at the Barbican on 11 December 1996. We are grateful to the Department for Education and Employment, who organised the seminar for us.

21. We commissioned:
     i. a study of ways of widening participation in higher education, from Professors Frank Coffield and David Robertson (Reports 5 and 6);
     ii. a study of rates of return to higher education from the Analytical Services Division of the Department for Education and Employment (Report 7);
     iii. a report on externalities from Professor Norman Gemmel (Report 8);
     iv. a report on higher education and the regions from Professor Brian Robson (Report 9);
     v. we ourselves organised seminars on learning and admissions, which took place on 5 March 1997 and 29 April 1997 respectively.

22. Where we found that other organisations were already interested in carrying out research into a particular subject, we sought to work with them rather than duplicate their work. Particular thanks are owed to the Higher Education Funding Council for England and the Committee of Vice-Chancellors and Principals in this respect. In some cases we contributed funding in order to extend studies to cover additional aspects of particular interest to us. In other cases, a member of our Secretariat was allowed to join the steering group for projects or to have early sight of the findings of them. Examples include:
     i. a jointly funded study to compare cost structures in a range of UK higher education institutions[4];
     ii. a jointly funded study to compare cost structures in a sample of higher education institutions in different countries[5];
     iii. studies on estates maintenance and information systems/management of IT as part of the Joint Higher Education Funding Councils (HEFCE and the Scottish Higher Education Funding Council) value for money initiative;

iv. study on the costs and benefits of non-traditional student participation in higher education, in relation to the student, the group, the institution and the state;

v. CVCP collaboration study.

23. The Higher Education Quality Council made a helpful analysis of European qualifications frameworks for us which can be found in Report 11.

24. Some of our most technically complex work was in the area of funding. We commissioned London Economics, working jointly with Coopers and Lybrand, to design and build a model on which we could test specific funding options and to assist us in identifying and testing a range of options for funding the activities of higher education and the support of students. Professor David Robertson was commissioned to examine options for learning accounts or a Learning Bank in parallel. Such work was supplemented by a range of small seminars to help us tease out the technical issues on funding learning, student loans and learning accounts/learning banks. The outcomes of that work can be found in Reports 12, 13 and 14.

Overseas evidence

25. There were a large number of countries which we would have liked to visit but, given the time constraints, we decided to confine our visits to a relatively small number of developed countries and to send only a small number of members on each visit. We arranged two visits to the United States because its system is so diverse and large and because it has a long history of mass participation in higher education. The Chairman went to Japan as another example of an economically successful country with a long history of mass participation. Members visited three of our European neighbours, France, Germany and the Netherlands, and two countries, Australia and New Zealand which are culturally like the UK and have recently introduced major reforms of higher education funding. In each case, we received excellent support from the British Embassy/and/or British Council in the country concerned to help us arrange an interesting and relevant programme. Our aim was, where possible, to have discussions with representatives of those responsible for policy-making at national or regional level, representatives of higher education institutions, employers and students, and to visit several institutions of higher education. This often resulted in a packed programme. Reports from our visits are in Appendix 5.

26. The visits were supplemented by other sources of information. Many of us had knowledge of other countries' higher education systems from our normal work. We sent questionnaires to a large number of embassies of overseas countries in the UK. Although we are conscious that the responses we received from them may, in some cases, represent official aspirations rather than the current reality, there was a refreshing degree of honesty and willingness to question current approaches in some of the replies. Summaries of what we learnt about the Asian 'tiger economies', and about some European countries which we did not visit, are in Appendix 5.

27. While we were undertaking our work, the Organisation for Economic Co-operation and Development (OECD) was making a 'thematic review' of the early years of higher education based upon detailed studies in a number of countries. One of their study teams visited the UK in September 1996 and their report (unpublished) has informed our thinking.

Visits to institutions

28. We visited a range of universities and colleges across the UK. For most of the visits we identified a particular aspect of the institution's work which we wanted to see and then invited the head of the institution to arrange a programme to include other areas which he or she felt we ought to see. In almost all cases we were able to meet a group of students as well as a range of staff from the institution. We appreciate the effort and thought which universities and colleges put into those visits and the warmth of welcome that we received everywhere. The places we visited were:

Birkbeck College
Bradford & Ilkley Community College
Cambridge University
Cranfield University
De Montfort University
Liverpool John Moores University
Llandrillo College
Mid-Warwickshire College
Northern College
Open University
Oxford Brookes University
Queen's University of Belfast
Robert Gordon University
Royal Northern College of Music
Sheffield Hallam University
Swindon College
University of Birmingham
University of Buckingham
University of Central England
University of Central Lancashire
University of Dundee
University of East London
University of Edinburgh
University of Paisley

University of Reading
University of Sheffield
University of Southampton
University of Stirling
University of Ulster
University of Wales, Bangor
University of Warwick
University of Westminster
University of York

Informal meetings

30.   Throughout the course of our work we had many meetings with individuals and organisations, some at our request and some at theirs. We have not listed the meetings but are grateful to those who have given their time so freely. We would like particularly to thank Professor Bruce Chapman, Professor Claus Moser and Professor Martin Trow, each of whom joined one of our meetings.

---

1   Harvey L, Moon S and Geall V (1997) *Graduates' Work: Organisational Change and Students' Attributes*, University of Central England, Birmingham
2   Belfield et al, *Mapping the careers of highly qualified workers*, HEFCE, to be published in late 1997
3   op cit
4   HEFCE. *Undergraduate Teaching in Higher Education: A Comparative Study*, to be published by HEFCE Summer 1997
5   *International Comparison of the Cost of Teaching in Higher Education* (1997) J M Consulting Ltd, Bristol

Chapter references

Chapter 1

1   A reference to the Committee under the Chairmanship of Lord Robbins, which reported in 1963.

2   Oral Evidence from the Higher Education Funding Council for Wales

Chapter 2

None

Chapter 3

1   Department for Education and Employment (DfEE)

2   Higher Education Statistics Agency (HESA)

3   Socio-economic group refers to the Standard Occupational Classification published by the Office of Population Censuses and Surveys (OPCS). The groups are: I – Professional; II – Managerial and technical occupations; IIIn – Skilled occupations, non-manual; IIIm – Skilled occupations – manual; IV – Partly skilled occupations; V – Unskilled occupations.

4   HESA

5   DfEE. The 'points score' is an aggregate measure of an individual's A level grades. Points allocated are: E-2; D-4; C-6; B-8; A-10.

6   School Curriculum and Assessment Authority, (1996) *Standards in Public Examinations 1975 to 1995*, London

7   HESA

8   **Full-time and sandwich first degree percentage drop out rates: 1984/85 to 1994/95**

Academic Year										
1984/85	1985/86	1986/87	1987/88	1988/89	1989/90	1990/91	1991/92	1992/93	1993/94	1994/95
15	14	16	17	14	16	15	17	17	17-18	17-18

Source: DfEE

9   HESA

10   DfEE

11   We were fortunate that while undertaking a study for the Committee of Vice-Chancellors and Principals (CVCP) on the economic impact of higher education, Professor Iain McNicholl conducted a survey of higher education institutions which included details of their workforce in 1996/97. We are grateful to the CVCP and Professor McNicholl for giving us access to his findings.

12   Committee on Higher Education (1963), *Higher Education Report of the Committee appointed by the Prime Minister under the Chairmanship of Lord Robbins 1961-1963*, London, HMSO

13   Enterprise in Higher Education was a programme funded by the former Employment Department.

14   Higher Education Funding Council for England (HEFCE), Scottish Higher Education Funding Counci (SHEFC), Higher Education Funding Council for Wales (HEFCW), Department of Education, Northern Ireland (DENI) (1993), *Joint Funding Councils' Libraries Review Group: Report,* Bristol

15   Edexcel was formerly the Business and Technology Education Council (BTEC). The Scottish Qualifications Authority was formed through a merger of the Scottish Vocational Education Council and the Scottish Examination Board.

16   Robbins (1963) op cit

17   Office of Science and Technology (1997) *The quality of the UK science base*, Department of Trade and Industry, London

18   PREST, CASR and the University of Manchester (1996) *Survey of research equipment in United Kingdom universities* for CVCP, HEFCE, HEFCW, SHEFC

19   HESA

20   HESA

21   OECD (1997): *Thematic Review of the First Years of Tertiary Education, United Kingdom*: (Unpublished Study)

Chapter 4

1   Nottingham Skills and Enterprise Network (1994) *Labour Market and Skill Trends 1995/96*, Nottingham

2   Nottingham Skills and Enterprise Network (1996) *Labour Market and Skill Trends 1996/97*, Nottingham

3   DTI (1996) *Small Firms in Britain 1996*, London

4   Nottingham Skills and Enterprise Network (1996), op cit

5   Evidence from the seminars with small and medium sized enterprises organised for the Inquiry

6   DTI (1996) *Small and Medium Enterprises Statistics for the UK 1994*

7   Council for Industy and Higher Education (1997) *SMEs and Higher Educaction: Higher Education A Framework for Future Policy* (Unpublished draft)

8   HMSO (1996) *Social Trends 1996*, London

9   The 1996 Chatham House Forum Report (1996) *Unsettled Times*, The Royal Institute of International Affairs London

10 Potter D (1996), *Paper for the Committee*

11 Potter D (1996), *Paper for the Committee*

12 *The independent*, (20 March 1997), quoting a study by McKinsey and Co

13 *Social Trends 1996* op cit

14 Committee on Higher Education (1963), *Higher Education Report of the Committee appointed by the Prime Minister under the Chairmanship of Lord Robbins 1961-1963*, London, HMSO

15 HMSO (1985), *The Development of Higher Education into the 1990s*, Cmnd 9524, London

16 Toyne, Professor Peter, (1993), *Environmental Responsibility*, HMSO, London

17 Ali Khan, Shirley (1996) *Environmental Responsibility A Review of the 1993 Toyne Report*, HMSO, London

18 DfEE (1997) *Projections of Demand for Higher Education in Great Britain*, unpublished paper sumitted to the Committee by Analytical Services Higher Education Division

Chapter 5

1   Committee on Higher Education (1963), *Higher Education Report of the Committee appointed by the Prime Minister under the Chairmanship of Lord Robbins 1961-1963*, London, HMSO

2   Department for Education and Employment, the Scottish Office, the Welsh Office and the Department of Education for Northern Ireland, (1996) *Purposes of Higher Education*. Unpublished evidence submitted to the Committee. Copies can be obtained from the Government Departments concerned

3   Belfield et al (1997), *Mapping the Careers of Highly Qualified Workers*, Birmingham, University of Birmingham

4   *The Development of Higher Education into the 1990s*, (1985), Cmnd 9254, HMSO, London

5   Enterprise in Higher Education was a programme funded by the former Employment Department

Chapter 6

1   This evidence included: a seminar for economists organised by the Committee and the Department for Education and Employment (1996) which discussed aspects of the labour market and ways of measuring the economic impact of higher education;
    Report 7, *The contribution of graduates to the economy: rates of return*;
    Report 8, *Externalities to higher education: a review of the new growth literature*

2   International comparisons about participation in higher education are difficult because of the differences in the way countries classify their provision at different levels, but see, for example, Department for Education and Employment, Cabinet Office (1996) *The Skills Audit* para 1.8, and OECD (1997) *Thematic Review of Higher Education* (unpublished)

3   OECD (1997), op cit

4   Confederation of British Industry (1996) *Input to the National Committee of Inquiry into higher education: Enhancing higher education*, p.2

5   Institute for Employment Research (1995) *Future employment prospects for the highly qualified*, sections 3.4–3.5

6   Social and Community Planning Research (SCPR) (1997) *Utilisation of graduate skills in the labour force*

7   Mason, G (1996) New graduate supply shock. Recruitment and utilisation of graduates in *British Industry National Institute of Economic and Social Research*, London, pviii-ix

8   Appendix 4, Consultation with employers, paragraphs 2.1 and 2.2

9   NUTEK (1996) *Towards flexible organisations*

10 Court L, Connor H (1994) *The US labour market for new graduates*, Institute for Employment Studies. This finding was also confirmed in our visit to the USA (Appendix 5 section 8)

11 Harvey, L et al (1997) *Graduates' work*, University of Central England Centre for Research into Quality, for the Association of Graduate Recruiters, p.1 (para 3) and p.35

12 Meeting with other officials at the Department of Health and NHS executive, 17 March 1997

13 Appendix 4, Consultation with employers

14 We also consider Belfield, CR et al (1997) *Mapping the careers of highly qualified workers* University of Birmingham. This studies two cohorts of those obtaining higer education qualifications in 1985 and 1990. We do not draw on this evidence here because the comparator groups used to calculate pay premia are drawn more widely than the other two pieces of research, and therefore the findings are not directly comparable with the research from IFS and Analytical Services.

15 Lissenburgh, S et al, Policy Studies Institute (1996) *The returns to graduation: how the labour market experience of recent graduates compares with non-graduates* report for the Department for Educaation and Employment

16 Blundell, R et al (1997) *Higher education, employment and earnings in Britain*, Institute for Fiscal Studies (IFS)

17 Court L, Connor H (1994) op cit, para 3.33

18 Report 7, *The contribution of graduates to the economy: rates of return*

19 The return to society as a whole differs from that for individuals in three ways. First government currently picks up many of the costs of higher education through free tuition and contributions to maintenance. These are components of society's investment, but the cost in not borne by the the individual. Secondly, society benefits from higher education to the extent that a graduate pays higher taxes, as well as earning a greater amount post-tax, the relevant return to society is thus the difference between the pre-tax incomees of a graduate and otherwise equivalent non-graduate. Thirdly, graduates may enhance the productivity of other people in ways not captured in their own incomes (one aspect of so-called externalities). See Report 8 summary

20 Report 7 paragraphs 3.23–3.34

21 Report 8, summary, 3rd bullet point

22 Report 8, paragraph summary, 10th bullet point

23 Report 8, paragraph summary, 12th bullet point

24 Analytical Services Higher Education Division, Department for Education and Employment (date), *Scenarios for demand in the longer term* (unpublished)

25 Institute for Employment Studies (1996) *University Challenge: student choices in the 21st centry* A report to the CVCP

26 Institute for Employment Studies (1996) *op cit*

27 Analytical Services, *Scenarios*, op cit (unpublished)

28 CVCP (1996) *'Our Unversities Our Future'* Evidence to the National Committee of Inquiry into Higher Education

29 Appendix 4, op cit Tables 14, 17 and 19

30 HEFCE, CVCP, SCOP (1996) *Review of Postgraduate Eduation*, HEFCE, CVCP, SCOP

31 Analytical Services, *Scenarios*, op cit (unpublished)

32 Confederation of British Industry (1996) Input to the National Committee of Inquiry into Higher Eduacation: *Enhancing higher education*

33 Appendix 4, op cit paragraph 2.16

34 OECD (1997), op cit

Chapter 7

1   Patterson, L (1997) Trends in higher education in Scotland, Higher Education Quarterly, Vol 51, No1, p44, quoted in Report 5, para 6, *Widening participation in higher education by ethnic minorities, women and alternative students*

2   See in particular Report 5, op cit. and Report 6, *Widening participation in higher education for students from lower socio-economic groups and students with disabilities*

3   See end note 3 to Chapter 3 in this annex for an explanation of socio-economic groups.

4   Oliver Fulton, paper for the widening participation seminar, 27 March 1997 (unpublished)

5   Equal Opportunities Commission, (1996) *Women and Men in Britain 1995: The Life Cycle of Inequality*, quoted in its evidence to the Committee, November 1996

6   Report 5, op cit, para 2.5

7   Institute for Employment Research, (1997) *The Participation of Non-Traditional Students in Higher Education*, The University of Warwick, Table IV.10

8   Metcalf, H (1997), *Class and Higher Education: the participation of young people from lower socio-economic groups*, Policy Studies Institute, Table 2 and p.5

9   Steedman H and Green A (1996) *Widening participation in Further Education and Training: A survey of the Issues*, Centre for Economic Performance, para 1.31

10 Higher Education Funding Council for England (1997) *The participation in higher education of geodemographic groups*, pp.2–3

11 Higher Education Statistics Agency (1996) *Students in higher education institutions 1994/95*, Table 11 records around 593,000 students on the first year of a programme, of whom around 16,000 (2.6%) are known to have a disability

12 Report 6, op cit, para 4.2

13 FEFC (1996) *Inclusive Learning*, p.6

14 Institute for Employment Research (1997) op cit, pp.146–148

15 Report 10, *Teacher education and training: a study*

16 Institute of Employment Research (1997) op cit, Table IV.10

17 Dr Gaie Davidson-Burnet, paper for the widening participation seminar, 27 March 1997 (unpublished)

18 David Raffe, paper for the widening participation seminar, 27 March 1997 (unpublished)

19 See, for example, evidence from various studies of successive sweeps of the Youth Cohort Study; (Gray, Jesson, Tranmer (1993), Ashford, Gray and Tranmer (1993) and Payne (1995) the Economic and Social Research Council's 16–19 Initiative; cited in Steedman & Green op cit, para 2.2.1–2.2.5

20 Steedman and Green op cit para 2.0–2.13

21 Stephen McNair, paper for the widening participation seminar, 27 March 1997 (unpublished)

22 Higher Education and Employment Division (1996) *Living with Diversity*. This paper summarises issues from the Guidance and Learner Autonomy Programme

23 Smith, Bocock and Scott (1996) *Standard systems, non-standard students: experiences of progression from Further to Higher Education*, Policy Studies in Education, University of Leeds

24 Smith, Bocock and Scott op cit, page ii

25 Report 6, op cit, para 3.26

26 Ursula Howard, paper for the widening participation seminar 27 March 1997 (unpublished)

27 Institute of Employment Research (1997) op cit, pxiii

28 Callender and Kempson (1996) *Student finances*, p.51

29 Including from SKILL – National Bureau for Students with Disabilities (1996), evidence to the Committee

30 HEFCE (1996) *Widening Access to Higher Education*, para 3(b)

31 FEFC, op cit, The Inclusive Learning report commissioned for the FEFC may be a useful precedent

Chapter 8

1   Boyer, E (1990) *Scholarship reconsidered,* New Jersey, Carnegie Foundation for the Advancement of Teaching, p.24

2   HEQC (1994) *Learning from audit,* London, HEQC
    HEQC (1996) *Learning from audit,* London, HEQC

3   HEFCE (1997) *The impact of the 1992 Research Assessment Exercise on higher education institutions in England,* Bristol, HEFCE

4   Gibbs, G et al (1996) Class size and student performance: 1984–1994, *Studies in higher education*, Volume 21, No. 3

5   Report 4, *Administrative and support staff in higher education,* (pp.261–273)

6   Entwistle N (1996) *Improving university teaching through research on student learning*, University of Edinburgh, Centre for Research on Learning and Instruction

7   Entwistle N, Presentation to Learning Seminar on 5, March 1997

8   House of Lords Select Committee on Science and Technology (1996) *Information society: Agenda for action in the UK,* London, HMSO

9   Coopers & Lybrand, Institute of Education, Tavistock Institute (1996) *Evaluation of TLTP*, HEFCE, DENI, SHEFC, WHEFC

10 Seminar on Admissions, 29 April 1997

11 CVCP (1997) *A summary of the work of the admissions review steering group,* London, CVCP

12 HEQC Evidence to the Committee (unpublished)

13 HEQC (1994), op cit
    HEQC (1996), op cit

14 Watts AG and Hawthorn R (1992) *Careers education and the curriculum in higher education*, Cambridge, Careers Research Advisory Centre

Chapter 9

1 Purcell, K & Pitcher, J (1996) *Great expectations: the new diversity of graduate skills and aspirations,* University of Warwick Institute of Employment Research

2 Committee on higher education (1963) *Higher Education report of the Committee appointed by the Prime Minister under the Chairmanship of Lord Robbins 1961–1963,* London, HMSO, p91

3 Dearing R (1996) *Review of qualifications for 16–19 year olds,* Middlesex, SCAA Publications

4 CIHE (1996) *A learning nation,* Evidence to the National Committee of Inquiry

5 Harvey, L Moon, S Geall, V (1997) *Graduates' work: organisational change and students' attributes,* Centre for Research into Quality and the Association of Graduate Recruiters

6 Dearing, R (1996) op cit

7 Hodginson, L (1996) *Changing the higher education curriculum towards a systematic approach to skills • development,* The Open University Vocational Qualifications Centre

8 CVCP (1997) *CVCP Key skills survey – a brief analysis of questionnaire repsonses,* CVCP (unpublished)

9 Harvey, L Moon, S Geall, V (1997) op cit, p.2

10 Westhead P (1997) *Students in small business: an assessment of the 1994 STEP student placement scheme,* Small Business Research Trust

11 Boud D Keynote speech at SEDA conference on assessment, May 1994

12 Brown S and Saunders D (1995) The Challenges of modularisation, *Innovations in Education and Training International,* Vol 32 (2) pp.96–195

13 McDowell, L (1995) Managing Assessment in a modular curriculum: issues, perceptions, responses and opportunities, *Modular higher education in the UK,* London HEQC

14 HEQC (1997) *Assessment in higher education,* London HEQC

15 Eds Hounsell D et al, 1996, *The ASSHE Inventory, Centre for Teaching, Learning and Assessment,* University of Edinburgh

16 Higher Education Quality Council (1996) *Graduate Standards Programme Draft Report,* HEQC, London

17 *National Record of Achievement Review* (1997) p.1 Report of the Steering Group

Chapter 10

1 HEFCE, SCOP, CVCP (1996) *Review of postgraduate education,* HEFCE, SCOP, CVCP

2 The Royal Society (1993) *Higher Education Futures,* London, The Royal Society

3 Dearing, R (1996) *Review of qualifications for 16-19 year olds,* SCAA Publications

4 CVCP (1996) *Our universities our future,* Evidence to the National Committee

5 NCVQ (1995) *GNVQs at higher levels: a consultation paper,* London, National Council for Vocational Qualifications

6 NCVQ (1996) *GNVQs at Higher Levels: Response to Consultation,* London, NCVQ

7 Harvey L, Moon S, Geall V (1996) *Graduates' work: organisational change and students,* The University of Central England, Centre for Research into Quality

8 HEQC (1994) *Choosing to Change: the report of the HEQC CAT Development Project,* London, HEQC

9 National Union of Students, Evidence to the Committee, cited in Report 1

10 HEQC (1994) op cit

11 HEQC (1995) *Choosing to Change: Outcomes of the Consultation,* London, HEQC

12 SACCA is a joint body of the Committee of the Scottish Principals and the HEQC through its Scottish Office

13 HEQC (1996) *Inter-institutional variability of degree results: and analysis in selected subjects,* London, HEQC

14 HEQC Graduate Standards Programme Interim report (1996) HEQC, p.6

15 HEQC Evidence – paragraph 9.3

16 CBI (1996) Evidence to the Committee of Inquiry, *Enhancing higher education,* cited in Report 1

17 HEQC (1995) *Learning from Collaborative Audit,* London, HEQC

18 HEQC (1996) *Quality assurance of overseas partnerships,* London, HEQC

19 Joint Planning Group for Quality Assurance in Higher Education (1996) *Final report,* London, CVCP

1   The term 'infrastructure' refers to buildings, equipment and facilities required to support research, such as information technology, library facilities and support services.

2   Office of Science and Technology (1997) *The quality of the UK science base*, Department of Trade and Industry

3   National Academies Policy Advisory Group, (1996) *Research Capability of the University system*, London, The Royal Society

4   Segal Quince Wicksteed (SWQ) Ltd (1996) *A study of selectivity*, Bristol, HEFCE

5   SWQ (1997) *Review of the dual support funding*, CVCP

6   The overhead contribution from the Research Councils cannot represent the actual indirect costs associated with a research project because:

    a.   there are other indirect costs, such as premises costs, which remain the responsibility of the institutions, (which are funded through the Funding body);

    b.   the overhead figure is allocated on the basis of funded staff costs and hence may not adequately take account of indirect costs associated with non-staff costs;

    c.   the overhead figure is an average (calculated on the basis of statistical returns) and as such does not take account of differences in indirect costs which may be associated with:

        i)   the costs of different subjects;

        ii)   different types of grant;

        iii)   different institutions.

7   Coopers & Lybrand (1995) *Review of the dual support transfer,* The Office of Science and Technology

8   House of Commons Education Science and Arts Committee (1990) *Report of Science Policy and the European Dimension,* London, HMSO

9   The RAE measures the quality of research in 'Units of Assessment'. These may, or may not, match with the departmental structure of institutions of higher education. Throughout this chapter, the term 'department' is used as shorthand for 'Unit of Assessement'

10   NAPAG (1996) op cit

11   PREST, CASR and the University of Manchester (1996) *Survey of research equipment in United Kingdom Universities,* CVCP, HEFCE, HEFCW, SHEFC

12   The Forum was established in 1996 and includes representatives of the CVCP, the Medical Research Charities, the British Pharmaceutical Industry, the Higher Education Funding Council for England and the Chairman of the Foresight Panel on Health and Life Science.

13   Council for Science and Technology (1996) *Evidence to the National Committee of Inquiry into Higher Education*

14   Joint Information Systems Committee (1996) *Five year strategy 1996-2001*, JISC

15   House of Lords Select Committee on Science and Technology (1996) *Information Society: Agenda for Action in the UK*, London, HMSO

16   House of Lords Select Committee on Science and Technology (1996) op cit

17   Frayling, C (1993/4) *Research in art and design*, Royal College of Art Research Papers, Vol 1, No 1

18   Frayling, C (1993/4) op cit

19   McNay I (1997) *The impact of the 1992 RAE on Institutional and Individual in English Higher Education: the evidence from a research project*, Centre for Higher Education Management, Anglia Polytechnic University

20   SQW (1996) op cit

21   The RAE grades the quality of departments on a scale of 1 (lowest) to 5* (highest).

22   1995-96 HESA data

23   National Science Foundation (1996) *Science and Engineering Indicators – 1996*, Washington D.C., US Government Printing Office

24   Office of Science and Technology (1996) *Science, Engineering and Technology Statistics 1996*, London, HMSO

25   HEFCE (1997) *The impact of the 1992 Research Assessment Exercise on higher education institutions in England*, Bristol, HEFCE

26   Comments made during institutional visits

27   DTI (1996) *UK R&D Scoreboard, 1996* Edinburgh, Company Reporting Ltd

28   OST(1997) *The Research Master's Pilot*, Office of Science and Technology

29   House of Lords (1996) *Academic research careers for graduate scientists*, House of Lords Session 1994-95 4th report

Chapter 12

1   Reich R (1991) *The Work of Nations: A Blueprint for the Future*

2   see, for example, Goddard J (1994) *Universities and Communities*, CVCP

3   Hill S (1997) *The Impact of the Higher Education Sector on the Welsh Economy: Measurement, Analysis and Enhancement*

4   Goddard J (1994) *op cit*

5   Florida R (1995) *Toward the learning region*, Futures Vol 27 No 5

6   Segal Quince Wicksteed Ltd (1990) *The Cambridge Phenomenon*

7   note by Dr John Bridge (Chairman, Northern Development Company) for Economic Role Working Group (unpublished)

8   Kanter R (1995) *Thriving Locally in the Global Economy*, Harvard Business Review September – October 1995

9   Kanter R (1995) *op cit*

10 Westhead P (1997) *Students in small business: an assessment of the 1994 STEP student placement scheme*, Small Business Research Trust

11 Goddard J (1994) *op cit*

12 HEFCE (1996) *Institutions' Strategic Plans: Analysis of 1996 Submissions*

13 Labour Party (1996) *A new voice for England's Regions*

Chapter 13

1   We have broadly interpreted the term 'Communications and Information Technology' to comprise those technologies which enable the processing, storage and transmission of both live and recorded information by electronic means

2   MacFarlane A, Presentation to the Scottish Committee, 16th September 1996

3   These costs have been provided by Dr Malcolm Read, Secretary of the Joint Information Systems Committee, and are based on a sample of medium and large institutions. They break down as follows:
    Central Initiatives: Central expenditure on C&IT such as JISC, TLTP, MANs, CTI, the SHEFC LTDI and UMI, and elements of related initiative expenditure such as Technology Foresight.
    HEI Central Spend: Expenditure by Computer Centre Departments. These figures have been provided by Computer Centre managers and are in line with HESA figures.
    HEI Departmental Spend: Estimated by Computer Centre Directors to amount to two or three times the Central spend
    HEI Overheads: C&IT-based central services such as libraries, and overheads costs such as space
    HEI Courseware: Courseware developed by institutions themselves and not part of any central initiative

4   An "Intranet" is the application of Internet technology inside an organisation. It can be made available across the Internet. The users of an extended Intranet form a closed user group or virtual private network and Internet users outside this group cannot gain access

5   Read, Slater et al visit to Harvard Business School, April 1997, Appendix 5

6   Read, Slater et al visit to Harvard Business School, April 1997, Appendix 5

7   E-mail correspondence between Dr Malcolm Read and Secretariat, 18/3/97

8   Joint Information Systems Committee (1996) Five-year Strategy 1996–2001, page 21 (JISC). Updated by Dr Malcolm Read, 1997

9   House of Lords Select Committee on Science and Technology (1996) Information Society: Agenda for Action in the UK, HMSO, p.88

10 Deloitte & Touche (1996), JISC: JANET Value for Money Study. (Deloitte and Touche), p.6

11 MANs are usually restricted to urban areas. MANs are already in place in Edinburgh, Glasgow, Aberdeen, the St Andrews Dundee area, Wales, Manchester, London and the East Midlands. MANs in Bristol and South West England will be up and running in 1997

12 Super JANET is the name of the broadband, or highspeed part of JANET. SuperJANET is envisaged as a network of networks, complemented by a number of Metropolitan Area Networks (MANs) serving areas where several higher education institutions are located closely together. Today, more than 120 higher eduction institutions have broadband access

13 Committee of Scottish Higher Education Principals (COSHEP) (1996) Submission to the Dearing Inquiry, p.7

14 Kemp P, Letter to the Principal of the University of Strathclyde, 30th April 1997

15 The UK pilot Site Licence Initiative is an attempt to help both institutions and publishers break out of the vicious circle of rising prices. The Funding Bodies pay an overall licence fee and the institutions receive the journals produced by the participating publishers free or at a small additional premium

16 Joint Information Systems Committee (1996) Background Paper to NCIHE, p.14

17 Further Education Funding Council (1996), pp.31 and 42, Report of the Learning and Technology Committee

18 Multi-service networking is the ability to mix video, voice, images, text and data on a single network link

19 As noted earlier we would recommend the extension of MANs only where technically and financially sensible. MANs must be cost-effective against other means of network provision and provide richer functionality. This is not possible in all parts of the UK as MANs tend to be provided by cable companies or utilities whose coverage is patchy. The costs given here are start-up costs, which tend to be high compared with recurrent costs; the latter would be met by the Joint Information Systems Committee (JISC) and the institutions as appropriate

20 This proposed extension of JANET to further education colleges is costed at a basic level

21 Cooper R (1996) Networking – the Key to Exploiting the Full Potential of Information Technology in Higher Education (unpublished), p.5; Potter D (1996) Information Technology and Higher Education: A Twenty Year View (unpublished), p.2

22 In February 1996 David Jinkinson, Head of Computing Services at Sheffield Hallam University, released the results of a snap survey of directors of the Universities and Colleges Information Systems Association (UCISA). Responses were received from 31 institutions, with ratios varying between 5:1 (in one institution) and 100:1 (in one institution). The average across all responding institutions was just under 15:1, and slightly better in pre-1992 universities than in other institutions

23 To get to a ratio of 8:1 would require another 75,000 workstations, which we have estimated, including network costs, peripherals and overheads, at c. £2,800 each – amounting to £210 million
    To get to 5:1 would take another 55,000 workstations on top of this, amounting to £154 million.
    We have spread this expenditure over four years

24 In 1998–99 we have assumed 40,000 students need computers at about £500 each, whereas by 2001–2002, 300,000 students will need computers at £500 each

Chapter 14

1 University of Birmingham Stress Survey, Autumn 1996

2 House of Lords Select Committee on Science and Technology, Academic Research Careers for Graduate Scientists, HMSO, 1995

Chapter 15

1 National Audit Office (1997), *Submission by the National Audit Office to the National Committee of Inquiry into Higher Education*, part 4

2 National Audit Office (1997), *Submission by the National Audit Office to the National Committee of Inquiry into Higher Education*, p.16

3 Report 1, Report on national consultation (1997), pg. 80

4 National Audit Office (1997), *Submission by the National Audit Office to the National Committee of Inquiry into Higher Education*, p.25

5 National Audit Office (1997), *Submission by the National Audit Office to the National Committee of Inquiry into Higher Education*, p.23

6 National Audit Office (1996) *The Management of Space in Higher Education Institutions in Wales*, HMSO, p.3

7 Evidence to the Staff and Cost Effectiveness Working Group received from Association of University Directors of Estates of the United Kingdom (AUDE) Dec 96

8 *The Review of the Academic Year*, A Report of the Committee of Enquiry into the organisation of the academic year, (1993) HEFCE

9 Final Report – Scotland, *Review of the Academic Year*, Scottish Advisory Group on the Academic Year SHEFC/COSHEP, Nov 1993

10 *Treasury Management Value for Money*, National Report (1996), HEFCE, p.17

11 *Procurement Strategy for Higher Education (1996)*, HEFCE p.1

12 CVCP evidence submitted to the Staff and Cost Effectiveness Working Group (unpublished)

13 *Energy Management Study in the Higher Education Sector National Report* (1996), HEFCE p.5

14 National Audit Office (1994) *The Financial Health of Higher Education Institutions in England* HMSO HC 13 Session 1994–95

15 National Audit Office (1997) *Submission by the National Audit Office to the National Committee of Inquiry into Higher Education*, p.23

16 HEFCE, *Undergraduate Teaching in Higher Education: A Comparative Study* to be published by HEFCE Summer 1997

17 Unpublished survey by the Universities and Colleges Information Systems Association for the Committee

18 Committee of University Chairmen (1995) *Guide for Members of Governing Bodies of Universities and Colleges in England and Wales*, p.3

19 National Audit Office (1997), *Submission by the National Audit Office to the National Committee of Inquiry*, para. 1.22

20 Second Report of the Committee on Standards in Public Life (1996) *Local Public Spending Bodies*, Cm 3270 HMSO, p.24

21 Committee of University Chairmen (1995) *Guide for Members of Governing Bodies of Universities and Colleges in England and Wales*

22 Chairmen of Scottish University Courts and Councils, Chairmen of the conference of the Scottish Centrally-Funded Colleges in association with the Scottish Higher Education Funding Council (undated) *Guide for Members of Governing Bodies*

23 Report 1, Report on national consultation (1997), p.64

24 Second Report of the Committee on Standards in Public Life (May 1996) *Local Spending Bodies*, Cm 3270 HMSO, p.30 recommendation 3

25 Second Report of the Committee on Standards in Public Life (May 1996) *Local Public Spending Bodies*, Cm 3270 HMSO p.32

26 Committee of University Chairmen (1995) *Guide for members of Governing Bodies of Universities and Colleges in England and Wales*, p.24

27 Report 1, Report on national consultation (1997)

28 For example following Cadbury (1992) *The financial Aspects of Corporate Governance* chaired by Sir Adrian Cadbury and Greenbury (1995) *Directors' Remuneration – Report of a Study Group* chaired by Sir Richard Greenbury

29 Seminar organised by Beachcroft Stanley's solicitors – 1997 (proceedings unpublished)

30 Surveys commissioned by HEQC, *Research Project on Student Compaints* by Dennis Farringdon (unpublished)

31 *Opportunity, diversity and partnership – the student agenda for Higher Education* (1997), NUS evidence to the Committee

32 Education Reform Act 1988, section 202(2)

33 Tight M (ed) (1988) Academic Freedom and Responsibility, The Society for Research into Higher Education, Open University Press, p.125

34 Second Report of the Committee on Standard in Public Life (May 1996) *Local Public Spending Bodies*, Cm 3270 HMSO, p.34

35 Report 1, Report on national consultation (1997), p.65

36 Second Report of the Committee on Standards in Public Life (May 1996), *Local Public Spending Bodies*, Cm 3270 HMSO, p.37

Chapter 16

1 including those in the higher and further education sectors; private providers and some commercial organisations offering what they referred to as their own industry-specific 'university;' legal advice about the status of institutions; and international experience; and a seminar for the Structure and Governance Working Group.

2 Committee on Higher Education (1963) Higher Education Report of the Committee appointed by the Prime Minister under the Chairmanship of Lord Robbins 1961–63, para 460

3 University of Middlesex evidence to the Inquiry, quoted in Report, *Report on National Consultation*, p.60

4 Organisation of Economic Co-operation and Development (OECD) *Thematic Review of the First Years of Tertiary Education*, (unpublished)

5 Ewart Keep, paper for the widening participation seminar, 27 March 1997 (unpublished)

6 Professor Brian Fender (14 May 1997) correspondence with Sir Ron Dearing,

7 OECD op. cit

8 Martin Cave, (1996) *The Impact on Higher Education of Funding Changes and Increasing Competition*, Higher Education and Lifelong Learning Conference, July 1996, p.84

9 Higher Education Quality Council submission to the Committee, p.20

10 OECD op cit

11 CVCP, (1996) *Our Universities Our Future*, submission to the Committee, p.14

12 Brian Fender, Chief Executive of the Higher Education Funding Council for England, (January 1997) paper for the Structure and Governance Working Group, (unpublished)

13 CVCP *Collaboration in Higher Education*, (forthcoming)

Chapter 17

1 HEFCE Circular 15/96, 'Analysis of 1996 Finacial Forecasts', para. 22.
Compared to the 78 institutions projecting deficits in 1999–2000, 26 actually recorded a deficit in 1994–95 and 48 were forecasting deficits in 1995–96

2 The expenditure on higher education programmes in 1995–96 in FE colleges, other than those franchised by higher education instituitions is estimated as follows:

		£ million
England	HEFCE grant	53.5[a]
	FEFC Funds	85.0[b]
	Mandatory Award Fees	58.0[c]
Scotland	SOIED	75.0[d]
	Mandatory Award Fees	25.0[e]
Wales	HEFCW grants	1.1[f]
	Mandatory Award Fees	0.6
Total		298.2

[a] HEFCE actual (FEFC academic year estimate was £59 million)

[b] FEFC based on 1995–96 units of funding for 80,000 students

[c] FEFC estimate from financial forecasts

[d] Derived from the higher education share (31.9%) of the total Scottish Office Education and Industry Department funding units to FE colleges

[e] Estimate based on number of full-time higher education numbers

[f] HEFCW grant on 500 full-time and 50 part-time higher education students in FE colleges

3 The mandatory award figures are taken from local eduction authority 503G return to the DfEE in England, from Student Awards Agency for Scotland and from the Department of Education, Northern Ireland

4 The figures include:
in England
(i)   all higher eduction in higher education institutions
(ii)   prescribed programmes of higher education in FE colleges
(iii)   mandatory awards tuition fees
in Scotland
(i)   SHEFC grants to higher education institutions in Scotland and mandatory award fees
in Wales
(i)   HEFCW grants to higher education institutions in Wales and to prescribed courses in two FE colleges
(ii)   mandatory award fees
in Northern Ireland
(i)   DENI grant to the two universities in Northern Ireland
(ii)   mandatory award fees

5 The proportion of research expenditure from the total of the funding in Table 17.1 has been calculated as follows:
Identified research grant plus identified teaching grant in 1995/96 (academic year) was £3,722 million to HE institutions.
Of this £803 million was for research (21.6 per cent). It is assumed that capital and other grants are distributed in the same proportion. This gives a total research grant of £950 million
Total public funding for higher education in 1995-96 academic year is two-thirds of financial year 1995-96 (£3,873 million) plus one-third of financial year 1996-97 (£1,898 million) see Table 17.3. This gives a total of £5,771 million. £950 million is 16.5%, which has been rounded to 17%.

6 International comparisons of costs of teaching in higher education, JM Consultancy, March 1997. The costs: of non-medical undergraduate teaching in English institutions lie between the highest (Netherlands and USA) and the lowest, Australia

7 Williams G, Institute of Eduations, 'Resources for higher education in OECD countries' (1996), Council for Industry and Higher Education (CIHE)

8 The HEFCE's estimate of the annual requirement for capital investment based on an institution's costs and financial forecasts, is about £750 million in *England* made up of
£400 million for refurbishment of the non-residential estate
£200 million to replace the existing stock of equipment
£100 million to make good the backlog of equipment identified in recent surveys (see end notes 16 and 17)
£50 million to enhance Communication and Information Technology provision
The HEFCE estimate that funding of some £550 million is potentially available to meet these costs made up of:
£250 million from research council and funding body capital contributions
£100 million from new borrowings
£200 million from cash flow
New borrowings are assumed to be limited by ablility to repay from operating cash flows. The more general contribution from the cash flow for operating activities assumes the relaxation in the planned reduction in funding levels in 1998–99 and 1999–2000 which we have suggested is required. The UK figures have been obtained by grossing up

9 This assumes that there is complete overlap with the requirements covered by end note7

10 These are financial year figures. In 1998–99 it is assumed that only two-thirds of the full-year expenditure will be incurred

11 The assumptions underlying the figures in this scenario will be available on publication of the report in a technical working paper from the DfEE: 'Projection of demand to study in higher education in Great Britain (GB) over the longer term; Tracy Spencer, and Christine Anderton, Higher Education Division Analytical Services, Department for Education and Employment

12 This is a GB actual figure and is slightly higher than the UK planned figure for 1995-96

13 Based on current year average grant plus loan for all eligible students (including those who recieve no grant and/or take up no loan)

14 'Costs structures in higher education', Report commissioned jointly by the Committee and HEFCE from Coopers and Lybrand (forthcoming)

15 Assumes that ultimately up to 50,000 part-time undergraduate students may be eligible for fee remission

16 PSI, Report 2, Full and part-time students in higher education: their experiences and expectations

17 Georgiou L, Halfpenny P, Nevada M, Evans J and Linder S, Survey of research equipment in United Kingdom universities, CVCP, June 1996

18 Georgiou L et al, Survey of teaching equipment in English and Welsh higher education institutions, to be published

19 Callender C and Kempson E, 'Student finances, income and expenditure and take-up of student loans, PSI, November 1996, Table 5.1

20 The rate has remained broadly constant since 1990 at about 18 per cent

21 Callender C and Kempson E Ibid (November 1996) Chapter 2 pp.35-38 and Table 2.13 and 2.14

Chapter 18

1 Evidence from the sample of students surveyed in Callender and Kempson (1996) *Student Finances: Income, Expenditure and Take-Up of Student Loans*, Policy Studies Institute, London suggests that the average sum received from parents/spouse was £874. Grossing this up suggests a total contribution of some £800 million, £100 million more than the assessed figure

2 This total is made up of £10.7 billion expenditure by higher education institutions, £2.1 billion public expenditure in support of students' living costs, £800 million parental contributions less an estimated £800 million to allow for double counting as a result of student maintenance support being spent in higher education institutions, giving a total of £12.8 billion. In addition, there is some £300 million expenditure on higher education in further education colleges.

3 US Department of Education, National Center for Education Statistics (1996) *The Condition of Education 1996*, NCES 96-304, by Thomas Smith, US Government Printing Office, Washington DC

4 There is some evidence to suggest that post-higher education earnings are lower for non-traditional students, although they still enjoy higher salaries than those without such qualifications (see Table 2.10, Report 6, 'Widening participation in higher education by students from lower socio-economic groups and students with disabilities') but research by the Institute of Fiscal Studies suggests that the returns to higher education qualifications do not vary according to background or ability (IFS (1997) *Higher Education: Employment and Earnings in Britain*)

Chapter 19

1 PCFC/UFC (1992), *Capital Funding and Estate Management in Higher Education*

2 Bates M, Review of PFI (Public/Private Partnerships) HM Treasury June 1997

3   The Joint DfEE/Higher Education Sector Working Group (1996), *PFI in Higher Education: Report to the Secretary of State*

Chapter 20

1   As at 31 March 1997. Repayments first fall due in the April after the borrower graduates or drops out of his or her course. Repayments can then be deferred for a year at a time if the borrower's income is below the repayment threshold

2   National Commission on Education (1993) *Learning to Succeed*, Heinemann, London

Chapter 21

1   Conceptual issues and the Australian Experience with Income Contingent charges for Higher Education, Centre for Economic Policy Research, Discussion Paper 350 ANA, September 1996

2   In particular Dr Nicholas Barr and Mr Iain Crawford of the London School of Economics since 1988

3   In particular in various papers by Dr Nicholas Barr et al at the London School of Economics

4   Age 60 for those aged 40 or over when they took out their last loan

5   Student Loans Company Customer Satisfaction Survey, Martin Hamblin Research, September 1996

6   Submission to the National Committee of Inquiry into Higher Education from Dr Nicholas Barr and Mr Iain Crawford, November 1996

7   Ibid

8   Existing student loans made by the Student Loans Company are within scope of the Consumer Credit Act 1974: this imposes specific duties on the lender to provide specific information to the borrower at specific times (Sections 75–78)

9   At present, when an employer defaults on payment, the employee is credited with the tax that the employer should have deducted from pay (whether it has been deducted or not). The employer is pursued for the liability. It is for consideration whether similar rules would apply in the case of loan repayments collected through the tax system

10   Report of the Commission on Social Justice, 1994

11   The Learning Bank: towards a strategy for investment in post-compulsory education and training, David Robertson, November 1995

12   Individual Lifetime Learning Accounts. A new infrastructure for the UK (to be published) J Smith and A Spurling. This provides an assessment both of policy and technical feasibility of establishing a system of learning accounts to promote lifelong learning

13   Student Finance Income and Expenditure and take up of student loans Callender C, and Kempson E. Table 2.10 indicates that gifts to students average about £450 in 1995–96

14   Called to Account, are compulsory individual learning accounts a wheeze or a nightmare? Mark Corney and Peter Robinson The Unemployment Unit, 322 St John Street, London EC1V 2NT (January 1996)

15   Lifetime Learning Accounts and Training Services: Issues for UK training policy. A report for the Institute of Personnel and Development (February 1997) Mark Corney (MC Consultancy) (unpublished)

Chapter 22

1   OECD (1997) *Thematic review of the first years of tertiary education: United Kingdom* (unpublished)

2   OECD (1997) *Thematic review of the first years of tertiary education: United Kingdom* (unpublished)

3   OECD (1997) *Thematic review of the first years of tertiary education: United Kingdom* (unpublished)

4   CVCP (1996) *Our Universities Our Future*, Submission to the Inquiry

5   SHEFC (1996) *Submission of Evidence from the Scottish Higher Education Funding Council*

Chapter 23

1   Figures from the Welsh Office show that in 1994 manufacturing represented 27 per cent of Welsh GDP, compared with 21 per cent for the UK as a whole. Their figures also show that VAT-registered companies with a turnover of less than £250,000 represented 82 per cent of all companies in Wales, compared with 77 per cent in the UK.

Chapter 24

None

Annex D

Glossary of acronyms

AHRC	Arts and Humanities Research Council
ALT	Association for Learning and Teaching
APL	Assessment of prior experiential learning
APT&C	administrative, professional, technical and clerical
AUDE	Association of University Directors of Estates
AUT	Association of University Teachers
BBSRC	Biotechnology and Biological Sciences Research Council
BTEC	Business and Technology Education Council
CAFAS	Campaign for Academic Freedom and Standards
CAT	credit accumulation and transfer
CBI	Confederation of British Industry
CDL	Career Development Loans
CIHE	Council for Industry in Higher Education
C&IT	Communications and Information Technology
CNAA	Council for National Academic Awards
CPD	Continuing Professional Development
CRE	Commission for Racial Equality
CRQ	Centre for Research into Quality
CST	Council on Science and Technology
CTI	Computers in Teaching Initiative
CUC	Committee of University Chairmen
CVCP	Committee of Vice-Chancellors and Principals
DENI	Department of Education for Northern Ireland
DfEE	Department for Education and Employment
DSA	Disabled Students Allowance
DTI	Department of Trade and Industry
EC	European Community
e-Lib	Electronic Libraries Project
EOC	Equal Opportunities Commission
ERDF	European Regional Development Fund
ESRC	Economic and Social Research Council
EU	European Union
FE	further education
FEFC	Further Education Funding Council
FTE	full-time equivalent
GCE	General Certificate of Education
GDP	Gross Domestic Product
GNVQ	General National Vocational Qualification
GTC	General Teaching Council
HE	higher education
HECS	Higher Education Contribution Scheme (Australia)
HEFCE	Higher Education Funding Council for England

HEFCW	Higher Education Funding Council for Wales
HEQC	Higher Education Quality Council
HERDF	Higher Education Regional Development Fund
HESA	Higher Education Statistics Agency
HMSO	Her Majesty's Stationery Office
HN	Higher National
HNC	Higher National Certificate
HND	Higher National Diploma
HRB	Humanities Research Board
IBSS	International Bibliography of the Social Sciences
IER	Institute for Employment Research
IES	Institute for Employment Studies
IFS	Institute for Fiscal Studies
IIP	Investors in People
ILAs	Individual lifelong learning accounts
IPDF	Industrial Partnership Development Fund
IPR	Intellectual Property Rights
IROs	Integrated Regional Offices (of Government)
ISI	Institute of Scientific Information
ITT	initial teacher training
JANET	Joint Academic Network
JISC	Joint Information Systems Committee
JREI	Joint Research Equipment Initiative
JSA	Jobseeker's Allowance
LEA	Local Education Authority
M	Masters
MA	Master of Arts
MANs	Metropolitan Area Networks
MBA	Master of Business Administration
MEd	Master of Education
MEng	Master of Engineering
Mpharm	Master of Pharmacy
MPhil	Master of Philosophy
MSc	Master of Science
NAO	National Audit Office
NAPAG	National Academies Policy Advisory Group
NASA	North American Space Agency
NATFHE	National Association of Teachers in Further and Higher Education
NCDS	National Child Development Society
NCVQ	National Council for Vocational Qualifications
NDCs	Networked Desktop Computers
NHS	National Health Service
NIACE	National Institute of Adult Continuing Education
NICS	National Insurance Contributions Scheme
NIESR	National Institute for Economic and Social Research
NUS	National Union of Students

NVQ	National Vocational Qualification
OECD	Organisation of Economic Co-operation and Development
OFSTED	Office for Standards in Education
ONS	Office for National Statistics
OPCS	Office of Population Censuses & Surveys
OST	Office of Science and Technology
OU	Open University
PEP	Personal Equity Plan
PES	Public Expenditure Survey
PFI	Private Finance Initiative
PGCE	Postgraduate Certificate of Education
PhD	Doctorate
PSBR	Public Sector Borrowing Requirement
PSI	Policy Studies Institute
QAA	Quality Assurance Agency
QCA	Qualifications and Curriculum Agency
R&D	research and development
RAE	research assessment exercise
RBL	Resource based learning
RDAs	Regional Development Agencies
RPI	Retail Price Index
SAAS	Student Awards Agency for Scotland
SACCA	Scottish Advisory Committee on Credit and Access
SARTOR	Standards and Routes to Registration
SCOP	Standing Conference of Principals
SCOTCAT	Scottish Credit Accumulation and Transfer Scheme
SCPR	Social and Community Planning Research
SEDA	Staff and Educational Development Association
SHEFC	Scottish Higher Education Funding Council
SLC	Student Loans Company
SMEs	Small and Medium sized Enterprises
S/NVQ	Scottish National Vocational Qualification
SPC	Student Portable Computer
SQA	Scottish Qualification Authority
SRB	Single Regeneration Budget
SSA	Student Support Agency
STEP	Shell Technology Enterprise Programme
STSS	Scottish Teacher's Superannuation Scheme
SVQs	Scottish Vocational Qualifications
TCS	Teaching Company Scheme
TECs	training and enterprise councils
TESSA	Tax Exempt Special Savings Account
TLTP	Teaching and Learning Technology Programme
TSS	Teachers' Superannuation Scheme
TQA	teaching quality assessment
TTA	Teacher Training Agency

UCEA	Universities and Colleges Employers Association
UCISA	Universities and Colleges Information Systems Association
UGC	Universities Grants Committee
UK	United Kingdom
UNESCO	United Nations Economic and Social Co-operation Organisation
UPA	Universities Personnel Association
USA	United States of America
USS	Universities Superanuation Scheme
VAT	Value Added Tax
UCoSDA	Universities and Colleges Staff Development Agency
www	World Wide Web

Annex E

Glossary of terms

1992 universities/Pre-1992 universities

1992 universities are those which gained the 'university' title following the Further and Higher Education Act 1992. Pre-1992 universities are those which had the title before this date.

Access course

A course which helps prepare applicants without traditional academic qualifications for entry to higher education programmes.

Access Funds

Government funds provided to higher education institutions to assist students in financial difficulty. Institutions distribute these funds according to their own definitions of financial hardship.

Age participation rate/Age participation index (API)

The number of those aged under 21 entering higher education as a percentage of the average of the number of 18 and 19 year olds. In Scotland, the API is defined as the number of Scotland-domiciled entrants to full-time higher education anywhere in the UK who are aged 20 or under expressed as a percentage of the 17 year old population from the previous year.

Assessment of Prior (Experiential) Learning (AP(E)L)

The process of assessing and sometimes giving credit for a student's previous experience and learning, for example gained in the work place, or other experience, not assessed or accredited by traditional qualifications.

Binary divide/line

The binary divide was the division of higher education into two sectors – the university sector and the 'public'/polytechnic sector. The Further and Higher Education Act 1992 abolished the binary divide.

Business and Technology Education Council (BTEC)

BTEC is a validating body which offers nationally recognised qualifications, including HNDs and HNCs (Higher National Diplomas and Higher National Certificates). Following merger with the London Examining Board, it is now known as Edexcel.

Committee of Vice-Chancellors and Principals (CVCP)

A representative body whose members include the Vice-Chancellors and Principals of all UK universities.

Communications and Information Technology (C&IT)

Those technologies which enable the processing, storage and transmission of both live and recorded information by electronic means.

Completion rate
The percentage of students who complete their programme of higher education. See also drop-out rate.

Continuing professional development (CPD)
Training and education undertaken by adults throughout their working lives.

Council for National Academic Awards (CNAA)
Established in 1964, the CNAA was responsible for the validation of programmes at public sector institutions (former polytechnics). The Further and Higher Education Act 1992 abolished the CNAA.

Credit accumulation and transfer (CAT)
Credit accumulation provides students with the opportunity to gain credit for their learning achievements which then count progressively towards an award. Credit transfer is an arrangement by which credits granted by one body are recognised by another.

Diplomate
Someone who has gained a diploma.

Distance learning
Learning through TV, radio, correspondence or via computer networks which takes place mainly at a distance from the educational institution responsible for the learning programme.

Drop-out rate/Wastage rate
The percentage of students who do not complete their programme of higher education.

Economically active population
Those in the population of working age (16-65) who are either in work or are looking for work.

Edexcel
See BTEC.

Enterprise in Higher Education (EHE)
An initiative funded by the former Employment Department. EHE's aims were to make higher education programmes more vocationally oriented and encourage students' personal development via the improvement of transferable skills. Funding began in 1988 and ended in 1996.

External Examiner System
A quality assurance system operated by higher education institutions on the basis of peer review. External examiners are academics from another institution who verify the standards of the awards being made with the aim of ensuring that they are comparable across the sector.

Externalities (to higher education)
Economic benefits of higher education to society which are not captured by the additional average pay received by graduates (the 'pay premium') and so reflected in the 'rate of return'. See Report 8 for more information.

Franchising
The process by which an institution agrees to authorise another institution to deliver an approved programme while normally retaining overall control of the programme's content, delivery, assessment and quality assurance arrangements.

Full-time equivalent (FTE)
Numbers of students are commonly given in FTEs. This simply means that students not studying full-time are given a weighting of less than one to reflect the amount of study they do in a given period of time. This helps to relate student numbers more accurately to, for example, resource needs and teaching time.

Funding Bodies
A collective term covering the Higher Education Funding Council for England (HEFCE), the Higher Education Funding Council for Wales (HEFCW), the Scottish Higher Education Funding Council (SHEFC), the Department of Education Northern Ireland (DENI), and, where appropriate, the Teacher Training Agency (TTA).

Further education
Further education is provision for people over compulsory school age which does not take place in a secondary school and which falls within the scope of Schedule 2 to the Further and Higher Education Act 1992. Further education may take place in sixth form colleges, further education colleges or higher education institutions.

Further education college
An institution whose primary mission is the delivery of further education.

Further education funding bodies
A collective term covering the Further Education Funding Council (FEFC), the Further Education Funding Council for Wales, the Scottish Office Education and Industry Department (SOEID) and the Education and Library Boards in Northern Ireland.

Further Education Funding Council (FEFC)
Established by the Further and Higher Education Act 1992, the FEFC is responsible for funding sufficient and adequate facilities for further education in England. The Secretary of State for Scotland has this legal duty in Scotland, and the FEFCW in Wales.

Graduate
Someone who has attained a degree.

Gross Domestic Product (GDP)
The total value of goods and services produced during a period of time, usually calculated for nations or regions.

Gross Domestic Product (GDP) deflator
A multiplier used to convert current expenditure into equivalent expenditure in a base year, on the basis of price movements in the economy.

Higher Education Funding Council (HEFC)
Created by the Further and Higher Education Act 1992, HEFCs are responsible for the funding of higher education. They also aim to secure value for money from public expenditure and encourage improvements in the quality of education through the publication of institutional and subject assessment reports. There are HEFCs for England (HEFCE), Scotland (SHEFC), and Wales (HEFCW). The precise responsibilities of the bodies differ, and more detail can be found in Chapter 22.

The Higher Education Quality Council (HEQC)
The HEQC is a private company owned by the Committee of Vice-Chancellors and Principals, the Conference of Scottish Centrally Funded Colleges (CSCFC) and the Standing Conference of Principals (SCOP). It aims to: provide information on the methods used to ensure academic quality and standards, and to offer judgements on their effectiveness; as well as to provide institutions with a provisional agenda on how to improve and enhance the quality of their educational provision. The HEQC does this by considering and reviewing the mechanisms and structures used by individual institutions to monitor, assure, promote and enhance their academic quality and standards, in the light of their stated aims and objectives.

Higher
The primary higher education entry qualification in Scotland. It is a one-year qualification, usually undertaken by school-leavers.

Higher degree
A qualification above a first degree such as a Masters degree or Doctorate.

Higher education
Educational provision above Level 3 (ie above A level and the Advanced level GNVQ) and its equivalents in Scotland.

Higher education institution
An institution whose primary purpose is the provision of higher education. This includes universities and colleges of higher education.

Higher National Certificate/Higher National Diploma (HNC/HND)
Sub-degree vocational qualifications awarded by Edexcel in England and by the Scottish Qualifications Authority in Scotland.

Home students

These are normally students resident in the United Kingdom.

Honours degree

A Bachelors degree with honours.

Income contingent loan

A loan where the level of repayments is based on an individual's income. There is usually no repayment until the individual reaches a certain threshold earnings level.

Incubator unit

A commercially semi-sheltered environment where people can develop a business idea, for example a campus-based business receiving support from a higher education institution.

Individual Learning Accounts (ILAs)

A combination of an accumulation fund; a distribution fund; a loan/overdraft facility and a repayment mechanism which together could be used by individuals to fund their post-16 education and training.

Initial Teacher Training (ITT)

A programme which leads to a qualification as a teacher at primary and secondary levels. It always has a school-based component.

Internet

A collection of thousands of networks linked by a common set of technical protocols which make it possible for users of any one of the networks to communicate with or use the services located on any of the other networks. The Internet refers to the INTERnational NETwork.

Investors in People (IiP)

The national quality standard for investment in training and development to achieve business goals.

Key skills

A term used in this report to cover communication skills, numeracy, the use of information technology and learning how to learn. See Chapter 9 for more details.

Level 3 qualifications

A generic term covering A levels, NVQ Level 3, Advanced GNVQs and equivalent qualifications. This level of qualifications is that traditionally required for entry to higher education.

Lifelong learning

The practice of students of all ages and backgrounds pursuing education and training throughout life.

Maintenance
Public money distributed to students by local education authorities (LEAs), on a means tested basis, to cover their living costs.

Masters degree (MA, MSc, MPhil, MEd)
Programmes predicated on the assumption that those who undertake them have completed a Bachelors Degree or achieved comparable attainment.

Mature students
Mature undergraduate students are defined as those aged 21 or over on 1 August in year of entry. Mature postgraduate students are aged 25 or over on 1 August in year of entry.

Means test
A way of assessing financial need on the basis of an individual's income and/or capital, or that of their family.

Modularisation
Modularisation involves dividing a programme of study into units (modules). The module should consist of coherent and explicit learning activities. Modules can vary in length. There is an agreed group of modules in order to obtain an award. In each programme there will usually be modules that are compulsory, with other optional modules taken from a wider choice.

National Curriculum
The framework for teaching and learning across a range of subjects and the associated assessment arrangements, laid down in Statute for all pupils of compulsory school age (5-16) attending state schools.

National Council for Vocational Qualifications
The agency responsible for designing and implementing the NVQ and GNVQ framework. It merged with the School Curriculum and Assessment Authority in 1997 to form the Qualifications and Curriculum Authority.

Ordinary degree
Except in Scotland, this usually describes a Bachelors Degree awarded without honours. In Scotland, it is a qualification usually characterised as having greater breadth than an Honours Degree and is a recognised exit point for students.

Overseas students
International students domiciled outside the European Union.

Pay premium
The percentage by which the average pay of one group exceeds that of another group.

Postgraduate Certificate of Education (PGCE)
A postgraduate qualification leading to qualified teacher status.

Postgraduate student
A student on a programme of study which normally requires a first degree as a condition of entry.

Private rate of return
The benefit to an individual from participation in higher education. Usually derived from the additional earnings which a graduate will accrue over a lifetime, with an allowance made for the costs they incur, including earnings foregone during their time in higher education.

Programme of study
The study undertaken by a student that leads to a higher education award.

Public Sector Borrowing Requirement (PSBR)
A measure of the extent to which the public sector has to raise cash, typically by borrowing, in order to finance that part of its expenditure not covered by revenue (eg taxation).

Quality Assurance Agency (QAA)
A new independent agency responsible for ensuring and enhancing quality and academic standards. It was formed in July 1997 from a merger of HEQC and Funding Council quality assessment functions.

Research Assessment Exercise (RAE)
A system used to allocate funds for research by the Funding Councils. The exercise is conducted every 4 years and assesses the quality of research in Units of Assessment based on historical information. Institutions submit evidence of their research activity since the last exercise. The quality of research is rated from 1 to 5* by subject panels.

Resource based learning
A form of learning which makes extensive use of learning materials (whether in print or computer-based) and requires the student to undertake a self-directed approach to their learning. See Appendix 2 for more details.

Sandwich programme
A programme which contains a substantial work-based element.

School Curriculum and Assessment Authority (SCAA)
A body which exists to promote higher standards of achievement in schools by developing the curriculum and its assessment, and improving consistency and quality in public examinations. SCAA merged with the NCVQ in 1997 to form the Qualifications and Curriculum Authority.

Semester
A portion of the academic year. There are usually two semesters in a year, but sometimes three.

Single Regeneration Budget (SRB)
A fund of public money used to encourage local partners to work together to regenerate local areas in England.

Small and medium-sized enterprises (SMEs)
Unless otherwise specified, this term is used loosely to describe organisations with fewer than 250 employees. More rigorous definitions are used, for example, in Appendix 4.

Social rate of return
A calculation which seeks to measure society's return on its investment in higher education. The investment is the cost borne by society; and the return is the graduate's additional productivity, for which their additional earnings are used as a proxy.

Socio-economic groups
These refer to the Standard Occupational Classification published by the Office of Population Censuses and Surveys (OPCS). The groups are: I – Professional; II – Managerial and technical occupations; IIIn – Skilled occupations, non-manual; IIIm – Skilled occupations – manual; IV – Partly skilled occupations; V – Unskilled occupations.

Staff-student ratio (SSR)
Expresses the number of students (normally calculated in FTEs) per member of academic staff.

Standing Conference of Principals (SCOP)
SCOP represents executive heads of colleges and institutions of higher education in the UK and promotes their interests to government, national and international agencies as well as to industry, commerce and the professions.

Sub-degree qualifications
Higher education qualifications below degree level, for example HNDs and HNCs.

Teacher Training Agency (TTA)
The body in England which is responsible for the funding of initial teacher training (ITT) provision and some other continuing professional development courses for teachers offered by higher education institutions. Its other responsibilities include accrediting providers of ITT, improving the quality and efficiency of all routes into the teaching provision, and ensuring an appropriate supply of high quality trained teachers.

Tertiary education
Usually taken to cover both further and higher education, but this term is variously interpreted. See Chapter 5 for more details.

Threshold standards

The minimum acceptable achievement (in terms of academic standards) for an award to be granted.

Top-up fee

A charge which could be levied by a higher education institution on students in addition to the existing recognised fees.

Training and Enterprise Councils (TECs)

There are 81 TECs in England and Wales which are responsible for funding all of the Government's training schemes.

Undergraduate

A student studying for a first degree, higher education certificate or diploma or equivalent.

Validation

The process by which a programme is judged to have met the requirements for an award by the relevant degree-awarding body, or the relevant examining board, or by an accredited institution.

World Wide Web

The World Wide Web (the 'Web') is a user-friendly interface to the Internet. The Web now connects a community which at the end of 1996 was around 50 million people and continues to grow rapidly. For the electronic community the Web is the equivalent of a town market place. Anyone who wishes can set up their own stall (ie establish their own 'web site'). There will be those who want to advertise on the Web, those who want to buy or browse, those who want to let others know what they have found. A number of different software systems ('browsers') have been devised and marketed to allow individuals to 'navigate' the Web to find what they are looking for.

Bibliography

A Guide to Funding Higher Education in England: How the HEFCE Allocates its Funds (1995-96)

Abecassis A (1994) *The Policy of Contracts between the State and the Universities: A Quiet Revolution*, in OECD, Evaluation and Decision-making in Higher Education

AGR (1996) *Skills for the 21st Century*, Association of Graduate Recruiters

Ali Khan S (1996) *Environmental Responsibility: A Review of the 1993 Toyne Report*, DfEE

Allen A & Higgins T (1994) *Higher Education: The International Student Experience*, HEIST/UCAS

Allen A & Higgins T (1994) *The Careers Adviser/Higher Education Interface*, HEIST/UCAS

Allen A (1995) *Higher Education Provision in the Further Education Sector: The Student Experience*, HEIST

American Pharmaceutical Companies: R&D and Manufacturing Investment in Europe (1995) Remit Consultants Ltd

An Overview of a New Policy Framework for Higher Education Transformation (South Africa)

Anderson M (1994) *Joint Funding Councils' Library Review Report*, HEFCE, SHEFC, HEFCW and DENI

Anglia Polytechnic University (1994) *The Future of The Classified Honours Degree*

Apple Computer UK Limited (1996) *Submission to the National Committee of Inquiry into Higher Education*

Armstrong H (Lancaster University), Bruce T (CVCP) & Jackson B (CVCP) *Cities of Learning? Papers from a Conference held on 20 & 21 April 1995*

ASCETT (1996) Annual Report 1996, Advisory Scottish Council for Education and Training Targets (ASCETT)

ASCETT (1996) *Education and Training; Intelligence Gathering; Best Practice and Benchmarking our International Competitors*

ASCETT (1996) *Learning For Life (Case Study 1)*

ASCETT (1996) *Learning For Life (Case Study 2)*

ASCETT (1996) *Recommendations from Initial Consultation*

Association for Learning Technology (1996) *Submission to the National Committee of Inquiry into Higher Education*

Association of European Universities (1996) *Restructuring the University: Universities and the Challenge of New Technology*

Association of Graduate Careers Advisory Services (1996) *What Do Graduates Do?*

Association of Graduate Recruiters (1995) *Skills for Graduates in the 21st Century*

Association of Scottish Colleges (1996) *Higher Education in Scottish FE Colleges (Issues for the Scottish Committee of Inquiry on Higher Education)*

Australian Government Publishing Service (1995) *Quality and Standards of Management Education*

Australian National University (undated) *Conceptual Issues and the Australian Experience with Income Contingent charges for HE*, Centre for Economic Policy Research

Australian Vice-Chancellors' Committee (1995) *Report of the Academic Standards Panel: Computer Science*

Australian Vice-Chancellors' Committee (1990) *Report of the Academic Standards Panel: History*

Australian Vice-Chancellors' Committee (1995) *Report of the Academic Standards Panel: Physics*

Australian Vice-Chancellors' Committee (1995) *Report of the Academic Standards Panel: English*

AUT (1995) *Higher Education: Preparing for the 21st century*, Association of University Teachers (AUT)

AUT (1996) *Efficiency gains or quality losses?: How Falling Investment affects Higher Education's Capacity to Contribute to the UK's Economic Success*

AUT Scotland (undated) *Higher Education under a Scottish Parliament*

Bach R (1970) *Jonathan Livingston Seagull, a story*, Pan Books, London

Bahram B (undated) *Music in Higher Education Symposium Report: "Funding for Teaching and Research in HE Music"*, Incorporated Society of Musicians

Baker K (1989) *Higher Education The next 25 years*, DES, HMSO

Baker K (1989) *Science Policy: The way ahead*, DES, HMSO

Ball C (1990) *More Means Different: Widening Access to Higher Education*, Industry Matters

Barnett R (1997) *A Higher Education Curriculum for a New Century*, Institute of Education, London

Barnett R (undated) *Towards a Higher Education for a New Century*, Institute of Education, London

Beachcroft Stanleys, *Education Law Bulletin*

Bell E, Dryden W, Noonan E & Thorne B (undated) *A Guide to Recognising Best Practice in Counselling*, Association for Student Counselling

Bienayme A (1989) *French Higher Education*

Birch W (1984) *An enquiry into the changing relationship between higher education and society*

Birch W (1988) *The Challenge to Higher Education: Reconciling Responsibilities to Scholarship and to Society*, The Society for Research into Higher Education & Open University Press

Blaug M (1990) *The Economic Value of Higher Education*, Netherlands Institute for the Advanced Study in the Humanities and Social Sciences, Institute of the Royal Netherlands Academy of Arts and Sciences

Bolton N, Stephens K & Unwin L (1996) *The Role of the Library in Postgraduate Distance Learning: A Research Project Funded by the British Library 1994–1996 Student Experiences: Evidence from a Questionnaire Survey*, University of Sheffield

Boxall M, Temple P & Whitchurch C (1991) *Cheques and Balances*, CUA

Boyle M (undated) *Managing Change through Student Involvement in EHE*

Bremer L (1995) *Financing and effects of internationalization in higher education*, NUFFIC

Brennan J, Little B (1996) *A Review of Work Based Learning in Higher Education*, Quality Support Centre, The Open University.

Brennan J, Lyon S, Schomburg H & Teichler U (undated) *Employment and Work of British and German Graduates*

Brennan J, Shah T & Williams R (1996) *Quality Assessment and Quality Improvement: An Analysis of the Recommendations Made by HEFCE Assessors*

Brice P (1996) *Checkout HE*, UNL

Brinkmann H (1994) *An Overview of German Developments* in Westerheijden D F et al, *Changing Contexts of Quality Assessment*, CHEPS

British Council and The Scottish Office (undated) *Guide to Education and Training in Scotland*

British Telecommunications plc (1997) *Evidence to the Information Technology Working Group of the National Committee of Inquiry into Higher Education*

Brown R (undated) A Single System?: *Speech by Dr Roger Brown Chief Executive Higher Education Quality Council*, SRHE Forum

Brown R (undated) *Quality Issues of Today and Tomorrow*, AUA Conference

Brown R (undated) *The Challenge of Quality in Higher Education*, HEQC

Bruce E M (1996) *Careers Curriculum Capability – Conference Papers*, Career Guidance and Capability Project, Leeds Metropolitan University

Bureau of Statistics (1996) *Education in the Republic of China*, Republic of China

Burke J (1995) *Outcomes, Learning and the Curriculum Implications for NVQs, GNVQs and other qualifications*, The Falmer Press

Buss D (1995) *The Impact of Modularity on Art and Design in Higher Education*, University of Plymouth

Cabinet Office, Office of Public Service & Science (1995) *The Director General of Research Councils' Review of the Science Budget Portfolio*, Office of Science & Technology

Cable Communications Association(1996), *Cable Industry Internet Offer for Schools: One Price, Unlimited Access* (press release)

Caesar's Bridge (1996) *Quarterly Newsletter of the European Schools for Advanced Engineering Education and Research*, 1196/2

Campbell I C (1996) *The Changing Face of Higher Education in the UK: A Revolution in Progress*, Institute of Psychiatry, University of London

Campbell-Savours D (undated) *The Case for the University of the Lakes*, Firepress Printers Limited

Carney M (undated) *Assessment in EHE*

Carney M (undated) *Employer Involvement in EHE*

Carney M (undated) *Teaching and Learning in EHE*

Carswell J (undated) *Government and the Universities in Britain: Programme and Performance 1960-1980*

Carter J & Withrington D (1992) *Scottish Universities Distinctiveness and Diversity*, John Donald Publishers Ltd

Cave M (1996) *The Impact on Higher Education of Funding Changes and Increasing Competition*, Brunel University

CBI (undated) *Thinking Ahead: Ensuring the expansion of higher education into the 21st Century*, Confederation of British Industry

CBI (1995) *Realising the Vision: A Skills Passport*

CBI (1996) *Human Resources Brief,* The CBI input to the National Committee of Inquiry into Higher Education (1996)

CBI/NatWest Innovation Trends survey (1996) Issue 7

CHEPS, HIS, CNAA (1992) *European Higher Education Systems*

Consumers' Association (1991) The Citizen's Charter: A Consumer Perspective

CIHE (1990) *Collaborative courses in higher education: expanding the partnership with industry,* Council for Industry in Higher Education (CIHE)

CIHE (undated) *Towards a Partnership: The Business Contribution to Higher Education*

CIHE and OST (1996) *University/Company Interaction: A Review*

Coffield F et al (1995) *Higher Education in a Learning Society,* School of Education, University of Durham

Coffield F et al (1996) *Higher Education and Lifelong Learning,* Department of Education, University of Newcastle upon Tyne

Coleman J A (1996) *Studying Languages A Survey of British and European Students,* CiLT

Commission on Scottish Education (1996) *Learning to Succeed in Scotland: A radical look at Education Today and A Strategy for the Future: Report of the Commission on Scottish Education*

Committee of Scottish University Principals (CSUP) (1992) *Teaching and Learning in an Expanding Higher Education System,* Edinburgh

Committee of University Chairmen (undated) Guide for Members of Governing Bodies of Universities and Colleges in England and Wales, HEFCE

Competitiveness: Creating the enterprise centre of Europe (1996) HMSO

Competitiveness Forging Ahead (1995) HMSO

Comptroller and Auditor General National Audit Office (1994) *The Financial Health of Higher Education Institutions in England,* HMSO

Computers in Teaching Initiative (1996) " . . . laying the foundations for change": *Annual Report 1994-95,* CTISS Publications

Confederation of British Industry (1995) *A Vision for our Future: A Skills Passport,* London

Connor H & Jagger N (1994) *The Labour Market for Postgraduates,* IMS, Report 257

Connor H and Pollard E (1996) *What do graduates really do?* The Institute for Employment Studies

Connor H, Court G & Morris S (1994) *The Training Benefits of Big Science IES,* Report 275

Connor H, Court G, Seccombe I & Jagger N (1994) *Science PhDs and The Labour Market,* IES, Report 266

Connor H, Hillage J & Moralee J (1996) *The Interface Between Employers and HEIs: A Research Review, Draft Final Report,* IES

Consortium of Telematics for Education (COTE) (1997) *Information Technology-Assisted Teaching and Learning in UK Higher Education: Main Report and Summary*

Cooke P et al (undated) *Innovating by Networking in North Rhine-Westphalia,* Interim Report to the European Commission DGXIII

Cooper R (1996) *Networking – The Key to Exploiting the Full Potential of Information Technology in Higher Education*, UKERNA

Cooper (1996) *Networking – The Key to Exploiting the Full Potential of Information Technology in Higher Education*

Coopers & Lybrand (1996) *Evaluation of the Teaching and Learning Technology Programme*

Coopers & Lybrand (1996) *Universities and Colleges Admissions Service: Study into the Administration of Mandatory Students Awards*

Coopers & Lybrand (1996) *The budgetary implications of education and training in the member states of the European Union: Part II – the national reports*, Draft report to DG XXII of the European Commission

Cormack R, Gallagher A & Osborne R (1996) *Higher Education Participation in Northern Ireland*, Centre for Research on Higher Education

COSHEP (1996) *Higher Education in Scotland – A Vision for the Future: Submission to the Dearing Inquiry*, Committee of Scottish Higher Education Principals

COSHEP (1994) *Higher Still: Opportunity for all Proceedings of the COSHEP Seminar University of Strathclyde 28 Oct 1994*

COSHEP (1995) *"A public and an economic good"*, Response to the DFE/SOED Review of Higher Education

COSHEP (1995) *First Annual Forum: The distinctiveness of Scottish Higher Education: the position today and future prospects*

COSHEP (1996) *Public Expenditure Survey 1996 Statement of Key Funding Priorities*

COSHEP (1997) *Statement on Higher Still and Higher Education*

COSHEP (undated) *Signpost to Higher Education in Scotland*

COSHEP/SHEFC (1993) *Review of the Academic Year, Final Report – Scotland: Scottish Advisory Group on the Academic Year*

COSHEP/SHEFC (1996) *Assessment Strategies in Scottish Higher Education, Third Progress Report to the COSHEP Steering Committee*

Council of Economic Advisers (1995) *Supporting Research and Development to Promote Economic Growth: The Federal Government's Role*

Council of Europe (1996) *Access for under-represented groups: Volume II Report on Western Europe*

Council of Europe (1996) *Participation in higher education in Europe*

Court G & Connor H (1994) *The US Labour Market for New Graduates*, IMS, Report 267

Court G, Jagger N & Connor H (1995) The IES Annual Graduate Review, 1995-96 IES, Report 296

Coyne W E (1996) *The UK Innovation Lecture 5 March 1996: "Building a Tradition of Innovation"*, DTI

Cozzens S E, Ziman J, van der Meulen B & Rip A (1995) *Using Basic Research National Bodies for Linking Basic Research with Socio-Economic Objectives in the USA, UK, The Netherlands, Germany and France An Occasional Paper of the Centre for Research Policy*, University of Wollongong

Crawford R ed. (1997) *A Future for Scottish Higher Education*, COSHEP

CSUP (1992) *Teaching and Learning in an Expanding Higher Education System The Committee of Scottish University Principals*

CSV (1995) *Learning Together – Student tutoring*, Community Service Volunteers

CSV (1995) *Learning Together – The Added Value of Student Tutors Volunteering in Schools*

CSV (undated) *A Guide to Community Service Learning*

CSV (undated) *It All Adds Up*

CUC (undated) *Guide for Members of Governing Bodies of Universities and Colleges in England and Wales*, Committee of University Chairmen

CVCP (1996) *Joint Planning Group for Quality Assurance in Higher Education*, Committee of Vice-Chancellors and Principals

CVCP (1996) *Learning for Change – building a university system for a new century*

CVCP (1996) *Our Universities, Our Future;* Evidence to the National Committee of Inquiry into Higher Education

CVCP (1996) *Sport in Higher Education*

CVCP (1996) *Universities in the United Kingdom*

CVCP (1997) *Guide to CVCP*

Daniel J (undated) *How Can Mass Higher Education of Quality be made Affordable?*, The Open University

Daniel J (1996) *How Can Mass Higher Education Of Quality Be Made Available*

Daniel (1995) *The Mega-Universities and the Knowledge Media: Implications of new technologies for large distance teaching universities*

Darby J & Martin J (1995) *Active Learning: Teaching with Multimedia*, CTI, Number 3

Darby J & Martin J (1995) *Active Learning: Using the Internet for Teaching*, CTI, Number 2

Davey B (1992) *The Student Charter Project Report*, Department of Employment's Enterprise in Higher Education Initiative

Davie G (1964) *The Democratic Intellect*

Dearden G, Evans N (1995) *Curriculum Opportunity: AP(E)L in Higher Education: The Characteristics and Achievements of some University Students*, Learning from Experience Trust (2nd Edition)

Deloitte & Touche, (1996) *JANET Value for Money Study*

Delors J (1996) *Learning: the treasure within*, Report to UNESCO of the International Commission on Education for the Twenty-first Century, United Nations Educational, Scientific and Cultural Organisation, France

DENI, HEFCE, HEFCW, SHEFC (1997) *Management Information for Decision Making: Costing Guidelines for Higher Education Institutions*

DES (1989) *Shifting the Balance of Public Funding of Higher Education to Fees: A Consultation Paper*, Department for Education and Science

DFE (undated) *Higher Quality and Choice The Charter for Higher Education*, Department for Education

DFE (1994) *Science and Maths – A Consultation Paper on the Supply and Demand of Newly Qualified Young People*

DfEE (1994) *Higher Education in the 1990s*, Department for Education and Employment

DfEE (1995) *Development Publications in Higher Education*

DfEE (1995) *HE Review – Continuing Education Data*

DfEE (1995) *Students' Unions: A Guide*

DfEE (1995) *The English Education System: an overview of structure and policy*

DfEE (1996) *Competitiveness: Creating the Enterprise Centre of Europe Learning and Skills Extract of Command Paper Cm 3300*

DfEE (1996) *Competitiveness: Creating the enterprise centre of Europe, Summary*

DfEE (1996) *Competitiveness: Occasional Paper, The Skills Audit: A Report from an Interdepartmental Group, Summary*

DfEE (1996) *Funding 16-19 Education and Training: Towards Convergence*

DfEE (1996) *Welsh Higher Education Credit Framework Handbook*

DFEE (1996) *Learning to Compete: Education and Training for 14-19 Year Olds*

DfEE (1996) *Lifetime Learning: A Policy Framework*, HMSO

DfEE (1996) *PFI in Higher Education*, Report to the Secretary of State, The Joint DfEE/HE Sector Working Group

DfEE (1996) *The Effects of Public Funding on Higher Education Institutions: Report to the Secretary of State*, The Joint DfEE/HE Sector Working Group

DfEE (1997) *Progression From Modern Apprenticeships into Higher Levels of Qualification*, Marque Associates

DfEE (undated) *Choice and Opportunity a Learning Future for 14-19 year olds*

DfEE (undated) *Competitiveness – Creating the Enterprise Centre of Europe; Learning and skills*, Extract of Command Paper Cm 3300

DfEE (undated) *Working with Higher Education: What's in it for your business?* HMSO

DfEE (1996) *Student Grants and Loans: A Brief Guide for Higher Education Students 1996/97*

Dodge J & Whitchurch C (undated) *Total Quality Matters*, CUA

Doing Well by our Children? Why Choice is not Enough (1991) Consumer Policy Review, Volume 1, Number 4

Dolton P, Greenaway D & Vignoles A (1996) *Whither Higher Education? An Economic Perspective for the Dearing Committee of Inquiry*

Drivers J (1995) *WFCHE: Capital Needs Study of Academic Accommodation*

DTI (1995) *Survey of Industry-University Research Links*

DTI, CBI (1994) *Competitiveness – How the Best UK Companies are WINNING*, HMSO

DTL (1996) *The UK R&D Scoreboard*, Company Reporting Limited

EBP National Network (1997) *Network News Leaflet*

Economic Research Council (1995) *Britain & Overseas: A Digest of News and Views on Britain's Economy and our Role in Overseas Trade and Payments*, Vol.25, No.4

Education Programmes Europe (1996) *European Education Programmes: Ford Automotive Operations*, I.T.D. Publications

Education Statistics for the United Kingdom 1995, HMSO

Ennis P & White J (undated) *An Auditor calls: Internal Audit explained. A guide for Budget Holders*, Association of University Administrators

ERC Centre for Business Research (1996) *The Changing State of British Enterprise*

European Commission (1995) *Structures of the Education and Initial Training Systems in the European Union*

European Commission (1995) *Structures of the Education and Initial Training Systems in the European Union (2nd edition)* EURYDICE

Evaluation of the National Record of Achievement in Scotland in *Managing HE*, GNP Booth Ltd

Everett M & Morris C (1994) *The Recruitment of UK Graduates to work in Continental Europe*, IMS, Report 248

Federal Ministry of Education, Science, Research and Technology (1996) *Basic and Structural Data 1995/96*, Germany

Federal Ministry of Education, Science, Research and Technology (1994) *The Fachhochschulen*, Germany

Federal Ministry of Education, Science, Research and Technology (1996) *Higher Education in Germany*

FEFC (1996) *Blackburn College: Report from the Inspectorate*, Further Education Funding Council

FEFC (1996) *Report of the Learning and Technology Committee*

FEFC (1996) *Inclusive Learning: Principles and Recommendations A Summary of the Findings of the Learning Difficulties and/or Disabilities Committee*

Fehrman C & Westling H (undated) *Lund and Learning: An informal history of Lund University*, Lund University Press

FitzGerald P (1994) *Higher Education: Making Reality of More for Less*

FitzGerald P (1996) *Survey of New Learning Methods: UK Business Schools*

Follet B (1993) *Joint Funding Councils' Libraries Review Group: Report*

Ford P et al (undated) *Managing Change in Higher Education: A Learning Environment Architecture*, The Society for Research into Higher Education and Open University Press

Forster F, Hounsell D & Thompson S (1995) *Tutoring and Demonstrating: A Handbook*, Centre for Teaching, Learning and Assessment

Forward Look of Government-funded Science, Engineering and Technology 1995 (1995) HMSO

Fraser W (undated) *Final Report*, Joint Planning Group for Quality Assurance in Higher Education

Frazer M J (undated) *Higher Education in Four Cycles*

Frazer M J (undated) *Higher Level Vocational Qualifications: The Role of Higher Education* QSC

Free Your Potential Employers guide 2nd edition, The Scottish Office

Freeman R (1996) The UK R&D Scoreboard 1996: *"Innovation – The Successful Exploitation of New Ideas"*, DTI

Association of MBAs: (undated) *Guide to Business Schools*, FT Pitman Publishing

Gallagher A M, Osborne R D & Cormack R J (undated) *Attitudes to Higher Education, Report to CCRU and DENI*, Centre for Research on Higher Education

Gallagher A, Richards N & Locke M (1993) *Mature Students in Higher Education: How Institutions can Learn from Experience*, CIS Commentary Series, No 40, Second Edition

Gareth W (1996) *Paying For Education Beyond Eighteen: An Examination of Issues and Options*, Council for Industry and Higher Education

Gellert C (1993) *Higher Education in Europe*, Jessica Kingsley Publications

Goddard J B (undated) *Universities, Communities and Regeneration: An Overview*

Goddard J, Charles D, Pike A, Potts G & Bradley D (1994) *Universities and Communities*, CVCP

Godwin S & Vosper D (1995) *Income Generation in the University and College Sector*, HEIST

Goodland S & Hirst B (1989) *Peer Tutoring: A Guide to Learning by Teaching*, Kogan Page, London

Goodland S (undated) *The Quest for Quality: Sixteen Forms of Heresy in Higher Education*, SRHE and Open University Press

Greenaway D & Tuck J (undated) *Economic Impact of International Students in UK Higher Education: A Report for the Committee of Vice-Chancellors and Principals*, CVCP

HM Treasury (1996) *Free Labour Market: Key to Job Creation and Opportunity for All*

Harri-Augstein E S & Thomas L F (1988) *Constructing environments that enable self-organised learning: the principles of Intelligent Support* from "*Experimenting with Personal Construct Psychology*", Routledge

Harri-Augstein E S & Thomas L F (1988) *Software for use in Self-organised Learning Environments: the practice of Intelligent Support* from "*Experimenting with Personal Construct Psychology*", Routledge

Harri-Augstein S & Thomas L (1995) *On Becoming a Learning Organisation*, SHL

Harri-Augstein S & Webb I M (1995) *Learning to Change, A Resource for Trainers, Managers and Learners based on Self-Organised Learning*, McGraw-Hill Book Company

Harri-Augstein S, Smith M & Thomas L (1982) *Reading to Learn*, Methuen

Harris M (1996) *Review of Postgraduate Education*, HEFCE, CVCP & SCOP

Harris R I D (1996) *The Impact of the University of Portsmouth On the Local Economy*

Hartingsveld L M van (1994) *Looking inside the Black Box: Aspects of Quality Assessment in Higher Vocational Education in the Netherlands*, in Westerheijden D F et al, *Changing Contexts of Quality Assessment*, CHEPS

Harvey L et al (1997) *Graduates' Work: Organisational change and student's attributes*, Centre for research into Quality, The University of Central England in Birmingham

Hay M & Abbott S (undated) *Investing for the future*

HEFCE (1995) *Average Units of Council Funding for Academic Year 1994–95*, Higher Education Funding Council for England

HEFCE (1996) *Funding Method for Teaching – from 1998–99*

HEFCE (1993) *Fund for the Development of Teaching and Learning: Phase Two, Circular 22/96*

HEFCE (1993) *Joint Funding Councils' Libraries Review Group: Report*

HEFCE (1993) *Teaching and Learning Technology Programme*

HEFCE (1994) *Introduction to the Higher Education Funding Council for England*

HEFCE (1995) *Higher Education in Further Education Colleges: Funding the Relationship*

HEFCE (1995) *Private Investment in higher education*

HEFCE (1995) *Review of Higher Education: Submission by the Higher Education Funding Council for England*

HEFCE (1996) *Best Practice in Collaboration between Higher Education Institutions and Training and Enterprise Councils*

HEFCE (1996) *A Guide to Funding Higher Education in England: How the HEFCE Allocates its Funds 1996–97*

HEFCE (1996) *Access to Higher Education: Students with Learning Difficulties and Disabilities, A Report on the 1993/94 and 1994/95 HEFCE Special Initiatives to Encourage Widening Participation for Students with Disabilities*

HEFCE (1996) *Analysis of 1996 Financial Forecasts*

HEFCE (1996) *Arrangements for Quality Assessment Visits between October 1997 and June 1998*

HEFCE (1996) *Average Units of Funding for the Academic Year 1995–96*

HEFCE (1996) *Challenge and Achievement: HEFCE Annual Report 1995–96*

HEFCE (1996) *Circular 9/96, Special Initiative to Encourage High Quality Provision for Students with Learning Difficulties and Disabilities*

HEFCE (1996) *Consultation 2/96 Funding Method for Research*

HEFCE (1996) *Differentiated Tuition Fees 1996–97*

HEFCE (1996) *Energy Management Study in the Higher Education Sector: Management Review Guide*

HEFCE (1996) *Funding Method for Teaching July 1996*, Consultation 1/96

HEFCE (1996) *Circular 21/96 Funding Method for Teaching from 1998–99*

HEFCE (1996) *Circular 8/96 Specification for Disability Statements required from Institutions*

HEFCE (1996) *Higher Education in Further Education Colleges: A Future Funding Approach*

HEFCE (1996) *Institutions' Strategic Plans: Analysis of 1996 Submissions*

HEFCE (1996) *Overseas Research Students Award Scheme (ORSAS) Policy Review*

HEFCE (1996) *Procurement Strategy for Higher Education September 1996*

HEFCE (1996) *Recurrent Grant for the Academic Year 1996–97: Final Allocations*

HEFCE (1996) *Review of Postgraduate Education*

HEFCE (1996) *Subject Overview Report QO 1/96 Quality Assessment of Chemical Engineering 1995/96*

HEFCE (1996) *Subject Overview Report QO 2/96 Quality Assessment of French 1995/96*

HEFCE (1996) *Subject Overview Report QO 3/96 Quality Assessment of German and Related Languages 1995/96*

HEFCE (1996) *Subject Overview Report QO 4/96 Quality Assessment of Iberian Languages and Studies 1995/96*

HEFCE (1996) *Subject Overview Report QO 5/96 Quality Assessment of Italian 1995/96*

HEFCE (1996) *Subject Overview Report QO 6/96 Quality Assessment of Linguistics 1995/96*

HEFCE (1996) *Subject Overview report QO 7/96 Quality Assessment of Russian and Eastern European Languages and Studies 1995/96*

HEFCE (1996) *Subject Overview Report QO 8/96 Quality Assessment of Sociology 1995/96*

HEFCE (1996) *Treasury Management Study in the Higher Education Sector: Management Review Guide*

HEFCE (1996) *Treasury Management Value for Money: National Report*

HEFCE (1996) *Widening Access to Higher Education A Report to the HEFCE's Advisory Group on Access and Participation*

HEFCE (1996) *Analysis of 1996 Financial Forecasts, Circular 15/96*

HEFCE (1996/97) Circular *Differentiated Tuition Fees*

HEFCE (1996/97) *Redistribution of HEFCE Funding for Teaching for the Academic Year 1996–97*

HEFCE (1997) *Fund for the Development of Teaching and Learning, Phase One*

HEFCE (1997) *Comparison of HEFCE Aggregate Student Returns and HESA Individual Student Data*

HEFCE (1997) *Mid-Year Financial Return*

HEFCE (1997) *Recurrent Grants for the Academic Year 1997/98*

HEFCE (1997) *Report on Quality Assessment 1995–96*

HEFCE (1997) *Subject/Programme Review in England and Northern Ireland between October 1998 and September 2000*

HEFCE, SHEFC, HEFCW and DENI (1996) *Research Assessment Exercise – The Outcome*

HEFCE, SHEFC, HEFCW and DENI (1996) *Research Assessment Exercise; Membership of Assessment Panels*

HEFCE (1996) *Strategic Plans and Financial Forecasts*

HEFCE (1996) *Method of Calculation of Holdback of HEFCE Grant 1996-97 September 1996, Circular 13/96*

HEFCW (1993) *The Council's Method for the Recurrent Funding of Teaching Consultation*, Higher Education Funding Council for Wales

HEFCW (1994) *The Assessment of Quality in the Higher Education Sector in Wales Future Directions*

HEFCW (1994) *Report of the Research Group*

HEFCW (1995) *Corporate Plan 1995–96 to 1998–99*

HEFCW (1995) *Higher Education Student Enrolments in Wales 1994/95*

HEFCW (1995) *Higher Education in Britain and Ireland Present and Future Policies: Wales*

HEFCW (1995) *Report of the Welsh Medium Provision Working Group*

HEFCW (1996) *HEFCW Annual Report*

HEFCW (1996) *Recurrent Grant 1996/97*

HEFCW (1996) *Teaching and Learning Practices*

HEFCW *Funding Outcomes 1994–95*

HEIST (1996) *Marketing Services for Universities and Colleges: Information Pack*

Hemmings P (1997) *Evidence to the Information Technology Working Group of the National Committee of Inquiry into Higher Education*, Research Machines plc

HEQC (1996) *Choosing to Change, Extending Access, Choice and Mobility in Higher Education*, Higher Education Quality Council (HEQC) (1995) *Graduate Standards Programme: Interim Report*

HEQC (1995) *Vocational Qualifications and Standards: In Focus*

HEQC (1996) *A Single System of Academic Quality Assurance*

HEQC (1996) *Academic Standards in the Approval, Review and Classification of Degrees*

HEQC (1996) *Graduate Standards Programme: Threshold and other academic standards*

HEQC (1996) *Graduate Standards Programme: Understanding Academic Standards In Modular Frameworks*

HEQC (1996) *Guidelines on Quality Assurance*

HEQC (1996) *Graduate Standards Programme: Threshold and other academic standards*

HEQC (1996) *Graduate Standards Programme: Understanding Academic Standards In Modular Frameworks*

HEQC (1996) *Guidelines on Quality Assurance*

HEQC (1996) *Threshold and Other Academic Standards: The Views Of Four Subject Groups*

HEQC (undated) *The Scottish Credit Accumulation and Transfer Framework – An Organising Framework for Higher Education in Scotland*

HEQC Scottish Office (1996) *Scottish Credit Accumulation & Transfer Framework An overview*

HESA (1995) *Data Report: Students in Higher Education Institutions, 1995–96,* Higher Education Statistics Agency

HESA (1995) *Higher Education Statistics for the United Kingdom 1992/93*

HESA (1996) *First Destinations of Students Leaving Higher Education Institutions 1994/95*

HESA (1996) *Higher Education Management Statistics – Sector Level 1994/95*

HESA (1996) *Resources of Higher Education Institutions Reference Volume 1994/95*

HESA (1996) *Supplement to Research Datapack 4. HE Management Statistics – Institution Level*

HESA (1996) *The Shape and Size of Higher Education in the mid-1990's*

Higher Education A New Framework (1991) HMSO

Higher Education and Disability: The Guide to Higher Education for People with Disabilities 1997 (1996) Hobsons Publishing

Higher Education and Equality: a Guide (1997) Equal Opportunities Commission, Commission for Racial Equality and CVCP

Higher Education Management Review (1995) Report of the Committee of Inquiry under the chairmanship of Mr David Hoare, Australian Government Publishing Service, Canberra

Higher Still (1995) Guidance Arrangements consultation document

Higher Still (1995) Implementation Studies in Schools

Higher Still (1995) Nomenclature

Higher Still (1995) Provision for Students with Special Educational Needs consultation document

Higher Still (1996) Responding to Consultation: Principles for the Post-16 Curriculum and Core Skills

Higher Still (1995) The Development Programme Plan

Higher Still (1995) The Interim Period

Highly Qualified People: Supply and Demand Report of an Interdepartmental Review (1990) HMSO

Hillage J, Hyndley K & Pike G (1995) *Employers' Views of Education Business Links,* IES, Report 283

Hirsh W, Jackson C & Jackson C (1995) *Careers in Organisations: Issues for the Future,* IES, Report 287

HMI (1991) *Aspects of Higher Education in the Federal Republic of Germany: The Fachochshulen*

Hodl E (1994) *Measures of Reform of Higher Education in Nordrhine-Westfalia,* in OECD, *Evaluation and Decision-making in Higher Education*

Hogarth T, et al (undated) *The Participation of Non-Traditional Students in HE,* University of Warwick

Hokkaido University (1995) *A Brief Sketch of Hokkaido University*

Holt T, Skene P & Priestley C (undated) *Discretionary Grants for Certain Students of Dance and Drama,* The Arts Council of England

Horsley M (1995) *Conservative Political Centre National Policy Group on Higher Education*

House of Lords Select Committee on Science and Technology (1996) *Information Society: Agenda for Action in the UK*

House of Lords, Select Committee on Science and Technology (1995) *Academic Research Careers for Graduate Scientists Report,* 4th Report, HMSO

Howieson C, Raffe D, Spours K and Young M (undated) *Unifying Academic and Vocational Learning: The State of the Debate in England and Scotland, Working Paper 1 of the Unified Learning Project*

Inclusive Learning: Report of the Learning Difficulties and Disabilities Committee (1996) HMSO

Industry and Parliament Trust (undated) *Employability Themes and Issues Paper*

Information Society: Agenda for Action in the UK (1996) HMSO

Institute for Employment Studies (1996) *The FE/HE Interface: a UK Perspective*

Institute for Employment Studies (undated) *University Challenge: Student Choices in the 21st Century (A report to the CVCP)*

Institute for Employment Studies (undated) *The Interface Between Employers and HEIs: A Research Review*

Institute of Manpower Studies (undated) *The US Labour Market for New Graduates; What do graduates really do?; The target for higher level skills in an international context; The IES Annual Graduate Review, 1995–96; University Challenge: Student choices in the 21st Century,* IMS

Institute of Physics (1996) *Degree Accreditation Scheme*

International Business Machines (1996) *Living in the Information Society*

Jackson C, Honey S, Hillage J & Stock J (1994) *Careers and Training in Dance and Drama,* IMS, Report 268

Jackson R (1996) *Academic Staffing: Problems and prospects,* DES, HMSO

Jallade J-P, Lamoure J & Lamoure Rontopoulou J L (1993) *Tertiary Diversification in France and the Conditions of Access,* in Gellert ed., *Higher Education in Europe*

Jenkins H (1995) *Education and Production in the United Kingdom: Discussion Paper No. 101,* Nuffield College, Oxford

JISC (1996) *Five Year Strategy 1996 – 2001,* Joint Information Systems Committee

JISC (1995) *Exploiting Information Systems in Higher Education: An Issues Paper*

JISC (1996) *Electronic Libraries Programme*

JISC (1996) *Five Year Strategy 1996–2001*

John Baillie 2nd & 3rd Memorial Lectures (undated) NATFHE

John Baillie Memorial Lecture – Designing a Coherent System of Post-16 Education and Training (undated) NATFHE

Johnstone M, McLaughlin P, Munn P & Sharp S (undated) *The 1993–94 Programme of Quality Assessments: Perceptions of Operational and Administrative Procedures: A Survey of Assessors & Institutions assessed carried out on behalf of the Scottish Higher Education Funding Council*, SHEFC

Joynson M & Wood J (undated) *This Committee Business*, CUA

Kapture-Blatt K (1996) *University Programs (Degree Programs for Ford Employees)*, Ford University Programs Group, Education, Training and Development

Kapur N (undated) *Kaleidoscope: Racial Equality in Graduate Employment* Henrietta Morrison

Kay, J (1993) *Foundations of Corporate Success, How business strategies add value*, Oxford University Press

Keen C & Greenall J (1987) *Public Relations Management*, HEIST

Keen C & Higgins T (undated) *Young People's Knowledge of Higher Education*, HEIST/PCAS

Keen C & Warner D (Eds) (1989) *Visual & Corporate Identity*, HEIST

Keen C & Higgins T (1992) *Adults' Knowledge of Higher Education*, HEIST/PCAS

Kerr G (undated) *People Managing*, CUA

Kouwenaar K (1989) *Higher Education in the Netherlands*

Labour Party (1996) *Aiming Higher, Labour's plans for reform of the 14-19+ curriculum*

Labour Party (1996) *Lifelong Learning: A consultation document*

Lambert P (1996) *Students as lifelong learners; factors considered in developing a multi-media guidance pack for adults choosing university*, Liverpool John Moores University

LaRocque N (1996) *Developments in the Higher Education Sector in New Zealand*, Social Policy and Government Services Branch, The New Zealand Treasury

Laurillard D (1993) *Rethinking University Teaching*, Routledge, London

Leigh C (1997) Best Practice in Collaboration between Higher Education Institutions and Training and Enterprise Councils, HEFCE

Letham R & Hill P (undated) *Appraising People*, CUA

Levey M & Mackenzie K (1993) *The Class of '92: Report on a Longitudinal Study Of Graduate Destinations*, Scottish Graduate Careers Partnership

Lewis R & Merton B (1996) *Technology for Learning: Where Are We Going?*, BP International Limited/University of Lincolnshire and Humberside

Liberal Democrats (1996) *The Key to Lifelong Learning Proposals for Tertiary Education in England and Wales*, Policy Paper 18

Lifetime learning: A consultation document (1996) DfEE, The Scottish Office & The Welsh Office

London Economics (1993) *Review of Options for the Additional Funding of Higher Education*

Lord Chancellor's Advisory Committee on Legal Education and Conduct (1996) *First Report on Legal Education and Training*

Lynn P (1996) *The 1994 Leavers (SSLS)*, The Scottish Office Education and Industry Department

Maassen P & Weusthof J M (1989) *Quality Assessment in Dutch Higher Education*

Maassen P, Goedegebuure L C J & Westerheijden D F (1993) *Social and Political Conditions for the Emerging Tertiary Structures in the Netherlands*, in Gellert ed., *Higher Education in Europe*

MacFarlane A G J (1996) *Future Patterns of Teaching and Learning*

MacGregor J (1990) *The Future of Higher Education*, The Bloomfield Memorial Lecture, DES, HMSO

Mallaband A (1996) *A Review of the Literature and Reports on the Use Made by Employers of Graduates and other Higher Education Leavers*, University of Sheffield

Marceau J F (1993) *Steering from a Distance*

Martin B (1995) *University/Industry Interaction*, Engineering and Physical Sciences Research Council

Martin B R (1995) *Technology Foresight: The Nurturing of the UK Skills Base*, Science Policy Research Unit

Mauch J E & Sabloff PLW (1995) *Reform and Change in Higher Education*, Garland

Marque Associates (1997) *Progression from modern apprenticeships into higher levels of qualification*, Final Report

McCallum D M (1985) *Future Strategy for Higher Education in Scotland*, HMSO

McEachan D (1993) *Graduate Employment in Scotland 1983–92*, Scottish Graduate Careers Programme

McNicoll I H (1995) *The Impact of the Scottish Higher Education Sector on the Economy of Scotland*, COSHEP

McNicoll I H (undated) *The Impact Of Income and Expenditure of the Further Education Sector on The Economy Of Scotland*, Department of Economics, University of Strathclyde

McPherson A (1994) *Is there still an untapped pool of ability?* Extract from *Insights into Education and Training Papers* selected by the National Commission on Education, Heinemann

McPherson A, Raffe, D & Robertson C (undated) *Highers and Higher Education*, Association of University Teachers (Scotland)

McVey B (1996) *The Business Birthrate Strategy*, Scottish Enterprise

Metcalf H (1992) *Non-Traditional Students' Experience of Higher Education: A Review of the Literature*, PSI

Metcalf, H (1993) *Non-Traditional Students' Experience of Higher Education: A Review of the Literature*, CVCP

Middlehurst R and Gordon G (1995) *Leadership, Quality and Institutional Effectiveness*, in *Higher Education Quarterly*, Volume 49, No. 3, July 1995

Ministry of Education (1993) *Everything you wanted to know about the Higher Education and Research Act*, Netherlands

Ministry of Education (1994) *The French Education System: Background report to the OECD*

Ministry of Education (1996) *Draft HOOP 1996 : Towards a Varied and Compact System of Higher Education*, Netherlands

Ministry of Education (1996) *Education Statistical Indicators*, Republic of China

Ministry of Education (undated) *Educational Report of the Republic of China on Taiwan – Perceptions of Education towards the 21st Century*, Republic of China

Monbusho (1995) *Ministry of Education, Science, Sports and Culture*, Government of Japan

Moser C (1996) *Our Educational Future: Priorities and Politics Lecture*, The Royal Society of Arts

Muller S ed. (1996) *Universities in the twenty-first century*, Berghahn Books, Oxford

NAPAG (1996) *Research Capability of the University System*, National Academies Policy Advisory Group

NATFHE (1996) *Fair and Equal Reward: NATFHE's HE Pay and Conditions Claim*, National Association of Teachers in Further and Higher Education

NATFHE (1996) *Forward Look of Government Funded Science Engineering & Technology: Summary*

NATFHE (undated) *A New Partnership for Company Training*

NATFHE (undated) *Access Funds: 1996-7 Allocation and Terms and Conditions for Payment of Grant*

NATFHE (undated) *Building a Learning Society*

NATFHE (undated) *Economic Impact of International Students in UK Higher Education*

NATFHE (undated) *Evidence to the Further Education Funding Council Committee Chaired by John Tomlinson*

NATFHE (undated) *Evidence to the Nolan Committee*

NATFHE (undated) *GNVQs and Lecturer Workload*

NATFHE (undated) *Governance, Democracy and Accountability in Higher Education*

NATFHE (undated) *Internationalisation of Higher Education*

NATFHE (undated) *Lecturers' Workload and Factors Affecting Stress Levels*

NATFHE (undated) *Opening up the Institutions*

NATFHE (undated) *Procurement Strategy for Higher Education*

NATFHE (undated) *The Future Organisation of Post-School Education and Training*

NATFHE (undated) *The Network Programme Report 1995 – 1996*

NATFHE (1995) *Governance in Higher Education*

NAO (1996) *Space Management in Higher Education: A Good Practice Guide*, National Audit Office

NAO (1996) *The Management of Space in Higher Education Institutions in Wales*

NAO (1996) *The Management of Teaching and Research Equipment in Scottish Higher Education Institutions*

NAO (1997) *Governance and the Management of Overseas Courses at the Swansea Institute of Higher Education, Report by the Comptroller and Auditor General*

National Commission on Education (1993) *Learning to Succeed, A Radical Look at Education Today and A Strategy for the Future*, Heineman, London

National Commission on Education, Council for Industry and Higher Education (1994) *Universities in the Twenty-First Century: A Lecture Series*

National Conference of University Professors (undated) *The Case for Universities, Policy Document No. 6*

NACET (1996) *Seen IT in the USA*, National Council for Educational Technology

NIESR (1996) *54th Annual Report 1996*, National Institute of Economic and Social Research

NCVQ (1995) *GNVQs at Higher Level: a consultation paper*, National Council for Vocational Qualifications

NCVQ (1996) *GNVQs at Higher Levels: Response to Consultation*

NCVQ (1996) *GNVQs at Higher Levels: Consultation report*

NCVQ (1995) *GNVQ: Assessment Review Final Report of the Review Group: Chaired by John Capey*

Newstead S E (1996) *The Psychology of Student Assessment based on the Presidential Address delivered to the British Psychological Society's Annual Conference,* Brighton UK April 1996

NIACE (1993) *An Adult Higher Education A Vision*

NIHEC (1995) *Report of the Sub-Group on Access, Participation & Student Migration: Statistical Supplement,* Northern Ireland Higher Education Council

NIHEC (1995) *Report Migration*

NIHEC, *Annual Report 1993–94*

NIHEC, *Annual Report 1994–95*

NUS (1993) *The Right to Accommodation*

NUS (1993) *The Right to Good Teaching*

NUS (1993) *The Right to Learner Agreements*

NUS (1996) *Funding Students and their Education*

NUS (1996) *Opportunity, Diversity and Partnership – The Student Agenda for Higher Education: Submission to the National Committee of Inquiry into Higher Education,* National Union of Students

NUS (undated) *Student Charter*

O'Neill I (1995) *Taught Postgraduate Education: The Student Experience,* HEIST

O'Neill I (1995) *Undergraduates' Perceptions of Postgraduate Education,* HEIST

O'Neill I (1995) *Alumni Relations in UK Higher Education,* HEIST

OECD (1994) *Evaluation and Decision-making in Higher Education,* Organisation for Economic Co-operation and Development

OECD (1995) *Education at a Glance OECD Indicators*

Office for Technology Development (1996) *Technology Strategy for Academic Advantage*

Office of Telecommunications (OFTEL) (1997) *Response to the National Committee of Inquiry into Higher Education*

Open University (1993) *Validation Service Handbook for Validated Awards*

Open University (undated) *One Source for Information on Distance Learning Worldwide*

Open University (undated) *The International Centre for Distance Learning*

Open University, *Policy on Access to Network Services*

OST (1996) *Forward Look of Government-funded Science, Engineering and Technology,* Office of Science and Technology, HMSO

OST (1995) *Progress Through Partnership: Report from the Steering Group of the Technology Foresight Programme,* Office of Science and Technology, HMSO

OST (1995) *Report on initial experiences with the "Realising our potential Award" scheme (ROPA),* Office of Science and Technology, HMSO

OST (1996) *Allocation of the Science Budget 1996–97,* Office of Science and Technology, HMSO

OST (1996) *Foresight: First Progress Report 1996,* Office of Science and Technology, HMSO

OST (1996) *Engineering and Technology Statistics,* Office of Science and Technology, HMSO

Paterson L (1996) Trends in Higher Education Participation in Scotland in *Higher Education Quarterly*, 8 August 1996

PFI (1996) *Risk and Reward in PFI Contracts: "Practical Guidance on the Sharing of Risk and Structuring of PFI Contracts"*

Phillips T (1996) *London: Countdown to the Millennium*, LWT

Pieda plc (1996) *Higher Education in Northern Ireland, Springvale Campus & Urban Regeneration Economic Appraisal*

Police Foundation and the Policy Studies Institute (1996) *The Role and Responsibilities of the Police*, Latimer Trend & Co. Ltd

Policies for the next Government: Science and Technology (1996) SBS Memorandum

Polytechnics and Colleges Funding Council (1992) *Capital Funding and Estate Management in Higher Education Universities Funding Council*

Potter D (1996) *Information Technology and Higher Education: A Twenty Year View*, unpublished paper

Private Finance Panel (1996) *5 Steps to the Appointment of Advisers to PFI Projects: Tips on the Selection, Appointment and Management of Advisers to PFI Projects*

Puttnam D (undated) *The Creative Imagination* in *What Needs to Change: New Vision for Britain*

QSC (1996) *UK Higher Education in the 1990s,* Quality Support Centre

Ramsden B (undated) *Ethnic Minority Students and Teacher Training*, HEBA

Rau E (1993) *Inertia and Resistance to Change of the Humboldtian University*, in Gellert ed, *Higher Education in Europe*

Rawlinson S & Connor H (1995) *Developing Responsiveness: College-Employer Interaction*, IES, Report 300

Realising our potential: A Strategy for Science, Engineering and Technology (1993) HMSO

Reflections on the Enterprise in Higher Education Experience at the University of Leeds 1991-96 (1996) *Facilitating Change in Student Learning*

Regional Economic Consortium (undated) *Partnership Pays, People Thrive, Business Profit; Building Closer Links between Work and Education*

Reich R (1991) *The Work of Nations*, Simon & Schuster, London

Republic of South Africa National Commission for Higher Education (1996) *Governance and Decision Making for the 21st century*, De Montfort University

RICS (undated) *Degrees and Diplomas Accredited by the RICS*, Royal Institute of Chartered Surveyors

Roberts D & Higgins T (1992) *Higher Education: The Student Experience*, HEIST/PCAS

Robertson D (1994) *Proposals for an Associate Degree – The Search for the 'Missing Link' of British Higher Education*, Basil Blackwell Ltd

Robertson D (1995) *Education Policy Universities and the Public Interest, Time to strike a new bargain?* in *Renewal*, Vol. 3 No. 4

Robertson D (1995) *Funding Policy in Post-Compulsory Education: Debates and Perspectives*, OU Course Reader

Robertson D (1995) *Funding the Learning Society Democratic Participation and Flexibility for Adults* in *Adults Learning*

Robertson D (1995) *The Learning Bank Towards a Strategy for Investment in Post-Compulsory Education and Training*

Robertson D (1996) *2005 – The Changing Face of Higher Education: Golden and Doomsday Scenarios*, HEFCE Workshop on *Higher Education 2005+*, Liverpool, 30-31 January

Robertson D (1996) *Credit transfer and the Mobility of Credentials in UK Higher Education: The Evolution of Policies, Meanings and Purposes* in *J Education Policy*, Vol. 11, No.1

Robertson D (1996) *Universities and their Cash Crisis* in *Parliamentary Brief*, Vol 4, No. 5

Royal Holloway Conservative Students (1996) *A Sensible Approach to Higher Education funding*

Royal Institute of International Affairs (1996) *Unsettled Times; The 1996 Chatham House Forum Report*

Royal Society of Edinburgh and Scottish Enterprise (1996) *Commercialisation Enquiry: Final Research Report*

Ruben, T & Winn S (1995) *Report 95/9: The financial situation of students at the University of Brighton 1994/95*, Health and Social Policy Research Centre

Sachs J (1997) *The Politics of Hope*, Random House, London

Sandison P C (1996) *The Struggle for a Market in Higher Education*, University of Bath, School of Education

SBS (1996) *Policies for the Next Government: Science and Technology*

SCAA (1996) *Curriculum, Culture and Society*, School Curriculum and Assessment Authority

SCAA (1996) *The Contribution of Design and Technology to the Curriculum*, School Curriculum and Assessment Authority

SCAA (1997) *Information Technology, Communications and the Future Curriculum*

Schuller T ed. (1995) *The changing university?* The Society for Research into Higher Education and Open University Press

Scotland's Polytechnic Colleges Group (1996) *FE 2000: A discussion paper – the role of the Scottish Further Education Colleges within HE*, Higher Education Scotland

Scottish Community Education Council (1995) *Scotland as a Learning Society: Myth, Reality and Challenge*

Scottish Education Department (1985) *Future Strategy for Higher Education in Scotland*, HMSO, Edinburgh

Scottish Enterprise (1996) *Prosperity for Scotland Science & Technology: Commercialisation Enquiry Final Research Report*

Scottish Enterprise (1996) *Prosperity for Scotland Science & Technology: Commercialisation Enquiry Draft Strategy*

Scottish Enterprise (1996) *The Business Birth Rate Strategy Update*

Scottish Enterprise (1996) *The Network Strategy: 'Our Purpose Is To Help Generate Jobs and Prosperity for The People of Scotland'*

Scottish Enterprise (undated) *Developing A Learning Technologies Strategy for The Scottish Enterprise Network*

Scottish Enterprise (undated) *Skills Strategy*

Scottish Enterprise and The Royal Society of Edinburgh (1996) *Technology Ventures Commercialising Scotland's Science and Technology*

Scottish Enterprise (undated) *Scottish Enterprise Annual Report 1995–96, Towards Jobs and Prosperity for Scotland*

Scottish Office (1994) *Higher Still: Opportunity for All*

Scottish Office (1995) *Statistical Bulletin Education Series*

Scottish Office (1996) *Scottish Certificate of Education Standard Grade*

Scottish Office (1995) *Statistical Bulletin May,* HMSO

Scottish Office Education Department (1992) *Upper Secondary Education in Scotland*

Scottish Tertiary Education Advisory Council of the Scottish Education Department (1985) *Future Strategy for Higher Education in Scotland: Report of the Scottish Tertiary Education Advisory Council on its Review of Higher Education in Scotland* HMSO, Cmnd 9676

SCOTVEC (1990) *Setting the Standard: in Scotland*

SCOTVEC (1996) *Responses to the Consultation Paper on SCOTVEC's Higher National Awards*

Secretary of State for Scotland (1995) *Further Education in Scotland 1995,* HMSO

SEDA (1995) *Annual Report for 1995,* Staff and Educational Development Association

Setting New Priorities for Higher Education Management (1996) IMHE General Conference 2/4 Sept 1996, The Regional University: Issues In The Development Of An Organisational Framework

Sharp C & Kendall L (1996) *Discretionary Awards in Dance and Drama: A survey of local education authorities,* National Foundation for Educational Research

Shattock M (1994) *The UGC and the Management of British Universities,* Society for Research into Higher Education

SHEFC (1993) *Collaboration in Higher Education Institutions: A Consultation Paper,* Consultation Paper 7/93, Scottish Higher Education Funding Council

SHEFC (1994) Circular Letter 35/94, *Collaboration in Higher Education: Responses to consultation paper 7/93*

SHEFC (1994) Circular Letter 47/94, *Courses Provided in Collaboration with other institutions*

SHEFC (1994) Circular Letter 58/94, *Collaborative Arrangements, Statistical Returns for 1994–95*

SHEFC (1994) *Merger Proposals from Scottish Higher Education Institutions*

SHEFC (1994) *Annual Report and Accounts 1993-94*

SHEFC (1995) *Addressing Technology Foresight,* Consultation Paper 2/95

SHEFC (1995) Circular Letter 55/95, *Use of MANs Initiative*

SHEFC (1995) Circular Letter 59/95, *Collaborative Arrangements, Statistical Returns for 1995–96*

SHEFC (1995) *Higher Education Institutions, Financial Statistics 1993–94,* Statistical Bulletin, No 6/95

SHEFC (1995) *Higher Education Institutions: Students and Staff 1993–94,* Statistical Bulletin, No 5/95

SHEFC (1995) *Non-recurrent Council Initiatives in 1995–96: Regional Strategic Initiatives Fund Circular Letter No. 56/95*

SHEFC (1995) *Review of Higher Education: Submission from the Scottish Higher Education Funding Council*

SHEFC (1995) *Scottish Higher Education Funding Council, Corporate Plan 1996 – 1999*

SHEFC (1996) *Enabling Strategic Change, Council Consultation Paper 02/96 Summary of Responses*

SHEFC (1996) *Access to Success For Students with Disabilities In Higher Education in Scotland*

SHEFC (1996) *Addressing Technology Foresight: Action Plan*

SHEFC (1996) *Council consultation paper 02/96, Enabling Strategic Change*

SHEFC (1996) *Students Eligible for Funding, 1995–96 (provisional)*, Statistical Bulletin, No 1/96

SHEFC (1997) *University Research in Scotland; Developing a Policy Framework*

SHEFC (undated) *Quality Assessors' Handbook*

SHEFC/COSHEP (1996) *Report of the SHEFC-COSHEP Joint Review Group on Quality Assessment*

Sims L, Woodrow M (1996) *Fast and Flexible: The AIRs Experience The Evaluation of the Accelerated and Intensive Routes to Higher Education*

Sizer J (1994) *Competitive Funding Models, Resource Management and Quality Assessment* in *Education Economics*, Vol.2, No.1

Sizer J (1996) *Enabling Strategic Change Seminar – Stirling Management Centre: 15 September 1996: Strategic Change Initiative: Outcomes of Consultation*, SHEFC

Sizer J and Mackie D (1995) *Greater Accountability: The Price of Autonomy* in *Higher Education Management*, Volume 7 No. 3

Skene C P (undated) *Business and Universities Growing Together, What are the Issues: Skene Young Entrepreneurs Award National Winners Booklet*

Slack J (1995/96) *The ABS Directory of Business Schools*, Butterworth Heinemann

Slowey M (1995) *Implementing Change from Within Universities and Colleges: 10 Personal Accounts*, Kogan Page

Smith D, Scott P & Lynch J (1995) *The Role of Marketing in the University and College Sector*, HEIST

Smither A & Robins P (undated) *Executive Briefing: Post-18 Education Growth, Change, Prospect*, CIHE

Smither A & Robinson P (1989) *Increasing Participation in Higher Education*, BP Educational Service

Society for Research into Higher Education (1996) *Further and Higher Education Partnerships, The future for collaboration*, Open University Press

Society for Research into Higher Education (1996) *Governing Universities, Changing the Culture?*, Open University Press

Society for Research into Higher Education (1996) *Working in Higher Education*, Open University Press

Society for Research into Higher Education (1997) *Repositioning Higher Education*, Open University Press

SOEID (1995) Statistical Bulletin Edn/F7/1995/19

SOEID (1996) *Higher Education Projections: A Paper by the SOEID for the Scottish Committee* (unpublished)

SOEID (1996) *Memorandum Governance of the Further Education Colleges in Scotland*

SOEID (1996) *Scottish Education Statistics*

SOEID (1996) *Scottish Higher Education: A general paper by the Scottish Office Education and Industry Department for the Scottish Standing Committee of the Committee of Inquiry into Higher Education*

SOEID (1996) *Scottish Higher Education: Public Expenditure and Value for Money* (unpublished)

SOEID (1996) Statistical Bulletin Edn/F6/1996/6

SOEID (1996) Statistical Bulletin Edn/J2/1996/12

SOEID (1996) *The 1994 Leavers: The Scottish School Leavers Survey*

SOEID (1996) *Upper Secondary and Post-School Qualifications and Assessment* (unpublished)

SOEID (1997) *Recurrent Funding for the University of the Highlands and Islands*

SOEID (undated) *Leaver Destinations from Scottish Secondary Schools 1994–96*

SOEID (undated) *Scottish Wider Access Programme: A Preparation for Higher Education: A Report by HM Inspectors of Schools*

Somekh B et al (undated) *The National Record of Achievement in Scotland; An Evaluation*, The Scottish Council for Research in Education

Southampton Institute (undated) *The Future of the University Sector: A discussion paper*

Spilsbury M, Moralee J & Evans C (1995) *Employers' Use of the NVQ System* IES, Report 293

Staff Development for Teaching and Learning: Towards a Coherent and Comprehensive Approach UK USDU Task Force Two Occasional Green Paper No. 8 (1994) The UK Universities' Staff Development Unit

Staffordshire University (1996) *The Dilemmas of Mass Higher Education 10-12 April 1996: Conference Report*

Standards in Public Life Volume 1 (Nolan Report) (1996) HMSO

Standards in Public Life Volume 2 (Nolan Report) (1996) HMSO

Stanhope A (undated) *Higher Education in Cornwall: A Summary Report*, Cornwall College

Staropoli A (1994) *Evaluating a French University*, in OECD, *Evaluation and Decision-making in Higher Education*

Statistics of Education, Student Support England and Wales 1993/4 (1995) HMSO

Student Awards Agency for Scotland (1996) *Access Funds: Guidance Notes for Institutions 1996/97*

Student Grants in Scotland, A Guide to Undergraduate Allowances 1996/97 (1996) HMSO

Student Grants in Scotland: A Guide to Postgraduate Allowances 1995/96 (1995) HMSO

Student Loans Company Limited (1996) *Annual Report 1995*

Sullivan R & Farrow A (1996) *Register of Members' Research Interests 1996*, Volume 1, SRHE

Superhighways for Education: The Way Forward (1995) HMSO

Survey of Research Equipment in United Kingdom Universities (1996) Prest

Taylor S (1996) *Scotland's Young People: 19 in '95 The Scottish School Leavers Survey (SSLS)* Social and Community Planning Research, SOEID

TECs Towards 2000 The Government's Strategic Guidance to TECs (1994)

The Cambridge Phenomenon: The Growth of High Technology Industry in a University Town (1985) Segal Quince Wicksteed Limited

The Carnegie Foundation for the Advancement of Teaching (1994) *The Academic Profession; an international perspective*

The Chartered Institute of Bankers (1995) Annual Review 1994 – 1995

The Construction Industry Board (undated) *Educating the Professional Team*

The Development of Higher Education into the 1990s (undated) HMSO

The Future of Britain's Universities: The Report of the CPC of the Sub-Group on Access, Participation & Student National Policy Group on Higher Education, (1996) CPC, National Policy Group on Higher Education

The Learning Society (undated) *An ESRC Research Programme on the Learning Society*

The Main Systems of Financial Assistance for students in Higher Education in the European Community (1993) Task Force on Human Resources Education Training Youth

The Ove Arup Foundation (1996) *Education for the Built Environment*

The Returns to Graduation (undated) HMSO

The Royal Society (1993) *Higher Education Futures*

The Royal Society (1997) *The Higher Education Sector: A Statement by the Royal Society*

The Royal Society of Edinburgh (1994–1995) *Annual Report and Accounts*

The University Research System in Japan (1995) Ministry of Education, Science, Sports and Culture, Japan

Thomas L F & Harri-Augstein E S (1993) *The theory and practice of conversational science: tools for the T-C practitioner* from *Self-Organised Learning*, Routledge, (2nd edition)

Tilak J B G (1995) *Cost Recovery Approaches in Education in India, NIEPA Occasional Paper 19*, National Institute of Educational Planning and Administration, New Delhi, India

Timpson A M & Baggini J G (1996) *Canadian Studies in the UK, A Directory of Canadianists Courses and Research*, British Association for Canadian Studies

TLTP (1996) *Institutional Case Studies*, Teaching and Learning Technology Programme

TLTP (1996) *Report of the TLTP Working Group on Open Courseware*, Teaching and Learning Technology Programme

TLTP (1996) *Science Case Studies*, Teaching and Learning Technology Programme

TLTP (1997), *Teaching and Learning Technology Support Network Case Studies II*, Teaching and Learning Technology Programme

Trow M (1992) *Thoughts on the White Paper of 1991*, Graduate School of Public Policy University of California, Berkeley, USA

TTA (1996) *Consultation Paper on Standards and a National Professional Qualification for Subject Leaders*, Teacher Training Agency

TTA (1996) *Consultation Paper on Training for Serving Headteachers*, Teacher Training Agency

TTA (1997) *Training Curriculum and Standards for New Teachers*

TTA (1995) *Allocations and Funding Study Report*, Coopers & Lybrand, Teacher Training Agency

TTA (1995) *Corporate Plan 1995 Promoting High Quality Teaching and Teacher Education*, HMSO

Tyneside TEC (1996) *Your Chances for Success*

UCAS (1994) *Statistical Summary 1993/94 Entry*, Universities and Colleges Admissions Service

UCAS (1994) *UCAS Annual Report 1993/1994*

UCAS (1995) *UCAS Annual Report 1995 Entry*

UCAS (1996) *Statistical Bulletin: Regional Progression of Accepted Applicants 1995 Entry*

UCAS (1997) *Statistical Survey 1996 Report (Qualified applicants: those who did not enter higher education)*

UCAS (1997) *Annual Report 1996 Entry*

UK Graduate Careers Survey 1996 (1996) *High Fliers*

UKERNA (1996) *Annual Report 1995-1996*

UKERNA (undated) *Broadband Networking in the Education Sector*

UKERNA (undated) *The Networking Programme*

Undergraduate Medical and Dental Education and Research: Fourth Report of the Steering Group (1996)

Universities in Germany (1995) Prestel, Munich

Universities in London (undated) A report commissioned by the Higher Education Institutions in London, Greater London Group

University Grants Committee of Hong Kong (1996) *Higher Education in Hong Kong*

University Grants Committee of Hong Kong (undated) *Higher Education in Hong Kong*

University of Edinburgh (undated) *Tutoring: A Handbook for Postgraduate and Other Part-Time Tutors*

University of Edinburgh, Institute of Education, University of London – Post 16 Education Centre, Economic and Social Research Council (1997) *Unifying Academic and Vocational learning; The State of the debate in England and Scotland*

University of Leeds & Leeds TEC Ltd (1995) *Joint Plans 1996-1999*

University of Luton (undated) *Work Based Learning in HE*

University of Manchester & UMIST (1995) *The Economic & Social Impact of Greater Manchester's Universities*

University of Newcastle (1993) *Assessment Issues in Higher Education*, School of Education

University of Newcastle upon Tyne (1996) *The Contribution of Universities to Economic Development: Progress Report*

University of Oxford (1996) *Commission of Inquiry: Consultative paper on the University's Objectives, Structure, Size and Shape*

University of Paisley (1996) *Geodemographic Analysis of First-Year Full-Time and Sandwich Students at the Universities of Edinburgh, Glasgow, Glasgow Caledonian, Napier and Paisley in 1995* (unpublished)

University of St Andrews (undated) *The University Court: A Handbook for Members* (unpublished)

Unwin L (undated) *The Role of Libraries in Postgraduate Distance Learning: Summary of Research Findings*, University of Sheffield

Unwin L, Bolton N & Stephens K (undated) *The Role of the Library in Distance Learning: Implications for Policy and Practice*, The British Library Board and South Bank University

Upper Secondary Education in Scotland: Report of the Committee to Review Curriculum and Examinations in the fifth and sixth year of Secondary Education in Scotland (1992) HMSO

Vroeijenstein T I (1994) *Preparing for the Second Cycle: External Quality Assessment in Dutch Universities*, in Westerheijden D.F. et al, *Changing Concepts at Quality Assessments*, CHEPS

Warner D and Palfreyman D (1996) *Higher education management: the key elements*, The Society for Research into Higher Education and Open University Press

Warwickshire Education Business Partnership (1996) *Working Together; The Newsletter of the Warwickshire Education Business Partnership*

Watson K (undated) *Alternative Funding of Education Systems: Some Lessons from Third World Experiments*, Oxford Studies in Comparative Education

Watts A G (1997) Strategic Directions for Careers Services in Higher Education, National Institute for Careers Education and Counselling, CRAC

Welsh Funding Councils (1995) *The Development of Quality Assurance in Wales*

Welsh Funding Councils (undated) *Review of Higher Education,* Department for Education

West E G (undated) *Britain's Student Loan System in World Perspective: A Critique*, IEA

Westerheijden D F, Brennan J & Maassen PA M (1994) *Changing Contexts of Quality Assessment*, CHEPS

Whitby Z (1992) *Promotional Publications: A Guide for Editors*, HEIST

White Paper (1995) *Competitiveness Forging Ahead*, HMSO

Wigglesworth, W R B (1996) *Telecommunications Charging Policie*s, paper presented to the IT Working Group (unpublished)

Williams G (1996) *Paying for education beyond eighteen: an examination of issues and options,* Council for I0ndustry in Higher Education, London

Withrington D J (1996) *The COSHEP/UCAS Entrance Guide to Higher Education in Scotland for entrance in Autumn 1997*, UCAS and COSHEP

Woodley A, Thompson M & Cowan J (1992) *Factors Affecting non-completion rates in Scottish Universities: Report to the Scottish Office Education Department*, Student Research Centre

Working Party on Governance: Report to the Board of Governors (1996) University of Portsmouth

Working Party on the Colleges of Higher Education and the Revision of GS 417 (1994) *An Excellent Enterprise: The Church of England and its Colleges of Higher Education*, Board of Education of the General Synod of the Church of England

Yorke M (1995) *External Examining in Art and Design*, GLAD

Yorke P (1992) *The Students' Charter*, Adam Smith Institute

Appendix 1

Report on Northern Ireland

Provision

1.   Higher education is provided by 2 universities (which, in their distinctive missions, exemplify the diversity of higher education), 2 colleges of education and, to varying degrees, in the region's 17 institutes of further education. Programmes in the latter are predominantly vocational eg HND/HNC and NVQ4, and cover a wide range of subject areas from Business and Related Studies, Health and Social Care to Engineering and Technology. Northern Ireland also constitutes a region of the Open University.

2.   Total student enrolments in 1994/95 were as follows:

	Full-time	Part-time	Total
Queen's University Belfast	11,026	3,009	14,035
University of Ulster	12,657	5,640	18,297
Colleges of Education	1,282	0	1,282
Institutes of FE	2,371	3,765	6,136
Total	27,336	12,414	39,750

3.   Some 85 per cent of students enrolled at the two universities come from Northern Ireland. Like the rest of the UK, Northern Ireland operates a policy of consolidation of student numbers through the setting of control totals.

4.   The universities are directly funded by the Department of Education Northern Ireland (DENI) on the recommendations of the Northern Ireland Higher Education Council (NIHEC). Funding is in the main based on the methodologies of the Higher Education Funding Council for England (HEFCE). The colleges of education are resourced on the basis of historical funding rather than on a student-based formula. At present the institutes of further education are owned and managed by the five Education and Library Boards (ELBs), which are responsible for funding their full range of functions, including higher education. There are plans for each college to become a free-standing corporate body, funded directly by DENI.

5.   The ELBs are responsible for making mandatory and discretionary awards to Northern Ireland students following specified programmes. Levels of grant and entitlement match those in Great Britain.

General

6. Since provision is an integral part of the UK higher education system and shares many of its characteristics, we believe that the overall thrust of our recommendations is also appropriate for Northern Ireland and is consistent with much of the evidence submitted by higher education institutions and other bodies there. With an Age Participation Rate of some 42 per cent in 1994/95 and with some 35 per cent of entrants from manual backgrounds, Northern Ireland is already well advanced in the direction of fuller participation and greater social inclusion which we recommend. However, whilst there has been a substantial increase in mature and part-time students, participation by these groups still lags behind the GB rate.

7. Our recommendations on teaching, quality and standards chime with the firm view throughout the evidence from Northern Ireland that the expansion of higher education, wherever it may be provided, must not be accompanied by a reduction in quality and that standards should be set and maintained. We envisage the National Framework of Qualifications and the writ of the new Quality Assurance Agency extending fully to Northern Ireland.

Higher education's regional role

8. What we say in Chapter 12 about the regional role of higher education is particularly apt for Northern Ireland. The universities in particular are rightly mindful of the national and international dimension of their work and, increasingly, of the possibilities for fruitful co-operation with the institutions in the Republic of Ireland. They are also very conscious, however, of their responsibility to act as a regional powerhouse, contributing to the advancement of every aspect of human capability within the region.

9. Given the compact scale of Northern Ireland, there is no reason why higher education there should not become a role model in this respect. The two universities are, for example, fully involved in the Northern Ireland Growth Challenge, a recent private sector initiative supported by the social partners. This has led to the creation of networks to promote the conditions for fast growth and development in their sectors of industry as well as to co-operate on wider issues germane to a best investment environment overall. The Growth Challenge and the Government's Industrial Research and Technology Unit joined forces to introduce the approach of the national Foresight Programme to key sectors of the Northern Ireland economy. Emerging from this work is a proposal to establish sectoral Technology Partnerships, whose functions would include:
   - strengthening links between Government, Universities and Business;
   - helping identify opportunities for collaboration and technology transfer and identifying 'brokers' who can assist in the process;
   - improving awareness of new technology developments, opportunities and best practice, especially among small and medium sized enterprises and through supplier chains.

The Universities would be involved in each Partnership Panel.

10. Northern Ireland has 30,000 companies but only 100 of them employ 200 or more people, and only 200 employ more than 100. Whilst the predominance of small companies, in terms of sheer number, is typical of all parts of the United Kingdom, it is particularly marked in Northern Ireland. Moreover, many of the 200 larger companies are branches of enterprises with headquarters located elsewhere and therefore with limited powers of decision.

11. The structure of the Northern Ireland economy has two implications:
    a) with a high participation rate in higher education, it is especially important that the UK-wide problem of a low take-up of graduates by small firms is tackled successfully, to the benefit of the graduate and the company. Research evidence covering manufacturing firms in Northern Ireland, Leicestershire, Wearside and Hertfordshire suggests that growth in turnover and employment in companies whose owner-manager was educated to degree level was higher. Better educated entrepreneurs were likely to implement business strategies embracing factors conducive to growth such as market research and product improvement.
    b) there is arguably a special role for the universities in providing an interface with small to medium sized enterprises so that they can be in touch with relevant technological developments and the economic potential of university research can be exploited for the development of new technology enterprises.

12. None of these considerations is specific to Northern Ireland, but this part of the United Kingdom is the one that for decades has suffered the highest levels of unemployment, and which because of its history of civil strife finds it correspondingly difficult to attract companies from overseas. It is therefore particularly relevant that public policy should recognise the distinctive needs of Northern Ireland and the vital role of higher education.

13. Each of the two universities can point to specific ways in which they have sought to contribute to the solution of these problems.
    ■ In 1984 Queen's University set up a holding company, 'Queen's University Business and Industrial Services' (QUBIS) to enable the commercially attractive aspects of its research work to be developed through wealth creating business. Companies employing some 200 graduate staff, with a turnover of £10 million, have developed from university research.
    ■ The University of Ulster has made a particular feature of sandwich programmes in which the student typically spends one year in employment either in Northern Ireland or abroad. These sandwich programmes now extend to some 1400 students. These students are encouraged to achieve an NVQ at Level 3 whilst in employment and not only to aim for a degree by the completion of their studies but also for a diploma in industrial studies offered by the University. Such practice makes a graduate more attractive to any employer, but especially to

small firms which expect all employees to be fully effective very soon after starting. When other placements of varying duration are also taken into account, some 22 per cent of the full-time undergraduate population benefited from some form of work placement in 1996/97.

- The Teaching Company Scheme is another mechanism for building bridges between newly qualified graduates and openings in small firms. The scale of teaching company schemes in Northern Ireland is four times the United Kingdom average. Even so, the maximum of 40 projects at any one time in Northern Ireland involving one to five graduates is not on a scale commensurate with the challenge.

14. Higher education's regional role should, of course, extend beyond a narrow economic development agenda and mobilise people towards the goal of strengthening the social fabric and fostering a sense of community. This is especially relevant in Northern Ireland, where we commend the interest within higher education in pursuing the American model of university-community partnership. American experience suggests that, if properly integrated into academic programmes, involvement in community/voluntary sector projects, with their emphasis on problem-solving, can (as with placements in industry) equip students with transferable skills.

Recommendation 89   **We recommend that higher education institutions in Northern Ireland, in close collaboration with all the relevant external players, steadily enhance their regional role, taking full advantage of the special potential for the development of strong regional networks.**

Capacity

15. Northern Ireland has a high level of achievement in education up to 18 which is reflected in the proportion of young people who are able to earn places at 18 and 19 in higher education. Including the 4 per cent that go to the Republic of Ireland, some 42 per cent earn university places, over one third above the average for the United Kingdom as a whole.

16. This high level of achievement is not matched by the provision of places in higher education in Northern Ireland. Some 40 per cent of the cohort goes elsewhere. This has certain advantages. Young people are taken into an environment where they can meet people from different backgrounds and can broaden their experience. It enables the very ablest to pursue their higher education in places of their choice which they judge give them the best possible opportunities. For others the range of programmes available, taking the United Kingdom as a whole, is wider than they could expect in Northern Ireland.

17. But there are disadvantages. Many who go elsewhere do not return and this means that Northern Ireland is losing a proportion of its abler young people. It has been calculated that over 11 per cent of the relevant age cohort is lost, representing for the most part the more intellectually able segment. There is also a cost factor in that these

students have perforce to live away from home. Moreover, Northern Ireland, which has a GDP some 80 per cent of the UK average, would benefit from the income generated from educating a higher proportion of its young people in its own institutions. The financial consequence of the large net outflow of students is estimated at a loss of some £45 million annually to the Northern Ireland economy.

18. The central issue in any policy towards higher education for Northern Ireland is therefore the extent to which it should have educational capacity equal to the take up of higher education. In both Scotland and Wales, the places available in local institutions could have met the locally generated demand for higher education. Providing for Northern Ireland on the basis of the Scottish ratio of places to population would require an extra 12,000 places. The figure to match the Welsh ratio is some 5,500 places.

19. Given the shortage of places, entry grade levels to the two universities are high. The less well qualified (many from lower income families) do not, unlike their GB counterparts, have local access to higher education institutions with lower entry requirements. The number of unwilling leavers would be even greater if, in circumstances of peace and stability, applications from outside Northern Ireland for places in the two universities were significantly to increase.

20. It is difficult to see why, as part of a long term policy, it would be other than desirable to put Northern Ireland into a position of broad equilibrium between supply and demand without of course denying students, and particularly those of outstanding ability, the opportunity of choosing to go to other parts of the United Kingdom. We support the conclusion of the NIHEC that students preferring to remain in Northern Ireland to pursue a programme of study offered by an institution there should not be obliged to go away because entry standards locally are so high as to exclude them when they could secure a place in Great Britain.

21. There are at least four ways in which this might be achieved.

Option 1

22. A new university campus could be established, as has been proposed by the University of Ulster for Springvale in Belfast. This was intended to be an institution built consciously across the Protestant/Catholic divide and committed to policies of close involvement in the community at all levels, with a conscious objective of lifting aspirations and attainment in an area of high unemployment. The full cost of such a project, accommodating say 4,000 students when fully developed, would be approaching £100 million, and, except to the extent that it came from private sources, this represents a heavy call on public funds. It is not for us to evaluate the feasibility of the project but we hope that the vision which prompted it will not be neglected. This was well captured in a lecture at the University of Ulster by the Chancellor of the City University of New York entitled 'Transformation and Redemption: the Urban University'.

'Universities that are truly inclusive, universities that engage everyone in society, have a special power to transform lives, renew cities and elevate society. They offer us "the only true way to emancipate ourselves from the divisions that limit our minds and imaginations"'.

Option 2

23.   The potential to expand numbers within the universities could be maximised by, for instance, the redevelopment of properties in the ownership of Queen's University, Belfast. We understand that, given its mission, the University's preference would be to concentrate the expansion on:

- postgraduate students;
- undergraduate students of good ability;
- areas where there is keen demand for places which Northern Ireland cannot meet, for example in dentistry and pharmacy.

24.   This would be a less costly option, put by Queen's at one-sixth of new build. To the extent that Queen's extended its postgraduate provision it would not address the need for more undergraduate places; and to the extent that it concentrated on abler students, it could upset the existing balance in terms of ability levels between Queen's and the University of Ulster, possibly to an extent that would depress the standing of the University of Ulster both in the province and more widely.

Option 3

25.   Extra places could be secured by using capacity more intensively and, for example, by progressively adopting a three semester year as was previously canvassed in a report by Lord Flowers. It would require very careful planning and it would not be equally appropriate in all disciplines or for all students. Nor is it an option without capital costs. But pilot experiences with introducing a third semester elsewhere in the UK and the intensive six week summer term introduced at the University of Ulster show that this is a practical possibility for development on some scale.

Option 4

26.   Institutes of further education could be encouraged to expand their own sub-degree activity, and the already developing practice of universities establishing collaborative relationships with the institutes could be progressively extended. This could, for example, entail further franchising of sub-degree programmes or the creation of partnerships of the kind recently developed in Fermanagh, in which various parties, including the local District Council and business groups, the local institute of further education and the University of Ulster co-operate in the delivery of programmes and the promotion of economic regeneration and development. Queen's, through its Outreach initiative, has developed partnership approaches with local Councils and institutes of further education, notably at Armagh and Omagh. The two colleges of education also have a contribution to make through diversifying away from their monotechnic status, as many of their counterparts in Great Britain have already done. With partnerships or under carefully specified validation and franchising arrangements, one could envisage the first or even the first and second years of a degree programme being delivered close to home.

27. There is already widespread acceptance within Northern Ireland that, at all levels and whatever the arrangements for the delivery of programmes, quality and standards must not be compromised. The recommendations in Chapter 10 will strengthen the safeguards against slippage.

28. The scope for developments of the kind considered under this Option without reducing the capacity to provide further education (which would be a retrograde step) has not been determined. This would need to be closely investigated before a judgement could be made about the potential scale and costs of this Option.

Conclusion

29. These Options are not mutually exclusive. They could be considered in various combinations. Detailed examination and costing is needed. In an era when the nation needs to maximise the education that can be provided within a given budget – so long as quality and standards can be assured – the relative costs of the options should be a major factor in devising the best solution.

30. However cost-effectively it is managed, the expansion of provision is likely to entail a considerable increase in public expenditure in Northern Ireland by way of additional investment as well as recurrent costs, although there will be offsetting savings in living away allowances. An evaluation of the importance of local expansion in the context of public expenditure priorities, which takes fully into account all the benefits (direct and indirect) as well as the costs, is therefore involved. There should be some public expenditure savings in Great Britain.

31. It is not possible to predict with any accuracy how much capacity is needed to bring overall demand for, and supply of, local provision into broad balance. On the assumption that, say, some 40 per cent of those who go to Great Britain each year for their higher education do so unwillingly, then about 5,000 extra places would be needed in institutions in Northern Ireland to deal with this particular issue. This is, however, likely to be a minimum figure since it assumes that the number of places occupied by students domiciled outside Northern Ireland does not increase and that there is no additional pressure on places in Northern Ireland arising from demographic change or higher levels of participation. It is not necessary , however, to identify the extra requirement precisely in order to make progress. Careful monitoring of demand for particular programmes of study against the capacity to satisfy it (on which some work has already been done) would reveal where provision might progressively be expanded.

32. A useful first step would be to lift quickly the Maximum Aggregate Student Number cap. This would encourage the institutions to identify their potential for increasing numbers without any – or certainly substantial – additional investment.

33. As Option 4 above implies, it should not be assumed that, in a mass higher education system, study for a degree is the norm or the best way of meeting labour market needs. Successful experience in Scotland, where over a quarter of higher education is now

offered in institutions of further education, demonstrates the value of sub-degree qualifications, particularly when there are well-established routes of progression into degree work.

34. Initial teacher training is one area where there is substantial unsatisfied demand for places. Student numbers in the two colleges of education in Northern Ireland are capped by reference to the local labour market. In the context of an overall expansion of higher education capacity in Northern Ireland, the case for constraining any aspect of provision on this basis is weakened.

35. The availability of a more substantial higher education resource within Northern Ireland should improve its economic prospects and enhance its attractiveness to inward investors. However, it is improbable that, at least in the short term, the increased output would be wholly absorbed within Northern Ireland, although job opportunities would be likely to be significantly better in conditions of peace and political stability. Whatever the strength of the local labour market, some will inevitably decide to pursue their careers outside Northern Ireland or seek experience elsewhere before returning later. More generally, however, if additional investment in higher education is to produce an adequate social as well as personal return, it is a corollary of expanding local provision that the job search should not necessarily be confined to Northern Ireland.

36. Whilst Northern Ireland has been more successful than the rest of the UK in expanding access to higher education for those from manual backgrounds – up from 25 per cent to 35 per cent of entrants between 1973 and 1991 – more remains to be done, particularly so far as young Protestant males are concerned. Survey data suggests that only 27 per cent of Protestant entrants to higher education are from manual backgrounds, compared with 43 per cent of Catholic entrants. Both percentages remained virtually stable between 1973 and 1991 and the rise in the overall figure for participation of those from manual backgrounds is largely due to the increase in Catholic participation.

Recommendation 90 **We recommend to the Government that options be examined for substantially increasing the number of higher education places in Northern Ireland in a cost-effective way which involves no compromise in quality and standards.**

Students' contributions to the cost of university education

37. It is often argued that students who come from homes where family incomes are low are likely to be more averse to pursuing university education if it involves an accumulation of debt and the responsibility to repay later. In the Northern Ireland context, with 40 per cent of students needing to find places in higher education outside Northern Ireland and with the additional costs involved in living away from home, it is sometimes argued that the disincentive effect of increasing the student contribution would be particularly great. Similar arguments could be made for other parts of the United Kingdom where there is no university provision within daily travelling distance

and there are many students who live in such areas, but the ratio of those obliged to study away from home to entrants domiciled in the region is particularly high in Northern Ireland. To the extent that there was a closer balance between the provision of higher education places (including close-to-home places) and those qualifying for them in Northern Ireland, the disincentive effect of an income contingent contribution by students to the cost of higher education would be reduced. That particular point is relevant to the case for increasing the provision of higher education in Northern Ireland.

38.   If the Government should decide to increase the student contribution (and we set out in Chapter 20 certain options) the method chosen could be significant for Northern Ireland, particularly pending expansion of local capacity. Average earnings in Northern Ireland are lower than in Great Britain and higher education attracts more students from poorer families. In 1986/87, almost 45 per cent of Northern Ireland students were on full maintenance grants compared with just over 29 per cent of English and Welsh students. In 1994/95, just over 47 per cent of students funded by the Belfast Education and Library Board were on full grants.

39.   The less socially regressive any change to current arrangements for funding higher education is and the more the repayment of the student contribution is contingent on the achievement of a decent threshold level of earnings, the smaller any disincentive effect, whatever the position regarding expansion of local capacity.

Options between 16 – 19

40.   The Dearing Report on qualifications for 16–19 year olds argues the case for the provision of an option which would combine depth in study with complementary studies in breadth. The proposal in outline was that a student taking the A level route would cover four domains of knowledge; that in each one of them the student would be required to achieve at least an AS, and that two of the four awards should be at full A level standard. In addition the student would be required to achieve an AS in the three key skills of communication, the application of number and use of information technology, with those competences demonstrated in the context of one or more of the student's chosen areas of study.

41.   While this option was welcomed by the Government and whilst the universities have long sought greater breadth in provision between 16 and 19, the practice of specialisation is so firmly established in university admissions procedures that schools are not willing to risk offering their students such an option lest their chances of acceptance in the university of their choice should be diminished.

42.   One practical approach to the adoption of the proposed diploma combining depth with breadth lies in a small group of universities deciding as a matter of policy that they would welcome such students.

43. In view of the long argued case for greater breadth in education between 16–19, it is for consideration whether the universities in Northern Ireland, together with schools and colleges – if they saw educational merit in the option – could adopt it as one of the recognised and valued bases for gaining university entrance in appropriate areas of study.

Recommendation 91 **We recommend to the Government and institutions that consideration be given to adopting the Dearing 16–19 year olds option as one of the bases for entrance to universities in Northern Ireland.**

Research

44. The research income of the Northern Ireland universities (£47 million) is derived as follows (1993/94 figures), with the corresponding United Kingdom figures in brackets:

Block Grant	Research Councils	UK Charities	Government and Health Authorities	Industry	Overseas and EU	Other
54% (37%)	7% (22%)	7% (14%)	13% (10%)	4% (7%)	12% (7%)	3% (3%)

45. A major difference in the pattern of funding is the relative importance of the block grant. This is partly due to the inclusion within the grant of NIDevR funding which was introduced in 1993/94 following the 1992 Research Assessment Exercise (RAE). In the absence of NIDevR, the block grant would have dropped from £25 million to £17 million. The then Minister at DENI, in a letter of 21 April 1993 to the Chairman of the NIHEC, which is responsible for advising on the allocation of NIDevR funds, defined its purpose as follows:
   - an improvement in the quality of the universities' research, and in the ratings achieved in the Research Assessment Exercise;
   - a greater contribution by research to the economic, social and cultural life of Northern Ireland and, in particular, greater success in relating research to the needs of industry;
   - an increase in the levels of research funding earned by the universities, including that from the Research Councils;
   - improved links with other universities, research establishments and with industry.

46. Phase 1 of a detailed study carried out (September 1996) for the NIHEC concluded that the two universities have made good use of the NIDevR funds and have taken effective steps to enhance their research capabilities in selected subject areas; and that the fruit was already evident in terms of academic research outputs and contributions to the local economy.

47. NIDevR was initially introduced for 3 years and later extended to 1996/97, when £9 million was allocated. For 1997/98, it has been cut by £4 million and by £6 million

for later years. These cuts entail a reduction of 16 per cent in the current year and of 24 per cent in subsequent years in the universities' block grant for research. There has been no corresponding reduction in regional research funding elsewhere in the UK. Indeed, since 1993/94, funding in Great Britain has increased by over 7 per cent in real terms, whilst in Northern Ireland (excluding the reduction in NIDevR) it has declined by over 10 per cent.

48.   Block grant is also disproportionately significant in Northern Ireland universities because of the low research income from other sources. The income from the Research Councils and Charities can be expected to improve as the universities, RAE gradings improve. It is not, however, simply a matter of gradings. The external income generated by researchers in Northern Ireland from all sources is in general lower than that generated by Units in the rest of the UK which have obtained similar grades. The structure of the economy, with its small firms, the prevalence of external ownership and the bias towards low-technology operations, reduces the short term opportunities for research sponsored by business.

49.   Overall expenditure on civil R&D outside higher education is low in Northern Ireland, amounting to 0.5 per cent of GDP (which is itself low) compared with 1.4 per cent for the UK (1993/94 figures). University research accounts for £47 million (64 per cent) of the total of £74 million spent on civil research in Northern Ireland, compared with 23 per cent for the UK. The significance of the research role of the Northern Ireland universities compared with their GB counterparts has been described in a review of the funding of university research in Northern Ireland by Segal Quince Wicksteed Limited as follows:

'In GB there are a wide range of organisations undertaking R&D and providing technical services including industrial research associations, contract research organisations, research council laboratories and government laboratories (either privatised or still within the public sector). This infrastructure does not exist in Northern Ireland. Virtually all research is undertaken by the universities (and to a limited extent by government departments) or by businesses on their own account'.

50.   We believe that research quality in Northern Ireland universities should continue to be assessed by the criteria which apply, through the RAE, to all UK universities. However, the amount of research funding to be disbursed by block grant on foot of these gradings or by some supplementary mechanism of the nature of NIDevR is a matter for DENI. We have no information on the rationale for the recent cut in the block research grant for the Northern Ireland universities but, given the acute concerns expressed not only by the universities but by local industry about the consequences of the cut, there is a strong case for an urgent and fundamental review of the amount of research funding which should be made available to the universities and on what basis, taking into account:

- the importance of a strong research capability as a factor in the region's economic strategy;
- the potential contribution by the universities to that capability;
- the need to reinforce the links, in terms of research and technology transfer, between the universities and industry;

■ the need to encourage the universities to increase the income earned from all external sources.

51. Phase 2 of the Study referred to at paragraph 46, which is in preparation, will make recommendations on the criteria which should be taken into account by NIHEC in advising DENI on the future funding of research in Northern Ireland universities and examine possible funding methodologies. We would expect it to serve the purposes of the fundamental review which we regard as necessary. Future policy considerations, whilst taking into account institutional and other differences, should also include the recommendations in Chapter 11 on improvements to the research infrastructure in top quality research departments; the need to bring greater focus to funding for applied research and regional development; and the streamlining of the RAE so as to release funds for scholarship and for personal research or professional activity in support of teaching.

52. The expansion of the higher education sector which is discussed in paragraphs 15 et seq would obviously have the potential not only to increase the academic research base in Northern Ireland but also to confer some of the resultant advantages of scale.

Recommendation 92 **We recommend to the Government that the scale and nature of funding for research in Northern Ireland universities should be assessed afresh in the context of the Province's strategy for economic development and of the recommendations in** Chapter 11.

The tertiary approach

53. Until recent years, thinking has been in terms of clearly distinguished institutions of higher and further education. This has many advantages, not least in ensuring that there is no mission drift in the institutions of further education for whom provision of higher education will often be attractive. The containment of higher education within institutions wholly dedicated to it facilitates the maintenance of quality and standards and also the association of teaching with research. It also makes clearer the distinction to be drawn between those studies which are of a nature to merit the award of a degree and other third level vocational and other types of study.

54. On the other hand, in an era of mass participation in education post-18, and in a society increasingly recognising the need for a lifelong commitment to education, there can be clear advantages for at least a proportion of students in having access to institutions whose mission incorporates those of further and higher education. These advantages are:
   a) an increased ability to gain access to the education required in the home area, thus reducing accommodation costs for full-time students, and the burden of travelling, both in cost and time, for part-time students;
   b) for students who do not seem ready for higher education, but who show their aptitude for study during a further education programme, the opportunity to progress without interruption within the framework of one institution through further to higher education;

c) the ability to address the needs of mature students who may want a programme that incorporates elements of higher and further education at particular points of their career;

d) the possibility of offering a wider range of services to local industry and commerce in the locality of the institution.

55. Given the growing co-operation between the further and higher education sectors, the progress being made in devising a credit accumulation and transfer system, and developments in technology, there has in effect been evolving a more open tertiary system, with the different types of institutions within it separated only by what has been described as a permeable membrane. We believe that the time is ripe to give the tertiary concept more formal expression so that post-18 education is seen as a whole and is planned as a whole. This is particularly important when the expansion of higher education provision is being considered.

56. We suggest that whatever machinery is devised should meet a number of criteria:
- it should enable distinctive issues and problems within the tertiary sector in Northern Ireland to be addressed and, where appropriate, distinctive solutions to be found;
- it should not diminish the present ability of the higher education sector to use the services of, or draw on the expertise of, relevant bodies in GB (eg the Funding Councils and the new Quality Assurance Agency) in the interests of avoiding unnecessary duplication or unnecessary divergence from UK-wide practice;
- it should locate outside DENI the responsibility for channelling public funds to the institutions, thereby paralleling the position in Great Britain;
- it should achieve these aims with a minimum of bureaucratic overhead.

57. Whilst there is a variety of possible models and the optimum solution will clearly be the outcome of a consultative process in Northern Ireland, the model which we propose is as follows:
a) the creation of a Higher Education Funding Council (HEFCNI) and a Further Education Funding Council (FEFCNI) responsible for the allocation of funds;
b) the creation of a planning forum for higher and further education, to be known as the Tertiary Education Forum;
c) all 3 bodies to be administered by a single Executive under one Chief Executive.

58. We envisage the two universities and the two colleges of education being within the remit of the HEFCNI, whilst the institutes of further education, in respect of all their activities other than work which is part of a degree programme, would be the responsibility of the FEFCNI. Whilst we see merit in all higher education provision, in whatever institution it is provided, being within the remit of the HEFCNI, we would prefer to see a boundary adjustment of this kind – or even the complete merger of funding arrangements – evolve as mutual confidence develops and from the experience gained in the close co-operative working which the new arrangements should encourage.

59. The Tertiary Education Forum would in effect consist of joint meetings of the 2 Councils, with such additional membership (particularly from outside academia) as might be necessary to enable it to form an overview of how the tertiary sector could best discharge its regional role. An important initial task of the Forum would be to consider the implications for Northern Ireland of our Report, including the vitally important issue of the expansion of local provision.

Recommendation 93 **We recommend to the Government that there be constituted in Northern Ireland a Tertiary Education Forum, a Higher Education Funding Council and a Further Education Funding Council.**

Titles

60. In Chapter 16 we considered the circumstances in which the 'university college' title might be used. The difficulties which have led us to recommend that the title be restricted have not arisen in Northern Ireland and it may be that there are special circumstances there which would justify some modification of our recommendation in its application to Northern Ireland. We certainly would not wish to inhibit the evolution of higher education there in ways which are responsive to local need and are fully consistent with our emphasis on the need to safeguard standards.

Conclusion

61. Participation levels demonstrate how much the benefits of higher education are prized in Northern Ireland. Our recommendations both generally and in respect of Northern Ireland should assist an already vibrant and innovative sector to continue to develop strongly, well-regarded nationally and operating within a flexible and accessible framework which enables local opportunities and priorities to be vigorously addressed.

Bibliography

Mohan J (1993) *Universities and their Communities, observations from the USA,* Notes for CVCP meeting 4 November 1993

Reynolds W A (1995) *Transformation and Redemption: The Urban University,* Speech at the University of Ulster at Jordanstown 6 February 1995

Northern Ireland Higher Education Council (1995) *Report of the Sub-Group on Access, Participation and Student Migration*

Armstrong D A (1996) *Education and Economic Development: Empirical Evidence and Regional Perspectives*

Gallagher A M , Osborne R D , Cormack R J (1996) *Attitudes to Higher Education: Report to CCRU and DENI*

Segal Quince Wicksteed Limited (1996) *Review of the Funding of University Research in Northern Ireland, Phase 1*

Index

i. All reports by us have been published in three media: printed text, CD/ROM and on the World Wide Web. This index relates to the Report of the National Committee only. For a user defined 'key word' search of all our reports the CD/ROM version has a built-in search engine to allow scrutiny of our text. The version placed with Educationline on the World Wide Web offers full search facilities based on the British Education Index. The website can be accessed via the following URL: http://www.leeds.ac.uk/educol/ncihe

ii. Given its prevalent use in our report, there is no entry in this index for 'higher education'.